Social Policy

SOCIAL POLICY:

Issues of Choice and Change

By MARTIN REIN

RANDOM HOUSE *New York*

For Mildred Rein

Library of Congress Catalog Card Number: 71–97583

Manufactured in the United States of America by The Haddon Craftsmen, Scranton, Pa.

Designed by Florence D. Silverman

9 8 7 6 5 4

Foreword

My first thought in re-reading these essays was to attempt to write a review of them from the standpoint of an American social scientist in the political and economic climate of 1957. This was the year of my first visit to the United States. Few people then, inside or outside the universities, had heard of the term "social policy," let alone its associated "social administration," which happens to be the title of my chair and the faculty to which I belong at the London School of Economics and Political Science. Vaguely, they were connected with either one of the less reputable moralistic interests of social work or with some peculiar British obsession about poverty and the poor law. Those were the days when sociology was struggling to join the "respectable sciences"; when economic policy was defined as that about which economists talk (still mostly about values and things which can be measured in terms of money); when debates about poverty, inequality, racism, black power, populism, and participation were barely audible; and when men thought that, given time, economic growth would resolve all the so-called residual problems of welfare.

My first thought, to write about the American discovery of social policy, social indicators, and social man since 1957 constituted, I eventually decided, a worthwhile task for someone else but not for me. There are many things I do not understand or cannot remember about the United States although I have visited it many times since 1957. And such a review might have been unkind to Martin Rein, a friend for seven years whom I first met on the campus of Brandeis University, who was interested in these questions before they were academically fashionable. In his Introduction to this book he writes, "What is needed in social policy is not so much good tools, but good questions." He was asking good questions at Brandeis and, as these essays amply affirm, has continued to do so.

The social scientist without an ideological frame of reference rarely asks good questions. If he does he then faces—as Martin Rein intellectually does—the difficult task of eliminating ideology from his answers. He has to be simultaneously both attached to and detached from social purpose—for that is what social policy is all about. He is, I think, as a social scientist, better equipped to achieve this balance in asking questions about social policy if he can appreciate the respective contributions and limitations of economics, sociology, political science, and public finance.

In many of the essays in this book, Martin Rein employs the analytic tools fashioned within these different branches of the social sciences. He came to this position, I suspect, not by some deliberate decision taken when he first began to puzzle about social policy but by a difficult process of intellectual growth. As he says, "The problems of our society cannot be contained within the terms of reference of the historical development and political struggles which have contributed to the development of the present distribution of functions within the social sciences." I believe this to be true, although I—and no doubt others—would qualify his statement by saying, "Some problems of our society . . ." in place of the inclusive all.

As we become more aware of the needs, relationships, satisfactions, and dissatisfactions of Social Man as well as Economic Man we are simultaneously recognizing the interrelatedness of the economic, the social, and the political. The recognition of interrelated welfares—where the individual's welfare depends not only on his own behavior, needs, and consumption but on those of others—forces us to recognize the interrelatedness of welfare choices where the structure of individual choices depends on the behavior and choices of others. Yet, an historical division of labor within the social sciences continues on its momentum, reinforced by more sophisticated methodologies, to emphasise the "separateness" of "disciplines" and thus to neglect an expanding area of values and choices, means and ends.

I believe that the study of social policy which, as Kenneth Boulding has argued,* can be theoretically distinguished from economic policy has developed in response to a need in society. These essays by Martin Rein attempt to analyse questions of social policy within a framework of argument which breaks down these historical divisions between the social sciences. They represent a significant contribution because by this approach the problems of value and choice in the area of social policy become more explicit. They do not provide the ideological answers for students but they should help them to think more clearly about the questions that need to be asked.

Richard M. Titmuss

London, England
April 1969

* K. E. Boulding, "The Boundaries of Social Policy," *Social Work*, 12, 1 (January 1967), 3.

Contents

Foreword   v
Introduction   ix

Part I: What Is Social Policy?

1. The Boundaries of Social Policy   3
2. Welfare Planning   21

Part II: Contradictions and Failures of the Social Services

3. The Social Service Crisis   47
4. Institutional Change: A Priority in Welfare Planning   70
5. The Strange Case of Public Dependency   85

Part III: Strategies of Innovation and Their Limits

6. Coordination of Social Services   103
7. The Demonstration as a Strategy of Change   138
8. Community Action Programs: A Critical Assessment   153
9. Organization for Social Change   165
10. Goals, Structures, and Strategies for Community Change   178
11. Social Planning: The Search for Legitimacy   193

Part IV: Choice of Social Objectives

12. Poverty, Policy, and Purpose: The Dilemmas of Choice   221

13. Conflicting Goals in Social Policy 249
14. Social Stability and Black Ghettos: A Conservative Choice 271
15. Social Work in Search of a Radical Profession 281

Part V: Case Studies of Choice

16. The American Welfare System 305
17. Social Services and Economic Independence 326
18. Citizen Participation and Poverty 353
19. Barriers to Employment of the Disadvantaged 374

Part VI: Social Science and Social Policy

20. Social Science and the Elimination of Poverty 417
21. Problems in the Definition and Measurement of Poverty 446
22. Research and the Development of Social Policy 461

Index 479

Introduction

I have drawn together in this book most of the essays that I wrote between 1963 and 1968; only one essay was completed in 1962. Although each was written independently of the others, in retrospect they seemed to contain some common themes. What binds the various pieces together is an attempt, still somewhat tentative, to understand what social policy is and how it might be studied. Because these articles reveal my own shift in emphasis and understanding over time, I offer a brief account of how they evolved.

My earliest inquiries consisted of a sociological analysis of welfare organizations—The Planned Parenthood Federation[1] and later The Massachusetts Society for The Prevention of Cruelty to Children.[2] I was especially interested in how the structure of an organization served as a strategy for achieving its mission. For example, local affiliates of The Planned Parenthood Federation by their reliance on elite boards and agency cooperation produced organizational inaction. I later extended this analysis to health and welfare planning councils, arguing that choice of a primary goal affects the choice of an appropriate structure. The study of protective services was my introduction to the incoherence of social service delivery systems. My account of social services crises published in *Trans-action* in May 1964 was a general view based on insights gained from this study.

At first, sociology seemed to offer the most relevant literature for pursuing such studies. But as I became interested in how organizations interacted and how organizational change was brought about, I found it increasingly necessary to extend my readings outside sociology. Political science seemed more relevant to my concern about the relationships among units of government, both at the same level and at different levels, and about the processes by which public decisions were made. Social policy seemed to be primarily about governmental decisions, which required an understanding of how government functioned. The debate about the feasibility of planning and the effort to make "muddling through" respectable was of marginal interest in sociological literature. But the analysis of organizational structure and decision-making processes was incomplete without attention to social welfare programs and the problems to which specific programs were addressed. Of course, this meant that it was necessary to have more detailed knowledge of specific social services—manpower, cash transfers, medical care, personal social services, housing, and so forth. The more deeply immersed I became in a specific program, the more it became clear that to limit myself to the literature within the relevant professional discipline restricted understanding of the programmatic issues. It was, for example, difficult to get insight into social work or education by reading only the literature in these fields or following what is taught in professional schools. A different perspective was necessary than that held by the profession, which regarded itself as central to rendering a specific social welfare program.

Moreover, if we focused instead on the problem, need, or preferences which the programs were set up to service, it became clear that the more important questions concerned how several programs affected each other, for example, the impact of housing on income or income on education. In addition, the solution of a problem did not necessarily require more resources for the relevant professional group. For example, to increase health may not require more doctors, or to expand education more schooling and teaching, or to enhance emotional well-being more social work and other forms of personal therapy. Particularly with the problem of poverty and the distribution of income, I found that economics and public finance seemed to provide more relevant ideas and substantive knowledge. It also presented a way of thinking about the consequences of programs and about the allocation of scarce resources among competing claimants. Economics emphasizes finding and perfecting the right methodology to deal with social and economic problems. It proceeded on the assumption that what was needed was a good tool, which could then presumably be applied to any problem.

Attention to outputs and problems required an appreciation of the goals of social policy. As I came to see it, social policy is all about multiple, vague and conflicting goals, and all are desirable and necessary. By trying to reduce social policies to a single goal of individual utility and by searching for a common metric to make multiple aims commensurable, economics appeared to abandon the central issue in social policy—the study of *social* purposes and how they can be realized. This has led me to the position, which I overstate to make explicit, that *what is needed in social policy is not so much good tools, but good questions.* I accept Professor Crozier's advice to the futurists studying post-industrial society. It is "a kind of folly" he asserted, to assume that "a rational view of the world based on the inevitability of scientific progress can cope with a fragmented, culturally diverse society full of complex emotional problems."[3] Science and technology cannot rescue us from the abiding issues of choice among conflicting but desirable social objectives. Indeed, by increasing wealth, technology and science exacerbate the problem of choice. Advances in methodological sophistication obscure the value dilemmas by creating an illusion of expertize.

Yet the logical implication of this compelling position seems equally unacceptable, for it implies that social science offers little to the evaluation of valuations (choice among values that are reflected in social welfare objectives). Accordingly, the social scientist seeking only to gather facts and to eschew the area of value assessment is forced to accept a technocratic framework, whereupon he is viewed as a policy scientist. This position is in favor today, but was spelled out in some detail in the early 1950s by Harold Lasswell, who stated, "that reliance upon the techniques and substantive contributions of these sciences diminishes policy makers' errors of judgment and gives greater assurance that the course of action decided upon will achieve the intended goals."[4] The scientist, according to this formulation, tries to see that the "course of action decided upon" will be best able to achieve the policy makers' goals. But if social policy is primarily about the clarification and explanation of submerged and conflicting goals then we must repudiate the technician's definition of the task of the policy scientist. Some social scientists, like Robert K. Merton, reject the technician's role.

> The scientist is called upon to contribute information useful to implement a given policy, but the policy itself is "given," not open to question. This often throws the scientist off the right track, for the data may indicate the need to devise a policy other than that which is "given." Acceptance of such conditions of research may become a threat to functions of scientist *qua* scientist. So long as the scientist continues to accept a role in which he does not question policies, state problems, and formulate alternatives, the more does he become routinized in the role of bureaucratic technician.[5]

Merton makes it clear that the task of the researcher is dispassionately and disinterestedly to ferret out the policy makers' values in order to understand how they inhibit the exploration of alternative options. He asserts that "the data" may suggest the need for new approaches. But clearly the data could not be secured or interpreted without a theory and a set of values that suggest relevant and significant information. In order to avoid the role of technician, the social scientist is forced to enter the area where values and facts become blurred and social philosophy and sociology begin to merge. The issue of whether "social science" is value free inevitably arises when the social scientist is forced to evaluate the valuations of the policy makers and comes increasingly to rely for his sources of data not only upon "facts" but upon what Weber called *verstehen*—the ability to project oneself into the object of study. Empathy provides the root for understanding and this insight is crucial for being relevant to policy.

Many social scientists reject Merton's formulation because they believe that it is inappropriate to explore the issues surrounding social purposes and social values. Weber believed that science "cannot provide any guides to personal conduct or any means of choosing among 'ultimate' alternatives. Before Tolstoy's questions—'What shall we do and how shall we live?'—it remains silent."[6]

The technician's role is, of course, extremely compatible with the view that science contributes little to illuminating the issues surrounding meaning, purpose, and choice in human affairs. The scientist's only task is to discover invariable relationships among events, not to act on or judge contemporary public issues. To depart from this safe and secure role enmeshes us in the unresolved issues of the relationship between social science and social purposes, for which we have developed neither theory nor methodology. The failure of social science to take up this challenge has contributed to the urgent need to develop the field of social policy.[7]

The student of social policy is thus forced to trespass on academic and professional domains in which he may have no special competence. Yet he cannot rely altogether on these disciplines to illuminate issues of social policy. Most academics study the social services in order to clarify the theoretical and methodological issues in their own fields, and only incidentally to build theory and deepen understanding about social policy, social action, and social purposes.

Typically we approach social policy as the economics, history, philosophy, sociology, or politics of social welfare services. (The use of the term "social welfare" can be confusing. I use it to include the broadest field of social intervention.) No framework exists to study social welfare as a whole, independent of these various disciplines. Each field by framing its special questions and exploiting its unique methodology sets the study of social policy in a different direction. Different policy questions seem to be more appropriate to some disciplines than to others.

All of this presents the student of social policy with an awkward predicament, which Arthur Seldon's critical review of Richard Titmuss' book, *Commitment to Welfare,* points out with great clarity.

> What is less clear is the analytical framework of "social administration" [the English term for social policy] within which the varied subjects—income maintenance, means tests, medical care, housing, education, the difficulty of reaching people "in need"—are examined. The nature of "social administration", its characteristic methods or principles, its differences from public administration and business administration are not clearly defined. Is it a science or an art? Is it social science or social work? Is it really an intellectual discipline with distinguishing characteristics?[8]

In the study of social purposes we confront the ancient problem of how fact and value affect each other. That is, in its analytic framework social policy is driven to the limits of social science and is thus open to Seldon's criticism.

The attempt to study social policy has much in common with earlier efforts to separate planning as a field for inquiry and professional training. Policy and planning have no serviceable theory and no developed methodology other than that derived from other academic disciplines. They differ in that planning is concerned with the process of decision and policy with its substance. Process and content might be reunited in what could be called "policy-planning." The efforts to teach planning only as a separate area have not, in my judgment, proved altogether successful because planning lacks theory, a clear method other than logical exposition, and the application of the process to substantive areas. On the other hand, the study of planning might languish if it were not pursued in its own right. It may, therefore, be argued that the present distribution of tasks among the academic and professional fields has been too rigidly made and has become increasingly irrelevant to issues of public policy, such as race, class, and the urban environment. The problems of our society cannot be contained within the framework of historical development and political struggles that contributed to the present distribution of functions within the social sciences. Whether we study "planning" or "policy," or whether we try another approach (for example, the study of urban areas, which focuses on the geographic unit rather than the intervention or the decision process), we can anticipate continued pressure to create a more relevant approach to our social and moral problems.

So far we seem to study social policy in terms of established disciplines without a unique approach to social policy in its own terms. The student of social work is confronted with a special unease because there is no developed social work approach to social policy. Some persons believe that social work provides the skills for understanding and identification of the needs of people. Yet the claim seems pretentious. The organizational auspices of social work often nurture more concern with control than compassion. Social work is more typically preoccupied with a narrowly conceived casework technology that inhibits broad understanding of the interaction between environmental forces and human behavior.

It is hoped that this book may serve as an introduction to a broad study of social policy, not from the perspective of any single profession or single academic discipline. The book is thus vulnerable to Seldon's criticism.

I want here to make explicit how these essays are related to each other and then to suggest how they might contribute to a more systematic study of issues in social policy. I am, of course, conscious that many of the ideas and even some of the specific examples will be repeated in different essays. Moreover, some of the essays could easily have fit into other sections. I do not offer a tight systematic argument, but only a tentative frame of reference that I have found useful in teaching students of city planning and social work. A summary of the six parts of the book will serve to present the main thesis.

Part I asks what is social policy and argues that it is the study of social welfare in its broadest terms. Part II examines the many contradictions and failures in the present system of social welfare services in the United States and the vigorous efforts to reform these services as undertaken in recent years. Part III explores a number of strategies of reform (demonstration, co-ordination, community action) and their limits (the lack of power, the lack of resources, the lack of commitment). But change without purpose is insufficient, so Part III also poses questions. What after all, are the social objectives of reform? What is social policy trying to accomplish? Part IV argues that policy is about ambiguous, multiple, and conflicting goals, all of which are desirable. Part V further develops the theme of choice of purposes as applied to the areas of manpower training, poverty reduction, cash transfers, and social service programs. The essays in Part VI ask whether social science can provide guides for making choices. I argue that social science offers a rational argument for choices made on other grounds; it does not provide rules for choosing.

I have reluctantly concluded the book with the position that although policy involves making choices about objectives, we have no scientific principles to aid us in making these choices. As I see it, policy choices are based on beliefs, on reason, on political compromise (discussed in Part IV). All are reasonable principles, yet they can and typically do conflict. My own bias is that one's belief system or ideology is crucial in making choices. Thus my profound conviction about the urgency of reducing inequalities guides my policy analysis and offers a standard for judging policies. And yet I wonder. For instance, as Britain confronts problems of race relations, they have begun to experiment with American approaches—community action, demonstration programs, etc. Ideology may be less relevant than the constraints of the problem. That is, within certain political and economic limits, there are few choices. Or rather, the choice may be between doing something effective, and doing something ideologically more comfortable, but futile. Still, ideology does affect style, which is also important when it affects the quality of performance. Here we face still another awkward dilemma, because most people do not know what they believe, especially when much of what they believe conflicts. But I cannot take the argument much further, other than to accept policies which are inconsistent because they are based on trade-offs among conflicting aims.

It is hoped that this book will be of some aid to teachers seeking to develop a course organized around the issues, debates, and outcomes of social welfare policy. Such a course would depart from traditional efforts to teach social welfare either descriptively (where detailed review of programs obscures issues of choice and the problems to be solved), or prescriptively (where goals are assumed to be non-problematic and only the means to implement policies are examined). In an effort to confront and understand the tasks of social policy realistically, there will be much ambiguity, untidiness, and ignorance. Hopefully this disorder will serve to excite the student's curiosity and lead him to accept the challenge of creating intellectual coherence in an increasingly important field. To provide some structure in this search I have listed six issues. The list is based on the assumption that the crucial questions concern what objectives are sought, how do social welfare services function, are they effective, and if not, how can they be changed. Social policy may be seen as a set of solutions that have developed over time by design, by accident, by compromise, and by precedent. These solutions are labeled social welfare services. They include at the least: education, medical care, income transfers, housing, and personal social services or social work.

The debate over issues in social welfare services will be agenda items for future choice. I assume that the agenda is relatively stable, for we are continually debating the fundamental issues of justice, stability, and social change. Each generation tends to focus on some items and neglect others and each era redefines its terms of reference. The list of issues is not so much based on a general theory of society but on a more pragmatic review of the recurrent concerns and debates about social welfare policy. The relative stability of these choices is an assumption whose validity needs to be tested by historical review. The list is suggestive not exhaustive.

1. *Social Policy*. What is social welfare policy? What are the boundaries between it and economics, between it and public policies? Is social policy compensation for inequities generated by the economic system, or must it embrace, as well, the social objectives of economic policy? What are the aims of social policy? Do goals such as freedom and consumer sovereignty, social stability, and redistribution conflict? When alternative goals and courses of action are presented, can "rules" or principles for choosing among the various options be developed? To what extent is choice determined by value preference, assessments of political feasibility, rationality, or some combination of these approaches?

2. *Organization and Delivery of Services*. On what principles are the various social welfare services and cash transfers distributed and financed: Free services *or* user charges; general *or* earmarked taxation; universalism *or* selectivity; centralization *or* decentralization; coordinated *or* autonomous specializations; reliance on the market by tax concessions and subsidies to individuals *or* direct provision by goverment or the voluntary sector? What level of resources is committed to each program and to social policy as a whole?

3. *Implementation of Services*. Review systems of control and accountability of welfare institutions; the basis of entitlement for benefits (determined by legal, contributory, or professional standards); obstacles to implementing established policies; the problem of underutilization (the effect of scarcity on use).

4. *Distribution and Allocation of Services*. How should expenditures be *distributed* in a single program, between, for example, prevention and treatment, or *allocated* within the social policy sector among housing, education,

medical care, cash transfers and so forth, and among sectors (economic, physical, and social) in order to achieve a given goal or to pursue multiple goals that are in partial conflict?

5. *Outcomes and Consequences.* What are the outcomes of social policy—intended and unintended (externalities)? Do social policies multiply or reduce inequalities? A review of outcomes confronts again the issue of the objectives of social policy—how are these defined and measured, and to what extent are they met?

6. *Change.* How is planned change brought about? What generalizations can be made about how social policy develops and how it can be changed? Is planning possible?

Most of these issues can be examined at different levels. In relation to all social services treated aggregatively, the essential question concerns the nature of the "welfare" or "social service" state. In relation to each of the services attention must be given to both the current picture and its historical roots. In their own right, drawing illustratively from each of the preceding, the focus should be on how choices differ in each sector (for example, we may elect to centralize the administration of cash and decentralize the administration of education).

We are primarily concerned with the differing conceptions of the purposes, principles, outcomes, and change in social welfare services. Courses in social policy should try to clarify areas of disagreement and crystallize the kinds of choice which policy must make. The decision to focus on areas of disagreement is based on the assumption that policy is essentially about the clarification of objectives (the choice of means in this context may be seen as a lower level goal). Everyone who sets out to teach social policy will want to do it in his own way. Detailed prescriptions are seldom useful. Yet is is hoped that the broad framework of ideas and the specific attempt to deal with some of these may prove useful for those who wish to use these essays as an introduction to social policy.

NOTES

1. Martin Rein, *An Organizational Analysis of a National Agency's Local Affiliates in Community Contexts* (New York: Planned Parenthood Federation of America, 1961).
2. Martin Rein, *The Network of Agencies Providing Child Protection Services in Massachusetts* (Waltham, Mass.: Research Center of Graduate School of Advanced Study in Social Welfare, Brandeis University, May 1964).
3. Henry Raymont, "Sociologist Sees Intellectual 'Peril,'" *New York Times*, December 15, 1968, p. 11.
4. Daniel Lerner and Harold D. Lasswell, eds., *The Policy Sciences* (Stanford, Calif.: Stanford University Press, 1951), p. 14.
5. *Ibid.,* p. 306.

6. Quoted in Harry Eckstein, "Political Science and Public Policy," in Ithiel de Sola Pool, ed., *Contemporary Political Science: Toward Empirical Theory* (New York: McGraw-Hill, 1967), p. 143.

7. Readers who wish to pursue this issue will want to read a thoughtful attempt to examine these questions in historical perspective. See, T. S. Simey, *Social Science and Social Purpose* (London: Constable, 1968). My discussion is indebted to this important book.

8. Arthur Seldon, "Commitment to Welfare: A Review Article," *Social and Economic Administration,* Vol. 2, No. 3 (July 1968), p. 98.

Part I

What Is Social Policy?

Chapter 1

The Boundaries
of Social Policy

What is social policy? Gunnar Myrdal has recently
observed that much "labor was often wasted on finding
precise definitions of our several social science disciplines
in the belief that this was an important activity." The
validity of scientific inferences cannot depend on their
definitions. He concludes therefore that the "one and
only type of concept which it is permissible to keep
vague is the meaning of terms such as economics, sociology, or psychology."[1] This generalization applies to
social policy as well. Accordingly, no formal definitions
are attempted here. Instead, we shall explore the boundaries of the subject—the relationship of social policy to
academic disciplines, to public policy, and to the social
work profession. Such an exploration will demonstrate
that the boundaries do not have clear perimeters, that
we cannot altogether eliminate the fuzziness of our
subject. But the search for order is valuable in itself,
for it will contribute to better understanding of the
substantive issues that the study of social policy confronts.

WHAT IS SOCIAL POLICY?

Social policy can be regarded as the study of the history,
politics, philosophy, sociology, and economics of the
social services. The definition of the term "social services" involves a stubborn ambiguity. The definition
should, at least, be broad enough to encompass services

3

such as education, medical care, cash transfers, housing, and social work. We are essentially concerned with how social services have developed and changed over time, the assumed needs and problems with which they cope, the ideas and principles by which they are distributed, the purposes and functions they are designed to fulfill, the experiences that emerge in the implementation of these ideals, and the consequences that emerge when services are organized and distributed along certain lines (i.e., who are their ultimate and immediate beneficiaries and what outcomes are related to the use or non-use of services). Finally, if these outcomes seem undesirable or inadequate, what changes are required, and how can these be brought about under particular historical, political, economic, and social circumstances.

This attempt to delimit the boundaries of our subject as the study of social services is by no means settled or even clear. Necessarily, the approach to social policy is much broader. We could include all activities that contribute to the health of a population or affect the equalization of income. Richard Titmuss has urged that we group together all activities that serve a common purpose. Social services would then be broadened to include all forms of collective interventions, such as fiscal, occupational, and social programs that contribute to the general welfare. The implications of this approach can be extended even further. A subsidized rural electrification program may contribute more than a cash transfer program to altering the level and distribution of income of those who live in regionally depressed areas. Accordingly, it is not the social services alone, but the social purposes and consequences of agricultural, economic, manpower, fiscal, physical development, and social welfare policies that form the subject matter of social policy.[2] This approach touches the boundaries of the broad area of public policy.

Anyone who has reviewed any programs addressed to a particular problem, such as poverty, recognizes the conceptual difficulties in delimiting the subject matter. This is hardly an academic exercise. If one wishes to know who are the major beneficiaries of social policies, the delineation of the field is crucial. The extent to which policies are redistributive or regressive depends on which programs we include and reject. To determine the extent of or the gap between resources and needs, a central preoccupation of policy-oriented research, requires a definition of social service resources. A narrow definition leads to resource expansion, a broader definition encourages redistribution or reallocation of these resources.[3]

Still another approach would consider the substantive issues once the primary focus of social economics. Social policy appears to be concerned with many of the problems that once intrigued social economics, but have since been neglected because they presented formidable methodological problems. In this sense social policy might be defined as neglected economics.

This economic approach to the study of social policy might embrace some of the following subjects. Of central concern would be the problem of social externalities, that is, the study of the uncompensated costs of production and consumption. Who are the causal agents of disservice and how can their victims be compensated?[4] For example, some of the twentieth century problems of Negro Americans may be seen in terms of the social costs of nineteenth century agricultural policies. Social policy also has a major commitment to the issues of redistribution and equity. Hence, it is forced to go beyond Wilfred Pareto's optimality, the principle that policy should leave no one worse off and at least some people better off, as each person judges his own utility. Thus, a social policy of redistribution is forced to confront these intractable and perhaps unsolvable problems of interpersonal comparisons of utility. John Dyckman asserts that "social planning for equity is planning for interpersonal comparisons. Since the economists have relinquished this area, it has fallen into the hands of sociologists, social psychologists, lawyers and others."[5] I offer one more illustration. Social policy is organized around the theory of benefits and their distribution, whereas economists have in the past paid more attention to the theory of taxation and its practical applications. Some of the best writing about benefit theory is found in the literature of public finance.

A compelling case can be made to define social policy as planning for social externalities, redistribution, and the equitable distribution of social benefits, especially social services. Increasingly the study of social policy must give major attention to these stubborn problems. This approach touches the boundaries between social policy and the academic disciplines. It would seem to require that one major social science serve as the master discipline, yet other fields claim a special role and competence in the study and practice of social policy.

Another somewhat narrower ground of contention with our definition of social policy centers on where to draw the boundaries separating policy, planning, community organization, and administration. A distinction is often made, at least implicitly, between policy analysis—accounting for the development of public policy and explicating the choices and assumptions underlying present or anticipated programs, without necessarily attempting to alter the direction of policy or make specific and detailed choices—and planning—converting value choices into concrete programs and plans for action by choosing among alternative patterns and levels of allocating resources to reach some predefined goal. Some have tried to combine these activities when they discuss policy planning. Community organization deals with the process of change either by drawing together diverse interests to facilitate reaching agreement on social objectives, or by organizing groups who are inarticulate and excluded from the decision process. Finally administration implements choices already made, but in the process of identification may shape the direction of policy, setting it upon a new or only slightly altered course. In summary, administration is concerned with converting choice into activity, community organization with the issues surrounding the process of decision making, planning with the substantive decisions, and policy with understanding the implicit rationale and value choice surrounding both the process and substantive issues of social services.

SOCIAL POLICY AND ACADEMIC DISCIPLINES

These observations make it evident that the definition of social policy is unsettled and the division of labor among its parts also remains unsettled. As urban social problems increase and expenditures for social services expand, interest in the study of social policy has been stimulated. Students and scholars of social policy in American universities are located in a variety of academic disciplines and professional schools, such as social work and city planning. As the demand for policy analysis increases, pressures to develop social policy as a separate discipline arise. We will therefore explore the boundaries which separate social policy and the academic disciplines, and will consider the response of policy analysts in professional settings to these boundaries.

Academic disciplines such as economics, political science, psychology, and sociology may be regarded as established domains having distinguishing characteristics within the social sciences. These separate and distinct disciplines, each with its own subject matter, methodology, and traditions, facilitate teaching and learning by providing a sense of order and form. More broadly, these domains may be regarded as a division of labor wherein responsibility is allocated within social science. But for many analysts, there is a "growing disrespect for the traditionally rigid boundary lines between separate disciplines of social science." In their work they have discovered that "in reality there are not economic, sociological, or psychological problems, but simply problems, and they are regularly complex."[6] If we accept this formulation, the special case of social policy is no different than the general case in the social sciences, for its proper study also impinges upon the concerns of all the established disciplines.

Although these academic disciplines also suffer from vagueness about their subject matter, time has helped them to establish a central puzzle to which they address themselves, and more often, a special methodology for securing answers to the puzzle. Economists, using the assumptions implicit in a price structure, have been able to make powerful generalizations about the meaning and nature of individual and collective values. They are concerned, as well, with rules for the allocation of scarce resources among competing claimants, and perhaps most fundamentally, with understanding the factors which contribute to economic growth. Political scientists are concerned with problems of power, authority, and accountability. They are further concerned with the forms of representative government and to a lesser extent with its purposes. Psychology has laid claim to problems of perception, learning, and human motivation. Finally, sociology has asked what produces order and stability in society, and increasingly, how societies, institutions, organizations, and groups evolve and change. From the work of scholars in these several disciplines a general conclusion can, with reasonable confidence, be made: the discipline is the master, and the central task of the scholar is to extend knowledge and to test the validity of the assumptions, principles, and insights acquired in relation to solving the central puzzle to which the discipline is addressed.[7]

Each discipline develops, as well, a spectrum of approaches relevant to both defining and unravelling its own central puzzle. The field of sociology can serve to illustrate the point. W. J. M. Sprout challenged the underlying assumption which served as the basis for T. M. Marshall's famous inaugural lecture "Sociology at the Crossroads," because he rejected the image of a body of men marching together who are faced with a decision at a cross-road. Sprout explains, "I do not see the situation quite like that. I see several bodies of men converging on an open space where they spend a good deal of time abusing one another."[8] Much of the contention and abuse derives from the different methodologies and hence the different problems with which the scholars of the field approach their subject. Sprout lightheartedly describes them as "fact-gatherers" (an industrious but grubby group whose efforts are obviously useful for rational policy-making because they are responsive to what they and administrators see as social problems), "method-men" (a sinister statistical brigade who are accused of letting their methods dictate the information they will obtain), "historical sociologists" (who are criticized by reformers for ignoring the urgent claims of the present), "bird-watchers" (who with their muddy boots and rural lisps provide us with case histories of strange social activities and with descriptions about life in the towns and villages of Asia, Africa, and other areas), and finally the "theorists" (who claim to be the true sociologists, although they, in turn, travel different routes and include the middle-rangers, the analytic, and the dynamic theorists).

This type of contention can be found in every academic discipline. There is, however, some evidence for what might be considered the emergence and domination of "hard," empirically based, statistically sophisticated methodology in all fields. Political science offers an illustration of the kind of abuse to which Sprout refers. The struggle has divided the discipline between a school of traditionalists and a school of behaviorists. The former is concerned with political theory (including the classic theorists such as Plato, Aristotle, Hobbes, Rousseau) and the latter with political science (with its emphasis on quantitative and empirical studies). De Sola Pool in a review of this conflict concludes that "the ideological struggle that led to this state of affairs is now said to be finished . . . Behaviorism is said to have won acceptance to the point where it is no longer an issue in the discipline."[9] Although empirical and quantitative approaches may have come to the fore in all of the social sciences, each discipline has adapted them to its special puzzle, with the result that we find survey research stressed in sociology, econometrics in economics, behaviorism in political science.

The distinction between academic disciplines and social policy (referred to as "social administration" in English universities) can now be drawn. Donnison offers the following instructive conclusions:

> . . . social administration cannot be studied in isolation from the major social sciences. Most of its body of knowledge could be incorporated in these disciplines (as applied economics, statistics, politics, and so on) with little strain and considerable benefit to them. It has scant theoretical structure. Its methods are dictated by the problem in hand and are not the preserve of its practitioners . . . It is not a "discipline." It is a "field"—the development of collective action for social welfare—in which scholars drawn from various disciplines try to clarify problems . . . Indeed, much of the best research in social administration goes on under other titles . . .[10]

It follows, then, that there is no special logic to justify the separate study of social policy other than the traditional arguments in support of creating opportunities for bringing the major disciplines together for collaborative work. The evidence that interdisciplinary research is fruitful remains inconclusive, despite the claims which have been made on its behalf. Nevertheless, those who are interested in social policy frequently have more in common with each other than they have with their respective academic disciplines. But the student who chooses the serious study of social policy as his field, without benefit of credentials in the established disciplines, finds it difficult to interpret to others and to himself wherein his loyalties lie, and to decide from which settings to pursue his inquiries. Professional schools, like social work and more recently city planning, have served as sources of professional identification for those who pursue the study of social policy. But the major commitment of these professions to clinical practice and to physical design has limited their adequacy as bases from which to work in this emerging, but amorphous field.

Myrdal appears to be arguing that he has grown disenchanted with the academic disciplines in the social sciences on much the same grounds that Donnison has argued that social policy is a field and not a discipline—namely, that the search for solutions to complex problems leads to regularly trespassing on the established domains of all disciplines. It might be argued that although we will continue to draw on the wisdom of older academic disciplines, social policy can be regarded as a discipline with a growing body of theory, methodology, and a special puzzle of its own. Titmuss supports this general view, in apparent disagreement with Donnison's conclusion. He explains that "in recent years the subject has in an empirical and confused way been slowly conceptualizing its major fields of research and teaching . . . I happen to believe that as a subject, social administration has begun to develop a body of knowledge and a related set of concepts and principles."[11] It might then follow that it should be thought of as a separate discipline, not necessarily tied to an established professional school. One disadvantage of this approach is that it might create an artificial split between action and research.

SOCIAL POLICY AS THE STUDY OF SOCIAL PURPOSES

Titmuss' approach to social policy (social administration) deserves elaboration for it serves not only to define one view of the field, but to clarify further the differences between the central puzzle and methodology of social policy and the academic disciplines. He states that, "Basically, we are concerned with the study of a range of social need and the functioning, in conditions of scarcity, of human organization, traditionally called social services or social welfare systems, to meet these needs. This complex . . . lies outside or on the fringes of the . . . free market, the mechanisms of price and test of profitability."[12] Thus, there appears to be general agreement that social policy is essentially concerned with the social services, which Titmuss defines here somewhat ambiguously as organizations that function outside of the market to meet human need. The definition of need and its relationship to preferences, on the one hand, and social problems as defined by others, on the other hand, are the crucial unresolved issues in this approach. So too is the definition of the social services. But these issues are not our major concern here; rather we are concerned to identify the central puzzle of social policy. It is here that Titmuss offers one important approach to staking out the field.

> It is the *objectives* of these services . . . rather than the particular administrative method or institutional device employed to attain objectives, which largely determined our interest in research and study and the categorization of these activities as social services. The study of welfare objectives and of social policy thus lies at the centre of our focus of vision. (Italics added)[13]

Social policy then, is concerned with social purposes. It is much less concerned with clarifying the costs and benefits of alternative means of fulfilling those purposes where there is already substantial agreement. It is not simply another tool for reaching decisions in a society committed to the view that ideology has expired through consensus, leaving only largely technical problems unresolved. Although policy analysts need a command of technical knowledge, we need not accept the technicians' approach to decision-making: "The belief that all problems have unique solutions deriving from purely technical considerations, so that as technology

advances the necessity for moral choices diminishes."[14] What is needed
then, is not so much good methods (as implied by the concept of policy
sciences), but good questions (as implied in a social philosophy). A sound
scientific methodology will, of course, be vital in answering relevant and
important questions.

In the early intellectual struggle over planning and the market economy,
the conservative opponents of planning feared most the danger of "scientism"—treating science as an "ism." This problem is again being discussed
today. "At times it seems we have fallen back on 'objective' social science
findings because our political ideology offers so few positive guides to social
reconstruction."[15] As our technology becomes more powerful and the problems of society more complex, the need for further sophisticated technology
seems to become more urgent. We tend to overestimate the contribution
of social science disciplines and accept technical decisions as we increasingly
abandon value, moral, and political choices. The important mission of
social policy is to identify the limits of social science for policy decision-
making. In a review of Max Weber's writing about the relationship
between social science and public and social policy, Harry Eckstein summarizes the argument as follows:

> . . . to the extent that life becomes "scientized" meaning recedes and men become
> estranged from the world . . . science cannot provide any guides to personal con-
> duct or any means of choosing among "ultimate" alternatives . . . Even when
> desirable ends have been chosen, it cannot solve or reduce such problems of con-
> duct as whether such ends sufficiently sanction undesirable but unavoidable
> means, or whether in choosing and pursuing desirable ends, the possibility of
> undesired repercussions should be taken into account, or how to deal with con-
> flicts among conflicting desirable ends.[16]

Eckstein concludes "that there is no policy science, no special scientific
training for decision-making."

Social policy research should probe the value assumptions underlying
the development of policy and explicate those areas where technicism
has become a substitute for choice. It cannot develop rules for choosing and
so cannot establish criteria for resolving conflict among multiple desirable
goals. It can foster a better appreciation of the links and the disjunctions
between programs and purposes.

According to this interpretation the central, although not exclusive, task
of social policy is to examine the social objectives of social welfare policies
as well as the social purposes of economic policies. This position grows out
of two considerations: the limitations of social science in making value
choices and the drift to technicism, with the result that science and technology become a surrogate for moral choice and political ideology. Social
policy is thus in the curious position of relying upon the tools of social
science to expose the limits of social science.

Needless to say, there is much controversy and disagreement about assigning so limited a role to social policy. There are those who claim that knowledge *does* (a factual statement), or at least *should* (a prescriptive statement), provide the major guidance for social policy decisions. In this view, the economists have pre-empted center stage with a dogged optimism that cost benefit analysis, regression analysis, linear programming, and other tools of research can and should play a major role in policy development. They do not see themselves as activists for particular programs and objectives but as dispassionate analysts of the least costly method for reaching defined goals. By a curious twist then, those who were the "dismal scientists" of the nineteenth century have become proponents of an ideology of euphoria which holds that most dilemmas of choice can succumb to economic growth combined with efficient rules for the allocation of scarcity. The problem of values has been de-emphasized and almost altogether replaced by a faith in the planning sciences.[17]

Today it is the sociologists who have assumed the mantle of the new "dismal scientists" of the twentieth century. At least a small band of insurgents have recently been much more reckless in challenging established arrangements in their disciplines. Reporting on a sociological meeting in California, *The New York Times* described "the rise of radical sociology." This movement toward radicalism, sometimes called the new sociology, has reopened the long-standing question of the relationship between social science and social policy. Many sociologists have, for example, been disturbed by the revelation concerning *Project Camelot*, in which anthropologists and sociologists participated in the 1964 United States Army project to study social breakdown in Chile. Many proponents of radical sociology (like Herbert Gans) have argued that one cannot escape value judgments by passively aligning oneself with the status quo. But as sociologists have raised these issues of values, of ideology, and of purpose, they may have diminished their claim to the knowledge and tools needed to influence the direction of social policy.

We cannot here resolve the contention regarding the promise and the limits of the contribution of social science to illuminating policy choices and establishing rules of choice, although the issue is crucial to understanding the boundaries of social science disciplines and the study of social policy. But we can explore the response to the boundary problems from the vantage point of those students who are trained outside the formal, established academic disciplines and who learn about policy from their bases in social work, city planning, and other professional schools. I think four generalized reactions can be discerned. It may be of some value to make these explicit so that students may understand that their reactions and apprehensions are shared by others who confront the problem of how to use social science without subordinating their concerns to the central puzzle in each academic discipline.

The first is a *confusion of identity,* especially for those who have drifted into social policy before acquiring credentials from the academic disciplines. Unlike their counterparts in England, they have no field like social administration to which they can owe allegiance. In American society they must align themselves with one or another of the established academic disciplines or with the professional groups wherein they have been trained. To the extent that neither are relevant to their present interests, they lack identity and a base within the university from which they can function. Centers for urban studies are now being created, which utilize the geographic unit rather than the social program (social services) as a point of departure. These centers are committed to action and research and may perhaps serve as home for policy analysts.

A second response is that of *humility.* Few students of social policy are bold enough to claim that they are "renaissance men," yet they must realize that policy questions have broad ramifications in virtually all the academic disciplines. It is natural to feel that it is impossible to master the substantive knowledge, the theory, and the methodology in all those fields that have a direct bearing on the subject.

A third response is a *sense of impatience.* Because each academic discipline is most responsive to its own central puzzle, its policy is often wanting. Scholars can produce a product which is somewhat arid and unilluminating of the issues of choice. For example, having mastered the intricacies and complexities of welfare economics, one may conclude that it offers little insight into the problems of maximizing individual and collective social welfare aims, and of choice among alternative means and ends.

The fourth response is one of *aggressive imperialism,* the desire to redefine the boundaries which mark off the established professions and to carve out an empire for the field of social policy. Evidence for this imperialism is found in schools of city planning, like that of the University of California at Berkeley, which are attempting to create centers for study and training in social policy. Further evidence of this desire to expand the boundaries can be found in schools of education, as at New York University, or in schools of public administration as at The J. F. Kennedy School of Government, which will offer advanced degrees in public affairs, or in schools of social welfare, as at Brandeis University. With this extension into the domain of the established professions, conflict is perhaps inevitable. Thus, students having these commitments to policy analysis confront an indifferent group of architects, or administrators committed to managerial science, or clinically oriented caseworkers who take issue with the new discovery of community organization and planning. Educators resent the neglect of techniques of teaching in favor of the broader issue of the purpose of education.

THE RELATIONSHIP BETWEEN SOCIAL POLICY
AND PUBLIC POLICY

A second boundary issue concerns the relationship between social and public policies. Most public policies today include social components and produce social consequences. Thus, the war in Vietnam significantly affects the deployment of additional resources in the social service sector. This is the clash between "guns and butter." The space industry will create external conditions that may contribute to future social problems. This is another example of the social cost of technological change. But even more immediate are such questions as how wages are established through management and labor negotiations, the redistributive effects of taxation and subsidy policy that provide concessions and transfers to special groups, or the impact of aggregative economic policies that establish the level of acceptable inflation upon unemployment rates. If we fail to establish the boundary between public and social policy, then the field of inquiry will be as broad as human wisdom and social experience itself. The pressure to establish boundaries, to make our subject matter encompassable is irresistible.

I think it is fair to say that few, if any, books on social welfare policy take such subjects as the social consequences of technological change, the distribution of wages, labor relations, taxation, or war as their themes. These are subjects of broad public policy which have clear relevance to social policy but cannot be equated with it. To try to create a more effective separation between these fields, social policy has been defined as intervention outside of the market system. This definition permits us to neglect preferences as revealed by the price mechanism and to avoid the test of profitability as a criterion of effectiveness. We can focus instead on programs which are responsive to human need and which contribute to building integration and a sense of community. Thus, social policy is regarded as "those aspects of social life that are characterized not so much by exchange in which a quid is got for a quo as by unilateral transfers that are justified by some kind of appeal to a status or legitimacy, identity, or community."[18] Such a definition offers only partial help in clarifying boundaries between social and public policy.

To define policy as an aid to social integration somewhat discounts the frame of reference used by writers like Myrdal, Galbraith, and more recently, Peka Kuusi, a Finnish sociologist. These writers underline the economically productive nature of social welfare policy. The human investment and human capital approach in the United States is a similar attempt to redefine the functions and boundaries of social policy, and in the process different sectors of social policy are isolated as implicit models for the whole of social welfare policy. In these new descriptions of social policy, education and retraining tend to be more central than the earlier emphasis on income maintenance and social casework. Even cash transfers can be justified as incentives which can alter the future income flow of individuals, for they facilitate an economic take-off. As the priorities within social policy are altered, policy functions and purposes seem to change as well.

More recently, even the idea that welfare policy is intervention outside of the market has been challenged. One reason is that we increasingly recognize that social services in fact respond to a market characterized by the rationing of always scarce resources. When the resource supply is fixed, it can be rationed by making less available to more people or more available to fewer people. The decision will affect the size and quality of a program. And it is a political decision to alter the level or total amount of resources. It has been argued that a large proportion of the Gross National Product (G.N.P.) would be spent by a country, for example, on medical care if this service were distributed through the market rather than through the public sector.[19] This implies that in responding to consumer demands the market is more efficient than public allocations, which require taxation and legislative decisions. In England conservative economists have argued that because public programs are compelled to ration scarce tax dollars, they tend to inhibit the growth in policy sectors, such as health and education. But if we wanted to alter the distribution of a service so that particular groups, such as the poor, would receive them, a public rather than market mechanism might be preferred. Although the arguments are inconclusive, they do illustrate the continuing debate about where to draw the boundaries between public provision and the market in the distribution of social services.

Industry and the market are being increasingly called upon as instruments to achieve social policy aims and objectives in other ways as well. Thus, industry in the United States ran most of the Job Corps under the poverty program. Both President Johnson and President Nixon have appealed to industry to redirect some of its resources to solving the housing and employment problems of our urban ghettos. Industry is being asked to redefine its entry requirements for new job applicants so as to take into account not only capacity for productivity but also social considerations. There is discussion about the need to offer federal subsidy to offset any cost to industrial productivity as a result of such policies. Finally, there is interest in directly subsidizing individuals to use market mechanisms by earmarked voucher schemes for rent supplements, educational vouchers, and so on. All of these activities only complicate our attempt to establish neat and tidy boundaries between social services and public policy. Certain needs like medical care and housing are supplied primarily by the market in the United States and by public sources in other countries. Unless we define social policy as programs only for the poor, if we are to take account of prevailing patterns, we must accept that the market is used as the mechanism for distributing social services and meeting individual and collective needs. How effective a mechanism it is and whom it reaches and neglects are important public policy issues.

There is another dimension to this review of the differences between social and public policy: it is assumed that social policy is responsive to human need whereas public policy has other immediate aims. Yet, the more we study the development of social policy the more it becomes clear that need itself is only a minor, and perhaps the least important, factor in understanding how services develop and are organized. For example, the professionals who run the social services play an important role in the development of social policy.[20] In their view of policy and in their role in creating laws for the purposes and organization of social policy, legislatures are often more concerned with issues of social control and social punishment than questions of social justice and human need. (Witness the restrictive policies of compulsory training and a federal eligibility freeze passed by Congress in the 1967 amendments to Title II, Part I of the Social Security Act.) When social policies are the domain of voluntary organizations, these bodies tend to seek client groups who can contribute most to the positive image that will enhance the organization's status, respectability, and survival.[21]

Thus, to define social policy as responsive to human need often reveals more rhetoric than reality and can contribute little to our understanding of the actual functioning of social policy in our society. The disparity between intent and performance is so apparent that it must be accepted not as an aberration but as a norm.

THE RELATIONSHIP BETWEEN SOCIAL WORK
AND SOCIAL POLICY

When measured by expenditure levels, social work plays only a minor role in the broad field of the social services. The high cost sector of social policy includes social insurance, education, medical care, and housing, and in these fields social work plays a small role. However, in that sector of social policy that the English call "personal social services" social work becomes central. A systematic exploration of boundaries must examine the relationships between social work and personal social services on the one hand, and all other social welfare services on the other hand. The failure to distinguish among them has caused considerable confusion. Only the briefest review is presented here to illustrate some of the boundary issues.

Social work is traditionally divided not by its purposes, but by its methods. Three major divisions are recognized—casework, group work, and community organization. The major commitment is to casework. Although community organization carries an important and growing share of the field, it nevertheless contributes only about 10 percent of the output of professional schools of social work. Its growth appears to have made the position of group work even more uncertain. But these labels convey little about the substance of the methods. No single explanation is likely to receive much widespread agreement. I regard casework as a method that, at the least, tries to combine counseling and guidance with environmental support from other social services. This unsatisfactory definition at least makes explicit the interrelationship between social work and other social services. Community organization may also be regarded as a form of social theory which depends on concerted action, on the assumption that people change as they try to change their world. But it ought to be seen as well as organized efforts to use a variety of methods to alter the social environment. This view makes the two methods complementary, for it rescues casework from the awkward position of trying to adjust individuals to an intolerable environment. These are the ideals on which the field is premised. Group work nestles uncomfortably between these approaches, and is necessarily becoming, I believe, an extension of clinical casework with a larger unit of intervention.

Social work as a whole can be conceived of as a way of preparing people for participation in society by providing them with information, guidance, and insight. As a service in its own right, it cannot be regarded as simply ancillary to other services. It might also be seen as a means for procuring the rights to services to which individuals are entitled by law or precedent. When one adds to this concept "aggressive procurement" we move into the arena of client advocacy and social reform. Here we confront another problem of boundaries—whether all of these activities are best carried out within a legal framework of advocacy or a social work framework of professionalism. Perhaps we are in the process of redefining professionalism to embrace advocacy as well. But the notion of protecting clients against an indifferent or hostile environment has always been the dominant rhetoric, if not the practice of social work. As the theme of protection is stressed, social work not only moves toward advocacy, but it presses into the broader areas of policy, planning, social reform, and social engineering. For only in these ways can the principle of protection be realized. In fact, social work is many things and its place within social policy depends on how its various practitioners seek to define and perform it. Social work becomes simply what social workers do.

Personal social services are equally difficult to define. They overlap considerably with social work, yet are broader. I should like to discuss these services here in terms of what larger functions they carry out. There is general agreement that personal services include liaison activities designed to provide advice, information, and referral to help individuals gain access to other social services and community facilities. They include as well services which are believed to promote social control, rehabilitation, and the restoration of individuals to earlier status. They also serve as surrogates for roles and tasks which are traditionally performed by families, including day care, homemaker, and institutional care. But social services acquire their special characteristics not only by what they do, but also by the groups they service. Services are typically directed at the marginal, excluded, and victimized man, that is, those who fall out, are left out, or are pushed out by other social institutions, including the market and the overall social service system. It is therefore useful to think of social services in terms of how they impinge upon the boundaries of these other services. In this sense, they may be treated as substitution, preparation, support, or amenities.

As *substitution,* they offer a less expensive (political and financial) approach to meeting need. Thus, a homemaker service may be in lieu of more expensive hospital, community, or institutional care. Remedial reading may be a substitute for smaller classes and better teachers. Remediation programs serve as an index of substitution. Generally such services substitute for more searching reforms. As *preparation,* they seek to enable individuals to make use of other services by providing them with information, advice, and counseling. As *support,* they first alter the individual's environment and then provide him the supports needed to function in a new setting. For example, a person may be given a job and then enabled to function better in it through training, health care, counseling, day care, and so on. Finally, services may be seen as *amenities* which enhance the quality of living. An example would be recreation. They can be organized to equalize the uneven distribution of amenities which separates income groups. The various activities may be the same, but in these four contexts their functions and purposes are different.

In summary, we are dealing with interrelated, but separate sectors—social work, personal social services, and social welfare (including cash and services). Social welfare is the broadest category embracing those forms of collective intervention which are concerned with medical care, housing, education, cash transfer, and personal social services. Personal services is one of the sectors within social welfare when it is defined as social services. We have tried to distinguish them from the other social services by suggesting that they are essentially linking, surrogate, and treatment programs. Some prefer to select from this definition only public outlays that act as transfers of cash and services. They would exclude transactions such as the purchase of services from the market, as in the case of medical care.[22] The Joint Economic Committee has an even broader definition, which includes programs that have an indirect or secondary effect on the development of human resources, such as rural electrification. Social welfare policy thus encompasses different activities: all social services including those distributed in the market; or only the public and private transfer systems; or policies, broader than social services, which include those economic and physical development policies directed at social welfare objectives. The broader the definition, the fuzzier become the boundaries separating public and social policies. We still lack criteria for deciding which particular programs are to be included in our definition. Preparation for education and access to housing are clearly social services, but is the Head Start program a personal social service or is it education. (Note: when this paper was written the Senate had voted to transfer the program from OEO to the Department of Education.) Shall we regard public housing as a personal social service when used as preparation and support rather than as an amenity? Social accounting schemes must resolve these issues if we are to be able to count the distribution of expenditures in each sector. Finally, when social work is narrowly interpreted as personal therapy, it is most clearly distinguished from personal social service; but as the "social" in social work is pursued, more than individual difficulties come into focus. Then we again touch the boundaries of personal services.

It should be evident from the above analysis that there is substantial difficulty in defining what social policy is in relation to academic disciplines, public policy, and social work practice. Just because the field cannot be defined, we must not conclude that it is unimportant, or that it doesn't exist. In 1968 over 163 billion dollars was spent on this sector of the economy that we cannot adequately define. More than 13.7 percent of the G.N.P. and 44 percent of total government expenditures is allocated to this amorphous area.[23] Nevertheless, the search for rational boundaries is important because it forces us to clarify the mission of social policy. What is social policy trying to accomplish and to achieve? The questions of values, purposes, and functions are the central underlying and abiding issues to which social policy must be addressed.

This leads us naturally into an exploration of the different models which influence the function and purposes of social policy. In Chapter 2, I argue that there are several models which inform the overall purposes of social policy. It may be regarded as allocative justice in which the principles of redistribution are central. Alternatively, policy may be seen as an instrument to achieve other goals such as economic growth, social stability, and physical renewal of cities. It may also be regarded as a social therapy designed to reintegrate individuals into communities from which they have become alienated and disengaged. Policy may be all of these. A dilemma arises when, in pursuing these different models at a particular moment in time, they lead in different directions because the goals which they embody tend to conflict. It is the boundary question which enables us to raise the more central concerns of goal and purpose and thereby help in clarifying the expanding field we call social welfare policy.

NOTES

1. Gunnar Myrdal, "The Problem of Objectivity in Social Research," Wilmmer Lecture, 1967, at St. Vincent College, Latrobe, Pennsylvania. Mimeo., p. 6.

2. See as an example, the definition developed by the Joint Economic Committee. The criteria for inclusion in the category of human resource programs are "that the programs are directed primarily toward the maintenance or development of people . . . or alternatively have as a secondary effect a substantial impact on the development of our human resources." *Federal Programs for Human Resource Programs,* Subcommittee of Economic Progress Joint Economic Committee, Vol. 1, 1966, p. 105. All of the policies listed above may have such secondary effects. By contrast, the definition developed by the Social Security Administration for their series on welfare expenditures is more narrowly drawn to include only programs which are specifically directed toward promoting well-being. In this report expenditures include "the major, public programs of income maintenance, health, education, housing, veterans' programs, and other welfare services directed specifically toward promoting the economic and social well-being of individuals and families." *Social Welfare Expenditures Under Public Programs in the United States,* 1929–1966. U.S. Department of Health, Education and Welfare, Social Security Administration, Office of Research and Statistics, Research Report No. 25, U.S. Government Printing Office, 1968, p. 8 and pp. 11–20.

3. For a further discussion of these issues see Chapter 23.

4. For an attempt to apply these ideas to social policy and law see Richard Titmuss, *Commitment to Welfare* (New York: Pantheon, 1968), p. 156. He argues that the "reasons for the lack of compensation for damages and disservices are many and various; they lie in our inability to identify the victims, to name and hold responsible the causal agents, and to measure in material terms the social costs of change and economic progress." Scholars have been concerned with legal aspects of externalties. See, Frank I. Michelman, "Property, Utility, and Fairness: Comments on the Ethical Foundations of 'Just Compensation' Law," *Harvard Law Review,* Vol. 80, No. 6 (April 1967).

5. John W. Dyckman, "The Organization of Metropolitan Social Planning," in *The Planning and Delivery of Social Services,* Summation of a Conference Sponsored by the National League of Cities and the Center for Community Planning, H.E.W., April 1969, p. 84.

6. Myrdal, *op. cit.,* pp. 5–6.

7. See David V. Donnison, "The Evolution of Social Administration," *New Society* (October 20, 1966).

8. W. J. M. Sprout, "Sociology at the Seven Dials," L. T. Hobhouse Memorial Lecture No. 32 (Bristol, Great Britain: Western Printing Service, 1962), p. 1.

9. Ithiel de Sola Pool, *Contemporary Political Science: Toward Empirical Theory* (New York: McGraw-Hill, 1967), p. vii.

10. Donnison, *op. cit.,* p. 610.

11. Titmuss, *op. cit.,* p. 23.

12. *Ibid.*, p, 20.
13. *Ibid.*, p. 21. See also, Thomas A. Reiner, "The Planner as Value Technician: Two Classes of Utopian Constraints and Their Impacts on Planning," in H. Wentworth Eldridge, *Taming Megalopolis*, Vol. 1 (New York: Anchor Books, 1967).
14. Jacques Ellul, *The Technological Society* (New York: Knopf, 1964), p. 253.
15. John W. Dyckman, "Societal Goals and Planned Societies," *Journal of the Institute of American Planners*, Vol. 32, No. 2, March, 1966.
16. Harry Eckstein, "Political Science and Public Policy," in I. de Sola Pool, ed., *Contemporary Political Science: Toward Empirical Theory* (New York: Mc-Graw-Hill, 1967), p. 143.
17. An exception to this generalization is found in a thoughtful article by Burton Weisbrod which deals with the economists' neglect of income distributional effects and support of allocative efficiency effects in developing cost-benefit ratio to determine whether a particular public program should be supported. He observes that "to date valuation of distributional effects of public expenditure programs has eluded economists." He believes that it is clear from research that if the issue were given serious attention it would be solved. Burton A. Weisbrod, "Income Distribution Effects and Benefit-Cost Analysis," in Samuel B. Chase, ed., *Problems in Public Expenditure Analysis* (Washington, D. C.: Brookings Institutions, 1968), p. 178.
18. Kenneth Boulding, "The Boundaries Between Social Policy and Economic Policy," *Social Work*, Vol. 12, No. 1 (January 1967), p. 7.
19. See, for example, Enoch Powell, *A New Look at Medicine and Politics* (London: Pitman Medical Publishing Co. Ltd., 1966).
20. See, Edward Banfield's study, *Political Influence* (New York: The Free Press, 1961).
21. See Charles Perrow, "Organizational Prestige: Some Functions and Dysfunctions," *American Journal of Sociology*, Vol. LXVI, No. 4 (January 1961).
22. Robert J. Lampman, "How Much Does the American Transfers System Benefit the Poor," in Leonard H. Goodman, ed., *Economic Progress and Social Welfare* (New York: Columbia University Press, 1966), p. 127.
23. Social Welfare Expenditures, 1967–68. *Research and Statistics Note No. 23.* (Washington, D. C.: U.S. Department of Health, Education and Welfare, Social Security Administration, Office of Research and Statistics, November 19, 1968).

Chapter 2

Welfare Planning

An inquiry into planning for the social services is handicapped by conceptual ambiguities as to the meaning of the terms "social services" and "social welfare." With refreshing candor, Donnison recently observed that "the distinctive feature of our subject is neither its body of knowledge (for most of this could be incorporated into other disciplines), nor its theoretical structure (for it has very little), and we are not interested in methodology for its own sake. We are concerned with an ill-defined but recognizable territory, 'the development of collective action for the advancement of social welfare'" (1962, p. 21).

But the global concept of "collective action for the advancement of social welfare" obscures the clashing conceptions of the political purposes of social services. At one extreme is the view that social services "assign claims from one set of people who are said to produce or earn the national produce to another set of people who may merit compassion and charity but not economic rewards for productive service" (Titmuss 1965, p. 14). So defined, social services are regarded as a burden to be carried by the productive institutions of society. Thus they constitute a residual function of government and philanthropy, and social service agencies should, ideally, strive toward self-liquidation. At the other extreme, Titmuss defines social services as "all collective interventions to meet certain needs of the individual and/or to serve the wider interests of society; [these] may now

Reprinted with permission of the publisher from the *International Encyclopedia of the Social Sciences,* David L. Sills, ed., Vol. 12, pp. 142-153. Copyright © 1968 by Crowell Collier and Macmillan, Inc.

be broadly grouped into three major categories of welfare: social welfare, fiscal welfare, and occupational welfare" ([1958] 1959, p. 42).

This discussion of the purposes of the social services has immediate import for planning, because estimates of total expenditures for social welfare clearly depend on the definition we accept. In the U.S. Social Security Administration's annual estimate of total welfare expenditures in the public and private sectors, social welfare is defined as "activities that directly concern the economic and social well-being of individuals and families" (Merriam 1965, p. 3). Consistent with this definition, Ida Merriam includes those agricultural programs that make surplus food available to needy persons (school lunch program, food stamp program, etc.). Lampman, on the other hand, employs a more encompassing definition of welfare in his assessment of the scope of money and nonmoney transfer payments. Public transfers include that portion of earned income (factor income) that is not a payment for current production having any value. Thus, in the agricultural sector he defines public payment for non-production as a welfare payment. Moreover, Lampman urges that the Social Security Administration's definition of public programs be expanded to include "subsidies and taxes which alter prices paid by the consumers and taxes that reduce disposable money income" (1966, pp. 3–4).

According to this more inclusive definition, the estimate of U.S. expenditure for "social welfare" in 1964 is about $97,000 million in transfer payments and transfer goods and services. By contrast, the more limited definition of the Social Security Administration leads to an estimate of $118,000 million. (No aggregate estimate is available for the conception of welfare favored by Titmuss.) This surprising finding arises because the broader view excludes health and education expenditures that are paid for directly by current users and are thus not regarded as extrafamily transfers. Lampman insists that the concept of welfare be limited to *public* transfer expenditures. He argues that there is no rationale for including personal expenditure for dental care while excluding personal expenditure for housing, as is done in the Social Security expenditure series. Direct payments by consumers for health services alone amounted to $17,000 million.

Not only does the size of the social welfare sector vary according to the conception of welfare we employ, but the pattern of distribution of welfare services is affected even more dramatically. In Lampman's pioneer study of the American welfare system (1966, p. 8), he estimates that almost 40 per cent of the total amount allocated for transfer payments, or $38,000 million, goes to those individuals who would be classified as poor before they received any transfer payment. Assuming that the poor contribute approximately $8,000 million in taxes and private contributions, he thus concludes that they receive a net benefit of $30,000 million.

In a more limited analysis of the distribution of housing benefits among

various income groups, Alvin Schorr comes to almost the opposite conclusion. He observes that in 1962 the U.S. federal government spent $820
million to subsidize housing for individuals who would be classified as poor;
this estimate includes direct subsidies for public housing and additional
housing payments for those receiving public assistance, as well as savings
from income tax deductions. By contrast, the amount the government
refrained from collecting in income taxes by granting tax concessions to
home owners (a predominantly middle- and upper-income group) is estimated at $2,900 million. Therefore, in regard to housing subsidies, the
federal government spent more than three times as much for those who
are not poor than for those who are poor. In this way, Schorr concludes,
the government "gives more to those who have more" (1965*a*, p. 437). The
main difference between the views of Lampman and those of Schorr is
their treatment of tax deductions. Lampman asserts that the distribution
of social welfare benefits must be seen both in relation to "who pays" and
to "who benefits." Tax deductions in his scheme are reflected in a smaller
"pay" figure, and they are of interest only to the extent that they alter the
burden on the rich as compared to the poor. By contrast, Schorr assigns
tax concessions to the benefit rather than the cost side of the ledger, which
permits him to compare the relative benefits of tax concessions between
those who are poor and those who are not poor.

The answer to the question of who benefits from America's welfare state
must remain inconclusive, not alone because of conceptual differences, but
also because of the limitation of available data on the cost of employee
fringe benefits and the size of tax concessions and how these are distributed
by income groups. As indicated above, there are two main positions regarding the redistributive effect of social services. On one hand, Lampman
suggests that, in the aggregate, welfare systems are redistributive and that
they work for the advantage of lower-income people. On the other hand,
students of British social policy, for instance, have concluded that the
major beneficiaries of England's welfare state are the middle- and upper-
income groups; thus Abel-Smith (1958) does not hesitate to assert that the
high-cost sectors of social services, such as education, health, and housing,
are instruments for the multiplication of advantage and privilege in an
advanced industrial society. The rediscovery of poverty in an affluent society
has riveted attention on the distributive effects of social policy: who are
the beneficiaries of public largess? This question provides a useful context
in which to begin planning. (There is little data available in continental
Europe, South America, or the developing countries for the study of
social policy; I have therefore been forced to rely heavily on the experience
of the United States and the United Kingdom.)

The Planning Process

Planning is traditionally defined as a method of rational decision making that counterposes means and ends in an attempt to assess how these can be best brought together at the least cost and with maximum effectiveness. This formulation tends to emphasize the technical problems of deciding on means; it implicitly assumes that the goals are clearly defined and capable of being measured. But this technical bias can be minimized, and the conception of planning recast, if one treats either the objectives or the implementation of the plan as problematic. The approach that focuses on implementation raises the question of feasibility and shifts the matter of planning away from the more dispassionate technical analysis of means and ends to a preoccupation with the realities of the environment as constraints on implementation. Similarly, the focus on objectives, including both the short-term and long-term aims of social policy, confronts the issue of ideology—the conception of the good society.

Planning can also be seen in terms of three interrelated stages: policy development, with an emphasis on the progressive modification of ends and means to achieve feasibility; policy implementation, concerned with the administrative circumstances that create disparities between purpose and performance; and policy evaluation, which attempts, through the rigors of social science technology, to document these disparities. The results of these evaluations in turn serve as an information input for the modification of established policy. Thus planning is a continuous and circular process, rather than an occasional event initiated to solve a specific problem.

The following discussion of planning will focus on the clarification of the goals of welfare and on the instruments for maximizing them; that is, it will deal primarily with substantive issues rather than with procedural questions. This approach will enable us to explore further some of the conceptual problems raised above in connection with the definition of welfare. Two interrelated tasks of planning—allocation and coordination—will be considered.

THE NATURE OF ALLOCATIVE DECISIONS

Allocation is concerned with the problem of how to divide limited resources among competing claimants. In order to simplify this analysis, we will consider these allocative decisions in relation to specific tasks, such as the apportionment of money among items in an annual budget or among the components of a development plan. Allocative tasks can be roughly sorted into three categories that vary according to the type of claimants involved: that is, resources are allocated, first, among the social, economic, and physical sectors; second, among the various sectors of the social welfare field; and, finally, among the various types of programs within a single specialized social sector.

Social, economic, and physical planning

First, we will be concerned with the social sector as a claimant for resources in competition with the economic and physical sectors. Consider the recent proposal in the United States for creating a demonstration cities program, in which 60 to 70 cities would request federal funds to develop a coherent attack on slums by combining physical and social renewal. According to the preliminary model programs for large cities, the estimated net cost of a neighborhood renewal program of 25,000 housing units is approximately $350 million, of which $100 million would be set aside to meet social costs—roughly a 3 to 1 ratio between these sectors. The expenditures set aside in the federal budget and in the demonstration cities program are examples of allocative decisions among different sectors of the economy.

How physical, economic, and social planning fit together will vary according to the prevailing conception of the *function* of social planning. At least four different views of the functions of social planning can be identified.

Welfare as a burden. One view of social planning sees welfare as a burden. According to this conception, since social welfare expenditure is heavily financed by taxation, we must pay special attention "to the specific sources of revenue used to finance it, to insure that the minimum of discouragement to enterprise and savings results from any given volume of welfare spending" (Burns 1954, p. 139). Eveline Burns suggests that we must be prepared to pay the costs of the depressive effect on enterprise and initiative arising from welfare expenditures, if these services enjoy a high community priority and are regarded as necessary. She exhorts the profession of social work to demonstrate that welfare services are indeed necessary but accepts the position that aggregate welfare costs inhibit economic growth. This view directs attention to the question of how much welfare we can afford without overburdening the economy.

Likewise, in developing countries some have felt that funds expended for the social sector detract from the maximum growth of the economy. Agricultural experts have sometimes said that it is almost immoral to spend money in the social sector when the country has insufficient food for its population. According to this view, agricultural development warrants the highest priority, and the allocation of funds for the social sector is at best a distraction that may be politically necessary.

Welfare as handmaiden. Recently, the conception of welfare as burden to economic growth is being replaced with a view that both economic and physical planning are best advanced by an investment in the social sector. One formulation of this view of welfare as "handmaiden" has been offered by economists concerned with investment in "human capital." Schultz suggests that inequalities in the distribution of personal income are most likely to be affected by such investments; he asserts that "the structure of wages and salaries is primarily determined by investment in schooling, health, on-the-job training. . . ." (1962, p. 2).

Physical planners have also become interested in a rapprochement with social planning. Although a physical plan may be immediately accepted as desirable and necessary, it cannot readily be implemented without the endorsement of citizens affected by it or without making provision for those who will be displaced by the renewal plans. Thus social planning has come to be defined in terms of the processes of relocation and citizen participation, namely, those activities that are necessary to facilitate the physical renewal plan. However, social planning for urban renewal and planning for investment in human capital are perhaps best seen as handmaidens for physical and economic development, respectively.

Welfare as complementarity. A third view holds that raising the level of living and increasing the investment in the social sector can only proceed in conjunction with greater economic growth; efforts to redistribute limited resources result only in the redistribution of poverty.

Interdependence arises when activities in one sector can serve either as objectives or methods for activities in another sector. Thus we sometimes may use primarily economic tools to achieve social objectives, as when we create employment opportunities and training opportunities in order to reduce youth unemployment and raise personal and family income, including those families receiving public assistance. Conversely, methods that are primarily social may be employed to promote economic objectives, as illustrated by the efforts to demonstrate that health improvement can make a major contribution to economic growth (see, for example, Mushkin 1962). Finally, complementarity is regarded as essential if more resources are to be added to the social services sector and if low-income groups are to receive a larger share of these resources. As Donnison states:

> An ominous feature of the present concern for equality is the tendency for some of its most forceful exponents to lay such stress upon the redistribution of the national income that its rate of growth is liable to be forgotten. . . . Redistribution can only be achieved by building more schools, hospitals and houses, recruiting and training more teachers, doctors and social workers, *and* by concentrating the increase in the areas where it is most needed. A high rate of economic growth can be achieved without alleviating social injustices, but injustices cannot be remedied without a high rate of growth. (Donnison 1966, p. 7)

Welfare as a means of social stability. The fourth view of welfare programs claims that funds earmarked for such programs are intended largely to reduce social deviancy and thereby to protect the political and economic stability of the community. Hence, according to this view, the resources of the "war against poverty" in the United States are increasingly being used as a means of tranquilizing the unrest in urban slums. For example, the riots in 1965 in the Watts section of Los Angeles, California, brought forth sustained efforts to bring large amounts of federal funds into the community for social welfare programs in order to avert future violence. The jobs and training generated in the United States by the Neighborhood Youth Corps will be made available to youths in the urban ghettos, based on the theory that the provision of summer employment opportunities can serve to avert or at least minimize the occurrence of riots.

Allocation among the Social Services

Allocative decisions must be made in regard to the distribution of resources among the various sectors that constitute the social welfare arena, such as health, education, housing, and income maintenance. Thus a developing country may need to choose between an investment of resources in the area of pensions for old people or educational programs for the young. It can, of course, attempt to distribute its resources according to some principle of balance that fixes the relative importance of these objectives, and so cuts short the debate over priorities.

The problems of choice are also confounded by the interrelationship among the social services. A study of social services in Mauritius illustrates how a policy of denying public assistance to the able-bodied unemployed created pressure on the medical system. Unemployed persons sought to acquire sickness certificates in order to qualify for welfare payments. Thus a policy choice in the area of public assistance had the effect of creating excessive demand on the medical care system (Titmuss & Abel-Smith 1961, p. 81).

Allocation within a Single Social Sector

Allocative decisions must also be made within any one specialized, functional area, such as health, education, or housing. Two types of problems can be broadly identified: the distribution of resources by domain and by clientele. Questions of domain concern the distribution of resources by type of service. For example, to what extent should resources be allocated for curative as contrasted with preventive programs? The question of clientele concerns the issue of determining who should be the major beneficiaries of the program. The development of universal programs designed to reach the total population does not avoid the need to make choices. It is widely acknowledged that upper-income groups avail themselves more of education and other high-cost social services (although the case for other sectors has not been as well documented) than do lower-income groups, "with the result that these services . . . represent in their mode of operation a redistribution of income away from the poor" (United Nations . . . 1965, p. 53). For example, as a rule of thumb, America spends less than half as much educating the children of the poor as the children of the rich (Jencks 1966, p. 18). Since universal programs result in inequalities, allocative policies aimed at redistribution may be necessary. This is becoming increasingly recognized in legislation, such as the Elementary and Secondary School Act of 1965, designed to distribute federal funds to schools with a substantial number of low-income families.

If we accept the traditional compartmentalization of programs as given, allocative decisions may typically be concerned with the distribution of resources by functional domain. However, allocations assigned in terms of traditional sectors have severe limitations; this approach often produces ineffective and inefficient solutions of social problems. Consider the following case-in-point. National levels of health, defined in terms of low infant mortality rates, are more highly correlated with measures of income, school enrollment, and calorie consumption than they are with the number of physicians in the country. This suggests that, to maximize health, it may be necessary to invest in nonhealth programs. "An extremely important requirement for improving health in a given country may be the improvement of the nutrition of children, if, as frequently happens . . . malnutrition . . . is leading to numerous diseases of adulthood, as well as to excessive morbidity and mortality among children" (United Nations . . . 1965, p. 55). Thus, if planning to maximize health takes into account only such matters as health facilities and health personnel, it may be ineffective or may achieve its aims in a very inefficient fashion.

POLITICS OF ALLOCATION

The problems of allocation are the abiding issues of social policy planning. They pose the fundamental questions of the purposes and effectiveness of the social services. However, while the allocative questions are the most crucial, they are also the most intractable and the least well understood. By and large, we have developed neither the administrative machinery nor the technology for making allocative decisions. So broad a generalization may seem arbitrary at a time when there is great investment and interest in policy-oriented research that goes beyond the traditional needs-resources approach into the more sophisticated cost-benefit analysis (Levine 1966). But most of these approaches fail to resolve at least two fundamental problems endemic to the social services.

First, programs for converting social values into economic terms continue to have a disingenuous ring to them. A cost-benefit analysis for an urban renewal program that attempts to convert the loss of aesthetic pleasure of enjoying greenery into some monetary equivalent must make assumptions that are arbitrary, forced, and, in the end, unconvincing. We have no universally accepted social arithmetic for converting values into dollars. Measures of social achievement lack a common scale of measurement that would permit us to add the benefits of programs, to delete the costs of various social problems, and to assign relative values, weights, and priorities to different social programs. In short, we have no rules to guide us in choosing among educational, health, welfare, housing, and other programs. Most attempts at planning for social services are forced to bypass the issues of priority.

The second problem concerns the nature of social objectives. Economic models tend to be fashioned on the assumption that economic policy is analogous to a theory of rational consumer choice; according to this theory economic man seeks to maximize his "utility" or preferences within the constraints of his income and the prevailing prices of the goods and services that he wishes to acquire. But the concept "need" does not lend itself to this type of rational calculation: what a man chooses is by definition his preference, but social needs imply necessities, and a man may not choose what he needs or what others think he needs. He may also lack the freedom to choose, because he lacks the necessary funds, information, or access to the services he requires. Moreover, the economic model is oversimplified, based as it is on the maximization of a single goal, which is defined as "utility" and measured by preference functions and indifference curves. Social life tends to be more complex than this. Allocative decisions involve the pursuit of multiple social goals, some of which are in partial conflict either with each other or with economic and physical objectives, but all of which, as this discussion of the goals of social policy has attempted to illustrate, are difficult to identify and select. Thus we cannot, in the end, develop a single best social plan. We are driven to the more unsatisfactory conclusion that there are only multiple plans, which will vary according to which items we accept as constraints for the achievement of certain objectives. For example, we can ask what level of inflation we are willing to accept in order to achieve full employment, thus treating price stability as a constraint and full employment as the goal; or we can ask the reverse question.

All of these problems confound the task of allocative planning. The secretary-general of the United Nations has effectively summarized these issues in a report to the U.N. Social Commission: ". . . social planning does not have the unity and coherence of economic planning. . . . Social allocation is ultimately a matter of judgment, operating among incommensurable values" (United Nations . . . 1965, pp. 37, 39). These judgments, of course, are not advanced as arguments against the systematic gathering of evidence and data, which can lead to judgments based on information.

But they do suggest that, in the last analysis, allocative decisions are based on value judgments—that is, there is no planning without ideology and politics. It is possible to identify at least four ways in which such decisions are made.

First, *tradition* plays an important role. In an analysis of the allocative process used by the United Fund organizations, Arthur Vidich observes that "the formula of tradition tends to work, as no unit is apt to feel unduly cheated if last year's proportions are carried over into this year" (1963, chapter 2, p. 6). Second, *preference* or *pressure* can play a significant role in the determination of allocative decisions. Since, as we have seen, there is no objective way to measure the relative need for housing as against education or health, knowledge of the preferences of consumers could, in principle, serve as one effective means for resolving these dilemmas of choice. Preferences can be secured either through some form of planning that is concerned with the channeling of the needs and aspirations of potential service users (i.e., planning for citizen participation in policy descisions) or through the use of survey research methods that attempt to gather information on preferences and then treat these as inputs for planning decisions. Thus, citizen participation in social planning and/or the development of measures of consumer preference can serve as purposive techniques for making allocative judgments. One of the unique features of the American "war on poverty" is the attempt to involve in policy making those who are potential consumers of antipoverty programs. There is, however, the unfortunate tendency in most planning efforts to involve the citizens only to the extent of asking them to endorse plans already prepared in advance rather than to use citizen groups for the initiation of policy ideas (Wilson 1963). There has been little attempt to use consumer preference surveys in the determination of policy. Admittedly, the development of such surveys poses a complex technical task, but their potential as an instrument of policy has not been exploited.

To the extent that preferences do play a role in policy development they usually emerge when organized interest groups for the aged, veterans, and other recipients of social services exert pressure on those who control allocative decisions. In the voluntary sphere, the selection of fund-raising programs that are likely to appeal to the community is, of course, one way of implicitly taking preferences into account, although these preferences are not necessarily those of the consumer. However, allocative decisions that are based on considerations of compassion, the popularity of the program, or community pressure may have little to do with the severity or pervasiveness of the social problems for which funds are raised, and they fail to take into account the needs of socially unpopular groups—that is, the ones that, like the American Indians, are unable to exert much pressure on their own behalf.

Allocative decisions are often avoided altogether, since policy, in response to different pressures, tends to develop piecemeal—a process that is often called proliferation by welfare planners. Proliferation, however, can itself be regarded as a strategy of allocation, particularly at the early stages in the development of new programs. Thus if we seek to expand the amount we spend in the area of, say, manpower training, we tend to proliferate many new programs and to create new agencies, which often lack adequate coordination with previously established efforts. Each program may even be supported under a separate piece of social legislation, as in the case of current training programs for disadvantaged youths in the United States. This form of allocation by accretion may seem a very irrational process after a sufficient number of these programs have been developed, but some pragmatists believe that it can also be an effective means of mobilizing resources for these services. Others, however, regard the way in which federal manpower programs have developed as the result of vested departmental interests and their clienteles (see especially Levitan 1966). Whether regarded as strategy or necessity, administrative dysfunctions arise when fragmented but interrelated services are not brought together into some coherent whole. This leads to pressure for coordination. But coordination increases visibility, and when new funds are sought in competition with other claimants there may be pressure to further fragmentize services as a technique for securing resources. However, specialization may arise from other pressures as well.

PLANNING FOR COORDINATION

The United States has an enormously complex and varied system for distributing social services. First, there is a three-tier vertical system, in which some services are distributed by sponsors administratively located at the national, state, or local levels. The three hierarchical tiers are bound together by financial, administrative, legal, and professional loyalties. The ties may be loose, as in the case of federated structures, where local operations are autonomous and create a national body to service their needs; or tight, as in the case of corporate structures, in which the locals are branch offices of a national agency. Within the boundaries of any one tier, there is a horizontally organized system, which can be sorted by auspices (public, voluntary, or private), or by functional specialization (health, education, housing, etc.), or by the type of clientele serviced (classified by age, problem, income grouping, etc.) and by the skill performed (teaching, medicine, social work, etc.).

Moreover, the instruments or means for carrying out these functions tend to take on varied forms. The government may directly operate services, or it may purchase them from voluntary and private agencies or professionals in the form of subsidies, grants, loans, or vendor payments. The latter procedure helps to support private and voluntary activity. The government may subsidize the facilities themselves, as in the case of low-cost housing programs; alternatively, it may provide individuals with subsidies, grants, or transfer payments so that they can purchase services in the open market, as in the case of unrestricted rent subsidies.

Even so condensed a summary of the organization of social services suggests its great variety and complexity. The components of the structure are not only complex but are also interrelated; programs cannot be treated in isolation, for they affect each other in at least two ways. First, the work loads of agencies in the same community do not vary independently. Thus, a protective agency, eager to conform to the principle that a child should not be removed from its own home, may assume that it has achieved its goal by decreasing its petitions to the courts, but as its court referrals decline, other agencies may begin to refer the cases of the protective agency to the courts, with the result that the total volume of court referrals remains unaffected. Second, many different activities are relevant to the solution of a single problem. Thus, as we have suggested, to promote the objective of health we may need to create indirect programs that are directed at expanding income, housing, education, nutrition, etc. The complexity and the interrelatedness of the social service system creates obvious pressures for coordination to reduce competition and promote coherence.

But the term "coordination" itself remains curiously vague and abstract, and it is more often used as a slogan than as a strategy for solving a specific problem in the organization of social services. Coordination strategies are, in the main, bound by a common problem: how to bring services into better harmony without reducing the autonomy of the component agencies and professions. In the following discussion of coordination, I will develop a typology of types of problematic situations that create the need for coordination and then examine the nature of the coordinative strategy that has been created, as well as the problems that are still unattended or are created by the very efforts at coordination.

In examining the problems of coordination, it may be useful to set our discussion within the market terminology of a supply system of social service agencies and a demand system of consumers or recipients of services—that is, a social service delivery system. This analogy should not be pressed too far, however, for many services do not follow a demand pattern and are imposed on individuals regardless of their preferences, as in the case of programs for delinquents or the mentally ill. Use of the term "service" minimizes the function of welfare as an instrument of community protection. Furthermore, "consumer demand" is too global a term, for it masks one of the most interesting characteristics of the delivery system: that the recipients of social services can themselves be classified, according to the agency which distributes the services, as clients, patients, customers, victims, or deviates. These labels also sort professional dispensers into a status hierarchy and thus can affect the quality and the nature of the treatment that individuals in similar circumstances will receive. Moreover, many services function not only as devices for meeting demand but also as rationing systems designed to limit either the volume or the quality and extensiveness of the service that each person receives. Services may ration scarce resources in terms of money, facilities, or professional skill. Despite these limitations, the above analogy is nevertheless useful because it permits us to classify coordinative problems as types of disjunctures between the supply and the demand system. Within this frame of reference, six "delivery problems" will be examined.

Service Inundation

The same client is often known to many community services, each of which may send a worker into the home of the family and may hold out to the family a set of expectations for desired social performance and exert sanctions for nonconformity. In the United States in the late 1940s, Bradley Buell's studies of "problem families" (Buell et al. 1952) directed attention to the issue of service inundation. He suggested that 6 per cent of the families in St. Louis were receiving more than half of the services offered by the community. However, in Buell's studies the term "services" was never adequately defined, for it included long-range continuing contact with the agency, as well as brief contact only at the point of intake. This ambiguity in the definition of services and the absence of data on types of services used make it plausible to suggest that Buell's findings can be restated as follows. A small proportion of families make contact with many agencies, most of which refer the family to other agencies, instead of offering them quality services. Thus families in need bounce from agency to agency, with no one assuming responsibility and accountability for them; the experience of these "multiagency families" reflects as much the fragmentation of the social service system as the pathology of the families. This fragmentation of services became the subject of debate within the social work profession in the early 1960s, and attention shifted from the problem of how the lack of coordination leads to clients becoming "overserviced" to how the same lack created the problem of clients who were "underserviced," or rejected and unwanted.

Strategies to reduce "inundation" appear to be concerned with rationalizing the function of the professional agents and with developing coordination through a more coherent personnel policy. Planning is thus directed chiefly at substituting simultaneous visiting for serial visiting and at cutting down duplication of effort by workers located in different social agencies who perform similar or related tasks (for example, when each agency secures its own family history to determine eligibility for a specific service, although one history could serve the needs of most agencies).

Two broad strategies for minimizing inundation can be identified—reducing the number of workers who visit the same family, or enhancing the communication among workers. The Service of Coordination in Paris pushes the first principle to its logical extreme. It achieves coordination by three simple but radical principles: only one social worker is assigned to a given family; each worker is responsible for all families in a defined geographic area; and no work is done twice (Schorr 1965*b*, p. 38). Thus, if a family caseworker believes that a family is in need of a supplementary financial allowance, she can secure the additional grant without a second investigation by a welfare worker. In 1967, the feasibility of reorganizing personal social services was being discussed in England by the Seebohm Committee. The changes most frequently discussed seemed to require combining the various separate departments and services into one ministry of social welfare, with status equal to that held by the existing ministries of education and health. This new ministry, or department, was to be organized on the basis of the skill to be performed, and was to be founded on the principle of merger rather than of coordination, so that the independence of established agencies could be respected. Exactly how the boundaries of such a welfare service might be drawn and which functions were to be included had not yet been agreed upon. However, it was thought that such a department would probably service other major departments by allotting social workers to courts, schools, hospitals, clinics, welfare departments, and other such agencies. One of the major purposes of this reform was seen as the coordination of scarce manpower skills (Titmuss 1966; Great Britain . . . 1966).

In the United States, numerous attempts at experimenting with similar programs can be identified. For example, under the auspices of the New York City Youth Board an attempt has been made to create an interdepartmental neighborhood service center. The organizing principle of this service, as described by its director, is the assumption by one worker of responsible concern for the total family (Lampkin 1961, p. 8). Most such efforts have succumbed under the pressure of established institutions after having survived, with little success, for only short periods.

Somewhat less radical than such administrative surgery are strategies that attempt coordination through increased communication. The social service exchange is an example of an attempt to create a central repository of information. Such exchanges operate under the assumption that if workers could identify the other community agencies that have contact with their clients, they would, in fact, contact them and work out some formal or informal coordination. When many voluntary agencies were distributing money rather than services, this seemed an efficient way of preventing the same person from securing aid twice. Case conferences provide another example of an organized structure whereby many workers from different agencies have an opportunity to meet to discuss their contacts with the same families. Often such conferences lead to a decision that one worker should assume responsibility for maintaining the ongoing contact with a family and so be able to keep the other agencies informed of the family's progress. (For a detailed case study of the inundation problem and the strategies used by community agencies to reduce it, see Willson 1961.)

These strategies seem to emphasize cooperation of workers rather than coordination of services. A major difficulty with these strategies is that many agencies that have significant contact with the family refuse, or are unwilling, to participate in joint deliberations or in the common sharing of staff. Nevertheless, the search for a polyvalent social worker continues as one strategy for reducing the inundation that specialization seems to create.

Problems of Access and Procurement

Whereas inundation involves multiple contacts by many agencies with the same family, the problem of access concerns the obverse problem of how to secure needed services within a highly fragmented and specialized service system, in which each agency defines its own service boundaries. When a family needs a nursing home service for an aged member, remedial services for a child having difficulty with reading, or a summer camp, it is likely to encounter the problem of access. In the situation where the consumers initiate the requests for these services, the social service delivery system comes closest to the demand situation of the market system; this is most likely to occur in cases where the recipients can be classified as customers, clients, or patients rather than victims and deviates. Access problems are exacerbated when a family has little income to purchase these services and must rely on the nonmarket system of public and voluntary social services.

Three broad strategies to facilitate access can be seen. Some coordinative strategies focus on an effort to educate the client, thus assuming that lack of access is a function of lack of information. Typically, they rely on devices such as information and referral services to inform consumers as to where available services can be secured. Scattered evidence shows that "arrival" rates from these referral services tend to be quite low (Furman et al. 1965). Such findings suggest the need for supplementary approaches.

A second approach is based on the assumption that although information is necessary, it is insufficient. According to this view, the referring agent must himself play a more active role as negotiator of the service jungle on behalf of the service conice that is requested. Some experimentation with knowledge of how the system works and with some power to accomplish his special aims. The political ward leader is a prototype of this kind of expediting agent, for he is often willing and able to apply pressure on appropriate agencies and to follow through to assure that his client receives the service that is requested. Some experimentation with indigenous workers serving as expediters has attempted to follow what is at least implicitly a similar model (Brager 1965).

A third strategy attempts to assure access by altering the structure in which social services are performed. In the United States, a new federal program providing neighborhood service stations, financed under the Community Action Program of the Economic Opportunity Act of 1964, has tried to create a new structure within the local community, in which many community agencies establish branch offices in the same facility. Thus a welfare department, an employment referral agency, a family guidance program, etc., will all locate their services in a single structure, providing something like a social service variety store, in which a range of services are available under a single roof. Ideally, a single intake worker is available to route the client to the appropriate service. This strategy is a form of coordination by physical propinquity; a client need only stop in one center to secure the necessary range of services he requires.

These coordinative strategies typically suffer from what has been called the problem of "green tape": where the total volume of services in a community remains constant, the strategy may only alter the pattern of claims (Rein & Riessman 1966). That is, it may provide preferential treatment for its constituency at the cost of assuring that some other individuals will not be able to secure access to these services.

Access for Community Agencies

The problem of access must be seen not only in terms of the desire for citizens to secure services but also in terms of the need of agencies to secure social services on behalf of their clientele, especially those who are victims and deviates. Community agencies that service an unwanted or unpopular population meet the problem of access when they try to secure for them the services they need. Such agencies find that in order to carry out their mission they require the cooperation of other community agencies. Thus a public welfare department must secure the cooperation of family counseling, employment, and health services in order to implement the national policy of reducing dependency. Similarly, a redevelopment agency involved in the problem of the physical renewal of the city may need a range of community services in order to make possible the relocation of difficult-to-place tenants, such as those with very large families or with special problems.

When an agency tries to secure different types of services on behalf of its clientele, these efforts may be labeled as "comprehensive planning." However, comprehensiveness is often the last stage in a series of earlier efforts to solve the problem of access. The agency may start first by referring its clientele to other community agencies; but if the referral process fails, it may find itself impelled to undertake these tasks in its own operation. Thus a settlement house may create a psychiatric clinic, a health service, or a remedial reading program. If funds are available, the agency may purchase the service from established community agencies, or alternatively, it may finance programs intramurally.

Occasionally, new structures are created to provide or facilitate services for an unwanted population. Thus the comprehensive planning financed in the United States under the Juvenile Delinquency and Youth Offenses Control Act of 1961 was oriented to securing relevant services on behalf of those who are in danger of becoming delinquent—that is, disadvantaged youths living in urban ghettos. In this context, the term "comprehensiveness" is best interpreted as the effort to get community agencies to provide services on behalf of the population of disadvantaged youths. Similarly, the 1962 amendments to the U.S. Social Security Act encouraged the creation of services for the underserviced population receiving public assistance. Planning for access could involve purchasing the needed services from established agencies. However, because resources are limited, such planning often relies on the use of small-scale demonstration projects, in the hope that the agency in which the demonstrations are placed will come, in time, to adopt the reforms it has started. Alternatively, it can work outside of established institutions (parallelism), or it can operate the services directly. All approaches have been used.

A major problem created by comprehensive planning is that it leads, in the short run, to competition for resources, as each community agency tries to provide the relevant services for a specialized population at risk— victims of relocation, the poor, disadvantaged youths, public assistance recipients, the mentally ill, etc. Without a major increase in the total amount of resources available, these agencies may find themselves in competition for limited personnel and facilities.

Resource Competition

One way of defining coordination is to say that it ensures that a varied range of services, frequently technically different or separately administered, are planned so as to operate as interrelated parts of a total treatment process in meeting family need or in remedying breakdown. It is surprising how little theorizing has been done about the kind of program scheduling that is necessary to contribute to meeting family need and to preventing social problems. Most sociological thought and research has tended to fragment the individual between the worlds of work, school, family relationships, community, and peer relationships. But much less work has been done on how the scheduling of events in these various worlds affects the capacity of an individual to function in one or another of them. Thus what is obscure in this approach to coordination is the failure to specify how varied services are or ought to be linked if they are to meet need or remedy personal and social breakdown. Without some scheme for ranking the relative importance of needs or problems, and without some procedure for determining the priorities to be allotted to various services, the task of integrative planning must proceed without benefit of theory and thus without benefit of any rules for reducing competition among claimants for scarce resources. Moreover, in the social services there is no theoretical analogy to the general medical practitioner who treats the "whole" person, exploiting the skills of specialists but retaining accountability for the total condition of the patient. While many professionals claim unique competence to manage the task of central coordination of social services, none have been assigned to fill this role. Thus to talk of "human need" or the "whole person" obscures the dilemma of choice confronted in developing strategies of coordination.

Clearly, what is needed is a system of priorities for allotting resources that is based on function, age, social problem, etc. Although we lack the means for resolving the value and jurisdictional issues of resource competition, we do have planning instruments that can either formally or informally perform the function of arbitrator and coordinator of competing requests for service. The U.S. Bureau of the Budget at the federal level is, of course, one case-in-point. Acting as the planning arm of the executive branch, it frequently interferes with the operation of specialized departments, encouraging them to cooperate and to avoid duplication of effort. But in the end the final allocative decisions are made in Congress through what is essentially a political process.

The Problem of Discontinuity

Social service can become disjointed or discontinuous if there is a failure to provide component services that are necessary to complete the cycle of change. This situation arises when programs assume coherence only when they are linked with other activities. An obvious case is that of job training, which includes the tasks of recruiting, screening, training, and placement. Unless these components relate to each other, the program lacks coherence. In practice, we often create separate agencies to carry out these specialized functions. Consider the case of manpower training for disadvantaged youths in the United States. The screening and recruiting tasks are, in part, the function of a community action program; a pre-skills training program (training-for-employability) might be carried out by the Neighborhood Youth Corps program or the Conservation Job Corps; the actual training task is often done by a program administered under either the Manpower Development and Training Act or the Urban Job Corps; and, finally, the job placement of graduates of the training program may be administered by the state employment office which, in turn, carries the dual responsibility of job placement and job development.

Problems of discontinuity can arise at any point where there is an inter-ruption in the flow of the person through the total system, starting with recruitment and ending with placement. One of the typical bottlenecks has been the transition from pretraining into training programs because of the lack of training facilities; and another has been the transition from training into job placement, often because of the failure of placement agencies to pay sufficient attention to the problems of job development.

Examples of discontinuity can be found in the flow of patients through a mental hospital program. Continuity of care is defined by Schwartz as "plan-ning of a patient's treatment so that the help given at any point is part of a total program. . . . A number of programs for in-patients, out-patients, and ex-patients have continuity of care as a goal, though phases of treatment are administered by separate agencies. It is rare for a single program to encompass all phases of a mental hospital patient's career" (Schwartz et al. 1964, p. 257). Continuity of care is indeed a crucial issue, since psychiatrists acknowledge that a patient's release from a mental hospital does not neces-sarily mean that he is cured. Thus post-hospitalization activities can be legitimately defined as parts of treatment. Indeed, the theory of community psychiatry rests on such assumptions.

Strategies to reduce discontinuity seek to maximize coherence among specialized agencies that perform part of what is, in effect, a single task. It should be noted that the goal of "coherence," which means the provision of closely related services, contrasts with "comprehensiveness," which em-phasizes the provision of a range of different services. In examining strategies to reduce discontinuity it is useful to specify at least three interrelated tasks: service entry; training or treatment; and reabsorption or placement. What-ever the ideals, planning for continuity tends, in practice, to focus on either the entry or the absorption problem. Thus job training programs for dis-advantaged youths emphasize recruitment, largely because training and placement opportunities have been limited. On the other hand, planning for mental health or the reduction of delinquency directs attention to the prob-lem of absorption, largely because of the concern about high recidivist rates.

The increased concern for community care, or outpatient treatment, makes the problem of absorption quite crucial for hospital and correctional in-stitutions. Ideally, the goal is to provide the full range of services. In the United States the Community Mental Health Facilities Act of 1964 has attempted to initiate planning that focuses on the creation of structures which can process individuals from diagnosis, through treatment, to rehabili-tation, and back to treatment institutions if necessary. They have encouraged the erection, where appropriate, of a single facility that offers inpatient, outpatient, and aftercare programs.

Planning for continuity can, however, create problems of duplication and fragmentation. Consider the following case-in-point. The U.S. Job Corps had, by the summer of 1966, encountered a projected average annual cost per person enrolled of about $7,500, and another $600 per person enrolled when the capital costs were taken into account. In order to protect this investment, it was considered necessary to create special placement counselors who would assist the graduates of the program in securing jobs. The Bureau of the Budget questioned whether these placement counselors should be assigned to the Job Corps or to the state employment service, and it was eventually agreed that they would be placed in the Employment Service but that the counselors would give priority to the graduates of the Job Corps.

Entitlement and Protection

One of the more intractable problems of delivering services rendered by bureaucratic agencies to clients is that of ensuring that clients receive the services that they are entitled to, and a related problem is that of protecting clients from unfair practices of the institutions which are designed to serve them. The entitlement question arises when individuals are denied services because of decisions that are based upon the judgment or discretion of the professionals who operate the services. For example, some potential clients are denied public assistance payments because they are judged to be "ineligible." The definition of eligibility is typically subject to a variety of interpretations.

The problem of protection arises when bureaucracies either abuse their power or carry out their mission in such a fashion as to inadvertently create difficulties. For example, many school systems have developed ability groupings, or a "track system," that sort individual pupils into four tracks—honors, college preparation, regular, and basic. The so-called basic track is designed for those individuals who have subnormal intelligence and a demonstrated incapacity to perform intellectual tasks. A recent restudy of 1,273 youths assigned to the basic track in Washington, D.C., revealed that 886 youngsters were placed in the wrong track; that is, they were found to be capable of doing "regular" work (Hechinger 1965).

A great deal of interest has been shown in creating instruments for assuring entitlement and consumer protection. I have defined these as coordinative strategies because they attempt to coordinate the preferences and rights of clients with the performance of institutions. For example, in the United States there has been some discussion about the feasibility of employing an ombudsman, who would act as an impartial agent to receive complaints made by clients against the service bureaucracies. Neighborhood legal services sponsored by the U.S. antipoverty program have broadened the definition of legal services for the poor so as to include not only protection in criminal cases but also protection from the operations of service agencies. For example, in New York City the Mobilization for Youth agency has developed a vigorous program that provides legal counsel for public assistance clients who have been designated as ineligible because of residence requirements; all of the cases that have been brought to court with the aid of this program were finally judged to be eligible for assistance.

Planning Structures

Coordinative planning requires a planning structure that can collect and organize the resources of various agencies to solve the many delivery problems. However, most planning structures have a common constraint, in that they cannot reduce the autonomy of community agencies, nor can they control the base budgets of agencies, although they can supplement these budgets as an incentive for cooperation. For example, the antipoverty program in the United States has created new community centers for comprehensive planning (community action agencies). These centers will function as funnels for federal funds that are now being made available directly to localities, as contrasted with the earlier pattern of grants-in-aid that were allocated through the states. However, the question of the appropriate structure for these new coordinative planning instruments remains highly controversial. Thus important policy issues have emerged in connection with several problems, which can be briefly summarized as follows: how to create a viable structure that can overcome the jurisdictional problems which arise in forging a coalition of established but autonomous service institutions; how to promote radical democracy which respects the preferences of service consumers; and how to create rational problem solving based upon research and planning. Moreover, when these three elements are combined, they tend to conflict. Most planning structures struggle only with the effort to reconcile the clash between established power and rational knowledge, since the consumer of the service is seldom formally involved in planning at the policy level. In contrast, these new community action programs are confronted with all three problems, but especially with the conflict between the established institutions and the consumers of social services (Marris & Rein 1967).

BIBLIOGRAPHY

Abel-Smith, Brian 1958 "Whose Welfare State?" in Norman I MacKenzie, ed., *Conviction*. London: MacGibbon & Kee, pp. 55–73.

Brager, George 1965 "The Indigenous Worker: A New Approach to the Social Work Technician," *Social Work*, 10, 2, 33–40.

Buell, Bradley, *et al.* 1952 *Community Planning for Human Services*. New York: Columbia Univ. Press.

Burns, Eveline M. 1954 "The Financing of Social Welfare," in Cora Kasius, ed., *New Directions in Social Work*. New York: Harper, pp. 131–158.

Donnison, David V. 1962 *The Development of Social Administration*. London: Bell.

Donnison, David V.   1966 "Social Work and Social Change," *British Journal of Psychiatric Social Work,* 8, 4, 3–9.

Furman, Sylvan S., *et al.*   1965   "Social Class Factors in the Flow of Children to Outpatient Psychiatric Facilities," *American Journal of Public Health,* 55, 385–392.

Great Britain, Scottish Education Department   1966   *Social Work and the Community: Proposals for Reorganizing Local Authority Services in Scotland.* Papers by Command, Cmnd. 3065. London: H.M. Stationery Office.

Hechinger, F. M.   1965   Tracking—Useful If Not Overdone. *New York Times,* Dec. 19, sec. IV, col. 1, p. 7.

Jencks, Christopher   1966   "Is the Public School Obsolete?" *Public Interest,* No. 2, pp. 18–27.

Lampkin, Lillian C.   1961   "Helping the Multi-problem Family Through Coordination of Services." Paper delivered at the Eastern Regional Conference of the Child Welfare League. Unpublished manuscript.

Lampman, Robert J.   1966   "How Much Does the American System of Transfers Benefit the Poor?" in Leonard H. Goodman, *Economic Progress and Social Welfare.* New York: Columbia University Press, pp. 125–157.

Levine, Abraham S.   1966   "Cost-Benefit Analysis and Social Welfare: An Exploration of Possible Applications," *Welfare in Review,* 4, 2, 1–11.

Levitan, Sar A.   1966   "Washington Notes," *Poverty and Human Resources Abstracts,* 1, 4, 17–20.

Marris, Peter, and Rein, Martin   1967   *Dilemmas of Social Reform: Poverty and Community Action in the United States.* New York: Atherton Press.

Merriam, Ida C.   1965   "Social Welfare Expenditures: 1964–1965," *Social Security Bulletin,* 28, 10, 3–16.

Mushkin, Selma J.   1962   "Health as an Investment," *Journal of Political Economy,* 70 (Supplement), 129–157.

Rein, Martin, and Riessman, Frank   1966   "A Strategy for Anti Poverty Community Action Programs," *Social Work* 11, 2, 3–12.

Schorr, Alvin L.   1965*a*   "National Community and Housing Policy," *Social Service Review* 39, 433–443.

Schorr, Alvin L.   1965*b*   *Social Security and Social Services in France.* U.S. Social Security Administration, Division of Research and Statistics, Research Report No. 7. Washington, D.C.: Government Printing Office.

Schultz, Theodore W.   1962   "Reflections on Investment in Man," *Journal of Political Economy,* 70 (Supplement), 1–8.

Schwartz, Morris S., *et al.*   1964   *Social Approaches to Mental Patient Care.* New York: Columbia University Press.

Titmuss, Richard M.   (1956) 1959   *Essays on the Welfare State.* New Haven: Yale Univ. Press. See especially "The Social Division of Welfare: Some Reflections on the Search for Equity," pp. 34–55.

Titmuss, Richard M.   1965   "The Role of Redistribution in Social Policy," *Social Security Bulletin,* 28, 6, 14–20.

Titmuss, Richard M.   1966   "Social Work and Social Service: A Challenge for Local Government," *Journal of the Royal Society of Health,* 86, 19–21, 32.

Titmuss, Richard M., and Abel-Smith, Brian   1961   *Social Policies and the Popula-*

tion Growth in Mauritius: Report to the Governor of Mauritius. London: Methuen.

United Nations, Economic and Social Council, Social Commission 1965 *Methods of Determining Social Allocation: Report of the Secretary General* . . . E/CN.5/ 387. New York: United Nations.

Vidich, Arthur 1963 "Analysis of Philanthropic Institutions and Psychology." Unpublished manuscript, prepared for a seminar on American Philanthropy, Brandeis University.

Willson, F. M. G. 1961 *Administrators in Action: British Case Studies.* Vol. 1. London: Allen & Unwin. See especially "The Administrative Consequences of Jim and Vera Fardell," pp. 279–345.

Wilson, James Q. 1963 "Planning and Politics: Citizen Participation in Urban Renewal," *Journal of the American Institute of Planners,* 29, 242–249.

Part II

Contradictions and Failures of the Social Services

Chapter 3

The Social Service Crisis

The purpose of this essay is to identify some of the problems in the organization of the local social service network and to comment on some of the defects in the present efforts to reorganize these services. *Local services* refers to the local setting where services are delivered by social service organizations to the consuming public, recognizing of course that local organizations increasingly have their source of authority and funding based in non-local systems. *Social services* refers to collective interventions which are outside the market place to meet the needs of individuals as well as to serve the corporate interests of the wider community. The activities of physicians, teachers, social workers, as well as other helping professions, are considered as social services.

The term *network* is used to designate this illusive and complex abstraction—the interaction of social service organizations. This term is unfortunate since it suggests a symmetrical web of interlaced strands designed to catch and to hold. In practice, services when taken as a whole may more typically be asymmetrical with gaps and discontinuities leading to the loss of those individuals which the net should hold. Nevertheless, the term can

Reprinted with permission of the publisher from *Trans-action*, May, 1964. This is a revision of a paper read at the Annual Meeting of the American Public Health Association, November 1963. I have benefited from the comments and criticisms of many people. I am especially indebted to Richard Titmuss for many unacknowledged insights into the operation of the service network.

be used to describe how a variety of community agencies, each performing different functions such as control, socialization, guidance, accommodation to and prevention of dependency and ill health, share either potentially, concurrently, or serially the same population.[1] Within the over-all network there are, of course, many subclusters of agencies organized to fulfill the various functions listed above. Boundaries among these agencies are constantly shifting and changing, as new agencies are formed and old ones merge. (The "death rate" of such organizations is believed to be quite low.)

The service network is various, complex, and contradictory. It is most difficult to make general statements about its operation without a long list of qualifications. What follows is intended as a series of suggestive hypotheses aimed somewhat one-sidedly at crystallizing problems, paradoxes, and contradictions. This is an unbalanced review of network characteristics, since achievements are largely disregarded.

CONFLICTING PERSPECTIVES

Perhaps the most salient characteristic of the organization of local services is that each agency performs a rather highly specialized function consistent with its own definition of its mission. There is, therefore, insufficient integration and, in fact, some conflict among the aims of the various agencies. It has long been recognized that the specialization of agencies increases the possibility that an individual with difficulty will fall into no agency's definition of its services. But less attention has been paid to the difficulties that arise when the same person is simultaneously or serially known to a net of local and non-local agencies each of which has different sets of values and goals. One consequence of this conflict is that some agencies within the network may act so as to negate the work of other agencies. This was dramatically illustrated by my study of protective services in one community. One agency, The Society for the Prevention of Cruelty to Children (SPCC), sharply reduced the percentage of cases it referred to the courts, but because other agencies (the police in particular) continued to rely on the courts as the appropriate agency for handling neglectful parents, this decrease in the percentage of court referrals by SPCC was accompanied by a proportionate increase in court referrals by other agencies. Thus, SPCC's change in policy had no effect on the eventual treatment handed out to children in its care. It is clear that one agency alone cannot really bring about change, since another agency may change in compensating ways, netting a zero in terms of effect on the community.[2]

The dispensers of the service define an individual's problems, the services he requires, and the appropriate moral attitude that should be taken in his situation. These decisions are made largely on the basis of the agency's function. Some evidence to support this generalization derives from the work of Scott Briar who has shown that in the field of child welfare, regardless of professional competence, an agency is biased in favor of offering its own services rather than referring its cases to other community agencies.[3] Experienced practitioners report similar observations. A fatherless family is likely to receive financial assistance if the mother applies to a public welfare department and substitute child care if she requests help from a child welfare agency.[4]

Even in a situation where agencies operate as gatekeepers and are expected to cooperate closely to achieve a common aim, differences among them in values and ideology persist. Stanton Wheeler reports significant value differences between the police and the juvenile aid officers, the judge and the probation officer, the social workers and the psychiatrists.[5] Barbara Wootton colorfully describes the confusion a child experiences when he is exposed simultaneously to the conflicting values of authoritarianism and permissiveness held by personnel employed by the school and by the child guidance clinic.[6] In our study of protective services, we found that agencies differ in the stress they place on parental accountability, long-range treatment, and the goal of intervention—the rescue of the child or the treatment of the mother. One consequence which arises from these functional and jurisdictional conflicts is that the resolution of differences is frequently not made with reference to the optimal situation from the recipient's point of view, but rather on the basis of the power and tradition of the agencies. Of course, not all differences get settled. Ultimately, as J. H. Robb incisively suggests in his provocative article, it is the individual himself who must reconcile these conflicting perspectives, although the process by which some aid is accepted while other aid is rejected is not well understood.[7]

In the end we must conclude that agencies do what they want to do within the limits of the resources which they command. Efforts to coordinate their work by the voluntary autonomous agencies do not have a distinguished history of success. D. Donnison has aptly described the situation in his study of a small Canadian community. He notes that the projects of voluntary service organizations "arise from a wish to serve, rather than from a problem to be solved."[8] Favored projects are those which lend prestige to the sponsoring group, attract public support, and avoid controversial issues. We are thus confronted with a paradox. We may assume that the public interest is best served by the efforts of autonomous organizations to maintain and enhance their positions within the service network. This situation is comparable to Dr. Mandeville's famous doggerels about the community of bees which prospered because each bee pursued its own independent task often with vanity and envy, vice and waste. More recently Kenneth Arrow has shown that it is logically impossible to promote the corporate good while maximizing the choices of individual actors. This conclusion suggests that if choices must be made in order to pursue the community good, the autonomy of individual agencies must be limited. But who shall define the community good?

COMPETING VIEWS OF THE SERVICE NETWORK

If we define the service network broadly to include the diversity of inter-related functions, it is possible to identify from the vantage point of different service dispensers four views of the service network: supply and demand, assistance in self-actualization, reclamation of the helpless, and promotion of conformity or adjustment.

The network may be viewed as a production-delivery system where *customers* purchase a product which is dispensed by a professional acting as a salesman or an intermediary. Recreation and group work services on all income levels may take on this character. Here some modified form of the law of supply and demand operates. Much of the publicity of these agencies is directed at recruiting customers although the expenditures incurred are likely to be budgeted as "community education." By contrast, the service network may be seen as a helping process aimed chiefly at the malfunction-ing individual. Recipients of the services are defined chiefly as *clients* or *patients* in accordance with the training of the helping professional. The service dispenser views himself as a therapist or at least takes psychiatry as his professional role model; he sees himself as providing some form of assistance in self-actualization. Alternatively, the service network might be viewed chiefly in humanitarian terms where the commitment is to the concept of personal care. The professional perceives his function as that of a caretaker (to use Erich Lindemann's term) committed to serving a helpless and deprived population. He enables the service recipient, in this case the *victim,* to win access to the social institutions which heretofore were inac-cessible to him. The organizational professional functions to mobilize and to organize certain specialized concrete services on behalf of the deprived. Finally the network may be seen largely in terms of social control—to bring the *deviant,* that is he who has broken moral and legal codes of behavior, to adopt more conforming behavior. This process of trying to encourage non-conformists to act like all others occurs within the context of a broader community which at least overtly espouses behavioral pluralism. Control agents are often unclear where deviancy begins and alternative cultural forms of behavior end—are households which are headed by females, broken homes? Does the term parental neglect refer to an acceptable pat-tern for rearing children among lower class families?

Thus the recipients of services may be defined as customers, clients or patients, victims or deviants. Services may in turn either be sold, offered, provided as rights, or imposed as obligations. Let us briefly further compare the concept of client with other possible definitions of the populations of individuals who receive services. A professional providing service to a client defines the illness of the person largely in personal terms, whereas the problems of victims are largely environmental. The professional is committed to aiding the individual who seeks help while the interests of the community are secondary. For example, the doctor and the lawyer have privileged communication with their clients. By contrast, the privileged communication of the social worker working with deviants as in the case of anti-social gangs is less clear, because community interest plays a central role. Finally, clients are different than customers because the professional is expected to know more about the individual's illness than the individual himself does, and the principle of caveat emptor is an abuse of professional obligation.

As various service dispensers seek to enhance their professional standing they attempt to redefine the population they service as clients, or to exclude non-clients (those who have little chance to become clients). Recipients of a service help to define the status of the dispenser. So too, does the nature of the service rendered. Those who service "clients" and provide therapy (especially modifying therapy rather than supportive therapy which takes on some of the character of care) enjoy the greatest professional prestige, while those who provide care to "victims" have the lowest prestige, and are even subjected to periodic public censure since it is sometimes assumed that the status of the victim derives from the treatment of the professional. Wootton observes that this practice is part of a much broader trend in contemporary society. "Over large areas the psychiatrist, along with psychiatrically-oriented satellites, has now usurped the place once occupied by the social reformer and the administrator, if not indeed the judge."[9] Yet one important latent function of defining social problems as personal illnesses is to convert the open value conflicts among different professional groups into a milder form of antagonistic cooperation. Each dispenser seeks to strengthen his bid for professional status by providing some form of therapeutic service. Thus professionals employ common terms of reference and are engaged in common search for the services of psychiatrists. Elaine Cumming's study of the police provides evidence for the extent to which therapy has even invaded the province of social control.[10]

One disadvantage of this process deserves comment. The notions of care and control imply a more corporate concept of community interests than do those of sales and therapy. When an individual is defined as in need of care and control there is the implication that some one group in society understands what is in his best interest. By contrast, clients and customers are more capable of acting in their own best interest. As all practice comes to be dominated by the model of professional practice based on the concept of clients and customers, with the goal of self-actualization through the purchase of service, care and control become less valued as activities worthy of professional pursuit. As a result professionals often shun working in welfare departments and correctional institutions, or once placed in these settings may define the social problems of dependency and delinquency in personal terms, at times neglecting the need for intervention at the environmental level. There is also danger that inappropriate services will be offered as professionals seek to develop a posture which reflects the hierarchy of professional values rather than individual needs. Many clinical practitioners, for example, have rejected the provision of concrete services in favor of counseling and long-range treatment.

By extending the concept of the population of recipients of service beyond the traditional definition of client, we can consider how individuals with similar problems encounter different fates not so much in accordance with their own problems as with the service dispenser's definition of them as customers, clients, victims, or deviants. As already suggested in the discussion of conflicting perspectives, the recipient of a service is exposed to differing images of himself, different definitions of his problem, different degrees of stigma, and also different kinds of treatment as he engages professionals representing one or another of these views. In an effort to understand some of the implications of these different perspectives let us consider three situations—in which deviants are classified as victims, clients as victims, or customers as clients.

The dominant view among many practitioners is that illegitimate births are a response to internal psychological conflicts—the reaffirmation of femininity, hostility to parental figures, and so forth. Consequently, the mother should be defined as a client. Some form of counseling service seems indicated in order to provide the client with support or insight so as to reverse the pathology or to redirect its expression into more acceptable forms of behavior. When viewed in moral terms, the mother is likely to be defined as a deviant. Punishment and deterrence become the major objectives of the action taken by control agents. Illustrative are the efforts to abolish welfare payments to mothers who continue to give birth to illegitimate children or to maintain benefit levels at only a fraction of accepted minimum standards. Illegitimacy may also be viewed as a product of social and economic inequalities in our society, a position which finds support in many studies. For example, Raymond T. Smith has shown that in the Caribbean, when economic stability is available to the Negro family, male desertion rates are low, family stability is enhanced, and illegitimacy is decreased.[11] When guided by this perspective the mother is more likely to be defined as a victim; the major concern is the provision of concrete services which will reduce inequalities and expand opportunity. In a confidence game in order to insure that "the mark," the victim of the game who may have been sold the Brooklyn Bridge, does not call the police, someone is left behind to help the mark work out his feeling of victimization. In a similar manner, social work appears at times to perform a similar function of inhibiting outrage and protest. Inappropriately defining the victim as a client may have the unanticipated consequence of "cooling the mark out," and one logical means to avoid this is to develop a program to transform victims to citizens is recommended.

Premarital sexual behavior may be defined as typical behavior (in approximately 12 percent of marriages in the United States, the woman is pregnant at marriage—the true incidence of premarital sexual experience is undoubtedly substantially higher); sexual behavior can be maintained and illegitimacy avoided by the purchase of services as a customer. These services may be preventive as in the case of the purchase of contraceptives, or remedial, as in the case of abortion.

It must be recognized that recipients do not always accept the label given to them by the helping professional. There often are situations where the service recipient defines himself differently than does the service dispenser. For example, individuals who make use of group work services may define themselves as customers, while the professional is likely to define them as clients. As customers they expect different treatment by the professional and greater flexibility in the use of the organization's services. After a teenage dance in a community center, the professional may stress the advantages in having the youngsters clean up because this will help to teach them responsibility. As customers, the teenagers may prefer to hire a janitor or they may expect the agency to provide this service as part of their membership dues. In such cases there can be open resentment about the professional's view of them.

The decision regarding the appropriate label to be given a service recipient is sometimes a political one. Is public assistance a form of public subsidization of low wages in an economy whose labor force is in transition and unable to generate sufficient jobs to keep all employed? Or shall the welfare recipients be defined as individuals with low intelligence and low motivation—personal defects rather than environmental defects? The issue is whether welfare recipients are to be seen as victims in need of social justice, deviants in need of punishment, or clients in need of rehabilitation.

THE NEGLECT OF THOSE IN GREATEST NEED

The service network is so organized that many in extreme need, particularly the poor, cannot find their way to it. If they do find their way to it, they often cannot meet the definitions of eligibility, or should they meet the definitions of eligibility, they may encounter disparities between their conception of their problems and that of the professional. The services originally designed to act as a mirror of community need act instead as a barrier, excluding those most in need of amenities, adjustment, care, and control.

In a searching and provocative analysis Richard A. Cloward describes the many ways the poor are disengaged from the local service network. His description of how private agencies pass on their "rejects" to public agencies is worth quoting.

> Thus private residential treatment institutions for juvenile delinquents, having made errors in intake, "pass on" their difficult cases to the public training schools; settlements and community agencies arrange to have the more difficult juvenile gangs worked with by public detached street workers; family agencies abandon so-called multi-problem families to departments of public welfare; private hospitals shrug off the chronically ill patient to the back wards of publicly supported custodial hospitals.[12]

A recent national study of the characteristics of applicants of family agencies provides statistical documentation of the processes by which some private casework agencies come to disengage themselves from the poor.[13] Evidence is offered for what Cloward calls "planned disengagement." The study notes: "The proportion of cases closing on a planned basis at the end of the first intake interview increases rapidly as social class declines." Evidence for planned disengagement is found in cases which go beyond the first interview. "Closings at worker initiative (this consists mainly of cases closed because the worker believes that modification will be unlikely), while unusual at any level, were more than twice as frequent at the lowest (social class) level than at any other." A form of planned disengagement also takes place as a result of the ". . . marked differences between client expectations and the services actually provided . . ." To classify such cases as having "unrealistic expectations of the agency's services" overlooks the limited kinds of services provided by the agency, and how these often act to screen out the poor.

One factor that obscures the extent of the rejection is the manner in which agencies keep their statistics. The screening, sorting, and rejecting of potential recipients is redefined as a helping process. By the use of nominalistic magic, rejects are defined as "serviced in intake"—cases which are seen only once may be defined as unable to use professional services. These administrative devices serve to hide the process of rejection by preventing the comprehension of the total amount of true rejections (see note 1).

As Cloward is able to show, a very similar process goes on in many public agencies. He accurately concludes that there is "something in the nature of professional technology that exerts pressure for disengagement *whatever the setting.*" Agencies neglect to service those in greatest need because there is pressure for them to accept "good" clients who will deliver all the rewards that professionals and agencies are accustomed to or need. A "good" client is one who is cooperative, motivated to use the service offered, able to change, and eventually able to express gratitude rather than resentment for the services that are made available to him. In short, professionals understandably prefer cases with good prognosis rather than the so-called hopeless case. Certain cases, including certainly many who are extremely disadvantaged, are characterized as "multi-problemed," "chronic," and are considered virtually "unreachable." Such labels reflect better the operation of agencies than the characteristics of the clients. In our study of SPCC, we found that the more frequently a case was referred for help, the less likely it was to be accepted. There are, of course, many reasons for this rejection. Perhaps, especially important, is the professional's judgment that little can be done to aid the family and priority should be given to less "hopeless" cases. Yet, there are some agencies—all too few in number— which are especially directed at helping just this specific kind of group. Pavinstadt's psychiatric project in Roxbury, Massachusetts, is one example where a team of psychiatrists, social workers, psychologists, anthropologists, and others have joined forces to find new ways of working with the most helpless. In addition, there are many non-professional agencies such as the Salvation Army and the Volunteers of America which take as their main task the care of the discarded and ignored groups in society.

PROFESSIONAL RIGIDITIES

There is growth in the guild protective organizations of the professional who manages agencies within the service network. There is danger that professionals may become preoccupied with the search for satisfaction in their work and social prestige which they hope can eventually become con- verted to higher incomes. As indicated, this concern with professional "hedonism" is one important force contributing to the failure to serve those in greatest need. Professional guilds protect the interest of professionals in other ways as well. A continuing shortage of professionals is maintained by limiting the scope of training and by over-defining the competencies needed to perform work functions. When a group of individuals who perform a service band together to control the body of persons who may legitimately perform that service, there is a set of almost inevitable consequences. There is a sense of loyalty to the colleague group, a striving to raise the prestige and rewards of the group as a whole, a tendency to define and limit the service and the clients who may legitimately be served; a corollary is that ancillary professions develop to handle the "dirty work" of the profession.[14] The danger in this process is that the interests of the recipients of the serv- ice become subverted to serve the interests of the professional dispenser of the service. This has been well described by Richard M. Titmuss in an analysis of hospitals in Great Britain. He observes:

> Board of Governors and Management Committees devote more of their time to conditions of work, questions of rewards, difficulties of status and dissatisfaction

among the staff than they do to the needs of the patients . . . one of the new problems is the danger that the hospital may tend increasingly to be run in the interests of those working in and for the hospital rather than the interests of the patients.[15]

INDIVIDUALISTIC BIAS

Agencies within the network define problems chiefly in terms of individual wants and needs. "We prefer today to analyze the infected individual rather than to eliminate the infection from the environment."[16] Intervention is consequently directed at individual behavior, while intervention at the level of the social structure is largely neglected. The skill of the professional is accepted as the major plank in a program for the solution of social problems. As a result, when we encounter maladjustment, we propose individual therapy; when confronted with the expansion of delinquency, we recommend more probation officers; in recognizing problems of ill health, we call for increasing the supply of physicians. In the stress on the one-to-one relationship there is an assumption that the specialized competence of the professional enables him to cope with the problem through dealing *only* with the individual.

In the study of SPCC we encountered many strong opinions regarding the proper way to manage the neglectful parent. Moral and psychological judgments were widespread, but the social milieu in which the family lived was virtually ignored, as all agencies evaluated the family in isolation from its environment. Professional workers at SPCC did not have systematic information about the occupation of the family's head, the source of the family's income, and the extent of the integration of the family into the neighborhood. The professional strategy of dyadic intervention appears to screen out information about the environment. Thus, despite the agency's simultaneous commitment to therapy and to social action, information regarding the environmental conditions which could contribute to the social action aims of the organization was not systematically gathered. There appears to be great pressure to define problems as inhering in the individual apparently because professional intervention takes place at this level. Even in programs geared to reduce youth unemployment, the emphasis is on personal failings; programs for job development are usually in short supply.

It is certainly true that there are many situations where professional skill on a one-to-one treatment level is called for. Many of the cases known to family agencies and child-guidance clinics undoubtedly fall into this category. These entail the failure of the individual to function satisfactorily in a relatively good social situation. The problem here is the inappropriate use of the therapeutic method in situations which call for other means of intervention. There are social conditions which place the individual in situations of hardship that prevent him from functioning properly, and in the face of which he is helpless. Mass unemployment, for example, would create such a destructive environment, and would call for intervention at the level of the *social structure*.

An analogy may help sharpen the point. Therapeutically oriented professionals might observe a traffic jam and deduce that its cause is inherent in the nature of the individual automobile. Some are not powerful or maneuverable enough. They might consequently attempt to solve the problem of the jam by working on one automobile at a time, trying to increase its power or maneuverability. The problem, in reality, is one involving arrangement and organization where the relevant variables are traffic flow, number of open lanes, the maximum number of available automobiles, and not the condition of individual automobiles. Effective intervention in such a case can only take place by modifying the overall pattern. The basic assumption of the individual bias, on the other hand, is that if every individual would behave with the maximum utilization of his energies, everything else would take care of itself. Yet clearly more efficient automobiles will not solve traffic jams.

PRESSURES FOR REORGANIZATION

The growing criticism of professional and organizational rigidities of social welfare services may well be one of the important bench marks of the 1960s. We are all too familiar with the attacks from those who oppose welfare services, but these critics are sounding another kind of alarm. Today the call for an "agonizing reappraisal" of the adequacy of our present welfare efforts is coming from friends and colleagues who have come to recognize that dedication to welfare aims and criticism of established means are not antithetical. Consider the following brief list of critics: Conant on education;[17] Peterson on health;[18] Gouldner on social services;[19] Titmuss on poverty and dependency;[20] Morris on social welfare planning.[21] These critics are striking out at the most vulnerable points when they direct their criticisms to professional vested interests, the quality of professional services, organizational illusions and deceptions, inequalities, and paralysis of action. Conspicuously absent from this list is a probing criticism of the field of mental health. To date, the monographs produced by the Joint Commission on Mental Illness are an enormous disappointment, as Elaine Cumming has so convincingly argued in her review of the Commission's work.[22]

It is not surprising that pressure for innovation and change is initiated by outside groups. Historically, this has almost always been the case. For example, the public health movement was promoted largely by lay groups in the face of vigorous opposition by physicians. Similarly, the juvenile courts developed from the interests of groups outside the legal profession; in public welfare, the Charity Organization Society (the mainstay of social casework before the Depression) was opposed to pensions for widows and the aged in the early part of the twentieth century. The vested interests of philanthropic societies which operated charity schools were a significant barrier in the struggle to establish a tax supported education system. Today, innovation is being stimulated chiefly by organizations outside of the local service network: by the Ford Foundation, the National Health Agencies, the Federal Urban Renewal Program, the President's Committee on Juvenile Delinquency and Youth Crime, and by the recent federal grants made to states to develop statewide planning in mental health. Local planning centers have developed in response to the work of these various funding organizations.

THE CAUSES OF SERVICE DEFECTS

Regardless of where the impetus for change may arise, community action to overcome the defects in the organization of services is likely to be influenced by the assessment of the *causes* of these defects. Although distinctions in causes are not readily disentangled, what follows is an attempt to infer the broad principles which underlie present thinking.

Social service can be viewed paradoxically as the last bastion of entrepreneurialism—any group can start a welfare agency and then proceed to compete for funds, professional personnel, and clients; and nearly any agency can claim to coordinate the work of other community agencies. This system of private, autonomous agencies has been defined as the essence of voluntarism and has been defended as basic to our democratic institutions. These agencies operate, so to speak, within a free market, where the outputs of each producing unit (agency) are not fettered by formal controls. This independent spirit is nourished by the lack of a positive national goal for social welfare (comparable to the Employment Act of 1946), to which all community agencies would be expected to owe their allegiance and to lend their support.[23]

Some scholars perceive the defects in the organization of services as stemming from the process of institutionalization. Agencies once bold and venturesome come to be dominated by caution and timidity. They desire chiefly to survive and to conserve and protect their domains. Thus the social movements of yesteryear become the preserving institutions of today. This process contributes to the displacement of organizational aims and leads organizations to become decreasingly responsive to the social problems which they were designed to cope with. Donnison suggests that welfare organizations undergo a process of evolution wherein they eventually come to have the following characteristics:

An interest in preventive rather than remedial work, an emphasis upon the family rather than the individual, the provision of comprehensive help rather than a specific service, an attempt to change people's behavior through education and counsel rather than an attempt to meet particular needs. This approach presents many difficulties. It makes it harder to limit and define the tasks to be performed, and to establish priorities between them. Close cooperation between the services becomes essential if their efforts are not to overlap wastefully. Close relationships also must be maintained with the people who use and support each service, for if they do not understand and accept the agency's function the work must fail.[24]

This pattern signals an advanced state of institutionalization; organizational commitment to social change is weak and emphasis is placed on educational and consultative services, which are publicly defined as preventive rather than remedial. Yet the need for change becomes acute when, as a result of this process, tasks become ambiguous, hard to limit and to define, and priorities become difficult to establish.

Some critics have focused on the continuing division of labor wherein tasks become increasingly more narrowly defined, and only highly specialized personnel and agencies are held to be competent to perform them. The results of specialization are dramatically exemplified in the splintering of agency functions. As new specializations are added, the need to find means for reintegrating them becomes more acute, with the result that there is increased pressure to develop more effective machinery for coordination and accountability.[25]

Finally, social welfare services may be seen as instruments which act as concealed multipliers of advantage and privilege. Advanced industrial society, according to this position, is characterized by income inequalities and sharp cleavages among classes. Welfare services act as mechanisms for the distribution of advantages rather than for the reduction of inequalities. Consequently, the most deprived tend to be overlooked and welfare services increasingly serve the more affluent middle classes.[26]

PLANNING GOALS

Each of these views of the social service network implies a different course of action: increased government control, loosening of organizational rigidity, coordination of splintered tasks, or social reform. These broad action alternatives are translated into specific action programs by adaptive mechanisms we have come to call social planning organizations. Sometimes the presumptive adjective "comprehensive" is added. These planning organizations have selected one or another specific defect of the social service network discussed above, against which their major program thrust is organized. Although the listing is not inclusive, three action programs are discernible to achieve the following objectives: the redefining of agency boundaries, servicing rejected populations, and reducing the individualistic bias.

Each course of action is based on an appraisal of network defects, which in turn, is related to assumptions about the basic character of our industrial society—voluntarism, specialization, inequalities (social stratification), institutionalization and the related issues of bureaucratization. We may well anticipate that all strategies of action which are based on modest action programs will encounter substantial impediments in their efforts to reverse or slow down some of the major social characteristics of industrial society.

In planning programs, we find one objective is the reexamination of the boundaries between residential and community agencies. This aim can best be seen in terms of the long-range trend in Western industrial societies away from the use of institutions as warehouses and toward relocating individuals in the community. One of the first signs of this trend was the abolition of almshouses and the provision of income, in cash and in kind, to enable people to live in the community—the historic transition from indoor to outdoor relief programs.

This change can now be recognized in varied programs, such as delinquency control, child welfare, hospital care, and mental health provision. Planning in these areas is directed toward forging new links between community-based agencies and institutions. National funding bodies have encouraged local planning organizations to prod mental hospitals to shift their caseloads to community-based mental health centers. Community-based organizations are being encouraged to service delinquents who have been released from correctional institutions, and to provide the kind of services which would keep a child in his own home and avoid his placement in foster care, children's insititutions or shelters. General hospitals are being encouraged to transfer their chronic cases to institutions which are more closely integrated in the community, such as convalescent and nursing homes. These institutions, in turn, are being encouraged, where medically feasible, to have their patients live in the community, and community-based organizations are being asked to provide services, such as meals on wheels, home nursing, and medical care, to enable the aged and the chronically disabled to live in the community. Has the trend gone too far? Some critics have felt that the return of the mental patient to the community may disrupt family life.[27] Planning for mental health (funded by NIMH) is a recent prototype of social planning to modify organizational boundaries.

A few brief comments are needed to introduce the second objective—the servicing of rejected populations. Each institution develops over a period of time an unwanted population which is marginal to the operation of that institution. This may be a recidivist population, as in the case of the courts and correctional institutions; or a population of persons who cannot use the institution's services, as in the case of school dropouts; or a population serviced by a single institution but shunned by other institutions and denied the collateral services they require, as in the case of public welfare recipients; or a population who should appropriately be serviced by an institution but is rejected outright by that institution, as in the case of alcoholics refused service by general hospitals although alcoholism is defined as a physical illness. These various unwanted populations share a common characteristic—they are all judged by the defining institution as having a poor prognosis. Therefore, planning is directed at encouraging various institutions to serve these marginal and unwanted populations. For example, funds are now available for welfare departments to purchase or develop their own services for individuals receiving public assistance.

A third objective, closely related to the second, aims primarily at changes in social arrangements rather than changes in the personality of the individual delinquent. However, the commitment is not only to secure services for rejected populations but also to introduce significant changes in the structure and program of service institutions. The major assumption in planning for the reduction of delinquent behavior has been that social institutions have thrown up barriers to the disadvantaged, blocking access to social achievement and leading youth to disengage itself from dominant norms. The work of the President's Committee on Juvenile Delinquency and Youth Crime is an example of this kind of social planning.

How can we assess the impact of these new efforts to cope with the discontinuities among fragmented and specialized agencies, the neglect of community agencies to service their unwanted and hard-to-change ·populations, and the individualistic bias in the definition of social problems?

Each of these thrusts is encountering difficulties. Reexamination of the boundaries between resident institutions and community agencies may lead only to juggling and to rearranging the parts within the service network rather than to a basic change in the linkages and accountability of community agencies. Each community approaches the task afresh, essentially directing its attention to who does what; that is, the modification of agency boundaries and the improvement of the routing procedure whereby clients are shunted by one agency boundary to another. But an enforceable plan which meshes the activities of pre-institutional, institutional, and after-care services is noticeably absent. So defined, we recognize a striking similarity between these new forms of planning and the more traditional planning of welfare councils, which were concerned with coordination, information, and referral, and avoidance of duplication; in short, the reallocation of function and resources within the local service network. The difference does not lie in the goals or the strategies of planning but rather on the amount and source of funds. More money is available for planning than heretofore and it is now non-local money from the federal government and national foundations.

Planning to reach individuals who have already failed and have been given up as candidates for help by the established institutions has stubbornly persisted in "creaming off" the most able and neglecting the most disadvantaged. Community Research Associates has developed an elaborate schedule to sift, sort, and label individuals receiving public welfare. Their scheme calls for a conscious policy of providing the least services to those who are most resistant to change (and probably most in need). California, in an elaborate program in training minority group members for entry into the aerospace industry, had developed such rigid standards that the target population was missed. Recently the Labor Department reported that retraining programs have failed to reach out to the hard core unemployed and have recruited the younger better-educated workers.

Planning tends in practice to avoid changing the system in favor of changing the individual. For example, an exhaustive survey of planning for unemployed youth conducted by the National Committee on Employment of Youth revealed a striking bias in favor of programs to "adjust the youth in the world of employment," an approach which takes as its major assumption "that unemployability inheres in the youths themselves."[28] Even programs specifically designed to change social institutions find that in the process of translating their theoretical rationale into specific action programs, attention to institutional change gracefully succumbs to programs aimed at changes in individuals, often without the full awareness of the planners; or if the focus on institutions is retained, attention shifts to the creation of new institutions rather than the improvement of the old.

Perhaps the most dramatic recent instance is the proliferation of new youth retraining programs throughout communities, while attempts to modify the vocational high schools are largely ignored. The Ford Foundation's Grey Area Projects, which are aimed at school reform, have not struck at the core of the school as an educational institution. Thus many of the projects they have funded have stressed earlier admission of children to school, usually to experimental nursery programs. In one city such experimental programs have been proposed for one or two schools in a deprived area, while most other schools do not even have kindergartens. On the other hand, some projects have popularized the idea of the community-outreach school which essentially is an after-school program wherein the school becomes the center for community activities. But aside from these before and after school programs, only modest attempts have been made at changing the school as a teaching institution. Money is poured into the schools for remedial reading programs while the basic approach to the teaching of reading which produces these disabilities is ignored.

More recently, in addition to proliferating services by creating remedial services, some planning organizations are supporting the creation of secondary institutions which duplicate the function of major primary institutions. For example, in one city, the Mayor's Office, the Ford Foundation, and other sources are supporting a new agency organized by indigenous Negro leaders, which in effect is attempting to create a separate school system with buildings, equipment, and staff that will parallel that of the publicly supported vocational schools. There are various rationales offered to justify the creation of dual institutions, but perhaps of special importance in the context of this analysis is an implicit theory of institutional change. This may be stated as follows: marginal programs funded over short periods of time for selected small populations will lead in time to major shifts in institutional aims, styles, resources, and effectiveness. Although the process by which this transformation is to occur remains obscure, it is nevertheless hoped that these projects may constitute the first link in the process of social change. Yet it is equally possible that these experiments may be short-circuited and remain largely ineffective insofar as the main issues are concerned. They may instead create the illusion of change rather than serving as the spearhead for innovation.

THE STRATEGY OF THE DEMONSTRATION: AN ASSESSMENT

How can we account for these limitations—the neglect of comprehensiveness, the "creaming off" the most able, the avoidance of institutional change? The equating of social planning with demonstration programs may be one possible cause. Because demonstrations enjoy such wide popularity, they deserve special comment. The "demonstration-research" project may be described as the major instrument for social planning in American communities today. Some national funding organizations are committed to local demonstrations on at least three grounds. The value of the following generalizations lies primarily in the framing of hypotheses and as a model for further testing.

(1) As a device to stimulate innovation and change in local programs so that they will reflect an environmental approach to social problems. However, the points of entry for the modification of social structure are left open to broad interpretation. To accomplish this task it is assumed that the planners of demonstrations will need to be innovative in that the demonstration programs will be based upon an understanding of the causes of social problems, rather than upon tradition, morality, and expediency. (By implication, this position assumes that present programs are not so constituted.) (2) To assure that demonstrations actually contact and service vulnerable groups, e.g., those who are already disadvantaged and those who are likely to become so. (3) To facilitate the implementation of those promising demonstrations, so that they will eventually be adopted as permanent programs by established community agencies.

However logical the interrelationship of these aims—innovation, servicing the vulnerable, and implementation of programs—however comprehensive and well-balanced the aims may seem, choices have been made, perhaps unwittingly, in the programs which are designed to effect them. A hidden scheme of priorities has been in operation with the result that the gap between the planning promise and the planning performance has widened.

In speculating about what seems to be more or less typical in existing demonstrations, we caution the reader that many demonstrations will undoubtedly be different. Although the evidence is as yet both incomplete and inconclusive (since not all the plans have been projected, nor have all the presently operating demonstrations been completed), there are indications that many "demonstration-research" projects may have unanticipated consequences and may lead to the neglect of the aims held by the funding body. In fact, the severest critics have traced this neglect to the concept itself. They have argued that, by their very nature, demonstrations contribute to the avoidance of comprehensive planning. They are fragmented in scope and narrow in focus, they act as a stop-gap to a more thorough, far-reaching, and encompassing effort to cope with social problems on a mass scale. This criticism has been advanced by planners of national repute such as Harvey Perloff, who has argued that programs like Mobilization for Youth, serving a limited population in a small corner of New York at a cost of more than twelve million dollars is essentially misplaced do-goodism which detracts from the major task which needs to be undertaken. He argues that social planning should be an integral part of organizations which can mold national policy, such as the President's Council of Economic Advisers.

Our criticism is not directed at the concept but rather at the way it is presently being interpreted. Sponsors of demonstrations are committed to achieving success and to assuring the eventual institutionalization of their experimental programs. They may try to create a "spread-effect" which might call either for exact duplicates of the program to be broadly adopted by other community agencies, or for a sponsoring agency to secure added funds to assure the continuity of the program after the demonstration is completed.[29] But, in either case, they are committed to a successful demonstration, a practice which leads to the recruitment of the "good risk client" and which, in turn, contributes to the creation of new categories of poor risk and failure—namely, those who cannot adjust to the traditional institutions, those who cannot adjust to social services, those who cannot adjust to the demonstrations. Thus, paradoxically, programs designed to reach the unreached have only augmented their numbers.

Although demonstrations aim to be innovative, those with which we are familiar have not retained the structure of institutions as targets of planned change. The reasons which underlie the avoidance are complex, yet it is essential that we attempt to understand this incapacity of planning organizations to respond to what is perhaps the major objective of the organization which funds their program.

One contributing factor is that national funding organizations pursue aims which in practice are difficult to reconcile. In the usual tradition of granting agencies, there is the expectation of local matching of federal funds. This position is defended on the grounds that it is naive to throw millions of dollars into a community where there is little interest in change, and where experimental programs are unlikely to become permanent. Community willingness to make financial investment is assumed to be the most reliable indication of commitment. Planning organizations have thus been forced to settle for those programs which are likely to win financial support from established community agencies. The process of winning such commitments is largely political, based on what the agencies are willing to try and what the planners are able to sell. Community agencies are not likely to buy programs which require basic structural change, particularly from outside organizations which offer only gilded glamour, with a glaring absence of effective sanctions. They are, on the contrary, more likely to support projects which require only modest organizational change and which, in turn, are likely to have visibly successful outcomes.

Technical ignorance and a vacuum in social policy are perhaps the most important reasons why institutional change is avoided as a planning objective. Do we truly know how to recognize the overall pattern of local community service? Do we really know how to redefine the boundaries of a cluster of community agencies with interrelated functions? Do we know what basic changes are needed in specific organizations, like welfare departments and schools?

Let us consider the first question in more detail. Substantial funds are available for local communities from different federal departments. The requirements of each funding group is likely to lead the local community to develop programs to coincide with the interest of the major funding source. Programs can be developed around the out-reach school, the welfare department, the health department, the mental hygiene clinic, and so forth. The traditional stand-bys—the settlement house and the welfare councils—are being financially starved and severely criticized as inadequate focal institutions for the coordination of local service programs. Do we have any factual data which can guide us in the selection of one or another institution as the appropriate focus for a community program? Do we know what consequences flow from linking organizations in different patterns or the consequences which follow when one or another of these institutions plays a more prominent role at the local level? Clearly, adequate information to guide social planning is simply not available. It must be acknowledged that a real theory of how to modify these social institutions is needed. Yet, surprisingly, planners have failed to appreciate fully these limitations in knowledge. This is dramatically illustrated in one city where the planning structure was developed to include two major groups: "knowers" and "sellers." The "knowers" were a small group of elite social scientists charged with developing a comprehensive plan, while the "sellers" were charged with the task of winning the commitment of agencies, convincing them of the merits of the plan. The scheme collapsed when it became increasingly apparent that the "knowers" did not really know and could not produce a package which the "sellers" could market.

Even more basic than the lack of knowledge is the lack of agreement on social aims—not the "preamble aims" of the good society and better life for all but the more concrete planning aims. For example, should a greater investment of resources (money, personnel, facilities) go to the underprivileged sectors of a community as a means of reducing present inequalities? To avoid confronting such issues of policy, planning organizations have diverted their interest to the issue of means. Perhaps the clearest example is the attention planners have given to the development of local citizen action groups. It is hoped that these groups will act as organized pressure bodies to produce institutional change. The Negro protest movement has, of course, accelerated the acceptance of this approach. Yet this formulation serves only to obscure the more difficult issues of the specific institutional changes which are to be sought. This vagueness in aims is justified as necessary for preserving the integrity of the grass roots organizations and for facilitating the growth of community competence to cope with problems. The means become elevated to ends, and attention is further diverted from a major commitment to institutional change.

Social science researchers have also been one further obstacle to the acceptance of institutional change as a central planning aim. They were brought into planning organizations to conduct studies which would help confirm or reject the basic underlying rationale of the funding organizations (that social institutions throw up barriers and block access for achievement, a process which contributes to increased disengagement and deviancy on the part of the rejected populations). Yet strangely enough, social scientists have acted to reinforce those pressures on planning organizations which have led them to avoid community institutions as prime targets of change. Instead they have favored the more traditional and tested approaches such as surveys of individual attitudes, self perceptions, role models, and so on. The indices they have proposed to measure the impact of the demonstration programs are largely those of individual social pathology—reduced rates of delinquent behavior, drug addiction, and so forth. They have avoided indices which would measure institutional change and have neglected institutional analysis in favor of a more individualistic approach. They have relied on the more traditional elements of their expertize (surveys of attitudes), and have only partly responded to the problems of the new settings in which they work.

Finally, the neglect of institutional change as a target must be seen in relation to the scope of the task. Earlier we suggested that service defects must be recognized as manifestations of the basic character of our industrial society—a private economy, where the specialized units of service are subject to problems of fragmentation, institutionalization, bureaucratization, and where institutions act to support and strengthen the prevailing distribution of advantages. We cannot expect that social planning organizations, often fighting for their own survival, will have the legitimation and the sanctions needed to support the kinds of institutional changes hoped for. Major programs comparable to the Social Security Act of the 1930s, which might act to modify our economic system, have not been proposed. Perhaps we are again witnessing private enterprise on trial, but such policies must in the end be political decisions for they help to defend our different views of the good society.

Although planning organizations cannot employ strategies of protest and although their bargaining power is relatively weak, they could employ a strategy of confrontation. We believe that nonsuccess-oriented demonstrations are needed, which would probe the basic policy issues, ask the tough questions, and would take as problematic (rather than given) the decisions of the established institutions.[30] In short, demonstrations could provide evidence for needed change in basic institutions. For example, success-oriented research in public welfare attempts to show that increasing professional staff, reducing size of caseloads, and so forth, could reduce dependency and contribute to the rehabilitation of individuals. Such a study would focus on the progress which clients have made. The Marin County welfare study is a prototype of studies which are designed to document the beneficial effects of intensive casework treatment. It shows that after several intensive interviews, welfare recipients are likely to go off welfare and stay off welfare roles, resulting not only in lower costs to the county, but in increased satisfaction to the recipient. By contrast, nonsuccess-oriented research would take the same study and use the findings to examine the structure of the welfare department and its basic social policies. Some observers who are presently undertaking such studies have suggested that the more deeply they become involved in their work, the more thoroughly they are convinced that what is needed is not tinkering with the welfare system but perhaps abolishing it altogether and substituting something like a negative income tax. This argument would substantially be strengthened if their studies showed little success on the part of clients. The research inspired by Richard Titmuss of the London School of Economics may also be classified as nonsuccess-oriented research in that it is designed to highlight the shortcomings in the operation of present social institutions in servicing disadvantaged groups. In short, it is research in the service of social criticism rather than in the service of social apology.

NOTES

1. Information on the number and type of individuals caught in this kind of net is in short supply. Bradley Buell's data suggesting that only a small percentage of

families in a community receive most of the services may be misleading. The term service—often interpreted to mean organizations—is not fully defined. In an article which appeared in 1948, Buell reported that the activities of more than one hundred agencies were classified into 34 different types of services. These include services provided by the agencies as well as referrals to other agencies. A situation where a small group of families receive a large concentration of services could arise where many agencies have high referral rates, short contacts, and a high rejection, low direct service intake policy. Unfortunately, Buell does not supply us with the supporting data on which his findings are based. The Buell generalization—6 percent of the community's families receive over half of the services—may be questioned on other grounds as well. It is unlikely that a study conducted in a mid-western city of 100,000 families, soon after World War II, a period of near full employment, can be regarded as a typical city as the author implies. Replications of this study are quite desperately needed. See Bradley Buell, "Know What the What Is," *Survey-Midmonthly,* October 1948; and Bradley Buell and Associates, *Community Planning for Human Services* (New York: Columbia University Press, 1952).

2. Martin Rein, *An Analysis of the Network of Community Agencies Providing Child Protective Services in Massachusetts* (Waltham, Mass.: Brandeis University, June 1962).

3. See Alfred J. Kahn, "Service Boundaries" and "Case Channeling" (mimeo.) for a penetrating analysis of interorganizational problems in the local service network.

4. This point was made by experienced administrators like Charles I. Schottland in personal conversation.

5. Stanton K. Wheeler (ed.), *Controlling Delinquency* (New York: Wiley, 1967). See also, Walter B. Miller's, "Inter-Institutional Conflict as a Major Impediment to Delinquency Prevention," *Human Organization,* Vol. 17, No. 3, 1959. This is a stunning and original analysis of the consequences for planning of conflicting intervention stances among community agencies in the area of delinquency.

6. Barbara Wootton, *Social Science and Social Pathology* (New York: Macmillan, 1959), pp. 330–331.

7. J. H. Robb, "Decentralisation and the Citizen," in J. L. Robert (ed.) *Decentralisation in New Zealand Government Administration* (London: Oxford University Press, 1961).

8. D. Donnison, *Welfare Services in a Canadian Community: A Study of Brookville, Ontario* (Toronto: University of Toronto Press, 1958), p. 152.

9. Wootton, *op. cit.,* p. 17.

10. Elaine Cumming *et al.,* "Policeman as Philosopher, Guide and Friend," paper presented at the annual meeting of American Public Health Association, November 1963.

11. Raymond T. Smith, *The Negro Family in British Guiana* (London: Routledge and Kegan Paul, 1956).

12. Richard A. Cloward, "Social Problems, Social Definitions and Social Opportunities," a paper prepared for the Regional Institutes on Juvenile Delinquency and Social Forces, April 1963, p. 34.

13. Dorothy F. Beck, *Patterns in Use of Family Agency Service: A Preliminary*

Report on a Census of the Characteristics of Applicants and Their Use of Casework Service (New York: Family Service Association of America, 1962).

14. My thanks to Robert S. Weiss, who in personal correspondence pointed out that *all* professional groups are subject to this type of professional unionization.

15. Richard M. Titmuss, "The Hospital and Its Patients," in Richard M. Titmuss, *Essays on the Welfare State* (New Haven: Yale University Press, 1959), p. 121–122.

16. Wootton, *op. cit.*, p. 328.

17. James B. Conant, *The Education of the American Teacher* (New York: McGraw-Hill, 1963).

18. Osler L. Peterson *et al.*, "An Analytic Study of North Carolina General Practice, 1953–1954," *Journal of Medical Education*, Vol. 31 (December 1956), Part II.

19. Alvin Gouldner, "Organizational Secrets," in *Social Welfare Forum, 1963* (New York: Columbia University Press, 1963).

20. See Chapter 5 for a review of Titmuss' position on dependency.

21. Robert Morris, "Social Work Preparation for Effectiveness in Planned Change," *Proceedings of the Eleventh Annual Meeting of the Council on Social Work Education,* January 1963.

22. Elaine Cumming, "A Review Article—The Reports of the Joint Commission on Mental Illness and Health," *Social Problems,* Vol. 9, No. 4 (Spring 1962).

23. One of the most incisive statements of this position can be found in the work of Arthur Vidich, "Analysis of Philanthropic Institutions and Psychology" (mimeo., an unpublished paper prepared for a seminar on American Philanthropy, Brandeis University, 1963).

24. Donnison, *op. cit.*, p. 151.

25. Alfred J. Kahn, *Planning Community Services for Children in Trouble* (New York: Columbia University Press, 1963).

26. Brian Abel-Smith, "Whose Welfare State?" in Norman MacKenzie, ed., *Conviction* (London: MacGibbon & Kee, 1958).

27. In a personal correspondence with David Kallen, of NIMH, the following observations were made: "Herein is a paradox which to me represents one of the most crucial issues. It seems to me to represent an attempt to get the community and the family to assume treatment responsibilities which, historically, they have abrogated in favor of other agencies. The sociological literature recently has expressed, correctly, a concern about the eclipse of community which is the result of urban industrial society. The eclipse, however, is of the geographically based community. The current planning efforts seem to be concerned with the hope that something that may not exist (the geographically based community) can reassume treatment functions that have been delegated to other sectors of the society. Certainly social work believes in the geographic community as an *ought,* and much social work effort is directed towards making reality of the oughtness."

28. Marsha K. Freedman, "Basic Issues Affecting Youth Employment" (mimeo., New York: The National Committee for the Employment of Youth, 1963).

29. See Chapter 7.

30. Marsha K. Freedman, "On the Uses of Demonstration Projects in Youth Employment," a paper presented at the 90th Annual Forum, National Conference on Social Welfare, May 21, 1963, Cleveland, Ohio.

Chapter 4

Institutional Change: A Priority in Welfare Planning

Social welfare agencies legitimate their mission by defining their function as that of meeting human need. The unmistakable implication in this formulation is that agencies are responsive to those social problems and conditions that can be objectively recognized and dispassionately treated without regard to the vested interests of the consumer, the distributor, or the sponsor of the service. The concept of vested interests is virtually absent in the lexicon of the professional; as Gouldner observed, "the dominant ideology . . . implies that the agency is a kind of a mirror held up to the community, that it merely reflects what happens to be there."[1]

Under many circumstances, welfare institutions do indeed serve as need-meeting institutions, reducing personal strain and relieving community problems. Our professional textbooks are filled with testaments to the relevance and importance of social agencies in meeting human need. Much less attention and thought has, however, been given to the more disarming question of the way in which community agencies create, as well as alleviate, problems.

There is nothing more subversive than a searching question. In this paper, we shall attempt to examine those

Reprinted by special permission of Child Welfare League of America from *Child Welfare*, Vol. 45, No. 1 (1966), pp. 259-268.

many anomalous situations in which institutional activity exacerbates rather than relieves problems. We have identified a half-dozen ways in which this process is likely to operate and have classified them rather loosely and preliminarily around the theme of "standards of performance."[2]

STANDARDS OF PERFORMANCE

Organization Standards and Societal Norms

Institutions serve many purposes, but we cannot assume, without reservation, that they all represent humanitarian and equalitarian aims, i.e., maximizing the development of individual capabilities. For example, social service institutions develop procedures for selection that also serve as instruments of social discrimination because they allocate persons to different career lines in accordance with their capacity to adapt to the ethics and values of business and industrial production. These standards of performance are based on a narrow range of acceptable styles and patterns of individual behavior. The role models required by our business and production enterprises are taken as the norm for assessing individual performance in the training experience provided by our school system, for example; those who fit the model and its requirements are encouraged to go on, while others—such as minority youth from the urban ghetto—are pushed out of the experience.

The social rights of the citizen to benefit from the facilities and resources that will enable him to maximize his potential for growth are not dominant values behind the operation of most social welfare institutions. These institutions seem more preoccupied with getting individuals to meet accepted standards, a process often referred to as "adjusting to reality." What applies to the individual in this situation applies even more forcefully to cultural and class minority groups.

Institutions of our culturally diversified society appear to be rather uniformly geared to the needs and preferences of only one segment of society —the idealized middle class. In part, uniformity of practice is a function of bureaucratic pressures that seek to maximize rationality, efficiency, and predictability by imposing a rigid and restrictive sameness on the activities of all parts of the system. These pressures for uniformity throughout the system give members of minority and low-income groups the feeling that these institutions are unrelated to their special needs. They are likely to feel depersonalized by what they interpret as institutional indifference or outright hostility.

Standards of Selection and Social Problems

Institutional behavior, as well as individual behavior, at least in part, contributes to and helps account for the rates of social problems. Nevertheless, most of the research directed at understanding social disorganization has sought to trace out the origin of these rates through the nature of human behavior, such as personal, familial, and peer-group pressures. There has been a curious neglect of the way in which the activities of organizations, rather than the behavior of individuals per se, help account for various official rates of deviant behavior. There is a stubborn resistance in social policy to the probing of the limitations and rigidities of institutional performance for an understanding of the origins of social problems.

In a thoughtful analysis of the role of the education counselor in the high school, Cicourel and Kitsuse document this tendency.[3] The study describes how counselors interpret and respond to the discrepancy between a student's capability (as measured by IQ tests) and his classroom performance. They found that counselors invariably viewed the problems in terms of the characteristics of students, i.e.:

> consequences of motivational and personal problems. Organizational personnel almost never questioned the inadequacies, defects, or failures of the "system." . . . That is, the efficiency of the tests used to identify ability, the courses designed to develop it, and the teachers assigned to evaluate the degree of development. [4]

This bias leads to a systematic neglect of the way in which the activities of organizations help account for various official rates of deviant behavior.

Present recording procedures suggest that there is an immediate and obvious relationship between widely used indices or rates of social disorganization and individual behavior. Making an important contribution to the understanding of social action by his insistence on the introduction of common sense into the analysis of social structure, Harold Garfinkel distinguishes between actual behavior and the selective recording of behavior in the form of official statistics and rates. The tendency to confuse the two concepts has muddled our understanding of social problems and has had unfortunate effects on the development of social policy.[5]

In order to understand why rates change, it is necessary to have a prior understanding of how organization personnel interpret, classify, and process similar behavior in different situations. Rates reflect, in part, the definitions that institutions develop for assigning individuals to different social categories; changes in these definitions can alter, even dramatically shift, the rates while the incidence of behavior in question remains unchanged. It is also of interest to note that slackening or tightening eligibility requirements—as, for example, in public assistance—affects not only the scope of economic dependency, but its character as well. When higher standards are used, recipients are more likely to participate in the labor force, and welfare is more likely to serve as a form of wage supplementation. The use of lower standards creates a picture of recipients as being largely outside the labor force. The public image and the self-image of the recipient shift with the standards we use; so, too, does the treatment accorded him. Punitive sanctions, for example, are less likely to be applied to those already active in the labor force.

One aspect of this complex process is of special concern here—the way in which similar categories of social behavior are differentially defined by the operating institution. Thus, an illegal act in a middle-income community is likely to be treated quite differently than a similar act committed in a ghetto community. Truancy, for example, may be defined as idiosyncratic behavior and dismissed; it may be defined as a symptom of a personal and emotional problem to be treated by a guidance counselor or therapists; or, alternatively, it may be seen as a delinquent act to be handled by the courts and the police department. A study in Philadelphia revealed that, in 1956, about 27 percent of all boys were destined to appear before a municipal court on charges of delinquency before reaching age 18. According to 1953 statistics, about 40 percent of Negro youth will become involved with the law before they reach 18.[6] In a discussion of social stratification and law enforcement, Cloward observes that our law enforcement institutions tend to function in a way that places

> the poor in greater jeopardy of being selected out for defining and punitive action. . . . Virtue is said to be the cause of high status. . . . This tendency to view the poor as morally inferior has enormous ramifications for understanding of criminal statistics as well as for statistics on other social problems. In effect, the poor are defined as more criminalistic; they are defined as less susceptible to rehabilitative measures, and thus they are subjected to more straightforwardly punitive measures.[7]

The arbitrary selection of standards for eligibility and the differential enforcement of established standards, which arises in part because of the tendency to equate moral qualities with social position, clearly raise questions about administrative justice, at least insofar as equality of treatment is concerned. They also raise questions about the way in which institutions contribute to personal problems by their delineations of the characteristics of social problems.

Standards and Stigma

Although the rates of deviant behavior are conceptually distinguishable from the behavior itself, they are by no means independent of each other;

institutional definitions constitute one complicating and confusing element in the behavior system of individuals and groups. The way in which an institution defines a person can affect his life chances and career alternatives in two interrelated ways: through self-definition and through social definition by relevant others. This is the problem of labeling. An individual's delinquent acts may start out as pranks and idle mischief, but the intensity and severity of the institution's response may lead the individual to act and to become the way he is defined, i.e., he takes as his definition of himself the way he is seen or defined by others.

Another equally cogent factor is the definition that other individuals ascribe to a person because of the nature of his contact with institutions. A recent study revealed that individuals with the same problem of adjustment were perceived quite differently, depending not upon their behavior, but upon the nature of the institution and the personnel from whom they received service.[8]

We are affected in what we are by how we see ourselves and how others see us. This self-fulfilling prophecy is the very essence of human behavior! In a probing discussion of the meaning of social psychology, Seeley notes:

> If a theory starts out from a naive preconception in physics, the data repudiate the theory if the theory is wrong. If a theory starts out from a naive preconception in social psychology, not only do the initial data tend to confirm it (since men are largely what they think themselves to be) but the preliminary confirmation, once published, tends to reinforce the inadequate self-conception and society-conception, and hence on subsequent tests to lend even greater plausibility to error.[9]

The problem of labeling is exacerbated when individuals are placed in the wrong rate-producing system because of shortages of facilities, differential access to resources and institutional rigidities. In theory, children requiring substitute parental care—not because of their behavior, but because of failures in their home situations—are placed in temporary shelters while awaiting placement in foster homes. But when shelters are overcrowded or children cannot adjust to them, they may be placed in detention centers designed to serve an altogether different function: protecting the community from harmful acts.

Or consider an even more dramatic example: Kahn reports that, "not at all atypically, one Massachusetts mental hospital found only 17 percent of the children in its wards to be psychotic."[10] Indeed, Szasz has charged that the label "mentally ill" is frequently assigned to those who are troublemakers. Psychiatrists thus serve as "policemen of the unconscious" as well as therapists of the mentally ill.[11]

Confusion Between Stated and Actual Standards

One of the most dramatic ways in which an institution can affect the behavior and career alternatives of the individual is through the process of purposive labeling, i.e., sorting individuals into various social categories. (This process is sometimes called diagnosis or testing, terms that suggest rigor and objectivity in the definitional process; but more often the labels so generated reflect a confusion between stated and actual standards.) An individual's social situation may come to be the decisive element in determining the diagnostic category applied to him. In one probing study of how schizophrenia was diagnosed, the investigator found that when psychiatrists were asked to judge identical behavior profiles, the occupation of the individual or of his parents decisively affected the diagnosis of schizophrenia.[12] Psychiatrists have learned only too well that schizophrenia is associated with lower-class behavior, and when confronted with an unknown cluster of behavior, there is apparently a strong tendency to rely on social class rather than any characteristics inherent in the behavior syndrome. This intrusion of class standards in the definitional process is of crucial importance because the experience that an individual has and the likelihood of his recovery is affected by the way he is labeled.

The most dramatic contemporary example of the confusion between stated labels and hidden standards is the IQ test. Over a quarter of a billion tests are administered each year in the United States by a variety of institutions interested in screening, labeling, and sorting individuals. These new instruments of social discrimination (the term is descriptive, not invidious) come to affect the life chances of individuals. Many who fail these tests take a first step on the road to becoming potential social problems. These tests, particularly those that measure IQ and vocational aptitude, are assumed to measure capacity inherent in the individual and unrelated to social definitions. (The case of mental deficiency, however, provides a dramatic example of how difficult it is to achieve this objectivity.) Yet who gets labeled as a defective is likely to depend as much on the tolerance of the tester as on the condition of the person who is being labeled.

Intelligence tests may be better measures of actual achievement than of innate ability. When the environment of an individual is substantially improved, dramatic changes in IQ level can take place. It has caustically been observed that "the usual intelligence tests employed by public schools are moderately good predictors of income level and minority status; whether they predict anything beyond social and economic deprivation remains to be demonstrated."[13] Although the IQ may represent a measure of environmental deprivation, it can best be understood as a subtle fusion of academic, biological, and social standards.

The instruments to measure intelligence and achievement further act to discriminate against those presently disadvantaged. They are often interpreted in a way that relieves the school of responsibility for its failure. Fortunately, there seems to be increasing awareness of this fact. Hillel Black, in his new book *They Shall Not Pass,* goes so far as to urge a United States Supreme Court test of the constitutionality of determining the educational futures of children of underprivileged backgrounds through the use of intelligence and aptitude tests.[14]

Standards and Professional Performance

Personnel in organizations often employ informal criteria for assessing and rewarding individuals, although they are not fully aware of the ways in which these criteria come to determine their reaction to the individuals they service. In his studies at the New York Medical College, Deutsch discovered that first-grade teachers were unwittingly rewarding children from middle-class households who displayed the proper attitudes of attention and verbal facility.[15] Smiles of encouragement were rarely directed toward children of lower-class backgrounds who had more difficulty responding appropriately. The net effect was an increasing apathy among the lower-class children and a remarkable discrepancy in their achievement levels by the end of the first grade.

Teachers were surprised and somewhat shocked to find that they had been making this kind of discrimination. After a period of training in the cultural styles of low income groups, they were able to achieve a satisfactory level of participation among lower-class children. As a result of this change in teacher behavior, no differences in achievement between middle-class and lower-class children were reported in the experimental group tested at the termination of the school year.

Teachers often unwittingly adopt the stereotypes of the instruments they use. A number of studies have shown that teachers do not expect low-income groups to learn; they maintain low levels of expectations even for those disadvantaged youth who have good school-achievement records. Riessman aptly termed this "discrimination without prejudice,"[16] but an angry Harlem account describes it as "cashing-in" (receiving salaries without performing the appropriate services).[17]

Standards and Organization Delivery

Unfortunately, an effective program, which achieves the standards it strives for, can end by creating bitterness and dissolution. Usually, what has been successful is the expansion of aspiration: people are taught to want a better life. But aspiration is not always accompanied by the delivery of those supportive services and opportunities that are necessary to complete the cycle of change.

Vocational-educational training in the United States, when it is successful in producing motivated graduates, may increasingly come under attack because of its failure to link the training experience with an opportunity for work placement. For nonwhite persons between the ages of 16 and 21, high school graduation has little effect on unemployment. (As a matter of fact, in October 1963, nonwhite dropouts had slightly lower rates of unemployment than nonwhite high school graduates, although the rates were very high for both groups—almost one in four were unemployed.[18]) Consider the training experience youth are likely to receive in the Job Corps under the present poverty legislation. This splintered program may have little momentum unless some mechanism is also provided for absorbing the graduates of the program into the community-based educational and occupational structures. To provide only one component of a cycle of social change is to develop an inauthentic and token response to the problems of job training for youth.

The high cost of the Job Corps ($11,251 per enrollee in the first year of operation) exerts great pressure to expend even more funds to protect the initial investment. Special counselors have been assigned to state employment services both to develop new jobs and to place the graduates of the Job Corps in them. Other training programs do not enjoy this privileged position.

These problems of reabsorption, or failure to deliver the resources necessary to complete the cycle of change, are quite pervasive among all institutions of socialization. In the case of correctional institutions for juvenile delinquents and adults, the effectiveness of treatment systems can be nullified because the offenders are unable to reenter the network of learning and performance opportunities that support a conventional career life. Similarly, release of patients from mental institutions into the community, even after a successful treatment program, can therefore be jeopardized by the failure to provide a coherent pattern of aftercare services. What is at issue is the failure to provide an integrated package of programs; instead, only disjointed and fragmented services are developed. These can expand aspiration and hope, but provide little structured opportunity to realize this hope in terms of further training, jobs, or a normal career in the community. The failure to deliver what is promised can lead to even more desperate apathy, retreat, and rejection of prevailing community standards.

By directing our attention to the way in which narrow, inconsistent, and uncertain standards reinforce rather than reduce social and personal problems, we have neglected to highlight explicitly a recurrent theme in our examples: Our social services are more responsive to the needs and preferences of the economically more advantaged groups in our society. Consequently, social services reinforce and strengthen present class boundaries. This situation prevails rather uniformly in all social welfare institutions, with the inevitable result that welfare institutions, which are designed to service the most disadvantaged, tend instead to cream off those who are most able to participate within the economy. We have developed what Myrdal has called a perversion of American social policy,[19] which leads to *creaming* and the neglect of those that are least mobile.

PLANNING FOR INSTITUTIONAL CHANGE

There is a restlessness in the 1960's that provides a sharp contrast to the quiet complacency of the early 1950's, when American social scientists were formulating a new natural law of income equalization and were predicting the emergence of a new social revolution. For more than a decade no major social legislation was passed. A social policy vacuum had developed in which optimism, based on the doctrine that economic growth would reduce social problems, bred indifference. Today, by contrast, social reform has (aside from the Depression years) never been so popular. It is reflected in a flurry of national social legislation: the Juvenile Delinquency and Youth Offenses Control Act, 1961; the Manpower Development and Training Act, 1962; the Community Mental Health Centers Act, 1963; the Economic Opportunity Act, 1964; and the 1965 Amendments to the Social Security Act. This is only a partial list of legislation deeply committed to creating institutional change in the areas of social welfare, education, employment, and mental health. Comprehensiveness, coordination, and increased relevance to the needs of the poor are the recurrent themes found in this legislation.

But while we have bent our energies to creative innovation, we have neglected to examine the new problems we encounter as we seek to resolve the old ones. A few years ago, Morris and I pointed to a fundamental problem in social planning that is today mushrooming into a full-blown crisis: Social planning is organized around narrow vested interests (in spite of what the professional may think), and each interest group sees itself as the center with all other services orbiting around it. As a result, we create separate planning for each service. Moreover, all of these interests "are necessarily in competition for limited funds and personnel. There is no definite allocation of funds and other resources for a balanced plan of action."[20]

The twin goals of comprehensiveness and coordination cannot be served by an aimless proliferation of planning efforts and bitter competition for scarce resources, and the goal that programs should be relevant to the poor may also be lost as the commitment to success produces creaming (searching for clients who make the program succeed rather than for a program that can help clients succeed).

Glazer's question sums up the issue very well: ". . . when planning is broken down as finely as this, is it planning or another form of chaos?"[21] Disturbed about the confusion of planning, he goes on to contrast the reforms of the 1960's with those of the early 1930's. Today we seem to have professionalized our social reform; the vested interests of the professionals, who have an immediate stake in the operation of programs, have provided the expertise and the driving force. But, we lack "public discussion in which issues are formulated, positions are taken, decisions made, reflecting more than a short range or at best a middle range response to crisis, present and potential."[22]

Narrow technology has led away from the kind of political dialogue that influenced development of the social services in the 1930's; unionization of the professional and aggrandizement of the administrators have replaced the support for reform once provided by organized labor and the intellectual. Narrowness of vision is not only caused by the absence of an overall philosophy about the place of social services in a complex industrial society, but it is also a product of our bureaucratic structure, which is the heritage of our past mistakes. Even the boldest ideas become dissipated when the problem of implementation is considered, e.g., in which part of the tangled bureaucratic web should the program be placed? The struggle over bureaucratic domain is replacing the interest-group conflicts of the past.

Although the social reforms of the 1960's are increasing in size, scope, and function, they may become self-stultifying without a more encompassing view of their direction, a more thoughtful appraisal of their impact, a more open view of alternatives, and a political debate regarding their purpose. Students of social welfare must increasingly examine the politics of social services. But our task here is more modest. We attempt only to identify and to comment briefly on those strategies of reform that may offer partial answers to the institutional deficiencies we have examined in this paper.

Parallelism

Parallelism is an approach that attempts to bypass the normal and established community institutions that are unable to respond to changing human needs and that seem to have lost their sense of purpose and commitment. Strategists who favor duplication of the established structures appear to have two somewhat divergent approaches.

Glazer, in an effort to assure that reform comes from the Negro community itself, seems to have lost heart about the value of directly operated government programs. He looks to private efforts for new sources of commitment and innovation. "The returns from such efforts," he concludes, "are often as surprising as the weakness of official and governmental efforts is depressing. . . . It is axiomatic to me that Negro organizations—whether they educate, train, advise, employ, organize or whatnot—can potentially do far, far more with Negro clients than can governmental organizations."[23]

An alternative rationale for the support of duplicatory planning is provided by Frankel's concept that calls for "deliberate planning to provide alternatives . . . we need to invigorate existing institutions by creating new ones whose function is to be a thorn in the side of existing bureaucracies—agencies that bear witness to what might be, that animate, enlarge, and discipline the public imagination."[24]

Duplication proliferates an already complex welfare structure, and the strategy of *purposive* duplication, whether motivated by the desire to prod or to replace, has apparent limitations. Although it may scck to avoid the arrogant assumptions of welfare colonialism, it is doubtful whether self-help programs can serve as adequate substitutes for a thoroughgoing reform of the vocational-education system. In addition, programs that define the poor as a separate class carry with them an invidious label, which may, in the end, only stigmatize the poor they seek to help. Will graduation from the Job Corps provide more acceptable credentials than graduation from an accepted educational institution? The alternative to parallelism, as Titmuss has proposed in a somewhat different context, is "to channel more resources to [the poor] through established, socially approved, 'normal' institutions: social security, tax deductions, education and training, medical care, housing and other acceptable routes."[25] His proposal brings us to our second strategy.

Redistribution and Social Choice

To create equality of opportunity, we must provide a proportionately larger investment in resources for the socially disadvantaged. Although the roots of the problem may be in institutional disfunction, as we have suggested, the remedies may be elsewhere. Jencks proposed that it might be important "to try raising school expenditures in one slum area to, say, double the level in nearby suburbs—just to see what would happen."[26] Thus, we may need to invest twice the amount in services and in staff if we wish these individuals to benefit, at least in the same amount as other sectors of society. These services should be available to the total underprivileged sector rather than to isolated subgroups among the poor.

Innovations sought by local community development projects cannot realistically be implemented without substantial federal aid, for financially starved communities cannot, by themselves, find the resources to develop the preschool nursery programs in urban ghettos or to expand per capita student expenditure so that they can obtain better qualified teachers and lower student-teacher ratios. The recently enacted Elementary and Secondary Education Act of 1965 is one attempt to redistribute resources to lower-income areas.

In addition to providing resources directly to service institutions, other reforms can be introduced that will distribute purchasing power directly to the individuals so they can then purchase services on the open market. This strategy is more directly concerned with challenging institutional performance than is the strategy of redistribution. By shifting the command of resources from the dispenser to the consumer, a new force for change may be unleashed, perhaps one that is powerful enough to establish a new center of gravity. This could force a realignment among agencies and produce changes within and among them. Institutions would thus be forced to become more responsive to the preferences of consumers.

Consider the implications of a reform that emphasizes cash allowances as well as free or subsidized services: A subsidy to provide a guaranteed college education for all, with the necessary financial support available directly to the individual consumer, is one example. Parents might be given educational subsidies in the form of vouchers; they would be required to exercise their option, and schools would be required to honor them. There is, of course, a partial precedent for this in the educational allowances granted to veterans after World War II. Some of the evidence suggests that this policy tapped a new level of socioeconomic participation in higher education. (It also spurred economic growth.) A policy of universal education based upon common citizenship rather than as compensation for military service could adopt the same principle.

Consider another example: By drastically raising the wage base in the Social Security system to 20 or 30 thousand dollars—while retaining the present formula, which weighs benefits in favor of low-income holders—it is possible to convert a regressive tax system into a genuinely progressive benefit system. Thus, a single reform can serve as an important instrument for income redistribution. The Social Security system can be extended to embrace income insufficiency as well as income interruption as we move toward some form of guaranteed income for all.

But redistribution, combined with a conscious policy of consumer sovereignty, departs from the prevailing orthodoxy of how to allocate services. Can the expansion of consumer choice serve as a strategy for promoting institutional change as well as enlarging freedom? Let us say that the proposal at least merits public debate to uncover the costs and benefits of such a policy. Leftwing critics of England's welfare state, like Abel-Smith, have proposed more freedom of choice in the social services:

> My bias in the future development of the social services is to argue for more benefits which people can choose how to spend, at the expense of some services now provided in kind, as long as the state ensures that the services are available and limits the adverse effects of the profit motive.[27]

The Strategy of Welfare Incrementalism

The third strategy of change may be described as welfare incrementalism. Illustrated by the theory on which the Community Action Program of the Economic Opportunity Act is at least implicitly based, four of its distinguishing characteristics can be isolated—localism, gradualism, comprehensiveness, and selectivity.

Although the resources and purposes of CAP programs may originate outside the local community, the strategy nevertheless depends on local initiative and direction. One of its major underlying goals is to revitalize local democracy by strengthening the competence of local institutions to perform their tasks, both singly and in concert. Innovative programs must emerge from the local strategy, for if change occurs at the insistence and under the direction of the Federal government, it may undermine the local initiative it seeks to promote.

Second, the strategy is gradual or incremental. Gradualism, as Lindblom has suggested, "involves the slow movement *away* from social ills as contrasted with fundamental change which seeks to restructure basic policy as it moves toward known and clearly defined goals."[28] The philosophy on which this approach to gradualism is premised leads to the development of social remedial programs based, as Titmuss has noted, on "separate laws for the poor [by which] administrators, psychiatrists, and social workers can help and counsel the minority poor to abandon the 'culture of poverty.' "[29] By contrast, a more fundamental approach redefines the problem of income deficiency as arising from the basic structure of society.

Third, the strategy is comprehensive; it rests on the assumption that the efforts of many institutions, each acting in concert with the other, must be brought to bear if lasting change is to be achieved. The reduction of poverty depends upon simultaneous intervention by many institutions—health, education, housing, etc. The specific manner in which the efforts of these institutions reinforce each other remains obscure in both theory and practice. Global terms like "linkage" and "coordination" provide the rhetoric that masks the ambiguity.

Finally, the strategy is selective. It seeks to service and to involve in policy decisions those who are in greatest need (in contrast with the principle of universalism, wherein services are allocated to all citizens).

An incrementalist strategy of reform may lack coherence because the components of the strategy tend to be in conflict. Comprehensiveness requires a coalition of institutional interests, but each member of a coalition seeks to maximize and defend the interests of the organization he represents. In the end, the allocation of resources is more a function of the relative power of participating groups than of a rational, coherent plan to introduce the changes that seem necessary. A representative structure of necessity is preoccupied with sustaining the coalition and avoiding jurisdictional conflicts.

In addition, gradual reform, which is to be brought about by working directly with the institutions to be reformed, must be limited to the kinds of projects the institutions are already prepared to undertake. Further, the programs that emerge from this strategy will be pressed to demonstrate their validity. The orientation to success may lead to "creaming," which in time leads to a modification or abandonment of the principle of selectivity; self-reform, based on gradualism, is limiting; and comprehensiveness leads more to consensus than to innovation.

All these strategies—parallelism, redistribution and choice, and welfare incrementalism—are important, but all have limitations and must be viewed against the broader framework of the purpose, direction, and meaning of social services. We must examine our strategies of reform against the more searching question: What purposes do we wish our welfare institutions to serve?

NOTES

1. Alvin W. Gouldner, "The Secrets of Organizations," in *The Social Welfare Forum, 1963* (New York: Columbia University Press, 1963), p. 170.
2. The term standards is used variously to refer to criteria used by organizations for screening and routing individuals to services, for professional norms of behavior, and for community values as they are reflected in the mission of welfare organizations.

   The following discussion draws freely on an earlier paper written in collaboration with Lloyd Ohlin [Lloyd E. Ohlin and Martin Rein, "Social Planning for Institutional Change," *The Social Welfare Forum, 1964* (New York: Columbia University Press, 1964), pp. 85–99].
3. A. V. Cicourel and John I. Kitsuse, *The Educational Decision-Makers* (New York: Bobbs-Merrill, 1963).
4. *Ibid.*, pp. 62–63.
5. Discussed in Cicourel and Kitsuse, *op. cit.*
6. Thomas P. Monahan, "On the Incidence of Delinquency," *Social Forces,* XXXIX (1960), 71.
7. Richard Cloward, paper presented to the Citizens' Advisory Council Meeting of the President's Committee on Juvenile Delinquency and Youth Crime, New York City, January 3, 1963, pp. 3–4.
8. Derek L. Phillips, "Rejection: A Possible Consequence of Seeking Help for Mental Disorders," *American Sociological Review,* XXVIII (1963), 963–972.
9. John R. Seeley, "Social Psychology, Self, and Society," paper presented at A. B. Helmsbey Lecture Series, Brandeis University, Waltham, Massachusetts, November 1962.
10. Alfred J. Kahn, "Case Channeling," p. C-6, and "Service Boundaries," p. B-14. Unpublished papers by Dr. Alfred Kahn.

11. Thomas S. Szasz, *Law, Liberty and Psychiatry* (New York: Macmillan Co., 1963), pp. 57–71.
12. Elliot Mishler and Norman Scotch, "Sociocultural Factors in the Epidemiology of Schizophrenia," *Psychiatry*, XXVI (1963), p. 328, footnote 55.
13. *The Administration of Services to Children and Youth in New York City* (New York: Institute of Public Administration, 1963), p. 19, note 16.
14. Reported in *New York Times*, November 17, 1963.
15. Personal communication from Lloyd Ohlin. Also reported in Ohlin and Rein, *op. cit.,* p. 93.
16. Frank Riessman, *The Culturally Deprived Child* (New York: Harper & Row, 1962), p. 16.
17. Kenneth B. Clark, *Dark Ghetto: Dilemmas of Social Power* (New York: Harper & Row, 1965), p. 49.
18. Vera C. Perrella, "Employment of High School Graduates and Drop-Outs in 1963," *Monthly Labor Review*, LXXXVII (1964), 526.
19. Gunnar Myrdal, *Challenge to Affluence* (New York: Pantheon Books, 1963), p. 42.
20. Robert Morris and Martin Rein, "Emerging Patterns in Community Planning," in *Social Work Practice, 1963* (New York: Columbia University Press, 1963), p. 170.
21. Nathan Glazer, "A New Look in Social Welfare," *New Society*, II, 58 (1963), 8.
22. *Ibid.*
23. Nathan Glazer, "Paradoxes of American Poverty," *The Public Interest*, No. 1 (Fall 1965), p. 81.
24. Charles Frankel, *The Democratic Prospect* (New York: Harper & Row, 1962), p. 161.
25. Richard M. Titmuss, "Poverty vs. Inequality: A Diagnosis," *The Nation*, CC, No. 6 (1965), p. 131.
26. Christopher Jencks, "Is the Public School Obsolete?" *The Public Interest*, No. 2 (Winter 1966), p. 21.
27. Brian Abel-Smith, *Freedom in the Welfare State* (London: David Neil & Co., 1964), p. 8.
28. David Braybrooke and Charles E. Lindblom, *A Strategy of Decision: Policy Evaluation as a Social Process* (New York: The Free Press of Glencoe, 1963), p. 102.
29. Titmuss, *op. cit.,* p. 131.

Chapter 5

The Strange Case
of Public Dependency

All of us are dependent during major and important periods of our lives. No one finds this strange or reprehensible. What does cause great, and rising, concern is *public* dependency.

This conception of dependency as a social evil is in part the legacy inherited from the early English Victorians. It is deeply ingrained in our philosophy of individualism and our commitment to industrialism. The critical social problem in the early nineteenth century was "pauperism," a condition defined as individual weakness of character which "poor relief" only encouraged. Nor have we today resolved the moral dilemma posed in the Victorian era. The fear that economic security robs initiative and promotes dependency is an abiding and disturbing issue in contemporary social policy.

In a period of unprecedented prosperity, with the predicted Gross National Product for 1965 almost 660 billion dollars, three very different factors intensify public concern over dependency: rising welfare costs, obtrusiveness of the urban poor, and rising unemployment.

The Social Security Administration estimates that the total spent on health, welfare, and education during fiscal 1963–64 was 71 billion dollars. This exceeds the total outlay for national defense. Today about 12 per-

Reprinted by permission of the publisher from *Trans-action*, March, 1965. I am indebted to Richard Titmuss for many unacknowledged insights about the problem of dependency.

cent of the Gross National Product is spent on social welfare. When public and private costs are taken together, expenditures exceed 108 *billion* dollars. The unrelenting *rise* in public assistance expenditures (which in the public mind is identified with the dole) worries critics even more than the total cost. Expenditures for public aid (including medical payments and other programs) more than doubled in the past decade and a half, rising from approximately two-and-a-half billion dollars in 1949–50 to more than five-and-a-half billions in 1963–64. But the critics seldom note that public aid expenditures as a percentage of Gross National Product remained unchanged at .9 percent, and the per capita cost increased less than almost every other kind of social welfare expenditure.[1]

More than 220,000 families have been displaced by "urban renewal" in the last fourteen years. This does not include those moved for "public improvements"—public housing, parks, highways, public buildings, code reinforcement. It is estimated—and estimates are usually conservative—that the next decade will see close to a million persons displaced.

Two-thirds of those uprooted by renewals have been Negro. Their ability to move in the city and to find suitable low cost homes is limited. Their plight has been graphically described as a black neck caught in a white suburban noose. Uprooted and transported, they have suddenly become prominent and visible.

They have been wrenched from their protective sub-cultures and exposed to the standards of a more demanding society. Chester Hartman, research fellow at the MIT-Harvard Joint Center for Urban Studies, after an extensive review of the literature on relocation concludes that "the deleterious effects of the uprooting experience, the loss of familiar places and persons, and the difficulties of adjusting to and accepting new living environments may be far more serious issues than are changes in housing status."[2] Those who are relocated may experience a greater sense of personal failure and have less ability to cope with their environment. A program intended to aid the poor may unintentionally serve to increase their dependency.

Unemployment continues high. Recovery from each recession finds it at a higher level than the preceding recession. Our traditional institutions seem unable to cope with our growing labor force and the technologically displaced. The private sector of the economy has had in the past five years a growth rate which has absorbed less than half of the increase in the labor force.[3] Some critics believe that we are in danger of producing in the future a social underclass, displaced victims of a society which no longer requires their labor and rejects them as useless.

Like our Victorian predecessors we want to reduce dependency (pauperism), and like them we tend to see it in individual and personal terms, a form of social pathology. We prescribe social services for those receiving public financial aid, rehabilitation to make slum dwellers more acceptable tenants, and training programs to make them more employable. But in our attempts to reduce these dependencies we neglect the idea that those receiving public aid have a *right* to adequate and decent levels of assistance. We tend to ignore the amount of low income housing actually available to the poor; and we neglect the development of policies to expand industries and services which can contribute jobs for the unskilled.

But what actually is dependency? What assumptions do we hold about it?

1. We believe that the dependents among us can be isolated and identified as somehow morally and socially, if not physically, less adequate human beings than the rest of us.
2. We believe dependency would disappear if only we would eliminate the personal inadequacies of the dependents themselves.
3. We believe dependency is bad. We must work to reduce it.

Here is the popular dichotomy: those who give and those who receive; those who take out of our economic system more than they put into it, and those who pay the difference. Broadly speaking, those who work or have wealth are considered to contribute more than they get. If these ideas shed light on little else, they do illustrate how our social thinking is tied to the ethic that the "improvident" poor have somehow brought their ills upon themselves.

Each of these assumptions warrants re-examination.

I believe it far more profitable to view economic dependence as biologists view ecologic dependence: we are all involved with one another. Life is interdependent—and the most fruitful understanding of it can come from examining degrees and conditions of interdependency, rather than from isolating debits and credits in a ledger which draws a dichotomy between the dependent and the independent.

UNIVERSAL DEPENDENCY

Over time, as well as at any moment, man is both dependent and independent. The two states are closely related. After an age when most mammals have passed into senility or death, man is still dependent, still undergoing the long training in education, socialization, and skills he needs to function adequately; and as society grows more complex the process of maturation takes longer and longer.

We all experience dependency at some time. Childhood, schooling, illness, old age, pregnancy, child-birth, and early child-rearing all include periods of dependency. Few people now believe that these dependencies are undesirable. Few argue that we don't need more well-trained physicians, scientists, and humanists, even though this means that many adults will not "produce" until they are thirty. We believe that the social benefits—

the "total production"—are well worth the temporary costs. Obviously then, not all dependency can be bad.

Generally, we are trying to extend socially desirable dependency to more and more people. Barbara Wootton has perceptively observed that economists make dizzy leaps between two rival assumptions about social dependency:

> First, the doctrines of scarcity economics (which have the merit of being agreeable to common sense) teach that thrift and work are the keys to prosperity: the longer and the harder everyone works, the better will it be for all. Then, with the swing to economics of depression, common sense is abandoned in favor of the paradox that it is not saving but spending, not working but withdrawal from work, which conduces to economic health.[4]

Many professionals believe that if we only knew what bothered the individual, and applied the right remedy to him, then we might be able to take him completely out of dependency and make him a right thinking, wealth-producing, tax-paying (rather than tax-eating) citizen, to use President Johnson's recent terminology.

No two schools agree on the exact composition of that elixir. Some favor a get-tough policy (Newburgh, New York), others prefer a more humanistic and therapeutic approach, stressing individual rehabilitation (1962 amendments to the Social Security Act). Both views share a common assumption, that the dependent has an inadequate personality—a position which has been correctly described as "fundamentally arrogant." This approach has, nevertheless, been made virtually the sole basis of many therapeutic professions. Dependency as well as poverty may not be the result of personal inadequacy nearly so much as it is the result of the structure of society.

If dependency is a fault of individual personality, and the dependent is a less adequate person, then the third common assumption follows inevitably: dependency is bad—let's get rid of it. However, if we view dependency in terms of social organization rather than individual pathology, we arrive at different social judgments and treatments.

Dependency is fundamental to life, part of its basic fabric. We must concentrate on its patterning and expansion, not regard it merely as an area of rot which must be cut out or at least "contained." It has long term causes and long term effects, and they must be analyzed. We need to develop a language of social growth and social costs, comparable to the concepts of individual growth and individual pathology.[5]

No act is, after all, without its consequences, no social act without its social costs. We often pay dearly for what seemed like a good policy at the time—and may even have been a necessity. Such socially unanticipated consequences—or "disservices"—greatly affect the amount and direction of dependency. They are the costs of progress.

According to William K. Knapp, writing on *The Social Costs of Private Enterprise,* economic disservices include "all direct and indirect losses suffered by persons or the general public as a result of economic activities."[6] The costs of extra washing and of respiratory troubles from industrially polluted air are such disservices as are other hazards to health and safety caused by business and industry. Often the organization of the market does not require a business to pay the economic costs to others of its actions. In the same way, the social costs of technological change are not borne by those who benefit most directly.

We neglect these disservices partly because we tend to regard industrialization in a society much as we regard puberty in a youth—we assume that once it is technically past it is all over, and growing up and adjusting is finished. Actually the tensions and problems associated with growth continue at each stage of development.

In the early stage of industrialization almost all other interests of our society were subordinated to it. It left a toll of human suffering so severe and widespread that, according to Karl Polanyi, if unchecked, it could have wiped out civilization.[7] With the movement from farm to industrial town came overcrowded slums, gross exploitation of labor, the brutalization of work, a declining standard of living (at least in the short run), and the incalculable psychological suffering as the centuries' old way of life broke down. Richard Titmuss notes: "Most of the long-industrialized countries of the West are still burdened by the as yet uncompensated disservices of the early stage of their economic growth."[8]

THE TROUBLE WITH PROGRESS

We are hindered by the new adjustments rising from what George Friedman calls "making industrial man into an object of rationalized production."[9] Close to a quarter billion tests are given annually to determine how well we can be made to fit into the increasingly specialized tasks of business and industry. All this testing and adjusting is going ahead despite the fact that, as a recent Russell Sage Foundation report says, "virtually nothing is known at present about the impact the testing movement is having on the society as a whole . . . (or) the individuals . . . directly affected."[10]

Tests increase "rationality" and "objectivity." Many executives and educators welcome the chance to reduce the unpredictability of personality to scores on a profile or holes in a card.

But those tested are not as enthusiastic. As one passes through the sorting process, his chances for work, education, status, fulfillment, and even social benefits are determined by a new form of social discrimination, most potent against those already disadvantaged. The reject will likely respond by retreating—turning his back on what he is not "fit" to obtain. A recent proposal has urged a United States Supreme Court test of the constitutionality of determining the educational future of children of underprivileged backgrounds through the use of intelligence and aptitude tests. *"Selection for excellence" is therefore becoming an increasingly effective way to create dependents.*

Another potent multiplier of dependency is automation. This is becoming an old, much documented story. In the last decade the population of the United States increased by 20 percent, production increased 43 percent, but the number of factory workers decreased 10 percent. We will need twelve million new jobs in the next decade—at present rates, which may decline, we supply six.

It is not because our economy is not working well (as during the depression) that these people become dependent—but because it *is* working well. Efficiency has made them superfluous or branded them incompetent. They did not pass the tests; they had the wrong skills or backgrounds; they were too old; they were in the wrong place; they could not adapt quickly enough. They no longer fit and are rejected. *Technical progress increases dependency.*

While industry often informs a man that he is too old to be hired at forty, medicine informs him that he can expect to live past seventy. A white girl born in 1959 has a better chance of reaching age sixty than her grandmother, born in 1900, had of reaching age five.[11] Should that grandmother, however, still be alive, she can look forward to another sixteen years. The aged population is increasing rapidly.

The young, too, are fruitful and multiply. Prosperity breeds optimism; prosperous women breed babies. More people marry, they marry younger, they have children earlier. Enough babies are born each year in the United States (and live past infancy) to populate Chicago, plus a couple of its suburbs. The young and old make up our two largest and most rapidly growing groups of dependents. Like the universe we are exploding in all directions.

And not only are the traditional killers of the very old and very young being overcome; we provide sheltered environments in which the deprived, rejected, handicapped, weak, and sick survive longer. We seldom make them well and competent (our illness patterns have shifted from acute to chronic) —we merely help them live longer. If anything, it has made them more dependent than before. *Medical progress increases dependency.*

Social disservices also occur in education and welfare—where social consequences are supposed to be anticipated. For instance, many believe that the best way to "anticipate" and "prevent" trouble is by early diagnosis and intensive treatment, but individuals singled out for such treatment often find themselves stigmatized and discriminated against—precisely what the treatments were supposed to prevent—and the programs boomerang.[12]

In England, epileptics avoid treatment for this reason—employable before "help" which labels them, they are often not employable after. In New York *potential* delinquents may find themselves bearing the onus of *actual* delinquents—and react accordingly. We are affected in what we are by the way others see us. Human behavior comes to conform with the assumptions we make about it. *Labelling increases dependency.*

We rehabilitate and retrain ex-convicts, ex-mental patients, and the unemployed to be able to hold jobs and fit into our society. We do not retrain industry, unions, government, or people generally to accept them. We run the risk of not delivering what we promise. Programs which are aimed solely at changing individuals and which neglect institutional reforms must encounter this difficulty.

The Job Corps, as organized, remains a splintered and isolated program; unless positive steps are taken to assume that its graduates really get more jobs or education or social and health services, it will have little effect. Established programs tend to stubbornly resist integration with new resources, and this contributes to one of the gravest deficiencies in these community programs. There is danger in starting a cycle of social change for which we provide no closure.

The higher the expectation, the greater and more complete the disappointment and feelings of hopelessness, worthlessness, and cynicism so characteristic of the American poor. The greater the leap between aspiration and reality, the more inevitable the fall. We may succeed in imbuing lower-class people with middle-class standards of success; and thereby do little more than deprive them of the supports of lower-class life.

The Job Corps, like all retraining programs, must decide whom to take and whom to reject. To assure the success and continued congressional support of this controversial program, a substantial amount of "creaming" may be unavoidable—accepting those who need the program least, but are most likely to succeed. But what will be the meaning for those who are turned away? What explanations will be offered to those not accepted? Titmuss has recently suggested that rejection from the Job Corps may mean ultimate rejection from the world of work, and this may prove to be more important than rejection by the armed forces, the colleges, or employers in business and government. And if we fail to provide those who have been rejected with physical and mental health services, we also exclude them from the world of clinical help. We thus assign them to a form of social death—scrap them as "social junk," to use Park's graphic term.

We give capital depletion allowances and pursue other policies resulting in the use of labor-saving devices and the reduction of low skilled jobs. But, for the most part we do not create national policies which encourage the development of labor-intensive industries such as health, nursing, education, recreation, and welfare—vital to the poor themselves as services. Shortages in these fields could be partly met if those jobs which needed less training were filled by those who had less training. But the people who take such jobs must feel that they have futures and can rise eventually to professional status. Little organized effort is being made to reduce the rigidities of procedure which block this upward mobility. Professional associations, as well as labor unions, attack it as a threat to "quality of service" and to professional privilege and position. *Retraining and professionalism themselves contribute to dependency.*

THE ODDS ON FAILURE

Since success is increasingly determined by who can get, or has, an education, future failures are being created earlier and earlier—and with less and less chance of reprieve. This trend is intensifying.

Not all failures come from lack of ability; a very great many are socially determined. Some persons never get adequate opportunities for education or training; others do not want—or do not know how—to take advantage of them. Alfred J. Kahn, professor at the New York School of Social Work, sums up:

> Of every one hundred children of high school age, eighty-seven enter high school and sixty-seven graduate . . . only thirty enter college and fifteen are graduated. . . . Of school drop-outs, one of three leaves during the eighth grade or before. . . .[13]

More than two-thirds of *all* children complete high school, but only 45 percent of *poor* children; 30 percent of youth on Aid to Families of Dependent Children (age 18-24) had not completed high school. Nor is the situation improving. A recent national survey dismally notes: "Little, if any, gain has been realized in the proportions of ADC children finishing high school since (a comparable) 1950 study was completed."[14] Eighty-nine percent of the bright sons of the well-to-do expect to go to college, but only 29 percent of the brightest sons of the poor. Among dullards (those with lowest quintile I.Q. scores) 56 percent of the prosperous expect college, but only 9 percent of the poor even hope for it.[15] Intentions must be distinguished from action. When actual enrollments rather than expectations are examined, the picture is even worse. Moreover, there is a strong and continuous trend downward—almost 1 in 4 heads of poor families have even *less* education than their parents, if those parents had nine grades or more—despite the urgent necessity for more education than the previous generation.[16] The final grim shadow for the future is cast by the 1965 report of the Council of Economic Advisers:

> Many individuals fail to develop their talent fully, often for economic reasons. In 1960, one third of the top 25 percent of youth did not go on to college; 5 percent did not even finish high school. This is a serious waste.[17]

The uneducated are even more handicapped in the search for jobs today than they were two decades ago. Since the median educational level of the entire male labor force has risen by more than 50 percent, the dramatic and disturbing results are clear. Today one third of all Negro youths age 16–21 who are out of school are also out of work.

A dropout who finds a job is, of course, "independent" early, and some might rejoice at this fact. But as a national survey shows, dependency increases soon, and greatly: 57 percent of dropouts under twenty-five were unemployed during the last five years, compared to 4 percent of college graduates.

The much-heralded theory of the poverty cycle assumes that poverty is self-perpetuating because deprivation in one generation leads, through cultural impoverishment, to family breakdown and indifference to educational achievement of children, to poverty in the next generation. A valid alternative analysis would focus not on personal defects but on institutional rejection, and the indifference which leads to development of protective sub-cultures which wall people off from the threatened destruction of their personalities.

Economic poverty begets educational poverty which begets economic poverty which begets dependency which begets economic and educational poverty—in a continuous closed circle of "begets." Children of poor parents study in larger classes with more difficult students in schools with less money under teachers who are paid less and are less well trained. Their education is inferior and they are little motivated or encouraged.

The rejects from our various selection processes form an army of outcasts, the socially disaffiliated. England has its "teddy boys," Russia its "hoodlums," and we our delinquents and skid row bums. All countries have "problem families."

Our rising affluence increases the army of those who prosper and belong; it also creates a permanent underclass who suffer from deprivation, failure, and loss of status.

What happens to the "socially disaffiliated?" According to sociologist Erving Goffman in his article, "Cooling the Mark Out," we create social ghettos where,

> . . . persons who have died in important ways come gradually to be brought together into a common graveyard that is separated ecologically from the living community. . . . Jails and mental institutions . . . certain regions and towns in California (set aside) as asylums for those who have died in their capacity as workers and as parents, but . . . still alive financially. For the old in America who have also died financially . . . old folks homes and rooming house areas . . .[18]

During a depression a "failure" can blame his plight on the "system"; during prosperity it is much more difficult to avoid blaming himself, and becoming hopeless and apathetic. The ethic of the prosperous—that their welfare is due entirely to their own virtuous efforts—is infecting the poor, in reverse.

How does a society respond to its socially deprived? Some writers, like Talcott Parsons and Bronislaw Malinowski, believe that social systems have built-in equilibrium mechanisms that make automatic adjustments to severe threat.

But they tend to ignore the time lag—the years during which much suffering and misery is endured, before "natural counter-forces" can deflect or gear them to useful purposes—if they ever do so.

As we examine the mechanism of response—the social services provided in America's Welfare State—it becomes apparent that there is a curious disregard for those dependents whose plight is most desperate. Two crucial policy questions must be examined: who gets what services? What is the quality of those services? Even a cursory examination of these questions led Gunnar Myrdal to conclude that there is "a preverted tendency" in American social policy so that those who need help most do not get it.

So pervasive has been our failure to cope with poverty and dependency that this tendency can be called the Iron Law of Social Welfare.

Medical care. James N. Morgan and his colleagues found in a national study that only one-third of poor families have hospital insurance of minimal adequacy, and three-fifths have no insurance at all. Using disability as a measure of need, only 24 percent of families with a person disabled were covered, compared to 76 percent with no one disabled.[19]

A recent report on the quality of medical care in New York City found that accredited specialists provide different care in different hospital settings. Ability and training alone do not assure quality services. How services are organized and, we expect, to whom they are offered, also affect the quality of care. Physicians consider out-patient clinics the Siberias of hospitals, and serve grudgingly; students and interns are seldom adequately supervised. There are too few physicians, too many sick, too little time, not enough concern for the patient.[20]

Welfare. Welfare programs are supposed to add to the incomes of those who do not have enough to live decently. But a University of Michigan study showed that half of the families in poverty did not receive any form of transfer payments, including social security. Daniel P. Moynihan, Assistant Secretary of Labor, has recently quipped that "social security is for winners, not losers," meaning those who have won some economic stability. Pensions help even fewer; only 11 percent of the poor had private pension help, compared to 40 percent of all families. Finally, only 23 percent of the poor receive public assistance.[21]

Child care. The iron law does not make exceptions for the young and weak. Alfred Kahn has recently documented the nature and scope of what he calls our "urban-child care crisis." He calls attention to the long term and sometimes unnecessary institutionalization of children; long term waiting in temporary shelters; frequent shifting of children from foster home to foster home. The handicapped, emotionally damaged, and non-white children are those most disadvantaged. The long term consequences of their neglect will be paid in the next generations.[22]

Education and housing. Education is the path upwards—and the poor, down farthest, get the worst, and have the least motivation to use what they have. In housing, the very large families and the "socially unacceptable" (unwed mothers, for instance) are hardest to place.

Mental health. The most skilled psychiatrists and psychologists have always worked with the least disturbed patients. Treating middle and upper class neurotics generally yields better results—and income—than treating lower class psychotics. One of the reports of the Joint Commission on Mental Health and Illness notes: "Usually the most difficult social and psychological problems fall in the area of no one's responsibility. The psychotics, sexual psychopaths, persons with suicidal or homicidal impulses, and persons presenting acute somatic symptoms are the groups left without any help short of commitment."[23]

Is the Iron Law of Social Welfare really iron—that is, inevitable? If so why?

REPEALING THE IRON LAW

I believe that the three chief factors that lead to denial of services to those in greatest need are professionalization, the rejection or inability of the needy to use the services, and the logical consequences of our social philosophy.

Professionals want to get satisfaction, pleasure, prestige, status, and income for their work. They want their efforts to succeed and to be acknowledged and appreciated. The most difficult, suspicious, recalcitrant, ignorant, impoverished, and hopeless cases afford little opportunities for such satisfactions.

We need more knowledge about the professions which are "increasingly becoming the arbiters of our welfare fate." Titmuss notes that, "We have to ask . . . questions about the ways in which professional people (doctors, teachers, social workers, and many others) discharge their roles in diagnosing need and in selecting and rejecting patients, clients, and students for this or that service."[24]

Professional associations will not readily pose these questions because they are organized by professionals themselves to serve their own interests. Change usually must come from outside, but often in cooperation with insurgent insiders. The public health movement rose over the vigorous opposition of physicians; and the juvenile courts developed in spite of lawyers, not because of them.

The poor and the dependent may be even less eager to work with professionals than the professionals are to work with them. Despite their physical presence in our cities they live in a far country with its own iron laws, which we must learn. As voluntary consumers of social services they will not willingly do things merely because respectable people think they should, nor deliberately seek out what looks like trouble or embarrassment. The barriers they create to social reformers are, as Herbert Gans has pointed out, "reaction(s) to the threat of humiliation."[25]

Professional and organizational commitment must precede the demand for responsibility, cooperation, motivation, and trust. Consumer rejection is most likely to be overcome only when we offer authentic programs with assured delivery, rather than promissory notes.

Our social philosophy states strongly that the greatest rewards should go to the most productive. "Who does not work, neither shall he eat." Those who do not produce are by implication, inferior. Our humanitarian values (no one should starve in the midst of plenty) may seem to be contradicted; nevertheless we increasingly demand of the needy that they be willing to conform and be "rehabilitated" from the sin of dependency to qualify for financial aid.

Many so-called welfare payments, like social security, are in fact rewards or delayed payments for productivity, not really welfare at all. Returns are related to earned salary; benefits are channeled through the wage system; the marginal groups follow the iron law and are excluded. When liens on property are required to qualify for public assistance, aid really becomes a temporary loan. One early reason given was ease of administration: the stable and employed are easy to handle and find. Another is the "foot in the door" tactic: it is felt to be politically sounder to establish a welfare principle with socially acceptable groups, and then hope coverage and benefits trickle down. But the trickle-down system has not always worked. For example, from its very inception workman's compensation was restricted to the aristocracy of the manual workers—the skilled laborer. Even today, 20 percent of workers, concentrated among the unskilled, are not covered. We often find it inexpedient to accept our social services for what they are. For instance educational programs of great national benefit appear coyly—and with inadequate coverage—behind the fig leaves of "GI Bills" for veterans or national defense scholarships.

In broad summary:

1. Our present welfare policy is not really designed to reach the neediest.
2. The poor have their own defenses against imputations of inferiority, and they resist assimilation.
3. Professionalization has hindered work with the poor.

To repeal the iron law we must develop social philosophy and techniques specifically designed for that purpose. We have the choice—the dilemma is one of ideology not technology.

Social welfare is a means to an end—and it is within our power and privilege to choose both the means and the end. Bismarck used social welfare to perpetuate an empire; in the thirties the United States used it to prevent social disruption. Today we employ it to preserve the middle-class ethic of rewarding the industrious.

We can continue along this path, or we can make welfare serve social justice and humanitarianism by using the criterion of *common citizenship,* in which need, not virtue, determines aid. If we choose the former, we had better think seriously about whether we really want to end the problems of dependency at all.

If we really mean to attack dependency:

1. Redistribution of income and benefits must be the fundamental principle which informs our social policy. We must invest much more work and money, absolutely and relatively, for the underprivileged. Post-hospital care, expanded job and educational opportunities—such services must be available to all of the poor.
2. Teachers, social workers, doctors, and others who choose to work with the poor, instead of being in effect penalized financially for their choice, should be given special rewards and incentives—including much more recognition.
3. When we think of the dependency of the poor, our attention is rigidly fixed on those who should be working and are not. We neglect the student preparing for a socially useful occupation, the mother caring for children, the aged who have earned retirement, the workers who are forced out of the labor force by technological change. We do not reject dependency—*only dependency of the poor.*

We need to extend the principles of socially accepted dependency to the poor. We also need to raise the "acceptable" school-leaving age, lower retirement age, and provide for periodic retraining. Dependency must become a social right which can expand freedom, and increase the range of human choice. Such a policy could well decrease future dependency and make old age less terrifying.

In the twentieth century, we may witness as dramatic a change in social policy direction as the shift from pauperism to poverty in the preceding century. We must in the next era develop policies based on: socially accepted forms of dependency; adequate rather than minimum services; compensation for those disadvantaged by rapid technological change. Such policies must be informed by a philosophy of redistributive social justice.

What would such a program look like? *The Economist,* a pragmatic scholarly journal in England, has proposed programs for the *radical reform* of the social services.[26] *The Economist* divided social services into two distinct objectives: (1) generous compensation for those damaged by rapid economic change; (2) a separate program for the relief of need. In specifics:

Unemployment pay should be increased so substantially that, for a short time, a man thrown out of a job should actually get more than he did while on the job to compensate for the pain in looking for a new job.

Mustering out pay (or pension) for men displaced by technological change, to be drawn for short periods (five years) even after they accept other jobs.

Housing subsidies to be attached to tenants rather than to houses—that is, a redistribution of subsidies to people rather than to structures.

Income guarantees unrelated to previous wages earned, so that the retired can maintain a standard of living much higher than known during their working years; an income consistent with the changing standard of living resulting from economic growth which will permit the poorest section of the old-age population to maintain a decent and adequate standard of living without recourse to public assistance.

A graduated social security tax which would be sharply progressive and have an income redistributive effect.

Higher family allowances, even above the guaranteed income level (or the prevailing wage scale), for poor parents with very large families.

The politics of who gets what and how, outside of the market, will become the salient issue of our vast social services in the generations to come. Solutions to the problem of dependency will be found only as we develop a social calculus which acknowledges our social costs and a constituency which can, in this new political game, make its weight felt to help pay them. We must search out, as Titmuss has recently suggested, "ways of extending the welfare state to the poor."

NOTES

1. Ida C. Merriam, "Social Welfare Expenditures, 1963–4," *Social Security Bulletin*, Vol. 27, No. 10 (October 1964), p. 8.
2. Chester Hartman, "The Housing of Relocated Families," *Journal of the American Institute of Planners*, Vol. 30, No. 4 (November 1964), p. 266.
3. R. T. Bowman and M. E. Martin, "Special Report on Unemployment Statistics: Meaning and Measurement," *The American Statistician*, Vol. 16, No. 4 (October 1962).
4. Barbara Wootton, "Is There a Welfare State?" *Political Science Quarterly*, Vol. LXXXVII, No. 2 (June 1963), p. 179.

5. Richard Titmuss (ed.), "The Social Division of Welfare," in *Essays in the Welfare State* (New Haven: Yale University Press, 1959), pp. 42–43.
6. William K. Knapp, *The Social Costs of Private Enterprise* (Cambridge: Harvard University Press, 1950).
7. Karl Polany, *The Great Transformation* (Boston: Beacon Press, 1957), pp. 68–76.
8. Richard Titmuss (ed.), "Industrialization and the Family," in *Essays in the Welfare State* (New Haven: Yale University Press, 1959), p. 108.
9. George Friedman, "The Social Consequences of Technical Progress," *International Social Science Bulletin*, Vol. 4, No. 2 (1952).
10. *Russell Sage Foundation, Annual Report 1961–62* (New York: Russell Sage Foundation, 1962), p. 9.
11. Frank W. Nottstein, "People Versus Resources," *Current*, 1962.
12. Jackson Toby, "Early Identification and Intensive Treatment of Pre-Delinquents: A Negative View," *Social Work*, Vol. 6, No. 3 (July 1961), p. 5.
13. Alfred J. Kahn, *New York City Schools and Children Who Need Help* (New York: Citizens Committee for Children of New York, 1962).
14. James N. Morgan et al., *Income and Welfare in the United States* (New York: McGraw-Hill, 1962).
15. Patricia C. Sexton, *Education and Income: Inequalities of Opportunities in our Public Schools*, (New York: Viking, 1961), p. 190.
16. Morgan, *et al., op cit.*, p. 208.
17. *Economic Report of the President*, 89th Congress, 1st Session, House Document No. 28 (Washington: U.S. Government Printing Office, 1965), p. 158.
18. Erving Goffman, "On Cooling the Mark Out," *Psychiatry: Journal of the Study of Interpersonal Relations*, Vol. 15, No. 4 (November 1952), p. 451.
19. Morgan *et al., op cit.*, p. 205.
20. Osler L. Peterson, "Medical Care in the U.S." *Scientific American*, Vol. 209, No. 2 (August 1963), p. 23.
21. Morgan, *et al., op. cit.*, see pp. 205, 216, 217.
22. Alfred J. Kahn, "The Social Scene and the Planning of Services for Children," *Social Work*, Vol. 7, No. 3 (July 1962).
23. Reginald Robinson, David F. DeMarche, and Mildred K. Wagle, *Community Resources in Mental Health* (New York: Basic Books, 1960), p. 287.
24. For a thoughtful analysis on the dangers of professionalism see, Richard Titmuss, "The Hospital and its Patients," in *Essays in the Welfare State, op. cit.* pp. 119–132.
25. Herbert J. Gans, *The Urban Villages* (New York: Free Press, 1962), p. 249.
26. "Social Services: The Radical Solutions," *The Economist*, Vol. 212 (September 26, 1964), pp. 1209–1211.

Part III

Strategies of Innovation and Their Limits

Chapter 6

Coordination of Social Services

PROBLEMS IN THE ORGANIZATION OF SOCIAL SERVICES

It is perhaps somewhat misleading to refer to the manner in which social services are distributed in the United States as a "system." Is this term appropriate for describing and understanding the multiple, contradictory, and conflicting goals of social services, or the indefinite boundaries which distinguish social from public services? What imagery should we use to describe these various services and their relationship to each other? The system analog suggests that the parts are interrelated, functionally intertwined, and mutually reinforcing, each unit contributing to some purpose broader than its own survival. To adopt this perspective is to confuse prescription with description and to blur the boundaries between myth and reality, practice and ideals. Moreover, unless we specify the purposes of the "system," we have not extended the discussion very far, for we have developed no standards against which to evaluate its output.

Perhaps we might prefer a geographic metaphor. We could then draw a map of services and their patterns of dispersal. But for other reasons we would be equally

This article is a revision of a paper "Coordination of Social Services" which was originally prepared for the Foster Care Conference sponsored by the Child Welfare League of America, Inc., in New Orleans, La., Oct. 29-Nov. 1, 1967. It is published in the Proceedings of the Foster Care Conference. This revision printed here with permission of Child Welfare League of America, Inc.

misled. In drawing a map, we must distinguish the boundaries of separate service regions and this is the greatest problem of the social services. Consider the example of the police department. It is clearly not a social service, since its primary mission is social control and social protection of person and property. However, the police can pursue many policies to achieve these aims, and some of these policies might justifiably be classified as social services. The Institute of Public Administration budget analysis of services to youth in New York City reports that the police department spent 1.7 million dollars for individual, family, and community services, or 7 percent of the total amount spent by the city government for such services to youth. Of even more interest is that the police expenditures for these services amounted to half the total amount spent by the New York City Youth Board and more than the amount spent by hospitals.[1] This anomaly arises because the goals of social service are varied; they serve many masters, including social control. They are not simply "humanitarianism in search of a method" as has been suggested.[2]

A good case could be made for viewing social services as a psychedelic mosaic—where the boundaries are vague, overlapping, and uncertain; reality and myth merge, and a participant's mood in observing developments of social policy shifts from euphoria to despair (as many who have been following the developments of the 1967 Amendments to the Social Security Act must surely feel).

But the analysis of problems in the organization of social services presumes that we have a clear understanding and a reasonable definition of the purposes of social services. A classic illustration is in the penetrating analysis by Richard Titmuss, in which he argues that services performing similar functions should be grouped together.[3] Thus fiscal welfare, social welfare, and occupational welfare must be seen as part of the same system. Activities included or excluded from this more embracing definition affect not only total expenditure, but the characteristics of beneficiaries and our ultimate assessment of who pays and who benefits from the services. By this redefinition Titmuss attempts to demonstrate that the major beneficiaries of the high cost sector of the social services are the middle classes. The failure to redistribute benefits is used as an argument for restructuring the boundaries between benefit systems. Specifically, tax concessions could be abolished or reduced and administratively brought together in a system of family allowances, thereby using the revenue system as a benefit system.

The reclassification of social service institutions by their function rather than by their traditional labels can lead toward startlingly different inferences about the patterns and problems in the social services. Consider the example of institutional care for children in the United States. A boarding school is primarily concerned with education, whereas a children's institution is primarily concerned with providing substitute social and economic care. But the boundaries between care and educational institutions are often vague. Many children in military schools are placed there "primarily" because they are difficult to manage and present behavior problems to their families. Similarly, many Indian children are placed in institutions defined as boarding schools, but which are in fact residential settings for dependent children where education is only an ancillary function. If we examine the characteristics of children in institutions in the United States, we find that they are placed most often because of behavioral and emotional problems. If, however, we include Indian children in boarding schools in our definition of residential care, the character of the problem changes rather remarkably. Then a third of all children in institutions are there for social reasons including family breakdown as well as economic dependency. If we include children in military schools, then the major problem reverts to that of emotional instability,[4] with one major difference; instead of the problem being concentrated among low income children it is now more normally distributed among other income groups in the population.

The issues of purpose and boundary are closely interrelated. These questions are neither academic nor rhetorical for they dramatically affect the way in which services are patterned and organized. But the boundaries of social service are not easy to define, since institutions serve multiple purposes and it is difficult to isolate their primary and secondary functions. Ultimately, the definition of the problems of organizing a system should evolve from an assessment of the institutions' performance in relation to their achievements. The failure to achieve goals generates the administrative problems in the structure of social services.

For the reasons stated above, agreement of purposes is indeed the most elusive and intractable issue in the social services. This is why I have decided not to start with a classification of goals, but with the common sense, traditional statement of the problems in the organization of services. This pragmatic approach, hopefully, will help clarify the issues from which the principles for organizing social services can be developed.

New delivery systems must solve the problems of the old. Since no one system will solve all the problems, we need to specify which problems we are concerned about and how restructuring and refinancing services will contribute to a reduction of these problems.

It is possible to identify four persistent problems in the organization and distribution of social services: (1) the dispersal of *similar* functions; (2) discontinuity of *related* functions; (3) incoherence when *different* functions are pursued without relationship to each other; and (4) consumer choice, which becomes a special issue when there are alternative programs to reach a similar aim. Most efforts to reform the pattern of delivering services are in response to one or another of these problems. No single reform is likely to be addressed to all of these issues. Each problem is briefly presented, followed by a more extended analysis focused on how each arises in the distribution of services for children. Similar issues arise and can be identified in other social services as well.

Functional Dispersion (Duplication). When there is a dispersal of a similar function among many different community agencies there is a duplication of service. Generally, when this problem arises we are discussing the dispersal of personal social services, which are somewhat broader than are the social work functions. The problem of duplication is essentially a question about what these social services are and on what principles should they be organized. We are, by and large, not seriously talking about the duplication in education, medical care, housing, or cash transfers. In these areas pluralism is regarded as the virtue of choice and not the vice of inefficiency.

Dispersal may be an effective strategy to secure resources for a new or unpopular function, as in the case of manpower training at the federal level. At some stage in the development of such programs, there is interest in collecting, coordinating, or integrating these tasks and dispersal becomes a problem. The rationale often lies not in a concern about inefficiency but in a commitment to growth; by collecting hidden resources, we increase visibility and power and thus enhance the capacity to win more resources.

Discontinuity. Many services are clearly related to each other for each contributes to the completion of a given task. Thus recruiting, training, and placing individuals on the job are related in the sense that the same individuals may be involved in all of these activities over time. The problem of discontinuity arises when the flow of individuals among related programs is interrupted. This interruption may be due to structural and administrative difficulties, as in the manpower system, or to philosophical, moral, and professional issues, as in the child welfare system. Flow can be inhibited by specialization or by non-decisions as these examples respectively illustrate. The non-decision system poses the most challenging conceptual problems in creating a system to solve or reduce discontinuity.

The flow of clients through the system of interrelated activities can be impeded for many other reasons. When scarcity produces a lack of resources, each service must limit the number of individuals it can accept. A backup occurs when individuals are halted at entry into the system. An entry backup can be in waiting centers, that is special institutions in which individuals await disposition for extended periods of time (overcrowded shelters and detention centers), or simply on waiting lists in the case of community care. Discontinuity may also arise where each agency's intake policies so define its boundaries as to reject graduates of other programs. For example, a child guidance clinic may not accept children who have been in mental hospitals, or an employment agency may not accept training program graduates with police records. In these examples the flow from institutional to community care or from one community to another is halted because of conflicting agency policies. Finally, flow may be interrupted when referrals are based on faulty information, or clients find it inconvenient to use the physical facilities of the next related program.

Incoherence. Specialized and differentiated services become fragmented when they cannot be combined in a coherent fashion relevant to the solution of a given problem. This difficulty arises when a single problem requires multiple interventions. For example, housing, medical care, education, and income may all be necessary in any coherent program to reduce morbidity and mortality. Since the time phasing required to bring these activities together is often not self-evident, the problems of incoherence and discontinuity can be separated. That is, distinctions can be made among problems which require simultaneous interventions, those which require serial interventions, and those which require both. So defined, incoherence refers to the problem of simultaneous interventions. This, however, can be reduced by planning for a mix of policies which take account of each other. But the intractable problem of incoherence arises when we recognize that multiple interventions also imply multiple goals. While we might be able to develop a comprehensive plan (policy-mix) for a given goal, we have not yet defined a comprehensive goal to which all comprehensive programs can be subordinated. We thus have two problems of incoherence: how to allocate and combine resources among differentiated programs to achieve a stated goal, and how to reduce the competition for scarce resources among different programs which embrace different goals.

OEO catalog of Federal Assistance Programs for June, 1967, lists a total of 459 programs to help people improve their social and economic position. These programs are administered by fifteen different federal agencies and departments. In most cases, the federal structure is paralleled by state and local structures. Incoherence involves the difficulty of concerting the efforts of different programs, having different goals, priorities, and administrative arrangements, on behalf of a common goal or a common population in a common geographic or target area.

Reduction of Choice. In many respects, social services can be regarded as social commodities that are distributed outside of the market system. Simply providing cash to individuals may not, however, convert a social and personal demand into a marketable product, because the market does not respond instantly to consumer preferences. Factors such as professional monopoly inhibit the ability of the market to expand supply even in the face of greater demands. The result, as in the case of medical care, is that demand only forces prices higher. Consequently, we need to *plan* for the diversity and distribution of services to satisfy the preferences of individuals. Public social services have traditionally been justified as social protection for fallouts of the economic system and noncompliers of the cultural system. These groups need help in adjusting to and making use of other institutions because they lack the capacity to choose; it can be extended to the concept of social provision to meet consumer preferences. But, characteristically, we have been fettered to the principle of efficiency and have neglected to take account of the role of consumer choice in public provision. Many services have developed in such a fashion as to narrow the range of choices and options available to individuals with low income and minority group status. We have, for example, created a dual delivery system in child welfare based on race, and in medical care based on income. Even within a given system, we narrow choices by preferring some services to others, as in the community care movement. We tend to support these services because we regard them as more humane, but also as financially less expensive. We thus scatter the population in our mental and medical institutions into the community but do not take adequate account of the increased cost to other institutions. The result can be not only less choice, but also unseen increased indirect costs because our social arithmetic is too narrowly conceived. For example:

> Considered only in financial terms, any savings from fewer mental hospital inpatients might well be offset several times by more expenditures on the police forces, on prisons and probation officers; more unemployment benefits masquerading as sickness benefits; more expenditures on drugs; more research to find out why crime is increasing.[5]

The attempt to match a specific service to a recognized need is dependent upon the knowledge that a particular need will be met best by a particular service. But this level of knowledge has not yet been developed in relation to most services. Thus, there is little justification for a policy of constraining choice so as to develop optimal programs for a given problem. Consider the case of retraining ghetto youth. Such a program could take place in either residential care or in the community. We do not now know which youngsters should be sent to which type of service. Various countries rely on different patterns and there is no ultimate test of effectiveness or need.

Without benefit of empirical evidence of program effectiveness or an accurate scheme of social accounting, I believe we need to create a delivery system based explicitly on the principle of widening choices for consumers rather than on economy or the dominant professional fad. Greater choices for consumers also means more choice for professionals when they must act in the "best interests" of some clients.

In other words, we may need overlapping, which makes more choices possible. I have tried to state the case for choice, not on the moral grounds of freedom which are self-evident, but on the more pragmatic grounds of uncertainty.

DISPERSAL OF SIMILAR FUNCTIONS

It will be helpful to view this delivery problem in a historical and cross-national perspective. Social work as originated in the Charity Organization Society was concerned with the duplication of cash. The rationale that defined duplication as evil was that if charity was uncoordinated, individuals could find it more profitable to receive benefits than to work. Thus it was assumed that "noxious charity" inhibited initiative, destroyed self-reliance, and eroded the incentive to work. It was argued that since the cause of pauperism was the character of the recipient and not his circumstances, indiscriminate giving only further weakened his character by providing him with an alternative to work. According to this view there was a danger that a liberal social policy could destroy the economic system by undermining incentives and threatening the will to work. To solve this problem, charity needed to be organized. In the context of the late nineteenth century, this meant, in part, the elimination of duplication of cash benefits and a division of labor between relief in the public sector and charity in the private sector.

Later, in the twentieth century, the number of private voluntary agencies distributing cash benefits decreased as a result of the depression and the assumption of this responsibility by government; and this definition of duplication passed from public concern. Today, duplication of income transfers in social insurance is viewed by some as an acceptable and, indeed, a desirable social objective. Individuals are expected to secure a minimum of benefits from the public sector in the form of social security, and to supplement these by private pensions. This theory of duplication has the curious effect of keeping benefit levels in the public sector minimum rather than adequate. This type of duplicatory system may be contrasted with the view that the public sector should provide adequate dynamized benefits that rise with changes in the price level and with economic growth. Thus the current debate about the duplication of cash concerns the relative mix and priorities to be assigned to the public and the private sectors.

Duplication of services emerged as a more central issue only after responsibility for most means tested cash programs were assumed by the federal government and the social insurance provision was universalized. To highlight the different forms that the concern about duplicatory services takes we contrast developments in England and the United States.

THE ENGLISH AND AMERICAN EXPERIENCE

In England, the classic argument in support of a reorganization of services was that it was necessary to solve the problem of duplication. In one influential study of child neglect in Manchester in the early 1950s, David Donnison reports the following case:

> The probation officer called to find the mother being interviewed by an education welfare officer, a mental health visitor, a child welfare officer, and the city counselor—all of whom arrived, by coincidence, at the same moment. At least four other visitors probably called on her during the same week.[6]

Note the shift of perspective as we move from duplication of cash to duplication of services. It is now the client who needed to be protected against inundation by community agencies, each of which sends home visitors to secure similar information and to perform similar helping functions. In the concern about cash it was the system which needed to be protected against clients who exploited the weakness of uncoordinated charity.[7]

The solution proposed was that of the case conference. The units that needed to be coordinated were the personnel in social agencies who made home visits. The strategy tried to promote cooperation among the personnel by securing agreements as to who should visit and when visits might be made. Agency representatives met periodically to discuss specific individual cases in an effort to reduce the problem of duplication, defined here as the inundation of clients by agencies performing similar functions.

But by the late 1950s the *Report of the Working Party of Social Workers* took the position that the problems of duplication had been over-emphasized. The report calls attention to a study of families conducted by the London County Council. Identified as "problem families" they were therefore most vulnerable to multiple visiting. It found that visits by more than two workers in a month occurred only in about 15 percent of the cases studied. "The crux of the problem," the report concludes, was not "so much multiplicity of visiting as multiplicity of independent and unco-ordinated visiting."[8] They recommended that the case conference be retained as an appropriate administrative structure, but that the goal of the conference be shifted from preoccupation with duplication to consistency of policy among the different agencies. The logic of this argument thus shifted the concern from cooperation among line personnel to consistency of agency policies.

Can we coordinate the perspectives and policies of different community agencies, each of which is concerned with different functions, such as social control, social provision, social therapy, and social protection? Or must the consumer alone reconcile these conflicting perspectives? This difficult issue was partially sidestepped by relying on the optimistic assumption that information would facilitate communication and informed discussion would lead toward a consistent policy. That communication might intensify conflicting perspectives of different agencies and thus exacerbate the problems of achieving consistency, was not considered and perhaps not even recognized.

But is it either possible or desirable to achieve consistency of policy among varying agencies? Professionals working in child welfare services have characteristically assumed that such consistency of policy is both. Problems are typically not defined in terms of a conflict of interest among contending parties—the community preference, the desires of natural parents, and the needs of children. We have assumed that policy can and ought to be consistent and harmonious. Common interests can be achieved through sound casework practice, open communication, and the education of the community by the professional (the community as client). We may, however, now be more willing to accept a conflict-of-interest framework. The Gault decision, in the United States, reversing our earlier philosophy, now requires that a child charged with a delinquent act have legal representation. The same principle will apply to court action in removing a child from its home for reasons of neglect. Since social workers have felt that they represent the "best interests" of the child, they were reluctant to view the practice of child welfare in terms of a conflict of interest, which requires advocacy on behalf of one or another of the parties.

By the early 1960s in England the problem of duplication was again the focus of public concern. Now, the effectiveness of the case method as a technique for reducing duplication was in question, and the definition of the problem seems to have shifted as well. The rationale for being concerned with the problem of duplication was not so much the protection of the client from inundation and inconsistency, but the expansion and more effective use of social work manpower. An editorial in the *London Times* summarizes this argument in its evaluation of the Scottish White Paper, which was concerned with the reorganization of social services.

> There is planned to be a radical reconstruction in amalgamation of the too many social agencies administered by different authorities, which have come to resemble the blooming of Mao Tse Tung's hundred flowers. In this field, too, a hundred factions have struggles competing for staff with basically similar aptitudes and interest. The too frequent result has been general understaffing of services and the emergence of some ingeniously competitive methods of attracting those rare birds . . . [changes] should lead, eventually, to a greater harmonization and consistency in training courses for those who wish to enter the social services. They should also create an advantageous career structure, and remove the necessity for early specialization.[9]

It was the similar aptitudes and interest of staff, each widely dispersed among many social agencies, each in competition with the other, that was regarded as the primary problem of duplication. According to this formulation the duplication of manpower had not produced competition, but had inhibited the development of an adequate career structure for personnel in the social services. To solve the problem of the duplication of manpower, the strategy proposed is the creation of a single department of social services, which would include child care, school welfare, probation, community care for the mentally ill, the sick, and the handicapped, old people's welfare, the provision of domestic help, and aid for homeless families. This new department could, in turn, service the courts, the hospitals, the clinics, the welfare departments, and other organizations very much like a health department with its staff of doctors and nurses services the schools and other community institutions.[10] There is, as might be expected, some ambiguity regarding the nature of the common skill that is to be gathered together from the various agencies. Is it primarily counseling, guidance, and linking services such as information about other resources, or concrete services like child care, home help, and legal protection? This raises a fundamental question as to the nature of social work itself. This question leads to different points of view as to whether the new department should be called a department of social work, or family services, or social services. As the problem is redefined, the strategy to bring services together has also shifted from cooperation of personnel, to coordination of policies, to integration of manpower. The strategy of integration based on a common skill may be interpreted as a move toward greater efficiency, but it was primarily seen as a strategy for expanding the manpower and the resources to be spent for personal social services. Proponents of this strategy believed that by collecting social work and other related skills into a single department, it would be possible to convert dispersed and latent power into a central and active power by increasing its visibility. Such a department could then more effectively compete for resources against other departments of local government, such as education and public health.

Developments in the United States have taken a somewhat different course. In the post-World War II period, concern about duplication grew out of the remarkable contribution of free enterprise in social policy. I refer to the work of private consultants who in studying social services have had an unusual influence on the thinking and development of public policies. One of the earliest examples is the work of Bradley Buell and his associates.[11] In the late 1940s, in their study of St. Paul, Minnesota, they made the startling discovery that 6 to 7 percent of the families absorbed 50 percent or more of all community services. To these families they gave the name "multi-problem," on the theory that multiple agency contacts must imply multiple family problems. If the findings of their study were conceptualized as multiple agency contacts, Buell might have been led to the problem of multiple visiting and thus the need for interorganizational cooperation. Instead, they focused on multiple problems, a condition of clients rather than of agencies.

The strategy evolved from these terms of reference was that of "case-sorting" based on the level of professional skill required and the allocation of personnel to the various cases so classified. The underlying assumption was that the effective use of skilled therapeutic personnel could "result in delaying, halting or curing the repetitious course of the disorder, and . . . this can make a measurable impact upon the community's total problem."[12] The strategy for solving the over-use of resources by a limited sector of the population was based on the belief that a better allocation of professional personnel alone could reduce community problems and lessen the demand for these services. A storm of controversy arose over the concept "problem families," the strategy of intervention, and its application to recipients of public welfare.[13]

By the late 1950s and early 1960s, the approach had dramatically changed from a preoccupation with the over-use of services to the abrupt discovery that services were being under-used. Poor families were now seen as being neglected and rejected by social service institutions. To understand this shift of focus we need to examine the various critiques of casework practice.

At one time it was felt that the caseworkers relied on a narrow conception that emphasized client readiness and willingness to use the formally scheduled office interviews. This had the effect of excluding low income families who could not conform to these standards. In response to this criticism, aggressive casework developed in the 1950s, where workers were encouraged to reach out into the community in search of their clients. But the results of these efforts were not altogether beneficent; for, as one critic observed, it leads to intrusion, direction, and coercion in the lives of clients.[14]

Several years later the criticism of casework practice was extended. The neglect by social work of the poor and the "problem family" became a public issue. In a thoughtful and provocative review of trends in family casework services, Cloward presented statistical evidence of the private agencies' disengagement from the poor. Indifference became perversity when voluntary agencies created an "illusion of service," since they continued, for purposes of fund-raising, to define their function as serving the poor.[15] Those in greatest need were most neglected as many welfare agencies "creamed off" the easy-to-reach and easy-to-serve cases.[16] With this redefinition of the problems in delivery of services, overuse seemed a less urgent issue.

Emphasis was increasingly placed on the provision of concrete services and on short-term help, rather than on the earlier model of long-term treatment, insight, and counseling with psychiatric practice serving as the prototype. To be relevant to the needs of the poor it was necessary to change the *content* of social work practice. With the rediscovery of poverty came the view that professional out-reach was itself insufficient. Now service delivery patterns focused on consumer protection, entitlement, the use of non-professionals, the decentralization of services, the creation of multi-service and one-stop centers. These different approaches were designed to link individuals more effectively to the basic services and to alter the responsiveness of agencies to the needs of low-income families through confrontation, pressure, and protest.

Both the Americans and the English seem to have shifted their emphasis from duplication and over-use to poor access and under-use. However, by the mid-1960s the two countries had developed quite different approaches to the reorganization of services. The 1968 Federal Task Force on Organization of Social Services in the United States reached the following conclusions:

> We should encourage the development of social services through government organizations, non-profit organizations, and private-for-profit organizations. At least as an experimental matter, these three systems should operate as parallel systems, competing with one another . . . and assuring rapid expansion of needed services.[17]

Obviously the traditional problems of dispersal and duplication were not being considered. Indeed, the recommendations of the Task Force would, by encouraging multiple auspices, contribute substantially to increasing the amount of dispersal in the service delivery system. One justification offered is that pluralism, by developing many potential constituencies, would contribute to the more rapid growth of social services. Not surprisingly the Task Force lists as a major priority the expansion of "services that ease and assure access for all to other services already available."[18]

By contrast the 1968 English Report of the Committee on Local Authority and Allied Personal Social Services (referred to as the Seebohm Committee, after the name of its chairman) reached virtually the opposite conclusions. The report called for an integrated approach as the foundation for an effective pattern of services. It proposed "setting up a unified social service department which will include the present children's and welfare services together with some of the social service functions of health, education, and housing departments. Such a unified department . . . should attract more resources and use them more efficiently."[19] It is striking how little attention is given to the traditional problems of duplication—simultaneous multiple interventions. Attention is called, however, to many problems which inhibit use, including discontinuous, inappropriate, and poor quality services, and difficulty in gaining access to services because consumers are "unclear about the pattern of services and uncertain about the division of responsibilities between them."[20]

It would appear from both the American and English reports that the dispersal of a similar function among many agencies is not regarded as a central problem. These reports are more interested in stimulating growth and use of social services. For a solution, the English look to a unified service and the Americans to a more pluralistic and competitive system.

The American experience has added at least one additional dimension to our understanding of how to link recipients to services. Under-utilization arises, in part, because of stigma and labeling, where service institutions invoke the principles of less eligibility in their treatment of clients. Stigma can also be present among recipients of services. Thus individuals need aid to secure services, and protection from the services which they already receive. A good deal of emphasis in the American war on poverty was given to aiding service users—the use of lawyers in fair-hearing procedures and the education of clients to the full range of services they are entitled to receive. The problem of under-use was seen as arising largely from the unwillingness of service institutions to reach out to the poor and to provide them with the services to which they were entitled. To procure services from recalcitrant and even hostile institutions, we organized community groups, emphasized consumer aggression, used non-professionals to embarrass bureaucracies and to insist on the rights of clients. Social action and citizen participation were emphasized as strategies to link individuals to services.

Both the American and English experiences are based on the premise that the pattern of access and availability of services influenced their utilization. Accordingly, both accept the necessity of decentralizing services through such techniques as "one-stop centers" or unified services. These centers provide a common physical structure in which to bring together many of the linking functions: counseling; information and referral for housing, medical care, and a variety of services; intake and recruitment for job training programs and employment services. All of these activities in varying ways link the consumer to the social service system and in this sense these functions can be seen as duplicatory and, therefore, in need of coordination. Decentralization and physical propinquity are strategies of coordination. However, much confusion results, since some neighborhood service centers see their function as rendering basic services (housing, medical care, skill training) and ancillary services (like home help). Most centers provide only a service which links individuals to these services. This approach has been criticized. Some observers have noted that "many of the problems that social workers deal with require not a 'diagnosis,' but prompt action to provide information, advice, or concrete help . . . Human problems cannot be 'diagnosed' by one unit and passed on to other services for 'treatment.' "[21] According to this analysis direct provision of services is needed rather than linking and referral services.

In summary, the rationale for the concern about duplication, that is, the problem of dispersion of the same function among different agencies, has shifted over time from protecting clients from over-use, to motivating them for use; from protecting society against the dangers of duplication of cash, to the protection of individuals from the institutions which were designed to aid them; from the reform of social work manpower skills, to their expansion. While the rationale has changed, the major strategy has consistently focused on personnel—the tasks they perform and their relationship to each other. The strategies of reorganization have varied from cooperation, to coordination, to integration of personnel. The problem of consistency of policy raised by the Younghusband Report has not been of major concern. We will return to it again in our analysis of the problem of incoherence in the organization of services.

DISCONTINUITY OF RELATED FUNCTIONS

Discontinuities arise when a variety of community agencies share the same clientele over time. The output of one agency is, so to speak, the input for another. Each agency represents a function relevant to completing the task, which the system as a whole is attempting to implement.

A number of attempts to restructure services can be understood as an attempt to address one or another of the problems of discontinuity. Comprehensive planning in mental health, for example, is an attempt to get at the question of boundaries by prior agreements among independent agencies. One approach calls for the integration of all interrelated activities under a single auspices.

An English hospital in Nottingham offers an illustration. "Here the hospital has in effect been given formal responsibility for the mental health of the city's population and is the administrative center of a comprehensive psychiatric program that includes a variety of out-patient families as well as in-patient service."[22] A special committee on criminal offenders in New York State proposed a similar plan of unification for the post-adjudicatory criminal system comprised of 56,000 persons referred to criminal institutions, 21,000 placed on probation, and 11,000 released on parole. The committee argued that "the separate concepts and resulting separate agencies responsible for probation, detention, and parole be merged into a single concept of different degrees of custody that would be administered by the new department." The report explained that "the major shortcoming of the existing . . . system was that the individual offender usually was transferred from one organization to another, which 'obviously precludes continuity of treatment.' "[23] However, integration may only shift the problem from inter-agency to intra-agency coordination, where presumably winning cooperation may be easier, a plausible but untested proposition.

However reasonable and logical unified approaches to the problem of discontinuities may appear, they are politically difficult to achieve and they run counter to the trend of increasing specialization and differentiations of functions. A more pragmatic approach accepts the established pattern of services and creates a specialized role of expeditor to facilitate the flow of clients through the system of interrelated services they may need. Information and referral systems, non-professional case aids and social workers located in a variety of health, educational, and welfare agencies may all contribute to reducing discontinuities. But these loose connective roles are inefficient. Arrival rates from referrals are low and no single center is held accountable and responsible for the service outcomes of these referrals.[24]

These choices can be more fully understood by contrasting the child care and the youth manpower systems. In the programs concerned with youth training are specialized functions of recruiting, testing, training for employability, training for skills, job placement, and follow-up evaluations to assure job continuity. The auspices of these different specialized agencies can be quite varied. Thus Community Action agencies are largely concerned with recruiting and employability programs, the Department of Labor's Manpower Development and Training Act program is concerned with skills training. Job placement is done by the State Employment Service and follow-ups might be undertaken by VISTA.

Each of these specialized but autonomous agencies is related to a common task. The nature of the task which the entire group of agencies (or system) is trying to accomplish is stable employment. Thus far we have only identified *serial continuity* in which the trainees move from one type of service to another over time. But it may be also necessary to have different services *simultaneously* available at any one stage in the process. An effective program of training for employability might require social services as well as health services, housing, and cash transfers. But the rationale for bringing these activities into a program to retrain disadvantaged youth is not that these youngsters have many problems which a just society should be concerned with, but that these activities contribute to the completion of the manpower system's task of training. Programs which contribute little to completing the task can be eliminated, since they have no independent validity.

Because clear hierarchy of purpose can, in principle, be established, the manpower-dominated model provides a cogent case for service continuity. There is, after all, no validity to recruitment without training, or training without employment. Moreover, the steps connecting the relevant activities are reasonably well understood. The implications of this approach can be radical. In order to solve the problem of discontinuity, we may move outside of the social service system directly into the market and insist that industry itself assure the graduates of training programs secure and stable jobs. If voluntary coordination proves ineffective, we may develop, as Haber has proposed, "federal or state authority to make these linkages compulsory."[25]

The problem of discontinuity can be approached by a variety of administrative forms including integration, referral, or some combination of both.

In the youth employment field, we find examples of efforts to create a single institution to embrace all the functions within a single agency. The Atlanta Employment and Evaluation Service Center provides such an example. Its primary purpose is "establishing a multi-discipline service program with adequate facilities whereby the functions of work evaluations, casework services, vocational counseling, job training and job placement, and subsequent employment can be . . . coordinated." Similar examples can be found in medical care where attempts are being made to bring together prenatal, paranatal, and postnatal maternity care in an effort to reduce discontinuities.

As we have suggested, integration as a strategy of reorganization is often politically difficult and financially costly. Hence we build into one agency a specialized task of routing its clientele to other community agencies in the determined hope that they will be accepted for service. This perilous journey through the established social service bureaucracy yields many casualties. A follow-up study of 140 emotionally disturbed persons who were "referred for service" shows that two-thirds failed to receive "significant help" and even these "were by no means provided with all the services required for the problems with which they were coping."[26] Referrals and even the purchase of services to assure continuity can be difficult when independent authorities are unwilling to subordinate their functions to the purposes of the referring agents. Invariably, all of the attendant problems of low arrival rates and poor communication accompany this approach.

New Haven's community action program offers an interesting attempt to organize services associated but still subordinate to the primary goal of training. At the heart of this program are the opportunity centers, with their focus on training and basic education. In addition, there is an administratively separate, unified Social Service Center that provides a variety of supportive activities such as counseling, day care, and so on. More than a third of those in the opportunity programs have been referred to the multiservice center because they are failing to perform adequately. Moreover, about 80 percent of all the clients of the center are also active in the opportunity programs.[27] Although administratively separate, a common auspices and a common commitment to manpower objectives presumably reduces the ineffectiveness of referrals.

This type of functional integration raises a fundamental question for social policy. One can make investment-type programs (education and training) the central focus for all other social services and this administrative arrangement seems consistent with a conception of social services as expanding personal choice and developing individual capabilities. In a similar fashion, if health is the central function, little objection is raised when all other social services orbit around medical care service, which may be defined as protection of individuals from the hazards of their environment. But when consumption programs like housing and income maintenance become the central focus, the relation of ancillary social services becomes obscure. If housing and income are provided for those who need it as a mattter of right, then ancillary or "supportive" social services ought not to be used as social control mechanisms to produce good tenants or reduce economic dependency. When social services saturate a public housing project there is danger that it may convert housing into a form of institutional care. Similarly, social services in a public assistance program may change assistance into coercion, if acceptance of service becomes a condition for getting assistance. Thus the preoccupations with social control and individual change seem to undermine the principle that housing and income are social utilities to which all individuals are entitled.

Turning from retraining to foster care, we confront conceptual problems of discontinuity which are more elusive. It is more difficult to define the completed task, to understand the activities which serially or simultaneously contribute to its completion, and to secure the power to subordinate the autonomy of agencies to a single authority responsible for and accountable to the completed task. There are three factors in the movements of individuals through this system over time: the condition that causes the need for substitute care, the response to the condition, and the nature of the completed task. Political, philosophical, and conceptual problems arise at each of these levels.

Let us briefly consider each stage. No adequate classification for the demand for foster care is available. Foster care is defined here to include substitute as well as supplementary family services. The administrative labels of dependent, neglected, and delinquent children are confusing for they more often describe the sources of financing than the condition of the child. Thus in New York City all Negro children who request placement must go through the Department of Public Welfare and are automatically classified as dependent, so as to assure federal financial participation in the cost of care. Unfortunately, the only national study of this problem has failed to come up with a more adequate classification of the reasons for care.[28] It is possible to redefine the problem by examining three demands for care. One is a *severance* demand, the request to sever parental rights. The most obvious example is, of course, a mother requesting that her child be adopted, as in the case of unmarried mothers. Many infants are in shelters only temporarily, before a severance demand is met when the child is adopted. The second is a *demand for emergency or temporary* care. The mother may, for example, be ill and require hospitalization on a temporary basis. Third is a *control demand* where the community or a member of the family tries to control the behavior of parents toward their children, or where the parents or the community try to control the behavior of the child. This is more complex because there is pressure simultaneously to rescue children as well as to control parental behavior.

The distribution of these demands is not well understood because of the financial and administrative considerations. A study by Ryan and Morris of all requests for child welfare services in thirteen public and private agencies serving the metropolitan Boston area indicates that about 30 percent of the demands are for severance. Among those situations where the condition of the parent is the major reason for making a demand (50 percent of all requests), more than one-fifth concern the behavior of the parent toward the child, and one-fifth concern economic circumstances of the family. In 20 percent of the cases, the behavior of the child is at issue, and almost three-quarters of these requests involve antisocial behavior.[29] Similar trends emerge in a study in New York City of families involved in a first request for placement from the Bureau of Child Welfare. The demand for emergency care because of physical illness of mothers accounts for 29 percent of all these requests.[30]

We next consider the kinds of decisions made by community agencies in response to these demands. Clearly the first decision is either to keep the child and offer it a "service" or to refuse to accept the child. This decision appears to be related to the nature of the service for which a demand is made. The Ryan and Morris study indicates that two-thirds of the demands to sever parental ties from unmarried mothers are honored (adoption). By contrast, only about one-third of all other demands are accepted.[31] It thus appears that we are dealing with at least two child welfare systems—children of unmarried mothers and children in families-in-trouble. In the latter category only a minority of children receive service, although over 25 percent are chronic cases with three or more previous agency contacts. Many agencies' energies seem to be organized around rejecting (25 percent of the cases were classified as rejected) or referring the client.[32] Less than one-half of the referrals result in acceptance.

Once a child is accepted, a second decision must be made concerning the nature of the services to be offered—foster care or supplementary services permitting the child to remain in his own home. The second decision seems to be as difficult to make as the first. The widely accepted model (when foster care is offered in control demands) is for the caseworker to work with the natural family and through therapy restore the viability of the home as the place to socialize the child. Casework then, in principle, makes it possible for the child to return home. But the Maas and Engler study, one of the few studies conducted in this area, indicates that contact is lost with the natural parent and that once a child remains in care for more than a year and one-half, he is not likely to return home.[33] But the study failed to separate emergency, severance, and control demands, and thus undoubtedly underestimated the extent to which children are lost in the foster care system. The Jenkins study in New York City shows that 7 percent of emergency demands as contrasted with 61 percent of control demands (of child's behavior) remained in care at the end of a two year period.[34] The fate of the child seems to be determined by drift rather than by the decision that long term, permanent care is necessary or desirable. It would appear that foster care is a difficult system to get into, but even more difficult to get out of.

In summary, once the decision is made to keep a child, another decision needs to be made as to whether or not a child should be returned to his home. This decision opens up three possible options: to return the child in the short run, or in the long run, or to sever the relationship altogether with the natural parents. It is the failure to define the completed task which creates this problem at this stage. The lack of knowledge, the lack of choice, and the lack of purpose appear to be endemic problems, which have produced a long-term permanent crisis in the child welfare system. Professional practice with its emphasis on process only exacerbates the problem by its reluctance to plan in terms of outcomes.

The reorganization of such a system poses more difficult conceptual problems than does the manpower system. For some planners increasing our knowledge about the performance of the system is the key to unraveling the puzzle. But the content and quality of research done is startlingly irrelevant to disentangling the dilemmas within the foster care system. Little factual information is available on the dynamics of demand, choice, and outcome. Although some scattered individual studies exist, no national information is available about each stage in the flow from demand to outcome.

Some critics believe that the problems associated with making choices contribute to the dilemmas of foster care. It is difficult to decide whether to separate a child from his parents on a permanent basis when the rights of parents and the "best interests" of the child may conflict. Moreover, a determined optimism among professional practitioners enables them to avoid the problem by placing their faith in therapy on the assumption that therapy can strengthen family life and resolve the problems which created the original demand for control. Based on this faith, a theology of professionalism has arisen: effective choices could be made if there were more professionals available with similar case loads "to work" with the natural family. But performance diverges from theory and, curiously, professionals seem more preoccupied with the development of the child than with the therapy of the parent. It is perhaps not surprising that contact with the family is lost and as the possibility of strengthening it becomes remote, so too does the possibility of returning the child.

The system of choice needs to be strengthened legally by combining professional and judicial advocacy. When temporary foster care decisions are made, the court must review them regularly and not leave the decision to the agencies alone. The present problem rests largely in the lack of an accountability system to periodically review the fate of the children. One ingenious proposal is that of dual guardianship as a strategy of accountability. According to this scheme a lay person would be assigned to monitor and to watch the movement of a child through the foster care system.

Choices cannot be made without some criteria or rules for choosing. These can only develop with clarification of the purposes of substitute and supplementary care. What is the nature of the completed task? By what standards should effectiveness be evaluated? Is the goal the rate of return of children to their natural parents, or the healthy development of children in long-term, short-term, and adoptive care? If practice-oriented research can be taken to represent, even partially, the major preoccupation of the field, then it would appear that much attention is given to such topics as the effect of the separation trauma and the impact of placement on the child's development.[35] Both research and practice seem indifferent to measures of the proportion of children who are returned to their parents and the factors which account for high and low return rates. Or should the completed task be defined as the *prevention* of the demand for care? Severance, emergency, and control demands imply a diversified range of problems that will not readily surrender to a single preventive strategy. But demand might lead to different strategies of prevention, as well as different strategies for accommodating to the demand once it is made.

Is it possible to organize a system based on indeterminate and multiple goals in which choices are morally and professionally difficult to make? New mechanisms of accountability will be ineffective if they also fail to make decisions easier. And we may have simply added another layer to an already complicated system. New structures, however ingenious, may not resolve the fundamental factors which inhibit the willingness to make a choice. The child welfare system poses a formidable challenge: how to organize a series of related functions in what might be called a non-decision system. Ethical, religious, and professional rules of choice are so fused as to make goals indeterminate and uncertain. Clarification of choice and purpose seems essential, but this will only solve the problem of continuity if we convert a non-decision system into a decision system. Such a solution obscures the dilemma, for it is not perversity which inhibits decisions, but conflicting goals. Can a system be devised that will reduce the costs of unclear and uncertain direction?

INCOHERENCE

Social services may be regarded as fragmentary, in the sense that each service fails to have a cumulative reinforcing effect on the other services. Programs are interdependent in that changes in the policies of one may
) all. Or the impact of one program on an individual simul-
ances the effectiveness of others that he may have contact
s continuity concerns the serial inclusion of related services

for the same individual, fragmentation concerns the simultaneous use of unrelated services that reinforce each other, forming some coherent pattern that produces a new level of social functioning. The problem in the organization of services is the failure of interdependent specialized services to reinforce each other.

Consider first the situation where a change in the policies or activities of one service affects those of other services. It is difficult to document the character and scope of service interdependency and to draw policy implications from such an analysis. Few studies have attempted to do so, but some illustrations are available. Donnison cites the example of a local housing department that evicted a family because the rent was ten pounds in arrears. The effect was to create homelessness, which then required that the children be taken into care at a cost of fifteen to twenty pounds per week for their maintenance.[36] An unpublished report by Packman in England indicates that in the six counties she studied, variations in child placement ratios (from 3 to 20 per 1000 child population) can be understood in relation to variations in the housing policies of these counties. A similar argument could be made for other programs. An increase in day-care centers can affect the demand for public assistance, the availability of home help can affect the volume of children accepted into foster care, or benefit levels can affect the proportion of children entering foster care because of their economic circumstances. When large numbers of children were suspended from the New York City school system in the 1950s, some observers felt that this policy had an impact on the intake of other agencies with the result that "detention and institutional space proved woefully insufficient; needed diagnostic facilities were not available and the ramifications affected many services."[37]

These examples all indicate an inverse relationship between the supply of services in one sector and demand in another sector. Resulting policy implications suggest that an increase in day care or medical care, for example, could have a spill-over effect, producing a decrease in the number of recipients of public assistance. But such inferences may be unwarranted. The demand for all services can increase, for only the tip of the "iceberg of demand" is visible. The availability of more services simply makes more of the iceberg known. The nature of the interrelationship among agencies is thus elusive and a review of past patterns may have little predictive value in understanding future demands for service.

A somewhat different type of interdependency is illustrated in a study of the Massachusetts Society for the Prevention of Cruelty to Children (MSPCC). No agency operates in a vacuum; its activities are affected by the community of agencies in which it is located. MSPCC was committed to reducing the proportion of its caseload that was brought to court and had been markedly successful in implementing this policy. However, in the past decade, the actual number of cases that ended in court remained virtually unchanged.

Other community agencies, especially the police, were bringing cases known to MSPCC to court. Thus the activities of one agency nullified the policies of another.[38]

Such interdependency poses the question of the consistency of policy among community institutions. Should the police and the protective agency hold a common philosophy? While it may be true that "truants persuaded by social workers to return to school are promptly excluded again by exasperated teachers,"[39] should child care, social work, and education operate on the basis of similar principles and goals. And if so on what criteria should a common policy among various agencies be established? Here, the argument for economy and saving of resources subtly arises once again.[40] It would be most convenient if the interests of humanitarianism and economy converged. The argument against the eviction of a family for non payment of rent was in terms of saving funds. Can the criterion of least cost serve as a guiding social philosophy to solve the problem of interdependency? Or should we accept a more pluralistic approach, where the purposes of agencies are given primacy even if they conflict? A coherent philosophy would not only be more difficult to achieve, but from the clients' point of view, there may be important advantages in retaining some confusion and competition. Donnison observed, "Perfect coordination may leave them dependent on one social worker who is expected by his colleagues in other services to give help on terms that will impose controls on deviant or disapproved behavior."[41]

Reorganizing specialized services should be viewed in historical perspective in order to see how a theory of poverty and dependency affects the principles on which services are organized. In England the minority report of the Royal Commission of the Poor Law in 1905 laid the conceptual foundation of the American system for delivery of services.[42] It repudiated the principle that services should be organized for the group in distress—the paupers. The minority report felt that a system of comprehensive services, providing the poor with medical services, education, cash, and so forth, simply laid the foundation for a dual delivery system, which separated those who were poor from those who were not. Services for the poor were of low quality, and when guided by the principle of "less eligibility" would stigmatize and degrade those it was designed to aid. To the Webbs the answer rested in the breakup of the poor laws and their replacement with universally available, specialized services organized on the principle of function—education, insurance and pensions, health, housing, and so forth. They had hoped that, in time, it would be unnecessary to have *any* program organized solely on the basis of individual economic circumstances.

By the 1960s we found that the legacy of differentiated and specialized become self-defeating and the pattern of residential segregation racial groups assured that even universally available services o a dual delivery system for the poor and the non-poor. As we rediscovered poverty, the arbitrary delineation of competence into functionally specific and professionally discrete activities, administered by independent agencies, became increasingly less acceptable. We proceeded to look for a new principle of combining specialized services to achieve comprehensive care.

In the search for a new Hegelian unity to bring these different services into a single framework, we have inadvertently recreated a modern poor law system; that is, one based on the principle that comprehensive services should be organized around the economic circumstances of the recipient. The alternative would be to accept the principles formulated by the Webbs in their famous Minority Report of the Poor Law Commission of 1909, which advised the breakup of dual-delivery systems. To implement the recommendations of the Webbs would require major reforms designed to produce basic changes in education, job training and placement, medical care, and the like, so that these institutions do not perpetuate advantages of the haves, but become instruments for the redistribution of privilege and opportunity to those who have been excluded from our economic and political system. We must, as Titmuss has urged, strengthen and reform "established, socially approved 'normal' institutions" rather than perpetuate the proliferation of dual delivery systems.

To appreciate why we have departed, in part, from the position of the Webbs, we need to examine our conception of poverty and its causes. Poverty is seen as having a circular etiology. "Men and women were sick because they were poor: they became poorer because they were sick, and sicker because they were poorer."[43] In the vicious circle argument, the causal link remains uncertain and indefinite. We do not know, for example, if poverty causes ill health or ill health causes poverty (the problem of drift). Moreover, poverty has multiple causes: cultural (the social costs of early slavery), structural (the breakdown of the opportunity system, etc.), and indefinite (it becomes increasingly difficult to identify the victims of poverty and their salient characteristics). Recognizing who is poor becomes even more intractable when we define poverty multi-dimensionally—as a condition that is more than the lack of income; the lack of dignity, amenities, and opportunities. Low income may not be correlated with all these defects. Since the poor are varied, no one policy can improve the conditions of all the poor. If the dimensions of poverty are equally varied, no single policy can touch all sides of poverty, even for one group among the poor. These arguments lead inexorably to the conclusion that multiple interventions are necessary. To avoid dissipating scarce resources, some strategy of coordination seems essential.

Thus far we have argued that to achieve a single goal—the reduction of poverty—multiple interventions are necessary. But the concept of poverty implies many different goals. Consider the goal in terms of some arbitrary level of ill health like morbidity and mortality rates, which are regarded as undesirable. More than medical care is necessary because health is also a function of such factors as the level of family income, education, housing, and food consumption. Consequently, both a mix of policies and comprehensive social planning are necessary. The task cannot be assigned to any one sector, for each sector lacks control over other sectors and tends to be biased in prescribing its own professional skills as the most appropriate. Seen in these terms, we can appreciate Melvin Webber's argument that "everything is everything else." And hence we must discover new ways of recombining specilized services. Webber goes on to explain that "the services we have delineated are not bounded regions of the system; they are more nearly like intertwined threads that interlace the system".[44] The boundaries of health, education, and welfare cannot be clearly distinguished, because they are so closely interrelated.

As long as we can agree on a common goal, there is a cogent case for reducing fragmentation. This is really a variation of the problem of discontinuity since the programs are related in that each contributes to completing a defined task. Difficulties arise when we recognize that not only does a single objective require multiple interventions, but that each intervention serves many goals.

To what goals or social problems is the recombination of fragmented and specialized services oriented? If we briefly review the experiences of the President's Committee on Delinquency and Crime, the Grey Area programs, the War on Poverty, and the Model Cities, it is possible to identify at least four competing and conflicting goals:

1. To improve the competencies of individuals and of local communities. According to this conception, it is important to organize services to enhance individual and group capability. Citizen participation is crucial to this goal, for to impose a set of benefits, no matter how beneficient, is simply paternalism or, in the language of an aroused Negro community, welfare colonialism. The rationale in support of this goal is varied and complex. Its roots lie deep in the tradition of popular and direct local democracy. But it has, as well, a sociological orientation, which assumes that an involved and engaged community is more effectively integrated and thus less susceptible to social problems.

2. To improve the competency of municipal government. The term competency suggests at least two different meanings. It means that cities have different problems and consequently no single overriding model will apply to all. Thus each municipality must learn to identify its problems and appropriately allocate its resources. The present grant-in-aid categorical system for financing welfare services is thus a major encumbrance, for it inhibits the decision-making process of the local communities in the allocation of their resources. The poverty program was a move toward some form of block grant under which it was possible for local government to make priority decisions regarding resource allocation. But by what rules

are resources to be allocated? Presumably this requires a high degree of technical competence and the reliance upon social planning.

Municipal competence also means political ability. This is a new art of statesmanship and grantsmanship. It is a political game and to win is to capture for your city a disproportionate amount of resources.[45] New Haven is a brilliant example of the art fully mastered. Acquiring skill in knowing the ever changing sources and criteria for federal financing of local programs can be a stimulating and exciting process, with high financial payoff for those who have mastered it. Clearly, however, allocative competence, political competence, and community competence all lead in different directions. The creative skills and information required for each is somewhat different and may even conflict.

3. To maximize economic self-sufficiency. Here we have a specific social problem—a single goal with multiple causes. No single program is capable of achieving this aim. Education, manpower training, housing, medical care—all seem relevant. How can we organize social services so as to maximize economic self-sufficiency? So great is our commitment to this goal that we seem to have forgotten that it is only one among many goals. Educational and developmental models are replacing earlier clinical and disease models on the assumption that we must find ways of combining social services with training so as to increase employability, which will, in turn, facilitate employment in the job market. If we accept this single-minded goal, then we can attempt to aggregate all governmental subsidies and decide what proportion of funds should go to cash transfers (if higher levels of living affect motivation), subsidies to education and training (for the short-run in the Job Corps and for the long-run as in Operation Head Start), and to supportive services (ranging from counseling and guidance to day care). All of these services are to contribute to the common goal of promoting economic self-sufficiency. So defined, the problem of fragmentation and incoherence is identical with the problem of discontinuity—combining services which are simultaneously or serially needed in order to accomplish a specific task.

4. To redistribute resources to the poor. This goal is to be achieved by creating new mechanisms of redistribution, which will discriminate positively in favor of the poor. This approach implies that a larger proportion of the increase in gross national product should go to the poor. In reaching toward the goal of greater opportunity we must also alter the level of living of individuals with low income. We may not be able to equalize opportunity without equalizing income and power. The criterion of social progress is the reduction of inequalities.[46] Although the goal of equity may be related to the goal of self-sufficiency, they are clearly different. To achieve a vertical redistribution of resources the emphasis on recombining isolated services is less crucial, for the components of increased well-being are themselves fragmentary.

The most characteristic problem of incoherence is priorities, where the multiple goals imply multiple interventions and it is not possible to subordinate one set of goals to another. All the activities are necessary but assigning relative significance to each is a hazardous and uncertain undertaking. These allocative problems exist because there is no specific completed task on which there is sufficient agreement, and no clear knowledge of which social services are needed or when (simultaneously or serially).

Present approaches to inter-sectoral planning differ from earlier thinking about coordination. They take the geographic area as the unit of planning—a neighborhood, a housing project, or some arbitrary number of city blocks. These areas may be either target areas, in the sense that some criterion of investment (usually based on need or inequalities in resources) serves as the basis for selection, or catchment areas, in the sense that they are administratively designated as one area from a universe of areas, all of which are to be included when the program is fully developed. Such areas can, of course, serve as the basis for allocation as well as coordination. The Elementary and Secondary Education Acts designated certain territories to receive more federal funds than others on the principle of positive discrimination in areas of high need. When *area* is used as a principle of coordination, it seems to lead to a decentralized, saturation approach—the more services and the closer their proximity, the greater the likelihood that they might be used. The federal program to relieve distress in the Watts area of Los Angeles illustrates the general strategy.

But the more difficult tasks still remain uncharted. Can we move beyond the principle of saturation in the allocation and coordination of resources? This task would require that resources be allocated to promote a "coherent integration" of social services. In the effort to solve the problem of fragmentation, we have only created a chaos in planning as programs have been spawned in mental health, community action, model cities, delinquency preventions, and so forth. But we have no comprehensive *plan,* which integrates all these problem-oriented comprehensive plans, nor are we likely to develop one. It is doubtful whether we can or should develop principles for organizing our specialized services. A United Nations' report puts the case as follows:

> In the social field there is . . . no single unifying quantitative goal that can be set—because there is no common measure of social values performing the role of money in economic analysis; and no aggregative concept like national income which can evaluate and synthesize the contributions of different programmes and sectors. Thus it is not possible to measure and compare by a common standard . . . a hospital and an institution for homeless children.[47]

How important is the problem of incoherence and the strategy of comprehensiveness? There are many parallels between the present debate about comprehensiveness and the earlier debates of the Commission of the Poor Law of 1905. Two alternative approaches can be identified. An income approach assumes a hierarchy of social policies and cash transfers, which is to be the primary instrument of provision. Public social policies should seek to convert need into a market demand, rather than to provide goods and services directly.

The second approach would build an infrastructure of specialized services that would be universally available but supplemented with the principle of positive discrimination. In this way, more resources would be available for each specialized activity, in the belief that unequal resources are needed to produce equal outcomes for low income groups. It seems perverse to be concerned with incoherence when the quality of services are so unequally distributed. According to the principle of positive discrimination, the geographic area can serve as the basis for distribution without stigma. Reorganization of services is a strategy for the distribution and expansion of resources to low income areas. Those who favor this approach would reject the view that a new form of poor law is required in which comprehensive services are provided for individuals who are poor. Saturation of specialized services in a given area is as far as they wish to carry the case for comprehensiveness.

REDUCTION OF CHOICE

The services of community agencies are overlapping in the sense that while they may be *different*, they are available to persons in *similar* circumstances. When agencies provide the *same services*, there is duplication; when the services are *different* but the conditions of the persons are similar, there is overlap. For example, high school youngsters with similar I.Q.s may elect to go to vocational school, a community college, work apprenticeship program, or a general college. Presumably, examination of a cross sample of youth in these institutions would reveal that a reasonably large proportion of those in similar circumstances, I.Q., incomes, and so on, can be found in all these settings. If this interpretation is valid then these institutions serve as alternative ways of meeting a given condition.

It might be argued that such overlap is a measure of dysfunction. Need should be precisely related to agency performance. Hence the programs listed above are not alternatives, but a hierarchy of service which relate ability to performance. In the case of an individual who commits a delinquent act, the behavior can be treated in different ways because the underlying causes may be different. It is widely accepted in social work that services should be organized to respond to the underlying causes of problems and not only, if at all, to the presenting situation. Based on this principle, the child who breaks a window might find himself incarcerated for many years if his act is interpreted as a symptom of more enduring pathology. Another youngster committing a similar act might be returned to his family if his action is interpreted as normal adolescent rebellion against authority. But this homey wisdom can be controversial when applied to services that have social control as their aim.

The model of matching services to "need" based on professional knowledge is called into question in a number of situations. It may be useful to review some of them. According to the recent Gault decision by the Supreme Court the choice of action to be taken in cases of delinquency is not to be made on the basis of professional discretion (based upon a differential diagnosis of individual needs) with judicial support for this judgment. The professional and the judge can no longer act, even in theory, in terms of the delinquent's "best interest": verification of the delinquent act is to be determined by the clash of contending interests, through our legal adversary system. This example illustrates only that we can undermine personal freedom if we "treat" based on presumed need alone and neglect to verify the condition in question. The judge will, of course, continue to have a number of choices for disposing of similar cases—probation, incarceration, or suspension, so that discretion is not altogether ruled out.

The position which holds that an understanding of individual need should determine service has been subjected to a variety of criticisms; based partly on review of actual practice and partly challenging whether sufficient knowledge is at hand to make such judgment. In a study of the intake procedures of Child Welfare agencies in Boston, Ryan and Morris conclude that:

> An overwhelming impression arises from these findings that the intake process is not the refined, highly diagnostic decision-making process that it is ideally thought to be. Decisions are made rapidly, with relatively little available information . . . and very frequently the decision is rejection or referral. When the decision is to accept, it often appears to be based on a rather standardized set of criteria, rather than on an individualized appraisal of the needs of the particular client.[48]

Scott Briar's research tried to determine the extent of agreement among professionals from five different agencies in arriving at placement choices for children. Three hypothetical cases were presented to these workers. The study shows that there was little agreement concerning the appropriate placement for these children.[49] He also found that the social workers' placement recommendations were directly related to the placement patterns in the agencies in which they were employed. When the social workers were employed in an agency that emphasized foster care they tended to recommend that; when employed in an agency that was largely committed to institutional care, this choice was preferred. It would thus appear that it is not the need of the client, but the service rendered by the agency which is the more determinative factor in the distribution of services rendered on behalf of individuals with presumably similar circumstances.[50]

In summary, there are moral, practical, and intellectual factors that impel us to exercise caution in accepting that services should match need. One policy implication is that we must unrelentingly commit ourselves to the development of research and practice which will better enable us to serve need. An altogether different inference can also be drawn; that we should expand the range of choices available to individuals. Thus the preferred distribution is not one which precisely matches needs and services, because knowledge of such a match is wanting. Rather it is a distribution which widens choices and expands options. Even when professional gate-keepers respond to differential need based on knowledge, they are limited in what they can do by the range of available community service. It makes no sense to prescribe intensive psychotherapy if no such service exists in the community, leaving aside for a moment whether this treatment would be effective or desirable.

These considerations convince me that a strong case can be made to widen the range of alternative community services available to individuals in similar conditions. And in this context it is informative to contrast the pattern of services which have developed in response to two different conditions—jobless youngsters with educational deficiencies and children in need of foster care. What services should be developed by the community in response to each condition?

Educationally disadvantaged youth could be assigned to the neighborhood youth corps, work experience programs such as the employability training programs sponsored by Community Action Agencies, Job Corps, skill training offered under the Manpower Development and Training Act, and so on. These specific programs differ in important ways: some are residential or institutional programs where the youngster leaves his family, while others are forms of community training; some make use of service institutions such as the school, while others utilize the employment market as a training ground; some emphasize preparation for work and training, i.e., employability, and others are more directly concerned with skill-training. Finally, some programs are income supplements which reduce the costs of deferred wages for individuals who would otherwise have to be in the labor force, while others are designed to strengthen the emotional experience of youngsters preparatory to both skill-training and job placement. On what principles should we determine the relative distribution of these varied services? I shall return to this question later.

In job training we are expanding the range of choices, moving toward further differentiation and proliferation of alternative community services. We are creating a wider variety of second-chance institutions, both in and out of the community. We are thus expanding the range of options. It could, of course, be argued that each type of service is designed to meet a specialized need and that in principle it is possible to determine whether a youngster requires one type of service or another. But I doubt if our diagnostic skill actually permits us to identify which youngsters could profit most from one or another of this impressive diversity of specialized services. We need not rely on the rationale of making treatment congruent with needs to support variety. Diversity has merit if it expands the choices of individual service users. Clearly, opening choices is a different goal than trying to fit individual needs into specialized programs. Yet another rationale for diversity is that it nurtures the development and expansion of resources available for new services.

By contrast, in the foster care field we are moving toward constricting the range of choices, substituting one type of care for another. Two examples illustrate this tendency to narrow choices—placement services for Negro children and minority groups and the shift from institutional to community care.

The grim story of minority children in need of placement has been chronicled in numerous studies in the past two decades. New York City may be typical of other large cities with a growing proportion of non-white children. In 1946 the Welfare Council's Committee on Foster Care for Children in New York City discovered that "Protestant agencies receiving public funds had 184 vacancies in which to place a capacity of 349 children." In 1955 the Deputy Mayor's report, *Children Need Families,* stated that "between 1946 and 1955 the number of Negro children awaiting long term placement had risen from 140 to 610, while the number of whites in the same predicament had fallen from 390 to 370." A 1961 report from the Department of Public Welfare, *Children in Temporary Care over Six Months,* states that the largest single group of children waiting in temporary care for more than six months were Negro, Protestant children, ages two to six.[51] To these studies can be added a report by the Department of Public Welfare, *Children in Shelter Care for over One Month,* covering the first six months of 1964. A comparison of the children who are rejected for long-term foster care by one or more agencies with those who are more readily placed, indicates that 40 percent of the Negro children were hard to place, by this definition, as compared with only 18 percent of white children.

Other large cities appear to report similar findings. A study of out-of-wedlock births identified from birth certificates in Boston reveals that 45 percent of white mothers had contact with maternity homes or child care agencies, while only 6 percent of the Negro mothers had such contact. The traditional interpretation of such findings are in terms of client apathy and underuse. But the study makes clear that it is not that the Negro unwed mothers failed to make contact with social agencies, for at every age level, the Negro is *more* likely to be known to hospital social service departments than are white mothers. The data suggest that the issue is the failure to offer services.[52]

The exclusion of Negro children may be reckoned as a permanent crisis in child care. In part public institutions have expanded their foster care programs to meet this crisis. The expansion of directly operated public services has contributed to de facto segregation in the public sector, to the extent that public services were responsive to the needs of unwanted or hard-to-place cases. We thus appear to have drifted into a dual delivery system so reminiscent of an earlier age that tried as a matter of policy rather than drift to separate the deserving poor to be serviced by the charity of voluntary agencies from the non-deserving poor to be treated in the public sector. The range of child care services available to Negroes has been limited, because of our commitment to the principles of sectarianism and to voluntarism. Because of the amount of demand, even if public agencies could win limited concessions from the voluntary-sectarian agencies (which paradoxically often draw their major financial support from the public sector), the problems of a dual delivery system would not be altogether avoided. More services to expand the volume of public care available to Negroes will simply exacerbate the problem of two classes of services.

It is widely believed that community care is to be preferred to institutional care. We have assumed, often with good reason, that the interest of humanity and the interest of economy in this case march hand in hand. This community care movement is widespread. It is one of the pervasive changes in social policy. Evidence of this change can be found in areas as varied as care of the mentally ill, care of the aged, child welfare, and correctional institutional care. The historical roots of this transition in policy lie in the Poor Law. In 1834 public policy tried to abolish outdoor relief (aid in the community) and made the workhouse (institutional care) a severe test of an individual's need for public aid. Subsequent events, buttressed by the growth of humanitarianism, forced a retreat from this conception of the function of institutions. By the mid-twentieth century the ideal was for services to be rendered to individuals in their own homes. Outdoor relief came to be preferred over indoor relief. The higher cost of indoor relief may have buttressed the psychological argument that made this alternative seem so appealing. When we compare the cost per child of different forms of care, we find that today institutional care is the most expensive. New York City, for example, spends the following amounts to maintain a child in care annually: $3,300 in a foster home; $6,500 in an institution; $11,000 in a residential treatment center; $15,000 in a city-operated temporary shelter.[53] In 1834 it was widely believed that when direct and indirect costs were taken into account it was cheaper to place individuals in institutions than to support them in a community. Yet one effect of such a policy today may be to narrow the range of choices available to families and to individuals.

I have argued that an effort should be made to secure a balance in the range of available services so as to maximize individual choice, whether this is determined by professional discretion (diagnosis) or by consumer preference. The logic of this argument implies that there must be built in underuse or "wastage" of resources, so that individuals will always have a choice without having to be placed on a waiting list. Some might reject this view of built-in wastage and prefer the simpler model, which suggests that services should not exceed demand. The assumption is that social services are very much like other market commodities, which respond to the demand for these services. But empirical studies in the use of hospital services suggest that the pattern for social services is more complex. It appears that the supply of service in fact may determine the demand. If we create institutions, they will tend to be used. Similarly if we build community care facilities, these will also be used. However, if we create neither of these services, the problems which gave rise to the need for them will find expression in yet another indeterminate way. Notwithstanding these very real difficulties, I believe that we should strive to expand, to diversify, and to proliferate the range of social services in order to maximize choice.

In order that attention to details not obscure the main themes, a brief summary may be useful. The problem of dispersal calls for strategies which rely on the cooperation of *personnel*. By contrast, discontinuities require coordination of *policies* among related functions to achieve some defined outcome, and incoherence calls for coordination of policies among unrelated programs, for which no single overarching goal or outcome can be specified. Constrained choices require greater freedom to select among alternative *programs*, by both present or future service users. Each problem in the organization of services thus implies a different target for action. No one pattern of reorganization is likely to solve all the problems presented.

NOTES

1. *The Administration of Services to Children and Youth in New York City,* Institute of Public Administration (1963), Table A-1, p. 56.
2. Nathan Cohen, *Social Work in the American Tradition* (New York: Dryden Press, 1958).
3. Richard Titmuss, "The Social Division of Welfare," in *Essays on the Welfare Service* (New Haven: Yale University Press, 1959).
4. Some observers have noted that children in military schools spend their summers in sleep-away camp, thus "a large number of them are really without parents who want them and simply rotate them between camps and private school." I am indebted to Joseph Reid, Director of the Child Welfare League of America, for this fascinating example of how definitions affect the character

of the problem. For some data which bear on these observations see, Donnell Pappenfort *et al.,* "Report Number Three of the Project on Physical Facilities for Group Care of Children" (Chicago: University of Chicago, Center for Urban Studies) (mimeo.) March 1968, pp. 9 and 22.

5. Richard Titmuss, *Commitment to Welfare* (New York: Random House, 1968), p. 106.

6. David V. Donnison, *The Neglected Child in the Social Services* (Manchester: Manchester University Press, 1956). See also "The Administrative Consequences of Jim and Vera Fardell," in F.M.C. Wilson, ed., *Administrators in Action* (London: George Allen & Unwin, 1961). The Fardell case provides a dramatic and unusually well documented case history of the multiple and conflicting philosophies of the agencies which a "problem" family and its children came to know over a period of two generations.

7. Redundancies have, of course, always been thought to imply waste and inefficiency in the sense of a maldistribution of services, whereby some receive many, while others receive few services. In this sense duplication may contribute to the creation of lacunae and discontinuities (the lack of follow-up and follow-through). These issues are discussed in the section dealing with discontinuities.

8. *Report of the Working Party of Social Workers in the Local Authority Health and Welfare Services* (London: Her Majesty's Stationery Office, 1959), pp. 248 and 319.

9. *London Times,* October 21, 1966.

10. David V. Donnison, "Social Work and Social Change," *The British Journal of Psychiatric Social Work,* 1967.

11. Bradley Buell's work was initially financed by a private foundation. He later became a private consultant selling the approach he developed from his research to state and local welfare departments. His critics have charged that his promotional activities have become a substitute for research and analysis.

12. Bradley Buell, "Conceptual Issues in Preventive Programming," quoted in Alfred J. Kahn, "Caseload Management: A Plan 'Package' " (mimeo.), p. 9.

13. See, for example, Irving F. Lukoff and Samuel Mencher, "A Critique of the Conceptual Foundation of Community Research Associates," *Social Service Review,* Vol. 36 (1962), pp. 433–443; and Henry Maas, "Family Casework Diagnosis: An Essay Review," *Social Service Review,* Vol. 36 (1962), pp. 444–450.

14. Alvin Schorr, "Trend to Rx," *Social Work,* Vol. 7, No. 1 (January 1962), p. 63.

15. Richard A. Cloward and Irwin Epstein, "Private Social Welfare's Disengagement from the Poor: The Case of Family Adjustment Agencies," in Mayer Zald, ed., *Social Welfare Institutions* (New York: Wiley, 1965), p. 623.

16. See, for example, Herbert J. Gans, "Redefining the Settlement's Function for the War on Poverty," *Social Work,* Vol. 9, No. 4 (October 1964).

17. *Services for People,* Report of the Task Force on Organization of Social Services (Washington, D.C.: U.S. Department of Health, Education and Welfare, October 1958), p. ii.

18. *Ibid.,* p. iii.

19. *Report of the Committee on Local Authority and Allied Personal Social Services,* Cmnd. 3703 (London: Her Majesty's Stationery Office, July 1968), p. 44.

20. *Ibid.*
21. D. Donnison and J. Stewart, *The Ingleby Report: Three Critical Essays,* Fabian Research Series 231, December 1962, p. 7.
22. Morris S. Schwartz and Charlotte Schwartz, *Social Approaches to Mental Patient Care* (New York: Columbia University Press, 1964), p. 158.
23. *The New York Times,* "State Group Urges Unification of 141 Rehabilitative Agencies," June 30, 1968.
24. For a thoughtful analysis of the problems of accountability see Alfred J. Kahn, *Planning Community Services for Children in Trouble* (New York: Columbia University Press, 1963), pp. 445–476.
25. William Haber, "Technological Change and Job Change," a paper presented at the *International Conference on Automation, Full Employment and a Balanced Economy,* Rome, Italy, June 1967, p. 11.
26. William Ryan, "Distress in the City: A Summary Report of the Boston Mental Health Survey 1960–62," in William Ryan (ed.), *Distress in the City* (Cleveland: The Press of Case Western Reserve, 1969).
27. *Unified Social Services, Monthly Report* (New Haven: Community Progress, Inc., April 1966) (mimeo.), p. 18.
28. Helen Jeter, *Services in Public and Voluntary Child Welfare Programs* (Washington, D.C.: U.S. Government Printing Office, Children's Bureau, Department of Health, Education and Welfare, 1962).
29. Ryan and Morris, *op. cit.,* p. 15, Table 2.
30. Shirley Jenkins, "Duration of Foster Care: Some Relevant Antecedent Variables," *Child Welfare,* Vol. XLVI, No. 8 (October 1967).
31. Ryan and Morris, *op cit.,* p. 81.
32. It is of special interest to note that one-third of non-accepted clients were referred, with "one-third of these referred back to the agency that made the original referral." Such procedures make vivid the imagery used by Elaine Cumming when she described the social services plan as a pin ball machine. *Ibid.,* p. 25.
33. Henry Maas and Richard Engler, *Children in Need of Parents* (New York: Columbia University Press, 1959).
34. Jenkins, *op cit.,* based on a reanalysis of the data made available by the author in a personal communication.
35. See Edmund V. Mech., "Practice Oriented Research or Separation in Child Welfare," in Miriam Morris and Barbara Wallace, eds., *The Known and Unknown in Child Welfare Research* (New York: National Association of Social Workers, 1965).
36. David Donnison, *Health, Welfare and Democracy in Greater London,* in Greater London Papers, No. 5 (London: The London School of Economics and Political Science, 1962), p. 5.
37. Alfred J. Kahn, *Planning Community Services for Children in Trouble* (New York: Columbia University Press, 1963), p. 516.
38. See Chapter 3, p. 49.
39. D. V. Donnison, "Consensus and Conflict in Urban Development" (mimeo.) The London School of Economics, 1968, p. 8.
40. For a discussion of the relationship between scarcity and coordination see, R. A. Parker, "Social Administration and Scarcity: The Problem of Ration-

ing," *Social Work,* Vol. 24, No. 2, April, 1907, p. 13. (Published by the National Institute for Social Work Training, London, England.)

41. Donnison, "Consensus and Conflict in Urban Development," *op. cit.,* p. 8.
42. See T. H. Marshall, *Social Policy* (London: Hutchinson University Library, 1965), pp. 32–44.
43. Gunnar Myrdal, *Rich Lands and Poor* (New York: Harper & Row, 1957), p. 11.
44. Melvin Webber, University of California at Berkeley, Department of City and Regional Planning, in an unpublished manuscript, 1966.
45. Full time county development coordinators spent half of their time securing, analyzing, and distributing information about federal grants and programs, according to a survey by the National Association of Counties, *American County Government,* publication of the National Association of Counties, Vol. 33, No. 6, 1968, p. 48.
46. Herbert Gans observed that historians of the 1960s may discover "that the social protest of the sixties has very little to do with poverty . . . [for] it has to do with inequality." "The Equality Revolution," *The New York Times Magazine,* November 3, 1968.
47. *Methods in Determining Social Allocations,* Report of the Secretary General, United Nations, Economic and Social Council, Social Commission, E/CN. 5/387, March 31, 1965, p. 37.
48. William Ryan and Laura B. Morris, *Child Welfare Problems and Potentials* (Boston: Committee on Children and Youth, 1967), p. 33.
49. Scott Briar, "Clinical Judgments in Foster Care Placement," *Child Welfare,* Vol. 24, No. 4 (April 1963), pp. 161–169.
50. *Ibid.,* p. 168.
51. These findings are quoted in *The Administration of Services to Children and Youth in New York City, op. cit.,* pp. 25–26.
52. James E. Teel *et al.,* "Factors Relating to Social Work Services for Mothers of Babies Born Out of Wedlock," *Journal of Public Health,* Vol. 57, No. 8 (August 1967).
53. Summaries of Participant's Comments at the Governors' Conference on Public Welfare, Arden House, November 2–3, 1967 (mimeo.). Comments by S. M. Meyer, Jr., President of Edwin Gould Foundation for Children.

Chapter 7

The Demonstration as a Strategy of Change

Programs of social change—like all government programs —usually come under political and budgetary scrutiny early in their lives. No matter how comprehensive and ennobling the proponents of a program say it is, the program must still run a political and economic gauntlet to prove its effectiveness and its value. With billions of dollars being allocated to meet changing social needs, we urgently need methods of effecting change that are speedy, appropriate, rational, and inexpensive. Many planning bodies, both in and out of government, believe that the "demonstration," or "demonstration-research," project is one of the most powerful methods of bringing about change.

A demonstration project is a small program, funded for a definite period of time (its counterpart in industry is usually called a "pilot project"). It has specific objectives and approaches which are subjected to critical scrutiny; it serves a select area and population with the fervent hope that the lessons it learns and "demonstrates," through the rigors of scientific research, will somehow lead to large-scale adoption and major shifts in the aims, styles, resources, and effectiveness of major social service organizations and programs.

Reprinted by permission of the publisher and co-author, S. M. Miller, from *Trans-action*, January/February, 1966.

It is seldom made entirely clear how this transfer will actually come about. This is probably its chief failing. When an industry runs a "pilot" program to test or gather information on a new process or campaign, it will usually follow through on its findings. If it fails to be responsive to changing preferences and new technology it may find its profit margin shrinking and its very survival threatened. Social service agencies, however, are not governed by the rules of a competitive economy. As a result they will seldom institute major internal changes—even when feasibility is demonstrated—without outside prodding from government agencies, foundations or other fund-givers or policymakers.

To add to or change existing services means to alter direction and effectiveness; therefore, the analysis of the demonstration project means analysis of social needs and of institutional resistances to change. To examine change is to assess present function—and it forces re-examination of the basic outlook and ideas of social services.

J. Kenneth Galbraith has called the demonstration "the modern device for stimulating action without spending money." It is the current "in" thing in social services. A conservative estimate of the cost of demonstration projects in 1964 probably runs about fifty million dollars. In a variety of guises they appear in the war on poverty, manpower retraining, welfare programs, public health, juvenile delinquency, vocational rehabilitation, public housing, education, and area redevelopment.
Examples:

1. In the slums of one city an advanced pre-school program has been set up for the benefit of a few children in a few schools in a neighborhood that does not have enough kindergartens. The hope is that its success, if any, may lead to a major change in the pre-school and kindergarten training for disadvantaged children in the area and throughout the city school system.

2. In a high crime neighborhood of another city, three social workers on special assignment set out to "reach" three juvenile gangs considered "unreachable" by the traditional settlement houses and the police. They were successful, as "special assignment" workers have been in other cities. But the program was dropped when completed, was never implemented, and most of the recommendations were not followed.

HOPE AND DESPAIR

The name itself—demonstration-research—is both a confession of despair and a profession of hope. There is despair because the needs and problems are so vast, the weight of past failure so oppressive, and what to do next so uncertain. But there also is hope that goals will be defined, the project might work, and research might lead to truth—and that when the right answers are found, rational man will adopt or expand them.

Demonstrations seem to be a way to get action. They spark flurries of activity; they are highly visible; things seem to be happening; private agencies and government bureaus that would not grant funds for operating projects will grant them for demonstrations.

The defects are equally glaring. Demonstrations are also a way to *dodge* action or *postpone* major change—relatively little money is spent, relatively few people are affected, the real problem is hardly touched. Public criticism concerning needed improvements is blunted, at least for a time. And if public interest has drifted when the demonstration finishes, the whole idea of squarely facing major needs can be allowed to die quietly.

This contradiction indicates uncertainty and lack of clear policy. We want to achieve desired social aims—but avoid unnecessary cost. How? We also know that institutions must change. But again how? For example, should school boards concentrate on integrated schools or quality schools? In dealing with poverty, should we concentrate on the young or the old? Since we have no national social welfare policy, the demonstration project, allowing trial without apparent commitment, is very attractive. Further, it can conveniently meet a major political problem by a token activity which may not solve it, but will not lose votes either.

The emphasis on research carries the aura and prestige of science and rigorous testing into social policy. (After all, if science can conquer space, why can't it conquer poverty?) The scientific aura often masks value judgments by seeming to transform them into technical questions. Is school integration really important because of its effect on learning, as many analysts believe—or because it fosters desegregation, as many others believe? The desirability of research should be recognized—but not overemphasized.

The major purpose of the demonstration is to test the validity of ideas which claim to improve the services and policies of established institutions (schools, welfare and health departments, training centers). As long as change is approached through experimentation and small scale innovation, judgment must be reserved, and condemnation for failure cannot be severe.

The demonstration project is an instrument of change; but it does not severely threaten the established institutions and it demands no immediate action. Peter Marris describes it as "the middle ground between conforming . . . and uncompromising reform."[1] The demonstration project may be seen as an attempt to professionalize social reform. By means of it the need for change is met in a way that established organizations can "live with"—perhaps even control.

In broad sum, the assets of the demonstration project are that it is fashionable, politically attractive, rationally appealing, inexpensive, and not binding.

THE LIABILITIES

Are we justified in placing so much hope in demonstration projects? Their very virtues are also their defects. Doesn't the professional control of discontent obscure the dramatization of issues that are often necessary for significant change? Reform can be self-limiting and incoherent if it proceeds only when it can secure the cooperation of the institution which it seeks to reform. The weaknesses of a broad commitment demonstration program become obvious in practice:

1. They often promote unequal distribution of money and resources.
2. They distract from national policy.
3. They overemphasize success and they tend to disregard or play down failure.

By their very limited and experimental nature, demonstrations favor some people, some organizations, and some locations over others. Some slum children get to go to well-organized nursery schools while those a few blocks away do not even have kindergartens; the poor young residents on the Lower East Side of Manhattan get aid programs from Mobilization for Youth which are not available to similar groups in the rest of Manhattan, much less the Watts section of Los Angeles.

Generally, this differentiation is defined as a social good; some help, somewhere, is better than none, anywhere; and it is only by contrast with a control group that the worth of an experimental program can be established. What happens nationally, however, is that whether people in similar situations get the help they need depends on local success in getting demonstration money from funding agencies, plus local willingness to invest the necessary resources, time, skill, and effort. The social services flourish in those cities willing and able to experiment; they languish in other cities. A new source of social injustice emerges—between those fortunate needy who happen to live in the cities rich in demonstration projects, and those who do not.

Since demonstrations emphasize local initiative, they work against the establishment of national standards and national agencies of assistance. Entrenched local interests often vigorously oppose liberal welfare benefits —many of the important changes in public policy have come about because it was necessary to deliberately overcome local interests that preferred low taxes to adequate welfare. Therefore, a program that serves a limited population in a small corner of a city at whatever cost (Mobilization for Youth in its first three years of operation cost more than $12 million) may be simply distracting from the major tasks needing to be done. Critics such as Harvey Perloff contend that social planning must be part of a national policy—controlled by a national planning organization like the President's Council of Economic Advisers. Local demonstrations can quickly become misplaced do-goodism. They can easily become permanent substitutes for vital broad-based programs. Demonstrations are now being used to train unemployed youths to qualify for jobs. As far as this goes, it is all to the good; but any retraining program with national meaning requires a major reform of public vocational high schools—not just demonstration-research.

A good idea, however well demonstrated, does not always drive out a bad one, or lead to more good ideas. It may, instead, prevent the use and adoption of better ideas which happen not to have been tested yet. Of course, action cannot be held up indefinitely in the hope of perfection; but we should not immediately adopt any idea because it is "better than what we have" if this means closing off potentially more promising avenues. (In fact, improvement should never stop at any terminal goal, no matter how good. The ideal is open end adaptability—*continuing* improvement to meet changing circumstances.)

Since demonstrations are by definition small scale interventions, they may be too small in scope to discover and bring about the major changes that might need to be made. For instance, a demonstration testing whether more social workers offering greater individualized services will rehabilitate and give more self-respect to relief recipients will not mean much if the welfare requirements themselves humiliate and degrade recipients by continued invasion of privacy and implied moral criticism.

While demonstrations can fail because they are too small in scope, they can also fail if too large. If too much money descends too quickly on a small operation dedicated to radical change, it can soon suffer hardening of the bureaucratic arteries and become a vested interest which will fight change.

YARDSTICK OF SUCCESS

The ultimate test of the success of a demonstration is whether it can actually influence long-term and large-scale policy. It is not enough to have proven that an idea will work if that idea then dies and is interred in a report. But the fundamental question of how a successful demonstration will lead to major policy changes is usually left obscure. The question is seldom even raised—yet nothing in planning can be more important. The comfortable slogan that "nothing can resist an idea whose time has come" avoids the crucial factor in social planning: How can success on a small scale become a means for change, improvement, and greater effectiveness in major institutions?

Three questions are fundamental to the strategy of the demonstration and must be answered:

1. What kind of influence do the promoters of the demonstration intend to have?
2. Whom do they hope to influence?
3. How will they exert that influence?

What is the demonstration demonstrating? Influence can be exerted and expressed in several ways:

Spread. Do the promoters want their project duplicated exactly elsewhere as needed?

Continuity. Do they want the original project continued on a more permanent basis—perhaps with more money and on an expanded scale? (Continuity is often used as a first stage, to be followed, hopefully, by spread. Usually there is more money available for demonstrations than program expansion; so administrators learn the art of grantmanship and keep applying for new demonstrations and the continuity of old ones as a means of expansion.)

Spillover. Is the purpose of the demonstration simply to attract attention to a problem—to show that *something* must be done about it (the solution not necessarily being the same as developed in the demonstration)? In spillover the demonstration serves merely as catalyst, not as model. The goal is the creation of a desire for reform and experimentation.

Those responsible for demonstration projects are often uncertain about *who* should do *what*. The President's Committee on Juvenile Delinquency and Youth crime, for example, tried on the one hand to impress a national audience with the necessity of learning and doing something about delinquency—and tried, on the other, to select projects that could make the greatest local changes. Consider the implications of this confusion. Money must come from somewhere, and on a reliable basis. If the demonstration is trying to convince Congress or the state legislature that delinquency, or a pre-school program for children, is a federal or state responsibility, then the state or federal governments should appropriate the money. If they are trying to convince local authorities that it is the community's responsibility to keep its own services going, then plans must be made to expand the local tax base or secure revenue from other local sources. It is difficult to see how all of these audiences can be satisfied simultaneously, without developing some priorities.

While vagueness reduces the need for immediate choice, postponement may only encourage, in the end, a monumental passing of the buck. Consider Project Head Start. If the summer demonstration program proved to be, as President Johnson suggested, "battle-tested" and "worthy," then, as Fred Hechinger, education editor of *The New York Times,* asked, "Why is it that so little effort is being made to move in the Head Start direction with local funds?"[2] This question certainly suggests a rather fundamental ambiguity as to who should do what.

TARGETS AND STRATEGY

Whom is the demonstration supposed to influence? Most people assume that they act from rational motives and that what they approve of is "objectively good"; but businessmen, politicians and professionals have different ideas of what constitutes "good." By what criterion do you judge the success of a demonstration in an urban school? Do you measure pupil performance? Adjustment? Cost? What audience was the project aimed for?

Questions of strategy must be answered, because the likelihood of failure to implement successful demonstrations is strong. Established institutions have a vested interest in their own survival, and a built-in resistance to serious change. To get institutions to recognize and incorporate reforms, demonstrations must first be successful. But a successful program is one that is accepted—and established institutions will not readily accept anything threatening. They favor change in small doses—regular, logical steps, built firmly on the foundations of existing programs. But the next "logical" step may never come to grips with the problem, and be far too conservative from any but a purely local viewpoint. Nevertheless, planning organizations and professionally inspired reform must often settle for those programs likely to win financial support from those with local influence. In the resultant political maneuvering and mutual accommodation, the innovations and the problem that needs solving may come out second best. The necessity to survive usually results in abandoning the strategies for promoting spread and spillover.

In practice, spread often occurs when national funders implement their own policy *before* the demonstration results are all in—and the pressure is strong for demonstrations merely to prove that they were right. The Amendments to the 1962 Social Security Act are a case in point—the policy of rehabilitation to reduce dependency was first inaugurated with only scattered evidence to support its validity; demonstrations were then set up to prove its worth. Preschool programs for the poor followed a similar pattern. The federal government has, unexpectedly, rescued these demonstrations by serving as a mechanism—through Operation Head Start—for encouraging spread. But frequently it has done so by undermining the very purposes of the demonstration—to implement policies already rationally tested. Thus we appear to have achieved spread, at the cost of rationality.

While funders of demonstrations have given little attention to the strategies of promoting spread and spillover, they have developed an approach for assuring continuity of the life of the demonstration. Three crucial elements of this strategy can be identified: *participation, money,* and *knowledge.* Let us examine these in turn.

Participation

Some projects try to develop a local board of directors with "clout"—power and influence. In theory, if the board becomes convinced of the correctness of a position, it will have the power and will to do something about it. The demonstration then becomes a strategy for educating the board. One difficulty with this premise is that people with power and influence are very often opposed to spending money for social welfare. They believe in fiscal containment—for them, holding down expenses is the greatest public virtue. They know that voluntary philanthropy cannot do the job alone, but they are philosophically unwilling to expand public participation, which must, in the end, mean increased taxation.

Why should anyone expect a powerful board of busy people to vigorously promote continuity? How much actual involvement can result from formal monthly meetings in which highly selective agendas screen out or postpone most controversy? Yet the belief that participation must lead to commitment remains a persistent and almost cherished myth about how to promote change. It reflects the professional bias which defines change as a process of self-education.

Money

What about financial involvement? Many funding bodies, like the Ford Foundation and various governmental agencies, require "matching funds," money that the community itself must put up as a sign of good faith and commitment. This is supposed to insure that the community will follow through on those demonstrations that work in order not to lose its initial investment.

In practice, however, funders often accept "matching" funds which do not match. A city may simply say that parts of its regular budget outlays for vocational schools, or playgrounds, are "matching funds" for a retraining or delinquency project—and the funder may accept this although in fact the city has spent nothing additional. The President's Committee on Juvenile Delinquency has accepted a Ford Foundation grant as a community's matching fund—and the Ford Foundation has in turn accepted the committee's grant to meet *its* requirement. The community involved here escaped unscathed financially. Such fiscal participation is unlikely to yield a deep commitment to the demonstration.

Besides, matching funds are only for the demonstration. What about the morning after the wedding? Who will pay for felicity during the long years ahead, at steadily increasing prices? Cities have limited tax bases. Boards shy away from projects with increasing budgets—the standard of efficiency is often measured by low cost and not high yield. Who will keep the project going?

If the who, what, and how questions are not answered with clarity and determination, a demonstration program, no matter how successful, can easily turn out to be a ritual where change is measured by activity, not by performance.

The Power of Knowledge

At its best, a demonstration is supposed to be planned, based on, and proven by the crucial ingredient of research. Sponsors have firm conviction that the results will be so definite, clear-cut, and dramatic that organizations will be impelled to find the opportunity to apply the innovations on a large scale.

Such hopes are like the search for the philosophers' stone. In practice, findings are usually inconclusive and non-dramatic; and even if they are overwhelming, there is no assurance they will change anything. Nonetheless, the bread-on-the-waters approach prevails, with firm faith that good ideas must inevitably prevail, and repay one hundred-fold.

Consider the early experience of the President's Committee on Juvenile Delinquency, which put great emphasis on research. Often the two research functions—policy making and evaluation—were confounded. The time needed to gather and interpret data that would influence policy was under-estimated—with the inevitable result that, since action had to proceed if the program was to survive, the research became an after-the-fact justification of decisions already taken.[3]

Often the whole point of the research was lost. The basic purpose was to test whether social institutions throw up barriers to achievement, and thereby bring about the very alienation and delinquency they deplore. But the researchers hired for the purpose wanted to be rigorously scientific; they fell back on standard techniques of examining individuals—the failings of persons rather than the failings of institutions. Relevance was sacrificed to rigor.

Under the best circumstances, evaluation of results is distressingly difficult. A demonstration project breaks new ground, or should. If it must include a great many unknowns, as in the case of comprehensive demonstrations, how then do you define exactly what is being demonstrated? Moreover, in the absence of clearly defined goals—the norm and not the exception in social action programs—how can effectiveness be measured? But even if the output measures could be clearly defined, often the time required to secure relevant information is much greater than the funders are willing to accept. For example, if we establish an innovative nursery program on the assumption that it will reduce delinquency or poverty, then a valid test requires that we should follow these youngsters through their school careers to adolescence or even to young adulthood. Even if we ask a more limited question about whether nursery programs facilitate later school adjustment, we would need to wait at least five years for reliable answers.

As a result of these difficulties, evaluation research alone can seldom serve as the primary justification for continuing a project. Perhaps this is just as well. Research findings are much more likely to show that expectations were unrealistic, rather than to prove them worthwhile. For instance, a decade and more than a million dollars have gone into research trying to evaluate how effective social casework is. Perhaps the only trustworthy inference to emerge is that more research is needed. Barbara Wootton has observed that the positive achievements of the social sciences have largely been negative: "Up until now the chief effect of precise investigation into questions of social pathology has been to undermine the creditability of virtually all the current myths."[4]

Experimental design is simply an inadequate research methodology for evaluating comprehensive demonstration programs, which are subject to the vagaries of political expediency.

We turn now from the strategy which the funders have used to promote continuity, to consider the often implied strategies by which demonstrations might produce institutional change. Clearly, all of these strategies—*infiltration, duplication,* and *pressure*—are not equally appropriate to the various aims of the demonstration—*spread, continuity,* and *spillover.* Selecting a strategy designed to achieve the objectives of the demonstration is obviously one way of strengthening it as an instrument of change.

Infiltration from Within

Sometimes a small demonstration is set up *inside* an established institution (the experimental pre-school program within an existing school system) in the hope that the larger will someday come to adopt the innovation of the smaller. How this will come about is not clear, but presumably by the force of good example, or by the tendency of a host organism to eventually develop toleration for a foreign body. Here again, if faith is placed in the power of knowledge to create change then results must be dramatic and unambiguous to be effective. Unfortunately they seldom are.

Also, the demonstration must be able to fit into the larger institution, while trying to change it. This is very difficult. If its concerns are peripheral to the host, it will have little influence. (A pre-school program tacked onto a school system which never had one will not affect the higher grades.) If its concerns are fundamental, it will be resisted. The host has control; it is composed of various sub-groups which have needs and interests which compete with the demonstration. In practice, in order to avoid confrontation, innovations usually get watered down.

Various methods may be used to keep the demonstration project from seriously changing the host organization. It can become a walled-off enclave able to go its own way as long as it doesn't bother people outside the walls, who go *their* own way. It can concentrate on remedial programs—remedies are always popular because they patch up old sores (and may even hide them)—rather than perform surgery. Indeed, as a general rule, any demonstration project concentrating on providing remedial service for an established institution has announced its inability to effect deep change, for instance, providing remedial reading services rather than changing the teaching of reading.

In short, as long as the host organization has control, significant change can be resisted. If sponsoring or funding organizations want it to achieve its goals, they should retain some control over its progress, but the more control they exercise the more alien the project becomes to the host.

Under some circumstances the infiltration tactic will work—a foreign body has been introduced into a system, and it must bring on some reaction. The energy, concern, enthusiasm and moral indignation of former Peace Corps volunteers in one school system has disturbed the old equilibrium and shaken up the teachers, destroying a few shibboleths in the process. They also, however, raised resistance and resentment, which in the end undermined the changes they wanted to bring about. The art, then, with such infiltration tactics, is to find the chemical balance that can release great energy and innovation without creating explosion.

Duplication from Without

One attractive way to get around an institution's resistance to change is to build a parallel institution which duplicates some or all of its functions, doing them better, in the hope that the established institution will modify its operation accordingly. Duplicate structures have the potential advantage of starting from scratch, unhampered by the dead hand of old practices and rigidities.

In Philadelphia, for example, Opportunities Industrialization, an organization led by Negroes, is attempting, with support from the Mayor, the Ford Foundation, and the Office of Economic Opportunity, to set up a system of vocational schools separate from and parallel to the public vocational schools. Recently the Ford Foundation announced a grant to the Church Federation of Chicago which will develop programs that duplicate the activities of a local Community Action Program.

But duplication is an open indictment of the old institution. Obviously, sponsors would not set up parallel facilities if they did not think the old needed change, or if they had much faith in its ability to change itself. The established institution may, therefore, consider paralleling as a declaration of war, inviting swift retaliation. The old institution usually has superior resources for combat and greater experience. Cooperation may be superficial; guerrilla war may develop. It can ask embarrassing questions at high levels—Why was the duplication thought necessary?—that can subject the demonstration to constant and pitiless criticism, exposure, and examination.

Duplication also bears the vice of expense. To set up a separate school system, for example, is enormously costly, especially if we want high quality. Nevertheless, its virtues should not be overlooked. As Charles Frankel says, we must have deliberate planning to provide alternatives. "We need to invigorate existing agencies to create new ones whose function is to be a thorn in the side of existing bureaucracies—agencies that bear witness to what might be, that animate, enlarge, and discipline the public imagination. Such agencies could give the public a better chance to choose what it wants and, indeed, to discover what it wants."[5] But if the strategy for promoting *spread* and *spillover* is not effective and only *continuity* is achieved, then duplication can further reduce the coherence of an already fragmented local system for delivering services to people.

Pressures from Without

Another way to get action toward implementing demonstration findings is to organize citizen groups—especially those with a personal stake in improving service—to put pressure on local officials or institutions.

Those affected usually know whether they have been getting the services they need, and can, if organized, be useful in seeing that they do get them. Saul Alinsky's Industrial Areas Foundation has been using such tactics for some time and it has inspired others, like the Syracuse Community Development Association, to use them. The Syracuse project is a federally financed anti-poverty demonstration program to develop techniques for organizing the poor. Organizers have " 'provoked' the poor to take action in their self interest . . . they have helped organize sit-ins, pickets, and campaigns to protest everything from garbage collections to welfare procedures."[6]

Social change through citizen action has become increasingly necessary and important. It has many advantages; but it has the great disadvantage that it may quickly build up a backlash of resentment that can make almost any cooperation or alternative strategy impossible. This happened to Mobilization for Youth when it organized and encouraged mothers to put pressure directly on school administrators for better conditions for children. The principals, enraged, counterattacked MFY, accusing it of irresponsible agitation. Future cooperation, obviously, became very difficult. The Syracuse project is at present fighting a decision of the Office of Economic Opportunity to cut off its independent financing and force it to apply for funds to the city's official anti-poverty program.

The purposes of the strategy are often obscured, for it is at once conceived as (1) a form of social therapy—people change when they try to change their environment; as (2) a form of protest whose chief aim is to promote institutional change and achieve a more equitable distribution of resources; and (3) as a way of promoting democracy itself—people should be involved in making decisions which affect their lives. But the tactics required to promote the goals of therapy, change, and democratic participation often conflict.

The use of citizen pressure, if it fails, may close off the opportunity for other strategies. Moreover, the bitter opposition which such programs create from established institutional powers may serve to reaffirm the powerlessness and helplessness of the poor, and thus defeat their very purposes.

IMPROVING THE ODDS

How can demonstrations become better agents of change? Here are some suggestions:

1. Funders should insist not only that the demonstration be relevant to the social *problem* involved, but that the staff also be clear on questions of social *policy. Few things are more subversive than a good question.* What proof is there of real innovation? Who supports the innovation? How exactly will the community employment and retraining program be reorganized? Are there enough resources and "clout" to push the program through in spite of resistance from established institutions?

2. Greater clarity of purpose is necessary. A major problem is not technology but ideology—what is the goal? Is it to achieve continuity, spread, or spillover? A demonstration that knows where it is going almost inevitably becomes involved in implementation, in making its recommendations effective. When purposes are unclear not only is direction and momentum lost, but outcomes are difficult to evaluate. How can "results" be judged unless the demonstrator knows whether he is (a) planning to provide choice, (b) planning for coordination, (c) planning for accountability, (d) planning for innovation, or (e) making a master plan, to be used as a model?

3. The funders must stay with the projects, not quit when the going gets rough. The demonstration cannot last or be effective if it is constantly swept with rumors that the funds will stop, and the backers quit backing. The best available evidence suggests that large scale community planning takes at least seven to ten years—there is no known way to hurry this process. Funders who give way easily to fads, impatience, or politics cannot give adequate leadership.

4. The funders must be more concerned with getting and maintaining quality. This may require more monitoring (though not meddling, admittedly a fine distinction). One way of building in accountability—a central necessity for improving social service—would be to set up a public

review board of experts, chosen for knowledge, perspective, and integrity.

5. New methods of reporting and accountability would be useful in many ways. *Merely requiring better reporting can make agencies more accountable, fostering reform and innovation.* Ernest Gruenberg describes a state department of mental hospitals that began to send out a monthly questionnaire to each hospital, asking how many patients were still being kept in straight-jackets—and found that the number declined sharply every month. Similarly, Peter Blau reports that when interviewers in an employment service were required to report how many Negroes got job referrals, the rate immediately went up.[7] In both cases all the administrators wanted initially was information; but reporting brought immediate reform. Projects should therefore be required to make reports which permit more accountability of the products they produce. Simply having to describe and break down the numbers and kinds of youths contacted and served or rejected in a delinquency or training program might give administrators a clearer idea of how effective they were, and inform those who shape policy whether the tough cases were being rejected in order to "cream" the easy. The statistics could also be used for large scale planning concerned with the entire lives of youths, rather than a specialized function.

6. Choices must be made. A program cannot promise, or achieve, everything. (This is related to the clarity and selection of goals and means.) The adoption of a policy is a commitment which itself shapes the development of an organization, and it must be carefully chosen. A proliferation of goals in a program usually reflects low confidence in major achievements. Multiplicity and alteration of goals often substitutes for effectiveness of action.

7. Demonstrations should call for continuous change. While the goal should be definite, it should indicate a direction, a focus, and not a terminus at which everything comes to a stop. As an experiment yields information, a feedback mechanism should operate which allows continuous modification. Mechanisms must be built which are continually sensitive and adaptive to new problems and new weaknesses.

8. Demonstration staffs must be prepared for, and learn to live with, conflict. They should not seek it out; they should try to minimize it; but they cannot do their job without challenging existing practices and stirring up resistance. Too little conflict may very well be proof of failure rather than success. Since they must work and contend with established institutions, they should have some sophisticated knowledge about the internal nature of organizations and professions. Organizations are not monolithic; even when they seem to be "consensus establishments," there is always a restless underground willing to go in another direction; and progress and cooperation depends on finding and strengthening those who support the demonstration policies or can suggest new directions.

There is no sure way of getting desirable results—each action provokes reaction and involves risk. But the primary talent in running a successful demonstration is not technical but administrative and political. It is not enough to know what is best to do—the administrator must be able to organize forces to get things done.

9. Research should be broadened to make it relevant to all social needs and to the whole service world. What is important here is not only the understanding of a single service, but of the overall pattern. Research can be vital in probing the consequences that flow from the present organization of social services. And since much of what we are doing is attempting to learn what is useful to do, research can help in the search for usable goals. This effort requires new kinds of links and tensions between programs and research.

Demonstration projects are not supposed to accept the easy answers. If they are concerned with usefulness rather than "success," they must ask the tough questions, probe for the basic issues, regard the accepted decisions with a skeptical eye. In the great debates on national social policy now under way, they can serve as "moral witness" to the accepted social and welfare services.

NOTES

1. Peter Marris, "Experimenting in Social Reform." An unpublished paper given at the annual meeting of the American Ortho-Psychiatric Association, Chicago, March 19, 1964.
2. Fred M. Hechinger, "Federal School Aid," *The New York Times*, March 22, 1964.
3. Peter Marris and Martin Rein, *Dilemmas of Social Reform* (New York: Atherton Press, 1967), pp. 191–207.
4. Barbara Wootton, *Social Science and Social Pathology* (New York: Macmillan, 1959), p. 326.
5. Charles Frankel, *The Democratic Prospect* (New York: Harper & Row, 1962), p. 161.
6. Reported in *The New York Times*, December 3, 1965.
7. Peter Blau, *The Dynamics of Bureaucracy* (Chicago: University of Chicago Press, 1965), pp. 74–80. See also Louis Schneider, "The Category of Ignorance in Sociological Theory," *American Sociological Review*, Vol. 27, No. 4 (August 1962), pp. 492–508.

Chapter 8

Community Action Programs: A Critical Assessment

Community Action Programs (CAP) are best regarded as experiments in professionally inspired social reform. The theory of reform in CAP springs from two sets of ideas, one concerning the causes of poverty and the other the means to overcome them. The ideas of CAP come largely from the experience of the Ford Gray Areas programs and the President's Committee on Juvenile Delinquency and Youth Crime. The validity of these ideas is still uncertain. They could either lead to a political alchemy as plausible but ultimately as sterile as the search for the philosopher's stone, or to a working theory of reform or social change. Five years' test in action suggests, from admittedly fragmented and isolated evidence, that both the strategies and the assumptions on which CAP rests need reinterpretation.

I propose to comment on each idea, its action implications, and the scattered evidence which leads me to conclude that the theory is misconceived. Finally, I hope to suggest an alternative function for Community Action Programs.

This essay is an expanded version of remarks initially made in Peter Marris and Martin Rein, *Dilemmas of Social Reform* (New York: Atherton, 1967). Reprinted with permission from Poverty and Human Resources Abstracts (PHRA), Volume III, No. 3 (May-June 1968) *Trend.*

THE VICIOUS CYCLE OF POVERTY

The theory of the poverty cycle finds support in the CAP projects and among scholars. An excerpt from the literature of the North Carolina Fund summarizes the main argument:

> We strongly suspect, for example, that simply strengthening the public schools will not benefit many of those who drop out of school early and follow the footsteps of their parents into poverty. Too many of these young people come from homes where the level of education, as well as of income and of general living environment, has been low for generations; where increasingly this cycle of poverty and frustration has blunted the desire of parents to give their children motivation for education; where the American dream of slum to affluence in three generations no longer has meaning. Children can make their way out of poverty, but only where there is motivation, sacrifice, and opportunity. Where those do not exist, there can be no breaking of the cycle.[1]

Poverty, then, is seen as self-perpetuating. The children of the poor and ill-educated start school at a disadvantage and soon fall behind. Their parents can give them little help or encouragement; school becomes a humiliating experience; the children cannot meet the teacher's demands and finally they lose their interest. They take the first opportunity to drop out. Without skills or confidence in themselves, they remain marginally employable. Some work off their frustration in crime and violence; most will always be poor. Robbed of the self-respect that comes from earning a decent livelihood, the young man cannot sustain the responsibilities of marriage, and so he bequeaths to his children the same burden of ignorance, broken homes, and apathy by which he himself is crippled.

The theory of the poverty cycle stresses the apathy of the poor. This concept of an incapacity to respond to opportunity handed from generation to generation is crucial to much of the argument by which Community Action Programs justify their methods. It is used to explain why people remain poor. Open to ambition, the argument runs, society has always assimilated poor immigrants and set them on the way to prosperity. It could do so still, if the poor were not too crushed. But the apathy and alienation of the poor inhibit their capacity to exploit available opportunities.

This argument found expression in Moynihan's recent controversial analysis of the Negro family: "At the heart of the deterioration of the fabric of Negro society is the deterioration of the Negro family (although its origins can be traced to slavery) . . . the pathology is capable of perpetuating itself without assistance from the white world." The inference Moynihan draws from these observations is that *"the cycle can be broken only if these distortions are set right"* (emphasis added).[2]

POLICY IMPLICATIONS

I believe one can draw off four important program implications consistent with the poverty cycle theory.

1. *Comprehensiveness.* The theory allows for a very flexible strategy since it sets no order of priority. If the causes of poverty are circular, then intervention at any point may be effective, and the more intervention the better. At the same time, neglect of any one aspect of the problem is excused by the indirect influence from action elsewhere in the cycle. The argument takes care of an apparent anomaly in the poverty program. It concentrates upon the needs of youth, yet many of the poor are neither young nor in search of employment—but include the retired, mothers struggling to bring up families on their own, and those fully employed heads of households who work year-round but do not earn enough to pull themselves out of poverty. This conception of the poverty cycle justifies acting upon the most malleable age groups. It is reminiscent of the New Poor Law of 1834, which was also preoccupied with how to get the able-bodied poor to work.

2. *Employability.* The logic of the poverty cycle argument forces the projects to focus not on job creation or on income, but on training programs to prepare youths to acquire motivation and demeanor before taking their place in the world of work. Consequently, these programs are less concerned with technical skills than with adjustment of individuals to the demands of employment. They reject social work techniques, hoping to inspire motivation and teach deportment through work experience. Employability programs set out to teach regularity, punctuality, neatness, how to approach a prospective employer, how to handle the conflicts and frustrations of work relationships, how to tolerate orders and respect the legitimate expectations of a boss. These assumptions have historical roots going back to the Charity Schools of the nineteenth century where education assiduously avoided training for occupational mobility and committed itself to character development. Employability training thus conceived is a door through which many youths must pass; it is an entrance to employment or vocational (skills) training (MDTA and Job Corps), or back to school. The Neighborhood Youth Corps and Job Corps in conservation areas and Work Crews financed by OMPER, the planning office in the Department of Labor, are examples of employability programs.

3. *Remediation.* These programs are similar in principle to employability programs but with techniques and activities appropriate to the world of school rather than to the world of work. The programs are designed to make children and youths better able to negotiate the requirements of the school system by overcoming their emotional frustration and cognitive deficiencies. Operation Headstart is, of course, the largest and best known

of the CAP programs aimed at strengthening the competence of children to function in school. To mention only a few, other programs include remedial reading, home visiting, and image building. The issue of the separation of church and state forces these programs to develop as supplementary to the normal school activities. Of the $321 million in CAP expenditures through 1965, $141 million was spent on Operation Headstart, with more money being spent for the summer crash program than its year-round counterpart.

4. *Participation.* These programs are designed to promote participation in social action in order to give families a stake in society. The assumption is that alienation results from disengagement in community activities. Poverty is the lack of power to command the events of one's life. It emerges as a result of "the personal sense of powerlessness felt by low income people," as a past director of Mobilization for Youth explained, and "is a major cause of their isolation and apathy." The redistribution of power is necessary to change people. Participation in social action generates power—the capacity to control and change events in one's life. As individuals acquire power and seek to change their world, *they* change as well. Thus, social action is a form of social therapy through self-help.

Employability, remediation, and participation strategies aim to reduce apathy, while comprehensiveness, which argues for multiple interventions, justifies all three. But if the importance of apathy is misplaced, the projects' framework of action breaks down. Pull hard enough at this thread, and the whole philosophy of community action unravels.

ASSESSMENT OF THE STRATEGY

The experience of the early projects suggests that apathy is not so crucial as was thought. As soon as the projects offered an opportunity that seemed genuine, there was more response than could be handled. Young men and women crowded the Youth Employment Centers in search of jobs and training. The Job Corps received 300,000 requests from youths and accepted only 20,000, redefining itself as a demonstration program, not as a mass training program.[3] Mothers hopefully brought their children to the nursery schools. Neighborhood protest organizations succeeded all too well, if the vigorous opposition they created can be taken as a measure of impact. And in the schools, remedial reading, which did nothing to change the demands of the system, still improved individual performance; given a chance, the pupils were ready to respond.

Many who came forward and had to be turned away never returned. Many more, perhaps, were too cynical or despairing even to inquire. But while there is still such a frustrated desire for a chance in life, and an eagerness to exploit any promise of help, the preoccupation with apathy seems almost perverse and surely misleading.

The projects do what they can to teach employability and remediation and to encourage participation. But the youths who participate in these programs become frustrated, not because they lack the motivation to seize upon the opportunity presented to them, but because the programs cannot fulfill the promise offered. While it is true that the youths lack the skills, the resiliency, and the tolerance of authority to meet the expectations of teachers and employers, more fundamentally, the opportunities which society holds out are too few. Graduates of employability programs have nowhere to turn. Even after training, they often cannot secure anything other than dead-end jobs. Each door they open leads nowhere. These projects are continually adding anterooms which disguise the ultimate frustration. The economy does not really want what those young people can offer. Therefore, the schools only half-heartedly encourage talents of so little potential use. The children of the slums respond to the projects because they recognize the sincerity of the intentions; they become discouraged only as it grows clear that the promise cannot be fulfilled.

Remediation programs prove equally frustrating. Scattered evidence suggests that children do learn when an investment is made in their education. But if the program lacks continuity, they do not sustain the gains made and are even more embittered than before. Deutsch's intensive preschool program for disadvantaged children produced impressive changes in the cognitive world of children, but preliminary evidence suggests that the children fall behind again after they enter the regular school system without continuity of this training.[4] It is doubtful that remediation which changes the performance of children can serve as a substitute for a high quality education. Indeed, to lure youths from their protective subculture and then fail to provide them with the necessary supports for the continuation of their first glimpse at success may produce intense frustration.

The experience of involving the poor in social action demonstrates that the poor can, and do, concert their efforts and, in the process, generate a new center of power. But we also learned that the institutions this new power challenged were indifferent, if not hostile, to self-help efforts which insisted on accountability. When attacked, organized power fought back effectively, and in the course of the struggle reaffirmed that the poor lacked power. If social action is ineffective, how can it reduce the sense of powerlessness necessary to overcome apathy? *Disillusionment is not apathy, and to confuse them only displaces the responsibility for failure.*

The poverty cycle seems, then, less intractably self-perpetuating than the CAP projects assumed. Poor parents may give their children little encouragement and few amenities to learn, and they may fail more than others to provide an emotional security from which their children can draw confidence. But this does not seem to rob the new generation of an eagerness to test, once again, the possibilities of the society which their parents failed to master.

THE VICIOUS CYCLE OF BUREAUCRACY

The proposals and strategies of Community Action Programs imply a theory of bureaucratic dysfunction. A morbid life cycle of bureaucracy seems to parallel the poverty cycle. An institution, in the interests of its internal organization and corporate survival, becomes preoccupied with loyalty to procedure at the expense of function. Rigid and self-protective, it becomes insensitive to those it serves. The regulations are faithfully followed, even where they frustrate the purpose for which they were drawn up. An elaborate ritual of service drifts into irrelevance. The institutions of education and welfare have grown especially insensitive and rigid. Their performance has inhibited access to opportunity for the poor. Moreover, jurisdictional problems inhibit an effective distribution of services.

This analysis attacks the way in which a bureaucracy functions, not the functions themselves. In the context of Community Action Programs, it implies that if the agencies would recommit themselves to serving the poor with more imagination and flexibility, they could meet their needs. Thus, for instance, schools fail to communicate their learning to slum children, because their language and conventions follow middle-class routines which their pupils cannot appreciate, and because the system is run for the mutual protection of staff, principal, and school administration. Vocational training colleges and settlement houses turn away those who need them most. Intent upon a tradition of training and programs which fits more middle-class users, they enhance the statistics of achievement and offer job satisfaction to the professionals who dispense their services. So the inherent conservativeness of bureaucratic organizations prevents their services from reaching the poor. To restore their relevance, they must be turned outward again to look afresh at the needs of the clientele they should be serving.

If this is so, it applies equally to any bureaucracy, whatever its functions. In fact, however, most social institutions do adapt to changing needs. Some, like middle-class suburban schools, innovate readily. Why should the institutions which serve the poor seem so outstandingly insensitive? Here apathy becomes crucial to the analysis: the poor, unlike other citizens, make few demands upon institutions, treating them all as part of a hostile environment from which they have retreated. They do not question the schools, but are resigned to the hours of classroom routine imposed upon their rebellious children. They do not visit settlement houses, or, once rebuffed, bother the employment service. They put no pressure on bureaucracy to adapt.

POLICY IMPLICATIONS

Armed with its theory of the dysfunction of bureaucracy, CAP was determined to change institutional performance so that it would be more relevant to the needs of the poor. It devised a programmatic strategy consistent with this theory. First, it emphasized innovation and experimentation. It was disturbed about professional disinterest in serving the poor and was drawn to programs which were ready to make use of nonprofessionals. It did so partly because this provided employment opportunities for the poor, but more fundamentally, because the infusion of indigenous personnel into self-regarding bureaucracies might force self-examination and propel organizations to change. Programs should also be innovative in the sense that they search out new techniques for reaching, training, and educating the poor. But the heart of the strategy assumed that the crucial reform needed was reorganization of the total framework of splintered and unrelated social services. While change in isolated bureaucracies was necessary, it was not sufficient. The total welfare delivery system needed to be integrated and made more coherent through coordination.

The theory of the poverty cycle led to an emphasis on comprehensiveness. This implies a broad range of activities. Since resources were limited, however, this meant that no single program would receive adequate funds. To rescue its own strategy from the dilemma of over-fragmentation, coordination became crucial. The rhetoric of CAP programs emphasized linkage, integration, coordination, coherence, etc.—to be brought about by centralized planning in CAP's. "The strengthening of the central planning capability and increased control over resource allocations are absolutely essential to effective local program development," the Chief of Research and Program Development for CAP resolutely declared.[5] Finally, the poor should be involved in policy decisions, not so much to reduce their apathy (which was the argument for social action), but to press for institutional change and to guard against the retreat into bureaucratic irrelevance. *Innovation, coordination,* and *participation* are the three major themes of the CAP program.

ASSESSMENT OF THE STRATEGY

To promote innovation, the projects naturally relied on small-scale demonstrations which permitted the time needed for experimentation. Commitment to comprehensiveness provided the rationale for experiments in many different areas. A review of expenditures confirms that CAP financed an impressive variety of programs. Aside from the employability and remedial education activities already discussed, they funded programs in housing and home management, family planning and health, consumer education, legal assistance, counseling, etc. The funds have not only been widely dispersed among different functional areas, but also among many institutions—new and old. Programs were either injected into established institutions or paralleled them. The justification of these strategies finds support in the theory of welfare incrementalism: small-scale demonstrations would create not only innovative programs, but continuity as well. Once tested, the experimental programs would spread to all other institutions which service the poor.

While CAP programs have sponsored significant innovations such as indigenous workers, participation, Neighborhood Service Stations, and the provision of legal service to protect the poor from the institutions designed to aid them, most programs are more accurately described as extensions of benefits already available to the middle classes. They are only new to the poor. Thus, continuity rather than testing innovations seems to be most crucial.

But how will the community be able to continue and spread these costly programs to their agencies? Who will pay for these reforms? Here the strategy is disturbingly silent. To add further complications, wherever the need is the greatest, the resources tend to be least adequate. Local taxation proves to be an inadequate basis on which to encourage continuity. When seen as extensions of amenities already available to the middle class rather than as innovations which depend on local taxation for full implementation, the crucial flaw in the theory becomes evident.

The fundamental problem is evidently not the manner in which institutions function, but their inability to function at all. The employment services do not have the jobs to offer, the schools cannot pay enough good teachers, the housing authorities cannot build decent cheap homes in attractive neighborhoods. The services themselves are as impoverished as those who use them. The CAP projects can only encourage agencies to make more imaginative use of what they have. However worthwhile, the improvement is bound to be marginal. Anything more must depend on a large-scale redistribution of resources.

Within this context, it is difficult to understand how participation of the poor in policy-making contributes to institutional reform. In theory, the poor could propose various programs which have been neglected by established institutions because of their indifference and disengagement from the needs of those they service. But it seems doubtful that they can implement their ideas for reform. Moreover, the question of who will pay for the innovations remains unsolved.

While the contribution of participation to institutional change is uncertain, this is not an argument against participation. This, at the least, has the symbolic value of extending a sense of dignity to the poor. However, not all observers ascribe so neutral a role to the participation of the poor. Cloward and Piven have argued that this gesture is by no means benign. Not only does participation "fail to produce significant changes in economic arrangements, but typically undermines the potentialities for low income influence as well."[6] This arises, in part, because participation is sponsored by a bureaucracy which intrudes its own agenda and thus neutralizes whatever potential influence low-income groups might have.

If the strategy of innovation and participation makes only an indifferent contribution, then coordination must play the key role in reducing bureaucratic dysfunction. While no one program can achieve much, many isolated programs combined into a coherent whole can accomplish a great deal. But Community Action Programs lack the power, the money, and the sanction to coordinate autonomous agencies which jealously guard their rights to independent action. I am increasingly convinced that the spirit of laissez-faire and rugged individualism is more alive in the welfare community than it is in the business community. *War on poverty* is itself a confusing slogan since it implies an enemy. The military metaphor breaks down as soon as one seeks to give this enemy an identifiable persona. Who defends poverty? The only recognizable villains are a rabble of racketeers—camp followers who surely could not challenge the will of a nation. Poverty cannot be projected as an external evil, but arises out of the structure of society itself. If a war at all, the attack on poverty is a civil war against narrow self-interest: the generals who lead the campaign are themselves confused by doubtful loyalties. Thus, the image of CAP's mobilizing resources against a common enemy misrepresents the nature of their function.

Early in the legislative history of this issue the question arose as to whether public schools had to go through the local CAP agencies to secure funds. Congress feared centralization, as the invective *poverty czar* suggests. Although the idea of a single local coordinating agency was challenged, CAP administration held fast to the principle. But in the end, the anarchy of local pluralistic democracy resisted the bid for rational centralization. It seems very doubtful that CAP agencies have won much control over resource allocation, which some federal officials judge so crucial for program development. They appear to function as conduits funneling federal funds through local agencies, unable to insist on either innovation or coordination as a precondition for the receipt of funds. Or, if they are able to bargain for innovation before funds are committed, they have no effective means of assuring that the projects will conform to what has been promised. Even if they do preserve the spirit of innovation, CAP agencies are eventually frustrated because they lack the resources to implement their reforms for more than a small segment of the poor.

Attempts to promote coordination and to redirect community resources run against stubborn problems which cannot easily be overcome. CAP agencies lack authority to integrate jurisdictions, and by pressing them to innovate and cooperate, often only make them more anxiously self-protective. They cannot appeal to any community of interests in a compelling enough manner to override more immediate loyalties to agencies or personal advantage. Therefore, they cannot be at once authentic spokesmen for the poor and the agents of established power.

In trying to serve as an instrument for resource allocation and coordination, it becomes increasingly difficult for the CAP projects to pursue their commitments to participation of the poor in policy development. The more the poor are directly involved in selecting policies which seem most relevant in their agenda of needed social change, the more likely they are to conflict with the agendas established by community agencies. The components of the strategy seem to clash. Coordination conflicts with innovation, and participation conflicts with both.

The problems of feasibility and coherence force us to return again to the crucial importance of resources. The insistence on innovation, integration, and participation poses intractable problems for the present philosophy and structure of CAP agencies. But even if these difficulties could be overcome, the fatal flaw in the strategy remains unsolved.

The poor urgently need more public money spent on their education and training, their housing, their health, and the welfare benefits which sustain mothers, old people, and the young. They need better protection under social insurance and minimum wage laws. And they need jobs which even an expanding economy is not likely to provide soon enough, often enough, or in the right place. At least for the time being, the full employment of young people from the slums in worthwhile careers depends upon the deliberate creation of opportunities where their talents can be used. They can be absorbed in the improvement of education and social services, in building new houses, in any of the undermanned, underdeveloped services of society where the highly trained skill of scarce professionals could be more efficiently exploited with the help of less sophisticated aides. But both the service and the jobs must be paid for chiefly from public funds. *As a cause of poverty, the weakness of the redistribution mechanisms in American society seems much more crucial than the shortcomings of institutional procedures.*

Community Action Programs as a Redistributive Mechanism

But paradoxically, an approach to reform apparently so misconceived, and so doubtfully successful in all its attempts has devised a sensitive and potentially powerful instrument of national policy. CAP could become a model of the redistributive mechanism which social reform in America has so desperately lacked. Since this program has arisen not from an ideal of national planning but from the tradition of community self-help, it preserves the spirit of local initiative and responsibility, while acting as the agent of the federal government. By putting the program under the control of an independent agency with its own board, it can create a means of distributing federal funds somewhat detached from the politics of city hall or any sectional interest, yet responsive to them all. And at the same time, CAP acts within the framework of principles laid down by its source of funds. It reconciles the inevitability of tackling redistribution at a national level with respect for the variety of local circumstances.

Seen in this light, the strategies of community action programs sort themselves into a new disposition. The coordination of local institutions no longer seems so urgent since the fundamental problem does not lie in this direction. Even innovation is probably less crucial than the spread of decent conventional practice. Until, for instance, there are enough teachers, well paid, well trained, and well equipped, the real weaknesses of orthodox education remain unknown.

It may help to summarize the steps of the analysis. First, poverty cannot be overcome by exploiting present resources more intelligently and persuading poor people to take advantage of them. However imaginatively used, the services, benefits and opportunities are still very inadequate. They cannot be increased out of local resources because the disparities of wealth tend to coincide with jurisdictional boundaries—the greater the need, the less taxable the population. And only a nationwide system of redistribution can collect revenue from the prosperous enclaves. However, such a federal instrument of social policy might deal clumsily with the variety of community circumstances and might affront the American tradition of diffuse democracy. Community Action Programs can be interpreted as a model redistributive mechanism which mediates federal action through a planning executive responsive to its own constituency. But if they are to function in this way, they must be free to arbitrate disinterestedly between national and local demands, pursuing long-term needs through the tangle of immediate pressures. They cannot, therefore, be identified with any government or lobby. Their ability to negotiate the political issues depends upon a professional neutrality which alone earns them the trust of all parties.

In conclusion, poverty is a national problem in the distribution of resources, not—as the CAP conceived it—a local problem in resource usage and exploitation. Once it has been shown that the poor are not indifferent to opportunities potentially available to them, but rather that the opportunities have yet to be created, the whole setting of community action programs falls into a different perspective. And from this point of view, the strategies of community action must also be reinterpreted.

NOTES

1. *The North Carolina Fund: Program and Policies* (November 1963), pp. 10–11.
2. Daniel P. Moynihan, "The Negro Family: A Case for National Action" (Washington, D.C.: Office of Policy Planning and Research, Department of Labor, March 1965), p. 47.
3. More recent data available in 1967 suggests a different interpretation. Sar Levitan ("The Job Corps," mimeo., 1968) observes that it was necessary to maintain "a continuous promotional effort to fill the available facilities—which by mid-1967 could accommodate a maximum of 43,000 youths." He estimates the size of the eligible population at about one million, out of school, unmarried youth from poor families.
4. Martin Deutsch, "Early Social Environment: Its Influence on School Adaptation," in *The School Drop Out* (Washington, D.C.: National Educational Association, 1964). When confronted with the findings that children lose in elementary school the gains they earlier won from their participation in Headstart programs, public policy developed in two different directions. One course of action tried to continue a high quality program into the elementary school level. Operation Headstart Follow-Through is an example. The other course of action was to try to preserve the gains made in Headstart by starting even earlier. Parent and Child Centers now offer, on an experimental basis, an educational enrichment program for children and their parents from the birth of the child.
5. Sanford L. Kravitz, "Community Action Programs: Past, Present, Future," in *American Child*, Vol. 47, No. 4 (November 1965), p. 4.
6. Richard A. Cloward and Frances Fox Piven, "Politics, Professionalism and Poverty," a paper prepared for Columbia University School of Social Work Arden House Conference on "The Role of Government in Promoting Social Change" (Harriman, N.Y.: November 18–21, 1965), p. 1.

Chapter 9

Organization
for Social Change

This paper is an account of the operation of a social welfare organization engaged in carrying out a controversial function. It seeks to examine the kind of internal structure which permits such an organization to retain its innovative goals, to pursue these goals vigorously, and to obtain the resources—money, clients, and personnel—which are necessary for the effective achievement of its goals.[1]

Such an examination is timely because conflict is often a precondition for promoting change. As organizations become increasingly involved in promoting community change and social innovation, they will need to develop structures which enable them to withstand opposition without sacrificing their goals. A variety of efforts both to promote change and to study the process of change have emerged on the current social welfare scene. Consider the following brief list: with the aid of Ford Foundation funds, Brandeis University is examining the response of existing social welfare agencies to the changed needs of the aged. Western Reserve University, concerned with the same problem area, is examining how priorities for services are decided. New organizations such as the Mobilization for Youth and sixteen similar projects throughout the country (all supported in part by funds from the President's Committee on Juvenile Delinquency and Youth Crime) are now being created

Reprinted with permission of the National Association of Social Workers, from *Social Work*, Vol. 9, No. 2 (April 1964), pp. 32-41.

with the specific objective of change through intervention, to expand opportunities available to disadvantaged groups. Organizations interested in promoting "the human side" of urban renewal, reducing racial discrimination in employment, reversing social disorganization in low-income communities, and so on, have come to recognize that politicalization of tenant groups, nonwhites, and slum dwellers—in other words, the mobilization of support at the grass roots level—is one means for promoting social change. Each of these various efforts challenges existing social welfare structures, and in so doing creates conflict and controversy. To achieve change, a better understanding of the organizational prerequisites required to initiate and sustain conflict is needed. This paper is an attempt toward understanding this question.

METHOD OF STUDY

Affiliates of the national Planned Parenthood Federation were selected as the organizations for analysis.[2] Planned Parenthood seemed most appropriate for a study of conflict because of its special problem: in addition to the normal obstacles confronting private agencies dependent on voluntary support, some of the procedures advocated by the Planned Parenthood Federation are opposed by an organized and influential institution in the community—the Roman Catholic Church.

The study was organized into three parts: history, statistics, and case studies of four affiliates of the federation. The first section provides a historical survey of the development of the national organization. Particular attention is given to shifts in goals, structures, and policies in response to the controversy engendered by the pursuit of its goals. In the second section, ratings of the relative effectiveness of its affiliates made by a panel drawn from personnel at the Planned Parenthood Federation were correlated with a number of internal and external variables in an effort to determine the degree to which these variables might be associated with the rating of effectiveness. Internal variables considered, among others, were the agencies' three primary resources—clients, money, and personnel. These objective measures, as well as the ratings by the panel at the national level, were considered as indicators of affiliate effectiveness. The external variables selected for consideration were measures of the affiliate's acceptance and opposition within the community. This was measured by referrals from other community agencies, by membership in a health and welfare council, by physical location of the affiliate (whether in the same building with another accepted health, welfare, or religious organization), and by the size of the Catholic population in the community.

The third section of the study, which supplements the historical and statistical material, contains intensive case studies of four Planned Parenthood affiliates, two judged generally effective and two deemed ineffective by a national rating committee. In each community the author interviewed executives of health and welfare agencies, executives of voluntary and governmental agencies outside the health and welfare field, members of the local Planned Parenthood Board of Directors, and the executives of the affiliate. In all four communities a total of sixty-seven local persons were interviewed. Each was in a position of community leadership by virtue of the office which he held.

Some limitations of this study should be noted. Inferences regarding the action taken by the four affiliates studied and the nature of the community response to these actions need not necessarily hold for other Planned Parenthood affiliates or other health and welfare organizations which are involved in controversial issues. The intensity of feeling and belief which are engendered by a consideration of birth control may make this a special problem. Second, generalizations from the case studies should also be circumscribed by the fact that the communities studied were all in the northeastern section of the United States where the studies were undertaken. There is evidence from this and other studies that community differences (regional, religious and ethnic subgroups, size and economic base) affect the pattern of agency interaction, the relative importance of public and voluntary organizations, and the willingness of organizations to become involved in controversy.[3] And finally, the ratings of affiliate effectiveness posed some additional limitations. Though the raters were in substantial agreement on the over-all ratings assigned to the various affiliates, analysis revealed that they did not regularly take into consideration characteristics they stressed as particularly important; also not all the criteria of effectiveness were applied consistently. Caution in the interpretation of these data is therefore indicated. This study must be treated more as a device for generating hypotheses than as a means of confirming them.

FINDINGS

Planned Parenthood follows what might be described as a locality-responsive style for the achievement of its designated goals. This term is selected because it captures the essential aspects of Planned Parenthood's operation, namely, that it has a structure and style of operating which is responsive to the needs, demands, and values of the community of local agencies in which it functions. The components of this strategy can be understood by considering the following dimensions of its organizational structure: sponsorship, source of authority, reliance on professional personnel, source of financial support, and stable pattern of interaction with other community

agencies. Let us consider each of these dimensions in turn. The pattern to
be described is an ideal type in that none of the four affiliates conforms
exactly to all the dimensions presented.

Family planning centers are largely sponsored by voluntary groups. Although a number of public agencies, particularly in the South, do provide
birth control services, these public agencies are not affiliated with the
Planned Parenthood Federation.[4] The boards of local Planned Parenthood
affiliates are comprised chiefly of local economic and social elites. These
elites have a substantial amount of interlock, i.e., overlapping memberships
on boards of other health and welfare organizations in the community,
including the community welfare council and the United Fund.

Affiliates have a strong local organization and are only loosely tied to
their national organization. This kind of tie to the national organization
has been identified by Sills as a federated structure in that it provides for
maximum independent decisions on the part of locally based affiliates.[5]
A national organization following this model only has authority which is
delegated to it by its affiliates. This contrasts with the corporate structure
which provides for centralized authority with minimum independent decisions made by the local affiliates. In the corporate structure, affiliates have
their authority delegated to them by their national organization.

Local affiliates seek professional personnel to act as executives of their
organization. It is believed that such personnel are able to facilitate Planned
Parenthood's acceptance by other agencies in the community. Professionals
trained as social workers are particularly valued for the contribution they
can make in promoting this acceptance and in furthering co-operation
among community organizations. (Over a third of the executives of local
affiliates in 1960 had some professional training and experience in the field
of social work. Social workers comprise the largest single professional group
of personnel employed by the local affiliates.)

Planned Parenthood has a narrow base of financing, relying chiefly on
funds raised from a select group of individuals in the community, client
fees, and board contributions. In two communities Planned Parenthood
affiliates received funds from the United Fund—even these obtain their
funds unofficially. Participation in federated fund-raising was perceived as
an ideal form of financing affiliate operations by some for at least the
major portion of the affiliate's needs.

Both the affiliates and their national organization place strong emphasis
on the policy of working co-operatively with other agencies. They are particularly concerned with gaining acceptance from other health and welfare
agencies. The federation singles out for recognition affiliates which are
successful in winning such co-operation. To win membership in a community welfare council is a desired prize. The degree of interagency co-
operation achieved by affiliates was one of the important criteria used by
raters at the federation who were assessing the effectiveness of its affiliates.

This criterion rests on the view that interagency co-operation, *per se*, leads to greater effectiveness and to greater capacity to obtain the necessary resources. Co-operation from established agencies is generally believed to have symbolic as well as instrumental value in that it serves to legitimize the operation of a particular agency.

When taken together, these dimensions of an organization's structure—sponsorship, source of authority, personnel, financing, and stable pattern of interaction with other organizations—form a strategy or a means for the achievement of an organization's aims. In this sense we view organizational structure as a strategy for goal achievement. This specific structure characterizes the Planned Parenthood style which we have designated as locality-responsive. Many other organizations, particularly those which function in the welfare field (family agencies, settlement houses, and so on), follow a similar style.[6]

EARLY HISTORY

The locality-responsive style, which characterizes the present operation of the federation, emerged as a result of an unusually bitter and prolonged tug of war within the birth control movement. The organization assumed its present form through a number of mergers. Analysis of the history of the federation and the four selected affiliates reveals a process of partial goal succession away from the controversial function of control of birth to the "safe" and "respectable" functions of child-spacing, premarital counseling, sex education, consultation on infertility, and even marriage counseling. Some Planned Parenthood affiliates have also developed relatively elaborate programs for cancer detection. One affiliate was spending almost one-fifth of its total budget on this program.

These shifts in goals were associated with shifts in the internal structure of the organization, in particular, its sponsorship and locus of authority. Lader, in his account of the history of the organization, comments on the increasing influence of social elites. He observes that women of social position "felt that the time had come to make birth control palatable to the rich and socially elect . . . as one of their expected duties along with settlement house and welfare work."[7]

This leadership stressed safety, respectability, and conservatism. Their national organization, the American Birth Control League, was organized along federated lines with representation from local affiliates. In 1928 Margaret Sanger, discontent with the league's policy of caution, withdrew and established a competitive national organization, the Clinical Research Bureau. Organized along corporate lines, policy-making in the bureau resided in the national body where decisions were binding on its constituent branches. The bureau's board did not include voting representatives from the branches. It functioned as a subcenter of power that could present a united front, particularly in times of crisis, and was organized so as to be able to serve as an instrument for social reform.

In 1939, the league and the bureau merged to form the Birth Control Federation. After the merger, the bureau abandoned its position of national leadership and was renamed the Margaret Sanger Clinic. It functioned as an affiliate of the newly created federation, which in 1942 was renamed the Planned Parenthood Federation of America. Again in 1962 the federation merged, this time with the World Population Emergency Campaign. The new organization carries the names of both organizations in its official title.

CONSEQUENCES OF PURSUING A LOCALITY-RESPONSIVE STYLE

It seemed indeed reasonable to accept Planned Parenthood's expectation that its most effective affiliates, judged by both objective and subjective standards, would be found in communities whose welfare and health leaders were most in sympathy with Planned Parenthood's objectives. It also seemed reasonable to expect that effective affiliates would be located in communities with the least opposition to their program, as measured by the low percentage of Catholics in the total population.

The statistical analysis, however, indicated that there was no significant relationship between any of the objective measures of agency co-operation, community acceptance, and community opposition, and the affiliates' ability to obtain the necessary resources—clients, funds, and personnel. In addition, none of these measures was correlated with the ratings of affiliate effectiveness by a panel of four judges drawn from volunteers and staff at the national level. Size of city was the only variable which was clearly associated with these two measures of effectiveness. That bigness and effectiveness seemed to be equivalent terms suggests that the federation, perhaps inadvertently, used a big-city image as a standard for its rating. Analysis of the rating of effectiveness used by David Sills in his study of the National Foundation for Infantile Paralysis reveals similar findings. This suggests that the equating of "goodness" and "bigness" may be endemic to the health and welfare field, at least so far as judgment ratings of effectiveness are concerned. Since the measures of effectiveness were so highly correlated with community size, the rather surprising finding emerged that Planned Parenthood affiliates did better in communities that have a large Catholic population. However, this finding is spurious. It emerged because Catholicism tends to be centered in urban, metropolitan regions rather than in small cities. When the size of the city is taken into account, the statistical relationship between Catholicism and effectiveness disappears.

Partly because Planned Parenthood was deeply concerned with the question of agency co-operation, and partly because co-operation is a "sacred cow" in the social welfare literature, some further observations regarding factors correlated with interagency co-operation will be briefly noted. First, the data show that membership in a community welfare council was *not* significantly associated with the percentage of referrals which affiliates received from other agencies. It can be inferred from this finding that an affiliate's membership in a council does not necessarily make other agencies willing to send it clients. Nor, it may be noted parenthetically, did such membership affect the affiliate's ability to raise funds. It is to be observed, however, that in such regions as the West and the Midwest where voluntary agencies are relatively few, where they have less historical and current significance in the total welfare picture, and where a lower proportion of Catholics is found, the relative percentage of agency referrals to Planned Parenthood was high. Agency co-operation, in the particular matter of referrals, appeared to be largely influenced by factors that vary by region. Clients, of course, come into an agency by many routes—case-finding, referrals from other agencies, self-referrals, or referrals from other clients. It might be expected that when all possible sources of obtaining clients are taken into consideration, affiliates that received a large number of agency referrals would have relatively higher client loads than those that received few referrals. At least the common emphasis on promoting agency co-operation is based on this view. The data show, however, that the percentage of agency referrals and the number of new clients served appear to have little relation to each other. Planned Parenthood apparently need not rely largely on other community agencies to secure its clientele.

CASE STUDIES

Next let us turn to an analysis of the case histories of the four affiliates of the Planned Parenthood Federation and consider both their internal operation and the way in which the community of health and welfare agencies responded to them. In this review attention will be focused only on the structure of the affiliate boards and the kinds of actions in which they were engaged.

On a local level, Planned Parenthood board membership is composed largely of the elites of wealth and status in the community. Their primary commitments appear to be to other organizations to which they belong— the hospital, the community chest, the welfare council, the Visiting Nurse Association, and so on. It is as a result of participation in these other organizations that much of their prestige accrues—thus they lend status to Planned Parenthood. Board members try to avoid taking action which might lead to conflict or inconsistency with these other commitments.[8] For example, in one community the board failed to act in support of a staff physician who lost his privileges in a Catholic hospital because of his affiliation with Planned Parenthood. In another community, board members who also served as trustees on the community council voted against accepting Planned Parenthood's application for council membership although they supported this action as members of the Planned Parenthood board. Perhaps the most dramatic incident of inaction and denial was the unwillingness of a currently inactive board member, a governmental official, to openly admit his association with the local Planned Parenthood board. Still another indication of board members' unwillingness to be publicly identified with Planned Parenthood is illustrated by the discontinuance of the practice of listing their names on official letterheads in several cases where such open affiliation proved a source of embarrassment.

In our study, the high-prestige nucleus of the agency boards was generally committed first and foremost to maintaining the current equilibrium within the health and welfare community of agencies. This group of interlocked elites had nothing to gain, and frequently much to lose, by promoting action that might cause conflict; they were thus content to do the best they could without launching aggressive appeals for community and agency support. Another consequence of the location of the board's primary source of prestige and commitment outside of the Planned Parenthood affiliate was that when conflict did arise, members were likely to respond in ways that favored their other attachments.

In all communities studied, we noted that board members of Planned Parenthood were thrust into the heart of community conflict despite their fundamental wish to avoid conflict and preserve existing relationships. These conflicts were created, time and again, when affiliates tried to gain acceptance from other agencies by seeking to become members of community welfare councils or by seeking to persuade local hospitals to offer contraceptive services, usually through some co-operative relationship with the affiliates. How is it then that boards managed to pursue those activities which enmeshed them in conflict despite their best efforts to avoid such conflict?

Frequently, these activities were initiated by segments of boards which may be called the "representative element." This term is used because these members are drawn from community subgroups (minority groups, religious bodies, professionals, and so on) in contrast to those who represent the elites of wealth and status. Community representatives were brought into the organization as a means of giving it a more democratic character. This broadening of representation was accomplished by means not unlike those used by a political party to achieve a "balanced ticket." But it was the elites who maintained the controlling interests in the boards. The representative members entertained hopes of impelling these Planned Parenthood affiliates to pursue dynamic policies and militant strategies directed at winning acceptance from other agencies. They do this either in the sincere wish to promote agency objectives or in the hope of creating rallying points of opposition to religious organizations that attempt to limit freedom in matters of conscience.

Sometimes Planned Parenthood's crises were thrust on the organization not by board members who sought action, but by members of the agencies' own professional staffs, spurred on partly by their professional commitment to agency acceptance and agency co-operation, and partly by the strong emphasis placed on interagency co-operation by the federation.[9]

Paradoxically, it was the boards' own ideological commitment to the importance of interagency co-operation that set the stage and made them receptive to activities which catapulted these affiliates into a sea of controversy. When confronted with community conflict, no matter what its source, the customary board response was to retreat, to take no action, and to avoid the issue as long as possible. This paralysis of action can best be understood, not by the vigor of the opposition, but by the inability of the affiliates to muster internal board support. Inaction, here, is a responsive mechanism to cope with crisis and preserve harmony.

Let us briefly recapitulate the study's findings. First, when affiliates of the Planned Parenthood Federation were compared with each other, community acceptance, interagency co-operation and community opposition did not appear to be relevant factors in contributing to affiliates' possession of resources, clients, and money. Even the panel's estimate of their over-all effectiveness as operating agencies was not, in reality, influenced by these standards though they were stated as a policy. Second, although interagency co-operation and acceptance did not appreciably affect affiliates' effectiveness as measured by these indices, local boards were nevertheless committed to pursuing a policy of winning agency acceptance. This emphasis apparently led the affiliates that were studied intensively to become involved in community conflict, to which their boards responded by withdrawal, indecision, and inaction. If we redefine effectiveness as the capacity to vigorously pursue stated goals, then the demonstrated caution and paralysis suggests that even the two affiliates rated favorably had ineffective boards.

A reasonable inference to be drawn from these qualitative and quantitative data is that Planned Parenthood is handicapped in the accomplishment of its objectives because it is operating with an organizational structure which is inappropriate to the specific objectives sought. In this context Thompson and McEwen in a recent analysis of goals and the environmental factors which influence their achievement note:

> competition, bargaining, cooperation . . . constitute procedures for gaining support for the organizational environment; the selection of one or more of these is a strategic problem . . . the organization that adopts the policy of competition when cooperation is called for may lose all opportunities to realize its goal.[10]

And we would add, conversely, that to adopt a strategy of co-operation when independent action is called for may result in a similar fate.

IMPLICATIONS FOR SOCIAL CHANGE

We have seen that the locality-responsive style which Planned Parenthood pursues is not congruent with the controversial goals it favors. By retaining this style we have seen Planned Parenthood dilute its goals, from birth control to child-spacing and marital counseling. The case studies have highlighted how efforts to gain acceptance produced fear, resentment, and conflict for other agencies and created embarrassment and conflict of loyalties for Planned Parenthood board members also active on other boards in the local community. The result has been withdrawal, indecision, and inaction. Planned Parenthood's commitment to a locality-responsive style seems to represent an unrealistic appraisal of the forces at work within its own organization and in its environment.

To what extent will these observations be supported if we extend our inquiry to other organizations that promote goals which involve them either in value conflict or in controversy rather than in the pursuit of integrative goals? Some value-conflict organizations promote *goals* which bring them into conflict with at least one major or dominant community group. (For example, racial integration, disarmament, and birth control.) Organizations engaged in controversy, by contrast, act as strong advocates of a particular point of view, but the ideals to which they subscribe are often widely accepted. (For example, equal rights, the reduction of disease, and medical care for the aged.) Disagreement prevails over the *means* employed to achieve these aims: national voluntary health agencies favor independent rather than federated fund-raising, unions and old age organizations favor an insurance rather than an assistance approach to medical care. However, organizations that merely seek to maintain or expand their operations are not ipso facto considered controversial, even though in the process of searching for scarce resources they may engender conflict. The definition of controversy presented here assumes organizational commitment to either goals or methods that are essentially innovative in character.

Variations in the proposed model may be indicated for the value-conflict and the controversial organizations. Nevertheless, we believe that encompassing both these types of organizations under the same frame of reference is useful. What is essentially needed is a kind of internal structure which allows an organization to take a strong independent stand when such a strategy is indicated. An organization which selects controversial aims does not need exclusively to follow a strategy of controversy. It may choose a range of approaches, from co-operation to bargaining to protest. Controversial organizations must, however, avoid organizational structures which act as constraints to paralyze their engagement in controversy at the point when such a strategy is indicated.

We would anticipate that examining a range of organizations operating within the same problem area would reveal that those organizations which are most capable of assertively pursuing their goals do not follow a locality-responsive style—they are not federated, locally based, or committed solely to a strategy of co-operation. What style then are they likely to follow? Guided by Sills's classic analysis of those factors which account for the unusual success of the National Foundation in winning support and avoiding displacement of its goals, we submit the hypothesis that a locality-independent style is most congruent for both controversial and value-conflict organizations.[11] Organizations which stress this style do not involve others in their decision-making. In this sense they function fairly independently of the community or group of organizations of which they are a part, and their center of control is non-locally based.

All organizations are co-operative with each other to some degree, and all agencies define their aims as being consistent with and furthering the common community good. Yet a key question remains. When should an agency do what it thinks it has to do with minimum regard for what other organizations believe or have to do? In the light of the above analysis, what organizational prerequisites are necessary for the pursuit of independent action? We use the same dimensions developed for our earlier description of locality-responsiveness.

Among agencies that follow the style of independent action, key board members (decision-makers) are generally non-elite. The term non-elite includes the functional equivalent of this term, that is, those who are discontent with either dominant values or accepted modes of intervention. In this sense even social and economic elites can function as non-elites. These agencies have a simple rather than a federated structure in that they comprise a group of homogeneous or like-minded individuals who share common goals and common values. "The old Townsend Clubs, an organization of older people run by older people for the benefit of older people provide an example of the simple structure."[12] In this sense the sponsors and the clients are very closely interrelated in that they are consumers of the services they seek to promote. Such organizations are part of stronger, more centralized national bodies and the local affiliates enjoy much less autonomy. Their authority is largely determined by non-local interests—a feature of their structure which permits them to resist local community pressure. Often their sources of financial support are outside the community, either within the broader geographic community where money is in relative abundance, or in national bodies like the federal government and large voluntary foundations.

These agencies tend to employ staff who are less concerned with the goals of community integration and interagency co-operation. Professionals drawn from social work and the public health fields are strongly committed to a co-operative rationality which stresses community integration, interagency co-operation, and avoidance of duplication. They find it difficult to work in such settings. Some professional groups, such as applied economists, political scientists, and lawyers, may be less committed to co-operation and more identified with the philosophy of pluralism which accepts the validity of competition. The lawyer, for example, although he may settle many cases co-operatively outside of court, defines the legal processes in terms of an adversary model where a conflict of interests is assumed. The lawyer represents one of the contending parties. He is guided in his actions by the ethics of his profession and by legal constraints. These represent the rules of the game.

This discussion has been concerned with the organization which is engaged in value conflict or in controversy. Another important area for study is the impact of controversy on the community. Taken from the perspective of established local agencies, foreign, non-locally based organizations in their midst are disruptive to an integrated local community. Established organizations have at times made vigorous efforts to assure the conformity of these innovative organizations, yet these overtures are often successfully resisted.[13] The nature of the long-range accommodations which communities and organizations make to each other is a matter which needs careful documentation. This and other questions will press for attention as new, non-locally based organizations continue to flourish in the local community. Of particular concern to social workers is the role they will play either as supporters of established community values or as supporters of social innovation. Changes in social work training will be necessary if we are successfully to enlist the participation of social workers in organizations committed to social criticism and to social change.

NOTES

1. This paper does not focus on leadership as a source of change. Although the importance of leadership is recognized, it is treated fully in the social work and social science literature.
2. Martin Rein, *An Organizational Analysis of a National Agency's Local Affiliates in Their Community Contexts: A Study of the Planned Parenthood Federation of America* (New York: Planned Parenthood Federation, 1961). A dissertation submitted in partial fulfillment of the requirements for the degree of doctor of philosophy, Brandeis University, September 1961.
3. Paul A. Miller, *et al., Community Health Action: A Study of Community Contrast* (East Lansing: Michigan State University Press, 1953). Christopher Sower, *et al., Community Involvement* (Glencoe, Ill.: Free Press, 1957).
4. Recently the Illinois Public Aid Commission voted to pay for doctors' services and for any contraceptives they prescribe for welfare recipients who voluntarily ask for birth control. The ruling of the commission is presently under attack. (*New York Times*, April 22, 1963). In 1958 the Pennsylvania State Board of

Public Assistance adopted a resolution permitting social workers to refer clients to either their own physician or to Planned Parenthood. However, in June 1959 it reversed this decision.

5. David M. Sills, *The Volunteers: Means and Ends in a National Organization* (Glencoe, Ill.: Free Press, 1957).

6. Roland L. Warren, *The Community in America* (Chicago: Rand McNally & Company, 1963). Our discussion of locality-responsive and locality-independent styles is similar, but not identical, to Warren's distinction between the horizontal and the vertical pattern.

7. Lawrence Lader, *The Margaret Sanger Story and the Fight for Birth Control* (Garden City, N.Y.: Doubleday and Co., 1955).

8. For a further discussion of the relationship between commitment and controversy, *see* James S. Coleman, *Community Conflict* (Glencoe, Ill.: Free Press, 1957).

9. For a discussion of cost as a factor in organizational relationships, *see* Paul E. White and Sol Levine, "Cost as a Factor in Interorganizational Exchange" (Boston: Harvard School of Public Health, 1962). (Mimeographed.)

10. James D. Thompson and William J. McEwen, "Organizational Goals and Environment: Goal Setting as an Interaction Process," *American Sociological Review*, Vol. 23, No. 1 (February 1948).

11. Under certain conditions, controversial missions which are needed but unwanted may be better handled by means of local authority. Selective Services and OPA (Office of Price Administration) were so managed. In this context, local authority can be trusted to respond to local atmosphere. On the other hand, local administration of national programs serves the function of attack avoidance, in the sense that should an attack be launched it would be directed at the local unit and not the basic idea of the program.

12. For a fuller discussion, *see* Chapter 10.

13. The difficulty in centralizing, and thereby controlling, organizations' access to community resources is well documented in a recent report describing the unsuccessful pressure extended by top business leadership to get independent health organizations to join the United Fund. For a full discussion of this incident, *see* Donald S. Connery, "Business and Charity: The Pittsburgh Skirmish," *Fortune* (April 1957).

Chapter 10

Goals, Structures, and Strategies for Community Change

The attempt to develop a systematic theory which describes and analyzes social work practice is gathering
momentum. The effort in community organization is no
exception. Valuable insights have been contributed by a
score of writers, drawing upon their unique experiences.[1]
The National Association of Social Workers and the
Council of Social Work Education are endeavoring to
define the foundations or boundaries of practice.[2] However, efforts to date have not yet reconciled in one scheme
the variety of practices encompassed by the term "community organization." Concepts drawn solely from practice descriptions must deal with welfare planning councils,
governmental commissions and interdepartmental com-
mittees, united funds, neighborhood councils, specialized
planning bodies such as mental health associations or
health councils, and the organizing activities of national
agencies as diverse as the Family Service Association of
America (FSAA) and the National Foundation, to say
nothing of community development.

The authors wish to express their grateful appreciation to Robert
S. Weiss for his many helpful suggestions. Originally presented at
the National Conference on Social Welfare, Dec. 23, 1968. Reprinted
with permission of the publisher and co-author, Robert Morris,
from *Social Work Practice* (New York: Columbia University Press,
1962), pp. 127–145.

This diversity in practice does not easily submit to an encompassing theoretical framework, except at the most general level. This chapter seeks to avoid global theories, and to understand the diversity by asking: How do the goals, structures, and strategies (in behavior) of organizations affect each other? It is our initial thesis that success in achieving a goal in community organization depends upon the use of a structure and a strategy appropriate to that goal; conversely, no method, however well implemented, is effective in all circumstances. Use of this simple guide depends upon a more penetrating analysis of each term: What goals do we mean? What alternative structures are available? What strategies can be drawn upon?

We do not lack broad goals for our social work efforts, but a great gap exists between the aim of all welfare, let us say, "a healthy society," and the more limited aims of a single voluntary family service or child-serving agency or department of public welfare. True, each of these agencies favors a good life for all, strong family and interpersonal relations, and a community with adequate resources to meet individual and group needs; but closer to everyday practice the goals of each are quite different in their operational aims, the types of problems the community calls upon them to handle, and the methods they use to achieve these aims.

Attempts to classify agencies in regard to either aims, functions, or methods may be found in the growing social work literature which is concerned with social problems and planned change. We shall consider the problem of organizational goals from still another perspective—the extent to which goals may be described as primarily committed to change in the sense of achieving predetermined objectives, or integration in the sense of conforming to common values.

This polarization has utility for describing the direct-service agency and its individual clients as well as those agencies engaged in community activities. To illustrate, goals of change have been equated with a belief that many acceptable solutions to perceived problems are possible for the individual; and integration has been equated with conformance to accepted solutions by the individual. An agency or society committed to change must necessarily hold as its norm the pluralism of many solutions so that an open arena exists where many agencies pursue their independent aims; one committed to integration necessarily singles out a narrow band of homogeneous standards which it urges its members to conform to and which are considered socially desirable goals.

In general, social work is committed both to pluralistic norms, captured in such concepts as self-determination, and to promotion of the acceptance of certain widely held social goals. Individual agencies, however, are more concerned with one or the other. Their methods and strategies are determined in part by such differences. Perhaps this explains the persistent differences in method and program between, let us say, a child-protective agency which encourages its clients to conform to child-rearing patterns which they do not accept and a family agency which attempts to help its clients realize the goals they do believe in; similar differences can be seen between a settlement house and the YMCA or Boy Scouts.

One type of agency, for example, encourages immigrants to adapt their cultures to the American way of life while retaining their cultural diversity or pluralism; another type stresses the melting pot and the integration of previous cultures into a single homogeneous culture.

Can the same concepts be fruitfully used to describe the field of community organization or community planning? Think of a variety of community organization agencies: welfare councils, mental health associations, a state interdepartmental planning committee in aging, the American National Red Cross, or the FSAA. Each one of these is a miniature welfare system, made up of many subunits called agencies, or chapters, or departments. Among such organizations it is possible to distinguish at least two basic aims, one dealing with pluralism or change and the other with integration or homogeneity. These goals are, in turn, associated with different organizational arrangements and require the use of sharply different strategies or means. The simultaneous pursuit of both integration and change leads to conflict. Decision as to which aim is primary is required or we run the risk of forsaking both.

In community organization, we deal with the relationship of relatively autonomous agencies (or subunits) to each other and to a larger welfare system. Community organization has been concerned chiefly with the evolution of acceptable common standards to which these agencies can conform—the general community need or interest, good practice, and so forth. For some agencies, adherence to these norms is primary. However, other agencies have only a secondary interest in such conformity; they are mainly interested in achieving their own self-established ends. The former are committed to homogeneous goals and integration; the latter, to heterogeneity and pluralism.

A welfare council must start with the relation of service agencies to each other and assume that there is an overriding community interest to which individual agency acts must or should conform. The FSAA depends on the local family agencies' acceptance of certain standards. The Department of Health, Education and Welfare's interdepartmental committee on aging operates on the premise that the Department's aims can be stated and that bureaus and agencies should subordinate their acts to these more general ends. In each case, the organization seeks integration between its general, homogeneous, conforming ends and the acts of its subunits. Promoting cooperation and coordination among these frequently diverse units is the measure of the achievement of integration. The encouragement of better working relationships among these subunits within the sponsoring organization is taken as prima-facie evidence that a greater welfare integration has been achieved and social goals reinforced. This agency integration, in fact, is seen as symbolic of community integration.

For this class of organization (or system of agencies), achievement of specific goals is, of course, desired (such as less juvenile delinquency, more casework, and so on); but this is secondary to, and dependent upon, the integration within. Such agencies usually express their goals in broad and diffuse terms. Such statements seem best to serve their integration aims, since they avoid the specificity which may breed conflict.

By contrast, the goals of other types of agencies are concerned with change and not integration; they emphasize their own specialized predetermined interest. They are committed to specific, limited, and concrete goals. They are less concerned with the impact of the achievement of their goals on other organizations. They are convinced of the singular importance of their selected goals, and the action they take to achieve them accounts for the greater expenditure of the organizations' resources.

Change-oriented organizations have the quality of a social cause. Within the health and welfare context we find such organizations as the Planned Parenthood Federation of America, Inc., committed to birth control, the National Association for the Advancement of Colored People (NAACP), committed to racial integration, the Children's Bureau, committed to the rights of children.

The specialized health drives found in any local community offer perhaps the most dramatic example of action taken by cause-oriented organizations. They consider the validity of their aims to be self-evident and the vigorous pursuit of activities that will contribute to their achievement to be natural and desirable.

Such agencies attempt to use their structure and personnel to reach these goals. In contrast, organizations concerned with integrative goals use their structure and personnel first to resolve differences or to coordinate various efforts.

To maximize the accomplishment of either of these goals, appropriate organizational structure and strategy are required. Our major premise is that certain strategies and structures are more appropriate for goals of change, and other structures and strategies are more consistent with goals of integration.

We need next to identify what we mean by "strategy," which is defined here as a settled course of action. The pattern which it selects from among a field of alternatives is employed by an organization in the belief that the chosen action will contribute most to achieve its ends. A strategy involves a set of basic assumptions about a style of action judged most appropriate to accomplish specific aims. It involves the broad directives, not the specifics nor the details which may better be described as "tactics." Strategy and tactics are instrumental, means-oriented approaches to achieve specified organizational goals.

In the relationship among various welfare organizations, it is possible to specify two different strategies which we term "cooperative rationality" and "individual rationality."

Cooperative rationality. This strategy comprises the following characteristics: consensus; legitimacy; rationalism; avoidance of controversy; and a fusion of ends and means. Each facet is interrelated; ideally, all the essentials of the strategy are present.

In the cooperative rationality strategy there is a search for unity in the interests of diverse groups; a search for common values with a tacit understanding based on implicit rules that nonshared ends, which can embarrass the participants or cause conflict, are assiduously avoided. One point upon which all groups of social welfare organizations can agree is the need to expand all welfare services, but they are in disagreement as to which services are more vital than others. They prefer not to set goals which commit them to the expansion of one program while others are sacrificed. Setting a common goal of providing more resources for everyone avoids the necessity of making specific choices. When choice is required, as unhappily it must be, then other strategies, such as compromise, competition, and bargaining, must be pursued. Cooperative rationality seeks to set goals about which all, or nearly all, participants are in agreement.

An essential component of the strategy is the art of arriving at interorganizational consensus. The health and welfare community, as we have said, is characterized by differences in goals and norms. This segmented character of social welfare organizations makes the search for consensus most difficult. Genevieve Carter, a close observer of social welfare planning, notes these diverse and partially conflicting values and comments on the problems they pose:

> This complexity, inherent in the planning council organization, becomes most apparent when you attempt to specify sub-objectives or goals of a planning council. We must keep these goals highly generalized, at least for interpretation purposes, because the more we specify the more we must reconcile the conflict of values within the organization . . . searching analysis is likely to upset our ideals which we need to keep intact in order to carry on with today's operations.[3]

Thus, an endemic problem limiting the effective use of this strategy is how to arrive at group decisions without becoming enmeshed in conflicts that will destroy the organization. A major task of this strategy becomes the achievement of internal integration. The completion of this task and the survival of the organization are, at least in part, testaments to the achievement of integration aims; failure to survive is evidence of nonintegration, rupture, and schism.

To facilitate reaching conclusions based on common aims and to avoid failure, a great deal of emphasis is placed on the use of process. This is a procedure for involving, in various ways, persons who have a stake in the decision outcome. Those who follow a cooperative rationality strategy accord the process of involvement a high degree of sacredness. In this view, involvement is equated with democracy; it is the foundation on which the strategy rests. The social work literature which supports this view cites the central role of open communication. The chief mechanism or vehicle to secure involvement, to permit open communication, and to reach agreement is the committee. The professional is seen as the enabler, the catalyst, the facilitator of the involvement process, an expert trained in the art of preserving democracy. Rossi refers to this professional as the engineer of consent.[4]

In practice, however, involvement seldom takes this turn. Agreement is usually reached by the selective and discriminative use of communication. A more realistic description of how consensus is achieved suggests that it is often necessary to make decisions on important issues outside the committee, not in order to undermine the democratic process, but to facilitate the process without destroying the committee through schism. These sessions provide settings for homogeneous subgroups, each of which meets to accommodate to internal differences among its own members. This harmonious climate permits a closing of ranks after alternative positions have been explored. At the committee meeting itself, a unified position is presented on behalf of each subgroup. Often there is an informal exchange among these subgroups prior to the committee meeting. Further, to achieve consensus, a selective agenda is developed to cover matters on which there is known agreement. Also, reports and studies are secured which focus on areas of agreement; taking votes is avoided till near unanimity is assured. Thus, in this view, the committee is not seen as a working group but as a platform from which a public reaffirms and thereby legitimizes decisions arrived at in private, and "in this essentially ceremonious and harmony-creating capacity the committee system serves a useful purpose."[5]

An integral part of the search for shared goals and the use of democratic procedures is legitimation by the community. This is achieved in part by the requirement that the set goals must favor no special interest, must be non-controversial, and must be in the community's best interest; that is, they must contribute to increasing community solidarity and to reducing community conflict and strain. Thus, the goals emanate from a now legitimate source—the community itself, further buttressed by the use of democratic process so important in our culture. Characteristic of this strategy is the indefiniteness with which the term "community" is used. The term is meant to cover all persons and interests, but it is not defined. Nor are mechanisms available which permit us to reach such an ideal community, so that it remains vague and general.

Several related tactics grow out of this key plank in the co-operative rationality strategy, namely, the use of community notables and appeal to grass roots opinion. In fact, the participation of community leaders is essential to legitimating the effort. In addition, citizen participation may also facilitate implementation of decisions. Participation by both segments of the community is considered tangible evidence of support, approval, and legitimation.

Fact-finding, study, and research are other essential dimensions of this strategy, since these scientific procedures are believed to offer objective approaches to identifying means of achieving the goals sought. Since the rightness of the goals is unquestioned, once revealed, the facts are believed to speak for themselves and, once known, will invariably lead to the action that they indicate.

Individual rationality. Individual rationality, by contrast, starts with predetermined, specialized, vested interests. This strategy is less responsive to the needs and wishes of other local community organizations; instead, its chief commitment is to the pursuit of its own interest. Whereas cooperative rationality appeals to one view of democratic principles, which asserts that legitimate values are those all hold in common, individual rationality places greater stress on pluralistic values and on the inherent legitimacy of each unique and special objective. Proponents of this strategy focus on a rationality of "realism"; it is rooted in a tough-mindedness which tries to respond to the world in terms of how it does function rather than how it *ought* to function. True, the aims are believed to be in the community interest and the aims are made legitimate by the support of various leaders, but this similarity to a cooperative strategy cannot obscure the fact that the interests are premised upon a prior belief in the correctness of each objective.

Starting with firm, specific goals, the sponsors ask, what is the most rational means of accomplishing their aims? Writers who have tried to develop decision theory state the problem in terms of the action that should be taken by an organization in order to maximize its stated value position, or, more bluntly, its stake.

A first premise in this strategy is that a group knows what it wants, or favors a particular decision among many possibilities. It selects one decision because it believes that this would contribute to achievement of its short- or long-term goals, enhancement or maintenance of the organization's ideology, control of resources, or stability of position. Thus, the organization may be said to have a stake in that decision. An organization seeks to get a decision implemented in a way that has most "payoff" for this stake. "Payoff" in this sense is the potential reward which accrues from a favorable decision.

In order to maximize its stake, an organization attempts to influence those who can control the decisions. This may involve going directly to the power or center of control, but more frequently health and welfare organizations employ a circuitous route. Intermediaries (as Banfield calls them) who are usually civic leaders act as allies or "fronts" for the organization which is anxious that a particular decision be made.[6] The key to the process is to convince or influence others that it is in their best interest to favor the decision that the organization supports and to act in concert with the agency to arrive at a favorable decision. Results are achieved by persuasion, coercion, or by any suitable means. The method used is, in part, contingent on available resources and the extent to which sanctions can be imposed (the distribution of rewards or deprivations in terms of prestige or economic gain). Depending upon what it can offer in a trade or an alliance, the organization will enter into coalitions. These coalitions are usually temporary, unstable, means-oriented alliances among groups with varying goals. There is a limited range of consensus among them.[7]

Briefly, then, we can relate goals to strategies. A strategy of individual rationality is best suited for goals of change, for new ideas where diversity or pluralism should be encouraged. Cooperative rationality is suited to conformity, when groups are asked to accept common goals and standards.

Action and decisions arrived at through an individual rationality generally are based on "compromises patched up among competing parochial interests."[8] By contrast, action sought by, or in, a cooperative rationality approach attempts to arrive at decisions which are based on common values held by participating groups.

The structure of an organization is another factor in bringing about community change. We have singled out for analysis two types, defined in terms of the degree of homogeneity of their members. Specifically, there is the federated and the simple organization. The federated structure is an association of agencies or autonomous substructures, such as members of a local welfare council or chapters of national organizations. Each of these agencies is a self-directing unit, neither wholly dependent upon, nor responsible to, the federated structure of which it is a part. They participate in the work of the federated body through representatives who link up the autonomous work of their organizations and the federation in which they participate. Subunits belong to the federation on a voluntary basis. They may withdraw at will, particularly if they feel that further participation may hinder rather than help their home agency. These organizations are primarily accountable to themselves and only secondarily to the federation. Participating units view any action taken by the federation in relation to its consequence for themselves.

The second type, the simple structure, is composed of a homogeneous group of like-minded individuals or organizations which share common goals and values. Its members are primarily responsible to themselves. The old Townsend Clubs, an organization of older people run by older people for the benefit of older people, provide an example of the simple structure. The National Foundation, the Association for Mental Retardation, and the NAACP are still other examples of organizations in which sponsor and client are closely interrelated. In this sense, the members are customers of the services they seek to promote. These groups have in common the fact that each one is concerned with furthering a particular program. They are also similar in that they draw their membership from persons who have a primary commitment to that specific aim.

This contrasts with the federated structure whose members try to incorporate loyalty to the federated body while maintaining a primary allegiance to their base organization. Frequently, the simple organizations take on the character of their cause. A single relatively homogeneous group of persons is responsible for setting the policy of the organization. They have similar ideological beliefs, a likemindedness of purpose in their commitment to the principles and goals of the interest which they are trying to further.

These two organizational structures, the federated and the simple, are in a sense ideal types and are seldom found in their pure form. In practice, a federated organization may be dominated by a single group which controls its economic resources. For example, business elements control some United Funds. The nature of the participation of constituent autonomous groups is largely influenced by the strength of this control. On the other hand, simple organizations frequently make every effort to include representatives of other groups within the community, in order to give the organization community sanction and dull the sharp edge of partisanship. The more such persons are included in the structure of a simple organization, the more it takes on the character of a federated structure; and similarly, the more the federated structure is controlled by a single group, the more it resembles a simple structure. Simple or federated structures form a continuum, and only at the extremes are they most clear-cut.

A useful way of distinguishing one type of organization from another is to recognize their primary goal orientations, of which two fundamental ones are change and integration. The utility of drawing this distinction between basic organizational commitments rests on the assumption that they are not compatible and that of necessity a choice must be made between them. What follows rests upon the validity of this distinction, which has been made in other contexts by other authors.[9]

An organization's structure and the major type of strategy it employs may be seen as critical to the realization of its goals. When structure and strategy are consistent with goals, the organization operates at maximum efficiency and has the greatest opportunity of achieving these goals. Inconsistency between structure, strategy, and goals may lead to ineffectiveness, dilution, and displacement of goals.

The table illustrates the ways in which structures, strategies, and goals interlock. It shows that a federated structure and a cooperative rationality strategy are most consistent with goals of integration. On the other hand, a simple structure coupled with an individual rationality is most congruent with achievement goals of change. We shall discuss the nature of this congruence, the consequences which follow from a "poor fit" between organizational structures, strategies, and goals, and some of the difficulties that reality imposes upon realizing these ideal types.[10]

Relationship between Goals, Structures, and Strategies

	Federated	*Simple*
Cooperative rationality	1	2
	Integration	Ritualism
Individual rationality	Survival	Change
	3	4

Cells 1 and 4 on the diagonal represent goals, while cells 2 and 3 on the diagonal involve potential goal displacements.

Cell 1: the integrative syndrome. In our highly complicated, industrial society, social welfare organizations are fragmented according to the specializations they are best qualified to offer. Along with varying technical competencies, these independent organizations hold different values, some of which are in partial conflict with each other. These organizations compete for scarce community funds or staff. It is difficult yet necessary to integrate these organizations in order to have a rationally organized community welfare system. The central task of an integrative organization is to locate homogeneous values which may serve as the basis for united action.

The federated structure, a prototype of which is a community council, is an appropriate structure for goals of integration since it assures representation from all the important segments of the community. However, while it lays the groundwork for integration, it simultaneously carries the seeds of conflict. Each member represents not only a differing value position, but has primary allegiance to his home organization. The degree of accountability to the home agency will affect the representative's ability to function independently of it, and will partly determine his receptiveness to the federated structure's goals. Similarly, his willingness to reach consensus with other representatives will depend upon the extent to which his values (the values of his subgroup) are strengthened by concerted action of the federated organization. As a result, it is rare for a council to press for specific priorities which will reduce support from important members, or to take social action not approved by nearly all of its important agencies.

Given this diversity of interests and allegiances, a cooperative rationality is ideally suited to reducing tension and strain and arriving at agreement. It is able to do this by avoiding predetermined objectives, involving all parties in the decision-making process, and engaging in a search for common values. Ideally, allegiance to member organizations and particularistic values will be minimized in the effort to pull together for the common good. To the extent to which home organizations represent different religious, economic, and political subgroup interests, the ability of the federated body to remain intact and to function harmoniously, at least symbolically, indicates that the corresponding subgroups in the community are also able to work together.

In this situation where the structure of an organization comprises conflicting interests the only action possible is action that derives from common values. Integration is, therefore, not only a necessary precursor of united action, but in itself becomes a goal of the organization. Thus, a federated structure and a cooperative rationality become essential for aims of integration, and structure, strategy, and goals reinforce each other.

To maximize the likelihood that consensus will emerge, integrative organizations limit their membership to agencies which subscribe to values and employ means that will promote harmony rather than discord. Thus integrative organizations shun the Planned Parenthood Federation in some Northeastern communities, or the NAACP in some Southern communities. Despite their own strong desire to be accepted by the integrating agency, these organizations are excluded because they embody values and aims not easily reconcilable with those of other member organizations. Exclusion of these agencies from the federated structure permits the pursuit of integration, for at least a limited group of agencies.

Cell 2: the problem of ritualism. When organizations employ inappropriate structures, or inappropriate strategies, or both, they are in danger of displacing or diluting their goals. Displacement of goals may take the direction of ritualism (going through acceptable motions but with limited or no results) as the table suggests. In the case of achievement-oriented organizations, this occurs in one of two ways. The action agency may develop a cooperative rationality or a federated structure or both. When both are present, the degree of ritualism will be greater.

An organization which is committed to achievement of action goals may become concerned with securing the aid of other community agencies, and in so doing it focuses on winning cooperation rather than accomplishing its aims. An ideology develops which suggests that cooperation has some inherent value. Slowly, goals change to adapt to cooperative means. Cooperation becomes an end in itself, and original aims are displaced or lost sight of.

Some affiliates of the Planned Parenthood Federation are examples of this process. They sometimes become overly concerned with interagency cooperation, a course which affords little instrumental value for this organization. To achieve cooperation, their goals have shifted from birth control to child spacing to premarital counseling. In this process of goal succession, which is more complex than we can describe here, cooperative rationality displaces action ends, and the agency is in danger of going through motions which end in inaction.[11]

On the other hand, ritualism may develop when a change-oriented agency shifts its structure from a simple to a federated type. This happens when its membership is recruited from different community subgroups (often in the name of being democratic) who have only minimal commitment to the objective. While these subgroup representatives may not be held formally accountable by their community subgroups, their very presence forces the change-oriented organization to consider the implications of action in terms of its effect upon these subgroups. And the potential for action is thereby reduced. If our formulation is valid, we would expect an organization like the Urban League to be most susceptible to the problem of ritual because it is comprised of representatives of both the white and the Negro communities. Fear of offending either subgroup can lead to inaction and avoidance of aggressively pursuing its aims.

An integration-oriented organization may also be prone to ritualism when it abandons its federated structure for a simple one in order to maintain harmony and to avoid internal conflict. When agencies of this type of organization are too disparate in their views to allow for easy common agreement, those that prevent consensus may not be permitted in in order to facilitate consensus. To illustrate, if a recreation or group work council excludes the Police Athletic League, church recreation centers, public playground agencies, and so on, because they lack professional social work staffs, the very purpose of the council is lost. A few councils are still dominated by a few agencies. When the very groups that must be integrated are excluded in order to reduce conflict, to the point that members are not truly representative of diverse community factions, and the organization begins to resemble the group of like-minded individuals that comprise the simple structure, the integrative aims are displaced. Litwak notes that "from this point of view the elimination of conflict is a deviant instance and likely to lead to the disruption of interorganizational relations."[12] We consider this to be ritualism since the organization is unable to fulfill its integrative aims yet cannot act as a change agency due to its overstress on cooperation and the avoidance of conflict.

The minimal role that public welfare agencies play in many community councils is perhaps the most striking example of the exclusion of an appropriate agency. A major organization that provides health and welfare services to the bulk of the clients in the community may belong and yet not participate deeply, while a number of minor organizations attempt to coordinate each other's work. This should not be taken as a blanket criticism of welfare councils, which are often critized for the wrong reason—that they are not action-oriented. Integration is important in our society, and becoming more so as we become more specialized. We are suggesting that council actions are ritualistic when they try to avoid integration, which is their task, by excluding groups which must be brought together.

Cell 3: the problem of survival. When, at the cost of its constituent agencies, an integrative organization exerts its primary energies in the direction of maintaining and enhancing itself we have goal displacement in the direction of survival. While the federated structure is retained, the interests of its affiliated members are overlooked. The integrative organization forsakes its cooperative rationality, at least for the moment, and pursues instead an individual rationality. It coerces, offers preferential treatment, or in other ways tries to induce selected organizations to affiliate with it. For example, organizations like Catholic Charities and the Salvation Army are permitted to join the United Fund with the unofficial understanding that they will be allowed to continue their independent fund-raising efforts. Or, the Red Cross is admitted and its budget allotment is determined largely by its previous fund-raising efforts. Bargaining power, rather than community need, or consensus, arrived at through interaction with member agencies, becomes the negotiable currency. The potential contribution of the Red Cross, or other national voluntary health organizations, to strengthening the United Fund is the primary criterion employed in making concessions to these organizations. On the other hand, organizations like the Cystic Fibrosis National Research Foundation and the Multiple Sclerosis National Society, which may be sorely in need of integration, are overlooked and disregarded because they have little financial support to contribute, and because they present little threat to the integrative organization. Community need is overlooked or minimized as the search for resources replaces the search for common values.

Cell 4: the change syndrome.   In a changing society, it is often necessary for some organizations to address themselves primarily to innovation. The very nature of innovation or planned change produces resistance in some quarters. To overcome such opposition, organizations must be willing to engage in controversy.

To do this, an organization must accept diverse and pluralistic value schemes as a given in reality. While it is not averse to common values, it starts with predetermined objectives which are believed to have special value. Success is measured by the degree to which these objectives are achieved. Unlike the integration orientation, which is concerned primarily with global values, goals arrived at through consensus and cooperation among members, a focus on achievement imbues an organization with concern for specific, clearly defined, and limited aims. These aims are often infused with a causelike quality, and their accomplishment becomes urgent and worthy of sacrifices.

To further these specific and urgent aims, a simple structure of like-minded individuals is most effective. Ideally, members owe sole or primary allegiance to this organization and are not in conflict with each other over goals, nor do they have divided loyalties to their other commitments.[13] The unity from within is essential in engaging in controversy with forces outside the organization. The aim here is not to represent community subgroups with differing interests, but to push for the agency's objectives in relative disregard for these groupings.

Since the very nature of the organization's goals may lead to controversy, an individual rationality is employed. The strategy of doing away with opposition by a search for a common denominator inherent in a cooperative rationality is replaced by recognition of conflict as inevitable and possibly desirable. Persuasion, use of sanctions, and any means compatible with demoncratic values are condoned. Both its simple structure, which permits accord on predetermined goals, and its individual rationality allow the organization to pursue its aims aggressively and without fear of internal disharmony. That such action-oriented agencies become embattled in bitter community conflict is well-documented in the *Fortune* article which describes Pittsburgh's attempt to develop a united fund.[14]

Thus we are able to see the necessity for change goals to be housed in a simple organization composed of like-minded individuals, operating within a framework which permits conflict with other community forces, and able to resist community sanctions and pressures which press the organization to identify with common values.

This has been a limited attempt to piece together a fragment of theory for community organization, drawing upon limited studies, logical analysis, and observation. Its validity and utility need to be tested in many situations. Two can be suggested: the attempt of welfare councils to move from co-ordination to active planning for urban renewal; and the efforts of the President's Committee on Juvenile Delinquency to extend resources and coordinate service while attempting to promote the "opportunity" theory.[15] As community health and welfare organizations become less concerned with integrative goals and more concerned with community planning, there emerges a growing need to adopt a different organizational structure and different strategy successfully to pursue these new goals. Our efforts are likely to succeed more rapidly if we can evolve practical theories to guide our actions rather than relying upon trial-and-error testing of methods.

NOTES

1. Carter, Kahn, Hunter, Wilensky and Lebeaux, Schwartz, Gurin, Seeley, *et al.*
2. See, for example, "Identifying Fields of Practice in Social Work," by the Sub-committee on Fields of Practice, National Association of Social Workers Commission on Social Work Practice, *Social Work*, VII, No. 2 (1962), 7–14.
3. Genevieve W. Carter, "The Content of the Community Welfare Council Research Job," in *Issues in Community Welfare Research,* Proceedings on the National Workshop on Community Welfare Research Personnel (Indianapolis: United Community Funds and Councils of America, Inc., 1958), p. 43.
4. Peter H. Rossi, "What Makes Communities Tick?" *Public Health Reports,* LXXVII (1962), 117–24.

5. Arthur Vidich, "Government Philanthropy and Private Philanthropy" (mimeo.), Brandeis University, n. d.

6. Edward C. Banfield, *Political Influence* (New York: Free Press of Glencoe, 1961).

7. A public strategy follows a similar process. This approach is often used when an agency has limited resources at its disposal and therefore limited capacity to develop coalitions. In this situation the organization reaches out to the public in the hope of winning support for its position. The major difference between an individual and a public strategy is similar to C. P. Snow's distinction between closed- and open-door politics. A public strategy is pursued by weak organizations which try to bring issues into the open because they feel that they can maximize their stake most in an open arena. A full development of this position can be found in Elmer Eric Schattschneider, *The Semisovereign People* (New York: Holt, Rinehart & Winston, Inc., 1960).

8. Banfield, *op. cit.*, p. 324.

9. Parsons distinguishes between expressive (integrational) and instrumental (change) roles within social systems, while Gordon and Babchuck separate voluntary associations along the same dimension. Warren's classification of horizontal and vertical structures within a community utilizes the differences in these two value positions. Here, we express the primary distinction between integration and change in terms of organizational goals. See Talcott Parsons, *The Social System* (Glencoe, Ill.: Free Press, 1951); C. Wayne Gordon and Nicholas Babchuck, "A Typology of Voluntary Associations," *American Sociological Review*, XXIV (1959), 22–29; Roland L. Warren, "Toward a Reformulation of Community Theory," *Human Organization,* XV, 2 (1956), 8–11.

10. This analysis is limited to an organization's internal machinery. We recognize, of course, that goal achievement is related to conditions outside the organization as well.

11. Martin Rein, "An Analysis of a National Agency's Local Affiliation in Their Community Contexts: a Study of the Planned Parenthood Federation" (New York: Planned Parenthood Federation of America, Inc., 1961; mimeographed), p. 117.

12. Eugene Litwak and Lydia F. Hylton, "Interorganizational Analysis," *Administrative Science Quarterly,* VI (1962) p. 397.

13. Sills's classic study of the volunteers of the former Polio Foundation explores the reasons for the unusual ability of one national voluntary health organization to get individuals to make such commitments. See David L. Sills, *The Volunteers* (Glencoe, Ill.: Free Press, 1957).

14. Donald S. Connery, "Business and Charity: the Pittsburgh Skirmish," *Fortune,* April, 1957, pp. 144–46, 250–57.

15. This theory holds that delinquency is engendered because opportunity for conformity to social and economic aspirations is limited. See Richard A. Cloward and Lloyd E. Ohlin, *Delinquency and Opportunity: a Theory of Delinquent Gangs* (Glencoe, Ill.: Free Press, 1960).

Chapter 11

Social Planning: The Search for Legitimacy

Where does the reform oriented planner get his authority to propose social change? A review of city planning experience suggests four sources of authority: expertise, bureaucratic position, consumer preferences, and professional values. In a parallel fashion, social reformers have looked to elite institutional interests, social science research, and client participation in their search for legitimacy. The dilemma is that individually each approach limits the effectiveness of planning, yet the various sources of authority are mutually exclusive and cannot be pursed together by one planning organization. The difficulties of this choice between approaches are central to the education of social policy planners.

All planning must in some fashion resolve the problem of legitimacy—what authority justifies its intervention. This is particularly true for those types of social reform and city planning that share a common ideological commitment to introduce *social innovation*—new programs and new ideas that will reduce or eliminate social problems.

What makes the intervention of the reformer and

Reprinted by permission of the *Journal of the American Institute of Planners* (Vol. 35, No. 4, July 1969), and the publishers of *Urban Problems in America*, edited by Daniel P. Moynihan, Basic Books, Inc., Publishers, New York, 1969.

planner meaningful and desirable? How is the need for innovative intervention justified and support for it secured? The problem of legitimacy is especially acute in American democratic society because the reformer-planner
has only limited power to implement his objectives. Lacking power, "the
ability to control external and internal environments and/or to counteract
the consequences of imperfect control,"[1] he needs, therefore, to win cooperation to achieve his aims. He must collect and harness fragmented power in
order to bring about planned change.

Some planning organizations hope to bypass this dilemma by repudiating
the mandate to innovate or to promote planned change. They define their
mission as providing only a forum to help others reach agreement through the
intervention of "enablers" rather than "planners."[2] In contrast, organizations
promoting planned change must seek the authority to impose limits on the
freedom of other organizations. They attempt to subordinate interests or
change functions and purposes of some organizations in order to promote
that elusive ideal we call the public interest. Yet, as soon as such organizations are powerful enough to be effective, they are also strong enough to
abuse their power. Efforts must then be developed to contain their power.
In a democratic society, great restraints are placed on the centralization of
power, while greater freedom is given to individual units. Still, when injustices exist, some centralized power is needed to correct them. How to
reconcile the clashing demands between the limitations needed to check
social abuse and the power needed to reduce human suffering with their
reduction in the freedom of action of others is a great challenge to democratic societies. The search for legitimacy is an effort to resolve this dilemma.

CITY PLANNING, SOURCES OF AUTHORITY

A review of the experience of city planners in the United States suggests
that they have relied on four different sources of authority to justify and
legitimate their intervention. These might be called the authorities of
expertise, bureaucratic position, consumer preferences, and *professional
values.*

The Authority of Expertise. This approach is based on the assumption
that planners have command of a technical-scientific body of knowledge that
enables them to challenge irrationality in the political process of city government, which has produced decisions based on "opportunistic bargaining
among vested political economic interests of great strength."[3] The early
planning movement was based on a doctrine which said that what planners
needed was great formal powers, independent of the political process, which
would enable them to act as an autonomous "fourth power" in city government.[4] In 1934, the first City Planning Commission of New York City was

comprised of a majority of members who "were committed to the premise that the Commission should be an institution of experts with an authoritative voice in the decisions of city government, yet be itself aloof and protected, without the necessity of bargaining with and making concessions to the 'politicians' and special interests."[5] Experience soon suggested that political autonomy leads to isolation and independence leads to impotence. Authority that is depoliticized, that is independent from the political process and based on technical scientific rationality, offers only the authority to propose, rather than the power to achieve.[6] Not surprisingly, the need for new sources of authority was soon recognized.

The Authority of Bureaucracy. During the 1940s, public administrators debated the possibility of separating politics and administration.[7] This debate centered around the issue of whether every administrative act also entailed a political consequence that obviated the purely technological solution. If politics cannot be separated from administration, then the planner secures his authority from politicians rather than technology. However, the more incomplete the control over the administrative process, the wider the influence of the professional, thus the planner's role in developing policy is ambiguous. According to this interpretation, the difficulty with the concept of planning as a "fourth power" was that the claims of the planners conflicted with those of the politicians.

In a recent analysis of this debate, Beckman took the position that this conflict of identity between the planner and the politician "can best be resolved . . . if he (the planner) is willing to accept the vital but more limited role that our system assigned to the public employee."[8] Beckman urges the planner to assist and serve the policymaker since the planner's "influence on public policy is achieved within the bureaucracy through competence. Planners and other staff advisers have influence only as they can persuade their political superiors . . . it must be remembered that in our system of government politics subordinates the public employee, grants responsibility and power to the politician, invests open authority in the voter."[9]

The planner who repudiates a decision of his superiors can try to persuade them to accept his opinion or he can resign in indignation. But in his role as an employee, the planner secures his authority from the director of a planning organization whose head is appointed by elected representatives who in turn secure their authority from voting citizens.

The theory about the relationship between the planner as a bureaucrat and the politician as the representative of the electorate often disintegrates in practice. The scope and complexity of public bureaucracies make them increasingly independent of review by elected officials. They control the information by which their competence can be challenged, and they outlast the politicians whose policies they execute. Moreover, elected officials serve the interests of certain groups better than the interests of others or of some hypothesized overall public interest. In theory an aggrieved citizen can protest directly to his representative against any intrusion of his rights or neglect of his needs. In practice, in a democracy, the needs and preferences of unpopular, unwanted, and powerless groups are neglected. Politicians are committed to political survival. They respond to the preferences of the constituencies that elect them rather than the needs of the inarticulate and hence unrepresented groups.

The Authority of Consumers. In the 1950s, the critique against the planner as a bureaucrat began to emerge in Herbert Gans', John Dyckman's, and Martin Meyerson's studies of recreation, education, and health care facilities. They came to recognize that planning which was responsive to professional discretion and to political leadership might in the process forsake the preferences, needs, and desires of the consuming population. What they seemed to be calling for was a new technology which could develop new standards by feeding new information into the planning process—namely data derived from social scientific inquiries about the preferences of present and potential service users. Gans, Dyckman, and Meyerson wrote that planning must be responsive to the consumer market. Explicit criteria as to how to establish procedures to resolve differences among the clashing preferences of different income or age groupings, or to resolve conflicts that might arise when consumer preferences clashed with the policies of planners, the established bureaucracy, or elected officials were not developed.[10]

Rapkin, Winnick, and Blank in their monograph on Housing Market Analysis developed a similar position, holding that the criteria for developing public policy should rest on the choices of users as these are identified through the mechanism of the market.[11] Turning to the ultimate consumer as the source of legitimacy for planning opened important ideological questions concerning the limits and possibilities of exploiting the market as a mechanism for assessing consumer choices. Davidoff and Reiner extended the general argument—"It is not for the planner to make the final decision transforming values into policy commitments. His role is to identify distribution of values among people, and how values are weighed against each other."[12]

By 1960, new forces emerged in the political process which gave currency and acceptability to the idea of consumer advocacy. A new body of literature and experience developed which sought to derive the legitimacy of the planner from the preferences of consumers, especially those who are politically inarticulate. Some planners were urging that a new source of legitimacy be found with the planner acting as a more direct advocate of the values, preferences, and needs of consumer groups—planning should derive its legitimacy from the needs of the people to be serviced. The planner could then offer his skills to a user-bureaucracy as contrasted with the supplier-bureaucracy to which planners presently offer their services.

These ideas found expression in the theory of advocacy planning which asserts that planners can derive their legitimacy from the clients to be served. Advocacy implies argument and contention on behalf of a point of view or of a specific proposal. Paul Davidoff in his influential article, "Advocacy and Pluralism in Planning," makes this position explicit when he urges that "the advocate planner would be responsible to his client and would seek to express his clients' views."[13]

All of these writers accepted the position that planners derive their legitimacy from the preferences, choices, and needs of the users, consumers, and clients who are affected by planning decisions. But they differ on this position's implications for action. A point of view oriented to clients can lead to social surveys of consumer choices, or to faith in the market as the ultimate mechanism for the expressions of choice, or to the defense of consumer rights within an adversary rather than a market framework. Each position has its difficulties. The preferences of all individuals as revealed from survey rankings of values cannot be aggregated into collective preferences without violating the choices of some individuals (following the famous Arrow paradox). Planning originated as an effort to supplement or supersede the market when it failed to meet individual needs or solve the problem of externalities. Faith in market freedom and choice for users did not contribute substantially to resolving these issues of public policy. As we have begun to experiment with advocacy, intractable problems have emerged.

One account of an advocate planner's experience suggests some of these formidable difficulties. First it proved very difficult to identify the client or community to be serviced. A community is heterogeneous, and efforts to locate a single-client-organization to represent it, as well as speak for its unrepresented elements, proved exceedingly difficult. But even if such a group could be organized, and its interests articulated, the planner discovered that local decision units can be parochial and even punishing to the poor with special problems, such as welfare mothers, skid row habitués, gypsies, and so on. Peattie offers the following grim observation: ". . . a consequence of giving every neighborhood in a city its advocate planner might be a general closing up of the city against the poor."[14] But even if the problems of locating the client and identifying and accepting his interests can be overcome, the advocate planner confronts a disturbing dilemma when he discovers that "the citizen client group seems . . . to serve a kind of legitimizing function which permits the planners to represent themselves as something more than merely proponents of another opinion."[15]

The Authority of Professional Values. Another source of legitimacy rests on the professional values to which the planner is committed as well as the technical competence he claims. According to this formulation, city planning is a value laden profession, and these values offer a course of authority—a sanction to plan. There is surely an uneasy nestling together of expertise and ideology, and a general reluctance to act on the authority of the latter is evident. Nevertheless, as the impossibility of separating values and technology is accepted, action based on values is taken. One form is the creation of a competing professional association committed to implementing different values. "It appears that the profession is being split into progressive and conservative wings: the former calling for social planning to reduce racial and economic inequalities, and the latter defending traditional physical planning and the legitimacy of the middle-class values."[16]

Increasingly planners are enjoined to act as insurgents within the bureaucracies where they are employed and to seek change in the policies and purposes of the bureaucracy according to the declared value assumptions. These values are procedural as well as substantive. Decision rules, such as involvement of those affected by decisions, illustrate the former, and goals, such as racially and economically integrated communities or reduction of inequalities, illustrate the latter.

Public opinion and official policies of the bureaucracy may be hostile to these values. The planner who acts as a rebel within his bureaucracy challenges its established procedures and policies. A declaration of open warfare forces the bureaucrat to resign on principle. As an outsider he may elect to infiltrate the bureaucracy in his role as consultant or researcher. Many private consultant firms and individual planners are committed to promoting their professional values as well as their technology. The bureaucrat may elect to stay and wage guerilla warfare, choosing points where the system is internally vulnerable, or he may develop coalitions with external groups to create internal change. He may lie dormant for years when levers for change are absent. Yet, every bureaucracy has insurgents who are ready to act as guerilla-reformers to shake up the bureaucracy.[17]

An unusual example of this procedure is the action of a group of young professional insurgent staff members of the New York City Planning Commission who call themselves the "urban underground." They attended a public hearing held by the Commission and "charged that the agency had disregarded its own planners' findings and had yielded to powerful real estate speculators in proposing to rezone a section of Manhattan for luxury housing."[18] What makes this experience so unusual is the concerted and open actions of these insurgents. The more typical pattern of bureaucratic insurgency of professionals is to try to promote change within the bureaucracy, that is to say, through closed door politics rather than open door politics.

This source of legitimacy poses awkward issues concerning the boundaries between professional and personal values, ethics of means and ends to be adopted, and procedures of professional accountability to judge when ethics have surrendered to expediency. But despite these and other difficulties, planners who repudiate the position that values and technology are separable are experimenting with this source of legitimacy.

STRATEGIES OF LEGITIMACY

Even this condensed review of the history of physical planning makes it evident that city planners have sought different sources of legitimacy: as scientific experts, independent of the political process; as agents of elected political representatives and the bureaucracies which are accountable to them; as translators and advocates of the preferences of user-groups; and finally, as implementors of professional values. Each source of legitimacy has its characteristic difficulties, as this brief review of the experience of physical planners as expert, bureaucrat, advocate, and insurgent has suggested.

But why must planners be forced to choose among these alternative sources of legitimacy? The position of planning could be substantially strengthened if it could simultaneously call upon professional technology, values, and standards, established political power, and the needs and wishes of client groups as sources of legitimacy. However, if these sources of legitimacy conflict when pursued together—and they nearly always do—then the planner must choose among them.

A review of the experience of what Reston called the "new breed of anti-poverty planners" helps to illuminate the problems which arise in adapting each source of legitimacy and in pursuing multiple sources of legitimacy which are in conflict. Federal legislation, such as the Juvenile Delinquency and Youth Offences Control Act of 1961 and the Economic Opportunity Act of 1964, provided the resources which made this form of social planning possible. More recently, through legislation made possible by the Demonstration Cities and Metropolitan Act of 1966, the style of planning has been extended to cope with problems of deterioration in the urban environment. The search conducted by these social planners and reformers for a relevant form of legitimacy is strikingly parallel to the search for legitimacy among city planners.

The city planner and this type of social planner share much in common. They both spend a great deal of their energies writing proposals in an effort to secure federal and state funds; they are both concerned with developing specific programs to implement ambiguous and ill-defined social objectives; they are both committed to drawing up both long-range and short-range plans; both are in principle committed to introduction of new ideas and to generation of social innovations that can lay the foundation for further experimentation; and finally, both hope to have the plans they developed implemented administratively. But, in the context of this essay, the important common ground they share is the search for legitimacy. How can their intervention be justified?

In the remainder of this essay three strategies are examined from the perspective of how they contribute to resolving the problem of legitimation of reform.[19] They are *elite consensus, rational analysis,* and *citizen participation*. Each strategy is crucial. None is sufficient by itself, for each has inherent limitations, but the efforts to pursue more than one strategy at a time often lead to conflict and contradiction. Thus in the effort to resolve one dilemma another is created.

The Consensus of Elites

One way of justifying intervention is to have it endorsed and supported by the leadership of the major institutions in the community. This strategy acknowledges the power of established institutions. One version seeks to influence power by boring from within, by co-opting the institutions to serve its purposes. The endorsement by established power legitimates the efforts of reform and change.

At one time in the social services this power of change was vested in the coalition of *voluntary* institutions that represented the elite of the community.

> Welfare services and planning became recognizably controlled by an essentially elite leadership in each community. . . . Associated with the socially elite were an economic elite. . . . These economic sinews became the foundation for the support of much of social welfare. It was only later recognized that this elite leadership was primarily white and Protestant, representing the early stratification of American society.[20]

These early economic and social elites often rejected the role of government in welfare, substituting voluntary health and welfare councils. They held an elitist view of democracy, assuming that they were best able to comprehend, to represent, and to protect the interests of the "total community."

Today, because of the changing role of government and the development of new centers of power, such voluntary bodies can no longer provide an adequate base for legitimate change. Consequently, planners have had to seek the participation of city government by forming a coalition of departments such as welfare, recreation, police, and the like, or a coalition of units of government such as the city, the county, the school boards, and the state. Legitimacy depends on bringing together a broad range of groups representing old and new sources of power—influential leaders, established organizational interests, and government.

A new factor is national influence on local action. In a penetrating analysis of the relationship between sociology and the welfare state, Gouldner calls attention to the manner in which social reform in the United States has changed in character. What is new is not the "plight of the cities," however increasing their deterioration, but rather . . . the locus of reform initiatives and resources is increasingly found on the level of national politics and foundations, rather than in the political vitality, the economic resources, or the zealous initiatives of elites with local roots.[21]

A broad based representative organizational structure that serves to legitimate reform may likely conflict with its very purpose—the search for innovation and change.[22] The greater the diversity of institutional interest that is embraced within such a planning structure, the greater can be the claim for legitimacy, since it can be claimed that most of the total community is represented. But as legitimacy is strengthened, innovation will probably be forsaken in favor of maintaining a consensus on which these divergent interests can agree. These new planning structures are continually beset with internal insurrection. In practice the commitment to shared goals seems less compelling than the preservation of organizational autonomy. Involvement of community leaders does little to resolve the problems of jurisdictional conflict; indeed, it may only aggravate the task. Voluntary planning bodies and the elite community leaders who represent them want more influence than they receive as only members (rather than convenors) of the coalition. Whereas they once enjoyed preeminence in the area of planning, they have now been cast aside and relegated to a secondary role by this new, more widely representative structure. Consequently, much of the energy of the planning organization is directed away from promoting innovation and change and toward solving the more intractable problems of sheer survival—maintenance of the coalition.[23]

The national reformers who made available the funds for these local planning organizations recognized this dilemma, but hoped that it could be solved. Essentially, their strategy rested on two related assumptions: that a marginal increase in funds can stimulate change, and that the involvement of voluntary and public bureaucracies is a necessary precondition for change. They hoped the power of federal money—small outlays with the anticipation of larger amounts of funds—and the process of participation would lead to change. They assumed that financially starved institutions would be willing to make changes in their operation in order to secure available and needed funds. Local reformers operating from these local planning organizations would play a central role in this process, for they could serve as interpreters of the institutional changes that would be required if funds were to be forthcoming. The professional reformer, enjoying a monopoly of knowledge and special access to nonlocal funders, could assert a substantial amount of influence on the direction in which the local coalition of elites would develop in order to obtain the wanted funds. *The fundamental premise in these negotiations was that because funds were so desperately needed by local institutions, they would be willing to participate in self-reform in order to secure them.* That the institutions might both obtain the funds from established and new sources and resist change was a contingency to which local and national planners seemed to have given little attention.

This second assumption rested on the faith that the process of involvement and participation might lead to self-education and the acceptance of the need to change. The implicit theory of bureaucracy on which this belief rests is that the sources of organizational rigidity are largely ignorance and faulty communication. If a context were provided in which institutional representatives could more freely communicate with one another, the validity of the need for change would more readily be recognized and accepted. Such a theory is, however, incomplete, for it ignores the existence of the more fundamental conflict of values and interests among institutions that more open communication might serve to exacerbate rather than to alleviate. The insistence upon participation of power in self-reform appeals to common sense yet it rests on inadequate assumptions about how institutions perform. In practice, organizations often agreed or participated to protect their interests rather than to promote the more illusive common goals on which the concept of the public planning rests. Thus agreement on a new form that committed organizations to involvement in a process did not equally commit them to accept substantive changes in their policies and programs. The latent conflict was only postponed. When it emerged, the coalition of autonomous participants was in danger of falling apart. As a result of these challenges, compromises were made to assure survival, and in the process innovation was sacrificed to achieve consensus.

Much as a representative structure may reduce innovation, participation by institutions in their own reform may lead to continuity of established policies. The funds made available by planners were simply not large enough to finance major reforms in these institutions. But even if sufficient funds were available, it is hard to see how planners could conceivably hope to initiate major structural changes unless the changes were in conformity with the institutions' prevailing interpretation of their functions and reflected directions the institutions were already prepared to take. Under these conditions it is the planners who have been co-opted by the institutions. *Involvement, although it facilitates legitimation, impedes innovation.*

An alternative to the theory that institutions change with self-education is derived from the assumption that institutions must be challenged, for they will not change of their own accord. The public health movement, which was promoted largely by lay groups, arose (with the support of some professionals) despite the vigorous opposition of physicians; similarly, the

Charity Organization Society (the mainstay and bulwark behind social casework before the depression) was opposed to pensions for widows and the aged in the early part of the century; and the Charity Schools opposed public education. According to this view, reform cannot depend solely upon the willing cooperation of the institutions to be reformed.

While it is useless to ignore the realities of established institutional power, a program of planned change runs the dire risk of losing its sense of purpose if it relies only on established leadership. Increasingly, planners find that the more they work with established institutions, the more compromises they have to make, the more difficult it becomes to ensure that funds are spent for innovation rather than for expansion of the status quo. This frustration has led to a tendency to bypass major service institutions. For example, we find in education the development of preschool programs, afterschool programs, summer school programs, tutorial programs which consistently circumvent the heart of the school's mission—everyday teaching—and create instead a whole series of special remedial programs. Remediation becomes a kind of index of the failure to achieve more basic structural change. It represents response to the more frustrating task of directly influencing the essential functions of the institution itself. Institutional resistance leads to program proliferation.

Many manpower training programs have ignored the state vocational training system and have worked through other agencies or set up their own agencies to provide special programs for work training. Here duplication and remediation do not represent a retreat but a strategy of confrontation. But to challenge institutions so frontally, a different source of legitimacy is necessary.

The Power of Knowledge

Another way of legitimizing planned change is to offer reforms as rational, coherent, intellectual solutions to the problems that are being dealt with. This tends to be the approach favored by academia and professional consultants. Knowledge in the rationalistic-scientific tradition in general and knowledge derived from empirical research in particular can provide a basis for legitimacy because, presumably, it can yield valid solutions. These, in turn, depend on a value-free social science capable of objectively probing the etiology of social problems and presenting programs for action based upon fact rather than upon institutional or other value biases. The analysis of social problems and the remedies proposed for reducing or eliminating them are viewed as technical rather than ideological issues. For example, the President's Committee on Juvenile Delinquency was especially committed to the importance of rational analysis as the basis for planning and program development. As a condition for receiving funds, national reformers required that communities attempt to conceptualize the problems of delinquency, poverty, or physical and social decay in the light of relevant data and social theory.

Reform stakes out a claim for legitimacy when it is based, not upon political consensus or ideological bias, but primarily upon the hard dispassionate facts provided by a rigorous social science analysis. Proponents of this position believe that science can and should "supercede moral and ideological speculation." Earlier expressions of this position can be found in the work of those committed to the idea of policy sciences (1940s) and the end of ideology thesis (1950s).[24] Consistent with this philosophy, the President's Committee promoted the ideals that not only are social plans to be based on a thorough, objective appraisal of the social problem, but the efforts at solution themselves are to be rigorously evaluated. With ruthless disregard for bureaucratic interests, those programs judged to be successful would be continued, whereas those falling short of the objective standards would be rejected and discontinued. Change is to be based not upon fads and vested interests but upon the evidence provided by evaluative research of program outputs. Science, rather than elitism, justifies intervention.

This strategy of reform has its own inherent contradictions. Perhaps not in the long run, since researchers can always justify their activities as ultimately contributing to truth and knowledge; but in the short run, it does indeed involve conflict, for gathering information is not without its costs. Consider the difficulty that many planning organizations have encountered in their efforts to study the conditions and problems of the Negro urban ghetto. Research, as one angry account has put it, can serve as "transparent dodges for the postponement of action, that those involved in the charade of research into the problems of disadvantaged youth are willing or inadvertent accessories to those who seem to perpetuate the clear and present injustices."[25] A disillusioned Negro community wants authentic action, not rhetoric, promises, or studies.

Although these resentments may not be altogether rational, they are surely understandable, particularly when we recognize that the preliminary research and analysis of so many of the community action programs became extremely esoteric, and in many cases never really issued any pragmatic proposals. Indeed, it is often difficult to find coherence among the social theory, the facts presented, and the programs that are developed to reduce the problem. This widespread disjunction between programs of reform and research and theoretical insights represents an important limitation of the contribution of research and theory to the reduction of social problems. Much of the research growing out of these planning efforts has not yielded new knowledge about the poor, nor has it yielded especially new insights into our understanding of delinquency, nor has it led to the kinds of new programs that need to be developed to tackle these problems. From these experiences it would appear that the contribution of value-free social science information to the development of social policy has been greatly oversold.

The rigorous testing of experimental action programs has also encountered fundamental obstacles. The most difficult problem the researcher found was explication of the social objectives for which the intervention was introduced. This was especially true for programs with broad, multiple, and partially conflicting goals directed at expanding opportunity or promoting organizational change. There were administrative as well as conceptual problems. It is difficult to include in most experimental social action programs the rigid controls that are necessary to provide the kind of clear-cut findings upon which it is possible to accept or reject particular techniques of intervention.

When this rationale of reform calls for comprehensive action involving many interrelated programs committed to broad and diffuse goals, a difficult research task becomes even more discouragingly complex. The demands of action are such that planners need to be somewhat opportunistic, flexibly adapting to shifting political coalitions that substantially alter the content on which their comprehensive program rests. But when the input variables are subject to significant change, the research task becomes even more tangled. As the limitations of the research design grow more apparent, it becomes hard to know what caused the measured outcomes. As a result, the interpretation to be drawn from the findings is open to serious question. Staunch supporters of particular programs are more likely to reject the research methodology and repudiate the criteria of evaluation, rather than accept the implications of negative findings that most evaluative research tends to yield.[26]

A strategy that relies upon the power of knowledge has other inherent limitations as well, for it can also conflict with other strategies of change. Research requires a degree of autonomy if it is to follow a problem, not yielding to political expediency and feasibility. But the ruthless pursuit of a problem without regard to the question of implementation may lead to a solution that, while it is rational, is not politically relevant. This, of course, is the fundamental dilemma of all rational planning, the attempt to reconcile the conflicting requirements of rationality and feasibility. Planning that disregards the question of implementation languishes as an academic irrelevancy; it may be right but not relevant, correct but not useful. While planning and research require close integration, they make competing claims for resources. Enterprising researchers have been able to secure a very substantial portion of total budgets available to planning agencies, while unwary planners are left with reduced resources to carry out their tasks. Irrelevancy can arise not only in the competition for resources, but in the conflicting value biases of the researcher and reformer —the different emphases they give to knowledge and action. Research can become preoccupied with a spurious rigor, leading to a kind of dustbowl empiricism that provides data overload. Without theory to guide in sorting the findings we have a situation where answers (data) are in search of questions. Bewildered planners are left with a maze of tables and data that yield no immediately coherent themes and that provide little information from which implications can be drawn. Reformers often hope that researchers will guide the development of planning policy by conducting studies that will help confirm or reject the basic underlying rationale of the organizations. Yet to develop new programs requires a leap from data to social inventiveness, rarely a product of formal research.

Even more than being a costly irrelevance, research can subvert the reformers' goals. The experience of the delinquency prevention programs offers an interesting example. The national reformers sought programs that would test the assumption that social institutions throw up barriers and block access to achievement—a process that contributes to increased disengagement and deviancy on the part of the rejected populations. Yet the methodological bias of researchers led the reformers away from their original commitment to institutional change and toward a redefinition of the problem in terms of individual rehabilitation. Thus, social scientists sometimes act to reinforce those pressures on planning organizations that prevent focus on community institutions as prime targets of change. Researchers usually favor the more rigorous, traditional, and tested approaches of their disciplines, such as surveys of individual attitudes, self-perceptions, and role models. The indices they have developed to measure the impact of demonstration programs have occasionally been behavioral but more often attitudinal. They have, by and large, avoided indices that would measure institutional change in favor of a more individualistic approach.

Research may conflict not only with the purposes of reform, but also with the search for elite consensus. Organizational studies that lead to the documentation of bureaucratic rigidities and social injustice may conflict with efforts to promote cooperation and secure consensus among institutions that are being researched. If research relentlessly pursues data on the operation of the bureaucracy, it will uncover findings that could become a source of embarrassment to cooperating institutions. Indeed, where such information is available, it is extremely awkward to know exactly what to do with it. If the information becomes public knowledge, it would only antagonize the institutions whose cooperation is so desperately sought. Yet, maintaining secrets is always hazardous. This may account, in part, for the fact that planners have rarely insisted that researchers study institutional performance.

Finally, research may not be able to answer the problems posed by the reformer. Consider briefly one such question that local, gradual, and comprehensive programs must confront. The hub of a comprehensive social welfare program can be developed around many institutions—the outreach school, the welfare department, the health department, the mental hygiene clinic, and employment centers. Some of the traditional voluntary services—settlement houses and welfare councils—are no longer regarded as adequate focal institutions for the coordination of local service programs. But do we have any factual data that can guide us in the selection of one or another of these institutions as the appropriate focus for a comprehensive community program? Should social programs center around health, housing, employment, education, reducing dependency? If all of these are legitimate, must we then abandon the search for a truly comprehensive program and settle for the present muddle of coordination, saturation, and concerted services?

Just as a broadly representative planning structure can subvert innovation in order to preserve the frail coalition of conflicting interests, so too can researchers subvert the reformers' mission if they become preoccupied with methodology and use their studies to promote their professional identities rather than the interests of the action program. The concern for rigor and professional identity may lead to neglect of relevant action problems. The concern for knowledge without explicit, carefully developed social purposes contributes to narrow technicism.

The Power of the People

Reformers can also claim legitimacy if their programs are endorsed, supported, and created by the recipients of the service. Such an approach has the advantage of avoiding the arrogant assumption that the technical expert or the elitist best knows the needs of the poor. It avoids the onerous charge of welfare colonialism or paternalism, wherein one group in society provides services on behalf of another. Recipients of the service are defined as politically articulate consumers, as citizens rather than as clients in need of therapy and care. Democracy is, after all, not only the search for elite consensus but also the mobilization of interest groups, each striving to pursue its own aims in the context of a pluralistic society. The American democratic system, according to this view, depends on rectifying "the basic imbalance between elites and non-elites by modifying the power differential between them."[27] It attempts to carry out this strategy by providing disadvantaged groups with more powerful instruments for articulating their demands and preferences. It helps them to organize protests in which their moral claim to justice and equal treatment can find expression. In addition to collective action it places before the poor the machinery of law through which they can act as plaintiffs against institutions that have bypassed their rights.

Strategies of planned change, which derive their legitimacy from the direct participation of local citizens and service users, have had a stormy history since they were launched by the President's Committee on Juvenile Delinquency and Youth Crime in 1962. These developments must be seen in the context of the civil rights revolution and the emergence of militant demands for black power. In response to pressures, representative communitywide structures were broadened to include individuals and groups that were the targets of change. The principle of "maximum feasible participation" articulated in the Economic Opportunity Act was administratively interpreted in many ways including direct participation of the poor on policy-making boards of Community Action Agencies.[28] In some cities, such as San Francisco (and later Oakland under the Model Cities Program), participation was interpreted as control, and the poor dominated the board with the mayor retreating to a subordinate role.[29] As organizational resistance to social change was encountered, participation turned from planning to social protest and social action, taking the form of rent strikes, boycotts, picketing, and other strategies of confrontation to promote change.[30] More recently, citizen participation has come to mean community control of social services, such as multi-service centers, health programs, and a decentralized public school system.[31] The Model Cities Program encouraged experimentation with advocacy planning, where local groups (Boston, for example) were able to buy given resources to hire their own planners to develop plans incorporating social and physical resources for the reduction of urban blight. Under the Nixon administration the Community Self-Determination Act of 1968 (before Congress as of this writing) may usher in yet a new phase of user control, for it is designed to create community-controlled business enterprises that would permit the people of the community "to utilize a share of the profits of (these) enterprises to provide needed social services."[32]

The acceptance of this argument leads to an anomalous position for it inadvertently supports a different interpretation of democracy for the poor than for other segments of society.[33] In the middle-income style of democratic involvement, citizens work through their representatives, whereas in low-income communities, democracy tends to be interpreted as a form of direct participation at the grassroots level. Community competence through self-help becomes defined as a therapeutic process for promoting social integration. Competent communities produce competent men, as each man is his own politician. Organizations are expected to develop spontaneously out of the mutual interests of residents working side by side on common problems. The rewards of participation are defined as civic pride, personal growth, and the reduction of community deviancy. The groups are not forged out of the more pragmatic interests in personal favors and economic advantages which more typically characterize the motives of those who join local political parties. The task might better be defined not as increasing the competence of low-income communities to manage their own affairs, but rather as creating more representative structures which will be more responsive to the special needs and interests of low-income groups. Paid politicians rather than paid community enablers may be necessary if representative rather than direct democracy is to be achieved. Direct democracy may thus be seen as a stage in the process of developing new political coalitions and new political leadership rather than as an ideal in the "good" community.

Richard Cloward and Francis Piven argue that fundamental conflicts between elite and low-income collective protests arise because they are based upon "quite divergent beliefs about the nature of social, economic, and political institutions and what it takes to change them."[34] The elitist approach assumes that institutions change by persuasion and education and that issues are largely technical and capable of analysis in terms somewhat analogous to a cost-benefit evaluation. Low-income collective protests, by contrast, view institutions as responsive to naked power and pressure; issues are defined in personalized terms; opponents are seen as culprits; and exploitation of the poor is rejected, whatever the benefits.

Efforts to organize low-income communities encounter difficulties in sustaining a high level of interest and participation, especially when programs have only marginal meaning for the residents and offer little opportunity for changes in jobs, housing, or other amenities. There is also the danger that issues are selected more for their capacity to rally interest than for their intrinsic merit. Protests can become ends in themselves instead of platforms for bargaining and negotiating. But without an issue for protest, organizations are likely to succumb to the meaningless ritual of organization for its own sake. Saul Alinsky's work is a prototype of one approach that attempts to sustain commitment by polarizing a community around an issue and then ruthlessly attacking the villain who is alleged to have created the problem.

While it has been exceedingly difficult to organize the poor on the basis of their poverty or social class in the occupational hierarchy, there is at least precedent for politicalization along ethnic and religious lines. Citizen participation reflects this aspect of American political life and extends it by inadvertently becoming a program for organizing the Negro community—the growing militancy of black urban action programs reflects the militants' discovery of the difficulties of securing authentic change. The heightened sense of relative deprivation converted the process from reform (defined either as therapy and self-help to achieve a competent community or as provision of opportunities through organizational change to promote mobility) to revolution, which found expression in riots and the repudiation of integration as a realizable social ideal. How established power will respond to violence and assault on its citadels is unclear. There is evidence of both blacklash and increased liberalization as the desire for social stability and social justice is joined and divided.

Lipsky has pointed out that "protest groups are uniquely capable of raising the saliency of issues, but are unequipped—by virtue of their lack of organizational resources—to participate in the formulation or adoption of solutions to problems they dramatize."[35] When protest groups are sponsored by social welfare organizations they rapidly lose their authenticity as grassroots movements. They drift into labor-saving self-help projects and cleanup and fix-up programs. It is rather startling to note how many bureaucracies attempt to organize low-income residents to promote bureaucratic goals. Sanitation departments create block groups; settlements organize neighborhood councils; the schools promote PTA's; and urban renewal in a similar fashion attempts to mobilize a community as a device for co-opting and reducing opposition to renewal plans. The professional comes to plan the agenda, and when the professional leaves, the organization collapses.

The process of involving the poor as a form of therapy and self-help on the one hand, and legitimation of the activities of the planners on the other hand, does not take adequate account of the potential role that citizen participation may have in politicalizing the poor. It can serve as well to create a new center of power by revitalizing the urban political machinery in low-income areas, replacing the atrophied structures that once helped generations of immigrants to adjust to American society. It is paradoxical that the targets of reform in one generation should become the ideals of the next generation: ethnic politics and the political machine were once seen as major impediments to good local government. However, many of the groups that do participate in these "establishment" sponsored programs are suspiciously regarded as having "sold out" their allegiance to the community from which they came. But this harsh assessment of betrayal fails to recognize that involvement, when seen from the point of view of its consumers, is a way of "buying in" to a system they aspire to be part of.

DILEMMAS IN THE SEARCH FOR LEGITIMACY

We have described, then, the three strategies that reformers and planners rely on to legitimate their actions. Each appeals to a different aspect of the democratic process: the need for consensus among elite institutional interests; the reverence for science and fact; and the validation of pluralism, diversity, and conflict on which democracy depends for its vitality. The dilemma seems to be that the reform that works with the establishment, which is searching for a consensus, tends to lose its soul and its purpose. It abandons its real feeling and commitment for the poor as it sacrifices innovation and reform for survival and growth. Yet, any program that is based solely on a fight for the rights of the poor and that fails to work with established institutions not only is likely to create conflict, but also may fail to generate any constructive accommodation that can lead to real reform. Organizing the poor on a neighborhood basis cannot achieve very much fundamental change. Vision is limited to issues around which local initiative can be mobilized; most typically there is failure to give attention to broad social and economic policy. Research can interfere with both functions, for it can be used, in Gouldner's graphic term, as a "hamletic strategy" of delay and procrastination, responsive to political realities, while avoiding action that will provide authentic services for the poor. Research can compete with reform for resources, and it may pursue competing aims. The documentation of social injustice, which seeks action by confrontation, may embarrass the bureaucracies and make cooperation with the reformers more difficult. But without research, without some kind of objective analysis of the consequences of action, social policy moves from fashion to fashion without ever learning anything. It is, after all, useless to continue to create innovations and to spread new ideas if one never checks to see whether the new ideas and innovations are mere fads or whether they do indeed produce any kind of demonstrable change.

How then can these dilemmas be resolved? The answer, I believe, is that they cannot, for the contradictions are inherent in the nature of American social life.[36] It is futile to search for paradigms and prescriptions that will clear the whole problem out of the way and ultimately demonstrate that the strategies are indeed consistent and mutually reinforcing, rather than fundamentally in conflict. The search for a welfare monism that rejects pluralism and conflict only fosters utopian illusions. When all three strategies are pursued simultaneously in the same organization, internal conflict develops over time.

Eugene Litwak has suggested that we typically resolve such conflicts by having the conflicting functions carried out by separate organizations.

> A society might stress both freedom and physical safety. These two values may conflict . . . yet the society seeks to maximize each. One way of assuring that each will be retained, despite the conflict, is to put them under separate organizational structures; i.e., have the police force guard physical safety and the newspapers guard freedom of the press.[37]

Fragmentation of function does not, however, resolve the dilemma; it serves only to exacerbate the problem of interorganizational relationships as lack of coordination becomes a perpetual crisis.

The government's delinquency prevention program stressed rational planning and the power of knowledge, the anti-poverty program sought to implement the ideals of "maximum feasible involvement of the poor," while the Model Cities Program seems to direct its energies, at least initially, to established power, and it was guided by the principle of "widespread" rather than "maximum" participation. This does not imply that each of the programs neglects the other strategies, but they do indeed seem to emphasize one at cost to the others. Typically, then, we pursue all the strategies in the same and in different organizations, but also at different points in history we stress one or another of them. We move to research when we become particularly conscious of a lack of knowledge, a lack of clear ideas. We move toward advocacy and direct action to help the poor when we are aware of the extent to which programs seem to be ensnarled in or captured by established power. We move toward established power when we feel that organized programs, whatever their merit, have succumbed to managerial inefficiencies and when direct democracy seems to threaten our commitment to representative government.

CONCLUSIONS

Physical and social planners have proceeded under the assumption that the consensus of values which binds society together offers the most compelling frame of reference for a "community regarding" planning process. However, when the divisions separating society become evident and the chasms dividing its groups become deep, planning at all levels comes to reflect these conditions. And although the need for disinterested planning becomes more urgent when the disharmonies in the society become more evident, it also becomes more difficult to perform as harmonizers and integrators. Rational planning is a myth when the value consensus on which it must depend is illusory and technology for eliminating arbitrary decisions is not available. But as the conditions of society become more complex and as each decision is a response to short range expediencies and accommodations of conflicting vested interests, the need to protect society's long-term interests becomes more insistent and the demands for rational solutions grow more urgent.

The crucial dilemma of planning cannot be altogether avoided: society's social problems require disinterested, rational, and politically independent solutions. However, we have no technology which lends itself to objective assessment, nor have we or can we ever devise a way to detach planning from political pressure, without at the same time converting the detachment into irrelevance. Nor is advocacy planning a solution, for one planner as advocate implies yet another (not necessarily a planner) as judge. A judge is not simply a mediator among conflicting interests; what makes his decisions just is their conformance to some normative standard, some moral value judgment.[38] But the society has created neither mechanisms of adjudication nor a body of law and tradition to provide us with norms and standards to judge conflicting social policies. This situation arises because the effect of social policies tends to be distributional in that they leave some groups better off and others worse off. Social planning impels us to go beyond Pareto Optimality as a criterion for public decision-making. Even the choices of means are never neutral insofar as ends are concerned.

Because the tools for intervention embody values no simple calculus for distinguishing means and ends are at hand. As a result, social science alone cannot help us choose among conflicting goals, nor can it offer criteria when public policy decisions require interpersonal comparison of utilities, nor can it offer criteria other than efficiency and effectiveness in empirical studies that try to bring together means and ends.

Since resolution of these fundamental dilemmas is not at hand, each source of authority that legitimates planning offers an alternative interpretation of its role. Thus one role can be seen as disinterested planning, which seeks to exploit whatever available consensus is at hand and to plan in terms of these areas of common agreement. Planning is then interpreted as a rational scientific process by which the relative efficiency of various means can be assessed when goals are known. Alternatively, as Reiner has suggested, the planner can be a rational goal technician, explicating the muffled goals among choices already made on other grounds.[39] Or, when agreement is lacking, planning can offer a forum through which the planner tries to forge harmony among conflicting interests. Or the planner may be seen as a bureaucrat acquiring his goals from elected officials' interpretation of his mission. When established political patterns are rigid, the planner may act as an advocate for rejected and excluded groups, organizing them to enter the political process. Or he may serve as a guerilla attempting to initiate change in bureaucracy by enhancing internal competence and responsiveness, having no explicit agenda of reform other than the wish to be relevant to current social problems.

From this review of the problems of legitimacy in social planning, two general conclusions can be reached: (1) The source of legitimacy in planning is neither self-evident nor narrowly restrictive. Indeed, there are multiple sources of legitimacy. However, they cannot all be pursued under the auspices of one planning organization and hence choice is required; and (2) Each source of authority has its characteristic weaknesses and strengths which present to the planner a set of intractable problems that are moral in character from which there can be no retreat into technology. These issues become explicit when one understands the implications and consequences of choosing among various sources of authority to legitimate planning.

Schools of city and social planning should not organize their planning curricula around a single source of legitimacy—physical planning around technology and social planning around advocacy. We must prepare students to understand that there are far wider choices to legitimate their work and roles. Meanwhile we need to probe more deeply the various dilemmas of planning, where each source of legitimacy is accepted, in order to extend our understanding of the moral problems posed for planners in a pluralistic society.

But since we have no final answers to the moral dilemmas presented by the conflicting values we seek to realize, teachers of social policy must accept the awkward conclusion that they cannot offer to their students a methodology and technology for doing policy analyses and reaching policy conclusions. We characteristically offer questions without answers. Rules and principles for choosing among alternative social objectives and competing sources of legitimacy are not at hand. Moreover, the search for decision rules ensnarls us in a preoccupation with technology which leads us to retreat from the fundamental moral and value problems that lie at the center of the study of social policy. If these generalizations seem valid, then we may reluctantly conclude that if our students, at the finish of their training, end up with no special competencies to undertake policy analysis it is because there are none available to master—other than the skills derived from the student's own intellectual resources or the special knowledge he has already acquired from the professional and academic discipline in which he has been trained. Social policy planning as a field of inquiry cannot serve as a substitute for professional and/or academic training but only as a supplement to it. But in building on this base of knowledge, we must not succumb to the temptation to take up the solvable problems and forsake the intractable dilemmas on the assumption that this is the orderly route to knowledge. Social policy is all about social objectives and the values that embody the choice of social programs. These are precisely the problems that touch the limits of social science and raise the spectre of that ancient but still inadequately explored terrain where facts and values merge. How and in what sense can science contribute to "the clarification and the formulation of values . . . and whether this requires the widening of the concept of social science to incorporate some of the attributes of philosophical criticism"?[40]

NOTES

1. David A. Armstrong, "Some Notes on the Concept of Planning" (Tavistock Institute of Human Relations, London, July 1964), p. 8. (Mimeographed.)
2. For an analysis of the dilemma that such organizations confront when they seek to promote change, or when they fail to embrace all relevant community interests in their forum, see Chapter 10.
3. Wallace S. Sayre and Herbert Kaufman, *Governing New York City: Politics in the Metropolis* (New York: Russell Foundation, 1960), p. 372.
4. This argument was again set forth when a group of planners was asked to advise on the development of planning in Puerto Rico. See, Rexford Gray Tugwell, "The Place of Planning in Society," A Series of Seven Lectures on The Place of

Planning in Society with special reference to Puerto Rico (Technical Paper No. 7, San Juan: Puerto Rico Planning Board, 1954).

5. Sayre and Kauffman, *op. cit.,* pp. 372–3.
6. See, Robert C. Fried, "Professionalism and Politics in Planning," *Journal of the American Institute of Planners,* XXXV, 3 (May 1969), 150–9.
7. For opposing arguments, see, Carl Friedrich, *Constitutional Government and Democracy* (Boston: Ginn and Company, 1946); and Herman Finer, *Theory and Practice of Modern Government* (Rev. ed., New York: Henry Holt and Company, 1949), pp. 871–85. For a useful summary of the debate, see, Glendon Schubert, *The Public Interest* (Glencoe, Illinois: The Free Press, 1960), pp. 120–1.
8. Norman Beckman, "The Planner as a Bureaucrat," *Journal of the American Institute of Planners,* XXX, 4 (November 1964), 324. See also, Alan Altshuler, *The City Planning Process: A Political Analysis* (New York: Cornell University Press, 1965).
9. *Ibid.,* pp. 326–7. Altshuler argues that since "political officials seldom give planners any clear instructions to guide the value-choice aspects of their work, much discretion remains with the experts." He thus appears to reject Beckman's formulation of the planner's role as bureaucrat. Altshuler's comments apply to any bureaucrat in the strict Weberian sense of the term.
10. Though they taught together and wrote a great deal on this theme, these scholars have not yet written up their work in a single report.
11. Chester Rapkin, Louis Winnick, and David Blank, *Housing Market Analyses: A Study of Theory and Method,* A Report from the Institute for Urban Land Use and Housing Studies for the Housing and Home Finance Agency, 1952.
12. Paul Davidoff and Thomas A. Reiner, "A Choice Theory of Planning," *Journal of the American Institute of Planners,* XXVIII, 2 (May 1962), 108.
13. Paul Davidoff, "Advocacy and Pluralism in Planning," *Journal of the American Institute of Planners,* XXXI (November 1965), 331–8.
14. Lisa R. Peattie, "Reflections on Advocacy Planning," *Journal of the American Institute of Planners,* XXXIV, 2 (March 1968), 84.
15. *Ibid.,* p. 86.
16. Herbert Gans, "Social Planning: Regional and Urban Planning," in *International Encyclopedia of the Social Services* (New York: The Macmillan Company and The Free Press, 1968), p. 131.
17. In the planning field, there has been at least one effort to create a loose coalition of insurgents who are seeking to change the policies of their own and other programs. Leonard Duhl calls this coalition a "floating crap game." The analogy is misleading though because the players are not in competition with each other but rather seek to support each other in their common mission. Professional associations, such as Planners for Equal Opportunity (PEO), may also serve as reference groups.
18. Martin Arnold, "Young Insurgents in Planning Commission Charge it Operates in Secrecy," *New York Times,* March 30, 1969, p. 34.
19. The claim to a source of legitimacy may be only illusory. Hence we need to pay attention to inauthentic claims to legitimacy. Under special circumstances, myths can be very important in convincing others that their claims should be heeded. This article does not systematically explore this important issue.

20. Robert Morris and Martin Rein, "Emerging Patterns in Community Planning," in *Social Work Practice, 1963* (New York: Columbia University Press, 1963), p. 156.

21. Alvin W. Gouldner, "The Sociologist as Partisan: Sociology and the Welfare State," *The American Sociologist,* III, 2 (May 1968), 109.

22. The use of the terms innovation and change may require some explanation. I find useful the distinction developed by Lake in his review of theories and research about social change. He states, "there is no clear distinction in the literature reviewed between a *strategy* of innovation and a theory of change. . . . When concepts are tied in with tactics and when time phasing activities are suggested, then the theories become strategies of innovation . . . a theory of change . . . is not accompanied by a program for inducing change." Dale G. Lake, "Concepts of Change and Innovation in 1966," *The Journal of Applied Behavioral Science,* IV, 1 (1968), 4–5. Kahn and his colleagues treat innovation as the procedures, roles, and activities that enable an organization to depart from fixed rules in the face of changing circumstances. For their discussion of innovative roles within an organization, see, Robert Kahn *et al., Organizational Stress: Studies in Role Conflict and Ambiguity* (New York: John Wiley and Sons, 1964), chap. 7. This paper is concerned with the efforts of some organizations to induce innovation in other organizations. This process I define as planned change or social reform.

23. For further evidence on the conflict between innovation and broadbased organizations in voluntary social welfare organizations and in health and welfare councils, see Chapters 9 and 10. For a review of the literature of international organizations that reaches a similar conclusion, see, Richard E. Walton, "Two Strategies of Social Change and their Dilemmas," *The Journal of Applied Behavioral Science,* I, 2 (April/May/June 1965), 167–79.

24. For a thoughtful review of these issues, see, T. S. Simey, *Social Science and Social Purposes* (London: Constable and Co. Ltd., 1968), p. 138.

25. Harlem Youth Opportunities Unlimited, *Youth in the Ghetto: A Study of the Consequences of Powerlessness and A Blueprint for Change* (New York: Haryou, 1964), pp. 2–3.

26. See, for example, Melvin Herman, "Problems of Evaluation," *The American Child,* XLVII, 2 (March 1965), 5–10; and U.S. Congress, Senate Subcommittee on Employment, Manpower and Poverty of the Committee on Labor and Public Welfare, *Hearings on S. 1545, Part 10* (Comments on Sar Levitan, "Work Experience and Training," staff paper), 90th Cong., 1st Sess., 1968, pp. 3072–81.

27. Peter Bachrach, "Elite Consensus and Democracy," *The Journal of Politics,* XXIV (1962), 451.

28. For a discussion of the critique of participation as policy-making, see John C. Donovan, *The Politics of Poverty* (New York: Pegasus, 1967), pp. 41–8.

29. James Cunningham, "The Struggle of the American for Freedom and Power," A Report Prepared for the Ford Foundation, August 1967. See, pp. 57–69 for an account of community action in the city of San Francisco.

30. For a thoughtful appraisal of the limits and strengths of protest, see, Michael Lipsky, "Protest as a Political Resource" (Institute for Research on Poverty, University of Wisconsin, April 1967). (Mimeographed.)

31. Hans Spiegel, "How Much Neighborhood Control?" in *Citizen Participation in*

Urban Development (Washington, D.C.: NTL Institute of Applied Behavioral Science, 1968), pp. 271–91.

32. U.S., *Congressional Record,* July 24, 1968.
33. See Chapter 19.
34. Richard Cloward and Francis Piven, "Low-Income People and Political Process," a Paper Presented at the Training Institute Program on Urban Community Development Projects (New York: Mobilization for Youth, May 1965).
35. Michael Lipsky, "Protest as a Political Resource" (Mimeo.), University of Wisconsin, Madison.
36. For a further discussion of each of these strategies and how they conflict, see, Peter Marris and Martin Rein, *Dilemmas of Social Reform: Poverty and Community Action in the United States* (New York: Atherton Press, 1967).
37. Eugene Litwak and Lydia F. Hylton, "Inter-organizational Analysis: A Hypothesis on Co-ordinating Agencies," *Administrative Science Quarterly,* 6 (March 1962), 396.
38. Gouldner, *op. cit.,* p. 113.
39. Thomas A. Reiner, "The Planner as Value Technician: Two Classes of Utopian Constructs and their Impacts on Planning," in H. Wentworth Eldredge (ed.), *Taming Megalopolis* (Vol. I, New York: Doubleday and Company, 1967), 232–47.
40. T. S. Simey, *op. cit.,* p. xi.

Part V

Choice of
Social Objectives

Chapter 12

Poverty, Policy, and Purpose: The Dilemmas of Choice

What programs should the federal government promote in order to reduce poverty?[1] Economists have addressed the problem of choice in terms of allocative efficiency: how to dispose of resources so as to optimize some desired social state. Economic theory, Dyckman suggests, may be regarded as "the search for the 'rule' which would locate the position in which the actor was 'best off.' "[2]

To aid in the discovery of a rule or a set of rules for allocating resources among a range of policy choices designed to reduce poverty, at least three different procedures can be followed. We could examine the characteristics of the poor on the assumption that in identifying who is, or is likely to become, poor we will come closer to an understanding of the kinds of programs we should invest in. We could investigate the causes of poverty in the expectation of attacking the root of the problem. We could weigh the differential contribution of intervention strategies designed to reduce poverty in an effort to select those which are most effective.

The authors wish to express their appreciation to those who critically commented on an early version of this material—Alvin Schorr, Sar Levitan, and Thomas Reiner.

Reprinted with permission of the publisher and the co-author, S. M. Miller, from *Economic Progress and Social Welfare* by Leonard Goodman (ed.) (New York: Columbia University Press, 1966), pp. 20–64.

221

All three approaches are useful and necessary. But they share a common dilemma—how to reconcile rationality, political feasibility, and value preferences. We shall briefly examine these problems as they emerge in a policy-oriented analysis of characteristics and causes.

Who is poor depends, in part, on how poverty is defined. The delineation of poverty would seem to be a matter of a straightforward, rational analysis. In practice, it is marked by value issues. If we accept a market-basket conception of poverty, then the poverty line would depend on the number, types, and quality of commodities we include in the basket, how these items are priced in the market, and their relative weights. Obviously, the higher the cost of the basket agreed on, the greater the number of people defined as poor and the more they will tend to resemble the population at large. A lower poverty level will, of course, classify fewer people as poor, and their characteristics will differ more from those of the general population. However, even without a change in the poverty level, the characteristics of the poor can differ depending on whether or not an absolute standard is employed. An absolute standard maintains one poverty line, say an income of $3,000 for all families. A variable standard, by contrast, adjusts for family size, age and sex of family head, and rural and urban differences. The latter dramatizes the problems of large families, children in poverty, those who are fully employed but with inadequate wages, and the Negro female household head with children. It decreases the relative importance of the aged and unattached individuals as groups in poverty.

Consequently, our analyses of characteristics depend not only on where we establish the poverty line, but on how we measure it. These seemingly technical decisions are partly political (the higher the poverty line, the greater the number of people defined as poor) and partly matters of value preference (poverty may be conceived in terms of a market basket, relative income shares, or a proportion of average income).

A second problem involves not the definition of poverty but the categories we select to group poverty-linked characteristics. Many classifications neglect the "fully employed," "families with children," and "social security beneficiaries." Current discussion, for example, neglects the fully employed who account for almost 30 percent of the poor. Smolensky corrects this relative indifference to the employed poor by asking: "To what extent do the data indicate that the persistence of poverty is due to . . . market failure and to what extent to social and political failure?"[3] Market failure occurs when a high proportion of the poor are in the labor force but earn inadequate wages; a large number of poor on social security reflects a political failure; a high preponderance of poverty among Negroes and among large families with children reveals economic and political failure and, some would argue, personal and social failure as well.

Classification schemes may conceal subtle yet no less important implications for policy. For example, an analysis which lists "children in poverty" may imply that the children of the poor should be rescued by training and rehabilitation programs, while the category "families with children in poverty" may highlight the importance of family planning. It may point to smaller numbers of family units rather than to the large number of children. Different schemes suggest different courses of action. No system of classification can be separated from the researcher's value preferences or political judgments about which dimensions of poverty are worth stressing. Some British scholars for example, are concerned with the following characteristic consequences of income inadequacy: diet deficiencies; height and weight of children; persons who are entitled to national assistance but not receiving it; misfits and "unfits" (our skid row population).

A third problem involves the limits of our understanding of how best to categorize the heterogeneous population that we define as poor. Most classification schemes contain overlapping categories, so that persons with multiple characteristics can be classified repeatedly. Morgan's attempt to list nonoverlapping characteristics leads to the anomalous position that the residual category is one of the largest, accounting for 20 percent of all poverty units. Moreover, about "40 percent of the poor . . . have no socioeconomic characteristics which would appear to be obviously debilitating" in terms of the poverty-linked characteristics used by Morgan and his associates. Smolensky interprets these findings as arising from "some unidentified agent which can produce poverty in urban slums of central cities."[4]

While rationality and value preferences enter into our definitions, measurements, and descriptive categories, policy decisions also confront the harsh realities of political feasibility. At times these clashing forces produce a surprising contrast between the programs we have decided to pursue and the characteristics of the poor. The present war on poverty, narrowly defined as the activities sponsored under the Economic Opportunity Act, is largely directed to the problems of youth in large urban ghettos.[5] But in 1964, 43 percent of the poor resided in rural areas; only 29 percent lived in urban slums; 70 percent were white.[6] These observations suggest that policy frequently bears a weak relationship to some of the most salient characteristics of the poor. Political feasibility can more than flavor the policy recipe. At times, this ingredient seems to be the most crucial of all, a fact which may help to account for our present preoccupation in the war on poverty with social and personal failures and our neglect of market failures.

Every student of social science is well impressed with the fact that a statistical relationship does not necessarily imply causality. Is the "culture of poverty" an independent entity that causes poverty, or is it an adaptive response to the state of want? Many have inferred that the Moynihan Report says that we must change the Negro family before opportunities can be effectively utilized by the Negro; for the pattern of family disorganization reduces the capacity of individuals to benefit from the resources made available to them. Critics regard this line of analysis as muddled, introducing a confusion between cause and consequence and creating, as Elizabeth Wickenden has suggested, a new scapegoat, the Negro mother. They stress the importance of environmental change, arguing that if an isomorphic relationship does exist between family and occupation, then it may be easier to change occupational opportunities. Shifts in family relationships will follow. To infer policy from presumed causality is to travel a hazardous road.

When we examine the causes of poverty, we begin to confront the limits of rationality in the social sciences. Consider only one other example. We know that mental illness and poverty are related, but we cannot agree on a causal link. We can and do argue that people are sick first, and as a result they drift through the social hierarchy into poverty. This is the famous drift theory developed by Faris and Dunham. Alternatively, we argue that people are poor first, that they try to better their social situation in the face of limited possibilities for mobility and the frustrations of failure, and that the process of striving leads to stresses which produce personal breakdown. There are, of course, those who question the validity of the data from which the initial inference linking class and illness is made.[7] They argue that the data reveal more about society's response to the poor than about the distribution of illness in the population. Studies which use only official rates of admission to mental hospitals largely reflect the class bias of our treatment procedures, which sorts the poor into custodial state hospitals while keeping those who are better off in nonresidential community treatment.

Is mental illness important as a cause or as a consequence of poverty, or is it merely an artifact introduced by our techniques of measurement and our concepts of mental health? The evidence is inconclusive. Personal moral preferences for the virtue of economic success, as well as the effectiveness of psychiatric interest groups, predispose us to link poverty with mental illness and emotional instability.

The analysis of the characteristics of the poor and the causes of poverty does not provide a firm basis for policy decisions. Does the study of intervention strategies constitute a stronger fulcrum for decision-making? This is the major focus of our discussion—the assessment of the strategy of employing competing policy alternatives as a way of generating rules for the deployment of scarce resources. We are chiefly concerned with probing the limits of rationality, examining the contribution of political feasibility to program development, and dramatizing the crucial, but often overlooked, importance of values in the choice among possible programs. Here, we develop neither specific guidelines nor principles of choice, nor an agenda of reform. Rather, we attempt to explicate the range of choice, indicating how people actually choose and how, perhaps, they might choose.

We propose a typology of six intervention strategies which may be sufficiently general and analytic to permit the exploration of the important policy issues concerning the deployment of resources. Startling new inventions or discoveries are unlikely to emerge suddenly. We are dealing, then, with a limited set of alternative interventions, although consensus on any single system of classification is unlikely. Our list of program strategies is neither exhaustive nor mutually exclusive, but it does provide us with a preliminary language for discussing choices. We distinguish six strategies: amenities; investment in human capital; transfers; rehabilitation; participation; and aggregative and selective economic measures.

1. *Amenities* are concerned with those services which contribute to strengthening and enriching the quality of life. They are services which modify the environment in which people live. Alfred Kahn proposes that we use the term "social utilities," comparing them to the more traditional public utilities necessary to sustain life in industrial society. Amenities are not conceived within a framework of disease and pathology but are regarded as the normal and accepted services which man requires to live in a changing society. Kahn summarizes his thesis as follows:

> Social change creates new prerequisites for adequate social life in industrial communities. Since these are recognizable as meeting functional requirements of the broader society, they ought to be socially created in the same spirit that earlier societies invested in public roads, the post office system, public health, and public education. The user is "citizen," not "client." There is no personal defect implied in the need for the service and no penalty involved in the use. [They are] designed to meet the "normal" needs of people arising from their situations and roles in modern social life [and] might be thought of as "developmental provision."[8]

2. *Investment in human capital* is a strategy which attempts to improve the economic capabilities of the poor by investing in them through such activities as "schooling, health, on-the-job training, searching for information about job opportunities and by investment in migration." (Health can be regarded either as an amenity or as an investment. We will discuss this ambiguity later.) Schultz has advanced the provocative hypothesis that "changes in the investment in human capital are the basic factors reducing the inequality and the distribution of personal income." One of the implications of this formulation is that "Modifications in income transfers, in progressive taxation, and in the distribution of privately-owned wealth are relatively weak factors in altering the distribution of personal income."[9]

Ambiguity is common in the purposes which educational programs are designed to accomplish. Nineteenth-century political economists regarded education as essential, but they saw it as a means of inculcating work habits and skills rather than as a route to occupational mobility. The charity schools of this period were designed to develop skills of character. The Job Corps and Neighborhood Youth programs seem frequently preoccupied with inculcating good work habits. Frequently, acquiring occupational rather than motivational skills seems to be deemphasized in practice.

3. *Transfers* involve changing the pattern of claims on resources through nonmarket mechanisms. Transfer systems redistribute income from one population to another—from the employed to the unemployed, young to old, rich to poor. Of crucial importance is the machinery of allocation. Subsidies or transfers could be provided in a form which would promote the self-respect of the poor by convincing them that they, like the farmer, are making a social contribution by accepting the subsidy. Recently, new tactics of allocation which reduce stigma have been discussed: the negative income tax; demogrants; insurance for fatherless families; children's allowances.

The current debate about providing protection against income deficiency contrasts with the social policy emphasis of the 1930s on maintaining the continuity of income despite the exigencies of superannuation, sickness, unemployment, and the other hazards of industrial life. Public income maintenance systems total $36 billion annually and reach over thirty million people. Such transfers comprise 6 percent of the national income and 40 percent of the income of the poor. Commenting on these data, Lampman observes that "most of such income goes to the non-poor and at least half the poor do not receive any of it. . . . To take all those in certain beneficiary categories out of poverty overnight would require only that minimum benefits be raised to the poverty income line."[10] But the willingness to devise new forms and benefit levels for reducing income deficiency continues to be regarded by many as only a stopgap program rather than a guaranteed right of all citizens.

There is a curious and disturbing bias in contemporary American public policy against the use of transfer payments as a way of reducing poverty. Levitan puts the case quite pointedly: "Most observers would, however, agree that it would be preferable to provide income to impoverished families through the creation of jobs rather than through providing cash assistance."[11] Herman Miller provides the rationale:

> If poverty is defined as the lack of income, the provision of adequate income for all means the elimination of poverty. But if we have raised incomes and have not changed the conditions we set out to change, our efforts can hardly be regarded as a complete success. In short, the burden of this argument is that the goals of the antipoverty program far transcend the mere raising of incomes.[12]

Yet when subsidy payments are made available to farmers to assure nonproduction, similar objections are not raised. In providing subsidies for the poor, we continue to be haunted by the Victorian legacy which asserts that income security, or guaranteed income, will serve only to encourage, reinforce, or cause the deterioration of morality, destroy the incentive to work, and lead men to desert their families in the confident expectation that they will be provided for. As a result, public assistance programs seem less concerned with adequacy of the benefit level and more with its deterrent effects. The prevailing orthodoxy, as reflected in both Title V of the Economic Opportunity Act and in the 1962 amendments to the Social Security Act, is committed to the reduction of public dependency. It is designed to change the source of income rather than to expand the amount available to families in poverty. These programs attempt to get certain people off the dole, Title V by work-training programs and the 1962 amendments by social services.

4. *Rehabilitation* is a strategy of changing people which involves the use of psychological and sociopsychological approaches to restore social functioning. The techniques range from general guidance and counseling to supportive or insight casework and psychoanalysis. A program of this type operates under a sizable grant given by the Office of Economic Opportunity to the National Urban League and several other national organizations for the purpose of launching a group counseling program in urban ghettos. It is assumed that rehabilitation can reduce poverty by overcoming family disorganization and containing social deviancy. The families aided will thereby win increased community acceptability, employers will be more willing to hire them, and they will gain greater competence as individuals and as families to use those institutions which faciliate mobility.

Rehabilitation seeks to change the person by providing him with support and insight rather than by altering his environment. It may encourage him to change his immediate environment without restructuring either the new or the old situation. It is directed at the fall-outs of institutions .and not at the performance of institutions. The environment is a "given," and the effort seeks to enable the individual to learn to adjust more effectively within it. In his description of social work, Philip Klein makes this incisive point: "It is the environment that is regarded as more static and adjustment is hoped for through the psychological flexibility of the individual."[13]

5. *Participation* involves those programs which promote social inclusion and try to reduce "poverty-related psychological and social problems" by providing families of the poor with a stake in society. Alan Haber elaborates the assumptions on which this strategy rests:

American poverty, while it involves considerable physical hardship, is primarily "social poverty." It isolates the individual from the social mainstream, denies him the respect and status of the "respectable" members of the society and excludes him from mobility opportunities into positions of "social worth."[14]

This approach has wide appeal. A New York *Times* editorial declares: "Obviously, no programs for combating poverty are going to have much appeal unless the poor acquire some greater sense of self-involvement in overcoming their personal and social afflictions."[15] But the strategy is ambiguous. Is it concerned with individualism and self-help, the sociotherapy of rehabilitation, or promotion of collective efforts aimed at the redistribution of power? A politically controversial program is strengthened by ambiguity, for each contending interest group can see in it what they wish. Clarity of goals may weaken its base of support.

The case for involvement of the poor is varied. It provides "immediate and compelling psychological returns"; it makes it possible for service bureaucracies "to fulfill their officially stated purpose";[16] it leads to political strength and the consequent redistribution of resources and activities in aid of the poor. The strategy requires that opportunities be structured for successful participation of the poor in decisions which affect their lives. For some, the dominant characteristic of the poor is a psychology of powerlessness.

Another variant of the view is suggested by Richard Cloward: "Economic deprivation is fundamentally a political problem, and power will be required to solve it." Without psychological overtones, he emphasizes the political powerlessness of the poor. Power can be expanded in many ways. One way is through programs designed to protect the legal rights of the poor by making legal counsel available to them, which, in the spirit of our legal adversary system, will defend their interests as the poor define them. Power can also be expanded by organized group action or by the participation of the poor in policy-making on the boards of antipoverty programs. Cloward has proposed before a congressional subcommittee that the preferred way to reduce powerlessness is to vest privately sponsored and ethnically based organizations with control over neighborhood community action programs. The poor could then exploit the potential power of a benefit system and make it into an influence system. It is "one strategy for increasing ethnic identity, group solidarity and formal organizational power."[17] These approaches attempt to promote social inclusiveness by changing the power-authority relationships between service distributor and service recipient.

6. *Aggregative and selective economic measures* lead to two different approaches for promoting the involvement of the poor in the market system and for assuring adequate incomes for those who do work. Aggregate measures are designed to dribble down to the poor the benefits of economic growth resulting from tax cuts, capital depletion allowances, and other incentives designed to stimulate production. Selective measures are designed to "bubble up" the poor into the economic mainstream by devices such as creating jobs for the underskilled, minimum wages, and other programs designed directly to benefit the poor.

Whether to favor aggregate or distributive policies or both continues to be subject to much disagreement. Much of the debate about economic policy and poverty revolves around different assessments about how to promote economic growth and full employment. Some economists focus on selective educational and training programs and the opening of special kinds of job opportunities, such as nonprofessional jobs, while others stress economic growth by heating up the economy. Will unemployment, especially of

Negroes and poorly educated youth, be responsive simply to economic growth?

There is also debate as to how to reduce fiscal drag. In recent years our revenue system has increased its income from the private sector by about $7 billion. Fiscal drag, which retards economic growth, can be handled in one of two ways: by cutting taxes—witness the $13 billion tax cut in 1964—or by increasing expenditures—for example, diverting excess federal tax funds to the states through revenue sharing.

Many of these issues are not narrowly economic, but represent value choices about the different ways in which we wish to achieve economic expansion and the reduction of poverty. Aggregative and selective measures represent not only different economic means but different objectives as well.

In summary, these intervention strategies can be conceived as attempts to change environment (amenities), to change occupational chances (investment), to change the pattern of claims on income distributed outside the market (transfers), to change people (rehabilitation), to change the distribution of power (participation), and, finally, to change the performance of the economic system (aggregative and selective economic measures). So defined, the inventory not only serves as a framework for policy choices, but also embodies different conceptions about the meaning of poverty which lead, in turn, to different interpretations about the measure of a poverty-free society. Means and ends thus become interchangeable, as each strategy implies its unique goal in the reduction of poverty.

We delineate below six goals of poverty reduction. We do not have an agendum, but agenda.

1. *Social decency.* Citizens have a right not only to freedom from want, which requires a minimum of income to protect them against deprivation, but to adequate services. By this definition, one cannot reduce poverty without providing access to amenities such as housing, medical care, recreation, and so forth, which comprise significant aspects of the quality and level of living. The lack of these amenities is, by definition, a state of poverty. For example, all individuals who lack quality medical care and adequate housing are defined as poor.

2. *Equality.* One theory holds that poverty will exist as long as the bottom fifth or the bottom tenth of the population receives a shrinking or a stable share of a growing economic pie. Here the solution lies in redistributing the position of the lowest income groups relative to the rest of the nation. The goal of poverty reduction is to improve the condition of the poor not only in relation to their own needs but in relation to other groups, so as to achieve a more equitable distribution of public resources. Consider housing. If we equate welfare benefits with tax concessions, as Titmuss has urged that we do, we come to the rather startling conclusion that the major beneficiaries of welfare policy are the middle- and upper-income classes. Housing subsidies granted to the upper-income fifth in 1962 were twice those given to

the bottom fifth ($1.7 billion to $820 million).[18] Good housing is justified not only as an amenity but also as a measure of equality—the poor should receive from the public at least as much as the rich. "We cannot," Titmuss insists, "delineate the new frontiers of poverty unless we take account of the changing agents and characteristics of inequality."[19]

3. *Mobility*. Poverty is also the lack of opportunity for mobility. Investment programs can be seen, as Plato suggests in *The Republic,* as the central casting system through which a society decides which men are made of gold, silver, or bronze. In a rigidly stratified social structure, those at the bottom, although they may be above the subsistence level, are still regarded as poor: they have no opportunity for mobility. Although enlisted men at the bottom of the military hierarchy may not be in want, and although they may receive amenities as a matter of right, they are, as William Grigsby has pointed out, nevertheless in poverty because they are forced into a social niche from which they cannot move. If the Negro enjoys an adequate standard of living but cannot move from a position at the bottom of the social hierarchy, he is poor. He lacks equality of opportunity for mobility. Thus, a measure of the reduction of poverty would be the absence of a a correlation between present occupational position and the social class of one's parents. The perpetuation of occupational privilege based on family position rather than merit indicates a lack of fluidity in the social structure.

4. *Social stability*. For some, the mere provision of income and services to the poor is insufficient; for they are concerned with the social problems associated with poverty and low income. Rehabilitation programs, despite the rhetoric of the helping professions which define their mission as self-actualization, serve frequently as an instrument of social control, encouraging behavior which conforms to widely accepted social values. These programs must also have some impact upon social problems like dependency, deviance, and mental illness, which are believed to march hand in hand with poverty.

This view frequently merges into a broader concern with social harmony and equilibrium. The concern is with insuring that the poor do not provoke deep disturbances of the consensus of permissible political action. For example, a reduction of poverty among Negroes that did not eliminate race riots would be regarded by some as meaningless.

5. *Social inclusion*. Individuals may be regarded as poor when they are excluded from participation in the major institutions of society. To reduce poverty we must open the opportunities for participation in the crucial institutions which shape policy that affects the lives of the poor. Services must be distributed so as to promote human dignity and preserve individual rights and self-respect. This goal can best be achieved, as Wickenden, Reich, and others have pointed out, by a rule of law, not by arbitrary, capricious, and unaccountable agency action. Procedures should assure entitlement

to services by legal safeguards and by institutionalized and protected rights. Improving the economic conditions of the poor without increasing their political power and personal control over their life space would not be considered, in this view, an effective reduction of poverty.

6. *Economic stability and growth.* For some, the attention to the problem of poverty is justified because its presence retards economic growth. Theorists of underconsumption argue that the growth of the economy requires that the effective demand of the poor be expanded. The poor are thus an important new market for our economic machine. Increasing the income of middle-income groups would swell savings, whereas, presumably, the poor would spend their additional income, profoundly expanding market demand.

Myrdal argues that:

> Never in the history of America has there been a greater and more complete identity between the ideals of social justice and the requirements of economic progress. The latter goal is not attainable if large-scale policy measures are not inaugurated to reach the former goal.[20]

Humanitarian and economic goals coalesce. But should they conflict, many would argue, the preservation of a healthy economy must be given priority. One conception of a healthy economy is that of price stability—the value of money is protected against inflation. We should be concerned with the reduction of poverty only as long as it supports economic growth and price stability.

Our analysis provides us with a framework for raising four fundamental policy issues in poverty reduction. These must be answered, however tentatively, before we can seriously undertake the task of establishing rules as to how scarce resources should be deployed among alternative courses of action.

1. *Investment multiplier.* The first issue we consider is the ambiguity in deciding which programs fall in which intervention category. In part, this is a value question: is the purpose of housing and health programs to provide amenities for those who are poor? Alternatively, it might be regarded as an investment program on the assumption that if we change the physical environment, people will change as well (good housing prevents crime and poverty). Or, it might be argued that by preventing and curing illness, people will be better able to secure and hold their jobs (health programs maintain employment). In part, it is a political question as well: will legislators accept a program of housing or rehabilitation if we do not argue that these services will reduce the scope of poverty?

The question is equally technical and rational. What is the evidence that housing and health programs prevent poverty? Does a given investment in housing or health have a small or a large effect on other aspects of poverty?

(A low return indicates a low-multiplier effect [inelasticity] for housing and health expenditures.) However, regardless of the answers to these questions, it is more important to discover whether most of the poor *are in fact* ill-housed or more physically ill than the rest of the population.

Schorr has made an impressive attempt to bring together the scattered evidence on the relationship between housing and poverty. He concludes that "the type of housing occupied influences health, behavior and attitude" as well as "family and social relationships." Housing affects behavior and attitudes in such a fashion as either to facilitate or to retard the movement in and out of poverty. He summarizes the case as follows:

> The following effects may spring from poor housing: A perception of one's self that leads to pessimism and passivity, stress to which the individual cannot adapt, poor health, and a state of dissatisfaction; pleasure in company but not in solitude, cynicism about people and organizations, a high degree of sexual stimulation without legitimate outlet, and difficulty in household management and child rearing; and relationships that tend to spread out in the neighborhood rather than deeply into the family.[21]

The argument is persuasive. Poor housing creates a variety of social-psychological states which "place obstacles in the path of improving one's financial circumstance." It is an independent cause of poor health, poor socialization of children, and poor motivation, each of which affects the capacity to earn an income or secure a job.

In opposition to the frequently glib emphasis on the disabling character of low-income styles of life, Schorr has been a persuasive advocate for what he calls the nonculture of poverty: malnutrition, poor health, and inadequate housing reinforce each other in causing poverty. From this point of view we must reexamine the bias of psychological assumptions about the life of the poor and commit ourselves to changing their circumstances by much larger investment in health and housing programs.

Despite its obvious attractiveness, Schorr's argument on the role of health (physical and mental) and housing remains inconclusive at best. Let us consider first whether housing and health affect each other, and then ask what each contributes to the problems of poverty. Wilner's large-scale and rigorous study[22] of housing and health in the city of Baltimore concludes that improved housing has little effect on physical illness, with the exceptions of childhood communicable diseases and accident rates.

Nathan Glazer challenges the validity of Schorr's position:

> We must root out of our thinking and our programs an assumption that lies deep in the heart of the urban criticism of Lewis Mumford and Jane Jacobs . . . the assumption that the physical form of our communities has social consequences. . . . I fear the confusion attendant upon . . . a program that hopes to achieve social ends through physical means. . . . The chief problems of our slums are

social—unemployment, poor education, broken families, crime. . . . Nor can they be solved by physical means, whether by urban renewal projects or even by programs that build housing directly for the poor.[23]

Glazer is obviously not opposed to good housing for the poor. He concludes, however, that "in terms both of their needs and of society's hopes for them, better housing . . . may not have a very high priority."

The contribution of housing as a social-psychological therapy affecting patterns of relationships, motivation, attitudes, and definition of self must remain, based on present evidence, a theory with inadequate empirical support. Indeed, Glazer suggests that a better case could be made for the proposition that social relationships have more effect on housing utilization than the reverse. Thus, the benefits of a high level of housing amenities may be nullified because of fragmental and incohesive family relationships.

While housing and health may have little effect on each other, what is the relationship of each to the poverty problem? According to the 1956 National Housing Survey, only one third of the poorest families with incomes of under $2,000 per annum, residing in Standard Metropolitan Statistical Areas, lived in substandard housing. Moreover, this group accounts for only about a third of the occupied substandard housing inventory. Thus, we come to the startling conclusion that two thirds of the poorest family units living in these areas reside in standard housing, and, conversely, most substandard housing is not occupied by the poorest groups. In his detailed analysis, Grigsby concludes: "It would seem that analysts who used the number of low-income families as a measure of housing need grossly exaggerate the housing problem of this group."[24]

When we turn to the relationship between morbidity and poverty, we find once again that anticipated relationships fail to emerge clearly. Surprisingly, the incidence of chronic and acute illness is fairly uniform at all income levels for the age groups fifteen through forty-four. While the rates are somewhat higher for older age groups, the differences are not impressive. On the basis of such evidence, Kadushin states:

> A review of the evidence . . . leads to the conclusion that . . . there is very little association between getting a disease and social class, although the lower class still feel sicker. Nevertheless, social scientists and public health experts have consistently refused to recognize that the world is changing.[25]

Persons of lower incomes complain more about illness and stay out of work longer for each illness but, Kadushin argues, we must distinguish more sharply the "split between exposure and reaction."

These data do not provide an argument against the development of health and housing programs for poor people. But they have led some critics like Glazer to conclude that "housing is not dynamic as an element in improving the general position of groups in society."[26]

But the argument of inelasticity is vulnerable on technical grounds. If housing and poverty seem unrelated, it may be an artifact of inadequate measurement. While the poor may live in standard housing, they may still be overcrowded and pay a disproportionately large amount of their total income for shelter. Those who occupy standard housing may be largely older people living in their own homes; their inclusion within the ranks of the poor may be due to our failure to include such assets in our measures of income. On the other hand, families with many children may be concentrated in substandard housing. Thus, the use of statistical averages may represent a distorted picture of the inadequately housed population.

Or consider the health figures we have cited. While morbidity rates among the poor may be low, infant mortality is high, the life span is shorter, hospitalization is longer and the consequences of disability more severe than among those with higher incomes. If we fail to find relationships among housing, health, and poverty, insufficiently subtle measures and unsophisticated methods may be the cause.

It seems perfectly reasonable to expect that in advanced industrial societies the relative contribution of poor health and poor housing to poverty may be different from, say, their apparently close relationships in Victorian England. But we have so little policy-oriented research that it is difficult to come to any firm conclusion about the argument for or against inelasticity. At this point, the housing explanation is only a suggestive hypothesis and is not sufficient to inform a policy choice.

While the inequitable distribution of medical care resources by income class may be rather easily demonstrated, it is not at all clear from available data that improved medical services for low-income families will lead to the reduction of poverty. We do know that lower income persons lose more work days due to illness or injury than other income groups, but it is not certain that working more regularly would catapult these groups out of poverty.

The expansion of housing can be supported on grounds other than its instrumental value in reducing poverty. Housing programs can be supported, as we have already suggested, on the grounds of equity. If tax concessions are equated with direct subsidies, the top-income fifth received twice as much as the bottom fifth. Or, as Grigsby observes:

> . . . the necessity to live in a slum environment when one can see on all sides vastly superior housing accommodations which are available to most of the population, may contribute to a feeling of being poor, or inadequate, or rejected, or part of an unfair social system.[27]

Inequalities and loss of dignity are the crucial aspects of poor housing and, as Schorr most recently observed, "it makes little difference whether housing is a result or cause of poverty; it is an integral part of being poor." Good housing and medical care are valid programs if poverty is conceptualized as the lack of these amenities: people are poor when they lack adequate housing and access to health services; by definition, adequate amenities mean reduced poverty.

2. *Effectiveness.* The second policy issue is that of effectiveness. A program is ineffective if it fails to achieve its purposes in its own immediate sphere of action. But this definition fails to take into account the profound difficulties in determining purpose. Anyone who seriously tries to obtain from an agency a definition of its goals is likely to discover that he has not raised a simple, information-eliciting question, but rather that he has challenged the agency's *raison d'être.* Few things are more disturbing to an agency than the determined search for clarification of its goals. Unless objectives are specified, evaluative studies are certain to be weak and inconclusive.

Given these qualifications, we may inquire: How effectively do present-day rehabilitation programs reduce deviancy? What can social science say? The contribution of social science in the broad field of social pathology has been largely negative. We explode myths rather than discover significant relationships. "The chief effect of precise investigation into questions of social pathology," Barbara Wootton observes, "has been to undermine the credibility of virtually all the current myths."[28] A recent review of the literature on delinquency by Kvaraceus comes to the grim conclusion that almost no strategy appears to be very effective.[29] Two recent studies support this conclusion. Meyer and his colleagues demonstrated that quality casework services did not prevent early departure from school or other disturbing behavior among teen-age girls.[30] Similarly, Walter Miller, after an exhaustive study of the effectiveness of group work, concludes that it is a dubious strategy for reducing delinquency.[31] Rehabilitative techniques can make groups more democratic; many youth are willing and even eager to be involved in socially sanctioned activities like sports and social dancing. But these activities have virtually no impact on the incidence of illegal acts. Miller concludes that delinquency is largely a function of age and sex, and as such is not amenable to sustained therapeutic efforts.

Not only do the various forms of rehabilitation fail to reduce deviancy, but they appear to contribute little to the strengthening of family functioning. The classic study of casework effectiveness based upon professional judgment of client growth (the Hunt Movement Scale) revealed that "the average amount of movement was about a half step on the 7-point Movement Scale." Wallace has recently reported that casework treatment resulted in little improvement in the functioning of multiproblem families. An experimental group of such families was given intensive casework services; two control groups were not. An imaginative battery of before-and-after measures was employed to detect change in the experimental and control families. No significant relationships were uncovered between the casework inputs and the performance of the targets of change.[32] If the relationship between rehabilitation and adjustment is tenuous, then so too, we expect, is the relationship between adjustment and the reduction of poverty.

Ineffectiveness does not automatically result in rejection of an intervention strategy. New grounds can be introduced to support a strategy; sometimes, the argument shifts to the amenity level. Whatever may be thought of

the scientific pretensions of psychiatry (and other variations), there can be no question as to its humanizing effect upon the treatment of socially refractory persons and particularly of offenders against the criminal law. . . . This humanizing influence is a good in itself, never to be discounted even if it should prove to be accompanied by awkward "side effects."[33]

While the instrumental value of rehabilitation programs in reducing social pathology and poverty is dubious, the ethical, moral, and humanitarian values of rehabilitation are not discounted.

Frequently, feasibility is the force behind a program which is not supportable on "scientific" grounds: "It is always easier to put up a clinic than tear down a slum," comments Wootton in her penetrating analysis of why "we prefer today to analyse the infected individual rather than . . . the infection from the environment."[34] We have developed a national policy to reduce dependency by the introduction of social services which have been widely interpreted as rehabilitative programs. Having accepted the validity of this doctrine and embodied it in our poverty and welfare legislation, we are now testing its effectiveness in a number of research-demonstration projects, thus inverting the rational process of policy development. The pressure to find support for existing policy will be difficult to resist. There will be a strong tendency to discredit or underweigh evidence which suggests that rehabilitation is ineffective. Thus, political feasibility will make rational analysis difficult.

Few studies have been conducted on the effectiveness of involvement and participation as sociotherapeutic techniques to affect the psychology of those in poverty. Nor has it yet been demonstrated empirically whether participation can produce bureaucratic responsiveness. The approach has been criticized on the grounds that while community action programs are by definition local, the bread-and-butter problems of employment, training, job security, and so on, are essentially national. But this criticism is too restricted, for it fails to deal with the issues of bureaucratic responsiveness and personal engagement.

The recent experience at Mobilization for Youth demonstrates that when poor people are organized for militant protest, conflict ensues as new power confronts established power. But the contest does not appear to increase organizational responsiveness. Indeed, protest organizations can become the victims of the very bureaucracies which they were attempting to make more responsive to their needs. In such situations the powerlessness of the poor is reaffirmed, and their disengagement may become more extreme than ever:

> Efforts to promote self-organization fail more often than they succeed. . . . First, poor people have learned cynicism from bitter experience. They do not widely and readily respond to efforts to organize them. Second, when they do seek serious ends for themselves, they threaten established institutions or interest groups. At that point, they are likely to learn once more that they are comparatively powerless. Third, the professionals who try to help them have, with rare exceptions, one foot in the "Establishment." The ethical and practical problems that arise in *their* marginal situation are not solved simply by an effort of will.[35]

3. *Coherence.* The third policy issue is concerned with two aspects of feasibility of investment programs—financial outlays and the difficulty of mounting authentic quality programs which can deliver jobs.

While a strong relationship undoubtedly exists among income, unemployment, and level of education, what is often overlooked is the scope of educational investment necessary before education produces benefits. Those who have completed a college education are better off economically than those who have not. But the differences between high school graduates and high school dropouts are not so large as might be expected. Both are falling behind the college graduate, and the high school graduate does not have a significant advantage over the dropout in job security or income. For nonwhite persons aged sixteen to twenty-one, high school graduation had little effect on unemployment rates. In October 1963, nonwhite dropouts actually had slightly lower rates of unemployment than did high school graduates, although the rates for both were quite high.[36] Similarly, the earning differentials between dropouts and graduates are unimpressive. For the males in the age group above thirty-four, the percentage differences between high school graduates and dropouts dwindled between 1939 and 1961. For example, in the age group thirty-five to forty-four, high school dropouts had 80 percent of the income of high school graduates in 1939; in 1961, the comparable figure was 87 percent.[37] The comparative advantage of a high school diploma is declining. A high dropout rate among nonwhites appears to be a realistic response to limited economic opportunities.

These data suggest that as educational levels increase for the total population, small increments are not likely to have the same yield in one generation as they did in another. Substantial educational investment may be necessary before an investment payoff emerges.

Consequently, the effectiveness of educational investments in reducing poverty will be determined by whether the investment in the poor is sufficient to move educational gains above the rising tipping point of significant change. Small-scale educational gains will be insufficient.

In training and retraining programs, the criterion of effectiveness is placement on a steady and adequate job. But few programs are able to provide either adequate training or the coherence between training and job that might produce substantial results. For example, a study of successfully released federal prisoners reveals that only 17 percent were working at a trade learned in prison. While the findings were intended to show that vocational education programs in prisons have little relationship to the success and failure of prisoners after release, they also reveal a strikingly low relationship between occupational training and occupational employment.[38] Cloward's review of youth training programs at Mobilization for Youth in New York City disclosed that of the 1,700 young people who applied for help, "roughly one in four eventually achieved competitive employment as a direct result of the program." Moreover, the placements were concentrated in marginal occupations, paying minimal salaries.[39] In another city, 24 percent of the graduates of Manpower Development and Training Act programs were unemployed.

Klarman observes that the argument about the economic benefits of a program of rehabilitation for those who are disabled and receiving workmen's compensation does not impress legislators: "Such skepticism may be warranted, for in the past the market economy has apparently not absorbed appreciable numbers of rehabilitated persons."[40]

Such scattered evidence on retraining suggests two related points. First, we seem to have done far better in reorienting, rehabilitating, and retraining individuals than we have at reeducating and reorganizing our economic institutions to receive them when they are ready. There is little use in retraining criminals, delinquents, the mentally ill, and the poor unless the economy is ready to absorb the graduates of these programs. When training has little relationship to placement, the coherence of these programs is very low.

Second, these training programs often lack authenticity and quality. Cloward's analysis reveals that the youths who graduated from the program failed to improve their level of reading and also failed to acquire marketable skills which would secure them employment in higher-paid occupations. (Good on-the-job training programs seem to produce lower levels of unemployment.) Training for character development or employability represents a low investment in human capital. At best, it is the beginning of an educational program and not its conclusion; it may only create a new group of more efficient competitors who displace others who are hunting for a limited number of jobs.

A coherent program would require not only expansion of, but major changes in, our educational, employment referral, and economic institutions. Without institutional change, highly promising programs may remain politically unfeasible or difficult to implement. When such programs fail, it often remains unclear whether the failure reflects the inappropriateness of the policy or the quality of the program offered.

Investment programs to increase labor market participation and to provide the skills necessary for upward mobility are seldom challenged on value grounds. On technical grounds, evidence is adduced to show that future earnings are related to present investments in education. But such programs often lack feasibility in terms of coherence and authenticity. Our model implies that major investments will yield large pay-offs. In fact, training for the poor frequently represents a marginal investment in low-quality training with inadequate assurance of a sufficient number of jobs to absorb the graduates. Technology and values encounter the stubborn realities of job scarcity and poor training.

4. *Value Conflict.* The final policy issue that it is possible to discuss in our limited space is the conflict among intervention strategies (and the goals they imply) and other policies which are strongly valued. It is naïve to assume that a community of interest prevails among contending individuals, groups, and goals on most issues. We ignore much of the conflict because of a tendency to believe that all the things we hold good must be compatible with one another. As always, the need for choice among competing values confronts us. We shall indicate four of these value conflicts:

a. The goals of high level employment and of price stability are in conflict. Samuelson and Solow suggest that a 5.5 percent level of unemployment was necessary to maintain price stability between 1948 and 1959. An unemployment rate of 4.5 percent yields a price increase of 1.5 percent per annum. "It may be doubted . . . that we can achieve both a satisfactory level of employment and price stability without major improvements in our anti-inflationary weapons."[41]

The British Labour Government recently discovered that its campaign promise to raise pensions was undermined by a monetary crisis which arose as a result of an unfavorable balance of trade. To strengthen its monetary and economic position, the Labour Government felt it could make only modest increases in pension allowances.

Tobin comments on a parallel situation in the United States:

It is not fanciful to link the plight of Negro teenagers in Harlem to the monetary whims of General DeGaulle. . . . Our own attachment to the dollar as an abstraction . . . makes us cringe before the European appetite for gold. We are paying much too high a social price for avoiding creeping inflation and for protecting our gold supply and "the dollar." But it will not be easy to alter these national priorities. The interests of the unemployed, the poor and the Negroes are underrepresented in the consensus which supports and confines current policy.[42]

He concludes that the case for price stability has been overdrawn.

b. The goal of reducing income inequality and meeting the income needs of poor people conflicts with the goal of promoting the labor market participation of the poor. Eveline Burns declares:

Workers whose normal incomes are very low and whose economic horizons are very limited may, if social security income is adequate for their modest wants, prefer benefit status to securing an income from employment, particularly if their normal type of employment is arduous or unpleasant, or if they are unmarried with no family responsibilities.[43]

c. The principles of deterrence and "less eligibility" in welfare are controls which have been devised to protect economic incentive—to insure that no individual prefers support to work. But these strategies conflict with the goals of economic stability and social rights. Obviously, the greater the differential between benefits and wages, the less effectively can welfare serve as a built-in economic stabilizer, preventing recessions and maintaining or expanding demand. Applying the means test as a deterrent and expanding the role of administrative discretion in determining eligibility and benefit levels conflict with the goal of reducing the sense of powerlessness of the poor and of promoting social rights as legal entitlements.

d. The goal of promoting social harmony and stability by the use of the instrument of law or programs of rehabilitation conflicts with goals of participation, social decency, and self-respect. To protect the expenditure of public funds, we have created not only "a law about the poor, but a law of the poor." The law for the poor is based on police powers and on society's presumed right to preserve public order and to protect one segment of the community from another. Because much of the life of the poor is public, they are more vulnerable to this form of control: the alcoholic who is drunk on the streets is more subject to public censure and control than the wealthy alcoholic who becomes drunk in the privacy of his home. Or consider another example: the right of states to exclude the entrance of poor persons from other states was justified on the basis of police power, not the power to regulate commerce. As ten Broek declares:

> Welfare programs founded on these conceptions and sustained by the police power focus on problems of behavior, utilize instruments of coercion and restraint, and are oriented toward keeping the peace and maintaining public order. They are designed to safeguard health, safety, morals, and well-being of the fortunate rather than directly to improve the lot of the unfortunate.[44]

This principle is implicit in many welfare rulings in such diverse fields as housing, mental illness, and delinquency. But the principle of preserving public order and protecting "the well-being of the fortunate" conflicts with the goal of reducing the powerlessness of the poor and protecting their legal right to assistance. The protection of constitutional rights and the use of police power compete in practice.

Participatory democracy conflicts with the goal of promoting social stability, at least in the short run. If welfare programs are designed chiefly to promote social control and to reduce conflict and tension in the community, then they are incompatible with the involvement of the poor in shaping policy, which may have the effect of involving them in boycotts, strikes, and other forms of protest which dramatize their grievances. If a major purpose of public welfare programs is to promote order and harmony through imposition (by kindness or pressure) of uniform standards of morality, then the requirements of social control and participatory democracy are antithetical.

Thus, the single, seemingly unambiguous aim of reducing poverty obscures the diversity of goals which derives from our varied conceptions of the nature of poverty. This diversity argues for many different types of intervention strategies. The dilemma of purpose arises when we encounter conflicts in the pursuit of these competitive goals.

The problems we have raised in our analyses of these four policy issues complicate the task of proposing specific recommendations on the deployment of resources. In summary, we have confronted the perplexities of inelasticity (low-multiplier effect), ineffectiveness, incoherence, and value conflict. But we cannot say with certainty whether these problems arise because we have approached the limits of present rationality (housing may be a cause of poverty, but our research has not been sufficiently subtle and sophisticated to demonstrate the fact), or the limits of feasibility (investment and rehabilitation yield poor results not because the ideas are invalid, but because the quality of the programs is low). Further, limited knowledge and uncertain acceptability complicate the issues of value choices. The problems of competing and conflicting preferences have not received the attention they require. The dilemma of preference may be stated as follows: how do we establish rules for the allocation of limited resources when we wish to promote goals which are in partial conflict?

Can a more sophisticated cost-benefit analysis rescue us from these dilemmas and enable us to deemphasize political decisions in favor of technical ones? Can we develop more effective decision models which explicitly recognize the pluralism of objectives and which make available to policymakers a clearer choice of the costs and benefits of pursuing various program combinations?

Without contesting the usefulness of cost-benefit schemes, such determined enthusiasm in support of policies without politics is overdrawn. For one thing, there are technical limitations. The cost-benefit model is most effective where it is least needed. "It will be most effective applied," suggest Lichfield and Margolis, "to those cases where we have repetitive events, simple goals, and well-defined products."[45] Webber observes "that our theory is still very primitive, that we still don't know how to discount future values or to estimate present benefits and costs [and] that we shall probably never find optima for total systems that are marked by multiple goals."[46] Limited information abridges the rational decision-making model and has led Lindblom and Braybrook and others to urge incremental and disjointed policy development. We now recognize that we cannot find the best answer, but only a better one than we now have.

But equal attention must be given to the play of values in rational model building. Model building tends to obscure value choices and disguises them as technical issues. In practice, one seldom finds multiple cost-benefit analyses, each leading to different conclusions as the operating assumptions of the model are altered. Nor has a great deal of attention been given to the definition of certain goals as constraints on others in the attempt to deal with goal conflict. But realism need not succumb to pessimism. The contribution of cost-benefit analysis is strengthened not only when value judgments are made explicit, but when different models are constructed to fit different assumptions. Thus, technicism can serve rather than replace common sense.

To highlight the importance of values in undertaking a cost-benefit analysis we will briefly comment on three decisions (value choices) which must be made in an evaluation of the deployment of resources in the war on poverty: the measure of a poverty-free society; the time period selected for the reduction of poverty; and the weight given to investment and consumption programs.

To decide on a measure of payoff we must agree on what we wish to optimize. Here we are immediately confronted with the uncertainty of purpose we have been discussing. What metric should we use? Most cost-benefit analysis attempts to convert utility and services into a monetary equivalent. But the measure of efficiency could also extend to the proportion of people served, the intensity of their difficulties, and type and quality of the service they receive. The choice of criteria is not only a technical decision.[47] What outcome standards shall we choose in the war on poverty —more income alone or more income with fewer social problems? More income with less income disparity between whites and nonwhites? Fewer families with children in poverty or fewer people in poverty? Shall we select one outcome alone or many? If the outcome criteria conflict, which shall we define as goals and which as constraints?

The time period selected also affects outcome measure, programs, and objectives. If priority is placed on the reduction of poverty within several years, then the importance of programs such as Operation Head Start becomes more limited. If the "culture of poverty" is deemed important, a longer time period may be involved; if poverty is defined as a lack of income, and aggregative or selective economic measures and transfers are regarded as sufficient to reduce it, then less time will be required.[48] When the benefits of a program do not accrue until a generation or more later, the rate of discount assumes special importance:

Money has different value when it is realized [or spent] at different times. Discounting converts a stream of costs or benefits into its present worth. The higher the rate of interest adapted for discounting, the lower the present value of a given money stream.[49]

The discount rate forces us to recognize that outcomes which mature at different points in time are valued differently. The relative emphasis on the immediate versus the more distant future is obviously an important value decision.

Finally, we must consider the relative weight to be assigned to consumption and investment programs. The efforts to deal with poverty can be classified as attempts to improve the *current* conditions of the poor (consumption) or to enhance their long-run economic prospects (investment). Consumption programs aim at directly increasing the income of those now poor through higher pensions, welfare payments, national minimum incomes, work-relief programs, and the like. Investment programs aim at improving the capacities and possibilities of gaining employment or at enhancing careers by training and education.

A high investment-yield approach puts policy-makers in search of populations which are most likely to change. To ask where to invest scarce dollars to achieve maximum payoff prescribes a success-oriented program. We would invest in those most likely to benefit. But this formulation undermines the commitment to work with the hard core of poverty. We cannot simultaneously hope to get the largest numbers of people out of poverty and, at the same time, concentrate on those least likely to be responsive. To work with the hard core affects the time requirements and the choice of outcome measures. Obviously, a mix of "cream" and hard-core groups is an answer to the dilemma. But how does one decide on the proportions?

These and other questions force value choices into the ledger of cost-benefit analysis. Who shall make these value choices? Mannheim suggests that this issue can be seen from two perspectives: ". . . in its religious and quietistic form, 'Who plans the planner?' or in its political and realistic form: 'Which of the existing groups shall plan us?' "[50]

Understandably, professionals and experts have avoided these questions. They have attempted to make their contributions to policy development in technical ways. This outlook increases the dangers of scientism, where value issues are treated in purely technical terms. In their study of how decisions about the location of low-income housing are reached, Meyerson and Banfield describe how the value question of where Negroes should live in the city is obscured by technical discussions of housing density, land use patterns, and the like.[51]

Our analysis leads us to conclude that we must politicize the process for making policy choices. This procedure does not necessarily require that all decisions be left for the electorate. Perhaps the best way to politicize policy-making is to create a pluralistic system where many interest groups have their own experts to develop policies which support their value biases.

We believe that an overemphasis on professional-technical reform poses a danger in a democratic society, the danger of scientism. "Welfare is concerned with social values," Titmuss reminds us. Indeed,

> it may be the embodiment, the carrier and the expression of a philosophy of everyman's place in society. There is no authoritarian role here for the expert . . . [but only] social servants, able perhaps to explain a little more clearly the choices available in terms of alternative policies and courses of action. These choices have continually to be made in the modern democratic state. We cannot make them for all time.[52]

We believe that it is crucial in American society to go further than choice clarification. It is also necessary to create new avenues for reintroducing interest-group planning in which ideology and not technology is the overriding issue. Technology should serve purpose. Our emphasis, consequently, has been not to ignore or even reconcile value and interest group conflict, but to make the clashes visible and significant. We introduce this perspective as a corrective to our current preoccupation with pragmatism. In the same spirit, Schorr observes that today "it is fashionable to deny an ideology," which he graphically defines as a passion for justice and charity supported by a systematic set of ideas.

The planner is not a value-free technician serving a value-free bureaucracy. We do not accept the assumption that there is no content in politics, but only efficient and inefficient decisions. Rather, we believe that planning is an instrument for maximizing different value positions. Paul Davidoff summarizes this argument as follows:

> Appropriate policy in a democracy is determined through a political debate. The right course of action is always a matter of choice, never a fact. Planners should engage in a political process as advocates of the interest of government and other groups. Intelligent choice about public policy would be aided if different political, social, and economic interests produced city plans. Plural plans rather than a single agency plan should be presented to the public. Politicizing the planning process requires that the planning function be located in either or both the executive and the legislative branches and the scope of planning be broadened to include all areas of interest to the public.[53]

We seek, then, multiple benefit-cost analyses, based on competing outlooks and assumptions, rather than spuriously solid analyses based on one thread of values. We are not in principle opposed to a systems approach. Our reservations revolve not only on the technical limitations—measuring those variables for which information is available rather than those which the model calls for—but also on its neglect of competing calculi of values.

At the present time, decisions in the war on poverty have strongly favored the investment approach, control, and stability. We should find ways of giving voice to interest groups with competing goals, of shoring up consumption and reducing inequalities of income, services, and participation.

Our personal convictions stress these goals. But, more importantly, we feel that a consensus should be a temporary result of action rather than the prime ingredient of action. We look forward, therefore, to a debate about objectives (and therefore about means) rather than to vague assumptions about national goals and misplaced confidence in our technical competencies.

NOTES

1. For a review of existing programs, see Sar A. Levitan, *Programs in Aid of the Poor,* Public Policy Information Bulletin (Kalamazoo, Mich: W. E. Upjohn Institute for Employment Research, 1965).
2. John W. Dyckman, "Planning and Decision Theory," *Journal of the American Institute of Planners,* XXVII (1961), 335–45.
3. Eugene Smolensky, "The Past and Present Poor," in *The Concept of Poverty* (Washington, D.C.: U.S. Chamber of Commerce, 1965), p. 42.
4. James N. Morgan *et al., Income and Welfare in the United States* (New York: McGraw-Hill, 1962), p. 195.
5. A report in the New York *Times* (December 22, 1965), describes the ill-fate of a $41 million program to aid the elderly poor: "An influential group within the agency favors youth-oriented antipoverty programs. The result is that projects in aid of the aged face a difficult obstacle."
6. *Dimensions of Poverty in 1964,* a description of the poor based upon the March, 1965, Current Population Survey conducted by the U.S. Bureau of the Census (Washington, D.C.: Office of Economic Opportunity, 1965), pp. 3 and 6.
7. S. M. Miller and Elliot Mishler, "Social Class, Mental Health and American Psychiatry," *Milbank Memorial Fund Quarterly* (1959); reprinted in Frank R. Riessman, Arthur Pearl, and Jerome Cohen, eds., *The Mental Health of the Poor* (New York: Free Press of Glencoe, 1964). Also see Chapter 21.
8. Alfred J. Kahn, "Investments in People: a Social Work Perspective," Urban Studies Center, Rutgers University, 1963, p. 6.
9. Theodore W. Schultz, "Reflections on Investment in Man," *Journal of Political Economy,* LXX, Supplement (1962), 2.
10. Robert J. Lampman, "Ends and Means in the War on Poverty," paper prepared for delivery at Morgantown, W. Va. (1965; mimeo.), pp. 12–13.
11. Levitan, *op. cit.,* p. 51.
12. Herman P. Miller, "Poverty and Income," American Statistical Association, 1965.
13. Philip Klein, "The Social Theory of Professional Social Work," in Harry Elmer Barnes, Howard Becker, and Frances Becket Becker, eds., *Contemporary Social Theory* (New York: Appleton-Century-Crofts, 1940), p. 766.
14. "The American Underclass," Institute of Labor and Industrial Relations, University of Michigan (1965; mimeo.). This paper is one of the most interest-

ing expositions of the poverty program. A similar analysis is developed in S. M. Miller, "The New Income," in S. M. Miller and Frank Riessman, *Social Class and Social Policy*. New York: Basic Books, 1968.

15. New York *Times,* November 9, 1965.

16. Warren C. Haggstrom, "The Power of the Poor," in Riessman, Cohen, and Pearl, *op. cit.,* pp. 205–23.

17. Richard A. Cloward, "The War on Poverty—Are the Poor Left Out?" *Nation,* August 2, 1965, p. 55; Richard A. Cloward and Frances Fox Piven, "Politics, Professionalism and Poverty," Arden House Conference on "The Role of Government in Promoting Social Change," 1965. In their provocative paper, the authors discuss the limitations of this strategy and conclude that "public programs for the poor not only fail to produce significant changes in economic arrangements, but they typically undermine the potentialities for low-income influence as well."

18. Alvin Schorr, "National Community and Housing Policy," *Social Service Review,* Vol. 39 (1965), p. 433.

19. Richard Titmuss, *Income Distribution and Social Change* (London: Allen and Unwin, 1962), p. 187.

20. Gunnar Myrdal, *The Challenge to Affluence* (New York: Pantheon Books, 1963), pp. 64–67.

21. Alvin L. Schorr, *Slums and Social Insecurity* (Washington, D.C.: Social Security Administration, U.S. Department of Health, Education and Welfare, Research Report No. 1, 1963), pp. 31–32.

22. Daniel M. Wilner *et al., The Housing Environment and Family Life* (Baltimore: Johns Hopkins Press, 1962); see also *Proceedings of the Working Conference on Housing and Health,* University of California (Berkeley: Institute of Urban and Regional Development, 1965).

23. Nathan Glazer, "Slum Dwellings Do Not Make a Slum," New York *Times Magazine,* November 21, 1965, pp. 57, 59, and 64.

24. William G. Grigsby, *Housing Markets and Public Policy* (Philadelphia: University of Pennsylvania Press, 1963), p. 27n.

25. Charles Kadushin, "Health and Social Class," *New Society,* December 24, 1964, p. 14.

26. Nathan Glazer, "Introduction," in Nathan Glazer and Davis McEntire, eds., *Studies in Housing and Minority Groups* (Berkeley: University of California Press, 1960).

27. William G. Grigsby, "Housing Aspects of Poverty," unpublished memorandum (University of Pennsylvania, 1965).

28. Barbara Wootton, *Social Science and Social Pathology* (London: Allen and Unwin, 1959), p. 326.

29. William Kvaraceus, "Prevention of Juvenile Deliquency: Evaluation of Different Types of Action," International Union of Child Welfare, Vaucresson, France, 1965. Cf. Bernard Berelson and Gary Steiner, *Human Behavior: an Inventory of Scientific Findings* (New York: Harcourt, Brace and World, 1964), pp. 287–94.

30. Henry J. Meyer, Edgar Borgatta, and Wyatt C. Jones, *Girls at Vocational High: an Experiment in Social Work Intervention* (New York: Russell Sage Foundation, 1965).

31. Walter B. Miller, "The Impact of a 'Total Community' Delinquency Control Project," *Social Problems*, X (1962), 168–91.

32. Report by David Wallace, School of Public Health, Columbia University, presented at a session of the Northeastern Conference of the Public Welfare Association, 1965. Evidence in support of the position that casework reduces dependency is also available. See, for example, *A Study of Marin County, California: Building Services into a Public Assistance Program Can Pay Off* (State of California: Department of Social Welfare, n.d.). The reason for the different findings is obscure.

33. Wootton, *op. cit.*, p. 334.

34. *Ibid.*, p. 329.

35. Alvin Schorr, "The New Radicals, Manqués," *Social Work*, IX (1964), 112.

36. Vera C. Perrella, "Employment of High School Graduates and Dropouts in 1963," *Monthly Labor Review* (1964), 526.

37. We are indebted to Pamela A. Roby for systematic recalculation of the data presented in Herman P. Miller, "Annual and Lifetime Income in Relation to Education: 1939 to 1959," *American Economic Review*, L (1960), 966; U.S. Bureau of the Census, "Consumer Income," Series P-60, No 39, February 28, 1963, p. 32. For other evidence of the small return from the completion of high school, see the cost-benefit analysis by Burton A. Weisbrod, "Preventing High School Dropouts," in Robert Dorfman, ed., *Measuring Benefits of Government Investments* (Washington, D.C.: Brookings Institution, 1965).

38. Daniel Glaser, *The Effectiveness of a Prison and Parole System* (New York: Bobbs-Merrill, 1964), as reviewed by Richard Korn in *American Sociological Review*, XXX (1965), 787.

39. Richard A. Cloward and Robert Ontell, "Our Illusions about Training," *American Child*, XLVII (1965), 6.

40. Herbert E. Klarman, *The Economics of Health* (New York: Columbia University Press, 1965), p. 47.

41. Alvin W. Hansen, *Economic Issues of the 1960's* (New York: McGraw-Hill, 1960), p. 4.

42. James Tobin, "On Improving the Economic Status of the Negro," *Daedalus*, XCIV (1965), 886.

43. Eveline M. Burns, *Social Security and Public Policy* (New York: McGraw-Hill, 1956), p. 57.

44. Jacobus ten Broek, "California's Dual System of Family Law: Its Origins, Development, and Present Status," *Stanford Law Review*, XVI (1964) and XVII (1965), 680–81.

45. Nathaniel Lichfield and Julius Margolis, "Benefit-Cost Analysis as a Tool in Urban Government Decision Making," in Howard G. Staller, ed., *Public Expenditure Decisions in the Urban Community* (Washington, D.C.: Resources for the Future, Inc., 1963), pp. 118–46.

46. Melvin Webber, "The Role of Intelligence Systems in Urban-Systems Planning," *Journal of the American Institute of Planners*, XXXI (1965), 294.

47. Janet S. Reiner, Everett Reimer, and Thomas A. Reiner, "Client Analysis and the Planning of Public Programs," *Journal of the American Institute of Planners* xxix, 4 (November, 1963), 270–82.

48. Weisbrod, *op. cit.*, p. 164.
49. Klarman, *op. cit.*, p. 165.
50. Karl Mannheim, *Man and Society in an Age of Reconstruction* (New York: Harcourt, Brace, 1950), p. 75.
51. Martin Meyerson and Edward C. Banfield, *Politics, Planning and the Public Interest* (Glencoe, Ill.: Free Press, 1965).
52. Richard Titmuss, "The Welfare State Objectives in Israel: Reflections on Britain," Anglo-Israel Association Pamphlet No. 7 (1965), p. 7.
53. Paul Davidoff, "Advocacy and Pluralism in Planning," *Journal of the American Institute of Planners*, XXXI (1965), 4.

Chapter 13

Conflicting Goals in Social Policy

The present effort to reexamine social policy by government and the private sector is based on the assumption that planning can proceed by identifying commonly shared goals. Men agree on ends, but disagree on means. Our only problem is to direct our attention to finding the best means. As science and technology produce better data, better theory, and better methodology, they can resolve or reduce the areas of contention about means. Behind this formulation rests a profound utopian belief that, in the end, political and moral problems about social objectives do lend themselves to technological solutions. Jacques Ellul, in *The Technological Society,* makes this position explicit when he asserts that "all problems have unique solutions deriving from purely technical considerations, so that as technology advances the necessity for moral choices diminishes."[1] Isaiah Berlin explains that the philosophical basis of such assertions rests on the utopian faith in some "world-transforming phenomenon, like the final triumph of reason or the proletarian revolution . . . that is the meaning of St. Simon's famous phrase about 'replacing the government of persons by the administration of things.' "[2]

This paper was first published in a National League of Cities' report entitled *The Planning and Delivery of Social Services.* April 1969. It was presented in September 1968 at a conference in Chicago sponsored by the National League of Cities and the Center for Community Planning, Department of Health, Education and Welfare.

249

I believe that this formulation is incorrect, for the most important issues in social policy concern its social purposes and hence there are no final solutions which enable men to choose among social aims, all of which are desirable and most of which conflict. But social planning today has accepted the ancient faith "that all the positive values in which men have believed must, in the end, be compatible, and perhaps even entail one another. . . . Somewhere, . . . and in some way, it must be possible for all these values to live together, for unless this is so, the universe is not a cosmos, not a harmony; unless this is so, conflicts of value may be an intrinsic, irremovable element in human life."[3] Even the most cursory review of the experience in social planning in the United States in recent years forces us to accept the position that "we are faced with choices between ends equally ultimate, the realization of some which must inevitably involve the sacrifice of others. . . . The belief that some single formula can in principle be found whereby all the diverse ends of men can be harmoniously realized is demonstrably false."[4]

I wish to review some of the conflicts in social policy and examine the various strategies by which we seek to resolve these conflicts. In this exploration, I will argue that the strategies for managing conflicts are themselves in conflict, and thus there are no ultimate solutions, no final rules for deciding among the various goods in life. Action must, therefore, forge a creative resolution of these dilemmas. It is useful, analytically, to distinguish between conflicting goals, conflicting means, and conflicting interest groups. We, therefore, review the consumer interests that policy should seek to satisfy, the variety of specific programs, and the aims they attempt to achieve.

WHICH CONSUMER INTERESTS ARE TO BE SERVICED?

If we wish to reduce poverty, which groups among the poor should we focus on and how shall we define their poverty? Titmuss has urged that the concept of poverty be seen in the context of social change. Hence we must understand poverty by taking account of the specialized institutions of power, authority, and privilege that generate new forms of inequality. "Each generation has to undertake anew this task of re-interpretation if it wishes to uphold its claim to share in the constant renewal of civilized values."[5] Although we continue to measure poverty in terms of subsistence, defined in terms of the minimum food requirements, the programs to reduce poverty are directed not at survival but at mobility; not to minimum protection but to maximum opportunity. But in the process of redefining poverty we must also redefine the groups to be serviced. Here choice is needed, not because servicing the needs of one group necessarily nullifies the needs of another, but because each group requires different policies, and each policy poses its own special dilemmas. In meeting the needs of one group, we generate conflict among other values we also cherish. I want to illustrate this thesis by examining three possible options. All are valid, but each leads to different policies that in turn embody different contradictions.

We might elect to work with the most deprived sectors of society; not the poor, or the near poor, but the very poor. For example, there are those who live at less than half of the poverty level. However, income is not an adequate measure of who are the helpless, the hopeless, and the most disadvantaged groups in society. Goffman once referred to these people as the "socially dead," as those who have lost a role they once enjoyed. And in a disturbing but perceptive metaphor he described them as "human junk who have fallen out of line in the march of industrial progress and who have been scrapped by the industrial organization of which they were once a part." If we choose to focus on this group, then we must search out "the social graveyards we have developed to hide the socially dead in institutions like mental hospitals, skid row. . . ."[6] This approach is still too limited because it leaves out those groups that never had a function. Among the most disadvantaged must be included not only the fallouts, but those who were never engaged.

Alternatively we could direct our energies toward those who have the most potential for being able to exploit present and future resources and who could best use these opportunities to alter their present status. We would be concerned with those who are most socially mobile, those who can most easily acquire the necessary social, intellectual, and occupational skills that would facilitate their move from one social category to another.

Finally, we can focus on groups that are falling behind the rest of society. They may not be the poor, at least according to the classic definition of subsistence poverty which stipulates the minimum needed to maintain mere physical efficiency or survival. These are the victims of inequality. "Inequality persists, however rich we become, unless we change relationships between people, between classes, and between races."[7]

Help given to the most disadvantaged confronts a curious dilemma. When we seek to make the level of provision adequate and we administer service with humanity and dignity, apprehension grows that intervention nurtures the very problem it is seeking to reduce. About 12 percent of the population in New York City is now on welfare. While the causes of this rise in the welfare population are subject to many interpretations, one compelling factor may be that humanity nourishes dependency. But the dilemma applies to all services that seek to be self-liquidating. Consider the case of services offered to those in mental hospitals. We could develop a mental hospital that meets the ideal of a therapeutic community, in which tension and competition are absent and in which individuals are respected for what they are rather than for what they produce. Under such circumstances, the services might be considered so desirable that the number of individuals who want to return to the "normal" community would be less than the number of individuals outside the therapeutic community trying to enter it. Thus, the goals of self-liquidation and adequacy seem to conflict, so the more we pursue policies that enhance the quality and adequacy of a program and the more attractive the program becomes, the greater the appeal it has for present and potential users. In the ensuing efforts to decrease the size and costs of the program, stigma intrude and "less eligibility" becomes accepted. The goal of making the program self-limiting is not easily forsaken.

Programs to promote individual mobility by "creaming off" the upper layer of talent and ability have a stultifying effect on those who are left behind. A "buy-in" for some individuals may prove to be a "sell-out" for the community from which they came. Facilitating individual mobility inhibits collective action because the group that is left behind, bereft of leadership, finds it difficult to act as a cohesive unit. A community that lacks the cohesion to act in concert is also vulnerable to increased alienation, deviancy, and disengagement of its members, and is widely believed to foster social disorganization. The inclusion of some in the larger society is thus purchased at the cost of the exclusion of many.

An editorial in *The New York Times* critical of the Republican position on poverty calls attention to this dilemma:

> . . . the American tradition enshrines individualism and self-reliance. Mr. Nixon's enthusiasm for "black capitalism" and for giving Negroes "a piece of the action" is in accord with that tradition. Yet if a financially successful Negro moves from Bedford-Stuyvesant to Long Island, he has improved his own situation—which is a commendable achievement—but he has left Bedford-Stuyvesant unchanged or even the worse for his departure. If the aim is to upgrade a blighted neighborhood or a demoralized school district or an area of high unemployment and crime, then the effort has to be communitywide and involve everybody in one way or another.[8]

To aid those who are falling behind the rest of the society poses an awkward dilemma that is derived, I believe, largely from uncertainty of commitment. The root of the muddle is uncertainty as to whether reducing inequalities is actually a desirable aim. Is it enough to improve the level of living of Negroes, or must we narrow the gap that divides the average income of Negroes from whites? Policies can both reduce poverty and increase inequality. It is crucial that this distinction be fully appreciated. Almost a quarter of a century ago T. H. Marshall in his classic essay, "Citizenship and Social Class," offered the following suggestive metaphor. Society is viewed as a building, and social policy can be directed at "maintaining the floor-level in the basement of the social edifice. . . ." The basement could be cleaned up and made more hygienic by assuring that no one falls below the floor of minimum protection in the basement. Such a policy leaves "the upper stories of the building . . . unaffected." By contrast, policies aimed at reducing inequality are "no longer content to raise the floor-level in the basement of the social edifice, leaving the superstructure as it was. It has begun to remodel the whole building, and it might even end by converting a skyscraper into a bungalow."[9] In a tall building like a skyscraper, the distance between the top and the bottom is substantial; in a bungalow it is markedly smaller. Both buildings may have a basement, but the distance between the top and bottom and between the middle and bottom levels is different. Inequality is concerned about this distance, and not alone about the conditions in the basement.

Nathan Glazer made a persuasive argument that we have substantially improved both the basement of social life for the Negro in America and improved his relative position as well. Yet "social policy faces a dilemma." Glazer unsympathetically complains that "most of us . . . believe that political and social attitudes reflect concrete situations—when things get better people become more satisfied and less violent—and that we change attitudes by changing conditions."[10] He is troubled about why improvement for the Negro is accompanied by increased discontent. In presenting evidence for improvement he is aware of the issue of inequality and he cites data to show that the gap between blacks and whites is narrowing and hence the Negro should be satisfied. Of course other analysts have questioned the very premise of decreasing inequality, an interesting example of the relationship between values and the measurement process.

Seeley tried to point out in his comparison between minority-status and poverty, "it would help the Negro-white problem very little if we were twice as nice to each other. The problem that is intolerable, personally poisoning, and socially destructive—is the *difference*."[11] All planning to reduce inequalities confronts the stubborn dilemma that it cannot specify the final outcome it seeks, other than to say less inequality is desirable. The failure to specify goals makes it possible for Glazer to complain that inequalities have indeed been reduced, but without allaying grievances, and for his critics to argue with equal cogency that not enough has been accomplished, and what has been accomplished has not been achieved at a fast enough rate.

But even when the distinction between deprivation and inequality is understood and reducing inequalities is accepted as the target of social policy, we find that in liberal democratic societies it is exceedingly difficult politically to redistribute resources and to reduce inequalities, which by definition require that someone benefits and someone loses. Democracy and redistribution as social goals seem to clash, for the many are unwilling to give relatively more at the margin to the few than they will be getting for themselves. Indeed. as the gap narrows, a restless working class reaffirms its commitment to keep the poor in their place. Still others believe that it is unfair for some to be permitted to take more out of public resources than they contribute to it in taxes. However, critics of this position point out that better measurement of the relationship between income distribution and social policy would confirm that the services that the poor receive are of low quality, and, because the taxes that finance social policy are often regressive, the poor pay heavily for what they get.

WHICH PROGRAMS CONTRIBUTE MOST TO THE REDUCTION OF POVERTY?

I should like briefly to review three programs and focus on how pursuing one can conflict with the implementation of the others. In recent years, we have successively been concerned with social services (especially manpower training and preparation for training), job creation, and income guarantees.

The classic conflict is between guaranteed income and employment. It is widely assumed that an effective income transfer scheme that supplements inadequate wages and provides a universal minimum floor of income protection would erode the incentive to work. On the assumption that income security conflicts with the will to work, social policy has elected to avoid the issue of insufficient income, the condition of those poor who work but cannot earn enough, and to focus on those outside of the labor force, the individuals and families whose source of income is interrupted due to death of the breadwinner, unemployment, disability, and so forth. Is the conflict between the employment system and the benefit system real or illusory? There is a curious lack of convincing data. The absence of data on so crucial an issue is all the more surprising since the incentive problem is an ancient one, dating back at least to 1795 when the Speenhamland system in rural England developed a policy to guarantee the right to live by a program of wage supplementation that was tied to the price of bread.

In the 1968 *Manpower Report of the President,* it was argued that, according to evidence from a 1961 study of cases closed on Aid to Families with Dependent Children, "26 percent of the white and 41 percent of the Negro children were in families where the mother had maintained some degree of attachment to the labor force during the periods of Aid to Families with Dependent Children."[12] Even though the AFDC mother's overall economic situation is presumably not improved by work, because for each dollar earned, a dollar in benefits is deducted, she nevertheless does work. The reasons for this are not altogether clear; both coercion and choice undoubtedly play a part.

Transfer income, in the form of means-tested cash benefits, and services are also widely believed to conflict. The elements that contribute to the conflict include a pattern of administration that distributes services based on professional discretion, and links entitlement to willingness to accept certain services, especially those aimed at supervising consumption and promoting economic self-sufficiency. The concept of rehabilitation, whether repressive or benign, appears to conflict with the principle of entitlement and the right to a benefit. Accepting this conflict, social insurance programs have avoided linking benefits to service. To protect entitlement, current welfare policy at the federal level has moved to separate cash and services at an administrative level, although both activities continue to be provided in the same department. However, as the social insurance program has won widespread acceptance of the principle that its benefits are a right, it has now begun to move in the direction of financing services from disability insurance funds and the pattern may be extended to other insurance risks as well.

The conflict between rights and services is not irreconcilable. It is a function of administrative intent. From its earliest inception in the Elberfield system in Germany in 1852, the provision of services in public assistance, then called the Poor Law, was used as a repressive measure. The supervision of consumption was intended to deter as well as to relieve necessity. It was an alternative to the nineteenth century workhouse test: need was measured by the client's willingness to lose his freedom by getting his benefits in an institution. "The only alternative mode of repression is to make things very uncomfortable for them by strict investigation and close supervision. This is the secret of the celebrated system in vogue at Elberfield and other German cities."[13] The Charity Organization Society faithfully pursued these ideals in its development of social casework. Current practice in welfare often continues to embody these principles, reflecting administrative intent.

Another recent conflict that has emerged centers on the observation that institutions which have acknowledged competence to contribute to individual development seem to be selective in the populations they service. They tend not to direct their capability to the needs of the most disadvantaged groups. On the other hand, if we choose to concentrate resources where need is most evident, we seldom find established institutions capable of meeting the need.

Help can be given to the most deprived areas and people by working directly with the residents and the users, giving them authority and power to build competent institutions. But involving people in policy determination and institution-building leads in the short run to wasted resources, ineffective planning, and internal conflict as groups vie for power. When professional confidence is shaken as a result of administrative instability or arbitrary action, service itself is forsaken. The crisis in the New York educational system is a case in point. But over time, new institutions are built and capability and competence are won. The struggle for control and power subsides, and in its wake, routinized career structures develop, loyalties emerge from accumulated experience, and new traditions and norms of expected behavior become established. The very qualities, however, that enhance capability, contribute to the tendency to neglect the most deprived areas and people. Capability and relevance appear to be in conflict. Although there are surely exceptions, where there has been a preservation of commitment, the conflict is often real and disturbing.

CONFLICTING GOALS

Conflicting goals exist at both local and national levels. At the local level, one of the most persistent dilemmas concerns the ideals of what is a good neighborhood. This seemingly abstract and philosophical question becomes concrete and pragmatic as soon as we try to develop a relocation program for those who are displaced from the ghetto by urban renewal and highway construction. Donnison explores some of the practical questions that need to be answered if a coherent community development program is to emerge.

> Should our strategy disregard class distinctions or deliberately seek to obliterate them; or should we recognize and accept the social ladder, and use it to promote social change? The problem confronts us as soon as we start rehousing people on a massive scale: decisions have to be taken about the quality and character of their houses, the rents to be charged for them, and the distribution of families among different neighborhoods. It confronts us again in the distribution of schools and the grouping of children between and within them.[14]

The questions posed imply that we cannot eliminate deprived neighborhoods unless we know what we wish to build in their place. We could, for example, keep facilities and structures in the area intact, but try to raise the average income level of its inhabitants. This policy would try to preserve the ethnic and racial enclaves that comprise our urban depressed areas. Alternatively, we would encourage individual mobility. This procedure would further confine and concentrate the most vulnerable, who cannot improve their situation, into a tighter ghetto, as it loses those who are most capable of improving their lot. In large cities that typically experience high rates of immigration, these communities continue to recruit the most deprived, serving as a port of entry for the mobile as well as a port of no-retreat for those who cannot make it. We might, instead, elect to integrate the deprived areas with the rest of the community, either by enabling individuals to live where they choose, by supplementing their income or supplementing their rents, or by making the deprived areas so attractive that they would be able to recruit those income and ethnic groups that can choose where they prefer to live. Such a policy of "upgrading" must find ways to keep in the community its present population, as the quality of homes are improved to make the area attractive to other groups.

Do we want to retain our ethnic and racial ghettos but raise their aggregate level of living, or do we want to disperse the ghetto by integrating it with other economic groupings? The variety of policies for neighborhood development seem to translate themselves into a single issue—do we want economically and racially integrated communities? Although distinctions of class and race will not be eliminated, what relationship should black and white have to each other in where they work, live, play, and educate their children?

We seem to have been singularly unable or unwilling to achieve communities integrated by race and class. Public policy is now confronted with a difficult choice as parts of the black community call for a policy of separatism. If we break up the ghetto, we rob the blacks of their one source of political power—strength in concentrated numbers. But if we elect to strengthen the ghetto by concentrating resources in it, by building black capital, by creating political constituencies for the preservation of separatism, by luring the black middle classes back into it and thus providing it with leadership, by increasing its wealth, by encouraging blacks to buy from black entrepreneurs, we then repudiate integration as an ideal.

I wish now to turn to conflicting goals of price stability and full employment as expressed at the national level. The liberal creed places its faith in the proposition that economic growth and full employment will contribute to the solution of urban social problems, especially the problems associated with poverty and race. But a rapid rate of growth combined with a full employment economy produces price instability. The desire to achieve both price stability and growth offers another illustration of the importance of conflicting, desirable goals.

The Council of Economic Advisers stated in its 1967 annual report that "improvements in the distribution of economic rewards and inequality of opportunity often occur in periods of high demand and relatively full employment . . . [and] it is during such periods that persons with educational, racial, locational, age, or physical disadvantages . . . secure their greatest relative gains."[15]

In 1968 we managed to bring unemployment rates down to the lowest point since 1953, but we only accomplished this with the fastest rise of prices since 1957. Hence the clashing goals of price stability and full employment emerge. The Council on Economic Advisers asks "is there a 'trade-off' between lower unemployment and price stability, [and] how do we choose between them?"[16]

In the answer provided by the 90th Congress, it would appear that full employment, with its assurance of the "greatest relative gains" for disadvantaged groups, must be forsaken. Public policy has moved in the direction of securing a 10 billion dollar income tax surcharge and a 6 billion dollar reduction in federal expenditures. If the policies to "cool off" the economy are effective, then according to estimates by some experts, unemployment would increase by a million and an economic recession could be anticipated.[17]

The interchange between Senator Proxmire of Wisconsin and Dr. Joseph Pechman, economist at the Brookings Institution, helps to clarify a number of inconsistencies between policies which seek to curb inflation and those designed to reduce poverty by either expanding jobs or by assuring incomes. Selected quotes follow:

> SENATOR PROXMIRE: I do not think you can possibly persuade the Congress to cut spending by $6 billion and increase taxes, and then turn around and say you are either going to adopt a program of creating a million more jobs in the public sector and a million more in the private sector for people who do not have jobs now, as the Kerner Commission says we must do, or do something which is more inflationary, pay people an income which is equivalent to a very simple job and they do not produce anything.
>
> So they are consumers to a greater degree, but not producers, which is the most inflationary thing you can do. . . .
>
> MR. PECHMAN: It will increase unemployment to some extent, but I do not think you are talking about the same groups. My own feeling is that any temporary increase in unemployment that you would get as a result of cooling off the economy would not greatly aggravate the situation of the poor, or at least not aggravate it as much as, say, the 5 percent increase in prices that you have had in the last year and a half.
>
> It is a problem of tradeoffs.
>
> SENATOR PROXMIRE: In the sense that the Negroes, for example, are last hired and first fired, marginal workers are generally the last hired and the first fired, too, you will have a million more people out of work and they are going to be the poor people; are they not?
>
> MR. PECHMAN: I would agree. . . .
>
> SENATOR PROXMIRE: Let me interrupt at this point to say that I was impressed by Dr. Mangum's indication that the thing our society or economy has done is that we have required the poor to be our price stabilizers. We do that as we cool off the economy and increase unemployment, the people who suffer are the people at the margin of work, the minority groups and the other people who do not have the skills and are laid off and cannot find jobs. . . .[18]

Mr. Pechman had argued, earlier, that the inflationary effects of income maintenance systems can be avoided by high taxes. The same argument would apply to the inflationary effects of employment.

> MR. PECHMAN: I assume you would be levying taxes to pay for it. You and I would be paying taxes. The poor would get higher incomes and would be spending what we might otherwise have spent.
>
> SENATOR PROXMIRE: So other Americans consume less so that the poor can consume more.[19]

Maintaining price stability conflicts with goals of reducing poverty, through guaranteeing either incomes or jobs. Both goals could be achieved, but not without opening new conflicts with other goals. Inflation can be reduced if we are willing to accept a reduction in freedom and choice, either through wage control, price control, or, as Pechman suggests, by the redistribution of consumption of the middle income groups, while expanding consumption at the bottom. Although the intellectual argument about tradeoff among these social objectives proceeds, the political outcome appears to be a program in which the poor bear the cost of maintaining the purchasing power of the rest of society. Paradoxically, in pursuing the question of what society can do for the poor, we discover the contribution that the poor make to the rest of society. That is to say, in debating a policy of positive redistribution from upper to lower income groups, we discover negative redistribution—the hidden transfers the bottom gives to the middle and top income layers. We should, perhaps, find ways to compensate the poor for the disservices they experience, when they pass on price stability to the rest of society.

A variant of the same conflict exists at the local level. Economic development of the city requires new capital, a favorable tax rate, low wages, flexible union rules, low welfare payments and hence lower tax rates, and government cooperating with business with a minimum of interference as to where business locates, whom it employs, or what it does. But economic development policies conflict with improving the conditions of the poor. The latter requires increased expenditures and hence higher tax rates; encouragement of labor intensive industries that create high employment levels but tend to have lower profits and, therefore, contribute less to municipal taxes; and recruitment of an unskilled labor supply that requires higher service outputs.

THE MANAGEMENT OF CONFLICTING GOALS

If we must reluctantly acknowledge that the goals of social policy are contradictory and conflicting rather than consistent and mutually reinforcing, how can we proceed in the task of making choices? Three broad responses to this query can be identified: by turning to rational, scientific decision making, to the economic market, or to the political arena. Each approach is reviewed.

Rational Analysis

This approach stresses that rational and scientific procedures can offer rules for choosing among conflicting objectives. The more systematic use of better tools will offer better solutions. The procedure that is widely believed to offer great promise in the human resource area is known as cost-benefit analysis or the rate of return on investment approach. A primary assumption of this approach is that "no public investment be deemed 'economic' or 'efficient' if it fails to yield overall benefits which are at least as great as those which the same resources would have produced if left in the private sector."[20]

As developed by economists, this procedure for allocation is a significant advance over the "windowless intellectual box prepared . . . by upright business accountants."[21] The great advance came with the insight about the importance of secondary or indirect benefits and the foregone principle of income, that the same resources when spent differently yield different benefits. Thus to choose one solution is to forego another. The major objective of this new form of social arithmetic is to improve the basis for major program decisions. Since August 1965, all Federal departments have been required to submit their budgets to a deliberate, uniform, and rational procedure known as PPBS—Planning-Programming-Budgeting System. William Gorham, former Assistant Secretary for Program Coordination in HEW, explains that the system tries to accomplish three things:

1. To display information about the functioning of actual government programs so that it is possible to see easily what proportion of Federal resources is being allocated to particular purposes, what is being accomplished by the programs, and how much they cost.
2. To analyze the cost of achieving particular objectives so that it is possible to rank the alternatives in terms of their relative costs.
3. To evaluate the benefits of achieving objectives as comprehensively and quantitatively as possible in order to facilitate the setting of priorities among objectives. The three activities are interrelated and build on each other.[22]

The radicalism of the whole approach relies less on its technological advance in the development of new tools, and more on the intrusion in policy development of a new set of questions.[23] Irving Kristol observes, "The economists are slowly replacing the lawyers as the theoreticians of public administration."[24] They have introduced a new set of questions into public policy for they have insisted, as the PPBS system illustrates, that departments should know what they are trying to do. "Certainly, many departments of government have never before asked themselves what they were about: a bureaucratic institution tends to take the value of its functions for granted, and concentrates on protecting and aggrandizing its jurisdiction."[25]

By posing new questions, such as insisting on clarity of aims; measures of performance; and alternative, foregone, and secondary benefits and costs, PPBS forces change in established procedures that is a welcome innovation.

But will it also be able, as Gorham suggests, "to facilitate the setting of priorities among objectives?" Gorham's own testimony before the Joint Economic Committee makes clear that in the task of choosing among alternative and conflicting objectives, cost benefit procedure cannot provide rules of choice. He asks:

> . . . [would] the total benefits from an additional million dollars spent on health programs be higher or lower than those from an additional million spent on education or welfare? If I was ever naive enough to think this sort of analysis possible, I no longer am. The benefits of health, education, and welfare programs are diverse and often intangible. They affect different age groups and different regions of the population over different periods of time. No amount of analysis is going to tell us whether the nation benefits more from sending a slum child to pre-school, providing medical care to an old man or enabling a disabled housewife to assume her normal activities. The "grand decisions"—how much health, how much education, how much welfare, and which groups in the population shall benefit—are questions of value judgments and politics. The analyst cannot make much contribution to their resolution.[26]

PPBS has other limitations that deserve at least some brief comment. First, it is difficult to get a common calculus or social arithmetic by which all goals can be reduced to a common monetary standard that is meaningful. The debate about the preservation of our redwood forests illustrates the issue. Redwoods are a source of lumber, leisure, and aesthetic pleasure. When competing goals cannot be reduced to a common standard, we face the problem of incommensurability. Second, the question about commensurable standards concerns noneconomic factors. For example: food programs or medical care may not have a high yield for work performance goals as compared to training. But even if well-being does not contribute to economic capability, it may be justified for its consumption value and the contribution it makes to improving the quality of life. The noneconomic impacts of public expenditures cannot be ignored. The approach tends to neglect a consideration of the administrative feasibility of implementing a given program, even if it is desirable. We do not have a calculus to take into account whether a program is effective, but whether it is likely to be carried out. The 1962 Amendments to the Social Security Act, which offered inducements to state welfare departments to provide social services to public assistance clients, is a case in point. Funds for services were used to determine eligibility as the directives of reform were simply ignored. Before we inquire if policies are effective, we must ask the prior question—have they been implemented? Third, the PPBS system ignores political costs and benefits in its calculus. A specific approach may have a higher marginal rate of return than another approach, but the pursuit of a lower rate of return may have a higher political payoff in terms of its capacity to survive or to finance the programs adequately over time.

Although means-tested programs are more poverty intensive than universal programs, their political costs may be very high. The next generation may discover that when programs are for the poor alone, they tend to be poor programs.

The Economic Market

Another approach for resolving conflicting and contradictory goals frankly acknowledges the limits of a rational calculus for collective choice and repudiates the belief that collectivities have goals. It assumes that only individuals have goals and that the individual is in the best position to make judgments about the allocation of scarce resources to achieve conflicting and contradictory objectives. These choices are made in a decision process of the economic market. Each individual, using his own personal cost-benefit ledger, reaches a decision that is his cluster of preferences of one set of values over another. Economists call these preferences "utility." Economic man tries to maximize this utility.

This formulation poses an ancient dilemma—whether social harmony and social justice can be achieved by reliance on a process in which each individual maximizes his own utility. If one holds the Hobbesean view of the nature of man that assumes that man is nasty, brutish, and selfish, then the dilemma becomes even more intractable. Nineteenth century economic theory tried to resolve the dilemma by assuming that there was no necessary conflict between individual preferences and collective needs. An "invisible hand" produces the coordination. The price system in the market is able to dispense with centralized authority and yet achieves coordinated decisions by a process of "spontaneous competitive controls." According to the "invisible hand" thesis, "prices are set by no one . . . they get set without anyone setting them."[27]

Community planners cannot rely on the hypothetical invisible hand when the outcome of individual utility maximization produces an offensive social product, such as racial discrimination in employment, housing, and education. Individuals prefer age, racial, and economic ghettos; this preference violates many planners' belief in a conception of a good society.

Despite the problems associated with individual utility maximization in a market framework, it nevertheless remains a persuasive argument about how best to resolve conflicting goals. Its appeal rests on the assumption that individual choice and individual freedom ought to be prime considerations in resolving clashing objectives. The market strategy provides an approach for converting informed preferences into real personal choices.

Present interest in restoring market choices and reaffirming the principle of consumer sovereignty can no longer be understood in terms of earlier political debates that divided the political left and right. At one time the conservative argument held that government was to be assigned a minimum role. The state, like the night-watchman, should be concerned only with the protection of property and with the safety of its citizens. The liberal position accepts the Galbraithian criticism that we have an imbalance between public and private expenditures and that we must redress the imbalance in favor of greater public outlays. The market is to be superseded when it is an inefficient instrument for meeting human needs, or at least it should be supplemented by public intervention when it works imperfectly. The result is both a larger public sector and a more centralized one, on the assumption that local government did not serve the interests of the low income population for whom public intervention was needed.

In recent years we find both liberals and conservatives interested in the expansion of consumer sovereignty, the use of the economic market as an instrument for choice among conflicting aims, and the dismantling or bypassing of public bureaucracy where feasible. The conservatives continue to argue that to accept choice by experts is to accept paternalistic government. But the liberals have joined the chorus of criticism against public bureaucracy and public planning. They have been angered by the findings of underdog sociology about the improper processing of individuals in caretaking and socializing institutions. They have also been disheartened by the failure of collective efforts to coordinate programs in the private and public sector and to marshal these resources to produce greater equality of opportunity and of conditions for disadvantaged groups. The result of this discontent has been to create a curious coalition of both the political right and left in search of ways to expand individual freedom and choice in the market.

In order to implement consumer sovereignty, people must be able to buy what they want. Thus, if consumers lack income, it is essential to provide them with funds, and if they lack the knowledge to choose wisely, then we must provide them with information. They also need access to a market that enables individuals to choose among social services and to purchase services rather than have them rendered free. Let us briefly consider each of these points.

To implement the principle of consumer sovereignty, a strategy of income redistribution is required. Conservative economists acknowledge the importance of income redistribution. Allan Peacock in England, for example, asserts that "the first essential, then is to provide the family with adequate means. . . . My view is that we should be devoting more attention to the distribution of wealth."[28] Some American economists have extended the premise, arguing that we need to dismantle bureaucracy and redistribute income simultaneously. An example may clarify the general structure of this argument. Consider the circumstances of the 380,000 Indians living on reservations in a program supervised by the Bureau of Indian Affairs. The Bureau employs 23,500 workers at an annual budget of about 250 million dollars, an amount that is equal to about 600 dollars per Indian family. On the average, Indians on reservations have an income of about 200 dollars per family. If the BIA were eliminated and its budget redistributed, family income among reservation Indians could be increased by almost one-third.[29]

Money without knowledge would be insufficient, however. The strategy of relying on the market also requires educated consumers. The Federal Government has created a special bureau that is concerned with the problem of consumer protection. The work of this bureau could cover the consumption of public goods, such as housing, medical care, education, social services, and so forth. The call for consumer information and protection in social services is a radical proposal, if creatively implemented.

We now have consumers' reports that evaluate the cost and the quality of consumer durables such as washing machines and typewriters. This idea could be extended to an evaluation of the quality of nursing homes, education, day camps, day care centers, and other social services. Authoritative public reports on the quality of public services made available to service users could create a new mechanism whereby service suppliers are held accountable to elite boards, elected officials, and professional review. Yet these procedures offer little protection and less openly available information. The distinction between consumer information and consumer protection must not be blurred. Educational programs may try to influence the decisions that consumers make. Information programs assume that consumers know best what they want and offer the facts to enable them to better implement their own choices. Programs for the poor tend to be educational rather than informational.

Several proposals have been made as to how the objective of expanding choice could be implemented. Voucher payments in education would, for example, expand consumer choice for a particular service. This approach does not provide resources for an individual to choose among conflicting goals, but rather expands his freedom in selecting the vendor for the choice of a specific goal. To enable individuals to choose among conflicting objectives requires a procedure that will give an individual, or family, an all-purpose cash grant that will enable him to choose and assign priorities among conflicting values. Such a grant would, in effect, provide an income guarantee for all individuals and family units. Much contention remains about the level at which all-purpose grants should be made. Presumably the level of the grant is not set at a minimum for subsistence, but at an adequate level to facilitate choice.

In addition to providing income redistribution, expanding information, and extending opportunities for choice, planners have increasingly attempted to secure systematic information about individual preferences as one ingredient in developing trade-offs among conflicting social values and goals. It is, of course, extremely difficult to obtain information about individual preferences and their priorities in the absence of a real market for choice. Individual behavior is not only a function of personal preferences, but of the range of available choices. Unless planners can specify the range of options, they may only constrain choices rather than discover preferences, for which it may be necessary to simulate or to create markets. However, by using this procedure, we learn only about past and present behavior, but not about the future. In addition, because attitudes and behavior diverge, the reliance on predicting future behavior by studying present attitudes about future wishes is uncertain. Arrow's work offers a logical proof that divergent individual preferences cannot be aggregated into a collective choice without imposition or dictatorship. Despite these difficulties, public planning may turn increasingly to the market to discover consumer preferences for conflicting goals.

The Political Arena

The third approach for resolving conflicting objectives may be seen as a variant of the economic market operating in the political sector. "Utility maximization by individuals coupled with bargaining and exchange may tend toward a sensible pattern of decisions and resource use. . . . In general the bargaining mechanism in the public sector has effects that are somewhat similar to those of the price and exchange mechanisms in a private sector."[30]

According to this view, conflicting goals are reconciled by a process of bargaining that seeks trade-offs among the various aims of different interest groups. Lindblom describes this process of bargaining as one of "partisan, mutual adjustment." In this process the expert himself is a partisan for some point of view. Everyone has a stake; there are no neutrals. The outcome of this struggle is a rational and a feasible solution to the conflicting interests and the conflicting values of the various interest groups that participate in the process.

When power is unequally distributed so that important interests are left out of the bargaining process, then it must be redistributed if the political market is to be viable. A democratic system thus requires that the interests of all groups, including the poor, the Negro, and other minority and disadvantaged groups, find expression within the political process. The theory that democracy is a process of bargaining among interest groups that produces a rational outcome can only be implemented when all interested groups are represented in the bargaining process. If the market process is to work, citizens' income and information must be redistributed. If the political process is to work, participation must be assured and the inequities of power among groups must be redressed.

The political administrator-manager maximizes his partisan interests when he acts in such a way as to assure his survival. To achieve reelection he must accommodate to the demands of the various constituencies. He can respond to conflicting interest groups or policies by adopting one of three approaches. He can ignore the conflicts by pursuing an inconsistent policy. At least in the short run, during the life of his political stay in office, he may be able to avoid choice while pursuing inconsistent policies. This argument in support of inconsistency must not be regarded as an irresponsible position. I believe that very often in public policy it is desirable to pursue an inconsistent policy. The only viable policy in race and welfare in the United States today may be inconsistency. We must thus seek to build up the ghetto, providing it with resources from which blacks in America can win political strength. At the same time we must pursue a policy of breaking up the ghetto, because the ideals of a segregated, apartheid society seem undesirable. In public welfare, as well, inconsistency is required. We must simultaneously attempt to make welfare self-liquidating and adequate. The former goal requires strategies which emphasize rehabilitation and less eligibility. The latter goal requires policies that improve the level of living of those who are on welfare by increasing benefits and enhancing the quality of services given in conjunction with cash payments. The more we achieve adequacy, the less likely is the program to become self-liquidating. Perhaps the only creative resolution of this dilemma is to pursue an inconsistent policy.

The second approach tries to develop a strategy for phasing in the various competing goals at different points in time. Political bargaining is, of course, one factor that contributes to the reliance on a pattern of decision that emphasizes giving attention to one goal or method and then to another. A harsher description of this process is that of faddism in public policy. But this process of bargaining or faddism can be seen also as an attempt to respond, to accommodate, and even to learn from external pressures. The process is extremely widespread. W. Arthur Lewis offers an illuminating account of how it operates in developing societies. The developments of social policy he describes are strikingly parallel to those in the United States. Lewis observes:

> The attitude to services has passed through a number of phases. When development planning began, at the end of the Second World War, the emphasis was on public services. This was defended by asserting that infrastructure was the key to economic development. After a while the assertion began to be doubted. Governments were expanding their public service commitments faster than public revenue, without this necessarily resulting in greater output of other goods and services. They were therefore now advised to concentrate instead on measures designed directly to stimulate the output of commodities in general and export commodities in particular. Production (meaning commodities) must come before consumption (meaning services). Development plans which concentrated mainly on public service programs were held inferior to those which were full of arithmetical targets for agriculture and manufacturing industry. Then came a counter-attack in which services were taken out of the category of "consumption"

and defended on the ground that they are "investment in human resources" and just as productive as "investment in physical resources."[31]

The third approach seeks a conscious policy of balance or mix among the conflicting objectives. One way to create a mix is to separate out the conflicting goals and treat each one as a constraint. For example, we may be willing to accept the goal of economic growth, if inflation is avoided and the benefits of growth also filter down to all groups in the society. Price stability and income redistribution are constraints on the goal of economic growth. To achieve such a mix, we may need to monitor the outcome of public policy and then take action that permits us to emphasize one or another of those objectives that are out of balance. Of course, this strategy does not tell us how we can decide which aim is to be a goal and which a constraint.

The goal-constraint approach tries to create mix and balance. The opposite approach calls for unbalanced growth. Here only one objective is pursued, while the others are forsaken in the short-run. When imbalance growth is carried out as a matter of systematic policy, it leads to the procedure described above, as the time-phasing of policies. While the distinction between mix and time-phasing becomes blurred, since all policies can be found operating at any moment in time, it is still useful because public policy emphasizes one or another of these approaches at different times.

CONCLUSIONS

The three strategies for managing conflicting goals—the rational, the market, and the political—have in common an emphasis on procedure. They are concerned with the process of decision and not with its content. I shall conclude with a statement about the limits and the contribution of research to the decision processes we have reviewed.

I believe that we need to guard against what might be called the crackpot rationality approach: the promise that policy sciences, armed with rigorous tools of objective measure, will rescue us from conflicting interests, conflicting means, and conflicting ends. This approach presents the danger of scientism—the use of science as an "ism." But this observation should not be taken to imply that information makes no contribution to the development of policy. Research can plan at least three roles: advocacy for choices already made on grounds other than research; specification that details a feasible, least-cost route to implement a given choice; and formulation to help determine what policies should be adopted. Research seldom contributes to the formulation of policy. It more typically provides an argument against potential critics and aids in developing specific plans. I believe that the resolution or management of conflicting goals is a process of bargaining and trade-offs that takes place in the market and in the political arenas. But how well does this system work? Here we need information on who benefits and who pays when all the intricacies of the exchange system get worked out. What happens to the programs we develop to equalize benefits? To what extent are they even implemented, and do they, in the end, multiply privilege rather than reduce inequities? We need to find a way of retrieving experience, of pragmatically learning about the actions we have taken and the programs we have developed. How to devise ways to integrate information, analysis, and action is a daunting task. It is one ingredient in the search for better ways to manage conflicting goals.

But I do not wish to overemphasize the contribution of research to the development of policy. Indeed, the efforts to rationalize the process can be stultifying. Albert O. Hirschman has argued about the importance of ignorance in planning.

> If, at the outset, the difficulties that were to beset a project had been foreseen, it would never have been undertaken. But when the difficulties arose human ingenuity solved them. Planners underestimate the capacity of society to meet problems: the benevolent hand of providence, therefore, conceals from them the difficulties in their way. . . . The most successful decisions have an element of gambling, an entrepreneurial brashness that refuses to be daunted by the endless, plausible possibilities of failure.[32]

These risks can be informed by analysis, but should not be bound by it. Parenthetically, I believe that one of the dangers of advocacy planning, which tries to help local groups develop social plans, is that the experts will fetter the creativity of neighborhood groups by exposing them to the complexity of the decision process. Sophistication may cause commitment to falter, thus inhibiting the vitality of protest and social action.

I believe that the crucial substantive issue is the redistribution of resources to the ghetto, although it is certainly useful to try to capture more federal funds for the city. Yet the emphasis placed on trying to secure these non-local funds and to concentrate these in areas of need may detract from the equally important task of getting the city to commit more of its own resources to ghetto areas. It is crucial to develop a system of accounts to document the trends in the redistribution of national and local resources. We need to monitor whether the poor and those at the bottom income level of society get more in absolute and in relative terms, or whether we have only made a gesture of action without materially affecting their level of living.

NOTES

1. Jacques Ellul, *The Technological Society* (New York: Knopf, 1964), p. 253.
2. Isaiah Berlin, *Two Concepts of Liberty,* An Inaugural Lecture, Oxford University, October 1958 (Oxford, England: Clarendon Press, 1966), p. 3.
3. *Ibid.,* pp. 52–53.
4. *Ibid.,* p. 54.
5. Richard Titmuss, *Income Distribution and Social Change: A Study in Criticism* (London: Allen and Unwin, 1963), pp. 187–188.
6. Erving Goffman, "On Cooling the Mark Out," *Psychiatry: Journal of the Study of Interpersonal Relations,* Vol. 15, No. 4 (November 1952).
7. D. V. Donnison, "Concensus and Conflict in Urban Development," London School of Economics, unpublished paper, n.d., p. 2.
8. "Poverty: The Republicans," editorial, *The New York Times,* September 17, 1968.
9. T. H. Marshall, "Citizenship and Social Class," *Sociology at the Crossroads and Other Essays* (London: Heineman Book Publishers, Ltd., 1963), pp. 90 and 100.
10. Nathan Glazer, "The Negro's Stake in America's Future," *The New York Times Magazine,* September 22, 1968, p. 30.
11. John R. Seeley, *The Americanization of the Unconscious* (New York: Lippincott, 1967), p. 284.
12. See Chapter 20.
13. T. W. Fowle, *The Poor Law* (London: Macmillan, 1881), p. 50.
14. Donnison, *op. cit.,* p. 10.
15. *Economic Report of the President* (Washington D.C.: U.S. Government Printing Office, January 1967), p. 102.
16. *Ibid.*
17. The policies of cutting the budget have not proved to be altogether effective, because the cuts were offset by a rise in expenditures in the six areas of the budget that Congress exempted from reductions. The net effect was to leave the Federal expenditure level unchanged.
18. U.S. Congress, Joint Economic Committee, *Hearings before the Subcommittee on Fiscal Policy,* 90th Congress, 2d Session, 1968, pp. 117–118.
19. *Ibid.,* p. 115.
20. U.S. Congress, Joint Economic Committee, *Economic Analysis of Public Investment Decisions: Interest Rate Policy and Discounting,* Report of the Subcommittee on Economy in Government, 90th Congress, 2d Session, 1968, p. 1.
21. Andrew Shonfield, *Modern Capitalism* (London: Oxford University Press, 1966), p. 229.
22. William Gorham, "PPBS: Its Scope and Limits: Notes of a Practitioner," *Public Interest,* No. 8 (1967).
23. At the level of tools there remains disagreement on the appropriate discount rate to use. Yet the final evaluation of an investment also depends on whether a high or low discount rate is employed. Variations in the rate can change the evaluation from where benefits exceed or equal costs to where costs exceed benefits. Joint Economic Committee, *op. cit.,* pp. 20–21.

24. Irving Kristol, "The New Regulators," *Fortune* (June 15, 1968), pp. 125–128.
25. Peter Marris, "The Strategy for Decision" (London: The Institute for Community Planning) (mimeo.), p. 8.
26. U.S. Congress, Joint Economic Committee, *The Planning-Programming-Budgeting System: Progress and Potentials*, Hearings before the Subcommittee on Economy in Government, 90th Congress, 1st Session, 1967, p. 9.
27. Robert A. Dahl and Charles E. Lindblom, *Politics, Economics and Welfare* (New York: Harper Torchbooks, 1953), p. 198.
28. Allan Peacock, *The Welfare Society*, Unservile State Paper No. 2 (London: Merritt and Hatcher, 1966), p. 17.
29. U.S. Congress, Joint Economic Committee, *Income Maintenance Programs*, Hearings before the Subcommittee on Fiscal Policy, 90th Congress, 2d Session, 1968, Vol. I: Proceedings (Washington, D.C.: U.S. Government Printing Office, 1968). p. 130.
30. Roland N. McKean, *Public Spending* (New York: McGraw Hill, 1968), p. 19.
31. W. Arthur Lewis, "Planning Public Expenditures," *National Economic Planning*, Max F. Millikan, ed., (New York: Columbia University Press, 1967), pp. 211–212.
32. Albert O. Hirschman, "The Principle of the Hiding Hand," *Public Interest*, No. 6 (Winter 1967), pp. 10–23.

Chapter 14

Social Stability and Black Ghettos: A Conservative Choice

"Welfare colonialism," once a cherished metaphor of radicals, has today achieved such widespread currency as to be a simple statement of fact. Nixon has even been forthright about it all. During the 1968 Presidential campaign, he suggested that all the black militants really want is "a share of the wealth and a piece of the action." This requires, he said, measures that would help produce "black ownership" from which would flow "black pride, black jobs, black opportunity, and, yes, black power."[1]

Humphrey supported a National Urban Development Bank in which federal funds would help finance high-risk ghetto business, which would help nourish developing black capital. A bipartisan group of senators in Congress (including Democrats Harris, Mondale, and Ribicoff and Republican Javits) have introduced and managed to get passed in the Senate the "Community Self-Determination Act," which is designed to create community-controlled business enterprises that would permit the people of the community "to utilize a share of the profits of . . . [these] enterprises to provide needed social services."[2]

Finally, we have the National Urban Coalition, affili-

Reprinted by permission of the publisher from *Politics and the Ghetto* by Roland Warren (ed.), (New York: Atherton, 1970), pp. 44–56.

ated with about fifty local coalitions. Each is designed to create a local alliance among business, religious, civil rights, and municipal leaders. The New York Urban Coalition has created a Task Force on Economic Development, which provides for two corporations; one offers managerial and technical advice to slum businessmen, and the other supplies short-term financing to ghetto businesses classified by banks as projects of high risk.[3]

In all these efforts, reports, and rhetorical flourishes it should be noted that the "blacks" and the "poor" are used interchangeably. This is a change from the rhetoric of the delinquency prevention programs (under Kennedy) and the poverty program (under Johnson), when it seemed politically unacceptable to have a national program for blacks; a war against poverty, it was believed, could appeal to all. We have now come so far as to admit in our language that most blacks are poor and many poor are black but we still blur the distinctions between the issue of race and the issue of class.

In a critique Nathan Glazer points excitedly to what he regards as one of the glaring omissions of the Report of the Commission on Civil Disorders; namely, its failure to take into account the middle-class Negro and the secure working-class Negro in its interpretation of the causes of urban unrest. "This is the missing man in the present crisis," says Glazer. "And yet he must be a key factor both in the analysis of the problem . . . and in the solution of the problem."[4]

The Glazer thesis about the missing middleman hints at the reasons why the political conservatives would advocate what appears to be a program based upon a more radical ideology. To see the matter more clearly, let me quote another sociological analysis, on the causes of ghetto instability, by Norton Long. Long's position can be briefly summarized as follows: in American society, many ethnic-commercial enclaves have created a government and economy of their own and from this political and economic base a social structure has emerged which assures social stability. However, the pattern in the Negro community is significantly different. Here a truncated occupational structure—with the top and upper-middle occupations cut off—has developed. It is dominated by lower-class Negroes and a noticeable absence of black commercial interests. And in this community all major forms of power reside largely in the white community. "The Negro middle class until recently has been escapist [and] . . . where it cannot physically flee it has sought physical co-existence and spiritual isolation. . . . The outstanding fact is that middle-class Negroes do not govern the ghetto. They are afraid of it." Black communities have witnessed the emergence of the lower class as the only authentic and indigenous culture made possible by the facts of a missing middle class—which even today absents itself from exercising leadership in community affairs—and control by an alien race. The combination of these ingredients has produced political instability and an economy of the "hustle," "cashing-in," the welfare dole.

In other words, "the costs of a purely lower-class culture of immediate consumption have been a failure to make use of the economic avenues of upward mobility."

This, then, is one interpretation of the causes of social unrest. The solution would lie in creating a black middle class. A transition of leadership is needed, not dissimilar to the colonial transition during which blacks are taught self-government by departing white rulers. "The key question is whether there exists or can rapidly be produced sufficient middle-class cadres to govern the black-governed city. . . . The greatest fear is clearly that the middle-class Negroes . . . cannot dominate the lower-class culture of Ghetto life." Presumably, then, the Negro middle-class leadership could more effectively police its own lower-class culture if it had both the authority and the capability of exercising that leadership. By altering the truncated structure in black communities, it would be possible "to break the debilitating dependence on white financing."[5]

The development of a Negro middle class appeals to anxious concerns about social stability, the containment of social pathology, the dangers of serious economic redistribution programs, control of lower-class culture, and the resort to interlocuteurs to enable whites to negotiate with blacks. There would appear to be a powerful, "conservative" network for black power.

A review of the rationale set out in Section 2 of the Community Self-Determination Act helps to make understandable why the argument for black capital has so much appeal to conservative thought. Here are some selected quotations:

> Programs and policies which tax some to support others offer no hope and no opportunity to those who have the capacity to become productive . . .
>
> Such a program should be designed to permit the people of a community to utilize a share of the profits of community-sponsored enterprises to provide needed social services, thereby reducing the burden of taxation upon the rest of society. . . .
>
> Order, stability, and progress can be achieved only when the people of a community actively participate in and are responsible for their own affairs in such areas as education . . . [and] economic development. . . .
>
> As that goal is approached, government incentives should be correspondingly phased out and government investments repaid, leaving the once dependent people to make their way as independent, unsubsidized participants in our national life.

The aims that inspire a conservative coalition to support black power and black capital are obvious. Taxation to pay for the benefits to the poor is viewed as a burden on society; hence, the poor should pay for their own services out of the profits of their community corporations. Federal financing of these corporations is only a temporary expedient, for the ideal is to make the program self-liquidating. Finally, the object is to promote order, stability, and progress. The assumption is that these goals reinforce each other. A compelling case could be made that token programs promote frustration and create instability. Note the list of limitations imposed on Community Development Boards. They "would not be authorized to issue or deal in securities, engage in acceptable financing, sell insurance, offer credit cards or make credit guarantees." These limitations seem designed to exclude Neighborhood Corporations from the high-profit sectors of business.

In some community action programs, we find codified a similar theory about how the restoration of leadership and authority would contribute to the creation of greater community cohesion, as the old ethnic leaderships are able to reassert their control over a more Americanized youth.[6] This theory of the causes of delinquency and crime saw the solution in a competent community in which established middle-class leadership would effectively be able to control its own affairs, including the policing of its youth. Competence could be achieved through the processes of community organization and citizen participation for the purposes of leadership development.

In short, an economically integrated community is more likely to be a socially stable one. Class, rather than race, seems to be more crucial in understanding the sources of social unrest. As individuals improve their economic situation, they abandon a community lacking stable leadership and, therefore, unable to control its members, especially its young. Clearly, as an abstract theory, there is much to commend this argument.

AN ASSESSMENT OF THE THEORY
AND THE SOCIAL POLICIES BASED ON IT

I wish to pose some questions about the validity, effectiveness, and relevance of the thesis, which must rest on the assumption that the principles of reform which applied in the past apply as well to events today.

The colonial model calls for a transition period during which leadership is transferred from the white to the black community. During this period, training for leadership is crucial. However, black leaders often criticize this approach because they feel that capability already exists in the ghetto. Perhaps the people are unlettered, but they are also shrewdly intelligent, with a demonstrated ability to adapt with creativity and ingenuity to an exploitative environment. According to this interpretation, social unrest is the product of a revolt against exploitation, rather than the result of the incompetence and indifference of the middle class in policing and governing its own lower class.

Yet, I would have to raise another objection concerning the motivation of some white political leaders in encouraging certain elements of the development of black power, namely the middleman. White America tries to create a black middle-class leadership to act as a broker, as a middleman between the white and the black community. White political leaders have no one to negotiate with during periods of confrontation. They are dismayed by the political style of black militants which demands morality and justice but lacks a concrete program with negotiable terms. The conflict between Ralph Abernathy and Bayard Rustin over the agenda of reform sought by the 1968 Poor People's Campaign is one example of different interpretations about the politics of confrontation. The insistence on leadership thus arises less from the desire to create an orderly transition from white domination to black control, than from the wish to create the machinery whereby a dialogue between the rulers and the ruled can be restored.

Thus far I have tried to ask whether the theory is valid and whether the colonial analogy illuminates or obscures the underlying motives behind urban social unrest. Even if we acknowledge the validity of the theory, we need to inquire if it can be effective in the political and economic environment of the 1960s. The issues involved will be briefly considered.

1. Class antagonism within the black community is very deep. Black anger against the "Uncle Toms" is quite different from earlier Irish anger vented against the "lace curtain Irish," who by "buying in" were seen as having "sold out." Hence, the middle-class broker role may be much harder to play today, both in terms of policing the lower class and negotiating with the white middle class. But it is not only that black leaders may not represent their constituencies; neither can white leaders deliver programs requiring state and federal resources that they cannot control locally. A loose association, like the Urban Coalition, of elite interest groups with representation from the black community cannot *assure* the implementation of programs, which the interchange among elites may inspire.

The rise of a Negro middle class, if also accompanied by the failure of the lower income groups to improve their situation, may create within the black community two groups as divided from each other as black are from white communities. It is unlikely that the rise of the Negro middle class will improve the relative position of the lower class as well. The appeals to individual mobility and collective advancement clash. As a result, the growth of inequalities can be expected, and accompanying it will be greater instability. The same arguments used in support of reducing inequalities when whites are compared with blacks hold as well within the Negro community. Reducing inequalities within the Negro community will contribute to a more just society and it may even be more crucial in producing tranquility than the creation of an elite middle class. Accordingly, the theory that the increased affluence of the Negro middle class will contribute to social stability seems a doubtful proposition. Some attempts to study political stability in developing societies have also demonstrated that a marginal increase in wealth, if not accompanied by the reduction of inequalities, can lead to political instability.

2. Cities in the United States are suffering financial, administrative, political, and economic crises, as deeply disturbing as the crisis of social unrest and rioting. Thus the transfer of power from whites to blacks may not be much of a prize today. Political control by blacks over a decentralized but financially starved school system or community action program, or even over city government, may serve only to intensify the sense of frustration. For example, black Mayors of large cities are discovering the disjunction between responsibility and power. Moreover, as the conflict between butter and guns continues (as witnessed by the 10 percent tax surcharge and the six billion dollar expenditure cut by the federal government), the amount of resources available for urban schools and poverty programs may (in the face of inflation and rising population) actually decline, thus forcing these benefit systems to act as rationing devices in the distribution of scarcity. The military budget in 1967 was 82 billion dollars a year, of which 30 billion dollars was for the Vietnam War. This level of expenditure generates one million military jobs directly and two million jobs indirectly, according to an estimate by Senator William Proxmire. Some economists feel that even in the post-Vietnam era this budget will not be substantially reduced. Accordingly, if no effective pressure for reducing military expenditure is developed even after the war, the clash between butter and guns may continue. Rationing of social services will, of course, result in further exclusion from institutions and intensification of the alienation which black control is designed to reduce.

But, curiously, social progress as well as urban failure makes the transfer to black power even more difficult. "Fifty years of social reform," Moynihan asserted, "has pretty well destroyed the basis of working class politics in this country."[7] He was, of course, referring to those reforms which were aimed at braking the power of political bosses to distribute patronage through their control of city jobs. The Civil Service Commission, for example, was designed, at least in principle, to assure that impartial criteria were used in the hiring of public officials. But the progress achieved by one generation is the target of reform of the next. Today, efforts are being made to reverse these gains, as we discover the socially useful functions of what earlier liberal reformers defined as corruption. Moynihan persuasively presents the case as follows:

Having destroyed the power of the local bosses, we learn that the people feel powerless. Having put an end to patronage and established merit systems in civil service, we find the poor unqualified and without jobs. Having banished felons from public employment, we find enormous numbers of men who need jobs have criminal records.[8]

There has occurred an assault on these liberal reforms. For example, the centralization of the school system and its administrative separation from city politics may have done much to reduce corruption in one era, but it has also created despair in another. Similarly, the long arduous struggle by labor to win job security and protection of working conditions for its members must be considered one of the great reforms in its day. Yet, as the Ocean Hill-Brownsville conflict illustrates, the achievements of the past inhibit the progress of today.

Or consider the reliance on credentials as the test of merit, that is, judging competence by formal academic achievement or scores earned on formal tests, rather than through performance. "Credentialism," as S. M. Miller calls it, is today being challenged as a criterion of exclusion rather than a measure of the quality of work performed. Employers have tended to over-define the competencies needed to perform occupational jobs. Hence our trained workers are more likely to experience frustrations which affect the quality of their work. The lowering of academic and social standards may thus enhance rather than erode the quality of employment outputs.[9] The hiring of non-professionals and the bypassing of the Civil Service requirements are also illustrative of this trend, away from credentialism.

3. The increased concentration of economic power will make it more difficult to promote the ideals of black capital self-help and self-sufficiency. The creation of black capital will largely be encouraged by stimulating the development of small businesses by reserving the Negro market to Negro businessmen. But the commitment to the resuscitation of small business in the ghetto will pose substantial problems. For one thing, all small businesses tend to have a high death rate, and there is every reason to assume that the rates of business failure within the Negro community will be as high, if not higher, than they are in the rest of the community. Second, as the size of the middle income group (annual family income of $7,000) expands to half of the Negro families, as it is now among whites, "the large national corporations will find the Negro market increasingly attractive. Thus, these corporations are not about to withdraw and allow the Negro businessman to treat the Negro market as his special preserve."[10] It seems doubtful that a clash between the needs of black and white capital will redound to the benefit of blacks.

There is also much discussion about locating more large industrial firms in the ghetto, and creating more jobs, as well as a black economic elite rooted not in the ownership of capital but in its management. It is doubtful, though, whether any of this will go very far. There has been a continued exodus of manufacturing industries from central cities for the past twenty-five years because it is simply not efficient for low capital, high labor intensive industry to function on the high land and tax rates in center cities.[11] And, finally, of course, account must be taken of the changing distribution in the occupational structure, which, while it has not altogether eliminated the need for unskilled labor nor created the disjunction of work and income which some have claimed, nevertheless has reduced the need for the kinds of skills for which the Negro is most heavily employed today. This trend will lead toward increased public employment rather than the development of black capital or decentralized private corporations.

But even if the creation of black capital, with its intended emphasis on self-help and self-sufficiency, were successful, it is much more likely to develop greater economic interdependency between the white and the black community and, hence, a more subtle form of economic control. In periods of rapid economic expansion (the gross national product increased by more than 40 billion dollars in the first half of 1968), industry may be willing to buy stability at a *token* level by encouraging the development of black capital through loan guarantees, technical assistance, and other devices. But as the size of the Negro middle class grows (Brimmer's argument) and/or as fluctuations in the economy produce periods of recession and a decline in industry profits, then economic realities may force a reassessment of the acceptability of the principle of black capital. In periods of economic decline, white economic domination of the ghetto may become visible, and anger will be directed not only against welfare colonialism and political control of the ghetto, but against white capitalism as well.

If this interpretation seems valid it would seem important to reach out to the economic citadels in the white community and tackle directly the problem of prejudice, especially at the levels of professional managerial and white collar jobs. The legal machinery needed to open up rather than wall off social equality is already in hand. A good deal of legislation already exists to assure Negroes the right to vote, the right to equality of treatment before the courts, the right to access to all publicly financed services, and the right to equal employment and open housing. But we have failed to provide the regulatory agencies with the power, the manpower, and the financial support which would permit them to implement these objectives.

Finally, we need to consider whether the missing man thesis distorts the priorities of public policy by directing attention to the problems of stability rather than justice. While it is true that liberals, militants, and conservatives have all expressed concern with black power, the goals they seek are, after all, quite different. One group is interested in a transfer of power. It wants different actors to fill the present slots in the structure which distributes positions of power, authority, and influence. The new actors ought to be middle-class blacks rather than middle-class whites. In the transfer power strategy, one major goal seems to be that of social stability and one major obstacle seems to be that of competence. There is fear on the part of whites that power will be transferred without capability. What is wanted by the whites is competent blacks who can act as power brokers negotiating with the white community in terms that will keep the ghetto cool.

But for other groups, more than a transfer of power to achieve social stability is being sought. Black power and student power have much in common in their search for a different society. They argue that the roots of American society which have produced the Vietnam War and the Negro crisis must themselves be poisoned. They want to tear out these roots and to plant afresh. But they are uncertain about what new seeds are requisite to produce blossoms of love, justice, and humanity. The older radicals assumed that the need for authority and bureaucracy would wither away in the good society. But if these are the very source of evil and the withering society is repudiated, then we are left with cynicism or ideals without a program. The former leads to dropping out and the latter to a revolution without a platform.

In conclusion, to break up the ghetto, social policy must emphasize the reduction of inequalities of income; full employment, based not on a national average, but on the disaggregated estimates for special groups (such as the ghetto residents and Negro youth); and, finally, a vigorous program to reduce "institutional racism rather than personal racism" by creating "social and economic institutions in which all peoples have a sense of identification."[12]

Even if the theory of the missing man is valid, which I doubt, it does not follow from it that workable solutions in a changing political economic and class situation can be derived by social policies designed to reinstate the missing man in an economically integrated community. There is often found an asymmetry in the development of policy, since the solution of the problems may be better achieved by methods other than those which attack the causes frontally. In the absence of evidence which can validate or refute the theory, it is perhaps best to pursue it, but along with other policies which are based on antagonistic assumptions. I would support, in short, a politics of inconsistency, directed at simultaneously breaking up the ghetto and strengthening it. The creative resolution of dilemmas cannot be reconciled with the ideological search for consistency, nor can it be allowed to rest on an arbitrary division of the world into the forces of good and evil.

NOTES

1. *The New York Times*, May, 1968.
2. *Congressional Record*, Senate, July 24, 1966.
3. *The New York Times*, June 11, 1968.
4. Nathan Glazer, "The Problem with American Cities," *New Society* (March 21, 1968), p. 3.

5. Norton Long, "Politics and Ghetto Perpetuation," in Roland Warren, ed., *Politics and the Ghetto* (New York: Atherton, 1969, pp. 31–43.

6. For a discussion of this theory, see Peter Marris and Martin Rein, *Dilemmas of Social Reform: Poverty and Community Action in the United States* (New York: Atherton, 1967).

7. Daniel P. Moynihan, "The Politics of Stability," a paper presented at the National Board Meeting, Americans for Democratic Action, September 23, 1967.

8. *The New York Times*, June 5, 1968.

9. "A hospital worker serving a local Negro administrator may demand no more in wages than he obtained from an absentee bureaucracy, but he may deliver more services. A pupil in a school administered by a board of local citizens may cost no more to educate than now, but the pupil may find the experience more relevant. His education, thus, may become more productive." Ghetto control of social services may not be feasible if non-professionals are not recruited to man the social services bureaucracies. Quoted in *The New York Times*, July 17, 1968.

10. Quoted from a commencement address at Clark College presented by Mr. Andrew F. Brimmer, a Negro member of the Federal Reserve Board. *The New York Times*, June 4, 1968.

11. For discussion of some of these issues, see Sumner M. Rosen's account of "Better Mousetrap: Reflections on Economic Development in the Ghetto" (New York: New York University, New Careers Development Center, 1968) (mimeo.).

12. *The New York Times,* April 28, 1968, quoting Bayard Rustin.

Chapter 15

Social Work in Search of a Radical Profession

There is a great deal of interest today in the radicalization of professions. A restless search for relevance to public policy is being undertaken in social work, psychiatry, psychology, city planning, sociology, and political science, to name a few fields. One form that the radicalization is taking is to question afresh the role of the professional association in the area of public policy. In the last few years, this reassessment has been most striking. At the 1968 National Conference on Social Welfare, for example, black activists pressed the conference to change its preamble, which defines the conference as a forum for discussion that "does not take an official position on controversial issues." The city planning profession has split recently into what Gans calls the "progressive and conservative wings: with the former calling for social planning to reduce economic and racial inequality, and the latter defending traditional physical planning and the legitimacy of middle class values."[1] Sociologists seem to be especially vigorous in calling for a radical sociology. Gouldner's review of Parsons' book *American Sociology* captured the discontent seen at the 1968 Conference of the American Sociological Society. He quotes one angry sociologist who asserted "the profession of sociology is an outgrowth of nineteenth century European traditionalism and conservatism wedded to twentieth century American cor-

Reprinted by permission of the National Association of Social Workers, from *Social Work*, Vol. 15, No. 2 (April 1970).

poration liberalism. . . . The professional eyes of the sociologists are on the down people, and the professional palm of the sociologists is stretched toward the up people."[2]

Gouldner and Seeley define a radical social science as one critical of the emerging forms of the welfare state, which they view as a new social control system seeking "conformity as the price of welfare." Reform should not be limited to "melioristic efforts within the system," they hold, but should "develop alternatives to the *status quo*."[3]

The furor about radicalization has also taken another form. It is directed not only at extending the role of the professional as citizen and member of a professional organization, but at changing the very essence of his professional activity. In this sense we are witnessing a search for radical professionalism rather than a quest for the professional who acts as a radical. Reassessment of the professional role is taking two major forms. The first is a reexamination of the profession's sources of legitimacy, a process that has been accompanied by a growing disenchantment with its avowed role as gatekeeper of tested knowledge. Some social workers are now trying to derive their legitimacy—their right to intervene—from the clients to be served rather than from the technology they have accumulated. It is not uncommon to find in the new professional literature a call for social workers to "join with . . . clients in a search for and reaffirmation of their dignity. . . . Let us become mercenaries in their service—let us, in a word, become their advocates. . . . Let our clients use us . . . to argue their cause, to maneuver, to obtain their rights and their justice, to move the immovable bureaucrats."[4] This principle of accountability to the consumer departs from traditional professionalism, which has always been colleague-oriented rather than client-oriented, a distinction captured by Everett Hughes who defined a professional as someone respected by his colleagues and a quack as someone respected by his clients.

The second broad approach to radicalizing professional activity has been to advocate intervention in larger systems, such as the community, rather than in the life of the individual. Today community intervention is an idea in good currency among the helping professions. Witness the growth of community psychiatry, community psychology, and community organization in social work. One need only read such journals as *Psychiatry and Social Science, American Psychologist,* or *Social Work* to recognize this shift to social action with neighborhood groups in the professions. This shift will be discussed in further detail later and I will argue that, by itself, community intervention represents an inadequate index of radical activity.

These two trends suggest a basis on which to elicit the creed of social work as a profession. But before proceeding the obstacles to formulating a professional belief system will be discussed. It is hoped that a review of these impediments will serve as an introduction to a discussion of the development of a radical social work creed.

OBSTACLES TO A PROFESSIONAL CREED

Throughout the social work literature, one finds references to social work as a value-laden profession. Hence it might seem an easy task to summarize the values that comprise its belief system and then to explore the relevance of this creed to today's urban problems. But the literature deals with values only globally; the discourse is confined to a high level of abstraction. For example, there is the widely held proposition that each individual has dignity and worth. Surely this is an important statement but, unless its implications and consequences are drawn for professional practice, it is not a useful framework for action.[5]

What is more, social work literature contains the implicit assumption that there is a consensus on professional values and one must join in this consensus as a precondition for professional practice. All values are presented as though they were mutually reinforcing. The possibility of conflict in values is never suggested although, in actuality, opposite sets of values are often embraced simultaneously. Timms, a prominent British social worker, notes that "caseworkers have asserted a faith in the potentialities of the human being to change himself and his society, whilst on the other hand, espousing a group of psychological theories which appear to place severe limitations on the capacity of individuals to change."[6] One obstacle, then, is to recognize that the values in a professional creed are problematic rather than self-evident and that they frequently conflict.

Another obstacle arises from the difficulty of defining the profession. What, after all, is social work? An exhaustive study of social work education in the early 1950s concluded that "social work and social workers should be looked upon as evolving concepts that are as yet too fluid for precise definition."[7] By the late 1960s this fluidity has hardly become solidified. Indeed, to the extent that social work is involved in a fundamental reassessment of its major organizing principles, it is even more fluid today than it has been in the past. Because social workers serve as policy planners, reformers, social critics, and clinicians, it is difficult to identify the single professional creed that binds together these diverse activities.

A further problem in identifying the professional creed arises from the inability to separate clearly the procedural and substantive aspects of professional activity. Social work, like other professions, was influenced by the pragmatism of John Dewey. Dewey stressed the continuity of experience and the importance of process. In accord with this formulation, means and ends became blurred, professional technology became defined in terms of process, and social workers came to emphasize method and neglect purpose. Therefore, it is exceedingly difficult to find out what social workers believe and what they are trying to accomplish. There is nothing more challenging to a social agency than to ask what its objective is. The emphasis on process rather than outcome tends to obscure the role of ideology. What social workers believe must be inferred from what they say and do.

The last obstacle to be discussed is the disparity between rhetoric and reality, between what professionals say and do. A failure to implement ideals can be identified throughout the history of social work. The field developed out of a deterrent ideology, which sought alternatives to sending poor persons to the workhouse and would permit them to stay in the community while at the same time keep welfare rolls low. The common premise underlying the celebrated Elberfield system in Germany, the work of Thomas Chalmers, and later the activities of the Charity Organization Society was the use of strict investigation and close supervision of paupers as a way of making life on the dole uncomfortable and intolerable. So harsh were the ideals of political economy on which the social work ideology of the nineteenth century was based, that it is not surprising to discover that humanitarianism and common sense inhibited their full expression. Reality and rhetoric diverge today as well. For example, social workers may believe that a precondition of good casework is full employment, a decent income, adequate social services, and a sound physical environment. But if this rhetoric were insisted upon, there would be no casework for the poor.

From a review of these obstacles, it seems reasonable to conclude that the search for a single, common professional creed is illusory. There are many creeds and many belief systems. The question now becomes: what are the critical components of the multiple belief systems? I think these may be found in an examination of the different orientations in social work to behavioral goals and change processes.

STANDARDS OF BEHAVIOR

Norms and standards can be examined from several perspectives—standards that judge client, professional, or organizational behavior. In this analysis, the primary focus will be on the standards or norms of acceptable social behavior to which social work clients are held accountable. From this focus we are examining the social purposes of social work practice. What then are these norms? Titmuss has astutely observed that "the attitudes that society adopts to its deviants, and especially its poor and politically inarticulate deviants, reflects its ultimate values. . . . We must learn to understand the moral presuppositions underlying our action."[8]

One of the principal moral presuppositions underlying social work practice in this country has been acceptance of society's linkage of work and income. With the exception of keeping women and the aged out of the labor force during the Depression, social workers have supported those policies designed to get the able-bodied poor to work. Industrial society is organized around the preservation of the middle class ethic that rewards the industrious. But are there criteria by which to judge men other than market-productivity standards? To respect the dignity of man and to assert that each man has inherent value must clearly repudiate these dominant norms.

The issue of conforming to established standards is crucial to the professional creed. It therefore requires further discussion. For example, school performance is judged by the individual's ability to meet competitive standards (based on mastery of a body of information) and on socialization for achievement. The ideal of helping people reach whatever level of performance they are capable of, that is, self-actualization without reference to minimum standards, is a radical ideal that challenges accepted social standards. Teachers and social workers know that educational attainment largely determines life chances and they strive to equip their pupils and clients to compete. Hence they are naturally attracted to those most likely to succeed, those whose achievements will reward the social workers' and teachers' efforts. It is after all not perversity but realism that leads professionals to make this assessment. The school cannot care equally for the education of every child, whatever his skill, unless society values all men for whatever contributions they can make. And thus, our performance-market-productivity-oriented society is not willing to insure this.

Social workers must choose whether to help individuals to meet prevailing standards or whether to challenge the standards themselves. If they choose to challenge values, they cannot do so by imposing new ones. As professionals they must show that established norms conflict with more fundamental values in the society or that they are inconsistent or irrelevant to the specific task at hand.

In most situations, there is an overwhelming urge to bypass the issue altogether by arguing that happiness and self-fulfillment can only be achieved when individuals conform to the standards of the society. Thus, helping people conform to the work ethic in our society assures their contentment because the conforming man is the happy man. This dubious proposition is lucidly challenged in *The People Specialists,* a book about the human relations movement in industry. Personnel men share much in common with social workers. The personnel movement has two conflicting roots—one in scientific management, which was concerned with the study of men at work to determine how their material output could best be increased, the other in social welfare, which was concerned with improving the workers' levels of living. Which aim were the personnel workers to accept: "to make workers more productive or to make them happier?" Personnel theory, like social work theory, proceeded under the assumption that to do one is to do the other. But as the author shows "there is no clear evidence to support any direct relationship between high morale and high productivity." Indeed, there is some contradictory evidence: "in most corporations maturity is not a prized quality. On the contrary, the infantile qualities of passivity, dependence, submissiveness seem to be the hallmarks of good employees."[9]

This is not an abstract philosophical debate. Most social work practice whether in industry, prisons, probation, public welfare, or mental health must accept the conflict between the individual's needs and the imposed and often arbitrary standards of society. When such conflicts arise, social workers must decide whether they support or challenge these established standards. Of course, some may try to define themselves as neutral arbitrators between contending parties. A radical ideal holds that the social worker must choose sides and is obliged to protect the individual against the system.

Industrial social work, which never fully blossomed in the United States, had to make 'such a choice. The difference between the French and Indian schemes illustrates the general dilemma. The French hired social workers on the assumption that happy workers were productive because they came to work regularly and were not distracted by marital, health, or other problems. In India it was assumed that the firm had more power than the individual and there was a natural tendency for power to corrupt. Hence the individual needed to be protected against this more powerful system. The social worker's role was to even out the odds.

INTERVENTION STRATEGIES

Theories of change can be divided into two broad categories.[10] There are those that accept social conditions as a constraint and conclude that change must start with the individual. They are based on the premise that if the individual himself would change, he could begin to alter the external resources in the social environment. In contrast, other theories treat external conditions as the targets of change, rather than as constraints. Their argument is that man cannot change until the world he lives in is transformed. His material circumstances must change first because man's emotional responses are adaptations to the external circumstances in which he lives.

Because what are implied are two alternative courses of action this distinction must be made as concrete as possible. As an example, the dichotomy just drawn will be applied to the area of manpower policy for disadvantaged groups. One approach emphasizes direct efforts to modify the attitudes of the disadvantaged before introducing them into job situations. This is based on the principle of preparing people in advance for a change in their environment. The other approach brings the subemployed into a job situation first, thus changing their occupational environment as a precondition for individual change. Social services are then looked upon as supports to help the individual handle the demands of his new environment. This shift from preparation to support is important in understanding the role of social services and social work in manpower training programs.

One further approach must be mentioned. It is the position that change in the character of the individual can be brought about by the process of social action. As man organizes to change his world, he changes himself. This change theory is more subtle than the others. It appeals to the conservative-traditional camp as well, where it is more popularly known as a self-help ideology by which individuals take action on their own behalf. There is radical and revolutionary support for it as well. In a thoughtful report on *Race Relations and Social Change,* Coleman explains the revolutionary argument for participation, as revealed in the writings of Sorel, Sartre, and Mao Tse-Tung:

> . . . Participation in revolutionary action transforms the previously apathetic masses, by giving them a goal and the hope of achieving the goal. The revolutionary action itself and the rewards of success it brings to hard work create men who are no longer bound by traditional customs, inhibited by ascribed authority patterns, and made apathetic by lack of hope. This psychological transformation, according to these authors, is a necessary prerequisite to the social and economic transformation. Applied to the case of Negroes in the United States, it would state that the real benefit of the civil rights movement is the psychological change it has produced and is producing in those Negroes active in it. A more radical application would be that only by engaging in a real revolution will Negroes be psychologically transformed in such a way that they can achieve their goals.[11]

But what if the external conditions do not succumb to action programs? This approach is not altogether explicit about this awkward question and how it might be resolved. One interpretation holds that even in failure, personality change can be achieved. The self-help position could argue that personal dignity is won by the process of striving to better one's conditions. Character is forged by the activity, rather than the outcome. The more radical position would appear to suggest that change can be brought about by the total submersion of the individual in the collectivity. Although his material circumstances may not be altered, his social-psychological environment has nevertheless been dramatically altered. Although social change approaches are often considered inherently radical, they are not. The purposes of social intervention theories, whether revolutionary or conservative, can be directed either at freeing men to build new standards or encouraging them to accept standards of prescribed behavior. It is for this reason that an intervention strategy, separated from the *purposes* of intervention, does not provide the basis for a creed.

Carried to its logical conclusion, this distinction between changing individuals and changing social conditions tends to break down. The assertion that the starting point for change is the individual is incomplete if it leaves out the political and hence environmental processes that have led to the creation of an organized effort to induce change in the individual. Moreover, the availability of an authentic helping person is in itself a change in the external environment if other human beings are accepted as environmental resources. Similarly, only considering a change in social conditions leaves out the intervening processes by which an altered world produces individual change. Why are some groups and individuals able to exploit changes in the external environment and others are not? Thus, when applied to specific situations, the distinction becomes less convincing. It is preferable to present a differentiated argument that specifies the conditions under which one or another theory of change is more appropriate. But in the absence of a scientific theory of change, passion and ideology have a rich soil in which to blossom. It is for this reason that in this paper these distinctions are treated as elements of an ideology.

A Typology of Social Work Ideologies

Standards of Behavior	Theories of Change	
	individual	social conditions
accept	traditional casework	community socio-therapy
	1	2
	3	4
challenge	radical casework	radical social policy

It should be emphasized again that the important generalization to be drawn from these observations is that both individual and social change theories can be used to accept or to repudiate established standards of behavior. Strategies of change can be used for different goals and, therefore, both goal and process became inseparable components of an ideology.

By dichotomizing each of the dimensions of standards and theories of intervention into a two by two table it is possible to identify four major professional creeds.

Traditional Casework

The literature of social casework abounds with references to helping the marginal, deviant, and mentally ill meet standards and, thereby, achieve self-actualization and fulfillment. That conformity is viewed as the road to self-fulfillment is evident.

As Kingsley Davis pointed out, advice about problems of living is given in terms of moral ideals rather than actual practice. It is assumed that "one can best secure mental health, best satisfy one's needs, by conforming."[12] The social worker is thus trapped into what Hughes has called the "fallacy of one hundred percentism"—the refusal to admit the possibility of less than complete acceptance of moral, legal, respectable norms for behavior.[13] It is not surprising then to find that Gordon Hamilton, a leading modern casework theoretician, describes the function of diagnostic casework as "adaptation to reality."[14] As Keith-Lucas pointed out, diagnostic casework "can be used to justify the caseworker's desire to urge or dwell on the moral standards of the community through identifying these with the client's 'reality.' "[15] Biestek makes the implications explicit: "the important fact to a caseworker is that these standards are realities in the client's life. . . . The client's personal adjustment must include a sound, realistic social adjustment, because as an individual he lives in a definite social community. . . . The function of the casework is to help the client accept and adjust to these standards."[16] Thus by falling prey to the fallacy of one hundred percentism, many caseworkers hold their clients to a higher standard of morality than the one to which the community itself adheres.

Throughout the literature of social work, a discerning reader can note that many social workers believe that the task of social work is "to reconcile the poor to their station in life . . . to plaster up the sores of an unjust society . . . to get the grit out of the administrative machinery—to persuade recalcitrant old ladies to go into institutions, to empty urgently needed hospital beds, to chivvy rent arrears from difficult tenants."[17] These are, after all, the various realities to which the clients of social work must adjust—the realities of the economy, racial injustice, and bureaucracy.[18] In an effort to discredit this interpretation of the social worker's function, Titmuss has pointed out that two questionable assumptions underlie the insistence on adaptation to reality.

> The first is that reality is something which the caseworker knows, but the client does not; the second is that if adaptation is genuinely to take place, reality must genuinely be accepted by the caseworker. The ultimate logic of this is to make the caseworker a prisoner of the collective *status quo*; consequently, she will have little or nothing to contribute to the shaping of the social policy. She will not, in fact, desire to do so.[19]

But this discussion of traditional social work is theoretical, being based only on what social workers say. Obviously, the literature may be subject to other interpretations. Only scattered empirical evidence is available on the attitudes and behavior of social workers, but these seem to support my exposition. I have found no study directly concerned with the issue of getting clients to meet standards of behavior; studies deal with agency rules or, more generally, with personal values.

In 1967 Rossi *et al.* analyzed welfare workers in fifteen cities who worked primarily with Negro clients. They reported that their sample "came out about evenly split on making decisions largely based on agency rules or largely on the circumstances of the client. However, the breakdown by race showed the whites considerably more rigid, with 54 percent (as compared with 40 percent of the Negroes) saying they usually obey the agency rules."[20]

Billingsley, in his study of professional child welfare workers in Boston, obtained data on the choices social workers make when their assessment of the needs of their clients conflicted with agency procedures. He discovered that "in spite of the social worker's intellectual and emotional commitment to meeting the needs of his clients," more than three-quarters complied with agency rules even when these conflicted with "the workers' own estimation of the needs of the client."[21]

McLeod and Meyer at the University of Michigan conducted a study in which they compared the values of professionals, non-professionals, and social work students on a number of value issues. One of these dealt with belief in change vs. tradition, that is, "the willingness to accept change as contrasted with the orientation that is committed to the traditional ways of the past." Their findings are suggestive. They found that the non-trained were oriented to the status quo (71 percent), but what was of special interest was the shift in values between those who were in training and those who were fully trained. Most students supported innovation while in training (54 percent), while most trained workers were committed to the status quo (52 percent).[22]

These findings are suggestive only, and it is hazardous to make firm generalizations based upon them. They do appear however to indicate that the dominant value commitment and behavior of professional social workers supports in theory and practice a posture of getting others to meet standards of acceptable behavior. They reveal the extent to which social workers personally comply with bureaucratic norms even when these conflict with clients' needs.

Radical Casework

Not all social workers are prisoners of the collective status quo when they work with individuals. Many overtly and covertly resist these pressures. Resistance to established norms can, as has been already suggested, take several forms. It can challenge the standards, either by appealing to other standards with which they conflict, or by showing that the standards themselves are inconsistent and lead to contradictory and unintended consequences. A latent functional analysis, when properly done, is, after all, a form of muckraking or social criticism. Gouldner's critique of practices in adoption offers an illuminating example.

> Adoption agencies require or recommend that adoptive parents be of the same religion as the mother of the adopted child, what proof is there that this practice is desirable or effective either for the child or for the parents? In this instance, it seems probable that the policy derives not from evidence of its effectiveness at all but from the pressure of various interest groups.
>
> It may well be most injurious to a child to be adopted by parents of a religious persuasion similar to that of his biological mother, if members of this denomination regard illegitimacy with moral revulsion. Yet, here, as in many other instances, agencies' practices are shaped by community pressures and legal requirements and do not rest on evidence of their effectiveness for the client's.[23]

Gouldner presents the hurtful consequences of certain adoption procedures in such a way that his statement becomes a useful instrument of social criticism. Critiques of this kind offer one framework from which a radical casework practice might emerge.

More typically, social workers try to activate those values that they accept as morally right and society accepts but fails to act on. They then organize their research and action to serve as moral witnesses, documenting the failure of society to implement the ideals it has already asserted in law or policy.

Another approach is suggested in the writing of Philip Lichtenberg. In a discussion of the prerequisites necessary for the cure of the psychotic, he asserts:

> If we compare the organizing principles relevant to a therapeutic community with those embodied in the present day organization of the society, we discover that the principles underlying the therapeutic community are superior. . . . Equality, cooperation, openness and frankness between persons at all levels of authority, two-way flow of communication with whatever hierarchies exist, control of the governed not only over themselves but over those who govern, preoccupation with one's true feelings rather than with masking one's attitudes, confrontation with poor communication so that it does not escalate difficulties, sexual freedom, etc., all of which have been found to be essential ingredients of [the] therapeutic community.[24]

It is the structure of the community that is faulty, since it lacks what the psychotic requires for his cure. Lichtenberg clearly insists that the world must be changed if the emotionally disabled are to be cured. Of course, Freud's work, which had an enormous influence on social work practice, is a brilliant example of a systematic critique of and challenge to society's standards of sexuality and its principles of individual responsibility.

Casework practice then can challenge the standards of society by showing that they are irrelevant or have hurtful consequences, that valid and relevant standards are not implemented, or that the standards men live by are faulty.

But the discerning reader might well ask: is radical casework an empty cell, logically plausible but nonexistent in reality? I resist accepting this formulation, for I am convinced that radical casework does exist. One form that it takes is when the caseworker acts as an insurgent within the bureaucracy in which he is employed, seeking to change its policies and purposes in line with the value assumptions he cherishes. Caseworkers can act as rebels within a bureaucracy, humanizing its established procedures and policies. One cannot read the literature in social casework today without finding some examples of radical casework. In the writings of Scott Briar, Henry Miller, and Irving Pilavin, one finds caseworkers repudiating the traditional norms of helping clients adapt to reality. They are at the frontier trying to find ways to make a radical casework live.[25]

Community Sociotherapy

Community sociotherapy has to do with the belief system which holds that such processes as organizing groups for self-help, protest, access to community facilities, or even revolution, can create a transformation of the individual personality. Participation in social action is viewed as a sociotherapeutic tool. Haryou, the Community Action Program in Harlem, put the argument as follows:

> If it is possible to establish a core program of social action, it would be reasonable to expect that the energies required, and which must be mobilized for constructive and desirable social change, would not then be available for anti-social and self-destructive patterns of behavior.[26]

The report claims, for example, that crime in Montgomery, Alabama, declined during the period of the civil rights protest.

This energy displacement theory was in an earlier period used to justify the notion that recreation reduced crime. It is a theory that explains how activism can be transformed into compliance. Other theories are also at hand, including claims for the positive effects on personal health of power, integration, cohesiveness, community competence, identity, and so forth. All of these have in common the proposition that as man tries to change his social condition, *he* changes in the process.

The attempt by sociologists to get social workers to use social action and self-help as strategies for promoting individual conformity has a long history. Part of the history that spans the twentieth century and has a consistency in ideology which would almost suggest a linear theory in its evolution will now be reviewed. The first example is drawn from Znaniecki and Thomas's study of the *Polish Peasant* written in 1918. The authors explain:

It is a mistake to suppose that a "community center" established by American social agencies can in its present form even approximately fulfill the social function of a Polish parish. It is an institution imposed from the outside instead of being freely developed by the initiative and cooperation of the people themselves. . . . Its managers usually know little or nothing of the traditions, attitudes, and native languages of the people with whom they have to deal and. . . . the "case method" which consists in dealing directly and separately with individuals and families . . . may bring efficient temporary help to the individual, it does not contribute to the social progress of the community nor does it possess much preventive influence in struggling against social disorganization. Both of these processes can be attained only by organizing and encouraging social self-help on a cooperative basis.[27]

The argument is clear. Organizing and encouraging self-help will reduce social disorganization. The failure to help the Polish immigrant conform to American standards, according to the author's criticism, is based on two factors—imposition by alien institutions, which today is called "welfare colonialism," and the individual case approach.

In the 1930s the prescription for action took an organized form in the Chicago Area Project under the leadership of Clifford Shaw and Henry McKay, when a social action program was launched to reduce crime and delinquency. Saul Alinsky was a student of sociology at the University of Chicago at the same time and, according to Morris Janowitz, "some of his notions of community action and organization are strikingly parallel to those developed in this project."[28] Perhaps so, but it seems that the distinguishing feature of this and the later programs the Chicago project inspired, is the absence of a political ideology and the commitment to sociotherapeutic aims. In the 1940s, New York University supported a project directed by Rudolph Wittenberg, that was designed to promote personality change through social action in East Harlem. In the 1950s, New York City's Youth Board Gang Project turned to community organization as a strategy to help create an integrated community that could reduce crime and delinquency. In the 1960s, community organization as sociotherapy can be found in Mobilization for Youth's program, which was originally conceived as a delinquency prevention program and was financed by the National Institute of Mental Health and the President's Committee on Delinquency and Youth Crime.[29]

The critique of social work in these examples was not directed at the purposes of intervention, but at its effectiveness. Sociotherapy was not a new ideology, but a new technology for getting marginal groups to meet standards. Znaniecki and Thomas's criticism is now the established orthodoxy accepted by community psychiatry and community psychology. Dumont, a psychiatrist at NIMH, commenting on the role of mental health programs in model cities, asserts that "community organization is itself a major mental health service, an end in itself."[30] Scribner, while stressing the varied interests of "social action" psychologists, makes evident their common commitment to "social action without . . . political movements as forces of change." While the purposes of change are varied, they all center on different aspects of the problem of compliance—"correcting deviant behavior which interferes with individual progress, . . . controlling mass hysteria . . . or changing child-rearing practices . . ."[31]

The concern for compliance through social action now seems to be taking a new turn. It is calling for an indirect strategy of involving the middle classes to control the lower classes, in whom it is assumed the roots of non-conformity to established standards grow. A change in social conditions is being called for to enable the middle-class Negro leadership to police its own poor more effectively. Apartheid in South Africa is justified on much the same grounds: by walling off the blacks from white society, black leaders must police their own lower class. Social stability is more effective when imposed by indigenous institutions than by welfare colonialism.[32]

Radical Social Policy

The link between social action and sociotherapy has been stressed here because I believe it is not widely understood and because it is the dominant pattern of the social environmentalist position today. But there is also evidence of a social action program that challenges the established standards of behavior and also tries to replace existing institutions rather than merely transferring organizational slots from white to black leaders. The three "Ws" dominated the intellectual leadership in welfare policy. Wilbur Cohen, Elizabeth Wickendon, and Winifred Bell were committeed to incrementalism as a strategy of change, and liberalism as a social philosophy. Cloward and Piven substituted a more radical approach to social policy in their work in the welfare rights movement. Their *immediate* aim was not to improve the social conditions of the welfare poor, for they were not trying to strengthen the welfare system, but rather to replace it.[33] They believed that this apparent conflict of aims between improving conditions which inhibit the urgency to introduce more fundamental change, and disrupting the performance of an intolerable system could be avoided in the case of welfare, because an improved welfare system would be politically unacceptable. Amelioration would lead to metamorphosis.

While these are important tactical issues, they should not obscure the essence of the radical creed, which is the commitment to reducing inequalities and altering social conditions—political, economic and social—as a precondition for individual change. Cloward and Piven are not primarily concerned with the problems of compliance, of getting individuals to meet standards, or promoting social stability. Rather, their emphasis is on altering institutions, redefining norms and purposes, and reassessing the standards by which professional performance is judged.

The ideals of a radical profession must be able to find expression in specific forms. Social workers already perform a great variety of professional roles as reformers and organizers, policy analysts, planners, researchers, consultants who are inside the bureaucracy, critics who are outside the established system, and "insider-outsiders," a role that enables them to be relevant, but critical. Like all creeds, it may contain inconsistencies and contradictions. When rigidly applied, it can become dogma and theology. The function of a belief system is not to provide answers, but to offer goals and objectives toward which one's professional activities can be oriented.

PROFESSIONAL CREED AND URBAN PROBLEMS

Of the four professional creeds discussed in this paper, I have given more attention to traditional casework and community sociotherapeutic ideologies because they are better developed and experience has sharpened the understanding of them. It is not altogether surprising that the more radical doctrines have failed to win wide support and hence remain at the margin of the profession. But the margin in one era may become the center of another.

Which of the professional creeds seems most appropriate to urban needs? America faces many urban crises—crises of race, class, managerial competence, and financing services. While the problems overlap and reinforce each other, they must also be distinguished from each other.

The problem of race cannot be solved without a redistribution of authority, resources, and power. The problem of poverty requires a redistribution of income and resources. The issues of race and class need to be sorted out and the tradeoff between income and power has to be clarified. The movement for school decentralization in New York City has by and large not demanded more resources for the ghetto, but only a different decision-making system.

What can be said about the relationship between professional doctrine and urban-racial problems? Which creeds are most relevant to this problem? In the search for a better solution to the problem of race, the liberal ideology, from which the spectrum of professional creeds previously examined are derived, has been assaulted. That the cherished beliefs about integration have been challenged is evident, but the insistence on separatism opens new issues. That the distribution of power among the social services is ethnically determined is a disquieting reality which has been long forgotten. Irish control of police, Italian control of sanitation, Jewish control of education, and perhaps Negro control over the new social services in community action agencies illustrate the neglected relation between service control and ethnicity. A redistribution of power may alter these established patterns. It has been relatively easy in ideological terms to accept a redistribution of power at the neighborhood level. A nineteenth century leader of the settlement house movement asserted, "Poverty, pauperism and other social evils could not be cured by alms, or by a redistribution of wealth, but only by creating genuine neighborhoods reestablished as a feature of civic life."[34] Many still believe that creed today; for them the neighborhood remains a tool for sociotherapy.

But the great racial crisis will emerge as blacks and other ethnic groups insist on a redistribution of power not by "turf", but by function. The struggle for power over education in New York City has already opened up the question of who controls the social services. For many blacks, control of the social services offers a much better leverage for the redistribution of power than does control over economic institutions. The accountability system in the social services has always been vulnerable. The demonstrated weakness of elite accountability, democratic accountability, and professional accountability are already evident. We may be witnessing a new demand for ethnic and racial accountability.

The traditional and community sociotherapeutic belief systems, on which professional social work ideology rests, will not be able to cope easily with ideological issues that the crisis of race has already presented. A more adequate creed will have to be developed if the profession wishes to be relevant to the issues of race.

Poverty cannot be dealt with simply in terms of overcoming apathy through more intelligent service or through social action programs, however dedicated. What is needed is a national redistribution of resources that deliberately redresses the imbalance of opportunities between rich and poor communities and between black and white communities. Sociotherapeutic approaches, whether individual or social, run the risk of deceiving themselves and others if they function without a complementary national reform.

A dispassionate analysis of current social policy would confirm my conclusion that social work programs have been used as a substitute for more searching policies to redistribute income, power, and resources. There is a perverse tendency in American social reform to repudiate social work, and then to embrace the very ideals that have been rejected. The Economic Opportunity Act stressed institutional change initiated by the poor. Sargent Shriver harshly reprimanded the social work community, at the 1965 National Conference on Social Welfare for social work's preoccupation with individualized methods and failure to reach the poor.[35] Yet as Kahn observed, "the heart of the community action program is in the field of individual remediation, help, retraining, counseling and aid. . . . social-change strategy, thus, continues to require case and individual elements, and political realities may even render individual services primary despite ideological commitment."[36]

Community sociotherapy and traditional casework appear to have a stubborn vitality. The more they are rejected, the more they seem to survive, flourish, and expand. In my judgment, the viability of the professional doctrine that emphasizes therapeutic solutions has produced a great dilemma in American society insofar as the solution of poverty is concerned, because it seems that our social policies have been based on it. Accordingly, we have tried to stimulate the economic participation of the poor through training to support the work ethic, employability and counseling programs and citizen participation, but have failed to develop an economic policy to achieve social objectives. In short, social policies have been generated to meet economic aims, but economic policies have not been used to meet social ends. Thus America lacks a policy of using up its available labor force or redistributing income among poor individuals and resources among low-income communities. Social work doctrine has inhibited the profession from openly repudiating the claim that casework can reduce dependency and social work can contribute to the reduction of poverty.

Social work, *by itself,* has almost nothing to contribute to the reduction of the interrelated problems of unemployment, poverty, and dependency. The social services cannot be the primary method for expanding employment opportunities and income among the poor.

Therefore if you interpret social work as a radical social policy committed to altering political and economic institutions which affect well being (on the assumption that social welfare activities to compensate individuals for the diseconomies generated by the political and economic system have been insufficient)—then it ceases to be social work. Individual social workers may, of course, function as reformers in the areas of employment, income redistribution, and political power—but these activities are marginal to their professional tasks. In this sense they are professionals who are radical rather than members of a radical profession. In recognition of this dilemma, some social workers have urged that the present profession be forsaken and a new one be built committed to the problem of inequalities of wealth, power, authority, and strategies of redistribution. These major unresolved problems of public policy also touch the limits of the contribution of social science to social purposes. Hence it is especially crucial that the problem not become subordinated to the methodology. But in this broader area of social reform social work will need to compete with new programs that have emerged and are variously called public policy, public affairs, social policy, or urban policy and that have developed at Harvard, MIT, Berkeley, Michigan, Buffalo, to name but a few. Can social work recruit able students, attract capable faculty, and win institutional resources and support to embark on this new venture and compete with these new centers of training? It clearly has not done so in the past. Whether history is a prelude to the future must remain an open question.

What can social work do short of repudiating its present mission? It can contribute greatly to improving the quality of urban life, humanizing institutions, and altering the priority of social values. It can perhaps implement these objectives by more broadly defining its present mission, and it must do so in terms of the way it interprets its clients' needs. A radical casework approach would mean not merely obtaining for the clients social services they are entitled to, or helping them adjust to their environment, but also trying to deal with the relevant people and institutions in their clients' environment which are contributing to their difficulties. That is to say, social workers must get the school to adjust to the needs of poor children as well as getting poor children to adjust to the demands and routines of the schools. They must force landlords to maintain their clients' housing as well as helping poor families to find somewhere to live. They must get public welfare agencies to change their procedures so as to make it easier to use welfare as a resource for help, as well as to help clients fulfill the requirements of the welfare bureaucracy. We need to develop casework in a hostile rather than benign environment, which is directed not so much at encouraging conformity (adjustment to reality) but to marshalling the resources of clients for self help and reform (challenge reality).

As social work moves away from altering the environment on behalf of a given client to altering the environment in general without reference to a specific client it moves to social reform and to the boundaries of its main concern. Action at the boundary is crucial and should be encouraged, but it should not lead, as it has done, to the neglect of its center. If we try to redefine the present margin so that it becomes the new center of social work activity then we accept the position that social work must move toward a radical social policy approach. A radical casework approach may prove, in the end, to be the more enduring strategy to pursue.

NOTES

1. Herbert Gans, "Social Planning: Regional and Urban Planning," *International Encyclopedia of the Social Sciences*, Vol. 12 (New York: Macmillan Co. and Free Press, 1968), p. 135.
2. Alvin Gouldner, book review of Talcott Parsons, ed., *American Sociology* (New York: Basic Books, 1968), *Science* (October 11, 1968), p. 247.
3. Letter by Alvin Gouldner and Jack Seeley to Frank Riessman, New York University, September 10, 1968. A conference on "Revitalizing Social Science," was held at New York University on October 14, 1968 to discuss the letter. This conference may be considered as a first meeting of representatives of the radical caucuses of the various social science associations. There is interest in creating a policy-oriented magazine and an organization. Unity on the left may be hard to maintain, as it always has been, but a start appears to have been made.
4. Henry Miller, "Value Dilemmas in Social Casework," *Social Work*, Vol. 13, No. 1 (January 1968), p. 33. Social workers are also dismayed by the criticism that casework *"systematically* excludes many of the persons most in need of

attention [and even] when properly applied to persons disposed to use it," is ineffective. See Scott Briar, "The Casework Predicament," *Social Work*, p. 6, same issue. To meet these changes, the field has shifted its emphasis from the application of tested knowledge and accepted standards of "sound" practice to experimentation. Demands for innovation, experimentation, and accountability to service-users all illustrate a willingness to challenge established standards of practice.

5. Consider the recent debate on whether war-injured Vietnamese children should be brought to the United States for medical treatment. The National Association of Social Workers' Commission on International Social Welfare asserted that such a plan disregards a basic child welfare principle that "children have the right to grow up in their own families in their own cultures." Such a conclusion, Kelman explains, has political consequences, for it supports the United States "government's desire not to call attention to civilian casualties of the war in Vietnam." Moreover, the preservation of life is a more important value, Kelman asserts, than respect for cultural diversity. Rose B. Kelman, "Vietnam: A Current Issue in Child Welfare," *Social Work*, Vol. 13, No. 4 (October 1968), p. 20.

6. Noel Timms, *Social Casework, Principles and Practices* (London: Routledge & Kegan Paul, 1964), p. 61.

7. Florence V. Hollis and Alice L. Taylor, *Social Work Education in the United States* (New York: Columbia University Press, 1951), p. 54.

8. Richard Titmuss, Foreword, in Noel Timms and H. F. Philips, *The Problem of the Problem Family* (London: Family Service Units, 1962), p. vi.

9. Stanley M. Herman, *The People Specialists* (New York: Knopf, 1968).

10. For this distinction I have relied on a paper presented by James S. Coleman, "Conflicting Theories of Social Change," delivered at the University of Chicago, October 23, 1967 (mimeo.).

11. James S. Coleman, "Race Relations and Social Change," July 1967 (mimeo.), p. 17.

12. Kingsley Davis, "Mental Hygiene and the Class Structure," in Herman D. Stein and Richard Cloward, eds., *Social Perspectives on Behavior* (New York: Free Press, 1958), p. 334.

13. Everett Hughes, unpublished lectures, Brandeis University, 1961.

14. Hamilton is sensitive to the awkward moral problem that arises when casework practice emphasizes adjustment. Therefore, she tries to distinguish between adjustment and acquiescence, emphasizing that casework helps "the client to identify what is real." But there is no systematic treatment of what is reality or how adjustment could be achieved without acquiescence. See also, Gordon Hamilton, *Theory and Practice of Social Casework*, 2nd revised edition (New York: Columbia University Press, 1951), p. 237.

15. Alan Keith-Lucas, *Decisions About People in Need: A Study of Administrative Responsiveness in Public Assistance* (Chapel Hill: University of North Carolina Press, 1957), p. 143.

16. Felix J. Biestek, "The Principles of Client Self-Determination," *Social Casework*, Vol. 32, No. 9 (November 1951), p. 374.

17. D. W. Donnison in a book review of Barbara Wooton, *Social Science and Social Pathology* (New York: Humanities Press, 1959), *The Almoner*, Vol. 12, Nos.

4, 5, and 6 (July, August, and September 1959), p. 172, notes that "the social workers who have to resist these pressures often work in isolated and exposed positions."

18. For a similar criticism, see C. Wright Mills's famous study, "The Professional Ideology of Social Pathologists," *American Journal of Sociology* (September 1949), pp. 179–180. Pathologists are sociologists who write textbooks about social problems. Mills believed that "these writers typically assume the norms which they use and often tacitly sanction them. There are few attempts to explain deviations from norms in the terms of norms themselves, and no rigorous facing of the implications of the fact that social transformations would involve shifts *in them*. . . . If the 'norms' were examined, the investigator would perhaps be carried to see total structures of norms and to relate these to distributions of power."

19. Richard Titmuss, *Commitment to Welfare* (New York: Random House, 1968), p. 42.

20. Peter Rossi *et al., Between White and Black: The Faces of American Institutions in the Ghetto* (Baltimore: Johns Hopkins Press, 1968), p. 144.

21. Andrew Billingsley, "Bureaucratic and Professional Orientation Patterns in Social Casework," *Social Service Review*, Vol. 38, No. 4 (December 1964), pp. 402–403.

22. Donna L. McLeod and Henry J. Meyer, "A Study of the Values of Social Workers," in Edwin J. Thomas, ed., *Behavioral Science for Social Workers* (New York: Free Press, 1967), Table 30–2, p. 409.

23. Alvin Gouldner, "The Secrets of Organizations," *The Social Welfare Forum, 1963* (New York: Columbia University Press, 1963), p. 167.

24. Philip Lichtenberg, "And the Cure of Psychosis Is for Us All" (Unpublished manuscript, Bryn Mawr College, 1968), pp. 12–13.

25. See, for example, Briar, *op. cit.*, pp. 5–11; Miller, *op. cit.*, pp. 27–33; and Irving Pilavan, "Restructuring the Provision of Social Services," *Social Work*, Vol. 13, No. 1 (January 1968), pp. 34–41.

26. *Youth in the Ghetto: A Study of the Consequences of Powerlessness* (New York: Harlem Youth Opportunities Unlimited, 1964).

27. W. I. Thomas and Florian Znaniecki, *The Polish Peasant in Europe and America*, Vol. II (Boston: Gorham Press, 1918), pp. 15–26.

28. Many of the observations in this section are based on an interview with Morris Janowitz. He later developed his insights in "A Note on Sociology and Social Work" (University of Chicago, undated), p. 3 (mimeo.).

29. For a further analysis of community organization as sociotherapy, see Peter Marris and Martin Rein, *Dilemmas of Social Reform* (New York: Atherton, 1967), p. 167.

30. Matthew P. Dumont, "A Model Community Mental Health Program for a Model Cities Area" (Washington, D.C.: Center of Community Planning, U.S. Department of Health, Education & Welfare, August 1967), p. 3 (mimeo.).

31. Sylvia Scribner, "What is Community Psychology Made Of?" American Psychological Association, Division of Community Psychology, *Newsletter*, Vol. 11, No. 1 (January 1968), p. 5.

32. For a discussion of the conservative argument see Chapter 14.

33. See, for example, Richard A. Cloward and Frances Fox Piven, "A Strategy to End Poverty," *The Nation*, Vol. 202, No. 18 (May 2, 1966).

34. Quoted in Roy Lubove, *The Professional Altruist: The Emergence of Social Work as a Career* (Cambridge, Mass.: Harvard University Press, 1965), p. 15.

35. Sargent Shriver, "Poverty in the United States—What Next?" *The Social Welfare Forum, 1965* (New York: Columbia University Press, 1965), pp. 55–66.

36. Alfred J. Kahn, "From Delinquency Treatment to Community Development," in Paul Lazarsfeld *et al.*, eds., *The Uses of Sociology* (New York: Basic Books, 1967), p. 497.

Part V

Case Studies of Choice

Chapter 16

The American Welfare System

Public attention is riveted today on the problem of
cash transfers. The rediscovery of the importance of the
direct cash grant in the relief of poverty represents the
final phase in the remarkable development of social
policies during the 1960s. To understand the shift, the
idea of money grants must be contrasted with the earlier
assumption that rejected cash transfers as a dole and
sought to "get the poverty out of the people" rather than
"the people out of poverty."[1] In the early 1960s policy
was first aimed at expanding opportunity through provision of services and citizen participation and then
reluctantly at the creation of jobs. The recent interest
in cash transfers has precipitated a lively debate about
purposes and form, and the nature of the constraints
that should determine these choices. A Presidential
Commission on Income Maintenance Programs, formed
to help clarify the choices and to offer recommendations,
represents a stunning change in national politics. Previously, this subject was almost the exclusive domain
of congressional, state, and local politics. During the
debate and exploration of new policy options, we have,
without specifically making any choices, dramatically
altered our public welfare system.

This essay examines the rediscovery of the importance

This paper was prepared for a conference held under the auspices
of the American Academy of Arts and Sciences Committee on
Poverty in May 1969.

of cash in the relief of poverty, the debate about reforming our present cash transfer policies, and the changes already made without having clarified the choices or the directions that these changes imply.

SOCIAL SERVICES AND SOCIAL REFORM

In the early 1960s, experimentation with the policies developed by the President's Committee on Juvenile Delinquency and Youth Crime and the Ford Gray Area Programs found expression in the philosophy of the Economic Opportunity Act of 1964, more popularly known as the War on Poverty. The poverty program called for a strategy to change people and the educational and training systems without altering economic policies that would expand the number of jobs and redistribute income. The poor were to be rescued from their poverty by structural changes in the social service system, which would make these institutions more relevant, more acceptable, and more accessible. The underlying theory about the cause and cure of poverty also called for involving the poor, on the assumption that participation would affect aspirations and provide, as the preamble of the Economic Opportunity Act asserts, "the opportunity for education and training" and "the opportunity to work."

The poverty program revealed how enormously resistant institutions are to change and how difficult it is to bring about change. But changes did, in fact, occur. As consumer demand was nurtured by reform, the diagnosis of apathy seemed less accurate for the poor than we had earlier imagined. Indeed, when people combined the problems of race and class an aggressive militancy developed which found expression in rent strikes, school boycotts, organizations for welfare recipients, and demands for participation (in some cities for control). As militancy increased, the opportunity approach to reducing poverty seemed to be threatened. We also learned that as institutions developed the commitment and capability to respond to the poor, they required resources to meet the demands for opportunity they had created. Paradoxically, in the early stage of the program, new institutions were given more resources than they could successfully manage, but as they came to acquire administrative competence they discovered that they lacked the necessary resources. Then a new program, Model Cities, was developed. Although more ambitious, it recapitulated the earlier frustrations of planning to prevent delinquency and reduce poverty. It also failed to provide the resources necessary to implement its ambitious plans. Finally, we learned that even when the demand for opportunity was met by training, education, citizen participation, and community control, increased employment and higher levels of living and income for the poor were still not assured. More than opportunity was needed.

POVERTY AND JOB CREATION

Without shifting from its emphasis on opportunity, public policy came increasingly to recognize that training without employment was inadequate. More jobs were needed. The Commission on Technology, Automation, and Economic Progress recommended creating 500,000 public service jobs and the National Advisory Commission on Civil Disorders proposed a program that would create a million new jobs in both the public and private sectors over a three-year period. These requests for job creation were not honored. There has, however, been a shift within manpower programs from institutional training programs in a classroom setting, supplemented in some cases by supportive services such as remedial education, health, child care, and counseling, to an increased emphasis on On-the-Job Training programs (O.J.T.) in which the federal government reimburses employers for the cost incurred in hiring and training unskilled workers. The cost of O.J.T. programs has risen from $44 million in 1966 to a projected $452 million in 1970. These figures represent an increase from 2 percent to 13 percent of total federal manpower outlays.[2] But we have been reluctant to create a direct program of guaranteed employment in which the federal government would act as "the employer of last resort." James Sundquist offers one interpretation of why a program of guaranteed employment has been resisted. He suggests that a public employment program assuring adequate wages and large enough to utilize the available labor supply would have enormous effects upon the wage structure of the private economy. He explains:

> The existence of an unemployment pool is a fact holding wages down. If public jobs were readily available at the statutory minimum of $1.60 per hour, then private employers would have to make their present $1.60 an hour jobs more attractive, and raising wages would be one of the means. The effects would ripple upward through the wage structure, and pay increases would in turn put pressure on price levels. Many families would be lifted out of poverty, but employers would find themselves with labor shortages and a profit squeeze, consumers would find themselves paying higher prices that would be blamed on "government spending" and public support for the program might be rapidly eroded.[3]

But O.J.T. programs in both public and private sectors can expand the number of jobs available to the poor. We are now pursuing several alternative forms, including direct contract with the business sector to cover the cost of training. In 1970, 140,000 jobs under reimbursement contract are being planned at an estimated cost of $3,000 each. The New Careers program under the Scheuer amendment in the Economic Opportunity Act in 1966 provides training opportunities for the poor in jobs in the public sector. This program seeks to create new jobs by restructuring job standards with annual expenditures of about $20 million and a maximum cost per enrollee of $5,000. A projected program, Industry Incentives, will provide monetary incentives for the location of plants in ghettoes as well as reimbursement of employers for the hiring and training of disadvantaged groups in these plants. Yet the impact of such small efforts on employment is likely to be minimal.

We thus appear to be developing a mix of job redistribution and job creation policies primarily through direct subsidy to government and industry for training costs, or to industry for the relocation of plants. We may in the future increasingly turn to tax incentives as contrasted with the direct contract approach, since we have not yet accepted the idea of government as the employer of last resort.

War and inflation have served as the proxies for an explicit American policy of "full employment." According to figures quoted by Representative Curtis in hearings on the Economic Report to the President in 1968, 600,000 men are in the armed forces because of the Vietnam war, and another million and a half persons are employed in munition plants. These figures suggest how the war has contributed to creating a tight labor market. It has also been estimated that if our efforts to reduce inflation by a 10 percent tax surcharge were effective, a sufficient amount of demand would be taken out of the economy to increase unemployment by 300,000 persons. If these estimates are valid, our tax policies would create unemployment about equal to the total in On-the-Job Training programs, which in 1969 are estimated to serve about 285,000 individuals. Policies to curb inflation and retrain the poor are in conflict. As Garth Mangum has suggested, we have used the poor as the price-stabilizers of society.

CASH TRANSFERS

While the opportunity approach to the relief of poverty through services and citizen participation continues, its future is uncertain as the Nixon administration charts its future course. We have seen how manpower policies have shifted their emphasis to On-the-Job Training in response to the need for better links between training and work. We have tried to explain why we have eschewed job creation programs which would guarantee work at adequate wages for all those who seek employment, and to suggest that concern about price stability and the end of the unpopular Vietnam war may have the effect of raising unemployment rather than decreasing it. Regardless of what future policies may be, it is clear that at the end of the 1960s public interest has shifted to the reform of our cash transfer system.

It is difficult to identify the origin of the interest in cash programs. It may be traced to debates in the late 1950s about the importance of automation and structural unemployment as factors in the high level of regional unemployment in depressed areas and ghettoes. The writers of the Triple Revolution offered a grim prognosis when they argued that work will be the privilege of the few and that technology will usher in the need for new mechanisms to distribute income outside of the wage structure. Although later developments did not support their argument, apprehension about automation did arouse interest in the guaranteed income.

The service-reform approach also contributed to the rediscovery of cash transfer through the creation of legal services and the support given to self-help and social action programs. Mobilization for Youth's storefront multi-service center confronted problems in New York City's welfare department. The lawyers associated with Mobilization's program began to specialize in welfare programs, and looked for test cases to challenge established administrative practices. One illustration of the impact of their work, as well as of the efforts of others, is suggested by changes in fair hearing procedures and their use. Clients in New York City whose cases are about to be closed may now request a hearing from the state, and according to a more recent ruling the case must remain open until a decision is rendered. In 1966 there were 386 requests for such hearings; in 1967 there were 3,332 requests. Neighborhood anti-poverty organizations and the Welfare Rights Movement also directed national attention to the efforts of those already on welfare to improve their conditions by getting special grants for which they were eligible but had not received.[4] The consequences of the activity in legal services and social action are of course difficult to assess. They undoubtedly made it easier for administrative policies to develop which reject the doctrine of less eligibility. At first, the demand for welfare did not increase in New York, but a greater proportion of those who applied were accepted. In 1968–1969, there was an increase in requests for services as well. A *New York Times* account reports that Governor Rockefeller conceded in private "that a reason for the rise in welfare and Medicare costs . . . is that the state never believed that all of the people who are eligible for [these] programs would learn about their eligibility and take advantage of it. In short, the original cost estimates . . . were based on a conspiracy of silence which was shattered by many grass-roots public information efforts, including that of the anti-poverty program."[5]

Legal services and local social reform, the creation of a national lobby for welfare recipients, the concern of some economists about the inequities and disincentives in the present welfare system, and the failure of the tax system to offer allowances to those with low income (tax exemptions) led to a growing interest in welfare reform. Other economists were less concerned with the reform of public welfare than with creating a new mechanism for the transfer of income to the working poor, to whom neither opportunity nor training seemed as immediately important as the insufficiency of earnings. In 1966 among the 29.7 million persons in families whose incomes were below the social security administration definition of poverty, 7.3 million were employed workers, of whom 6.7 million earned less than $3,000 from year-round, full-time employment. Concern about the inadequacy of income of this neglected category led economists like Robert Lampman to try to devise a new income-transfer scheme. The special situation in New York City, with close to 13 percent of its population receiving public assistance payments, also directed national attention to the ancient paradox that affluence and dependency march hand in hand. These and other forces helped direct national interest to the creation of new instruments of reform for transferring cash from one group in society to another.

CHANGE WITHOUT CHOICE

While the national attention caused continuing intellectual debate about the choice and design of the cash transfer system, significant changes in our present cash transfer schemes have already emerged. These changes are not always due to clear choice of direction and policy. We may be drifting toward new policy choices based on a series of incremental changes in present programs. Two major changes will be analyzed. First, welfare is becoming increasingly a substitutive system, in the sense that liberalizing and improving welfare serve as a *substitute* for the development of other sectors of social and economic policy. Second, public welfare increasingly serves as a *supplement* to the low wage sector and to the social insurance programs. But the practice of substitution and supplementation contradicts an earlier commitment to the withering away thesis.

The withering doctrine was first enunciated in Britain in the Minority Report for the Poor Law Commission of 1909, of which the Webbs were the primary architects. They believed that the break-up of the Poor Law (public assistance) could be achieved by creating cash transfers and social services which were universally available without a means test. Universality would produce high quality and adequacy of benefits, because the middle classes would have a stake in building up the quality of these programs. The Majority Report, by contrast, held that there would always be a residual group in society for whom a program of last retreat would be needed. Means tested programs could thus never be eliminated. Public policy is once again revisiting this ancient debate. Should we direct public policy to the break up of the Poor Law through the use of non-means-tested schemes? Is all means testing to be equated with the Poor Law, so that expanding selectivity contributes to strengthening the Poor Law in a new form? Current experiences suggest that we may have reversed our earlier commitment to the withering away doctrine which assigns a residual role for means tested welfare policies.

Substitution refers to the reliance upon assistance programs in lieu of efforts to broaden non-means tested contributory social insurance systems or to develop non-contributory universal programs like children allowances as the mechanism for redistributing transfer income. The Social Security Act of 1935 clearly intended social policy to develop in such a fashion that assistance programs would be limited to a small residual population who for varying reasons were excluded from coverage in the social insurance system and who failed to benefit from general economic prosperity. Orderly progression in the development of social security systems was assumed. A national, compulsory, contributory social insurance program would become, in time, the major instrument for income redistribution between generations and between income groups, by weighing benefits slightly in favor of low income earners. As the system developed the need for all other transfer systems should gradually wither away.

In at least two important areas we have come to rely on means tested assistance programs as the instrument for the provision of transfer income rather than on the insurance mechanism. This appears to be the case in income loss due to long-term unemployment risks and may be the case in the development of social services. These examples of the substitution of assistance for insurance or other forms of universal provision will be briefly examined.

In the wake of the economic recession of 1960, President Kennedy proposed legislation to extend ADC on a temporary basis to children of unemployed parents, and, as an emergency measure, also to extend unemployment insurance to individuals who had exhausted their unemployment insurance benefits. The opportunity to widen insurance coverage to include the long-term unemployed as a permanent feature of the system was not exploited. Instead the assistance program was to be expanded to include new risks that had been covered only in the insurance system. The assistance mechanism was extended to pick up the fallouts of the insurance program. In so doing it altered a fundamental doctrine of the New Deal legislation which drew a distinction between the unemployed and the unemployable. The loss of income due to unemployment was one of the risks which unemployment insurance was designed to cover. Federally aided, means tested assistance programs were designed only for selected categories of unemployables: old age, blindness, physical disability, and the absence or disability of one or both of a child's parents. The economic recession in the early 1960s brought pressure to liberalize public assistance rather than to develop a more comprehensive, permanent program for long-term unemployment insurance. James Sundquist summarized the logic behind these developments.

In each recession, of course, a major new category of needy families appeared—families of men still jobless after their unemployment insurance had expired. The anomaly was that if the family remained together it was ineligible for federally aided assistance, but if the father disappeared his wife and children would apply for aid to dependent children (ADC).[6]

Common sense and public policy have always insisted upon the distinction between those who could work and those who could not. Social programs were devised to reflect these distinctions. But the dichotomy between unemployed and unemployable, because it fluctuates with market conditions, is inherently vague. It was also widely believed that the efforts to implement this artificial distinction contributed to the break up of the family, by providing individuals with an inducement to accept this label, which would make them eligible for benefits. To preserve the family, the new AFDC program was first expanded to include male unemployed heads. More recently, President Nixon recommended to Congress that the program be further extended to the category of all poor families with children (Family Assistance Program). This could add 12.4 million persons to the 10 million persons now on welfare. Thus a policy to promote family stability and to reach the working poor was purchased by sacrificing the principle of the break up of the Poor Law. In order to rescue the principle that assistance should be a residual program, which would wither away with the growth of insurance programs, a new doctrine of making welfare self-liquidating was introduced. Social services broadly defined are seen as a means of reducing the welfare burden. A report of the House Ways and Means Committee asserts this aim with vigor and clarity.

> The new approach . . . places emphasis on the provision of services to help families become self-supporting rather than dependent on Welfare checks. The bill would . . . provide incentives to recipients . . . to improve their condition so as to render continual public assistance . . . unnecessary. . . . Experience has shown that adequately trained personnel can be one of the largest factors in reducing ultimately, the cost of the public assistance program.[7]

In 1962, building on the 1957 Amendments to the Social Security Act, the idea that welfare clients could be rehabilitated to economic self-sufficiency through social services was reintroduced. Further elaboration of this general thesis was included in the 1967 Amendments to the Social Security Act. It is based on the assumption that individual handicaps, such as the lack of work skills and education, or the lack of motivation, or the lack of knowledge about the availability of jobs, or the lack of health, inhibits self-sufficiency. Remedies were therefore directed at changing individuals and not at altering labor market conditions. We have now forged a system with the following main characteristics: *education and manpower* retraining to teach literary and occupational skills, *social services* to provide counseling and concrete services, such as day care to facilitate the transition from welfare to work, combined with an *incentive* to improve the level of living for those who work. This system of incentives includes an earning disregard of the first 30 dollars per month of earnings plus a marginal tax rate of two-thirds on other earnings. Finally to these inducements has been added a compulsory feature, which requires welfare mothers to accept training and/or work. In addition, a federal freeze on AFDC benefits above a fixed proportion was introduced to induce states to develop program training, social services, and income incentives which were regarded as the best available means to rehabilitate welfare clients. By liberalizing public assistance the theory that residual programs would naturally decline with economic growth and the full development of social insurance was forsaken and a new one accepted which called for active measures of self-liquidation through rehabilitation, compulsion, and fiscal penalties to the states. Growth was a precondition for the future decline of assistance when the effectiveness of these active welfare policies decreased future case loads.

President Nixon's proposals for welfare reform embody all of the principles set out above, but extends them not only to the unemployed male headed family, but to all the employed poor as well. In effect the WIN program is being extended to all the poor. The incentive to work is strengthened by a $60 earning disregard and a 50 percent reduction in benefits as earnings rise. The present provision which compels persons to accept work or training is reaffirmed. The program tries to alter the handicaps of the labor supply system and leaves untouched the structure of the demand system in terms of wage levels and the volume of jobs. It is predicted that such a program, despite substantial initial investment, will become self-liquidating and "will lessen dependency rather than perpetuate it."[8]

The size of these new additions can be estimated only in general terms. The unemployed parent segment of AFDC that permits federal reimbursement to states that provide cash transfers for unemployed parents included in 1966, 65,400 families, who make up a total of 325,000 persons. With 5.7 million persons receiving AFDC, the size of the unemployed parent segment remains small. However, between 1960 and 1966 the number of AFDC recipients increased by 1,586,000 persons and 21 percent of the increase in this program is attributable to the new unemployed parent program.[9] President Nixon's proposal to add the employed poor would double the number of eligible persons and increase costs by 4 billion dollars.

The 1967 Social Security Amendments authorized a major expansion of manpower training and social services, especially day care, for the purpose of increasing the earning power of AFDC recipients. The major focus of WIN (Work Incentive Program) program is on female family heads.

The program has three priorities. They are respectively: direct referral to jobs (14,000), training (132,000), special work projects (30,000), based on 1969 estimates. The program seems to be *primarily* oriented to training female heads in AFDC. The Bureau of the Budget estimates that 80 percent of enrollees will be women. Cost estimates are illuminating. Training cost per enrollee, based on man-year costs per trainee, are projected for 1969 at $1,060. The cost of basic services for enrollees of the special works project are estimated at $108 per enrollee. Preschool day care is estimated to be $1,200 per child and $600 per school age child. When the costs of these services are added, taking account of the status of the recipient and the nature of the manpower program to be offered, the federal costs of the WIN program are estimated to be $126.5 million in 1969 and $1,612.6 million for 1970. Net costs are estimated at $107.0 million and $705.1 million for each of these years.[10]

Manpower, social services and means tested welfare programs are thus being drawn together. In the efforts to get the welfare poor to work they will be even further expanded. For example, President Nixon is planning "to provide child care for the 450,000 children of the 150,000 current welfare recipients to be trained."[11] The WIN program and the new Family Assistance Program set the framework for an expanded social service system (including child care, manpower training, counseling, etc.) to be limited to those eligible for welfare.

Two federal Task Forces have recommended that we not move in this direction. They proposed that services be separated from cash and that they be distributed through administrative machinery which would make them available to the total community. The Department of Health, Education and Welfare has partially responded to these recommendations and has at the federal level administratively separated the Bureau of Individual and Rehabilitative Services from the department which disperses cash. But despite these changes no national program independent of the Poor Law has been established for the distribution of social services.[12]

Nor is the incentive system, known as the thirty and one-third scheme ($30 disregards on earnings and a marginal tax rate of about 63 percent on earned income) a costless program. An estimate of the total annual additional costs as a result of the application of the incentive policy to AFDC and general assistance cases, in one large state, Pennsylvania, is $2,136,000 or about 1½ percent of annual total costs for the preceding fiscal year.[13]

In summary, public assistance has become a substitute for an extension of unemployment insurance to the long-term unemployed, and as such has been one factor contributing to the recent precipitous rise in welfare caseloads. The inclusion of the able-bodied unemployed seems to have replaced the idea of an automatic decline in welfare to be brought about by economic growth and the expansion of social insurance. The inclusion of working poor following President Nixon's proposal creates a national system of wage supplementation for marginal, low wage, low status jobs. We now have an active welfare policy designed to reduce economic dependency. The main elements of this policy are training, services, and income incentives. Estimated costs are still modest. While these policies are now directed at the welfare poor, they may as the Nixon administration has proposed be extended as a national policy to all the poor. If poverty becomes a test of access to training and services, it may inhibit rather than stimulate the development of a national, non-means tested social service program financed from either social insurance funds or from general taxation.

WELFARE AS A SUPPLEMENTARY SYSTEM

Welfare may be regarded as a *supplement* to wages, social insurance benefits, and means tested in-kind services. But the converse may also apply, because wages, insurance benefits, and services may serve as *supplement to welfare cash grants*.

Consider first the example of the relationship between work and welfare. Welfare and employment are widely regarded as alternative rather than complementary or overlapping sources of income. The AFDC caseload is generally seen as made up of nonworking mothers. This is consistent with the theory of public assistance embodied in the original Social Security Act of 1935, which assumed that social insurance protected members of the labor force when their income was interrupted, while federally financed social assistance aided the unemployable. But, in fact, AFDC mothers are frequently active members of the sub-employed labor force—the under-employed and low wage workers. Public assistance often serves as a form of wage supplementation for the low paid, partially employed worker. In states which do not meet full need as defined by states' standards, welfare recipients are permitted to supplement inadequate benefits through employment. We thus have what might be considered a double Speenhamland System, where welfare supplements low wages and low wages supplement insufficient benefits. Welfare status, therefore, does not necessarily represent a sharp break with the labor force, as the theory of assistance would imply.

In the rural South the link between work and welfare must be seen in relation to the seasonal manpower requirements of an agricultural economy. It is reputed that virtually all welfare ceases during the crop season. But individuals must also have their needs met when no work is available. To supplement the needs of those employed in this agricultural economy, welfare benefits are available when work is not. In this situation, welfare supplements wages serially, over time, rather than simultaneously by overlapping at a given point in time. Other industries with seasonal employment may follow a similar pattern. But little systematic inquiry has been undertaken into the relationship between work and welfare from the point of view of the requirements of the industry rather than the work pattern of the recipient.

Welfare also supplements other sources of income. The trends in one large city, Philadelphia, will illustrate how the supplemental character of the welfare system has grown. In 1961, 34.4 percent of the families had other sources of income; by 1967, the figures had increased to 42.9 percent. In 1961, earnings from employment of the mother, father, and children accounted for 5.6 percent of all other sources of income; the figure increased to 9.0 percent in the 1967 study. A breakdown of the families with cash income suggests that about half of this income is derived from the contributions of the absent father. Between 1961 and 1967 this figure declined from 57.1 percent to 51.5 percent.[14]

However, generalizations based on one city are hazardous. An examination of the pattern in New York City, from monthly statistical reports, suggests almost the reverse pattern. In 1961, 55.5 percent of families, ADC and TADC combined, received income from no other sources than welfare; by 1967, the figure increased to 66.1 percent.[15] The contributions from relatives declined in New York, while they increased slightly in Philadelphia. Income from all other sources increased in New York City from 9.6 percent to 11.2 percent.[16] For further analysis, we await the findings of the national study.

Old Age Assistance offers the most dramatic illustration of how assistance supplements social insurance. In 1966, 48.6 percent of the 2.1 million old age recipients were also receiving Social Security benefits and 7.1 percent of all social security beneficiaries were receiving welfare.[17] In England, such supplementation is now a matter of national policy and the National Assistance program was renamed Supplementary Benefits. In both countries the United States supplementation is still regarded as an index of the failure of social insurance to provide a minimum floor of protection.

BENEFIT LEVEL AND WAGE LEVELS

The work and welfare systems are likely to become even more interdependent in the future, partly as a result of national policy to draw the AFDC mother into the labor force. The Work Incentive program (WIN), is only the most recent effort to use training to promote economic independence. It was preceded by the Work Experience Program of the Economic Opportunity Act of 1964, Title V, and by Community Work and Training Program under the 1962 Amendments of the Social Security Act.

The efforts to reduce economic dependency through training are likely to increase the extent to which the benefit and wage sectors will be supplementary to each other. The evidence to support this is fragmentary, but suggestive. A comparison of the increase in wage levels and benefit levels suggests that benefit levels in selected public assistance categories are rising faster than wages and that the gap between the systems is not narrowing. Moreover, in some states benefit levels for those who participate in training can be substantially higher than the wages that can be secured from many jobs in the economy. Each of these themes will be briefly amplified.

The data in Table 1 suggest that increases in benefit levels differ by the category of assistance and by the level of benefits paid in different states. Low benefit states are above the national average in the increase in benefits

Table 1[1]

**Increase in Average Monthly Benefit Levels per Recipient
for Public Assistance by Category, 1961–1968[2]**

| *Public Assis-
tance Category* | *Increase in
Highest States* | *Increase in
Lowest States* | *Increase in the
National Average* |
|---|---|---|---|
| OAA | 118.0 | 113.6 | 116.2 |
| AFDC | 126.1 | 118.6 | 123.2 |
| GA | 141.4 | 130.6 | 138.2 |
| AB | 122.9 | 127.2 | 124.7 |
| APTD | 122.9 | 124.1 | 123.4 |

[1] Mrs. Marilyn Smuck helped in compiling this table.

[2] Index for 1961 equals 100. Benefit levels for July and August were averaged. The states were equally divided between high and low states for each category and for each year.

for the blind and disabled. By contrast, the high benefit states are increasing their benefits more rapidly than the national average in their programs for aged, dependent children, and general assistance. In the 1961 to 1967 period, average earnings in metropolitan areas for men employed in skilled maintenance and unskilled plant jobs increased between 19 and 22 percent. Surprisingly wages for the unskilled increased slightly faster than wages for the skilled.[18] Skilled maintenance men in manufacturing increased their earnings 19.3 percent and 20.3 percent for all industries, while unskilled men increased their earnings in manufacturing by 20.1 percent and 21.8 percent in all industries. AFDC benefit levels both nationally and in the high benefit states increased faster than wage levels in metropolitan areas, for skilled and unskilled occupations. Only in the low benefit states did the increase of 18.6 percent in benefit levels for AFDC lag behind the increase in wage levels.

As long as benefits and wage levels do not overlap, the more rapid rate of increase of benefit levels has no appreciable effect on the extent to which these systems supplement each other. The separation between benefits and wages can, of course, be achieved either by policies designed to keep benefit levels low or wage rates high. The low benefit approach has a history going back to the principle of the New Poor Law of 1834, which held that no income derived from welfare benefits should exceed the amount that the lowest paid independent worker in the community could earn. This famous doctrine of "less eligibility" was clearly intended to serve as a deterrent, discouraging individuals from choosing benefits as a substitute for wages. But this preoccupation with setting benefit levels so low that they act as incentive to work clearly and dramatically conflicts with the competing principle that individuals should be assured a minimum floor of income protection, and that the poor should share in the increased affluence of the society.

If American public policy seems to reject the principle of less eligibility, it is equally reluctant to commit itself to raising wage levels at the bottom. Recent data on the distribution of income in New York City dramatically document the proximity of welfare benefits and wage levels. In August 1968 welfare benefits levels were increased by an average of 7 percent for AFDC cases, an amount equal to about $250 per year for a family of four persons. The effects were stunning. "That slight dollar increase immediately caused an increase of 300,000 in the number of eligibles. . . . After the August increases, close to half of the city's minority populations lived in . . . families" [that were eligible to receive welfare payments].[19]

Economists are especially apprehensive about a policy which would raise minimum wages because they feel that it would have the perverse effect of drying up the volume of low wage jobs and thereby reducing for the poor the option of choosing between work and welfare. Instead, as we have earlier suggested, public policy is committed to decreasing welfare rolls through rehabilitation, which emphasizes the importance of cash incentives combined with services and training. We have repudiated the coercive approach of encouraging economic independence through less eligibility and have favored policies that encourage independence through incentives and training. Curiously, like the Webbs, we are prepared to compel people to accept rehabilitation. Thus a contradiction between coercion and therapy emerges in these policies.

It may be useful to reconstruct the logic in support of each of these approaches. Economists argue that the present welfare system has a perverse dis-incentive effect on the will to work, because it contains a 100 percent tax on earnings above the benefit guarantee, such that for every dollar earned, a dollar in welfare benefits is lost. The result of this policy is that an individual is economically no better off when he elects to work. Aside from coercion and deterrence, which offends our commitment to freedom and choice, what strategy will best nurture the will to work? The incentive approach asserts that people will naturally choose work if they will be better off financially. According to this point of view, if we reject coercion, then we must create a positive incentive to work which makes it possible for individuals to be better off economically as a result of their labors. But others argue that this is too limited a view. People work for many reasons. Even low wage workers with boring jobs may elect to work rather than to secure benefits in order to introduce diversity into their lives. Thus, many women on AFDC prefer work because it provides them with an opportunity to avoid the monotony of being at home and the burdens of child rearing. These individuals may elect to work even if their economic position is not improved. Training and child care provide the opportunity and encouragement to acquire the work skills which may alter the *source of income,* if not the *level of income.*

A third point of view holds that some people accept work over benefits because of their life style and personal and social values. Some individuals are even prepared to be economically worse off working than they would be if they accepted benefits because it offends their personal values and life style to receive benefits. Alternatively, some individuals, although they might be better off at work, may prefer instead to secure benefits. Some planners hope to instill those values in individuals which will make them prefer work, even if it leaves them marginally worse off economically. Proponents of this position see the incentive problem in social-psychological terms, rather than in economic terms. They hope to devise a program of services and training which is designed primarily to change life style and personal values.

In summary, there are three points of view about how to encourage economic independence. One position argues that individuals must be better off economically at work than on welfare; the second holds that an individual should be no worse off economically, but that he can secure other secondary gains; the third asserts that individuals might even accept being even slightly worse off economically, if they could acquire the values of a work ethic which supports economic independence. Each approach appeals to a different theory of human motivation.

The validity of these competing theories is not at issue here. The service and training approaches have been tried, often yielding indifferent results. Faith is now being placed on the special contribution that economic incentives have on the will to work. It is therefore useful to explore the consequences of grafting an economic incentive system onto the present welfare system, without an accompanying public policy directed at raising the wage level of unskilled and semiskilled jobs. Essentially, the incentive system encourages individuals on welfare to seek employment by disregarding the first $30 that they earn in determining their benefit level and by taxing additional earnings at a marginal tax rate of 66⅔ percent. This system has the peculiar effect of making people economically better off if their income is derived both from work and from benefits. Consider the following example: in Pennsylvania the maximum total allowance for a family of four on public assistance is $259 per month or about $3,120 per year. As a result of a recent change in policy aimed at reducing inequities among program categories, this schedule of allowances applies to all federally aided categories and to general assistance. If the head of the household were to participate in a work incentive program, to this basic grant would be added on an annual basis an additional $360 for the income disregard, $240 for employment related expenses, a maximum of $1560 of earnings at a marginal tax rate of 66⅔ percent, and a break even point of $4,680. This $2,160 could be added to the allowance of $3,120 for a maximum total of approximately $5,280. By contrast an individual who earns the minimum wage and works year-round at 40 hours per week would find his net earnings to be substantially lower. His $3,328 annual income is subject to a 2 percent city wage tax and about a 5 percent social security tax, yielding a net income of $3,105. To this amount must be subtracted his work expenses of $210 thus leaving him with a net of about $2,865.

Thus those individuals who earned at the minimum wage level would end up with about $2,900 as compared with the $5,280 that an AFDC parent could obtain if she secured benefits and found work which enabled her to earn up to the break even income level. In order for an individual to be better off economically while receiving no benefits she would thus have to earn at least $5,280 per year. Only 1 percent of women and 23 percent of men on AFDC and AFDC-UP who completed MDTA programs, through October 1964, earned more than $2.50 per hour or about $5,200 per year.[20] In the example used, benefits supplement wages for a family of four up to an earning level of slightly over $100 per week. Accordingly, the incentive system has the effect of making most individuals economically better off if they are in both the welfare system and the employment system.

The implications of this analysis seem to me to be compelling. As long as we rely on an incentive system combined with a service and training strategy, which is not supported by a systematic policy to raise the wage level of the low earning sector, then we have in effect elected a policy which encourages an overlap of supplementation between the wage and the benefit sectors. I believe that this is a dramatic example of a change without a clear choice. We have drifted into this set of changes without a searching reexamination of the assumption that the economy can generate jobs at high enough wages to meet family needs.

The traditional economic theory of the relationship between work and welfare may be summarized as follows: Society may be seen as a self-regulated economy where the natural forces of the market combined with aggregative fiscal policies produce a set of labor market conditions which offers an adequate livelihood for every able-bodied man who wants to work. A properly operated economy should provide an economic function for all of its able-bodied labor force and for those who are dependent on them. Society can be divided into two classes of people: the able-bodied and those dependent on their earnings; and those dependent groups who have no able-bodied breadwinners to support them, including the sick, aged, children, and physically disabled. Just as an economic policy was needed to heat up the economy when it was unable to use up the available labor supply, or to cool off the economy when employment became too tight, prices rose, and produced inflation, so a social policy was needed to pick up the responsibility for those who were economically dependent and without an able-bodied breadwinner. By the late 1930s we agreed that a scheme of national protection was needed under which people contributed to a national fund which protected them and their dependents from income loss for a specified list of risks, and that a federally aided system of public assistance was needed for those who were out of the labor force and in economic need.

This implied a philosophy that the able bodied who failed to find protection for their dependents or income for their needs were unworthy or incompetent. If this view is not accepted, social policy needs to be directed at teaching the poor to limit their needs by controlling family size, or expanding their earnings through education and training. To be able bodied and to be poor seems a contradiction in terms. But if the economy does not always provide an opportunity for those able-bodied poor willing and able to work to earn enough income to meet their needs, this reflects a weakness in the economy rather than in the character of the able-bodied poor. If this question about the inadequate functioning of the economy is accepted, we need to examine why our economy is not able to provide work at high enough wage levels to meet family needs. To focus only on full employment obscures the question about the quality of that employment. This dilemma concerns wage levels rather than employment levels.

To raise minimum wages threatens the volume of jobs. Yet to neglect to raise them leaves a family of four earning at this level in a city like Philadelphia with a net take home pay (after taxes and work expenses are deducted) of less than $2,900, an amount lower than the poverty level of $3,500 for such a family. This makes low wage jobs not worth offering. Many jobs at or near the minimum wage are not filled, because they offer earnings at less than the minimum people are willing to accept. Moreover with increased affluence we have been prepared to raise the budget allowance for a family of four on welfare at an even faster rate than minimum wages. Durbin shows that in New York City between the years 1962 and 1967 minimum wages rose 30 percent, while the welfare budget allowance increased by 45 percent.[21] While minimum wages did rise faster than the 19 percent increase in average wages in manufacturing in New York City during this period, benefit standards rose even faster. (As we have seen this applies nationally as well.)

The English have tried to resolve this awkward policy problem by a system of wage stops, which prevents a worker entitled to welfare benefits from getting more in benefits, regardless of his needs, than he could have earned when he was employed. Here is the principle of less eligibility at work in the mid-twentieth century under a Labor government. The emphasis on incentives in welfare policy in the United States has, I believe, driven us to a principle of wage supplementation. We have, by and large, rejected the English version of less eligibility, which is the wage stop, and we have also avoided a serious discussion about the consequences which follow from increasing welfare benefits faster than wage levels. The difference between an employment or job policy and a wage policy in the low minimum wage sector has been obscured. We have drifted into a program of supplementation without a clear choice in support of it. Cloward and Piven have recognized the ambiguity and are seeking to exploit it creatively as a strategy of change through confrontation. They are calling for a new effort to organize the employees in the low wage sectors to secure the benefits they are entitled to under welfare.

They argue that the Home Relief system can serve as the mechanism for wage supplementation in New York City for a substantial number of families. A family earning at minimum wages is entitled to a wage supplement of from about $1,000 per year to $3,800 depending on the number and age of the children. Workers earning at higher wage levels are also entitled to wage supplements ranging from $360 to $760 per year based on the number and age of their children.[22] By this strategy they want to have benefits supplement wages. The foregoing analysis focused on wages as a supplement to benefits, but the principles and issues are similar.

"BENEFITS IN KIND" AS WELFARE SUPPLEMENT

While public attention is debating the means tested cash transfer system, a means tested "benefits in kind" system has emerged with estimated annual expenditures in fiscal year 1969 of about $6.3 billion (see Table 2). These benefits in kind are supplements to both the welfare system and the low wage sector. It is increasingly difficult to distinguish between a supplementary and a substitutive system. For example, when Governor Rockefeller cut the New York State welfare budget he sought to include the value of food stamps as a substitute for the lost welfare benefits. The rediscovery of hunger, the preoccupation with reducing welfare through rehabilitation, and the commitments to provide medical care for the poor suggest that means tested, in-kind programs are likely to grow at an even more rapid rate than have means tested cash transfers.

Table 2

Benefits in Kind: Outlays for Selected Programs

	Outlays (millions of dollars)		
Type of Means Tested Benefits and Programs	*1968 actual*	*1969 estimate*	*1970 estimate*
Medicare	$3,686	$4,612	$5,797
Food and Nutrition	913	1,221	1,445
Food stamps	187	273	338
Child Nutrition	217	246	367
Special Milk	104	104	15
Removal of surplus commodities	385	598	725
Housing:			
Public Housing	290	335	456
Rent Supplements	2	14	30
Training[1]	—	84	172
Child Care[1]	—	31	95

[1] Estimates for child care and training for welfare recipients in the WIN program is based upon data presented in "Program Memorandum on Income Maintenance and Social and Rehabilitation Services of the Department of Health, Education and Welfare," *op. cit.*, Section 11, 1.7. The HEW estimate of costs is at variance with the estimate in the Special Analysis which projects total outlays for WIN program in 1969 at $90 million and 50,000 children are expected to receive child care services.

The table is reproduced in the *Special Analysis, Budget of the United States*, Fiscal Year 1970, Table M-9, p. 185.

CONCLUSIONS

This discussion has examined the development of public policy during the 1960s that has come to assign priority to a cash transfer policy. This, in turn, has launched a national debate about the choice that new or reformed cash transfers might take. While we are debating these choices, we have introduced changes in our cash transfer system (and especially in the means tested sector of this system) without explicitly having accepted the choices in philosophy which these changes imply. We have, on the one hand, a debate about policy choice in which there is little change; and, on the other hand, we have introduced changes without explicit policy choices to support them. The changes we have already adopted, often without careful scrutiny as to whether they support our explicit policy choices, warrant serious reexamination. Would we explicitly choose the changes we have made? I list only one issue in doubt.

In some states we have already assured benefit levels in public assistance at or near the poverty line and added an incentive scheme to this guarantee. This change in policy tends to lead to the curious outcome that families are likely to be economically better off when they are *at work and on welfare*. To avoid this dilemma, we need policies which are not only directed at altering the capability and motivation of the supply of manpower, but are directed as well at the supply system. A wage level policy is needed which seeks to raise the wages in the marginal, low wage economy and to make work an alternative rather than a supplement to benefits. Under what circumstances then do we subsidize the low wage earners with means-tested benefits, or universal children allowances which supplements wages by taking account of faimly size or subsidize the industries in which they are employed? The impact that improvements in low wages will have on the volume of jobs and on the rest of the economy is a critical issue, more informed by passion than understanding. We have been reluctant to debate a wage level policy, yet this remains the basic issue as means-tested cash transfers are used to supplement low wages and as the welfare poor are encouraged to become the working poor as well.

NOTES

1. See, for example, James Reston, editorial in *The New York Times*, describing the philosophy of the Poverty Program (The Economic Opportunity Act of 1964), January 16, 1967.
2. Special analysis, *Budget of the United States*, fiscal year 1970 (Washington, D.C.: U.S Government Printing Office, 1969), p. 139.
3. James L. Sundquist, "Job, Training, and Welfare for the Under-Class," in *Agenda for a Nation* (Washington, D.C.: Brookings Institution, 1968), p. 61. Rehn and Lundberg in "Employment and Welfare: Some Swedish Issues," *Industrial Relations* (February 1963) argue that while an indiscriminate job creation policy does have an inflationary effect, a well-planned job creation policy together with a comprehensive manpower policy need not.
4. The data on fair hearings are cited in Larry Podell's Testimony before the Adams Committee, a Joint-Legislation Committee to revise the social service laws in New York, 1968.
5. Sidney H. Schoenberg, "In New York, the Ax is Heaviest on Welfare," *The New York Times*, Section 4, April 6, 1969.
6. James L. Sundquist, *Politics and Policy: The Eisenhower, Kennedy, and Johnson Years* (Washington, D.C.: The Brookings Institution, 1968), p. 126.
7. Report of the House Ways and Means Committee to accompany H.R. 10606, No. 1414, 87th Congress, 2nd Session, March, 1962, p. 3.
8. "Excerpts from Nixon's Message to Congress on Welfare," *The New York Times*, August 2, 1969, p. 18.
9. See Irene Lurie, "An Economic Evaluation of Aid to Families with Dependent Children" (Washington, D.C.: The Brookings Institution, September 1968) (mimeo.).
10. "Program Memorandum on Income Maintenance and Social and Rehabilitation Services Programs of the Department of Health, Education and Welfare,"

Fiscal Year 1970–74. November 1968. Part II, pp. 3–6. U.S. Dept. of Health, Education and Welfare, Office of the Asst. Secretary (Planning and Evaluation).

11. *The New York Times,* August 2, 1969, *op. cit.,* p. 18.

12. *Services for People,* Report of the Federal Task Force on the Organization of Social Services, Washington, D.C.: U.S. Dept. of Health, Education and Welfare, 1968 (mimeo.). In April, 1968 only 24 states were paying four-person AFDC families 100 percent of cost standards of basic need. But in other states, work is a supplement to low benefits. Some of the states, where only a portion of the official standard of need is paid in the form of welfare benefits, individuals are permitted to work to make up the difference. These practices deserve serious study as public policy accepts the principle of supplementation.

13. The estimate is based on the February 1969 experience and projected for the balance of the year. The federal share of the AFDC costs was $998,500 and the state share $815,900. General Assistance costs were $322,000, for which there was no federal reimbursement.

14. "Characteristics of the AFDC in Philadelphia," December 1967 (mimeo.), Table 14; and "Study of Characteristics of Regular Segment of Aid to Dependent Children Families," March 1962 (mimeo.), Table 10. The data are based on a 3 percent sample in 1961.

15. Comparisons are even more difficult because the Philadelphia study is based on AFDC cases in 1961 and on AFDC and TADC cases in 1967. The proportion of TADC included in 1967 is very small.

16. Elizabeth F. Durbin, *The Effect of Welfare Programs on the Decision to Work,* prepared for Project Labor Market, New York University, Graduate School of Business Administration, August 1968, Table E-2a.

17. Special Analysis, *Budget of the United States,* Fiscal Year 1970, p. 184.

18. *Wages and Related Benefits,* Part II: Metropolitan Areas, United States and Regional Summaries, 1966–67. Bureau of Labor Statistics, U.S. Department of Labor, Bulletin No. 1530–87, July 1968, p. 77.

19. David M. Gordon, "Income and Welfare in New York City," *The Public Interest,* No. 16, Summer 1969, p. 82.

20. These findings are cited in Leonard Hausman, "The AFDC Amendments of 1967: Their Impact on the Capacity for Self-Support and the Employability of AFDC Family Heads," Proceedings of 1968 Annual Meeting of Industrial Relations Research Association, May 1968, p. 507.

21. Durbin, *op. cit.,* Table D-3. Average monthly direct grants increase for all assistance categories by 37 percent and 32 percent for ADC, 44 percent for TADC, and 28 percent for Home Relief.

22. Richard A. Cloward and Francis Fox Piven, "The Poor Against Themselves," *The Nation,* November 25, 1968.

Chapter 17

Social Services and Economic Independence

SOCIAL SERVICES RISE TO PROMINENCE

The 1960s have witnessed an accelerated growth in the development of social service in the United States, inspired largely by federal legislation directed at delinquency, unemployment, poverty, and urban decay. Because the social services are so difficult to define, estimates of the amount we spend for them are uncertain. In a yet unpublished series, the Social Security Administration has attempted to specify program components in addition to education, housing, and medical care, and to estimate the expenditures for these other public welfare programs. They have included in their figures vocational rehabilitation, institutional care, school meals, child welfare, special OEO programs (excluding Head Start), and, finally another residual category, "social welfare not elsewhere categorized." Federal outlays for social services, so defined, increased from $450 million to over $1 billion between 1960 and 1966. The $1.04 billion spent by the federal government in 1966 represents 44 percent of the $2.3 billion spent by all levels of government in that year for social services.

This paper was first published in a National League of Cities' report entitled *The Planning and Delivery of Social Services*. It was presented in September 1968 at a conference sponsored by the National League of Cities and the Center for Community Planning, Department of Health, Education and Welfare.

The prominence of the social services is, however, not completely due to their expenditure level. The marginal rate of increase of funds for new and established programs available to communities lacking resources and hence eager to capture federal funds,[1] combined with the requirement that the receipt of these funds be contingent upon the commitment to experiment and to innovate, did, of course, contribute much to the visibility of the social services. But the primary factor that thrust the social services into prominence during this period was, I believe, a reinterpretation of their mission and the unobtrusive inclusion of this new function in diverse types of social legislation directed toward different problems and populations.

Much, but not all, of the social legislation in the early 1960s can be so interpreted. The Area Redevelopment Act of 1961; the Manpower Development and Training Act of 1962, and especially its amendments since that date; the amendments to the Social Security Act of 1962 and 1967; the Economic Opportunity Act of 1964; and the Demonstration Cities and Metropolitan Development Act of 1966 illustrate a converging commitment to a single strategy—the use of social policy to promote labor force participation. Thus, to partially solve the problems of depressed areas—unemployment, public welfare, delinquency, poverty, and urban decay—we have pursued the goal of promoting economic self-sufficiency by placing our faith in social "investment" programs.

The influence of the investment strategy in the 1960s has been pervasive and persistent. It can be found everywhere among the wide range of social welfare programs. Amenities like child care, once seen as a tool to enrich the psychological and social development of children, have become instruments for getting welfare mothers to work. Counseling and therapy to enable man to enjoy life better and give it meaning and dignity have become work preparation, a strategy to expand the employability of ghetto youth. Counseling has recently been extended to cope with the employability problems of adults in the ghetto. Education, as a means of enhancing the quality of life, is narrowly defined as a means for increasing income and achieving occupational mobility. Even cash transfer programs to welfare recipients are interpreted not only as means of meeting need, but as techniques for promoting self-maintenance.

WHAT ARE SOCIAL SERVICES?

Much confusion surrounds the meaning and usage of the term "social services." The following indicates how the concept is used here. We have a federal Department of Health, Education and Welfare. Welfare, in this context, is defined as a means-tested, cash transfer program. When the cash component of this program is removed, a variety of activities remain. These might be called the little "w" in welfare, while the big "W"—in terms of expenditures—is cash benefits. These little "w's" are intended to perform a variety of social service functions. One of the most widely accepted functions is "to help individuals to overcome the obstacles that stand in the way of their use of . . . other services."[2] This linking and connecting function is one recurrent theme. One way to approach a definition of the social services is to explore what they do, for which groups, and for what purposes. Although the main focus of this paper is directed to the questions that surround the purpose of these services, a brief comment about the functions and the group serviced may be useful. I have classified the functions of the social services in terms of five "P's":

Preparation: The use of counseling, guidance, and information to enable individuals to make use of other available institutions.

Procurement: The process of referring individuals to other community resources.

Provision: The rendering of concrete or "hard" services—such as day care, homemaking, meals on wheels, etc.—that facilitate the use of other programs and extend well-being.

Participation: The planned involvement of consumer groups to serve: (1) as a source of information concerning their own needs and preferences; (2) as a strategy of pressure to produce institutional change; (3) as a means of encouraging conformity to accepted norms, without coercion; and (4) as encouraging the use and legitimatizing the function of the social services.

Protection: Assuring that individuals are protected against arbitrary exclusion from programs to which they are entitled, protected against programs that may unintentionally inflict hurt, and guaranteed quality and equality of services.

Programs to carry out each of these functions can be used for many purposes. Participation can be used to indoctrinate, to control, to socialize, and to change. Individuals can be prepared "to adjust to reality" as well as to change it, or they may be encouraged to accept emotionally their exclusion from services, or they can be organized effectively to demand their legal right to these benefits. The social services are not inherently benevolent for they can serve many masters. Moreover, it is important to distinguish inputs from outputs. Services may not achieve the purposes for which they were intended—they may prove a source of hurt as well as a source of help. Intent is, after all, not an index of performance. Although these services have been traditionally directed at marginal groups that fail to perform at the level of some institution's standards of adequacy, most groups in society can, at some point, profitably make use of each or all of these functions.

Medical care, education, housing, and cash transfers are not social services in the sense used here.[3] However, when these programs are used as aids to enable individuals to make better use of other programs, they come to take on the characteristics of a social service linking individuals to services and services to each other. A medical care program in a school, or a housing program as a component of a manpower program, may be regarded as a social service when it better enables individuals to consume education and manpower training services.

Finally, we tend to redefine, over a period of time, the boundaries between social services and social welfare. Head Start, a program designed to link ghetto children more effectively into the early grades of school, may be regarded as a social service. Should the program become nationwide in scope as a compulsory kindergarten program, then we will redefine the program as education. This process, of course, tends to reinforce the residual character of social services. Perhaps at some future date, if children have difficulty in utilizing these new kindergarten programs, new social services will emerge to aid the dropouts of this program.

The boundaries that distinguish social services from social welfare programs are vague. Social services at least have certain features in common because they link individuals to other services, they are concerned with the capacity to consume, they extend the level of living by redistributing amenities to disadvantaged groups, they serve as proxies for cash, and they are sometimes used as levers for change.[4]

WHY THE SOCIAL SERVICES CAME TO PROMINENCE

What factors have brought about the emergence of the social services? This is an intriguing question that will perhaps preoccupy historians in the future, but I would like to offer some provisional interpretations.

First, the opportunity theory of delinquency and the investment theory of economic growth were joined by individuals influential in the development of federal social policy. The sociological theory held that delinquency was brought about when aspirations could not be fulfilled because opportunities were blocked. Access to employment and education was the key to unlocking the door that was inhibiting full participation in society. Later the argument was loosely extended as the rationale for a strategy to reduce urban race riots on the assumption that it was the marginal and excluded individuals who participated in these disturbances.[5] The economic theory attempted to account for the dramatic evidence that conventionally measured inputs in production left unexplained a very large fraction of the measured growth in national products. This set off a variety of attempts to identify, specify, and measure components of "the residual."[6] Out of these efforts came the human investment approach with its emphasis on

the importance of education and other social services as factors that contribute to national income growth. In the introduction to a three-volume
study of all federal government programs that are directed to supporting or
developing people in the United States, we find the following vigorous
statement about the importance of social policy to economic growth: "It has
become evident that the concept of investment in human resources . . . is
essential to analytical efforts to account for economic growth and the productive achievements of technologically advanced countries."[7]

Perhaps this juxtaposition of opportunity theory and human investment
theory is artificial. Perhaps the observation that there was a joining of the
concerns of delinquency and economic growth, in which both relied on a
common strategy of promoting education, is irrelevant. Yet, concerns about
the causes of the residual of economic growth and the residual population,
outside of the norms of conventional society, seemed to have reinforced
each other and provided a rationale in which social and economic policies
appear dependent upon each other. Myrdal eloquently offered the rhetoric
for such an alliance when he asserted that now, as never before, the interests in humanity and growth have converged.[8] As social and economic
objectives reinforce each other, the requirements of social justice and
economic growth march hand in hand.

The investment approach was widely believed to represent a departure
from the traditional view of social welfare that saw welfare as an economic
burden, draining off resources from the productive members of society
to its nonproductive members. It was assumed that the provision of economic
and social security eroded the incentive to work and paralyzed the initiative
to participate in the economic life of the community. During the depression
of the 1930s, we came to accept a new role for social welfare. It was considered not as a burden, but as a creator of consumption, expanding economic demand by providing cash to families so that they could continue their
roles as economic consumers, even though no longer able to earn an income.
So defined, social policy was directed to safeguarding the consumption needs
of the noneconomically active population, especially through transfer payments to the aged and handicapped and their dependents.

But the most recent formulations depart from earlier social policies that
served as social bandaids, tending the wounds of those who were fallouts of
the economic system. These interventions occurred after the market had
generated disparities between need and income. The investment strategy
attempts to alter the source and amount of income and the occupational
position of individuals, both before and after they enter the market system.
It assigns to social policy a new role as investor in human resources, stimulating aggregate growth by the direct investment in human capital that
yields a return of enhanced human productivity, not by the "under-con-
sumptionist's" argument of expanding demand by contributing to the marginal propensity to consume.

A second factor contributing to the emergence of social services in the 1960s may be in a carry-over of the interpretations about poverty and its causes that were widely held in the preceding decade. In the 1950s it was assumed that economic growth was redistributing income and that the traditional economic problems had largely been solved. Capitalism has tamed the business cycle, and severe economic depressions are no longer with us. In this mood Arthur Schlesinger asserted in an article in *The New York Times Magazine* in 1957, "The major problem of economic structure seems to be solved." He went on to complain that we had inherited a misleading legacy from the New Deal, the assumption that the essential problem of liberalism was the fight against poverty. The villain of the piece was not "the conspiracy of wealth," but "the conspiracy of blandness."[9] The social costs of affluence—blandness, conformity, mass society—were the pressing challenges of the period.

Social policy during this period languished on the optimistic assumption that a social revolution created by economic growth would equalize incomes and hence reduce the need for public intervention. When we entered the 1960s and discovered poverty in an affluent society, we treated it, to use Galbraith's term, as "case poverty."[10] The shift from a mass unemployment economy, to an economy in which unemployment and underemployment are based to a great extent upon class and race, is often advanced as one persuasive argument to support the need for social policy. Then Secretary of Labor Willard Wirtz asserted at the Senate Hearings on the War on Poverty that unemployment is a personal and not an economic problem. On this assumption, investment programs designed to rescue the poor from their culture of poverty, apathy, and alienation seem valid.[11] This interpretation of the causes of disengagement from the labor force has been developed in various theories about the culture of poverty. Changing people was, accordingly, assumed to be important, and this could best be achieved by changing the institutions that serviced the poor by altering the tasks and how they were performed. Many of the programs that emerged appear to share this common philosophy.

A third factor contributing to the prominence of the social services was the pragmatic commitment of social reforms to exploit the resources at hand, rather than to wait for fundamental changes and thereby postpone immediate action. In the 1950s it was fashionable to believe that residual poverty would disappear with economic growth. No one was very concerned with poverty. But as soon as poverty became a national issue, and the inadequacy of the social services was seriously considered, anxiety about structural unemployment also rose.

In 1961, the average unemployment level was at 6.7 percent, but Negro unemployment was two times the national average, unemployment among youth three times the average, and unemployment among Negro youth four times the average figure. Concentration on the organization and development of social services served as the rationalization for an inability to tackle, especially in urban areas, the more fundamental questions about job creation and more resources for the high cost social welfare programs. There was, however, more success in introducing fiscal policies to stimulate aggregate demand. Moreover, an economic policy to create enough labor demand to employ the available labor supply requires accepting some inflation, a tighter balance of payments, and the reduction of freedom for both business and labor through the imposition of national standards of prices and wages.[12] Thus, many were unwilling to pay the price, even if it had been politically feasible.

In summary, theoretical, historical, and philosophical ideals seem to have been drawn together in thrusting the social services into prominence. The theory of investment supported the repudiation of amenities, caretaking, and consumption programs; and the elevation of opportunity programs, which sought guided occupational mobility as a social objective, stimulated economic growth and promoted social stability. Such a program further supports the American interpretation of social justice that places its faith in programs designed to equalize the opportunity to be unequal, rather than in programs designed to alter the proportion of personal income received by the bottom 20 percent of the population. Opportunity equalization, rather than income equalization, is the goal of the good society. Finally, partly for historical reasons and partly in accommodation to judgments about what was politically feasible, we sought to promote the goal of economic independence and the reduction of poverty and unemployment through social policies that emphasized the social services, rather than through selective economic policies. Thus, we focused on the economic and social objectives of social policy rather than on the social objectives of economic policy.

WHY THE ESTABLISHED PATTERN OF SOCIAL SERVICE NEEDED TO CHANGE

A new and important role for social services could only emerge if the structure and function of the established service institutions would change, or if new services could be grafted on to the old. We review first the criticism directed against social services in the early 1960s, and then examine the principles of reform that were sought.

There was concern that the social services were inappropriate to the needs of the poor, which were defined as employment and education. As a result, there was a widespread pattern of underutilization of services, because the poor repudiated services that were not relevant to their needs and institutions rejected the poor for their inability to use what was offered to them.[13] These criticisms can be reviewed in three main areas—the distribution, the relevance, and the performance of the social services.

Distribution

At the heart of the criticism was the failure of institutions to reach the poor and the disadvantaged groups in society. While Bradley Buell and other critics of the early 1950s focused on how a minority of the poor had captured most of the limited community resources—6 percent of the families were using 50 percent of the resources[14]—the reformers of the 1960s riveted their attention on the interplay between the apathy, indifference, and alienation of the poor and the process of labeling, neglect, and rejection by social institutions. This complementary pattern led to underutilized services. Cloward documented the planned disengagement of family casework agencies from the poor;[15] Gans criticized the membership bias of settlement houses;[16] Cummings showed that for mental health services "the poorer, the more ignorant, and the sicker the patient, the more eligible he is for treatment by the less trained and less professional practitioners";[17] Rein, drawing on his research on child welfare, presented the case that professionals in the social services had succumbed to the pressure to work with "good" clients and had neglected those in greatest need.[18]

What all these critics shared was the belief that social welfare programs tended to work with the more advantaged groups and neglected the poor. This process of "creaming" resulted in the underutilization of services, and so a strategy to enhance utilization was sought. Whereas the critics in the 1950s saw the problem essentially as one of the overuse of services, for which they proposed a more effective deployment of professional personnel by reallocating case loads, the critics of the 1960s saw the problem as one of underuse. They were disturbed that professionalism contributed to the creation or reinforcement of this pattern and placed their faith in structural reform—altering the pattern of allocating and delivering social services—as well as changing the content of the services.

Relevance

Disengagement was attributed largely to the failure to be relevant. Two themes for comment seem to lie at the base of much of the criticism of relevance. First, there was a concern about the maldistribution of "soft" and "hard" services. That is to say, diagnosis, counseling, and passive referral came to dominate the social services, while the provision of physical resources and individual advocacy were neglected in the struggle to secure resources from other agencies. The study, *Girls at Vocational High School*,[19] though written in a somewhat later period, helps to make explicit and vivid the general line of this criticism. Girls with severe reading handicaps were not referred to reading clinics for concrete help in reading. The emphasis was placed on helping them to overcome the "emotional difficulties" that inhibited their capacity to read.

The second criticism was that social services failed to play a role ancillary to investment programs. They did not prepare people to make use of educational facilities and training programs that would enhance their capacity to secure better jobs. They were too narrowly tied to an older conception of diagnosis and treatment, bearing the mark of a medical, clinical model that viewed dependency and deviancy as personal pathology requiring individual treatment.[20] To replace this "sickness" model, a developmental model was sought in which the crucial developmental phases were the transition from the home into the school and from the school into the world of work. Here the influence of the human resource approach is evident.

A brief look at the distribution of social service personnel by employment in ancillary or autonomous settings may help to shed further insight into the nature of this criticism. (Public assistance is excluded, since it is not primarily a "service.") If we accept as a working definition that ancillary settings are those that help individuals make use of other institutions[21]— such as the courts, schools, and rehabilitation, medical, and psychiatric agencies—then we can make a preliminary estimate of the concentration of personnel in these settings. Approximately one-third of all personnel, including those who are graduates of schools of social work, are based in ancillary settings so defined. The trend over the past decade is an increase in the employment of social service workers in these settings, from 25 percent to 31 percent. The largest rate of increase between 1950 and 1960 for all personnel occurred in the courts and in psychiatric settings; the most rapid rates of increase of professional social workers were in school, rehabilitation, and psychiatric settings. Although schools and rehabilitation show a high growth rate, combined they nevertheless account for only 5 percent of the distribution of all the professionally trained personnel in 1960.[22] In summary, only a small proportion of social service workers, including those who are professionally trained at schools of social work, are employed in ancillary settings, and they are concentrated in settings concerned with pathology and deviance.

There is a surprising similarity between trained and all social service workers—55 percent of both groups are employed in autonomous settings. Professionally trained personnel are concentrated in family casework, mental health, and child welfare. All social service workers tend to be employed primarily in child welfare and recreation. Programs that might be described as consumption programs, although they are concrete services, are not relevant to an "investment" approach. While there is some overlap, professionals, on the other hand, tend to work with emotional disabilities and dispense "soft" services that, by and large, lack a framework linking emotional disability to work disability. Neither the professionally trained nor the non-trained are oriented to a "human resources" strategy.

Performance

The third criticism directed at the social services was that they were not only rigid and indifferent to the needs of their clients, but actually harmful to them. A cultural gulf between the professional and the consumer had developed. Social service workers, like ghetto teachers and welfare workers, supposedly held their pupils and clients in low esteem. This process of labeling served to reinforce or create alienation. The evidence suggested that teacher expectation affected student performance. Rainwater has recently described the task of social workers as that of dirty workers who "carry out society's covert orders to control and cool out those who must be excluded from ordinary society."[23]

One example is the use of social service workers to exclude unwanted people from public housing projects in New York City. Workers were asked to evaluate families whose members fell into any of twenty-one behavior categories and were regarded as "potential problems." The Housing Authority "conceded that the evaluation process took so long that if an applying family was referred to the social service division its chance of getting an apartment was remote."[24] Intake interviews may be seen not only as a process of intake and acceptance, but as one of exclusion. The process of determining eligibility for services, one of the traditional tasks of social service workers, must be understood as a decision to reject as well as to embrace. Referral may be seen as a tactic for the management of rejection. The objects of criticism were the commitment of the professionals and the policies of the organizations that employed them. This stinging indictment of the social services is illustrated in the statement Sargent Shriver made before the House Education and Labor Committee, where he described them as "hostile, uncaring, and exploitative institutions." The Negro community as well, accused them of "cashing in" and "cooling out," which combined to create a grim welfare colonialism where white imperialists exploited black colonials.

WHAT WAS PROPOSED

The basic premise of this analysis of the distribution, relevance, and performance of social services was that the crisis was largely political, administrative, professional, and structural. These difficulties could be overcome by "technical know-how, project innovation, self-help, and consumer aggression."[25] Hence innovation, social experimentation with professional tasks, and organizational coordination became central. What was called for was the reform of the delivery system. The vocabulary of reform was inspired by the model that most closely corresponded to the new direction that reform in the social services was urged to take—making poor people more productive through opportunity programs. Thus, the language of the market became widely accepted in the social services, as we came to talk about "delivery systems," "packaging services," "supply and demand," "investment and consumption." Even the professionals came to be described as "social brokers" or "investment counselors in human resources."

The reformers sought to make social services concrete and accessible. Neighborhood centers, inspired by Mobilization for Youth, became the prototype. They tried to make their services both more concrete and more acceptable, assuring that referrals were not polite rejections, but that they might serve to initiate a process that culminated with individuals actually receiving relevant and wanted service. Citizen participation emerged as one strategy by which intransigent service bureaucracies could be pressured into change. The use of nonprofessionals was also encouraged as a strategy of change, although it was inspired by other ideals as well. Legal services were also established to reduce institutional exclusion and to widen, under law, the principle of the right to benefits. Thus, to stimulate greater use of services, a pattern of decentralization supported by law and pressure was developed.

New Haven's Unified Social Service Center provides an illustration of the effort to coordinate services by making them ancillary to manpower training. At the heart of this program were the opportunity services of education and training. Eighty percent of all clients known to the multiservice center were also active in the opportunity program, and more than one-third of those in the opportunity program had been referred to the multiservice center because they had failed to perform adequately in the program.[26]

In this context social services are rendered in an effort to reduce the failure and dropout rate from the opportunity centers. They serve as a handmaiden to training. (Some family casework agencies inspired by such examples, have attempted to move in a similar direction by rendering their services in cooperation with training programs.) The assumption is that training without counseling and supportive services is less effective, that counseling will enhance a person's capacity to complete training and to obtain and hold a job.

Whereas these earlier experimental programs tried to link services and training, later programs attempted to draw together social services and employment. The "Jobs Now" program in Chicago illustrates the kind of ancillary role social service can play in industry. Industry agrees to redefine its entry requirements (hiring policies) and is willing to alter its tolerance levels (firing policies) on the condition that social services are available to provide support, education, and counseling to the marginal workers who are employed by industry. Thus, ancillary services may operate in at least two ways: as a strategy of preparation designed to facilitate the entry of individuals into the work, training, and educational systems; or alternately, as a system of support for individuals who are part of these systems, but are having performance difficulties. The ancillary roles of preparation and, to a much lesser extent, support are examples of the new direction that social services were called upon to take.

In addition to the emphasis on innovation, access, participation, coordination of training, and employment, new forms for reallocating social services were sought and several other principles emerged. Selectivity of a geographically delimited target area—poverty areas rather than people in poverty—was made the unit for program and provision, in an effort to implement the principle that Titmuss has called "Territorial Welfare Justice."[27] It is assumed that a broad social deficit exists among residents throughout the area. Hence it is possible to make services universally available, thus making it possible to avoid individual tests of means and needs, because these areas had, by definition, already fallen behind the rest of the community. To equalize opportunities for its residents, unequal amounts of additional resources were to be made available on the theory of positive discrimination. Commenting on the Poor Law of 1909, the Webbs observed that "it is a simple axiom that the addition of equals to unequals produces unequals, whilst it raises the standard of living of all."[28] The principle of positive discrimination seeks an unequal input to produce a more equal outcome. But where were the resources to come from? One assumption was that resources were already at hand, but they were dispersed, fragmented, and poorly coordinated by a system of government and a system of administration that almost inspired the disorder of pluralism as an ideal. Federal, state, and local resources, already available but widely scattered, should be collected and concentrated in these poverty areas. The principle of saturation and decentralization may be understood as strategy for redirecting rather than creating new resources. But increments to resources alone would not be sufficient if the various programs failed to reinforce and support each other. Repackaging of services was also needed. New ways were sought to bring different services together into different combinations. However, the passion to create new systems of delivery was directed more at new forms of linking consumers to services rather than at linking services to each other. The federal government failed to create new models that might serve as a basis for experimentation. Programs were to take account of the consumers' point of view. Power and authority to make programmatic decisions were to be redistributed between the citizen-consumer and the service bureaucracy.

These principles were not altogether internally consistent. Intensive poverty programs concentrated in low-income areas may be efficient by selectivity, but effectiveness may depend on the amount and quality of service rather than on the pattern of organization. Efforts to be responsive to the consumer often proved, at least in the short run, to be inefficient, as the development of services was inhibited in the struggle for authority and control. To require a consistent strategy was too demanding a task; the reformers were more preoccupied with innovation and activity than with coherence.

ASSESSMENT OF THE CRITIQUE AGAINST THE SOCIAL SERVICES AND THE STRATEGY OF REFORM

The criticism that the social services lacked relevance to the poor, were of low quality in their performance, and failed to reach those in greatest need was compelling. Equally convincing in the light of this assessment was the agenda of reform with its emphasis on innovation, participation, access, and service ancillary to training and work (investment), selectivity, saturation, positive discrimination and repackaging of overspecialized programs. But the diagnosis and the reform, while generally accurate, were incomplete and hence misleading. In this examination of the critique of the social services, four issues are reviewed: the effort to change people without changing their environment, the lack of resources, services as a substitute for national policies, and the investment bias.

The approach assumes that it is possible to change people without changing their circumstances. Accordingly, the central problem was seen as changing service institutions and changing the ability of the poor to use them. Thus, the strategy was directed, as Reston phrased it, at "taking the poverty out of the people." But such an approach must be based on the belief that "the poor can be changed [by learning productive skills, by learning how to use their money wisely, by developing better attitudes, etc.] while they are still poor and that once they have changed they will then be able to . . . do away with their poverty."[29]

However plausible, this assumption, although supported by the charge that people have failed to change institutions to perform their mandate, is vulnerable to the criticism that it has confused cause and effect. That is to say, are the characteristics of the poor the cause of their poverty, as the culture of poverty thesis implies, or are these characteristics an adaptation to the circumstances of deprivation, both absolute and relative, and of exclusion, which is what we mean by poverty? A strategy to alter the flexibility and responsiveness of opportunity generating institutions—training and education—seems less urgent than programs more explicitly directed at altering the resources of the poor. The emphasis on "self-help"—education, information, training, and participation—and the neglect of "care-taking" programs aimed solely at mitigating poverty is an incomplete and misleading reform. Rainwater in a review of the debate between a service and cash strategy argues:

> . . . the resources which income from employment or income maintenance provide, . . . would radically alter the situation to which lower class people have to adapt. As that resource base improved, and as consequently the lower class individuals involved experienced themselves as less and less excluded from conventional society, we could expect that their adaptations would change.[30]

The glaring omission of the program for the poor was the failure to pay attention to the importance of the level of income, whether the source be employment or public transfers, as a direct means to alter not the opportunities, but the circumstances of the poor. Social services were assumed to have a significant role to play in linking and preparing individuals to exploit the education and manpower training opportunities that are available. But this argument is valid only to the extent that dependency and unemployment are aggravated by ignorance, incapacity, or indifference to training and educational opportunities, and to the extent that poverty is worsened by the incapacity to consume, or what Rountree called "secondary poverty," rather than by the lack of resources, "primary poverty." The rationale for a social service strategy thus requires that the problems be seen as personal and structural, in the sense of the failure of service institutions to offer genuine opportunity. That is why so determined an effort was made to see apathy and alienation and the conservatism of the local institutions as the primary causes of dependency and poverty.

If we concede, as I believe we must, that the dichotomy between changing circumstances and changing opportunity is overdrawn and a strategy that combines them both is necessary, then the resource base to carry out the service institutions' functions must be adequate. Here the strategy of reform was especially vulnerable. When the war on poverty was launched, the Economic Opportunity Act made available $1.3 billion annually for the first three years of the program, but with 34 million poor people, this meant that the fight against poverty was based on an average annual expenditure of less than $40 per poor person. "Obviously," as Sar Levitan dryly observed, "this amount fell far short of the President's commitment to wage 'unconditional war on poverty.' "[31] But expediency soon surrendered to ideology, as the possible became the desirable. In order for a billion dollar program to reduce a $12 billion poverty income gap (the aggregate amount of money needed to make the poor nonpoor when poverty is defined as a lack of subsistence income), it must be assumed that the social services have a high multiplier effect in reducing the gap between income and need. Many must have believed this to be true, for Shriver confidently predicted the elimination of poverty in ten years. The intellectual basis for this belief was the argument advanced by Myrdal that because poverty is caused by a "circular and cumulative process, continuously pressing levels downward, in which one negative factor is, at the same time, both cause and effect of other negative factors," then it would seem reasonable to expect that positive intervention at many points in the cycle of poverty will produce final effects of much greater magnitude than the reforms themselves.[32] In other words, a small increase in resources could create a big change, for the root of the problem was largely administrative, professional, and structural.

In answer to the question of why were the poor left out of the social service world, the theories advanced stressed that the poor were either alienated, uninformed, or unwanted. Each theory leads to different policy implications. One position stresses the condition of the potential consumer. He is defined as alienated, apathetic, and disinterested in availing himself of services. Citizen participation is crucial here on the assumption that it is an effective form of therapy—as people try to change their world, they change in the process. Social action is a strategy for promoting engagement and reducing apathy. Or perhaps the alienated consumer may require supports to assure that he is sufficiently motivated to use the service; then nonprofessionals, capable of providing peer supports, may be regarded as one approach to the problem of underuse.

The cause of underutilization might also be the uninformed consumer. Information, then, is the crucial ingredient needed to expand utilization. But if the causes of underutilization are seen as arising from the policies and practices of rejection by the service distributors, we must then either develop other personnel to cope with the unwanted, rather than with the ignorant or the alienated, or modify those attributes of the poor that lead to their rejection. We may accordingly be led to seek reforms to change organizational policies and practices of the agency—for example, by decentralizing services, reallocating authority, or by replacing the institution altogether, as in the case of the present debate about alternative approaches to public assistance. At the same time we can work to modify those class differences and racial stereotypes that create a cultural gulf between caretakers and their clients. The task is defined as a need for internal reform of a specialized service, as well as the reorganization of the relationship between consumer and service units.

If, however, we were to define the problem of underutilization as one that arises from scarcity where each agency is forced to ration limited resources either by serving many and giving little to each, or by serving few and providing more for each, then the allocation of more resources is the relevant strategy to solve the problem of underuse. Indeed, a more aggressive program of linking consumer to service may result only in altering the pattern of claims for these services and not the amount of services.

Internal reform and the expansion of resources may be seen as alternative strategies for coping with underutilization. New programs and structures do not seem so urgently needed. We need simply to extend to the ghetto the amount, the pattern, the quality, and the procedures of accountability for service outcomes that already exist in other communities. So defined, the problem is one of commitment, not of structure.

If we accept the assumption that the problems of marketing social services are similar to those involved in the marketing of other commodities, then we need to pay attention to three phases of the process: production costs that convert resources into a product; distribution that packages and markets the product; and consumption, where the consumer is motivated to purchase the product and presumably then to put it to some use. But the diagnosis of the malaise in the social services has been focused on the latter phases, to the neglect of the initial phase, that is, the costs of production. The efforts at reorganization focused on promoting changes in the delivery and consumption patterns among the users and distributors of social service. The assumption that repackaging alone could enhance the quality and effectiveness of services was both logically and pragmatically wrong. Neglected is the need for a dramatic increase in social resources to be distributed to an expanding market made possible by stimulating demand.

A review of the experience at the neighborhood level, where the program reached the consumer, provides evidence of the crucial importance of resources. The experience in New Haven, one of the best administrated community action programs, revealed that "as soon as the projects offered an opportunity that seemed genuine, they encouraged more response than they could handle. . . . Youth employment centers . . . were scarcely opened before their facilities were overtaken by the demand they brought to light. After three years of continual expansion, Community Progress Inc. . . . was still able to provide some service to only half of those who applied."[33] If C.P.I.'s rate of expenditures, in a program reaching only half of the poor, "were projected on a national scale, a sum of $10 to $13 billion annually would be required." Mitchell Sviridoff, then director of Community Progress Inc., has estimated that to reach all of the poor families in New Haven the cost of the program must be increased threefold. "The cost of community action alone would reach $30 to $40 billion."[34]

Not only was the resource base inadequate, but the timing and the marginal rate of increase of resources served only to exacerbate the problem it had set out to relieve. When the programs were getting launched, large amounts of resources were given more quickly than could be utilized, a phenomenon known as "the year end dumping of federal funds." As needs were uncovered and as capability increased, the funds were cut back. Community action agencies were forced to ration these scarce resources and one might anticipate that they will in time, under this duress, develop tactics of exclusion and rejection of the poor very similar to those that they set out to change in the established institutions.

Although too few resources were given to the social services, too much was also expected of them. The social services were called upon to perform their task of preparing people for work in the absence of a national manpower policy and a national income-maintenance policy. This vacuum in national direction has important consequences in limiting the effectiveness of social service intervention. Not surprisingly, the lack of jobs and income was accepted as a reasonable constraint. The social services proceeded to emphasize the other aspects of poverty, dependency, and personal defects that belong more to their traditional sphere. Although it is true that all programs must accept some practical limit to their aims and work within the context they are given, we run the risk of deceiving ourselves and others by distorting the societal functions of social services when such services are not joined to the wider issues of work and income.

Consider the national concern for the problem of insufficient food for the poor in the United States. "It is intolerable to expect children to get any benefit from free education while they go hungry," a recent editorial in *The New York Times* angrily asserted.[35] With 12.5 million children under 18 living in poverty, fewer than 2 million children, or about 4 percent of all children enrolled in public schools get free or reduced-price lunches. In this context, food may be regarded as a concrete social service, at least to the extent that it enables individuals to make better use of education. To solve this problem of hunger, a national school lunch program or a national food stamp program designed to redistribute available food resources may seem appropriate. But if political obstacles prevent the development of such a national program, then the social services will come to emphasize budgetary management—the art of spending available money more effectively, without a complementary policy that makes available more food or more money. Consumer education must be rejected when it serves as a substitute for a national policy that would alter the size of the population that receives food "free or at reduced prices."[36]

This example of hunger is, of course, only an illustration of the broader tendency to expect too much of social services when they act as a substitute for needed resources. Yet, there is a pervasive use of social services as a means of linking and preparing individuals to exploit opportunities on the assumption that resources are available. The poverty program sought to prepare people for training, only to discover that training is ineffective without jobs. The efforts now being launched to reduce dependency through the use of training services and earning incentives will encounter the same stubborn difficulties if available employment opportunities do not improve the level of income of those on welfare. The social services are then called upon to use carrots and sticks in motivating the welfare poor to work, but without benefit of national commitment to produce adequate jobs that can alter the level of earning as well as the source.

What is at issue is not only an inappropriate mission for the social services, but a distortion of their purposes. Hence, there is a danger that "services" will become "disservices" and "welfare" will become "ill fare." There is, after all, nothing at all inherently beneficent and humanitarian about social services. When they are called upon to serve as a substitute for a national policy to provide income, jobs, or food, they can become instruments to hurt as well as to heal. To stress preparation without resources must in the end only intensify the sense of frustration and despair. Few examples of the humane rationing of scarcity for the poor are available. That the welfare structure has proved to be demeaning and destructive is an indictment that has now become part of the established orthodoxy as America searches for a more adequate cash transfer program.[37]

Are we overstating the case of scarcity and the absence of a national program? What recent progress has been made toward full employment and income redistribution? We have witnessed, during the 1960s, a great deal of interest in manpower policies that seek to influence the supply and distribution of workers and jobs. Although it is true that in the past half dozen years manpower policies have "shifted from an emphasis on manpower as an economic resource to manpower as special training for disadvantaged groups," nevertheless expenditures for these programs are below $2 billion yearly and they reach an average 300,000 persons annually. In 1966–67, new legislation and programs have "provided authorization for about 475,000 public service jobs (nearly one-half of them part-time)."[38] Clearly we have made some advances, but the focus on selectivity of target groups and target geographic areas has not contributed to a policy of guaranteed employment for all those who wish to work. The situation at the time of the 1967 Detroit riots illustrates the problem. The Michigan State Employment Service estimated that 56,000 were unemployed with an additional 70,000 underemployed, yet "all the manpower and anti-poverty programs in the City were employing or training a total of only 7,000 persons."[39] A token program should not be confused with a national commitment to provide full employment.

The federal government is even more deeply involved in cash programs. Between 1960 and 1966 federal cash benefit programs for individuals increased by 55 percent, from $22.5 to $34.8 billion. However, the proportion of total federal expenditures that went to the poor declined slightly, from 37 percent to 36 percent, with projected estimates for 1968 showing a further decline to 35 percent. Public assistance outlays in 1960 account for only 9 percent of all federal expenditures for cash transfers, and projections indicate that these will also decline to 7 percent in 1968.[40]

We have neither moved toward guaranteeing work—a national policy to use up the available labor supply—nor guaranteeing income, with the result that the proportion of total personal income received by the bottom 20 percent of the population has remained unchanged at about 4 percent of the total during the past several decades.

The reforms overstressed the unique emphasis of the investment approach in social policy. A persuasive case can also be made in support of the position that the emphasis on preparation for work and skill development, the reduction of dependency, and the expansion of economic opportunity, represents a continuity in the history of social policy, and especially in the history of social services and social work. In this sense, the Poor Law of 1834 and the Economic Opportunity Act of 1964 represent continued efforts to utilize services as an instrument for promoting economic self-sufficiency. The earlier programs rested on the theory that the will to work could be nurtured by the principles of disenfranchisement: political—the loss of the right to vote, personal—the loss of personal freedom by the workhouse test, and social—by assuring that benefit levels were lower than those of the lowest paid wages. Shame and other deterrents were used to induce the poor not to be dependent. Present politics are still constrained by past tradition, but we have also grafted onto the old a new emphasis on training, education, and the redistribution of dignity, social honor, and even power as strategies to encourage work. The common theme that binds together the traditional and the new social legislation is that of motivating the able-bodied poor to work.[41]

Even the most cursory review of the history of social work suggests how central to the values of the profession has been its commitment to reinforce the work ethic of those who were economically marginal.[42] From its origin in the principles and practices of the Charity Organization Society, to halcyon days of the golden age of social reform at the turn of this century when the settlement house movement flourished, and then to the 1962 Social Security Amendments, social work values have supported policies and programs designed to get the able-bodied poor to work. The social services in general, and social work in particular, have historically been used as strategies to stimulate economic activity and promote economic independence. With the rise of federally financed cash transfers, however, and even before the great depression, social service drifted from this historical function. The psychiatric deluge inundated the social service field, but it also washed away the profession's narrow confinement to the goals of social control and the reduction of dependency. Social work reached out to middle class groups for whom the problems of conformity were subordinate. Even public welfare stressed the rights of mothers to cash benefits. It was believed that women should be in a position to choose between work and welfare. Many believed that the proper place for women with young children was at home raising them, rather than in the market providing for them. Economic conditions reinforced this liberal philosophy, for the urgent need of public policy during the depression was to encourage withdrawal from the labor force rather than increased participation in it. The "new" emphasis on training and employment was a more conservative call to return to the historical legacy that social work had forsaken.

The human resources approach regards people as productive assets, "in which investments may be made and from which tangible, salable returns may be expected." Weissbrod has pointed out, however, that "economic efficiency as a central goal in evaluating human resource programs is in danger of being overextended." Evidence is growing that education, which by our definition is not a social service, may not be profitable for special groups such as those anticipating dropping out of high school, those with seriously deprived backgrounds, and those with low ability. If future empirical work supports the findings that human resource programs have a low investment-efficiency yield, should we abandon these programs for the poor, should we pursue inefficient programs, or must we redefine the social goals that such social welfare programs should serve? Some economists are now saying that we have "paid virtually no attention to the income-distributional effects of . . . [human resources], . . . or to their contribution to other social goals."[43] All of these issues apply as well to the social services.

In a thoughtful review of the relationship between economic and social policy, Kuusi observes that the "fundamental specific function of social policy is not the promotion of economic growth. Its task is to insure the consumption possibilities of the weakest section of the population."[44] The Joint Economic Committee's report also cautiously notes that "appropriate weight needs to be given to non-economic objectives, which economists often lump with consumer satisfactions."[45] Distinguishing between expenditures for consumption and investment poses obdurate conceptual problems. The report offers no criteria for establishing that "appropriate weight." In current practice it seems clear that improving the opportunity for mobility, rather than improving conditions, is the dominant refrain.

The implications for social policy are compelling. Social and economic policies must be separated and social policy must be used to serve social objectives, including extending the quality of living for all members of the society and narrowing the inequities in the distribution of social services, so that the bottom 20 percent of American society receives, at the outcome, a more equitable share of available services. The quality of living, at least in part, depends on the redistribution of amenities and power, which in turn implies a different ranking of social objectives. The quality of life can be extended by using social policy to provide amenities. In the social services, the goals to enjoy, to live, to choose, to develop should be given greater weight than the goals to conform and to produce. The goal of promoting economic independence and productivity cannot be achieved through social policies that emphasize social services, but rather through economic policies. We have neglected the social purposes of economic policy, while urgently insisting on the economic purposes of social policy. In assessing the contribution of social policy to the reduction of inequalities and improving the level of living of workers in England, Barbara Wootton was able to demonstrate that income equalization in the post-World War II period owed more to the pattern of full employment than to the emergence of the "Welfare State."[46]

THE SOCIAL USE OF THE SOCIAL SERVICES

Although the diagnosis of the malaise in the social services is severe, and the reforms proposed are imaginative and bold, they are vulnerable to the criticism that this examination of the critique of the social services has tried to demonstrate. The new reforms embodied in federal legislation to reduce delinquency, poverty, and dependency assume that it is possible to change people without changing their circumstances; that a marginal increase in resources yields a large output because the problems are at root professional, administrative, and structural; that service programs are valid in the absence of a national commitment to redistribute income and to assure full employment for selected groups; and that the new reforms represent a departure from, rather than continuity with, earlier policies for social services. If we have embarked on social experimentation, then the experience of the last half dozen years has made it evident that each of these assumptions is tenuous. As a result of the weaknesses of the underlying rationale, the efforts to enlarge the scope of the social services have succeeded only in narrowing their social mission. Inadvertently, the economic purposes of social services were stressed, such as strategies to get the able-bodied to work, while the social purposes of economic policy were almost altogether neglected. Moreover, too much was expected and too few resources were made available.

Although clarity of purpose was often absent and promise outreached performance, much was accomplished. Although the programs could not provide the needed resources or inspire a national commitment to the ideals of income redistribution and full employment, they did contribute much to the development of new political constituencies that are today transforming professional reform into interest-group politics. Unpopular and unwanted groups are acquiring new power alone and in concert with other groups. They may provide the source of pressure and power that will produce the commitment, the will, and the resources needed to alleviate the problems of race, poverty, dependency, and unemployment.

Whether this struggle is won or lost, we will still need to understand what is a proper use of the social services. A viable role must proceed with the clarification of social objectives. If society wants to reduce poverty, dependency, and unemployment, then the social services have almost nothing to contribute. Full employment and income redistribution are the only viable strategies. If this line of reasoning is valid, then educators should reject the money authorized by the 1967 Amendments to the Social Security Act for the training of social workers to help reduce dependency. Pragmatists and incrementalists will be shocked by this suggestion, since they have for years argued, at least implicitly, that more services are better than less. By implication, the social purposes for which services are to be used are less important. They were confident that once services were available they could be redefined to serve other ends. But this strategy of stimulating growth, while discounting the social mission in the social services, has not proved successful. As a result, those who once supported the 1962 Amendments to the Social Security Act repudiated them in 1967. Even more serious is the failure to recognize that growth is purchased as a substitute for the more demanding, costly policies that are necessary to improve living standards of the poor. The social services appear to have become the primary method for encouraging work and expanding income among the poor.

If, however, society is prepared to alter first the environment in which people live by giving them adequate income, or by placing them on a job, then social services have a minimal role to perform in supporting individuals while they make the transition. I believe that in time most people will make the transition themselves, if the programs to change their environment are authentic. Some individuals will surely need help and so social services as supports to facilitate transitions are valid. But available evidence suggests that the importance of these supports may be exaggerated. For example, the Greenleigh study of personal problems of slum residents in Detroit and the West Side of New York shows that 85 percent of those interviewed had either no problems or only minor problems that were amenable to short term solutions in a period of less than three months.[47] It would appear that when the homes of the poor are taken away to make possible the progress of many at the cost of some, the major problem they confront is the need for another home at a rent they can afford to pay. The crucial program needed is low cost housing provided either by subsidizing the consumer or his dwelling. Prior to these studies it was widely believed, and that was in part why the studies were undertaken, that those who live in slums had emotional, personal, and behavioral problems that inhibited their ability to make the transition into decent physical accommodations. Hence, a social service program to change the capacity to use new facilities was regarded as indispensable if a relocation program was to be successful. However, the lessons to be learned from these inquiries are clear. The major need is for housing and not for social services to link those displaced by renewal to other community services, or to counsel, to teach, or to motivate them to use facilities that public policy is unprepared to provide.

But if the goal of public policy is to extend the level and quality of living of ghetto residents and to redistribute amenities—defined perhaps as those goods and services that have a low income elasticity of demand in the budgets of average households, or more simply, as the equitable distribution of total expenditures for consumption items like vacations, legal protection, and child care arrangements—then the social services have an important role to play. A different mix of these amenities will be needed, depending on the special groups that become the focus of local policies. An international review of the relationship between social security and social services confirmed what common sense would indicate, that the sick, the aged, the young, and those who lack intact families make use of different services. It is therefore difficult to recommend services without specifying the group to be serviced. Nevertheless, some general statements can be made.

For example, the social services could profitably pay even more attention to their protective functions. It has always been claimed that they have a humanizing effect on the institutions in which they function—the courts, the schools, the hospitals, and the prisons—by extending the humanity and compassion of these institutions, even if these ideals have been no more than the vague hopes of utopian visionaries. I think it is important that we go beyond this diffuse humanizing function of social services to develop new instruments that will ensure entitlement, access, and redress of grievances. New forms of social services must be developed for the alienated, for the uninformed, and for the aggrieved.[48] Legal service programs inspired by the Office of Economic Opportunity have done much to redefine social services from a consumer point of view, and to document the inequities in the present dual system of law and social welfare service we have created for the poor and nonpoor. As we discover the rights of the poor, we also discover the need to protect the rights of all citizens from professional discretion and bureaucratic indifference.

In a thoughtful review of the analysis and recommendations of the Seebohm Committee report on personal social services in England, Peter Townsend offers a second general conclusion that applies to all groups who make use of social services. In the social services, he argues, it is "the provision of physical services and resources and the representation of the individual and the family in the struggle to obtain resources from other departments and not the practice of individual casework [that] becomes paramount. The concern should be with the quality of life and the integration and development of the local community."[49]

In conclusion, then, I believe that a positive role for the social services should proceed by first redefining goals so that greater emphasis is given to extending the quality of life and redistributing services. In the absence of national manpower and income redistribution policies, social services should deemphasize the role of preparing, counseling, and linking individuals to investment programs and give priority to providing concrete services and protection that ensures entitlement. When jobs and income are assured, then social services can play a minor role in supporting, preparing, and enabling individuals achieve economic independence. Social services cannot serve as a substitute for a national commitment to assure full employment and adequate income. Wherever it is feasible, the social services should emphasize participation as social action to help develop the political support among consumer groups that will help to realize the objectives of redistribution.

A policy of redistribution requires that the outcome of social services go beyond equalizing opportunities; it should also serve to equalize conditions. To the extent that the social services reflect consumer demand and have an economic value that would be purchased in the market in the absence of public provision, they may be regarded as extensions of income. Redistributing social services also redistributes income. Social services will not make a major contribution to this process of income redistribution, but they do have some role to play and this role should be made an explicit social objective. Surprisingly, they may contribute more to the redistribution of power and prestige than of income by enabling minority groups to control what has been dispensed on their behalf. Thus, the goal of the social services should be explicitly to redistribute income, power, and prestige under the assumption that we will have a better society when the disparities among freedom, mobility, income, and personal dignity are leveled.

NOTES

1. This was a frenetic period of growth in social legislation. During an eight month period in 1965, the Administration proposed and the Congress adopted, at least thirty major pieces of legislation establishing new programs or significantly expanding existing programs. William Gorham, "Sharpening the Knife that Cuts the Public Pie," Lecture No. 2, Washington, D.C. Dept. of Health, Education and Welfare Forum, December 20, 1967, p. 3.
2. Helen L. Witmer, *Social Work: An Analysis of a Social Institution* (New York: Rinehart, 1942), p. 486. The entire book is devoted to the problem of how to define social work. The study is especially relevant to our present inquiry. Although social work is only marginal to social welfare programs, such as education, medical care, social security, and housing, it is central, though not identical, with the social services.
3. The U.N. uses the term to imply precisely the opposite meaning than that proposed here. They distinguish between social welfare and social services and urge that social services be "given a wider meaning including all or some— depending on the country—of the following fields: health, nutrition, housing, education, social security, manpower policy, social welfare, social defense." *Reappraisal of the United Nations Social Service Programme,* Report by the Secretary General (E/CN.5/ac 12L.3, March 29, 1965), Addendum February 17, 1965, p. 20.
4. If social services are seen as residual, linking, and adjustive, then they are vulnerable to the charge of helping people to adjust to intolerable circumstances. Consequently they are impelled to broaden their functions to include the principle of the mutual adjustment of people and institutions. Social reform

and protection are thus added to social adjustment as ways to avoid victimization of those who are to be service beneficiaries. The definition is broadened to include social reform—institutional change; social provision—use of concrete and other services; social preparation—helping individuals use other services through information, counseling, and referrals; and social protection—legal and consumer protection to insure entitlement and to protect social rights. These various functions may conflict with each other, especially when they are administered by the same organization.

5. For a devastating critique of the theory that the social riffraff cause riots see, Robert M. Fogelson, "White on Black: A Critique of the McCone Commission Report on the Los Angeles Riots," *Political Science Quarterly*, September 1967.

6. Mary Jean Bowman, "The Assessment of Human Investments as Growth Strategy," *Federal Programs for the Development of Human Resources*, U.S. Congress, Joint Economic Committee, 90th Congress, 2d Session, 1968, Vol. 1, p. 85.

7. *Federal Programs for the Development of Human Resources*, U.S. Congress, Joint Economic Committee, 89th Congress, 2d Session, 1966, Vol. 1, p. 4.

8. Gunnar Myrdal, *Challenge to Affluence* (New York: Pantheon, 1962).

9. Arthur Schlesinger, Jr., "Where Does the Liberal Go From Here?" *The New York Times Magazine*, August 4, 1957.

10. John K. Galbraith, *The Affluent Society* (Boston: Houghton Mifflin, 1958).

11. U.S. Congress, Senate Committee on Labor and Public Welfare, *Examination of the War on Poverty*, Hearings before the Subcommittee on Employment, Manpower and Poverty, 90th Congress, 1st Session, 1967.

12. For a description and a justification of the position that we should accept the "small accompanying costs" of unemployment and reject the "oppressive" costs to economic and social stability that a policy of full employment would entail, see Daniel P. Moynihan, "The Crisis in Welfare," *Public Interest*, No. 10 (Winter 1968).

13. Other countries have criticized their social services program, but on different grounds and with different implications for policy. For example, the Seebohm Committee in England, in establishing its claim that there was a need for organizational change in the personal social services, lists the following shortcomings: inadequacies in the amount of provision, poor coordination, difficult access, and insufficient adoptability. The cause of these shortcomings are seen in terms of lack of resources, inadequate knowledge and divided responsibility. *Report of the Committee on Local Authority and Allied Personal Services*, Cmnd. 3703 (London: Her Majesty's Stationery Office, July 1968), pp. 29–35.

In the American contest much less emphasis was placed on the amount of resources. Indeed it was felt that more resources would only be misspent, since the problems were seen as arising from professional, structural, and administrative rigidities.

14. Bradley Buell, *Community Planning for Human Services* (New York: Columbia University Press, 1952).

15. Richard A. Cloward and Irwin Epstein, "Private Social Welfare's Disengagement from the Poor: The Case of Family Adjustment Agencies," in Mayer Zald, ed., *Social Welfare Institutions* (New York: Wiley, 1965).

16. Herbert J. Gans, "Redefining the Settlement's Function for the War on Poverty," *Social Work*, Vol. 9, No. 4 (October 1964).

17. Elaine Cummings, "Allocation of the Care to the Mentally Ill, American Style," in Mayer Zald, ed., *Organizing for Community Welfare* (Chicago: Quadrangle Books, 1967).

18. See chapter 3.

19. Henry Mayers *et al., Girls at Vocational High School, An Experiment in Social Work Intervention* (New York: Russell Sage Foundation, 1965).

20. For a criticism of this ideology in the social welfare and clinical fields, see Leonard Cottrell, "Social Planning, the Competent Community and Mental Health," in *Urban America and Planning of Mental Health Services*, Group for the Advancement of Psychiatry, Vol. V, Symposium No. 10, November 1964, pp. 395–398.

21. See Witmer, *op. cit.*, for her famous definition of social work.

22. U.S. Department of Health, Education and Welfare, *Closing the Gap in Social Work Manpower*, Report of the Departmental Task Force on Social Work Education in Manpower, November 1965, p. 34.

23. Lee Rainwater, "The Revolt of the Dirty Workers," *Trans-Action*, November 1967, p. 2.

24. *The New York Times*, May 12, 1968.

25. Richard M. Titmuss, "Universal or Selective? The Practical Case Against the Means Test," *New Statesman*, September 15, 1967, p. 308.

26. "Unified Social Services," Monthly Report (New Haven: Community Press Inc., April 1966), p. 18 (mimeo.).

27. The concept of poverty areas extends the definition of the slum to include not only the condition of the physical environment as measured by the quality of housing, but by the circumstances of the people who live in these areas as well. For a definition, see U.S. Bureau of the Census, *Current Population Reports*, Series P-23, No. 19 (Washington, D.C.: U.S. Government Printing Office, August 24, 1966), p. 3.

28. Sidney and Beatrice Webb, *English Poor Law Policy*, 2nd edition (London: Longmans, Green, 1913), p. 264.

29. Lee Rainwater, "Poverty and Deprivation in the Crisis of the American City." A statement presented to the U.S. Senate Committee on Government Operations, Subcommittee on Executive Reorganization, Washington, D.C., December 6, 1966, p. 19.

30. Lee Rainwater, "Policy Research, Applied Research and Lower Class Culture." Paper presented at the 20th Annual Meeting of the Society for Applied Anthropology, Washington, D.C., May 1967, p. 13.

31. Sar A. Levitan, *The Design of the Federal Anti-Poverty Strategy*, University of Michigan: Institute of Labor and Industrial Relations, March 1967, p. 8.

32. Gunnar Myrdal, *Rich Lands and Poor* (New York: Harper & Row, 1957), pp. 19–20.

33. Peter Marris and Martin Rein, *Dilemmas of Social Reform* (New York: Atherton, 1967), p. 89.

34. These figures are cited in James L. Sundquist, *Politics and Policy* (Washington, D.C.: The Brookings Institution, 1968), p. 154.

35. *The New York Times,* May 6, 1968.

36. I wish to express my thanks to Alvin Schorr for suggesting this example to me.

37. A recent criticism came from twelve of the foremost industrial and financial leaders in the country. See, for example, the report of the Steering Committee appointed by Governor Rockefeller for the Arden House Conference on Public Welfare that commemorated the 100th Anniversary of the New York State Board of Social Welfare.

38. Garth L. Mangum, "Government as Employer of Last Resort," *Federal Programs for the Development of Human Resources,* U.S. Congress, Joint Economic Committee, 90th Congress, 2d Session, 1968, Vol. 2, p. 436.

39. *Ibid.,* p. 444.

40. Michael S. March, "Federal Programs for Human Resources," *Federal Programs for the Development of Human Resources,* U.S. Congress, Joint Economic Committee, 90th Congress, 2d Session, 1968, Vol. 2, p. 125 and l. 136.

41. *Federal Programs for the Development of Human Resources,* U.S. Congress, Joint Economic Committee, 89th Congress, 2d Session, 1966, Vol. 1, p. 4.

42. Roy Lubove, "Social Work and the Life of the Poor," *The Nation,* May 23, 1966, pp. 609–611.

43. Burton A. Weissbrod, "Expenditures on Human Resources: Investment, Income Distribution, or What?", *Federal Programs for the Development of Human Resources,* U.S. Congress, Joint Economic Committee, 90th Congress, 2d Session, 1968, Vol. 1, pp. 80–82.

44. Pekka Kuusi, *Social Policy for the Sixties, A Plan for Finland,* Finnish Social Policy Association, 1964, p. 93.

45. *Federal Programs for the Development of Human Resources,* U.S. Congress, Joint Economic Committee, 89th Congress, 2d Session, 1966, Vol. 1, p. 4.

46. Barbara Wootton, "Is There a Welfare State? A Review of Recent Social Change in Britain," *Political Science Quarterly,* LXXVII, 2 (June 1963), p. 181.

47. Greenleigh Associates, "Home Interview Study of Low-Income Households in Detroit, Michigan," February 1965.

48. This idea is developed further in an article by Martin Rein and Frank Reissman, "A Strategy for Anti-Poverty Community Action Programs," *Social Work,* April 1966.

49. Peter Townsend, "Family Welfare and Seebohm," *New Society,* August 1, 1968.

Chapter 18

Citizen Participation and Poverty

This paper examines the changing character of maximum feasible participation of the poor as it has evolved over the past several years, both prior to and since the inception of the Economic Opportunity Act of 1964. Though participation of the poor can be justified on a variety of grounds, none is more compelling than the assumption that such participation contributes to the reduction of poverty. Indeed, much of the justification for the strategy of involvement grew out of a set of implicit assumptions about how poverty and participation are linked to one another. As these assumptions, both about the meaning of poverty and the contribution of participation to its reduction change, then the forms of participation change accordingly. This observation should not be taken to imply a causal argument that theory leads to action. It is perhaps more accurate to suggest that in the current history of citizen participation accident, discovery, error, and other forces contributed to the various forms of participation which have evolved.

Social policy tends not to develop in a tidy fashion. The forms of citizen participation evolve from a whole set of contradictory, conflicting, and accidental forces. There is no legislative history as to the meaning and intent of Congress in providing for maximum feasible involvement of the poor in the Economic Opportunity

Act's definition of community action.[1] There is, however, an administrative history, i.e., a history based on experience.

The different forms of citizen participation embody conflicting values. No effort has been made to resolve these different perspectives. In characteristic fashion, we pursue contradictory programs, *choosing ambiguity as a way of maintaining political viability.* (Note the same reluctance to make key decisions in other OEO programs such as the Job Corps; it was never quite decided whether the program was designed primarily for those who are most deprived, those with the best potential, those who could not read, those who lacked motivation, or for those who are fully motivated but need vocational training.)

Citizen participation is largely a slogan. It has various meanings and forms which co-exist and yet partially succeed each other. Its major forms are still being forged, for no resolution satisfied the diverse interest groups or the expectations invested in it. As the problems of one approach become evident, another model emerges to prominence.

In this chapter then, we examine the various interpretations of citizen participation as socio-therapy, as social action, as employment, as rights, as involvement in policy making, as the redistribution of political power, and try to show how these are believed to be linked to the reduction of poverty.

POVERTY AS POWERLESSNESS AND APATHY

Poverty may be seen as caused by the spiritual emptiness of ghetto life and by the apathy of the poor who, alienated from the norms of society, retreat into a protective subculture characterized by social disengagement and indifference. This subculture is often referred to as the culture of poverty. Kenneth Clark has described the stagnation of the poor as their most striking characteristic. The poor have a pervasive sense of futility, which, according to Clark, is not even positive enough to be called cynical. It follows that it is hard to disillusion the poor, for they start with few illusions. Equally, it is hard to engage the poor, for they start with few hopes. It is this theme which explains why Haryou, the predecessor to the community action agency in Harlem, assigned crucial importance to the idea of culture building. The destruction of culture can be understood, as the sub-title of their planning report suggests, as "the consequence of powerlessness." The lack of power derives from the dependency of the Negro to control the events which shape his life. In a discussion of the Negro's crippling dependency on the white community for the solution of the problems of inadequate education of the children of the ghetto, the Haryou report redefines the traditional view of the problem:

. . . and then the black man goes back home again and says, "I can't solve my problem unless I have a white person at my side; but I can't fight and make a change in this system unless I have a white person at my side; I can't be a man and not ask but take what is mine unless I have a white person at my side." And so he sees that he is in fact, less than a man. To reduce the demoralizing consequences of this form of welfare colonialism, the vitality, anger and energy of youth must be harnessed. Haryou must not attempt to teach the young person . . . but Haryou must be taught by the young person in Harlem.[2]

The confidence and self-respect of the Negro was to be achieved by his own involvement and participation in shaping and creating his own life; it was the young who would provide the source of leadership. Poverty is caused by powerlessness, and the means to overcome poverty is self-help and participation. The more the Negro himself operated the strategic institutions in ghetto life, the more he would be able to reject welfare colonialism and substitute a vitality of independence and self-respect; the more would poverty defined as powerlessness decline.

This point of view stresses that poverty is not so much a lack of material advantage, in the sense of insufficient economic resources, as it is a lack of power. It assumes that there was something wrong with the poor which left them unprepared to exploit the resources and opportunities available to them. Hence, what was needed was a program to prepare the poor so that they could more effectively use available community institutions and resources. To achieve this aim, the war on poverty created remediation, employability and citizen participation programs. All of these programs share a common rationale—the reduction of the dependency and the apathy of the poor, which would, in turn, give the poor opportunity to participate in the mainstream of American society. The hallmark of OEO programs is training—training for work habits, training for skill development, training for citizenship, training for participation.

But there is a mischievous quality about the term "opportunity." The theory of opening opportunity not only implies the chance to get ahead, but it also implies a strategy of promoting conformity without coercion. Even the opportunity to overcome powerlessness is seen within these terms of reference. The link between power and conformity is contained in the program ideal of trying to promote a competent community. Residents of a community should be able to solve their own problems and control their own destinies by being able to influence the institutions which service them. When resident groups lose the capacity to solve their own problems or the capacity to modify institutional performance in accordance with their needs, one frequent result is a breakdown in the institution of authority. This weakness in turn leads to a breakdown in the mechanisms of social control. The grim product of the incompetent community is the collapse of its control system which leads to the expansion of crime, delinquency, and social deviancy.

This line of argument holds that poverty and delinquency are created by apathy, and by the incompetence of the residents to manage their own affairs and to encourage institutions to develop appropriate solutions to solve emergency problems. Thus, personal incompetence reinforces institutional incompetence. The apathy of the poor prevents them from demanding that the institutions which service them accommodate to their needs. The plight worsened and their capacity for effective action further weakened, a vicious cycle of poverty reinforces a vicious cycle of bureaucratic dysfunctions. To break the cycle, the vigor of local democracy must be restored, and this could best be accomplished by expanding the freedom and the competence of local residents to respond to their local problems. Citizen involvement in local decision-making, through competent local leaders, who understood how best to command the events and institutions which shape their lives, was a major ingredient of the strategy of building a competent community.

This interpretation of the dynamics which link personal and institutional incompetence was accepted by the federal panel which reviewed and passed on local projects requesting funds under the Juvenile Delinquency and Youth Offences Control Act of 1961. There was latent disagreement on the panel between the views of Lloyd Ohlin who focused on the use of established power to change institutions and Leonard S. Cottrell, Jr., who felt that whenever you could restore the competence of a community of people to act in concert on a community problem "you would lower the rate of delinquency."[3] Community organization as a strategy to reduce delinquency and crime had a long history in sociological thought. The Chicago School stressed it, and many projects in the 1930's were inspired by this theory.

NEIGHBORHOOD ORGANIZATION FOR SOCIAL THERAPY

While neighborhood groups can be organized as a means for reducing apathy and promoting conformity among the poor, they can also be organized to promote institutional change. The differences between social action for institutional change and neighborhood organization as a form of sociotherapy need to be clarified. To use the form of one to achieve the goal of another can pose a very awkward dilemma. The experience of Mobilization for Youth in New York highlights this problem. Mobilization's prospectus makes the following point:

> Most efforts to organize lower class people attract individuals on their way up the
> social ladder: persons who are relatively responsible about participation, articulate

and successful at managing organizational "forms" are identified as a lower class status rather than those who actually reflect the values of lower-class groups.[4]

The Mobilization proposal was clearly critical of this state of affairs and tried to attract the truly indigenous leadership in the community. But this argument can have curious implications, as Daniel P. Moynihan caustically charged in an address at a conference on poverty in Berkeley.

> Note what is to be remedied: instead of getting hold of local people who are relatively responsible about participation, articulate and successful at managing organizational "forms," Mobilization for Youth is getting hold of a lower level, true and genuine leader who is what—inarticulate, irresponsible and relatively unsuccessful? . . . I am sorry but I am suspect of that proposition.[5]

But if the major task is to reduce poverty by reducing alienation, deviancy, and the personal sense of powerlessness which is caused chiefly by isolation and apathy, then the paradox disappears. For the argument then is that people change as they try to change their world. If institutions change so as to be more relevant to the poor, and if, in the process of altering the performance of institutions, the poor change through the process of social engagement and social confrontation, then much could be accomplished in reducing both the vicious cycle of poverty and bureaucracy. In this perspective, neighborhood organization is essentially a form of therapy and only secondarily a means of changing institutions. Moynihan's argument thus becomes irrelevant to this view; for who else should be involved in therapy other than the inarticulate, the irresponsible, and the unsuccessful?

It is crucial to separate out the two agendas of reform, that of changing people and that of changing institutions. Whether each approach supports the other remains a question to be determined empirically. Philosophically, the distinction is crucial.

In a thoughtful paper on mental health programs in model cities, Dumont reaffirms Mobilization's position on the appropriate population to be involved.

> From a preventive aspect, the community organization efforts will be directed toward the development of neighborhood and community groups among the as yet unaffiliated and disorganized people in the area; welfare recipients, public housing residents, tenement dwellers, the hard core poor who have the most severe and the most extensive psychological and social pathology.[6]

The socio-therapeutic ideals which lie behind this assertion are clear. Dumont goes on to explain that community organization "is itself a major mental health service, an end in itself."[7]

More recently the effort to link participation and conformity has been loosely extended to apply not only to individual and collective deviancy (delinquency, crime, and gang fighting) but to urban racial riots as well. The competent and conforming community according to this formulation does not call for organizing the poor, as do Cottrell, Mobilization for Youth, and Dumont, but for the restoration of power and authority to the middle classes.

Nathan Glazer recently commented that one of the glaring omissions in the analysis of the Kerner Commission Report is its failure to adequately take account of the middle class Negro and the secure working class Negro in their interpretation of the causes of urban unrest. "This is the missing man in the present crisis. And yet he must be a key factor both in the analysis of the problem . . . and in the solution of the problem."[8]

Norton Long's paper on "Politics and Ghetto Perpetuation"[9] provides an interpretation of the role of the missing man in today's urban social unrest and the policy implications which derive from the analysis. Long's paper is an attempt to formulate a theory about ghetto instability. Long's position can be briefly summarized as follows: In American society other ethnic enclaves have created a government and economy of their own and from this political and economic base a social structure has emerged which assures social stability. However, the pattern in the Negro community is significantly different. Here a truncated occupational structure has developed which is dominated by lower class Negroes, certainly a noticeable absence of commercial interests and with control largely residing in the white community.

> The Negro middle class until recently has been escapist (and) . . . where it cannot physically flee it has sought physical coexistence and spiritual isolation. . . . The outstanding fact is that middle class Negroes do not govern the Ghetto. They are afraid of it. We thus confront a community with a unique lower class culture made possible by a missing middle class and control by an alien race. The result of the failure of self-government has been a distrust of leaders and the emergence of the lower class as the only authentic and indigenous culture. The combination of these ingredients have produced political instability and an economy of the hustle, "cashing-in" and the welfare dole and a social incapacity to mobilize resources. The costs of a purely lower class culture of immediate consumption have been a failure to make use of the economic avenues of upward mobility.[10]

This, then, is an interpretation of the causes of social unrest. The solution lies in creating a black middle class. A transition of leadership is needed, not dissimilar to the colonial transition, when blacks were taught self-government by departing white rulers. "The key question is whether there exists or can rapidly be produced sufficient middle class cadres to govern the black governed city . . . the greatest fear is clearly that the middle class Negroes . . . cannot dominate the lower class culture of

Ghetto life."[11] Presumably then the Negro middle class leadership can more effectively police its own lower class culture if it had both the authority and the capability of exercising that leadership.

In summary, the socio-therapeutic rationale for citizen participation, with its emphasis on both personal and collective controls, can lead to efforts to organize the poor or to organize the non-poor. The rhetoric of powerlessness and apathy apply to both approaches. These views share in common, however, the commitment to produce conformity through participation.

The major emphasis of the socio-therapeutic approach places the burden of responsibility for change upon the individual, rather than upon socio-economic institutions. But the formulation is incomplete. While competent men make competent institutions, the converse is equally compelling, for the quality and capability of the institutions affect the competence of those serviced by them. Within these terms of reference, citizen participation as social action and protest against the incompetence of institutions emerged.

SOCIAL ACTION AND PROTEST FOR INSTITUTIONAL CHANGE

How can institutions in a democratic society change? The President's Committee on Juvenile Delinquency and Youth Crime had hoped that a coalition of power (established institutions) and knowledge (research) would serve to change institutions so that they would provide increased opportunity for the poor. This was essentially an elitist approach. Like C. Wright Mills' criticism of the power elite, it argued that the wrong elite were in power, rather than that elitism was an inappropriate source of power.

This approach was a form of sophisticated naiveté; it assumed that a marginal increase in funds and the involvement of some established power groups would be sufficient to provoke change in long-established institutions. The idea of participation was crucial in this formulation, for it assumed that the institutions must be involved in their own reform. In order to prod the institutions into becoming involved in a process of self-examination, new funds were made available.

But this interpretation of how institutions change was incomplete. First, it assumed that bureaucratic rigidity, not the insufficiency of resources, was the root cause of institutional incompetence. Accordingly, the major agenda of reform sought to increase the flexibility of institutions so that they could more appropriately and creatively service the needs of the poor through small scale demonstration projects. More resources were needed to convert the demonstrations into a regular program, but these were not forthcoming. The difficulties of transforming Headstart from a summer to a year round program is a case in point for it raised problems of teacher availability and the cost of full year salaries and facilities when school buildings were in use.

Secondly, even when resources were at hand it proved difficult to get professionals to become client oriented. The hallmark of professionalism is responsiveness to the standards of colleagues, rather than to the preferences of clients. To change professional performance required shifting the reward system and criteria by which professionals judge quality. This demanded not so much changing the attitude of individual teachers; it required, instead, changing the view of those who teach teachers and the criteria by which a given educational system allocated rewards—wages, promotion, recognition. Institutions resisted change. Experience in trying to change institutions affirms that we know more about the forces which inhibit change than those which help to bring it about.

As limitations of the elite approach (with its emphasis on experimentation and self-study by institutions) became evident, the strategies of pressure and protest developed. It was out of the frustration of trying to change institutions that the possibility of using consumer groups emerged. Social action to promote change came to rely increasingly on organizing the poor for conflict, confrontation, and protest. The tactics of public shame, made possible by widespread newspaper coverage, were used as a source of power to promote change. Rent strikes, picketing of the schools, and other forms of militant social action were encouraged by many federally financed community action programs as a way of reducing poverty by changing service institutions. But the strategy of social action as social protest was vulnerable. The experience in San Francisco helps to illuminate its underlying dilemmas.

The San Francisco Community Action Agency put its faith in organizing power. It hoped to apply massive pressure to produce massive change in institutions. The city-wide agency delegated much of its power to neighborhood boards. "Resident boards in the poverty areas gained unprecedented power over program, personnel, and budgets."[12] The director of the city-wide C.A.A. explained that this strategy sought "to mobilize resident power to be able to reshape the big money institutions like the schools, employment services, and welfare to be more responsive to the poor."[13] The Western Addition Neighborhood, an area of 300 blocks with 88,000 residents of whom 50% were white and 40% were poor, devoted all its energies to this approach. The area was sub-divided into 32 sub-areas, each sub-area had its own community council, block captains and representatives to be sent to an area board. All of this involvement was to be accomplished by fifty full time and seventy part time organizations. All the organizers were black.

But the strategy collapsed. The institutions did not respond to pressure by offering massive services or fundamental changes in policy. Moreover, massive pressure could not be generated. The efforts to organize the 32 areas proved to be very difficult as internal tension between established ghetto power and black militants was created. The focus on acquiring power through community organizations yielded no tangible and visible services.[14]

The strategy failed because it could not mobilize the poor and deliver concrete services; in other communities, the strategy failed precisely because it did deliver services and it could concert the will of the poor. When protest secures a concrete service, the very success of the effort sometimes leads to the reduction in discontent and membership interest which threatens the stability of the group. Often the victory is illusory because it represents only a gesture, a token response by institutions to win peace rather than to provide lasting reform. But where social action is effective and militancy produces institutional discomfort, then a power struggle ensues. Accommodation and bargaining by established power groups is superseded by direct assault. When established power was threatened, it often fought back by striking where the protest was most vulnerable—at the source of funds which paid for organizing the poor.[15]

As the tensions in the social action strategy developed, some of the other available interpretations about the meaning of citizen participation seemed more appealing. Although protest continued, other strategies became important. Employment of nonprofessionals represented an example of attempting to deliver service and work for ghetto residents. New sources of power were sought and the power of the law was employed as a base to promote institutional change and to protect consumer rights.

INDIGENOUS WORKERS

Another of the ways that citizen participation became widely interpreted was in terms of the employment of the poor. The indigenous worker nonprofessional idea was a marvelous invention. It beautifully exploited the ambiguities in the philosophical choices concerning the causes of poverty. Why were indigenous personnel needed? One ready common sense answer was that the poor needed jobs. Training alone often led to blind alleys where there were insufficient job opportunities for the number of graduates of these programs.

From the time of the initial proposal for an Economic Opportunity Act, Secretary of Labor Wirtz consistently opposed the community action idea of helping young people develop their capabilities via a variety of new and immediate training, remediation, and participation programs. He saw poverty as a lack of money; money depended, in the end, primarily upon jobs. Community action, preoccupied with training, created no large numbers of new jobs. Jobs provided the opportunity for reducing poverty by providing the poor an independent source of income.

What was needed was a program of job expansion. Employment of indigenous personnel offered such an opportunity. But in order to avoid the charge of creating a large public works program, the same strategy of employing indigenous personnel could be used to satisfy the other goals of changing institutions and changing the poor. Some hoped that by introducing indigenous personnel into organizations, it would deossify rigid and irrelevant organizations. Moreover, agency workers drawn from the neighborhood were in an especially strategic position to encourage the poor to make use of existing institutions; and in the process of changing others, indigenous workers would change as well.

The program of indigenous personnel thus offered an excellent opportunity to draw together several different meanings of citizen participation. It stood simultaneously for jobs, for institutional change, and for personal therapy. This helps to account for the popularity of this form of citizen participation and its likely desirability as a form of involvement. A recent OEO report indicates that as of September 1966, approximately 132,000 nonprofessional positions have been authorized, including 25,000 positions which remained unfilled.[16]

The use of nonprofessionals, however, has raised a number of issues. There has been a great deal of creaming because many of the nonprofessional roles are being filled by people who are middle class, like housewives who have college degrees, rather than by poor people. There is a tendency to recruit those among the poor who are better off, rather than to try to recruit those who are the most disadvantaged of the disadvantaged. We always have levels of disadvantage; most of our social policies skim cream off the top and neglect the bottom, with the result that the conditions of those left behind further deteriorate.

Some professionals have observed that nonprofessionals often render low quality service, and that training is essential to improve performance. On the other hand, upgrading is limited; i.e., nonprofessionals lack opportunities to move either into the higher levels below the professional level, or to have a new route into professional life. While nonprofessional activities could become a new kind of credentialing activity, it is more often just a dead-end stage.

The nonprofessional role is frequently treated as the bottom of the status hierarchy within the social services rather than as a part of the fellowship of social service workers. Black people at the occupational bottom are labeled nonprofessionals and are looked upon as the peons of social services with a limited role and with little power within the agency. There is no active, urgent concern to change their situation, although the new organization of nonprofessionals may change this situation. Professional equality does not extend to the new kind of nonprofessional worker. Rather than the colleague principle, the principle of hierarchy is still insisted on in most agencies.

It is not unreasonable to suggest that much more hierarchy is exhibited in the organization of services in social agencies than in most other organizations. A consequence is that the social service nonprofessional is usually

(1) Business wk
   may 13, 91   Hall

(2) America
   June 1, 91 Best

confronted with a difficult task in winning respect and compensation for his achievements. In some agencies nonprofessionals are trying to reverse this pattern, but this is not the national practice.

A possible danger in the nonprofessional role today is that there may be developing a low paid black civil and nonprofit service supervised by white professionals receiving high pay and status. This race-occupational division may become more acute rather than less with time.

PARTICIPATION AS LEGAL PROTECTION

Legal protection against administrative discretion merges with ideals of participatory democracy. Both are preoccupied with issues of the rights of marginal groups against dominant established interests. Appeal to law can serve as an instrument of reform and protest, challenging established procedures. Although militant social protest was vulnerable to challenges on the basis that its activities were inappropriate to its mission (federal funds should not be used to promote confrontation, boycotts, and protest) the law was neutral in relation to auspices, for "the law lends itself impartially to manipulation by militant radicals or repressive conservatives."[17]

When Mobilization for Youth came to recognize the limits of a cooperative strategy, it used these limits to justify a more aggressive approach of protest and confrontation. But it soon came to realize the limits of protest as well, when after the death of President Kennedy it lost its political support. The counter-attack by the schools, the police, and other institutions sorely threatened its survival. Cloward and Piven's experiences at Mobilization undoubtedly influenced their decision to turn to law as a source of support in redressing the grievances of the poor and promoting changes in institutional policy. Mobilization's neighborhood legal service came to specialize in welfare problems focusing on those administrative practices which rejected individuals who applied for welfare. They sought out test cases which could challenge the established principles by which exclusion was made possible. And so law was used as an instrument of reform.

Cloward developed another idea about how to combine law and protest. In an influential paper[18] he demonstrated that there was a high rate of under-utilization of welfare in New York, i.e., many individuals entitled to benefits were not receiving them. He argued that if non-users became users, the welfare system might collapse under the weight of the added costs. The Welfare Rights Movement was an attempt to organize the eligible non-recipients of welfare. Soon after it began, its strategy shifted from recruiting clients to getting benefits for those who were already clients. The vigorous and militant program of the Welfare Rights Movement in New York City was directed at the special grant allowance program, but supported the legal right to benefits. The protests were successful in raising the cost of the special grants for items such as household furniture, clothing, etc., from $3 million per month in 1967 to $13 million per month in 1968. These efforts did produce a change in policy from discretionary allowance, where some got more, to a flat rate where all families got $100 per year, an amount less than the average size of the special grant allowances. Organizing for entitlement did not collapse the welfare system, but it did pressure it to change. A policy change in support of flat grants was the product, but the victory was soon seen as defeat. While it reduced administrative discretion and promoted more equality of benefits, it also reduced the size of the benefits for those who had learned to make the system respond to their needs.

The pressure for legal protection against administrative discretion and the effort to use law as an instrument of reform found expression in other areas as well. Interest in grievance, access, and information about rights and services developed from the consumer's point of view. The need for forms of accountability became evident. Public discussion was opened about the need for new services for the aggrieved (*ombudsmen*), for the alienated (neighborhood service centers which facilitated access), and for the uninformed (information and referral schemes, which might provide not only information on what and where services were available, but the more radical program of assessing the quality of services such as private medical care, nursing homes, and public schools).

PARTICIPATION AS POLICY DEVELOPMENT

The idea that the poor should be involved in shaping policy was entirely consistent with the ideals of the revitalization of local democracy and the increase in the competence of local leaders in managing their own affairs. This view of participation represented a form of radical democracy in which both institutional representatives of established power and the consumers of the service (not in their role as clients, but as citizens) would shape policy. The involvement of the citizen in creating policy presented no conflict with the ideals of a competent program, for the poor were to be involved in making allocative decisions. Such decisions, by their nature, involved matters of judgment and preference; they involved such questions as the relative emphasis to be assigned to programs for young children, youths, and adults, and the relative weight to be given to health, recreation, legal, and training services.

But local and national priorities are not always smoothly aligned and mutually reinforcing. Indeed, more typically they are in conflict, as in the case where a community is eager to spend its funds on recreation, while OEO rejects this type of program on the ground that recreation contributes little to the reduction of poverty. OEO, on the other hand, may be interested in promoting legal services for the poor as part of a national decision to spend funds in this area, but legal services might have a low priority on a local agenda. Thus, there might be a conflict between national and local priority systems, and assignments may conflict. To the extent that the national agenda intrudes into local decision-making, it undermines the ideal of developing the competent community. The more intrusive, insistent, and effective is the federal government, the more likely is this new form of cooperative federalism to increase the sense of local impotence.

This issue has not received the attention it deserves. Instead, the emphasis on involving the poor in policy-making has centered on the procedure for selecting the poor, rather than on the kinds of decisions which they are to make. Elections become the crucial battlegrounds of public policy with great debates about the most appropriate form for electing and selecting the poor on policy-making boards.

How to elect the representatives of the poor was indeed a troublesome issue. A variety of procedures were followed, including appointment by the mayor and elections. The low turn-out rate in many of the elections has been used as an argument to reaffirm the notion that the poor are apathetic and that stagnation is intense. Voting is regarded as inherently good; for many it was regarded as a form of socio-therapy on the assumption that voting strengthens the bonds of social cohesiveness.

Consistent with this assumption was the treatment of elections as only a symbolic gesture of engagement, rather than as a political act. The analysis of the low turn-out rates was strikingly apolitical, emphasizing psychological withdrawal. Had elections been accepted as political acts, the low turn out might have been interpreted quite differently. For example, it could have been pointed out that most elections were without constituencies, without issues, without rewards, and without trust since they were often held under OEO auspices, which in many communities represents the establishment.

As the debate continued, the meaningfulness of participation in formal city-wide Community Action Agencies came increasingly under question. A resilient system proved very creative in devising new administrative arrangements which devitalized the organizational structure in which the poor were advised to participate. Those who were strong advocates of participation were concerned that the procedure led to creaming off the most militant leadership in the ghetto, i.e., the leadership became co-opted, or to put it more harshly, they "sold out." Others cogently argued that they were not selling out, but simply buying into the system.

The same issues have remained alive in the implementation of the meaning of citizenship participation in model cities programs. The shift in rhetoric from "maximum feasible participation" under OEO to "widespread participation" in model cities may be interpreted as a desire to abate the intensity of engagement. But once the ideals of citizen involvement were unleashed, they were hard to contain, even in a program which set out to do so. Administrative interpretation of guidelines depended on the political climate; and as demands in Negro communities became more radical, the concern for involvement in policy shifted to control of policy.

The demand for the transfer of power took two forms, aside from the more political approach of running candidates in an attempt to win political control over the city. One form is economic development through devices such as community corporations; the other is control of the social service system by the decentralization of authority and power.

THE TRANSFER OF POWER

The theme of involvement in the policies of community action agencies soon spread to involvement in other programs as well. Requirements for citizen involvement can now be found in the amendments to the Social Security Act, in recent legislation concerning the treatment of delinquents, in local legislation, and in the voluntary sector (e.g., students demand a role in policy making in the university and clients want to influence the policies of social service agencies).

The transition from involvement in policy to control of policy was perhaps less awkward than was the early struggle to win a role for local residents in the decision machinery of social service bureaucracies. The concern with law and participation had focused on the failure to give due regard to the rights of individuals, to fully implement entitlement, and to assist the aggrieved individual who was hurt by the administrative service system. Thus the concern with law and participation was primarily directed at seeing that the rules were enforced or at changing the rules by court action. By contrast, the concern with the transfer of power was directed at the issue of who should set the rules, and especially the role of consumers as rule setters.

The emphasis on the transfer of power cannot altogether be understood without recognizing the difference between issues of race and class. While policies directed only at issues of class (poverty and low income) can assign priorities to programs which emphasized service (e.g., jobs or income), policies concerned with race must today give attention to the questions of integration and separatism. The separatist black power advocates have been most preoccupied with the case for a transfer of power. The separatist hope is outlined by the following comment:

> [to achieve for their followers] group and even private political power, self-esteem and dignity, and a modicum of territory or turf over which proprietary control can be exercised. . . . This position says that if you get jobs and income without getting power, the political and economic power of the whites will be used to take the income away from you in taxes, rents, high prices. . . .[19]

The call for a transfer of power has taken two forms: community corporation and decentralization. We briefly review each.

COMMUNITY CORPORATION

"A corporation is a means which permits the blending together into one self-contained entity multi-source capital in various forms with management obtained from nonowner sources."[20] The sources of capital and management can be blended together in various combinations from public, private, and corporate areas. These types of nonprofit organizations can be identified: those organized for a private purpose (social, paternal, civic, patriotic, etc.), those created for quasi-public purposes (but outside the usual governmental machinery in order to exploit the flexibility and managerial techniques of private enterprise and also "to make possible greater citizen participation"), and finally the government corporation or public benefit corporation (e.g., T.V.A. or the proposal to change the federal postal system into a public corporation).

In a thoughtful analysis of the quasi-public, nonprofit corporation, Leshner notes that since 1932, new social legislation brought government into the position where "it not only invested the capital but took over the management in toto."[21] During this period in fields such as public assistance and child welfare, progressive reforms called for a transfer in administration from the voluntary to the public sector. The mood of the 1960's seems to have reversed the trend because "problems have developed . . . in the area of administration. The increased size of government makes more difficult citizen participation and citizen communication."[22]

Without accepting the thesis that administrative problems are chiefly problems of size, it is evident that in the past several years, a great deal of interest and some experimentation with the idea of a community corporation has emerged. In 1964, OEO granted $185,000 to the East Central Citizens Organization (ECCO) in Columbus, Ohio, to cover the organizational and administrative expenses in developing a community corporation. The corporation is controlled by the residents of the community and it is organized to provide services to the community, such as job training, day care, recreation, and housing rehabilitation.

Senator Robert F. Kennedy developed the Renewal and Rehabilitation Corporation in the Bedford-Stuyvesant section of Brooklyn, New York. But the original corporation, dominated by established social welfare agencies and civic groups, did not permit control by grass roots organizations. As a result of pressure, a new corporation was created. But according to one review it remains "doubtful that it will give a significant measure of control to the poor in the community."[23]

These local experiments, reinforced by pressure from black separatists, have contributed to the newly proposed Community Self-Determination Act of 1968. The Act is supported by a curious coalition of black militant leaders at CORE, intellectuals at the Kennedy Institute of Politics at Harvard University, and by lawyers and businessmen. The legislation is inspired by the ideals of corporate capitalism and the Israeli kibbutz. "Both—through loans, technical assistance and profit making . . . [hope to] achieve self-sustaining growth."[24] Yet even a cursory examination of the legislation suggests how strongly the conservative creed for urban America influences the basic principles on which the legislation rests.

The legislation calls for the development of Community Development Corporation (C.D.C.) to manage and to own business enterprises. A network of Community Development Banks would provide the necessary investment funds. Federal tax incentives would encourage private business to enter into turnkey agreements with the C.D.C. to turn over the business to the C.D.C. as a subsidiary. This complex structure of national boards, banks, and local corporations would hopefully generate profits to be used to finance community social services wanted at the local level.

A review of the supporting rationale set out in Section 2 of the Community Self-Determination Act[25] helps to make understandable why what might appear as a radical argument for black capital has so much appeal to conservative thought. The aims which inspire a conservative coalition in support of black power and black capital are clear. Conservatism views taxation to pay for the benefits to the poor as a burden, hence the poor should pay for their own services out of the profits of community corporations. Federal financing of these corporations is a temporary expedient; the ideal is self-liquidation as succes fosters pragmatic extinction. Finally, the goal is to promote order, stability, and progress. The assumption is that these goals reinforce each other. Yet a compelling case could be made that token programs promote frustration and thus create the instability they are designed to overcome. Note as well the impressive lists of economic limitations imposed on Community Development Boards. They "would not be authorized to issue or deal in securities, engage in acceptable financing, sell insurance, offer credit cards or make credit guarantees."[26] It would appear that the effect of these limitations seems to be directed at keeping the corporations away from the high profit sectors of business.

DECENTRALIZATION

The use of profits of community corporations to purchase social services and thereby transfer decision power from the public supplier bureaucracy to the user-bureaucracy appears to be limited to the class of services which the English call personal social services. In reviewing the functions of the

Community Development Corporation, the Community Self-Determination bill lists the following services: "basic education, child welfare, day care, pre-school training, health, consumer education, home ownership counseling, college placement assistance, job finding, recreation, legal aid, etc."[27] The common theme which binds together what might appear as a random classification of services is the emphasis on activities which facilitate access to, or better prepare individuals to make use of, other institutional services. Although health is listed as a service, it is likely that what was intended was only medical diagnostic and referral services, rather than high-cost hospital, surgical or other direct physician services. The services then are directed at the low-cost sections of social welfare. The profits of local economic development could not, after all, realistically cover the expenses of such high cost services as education, medical care, and income maintenance.

In the high cost section of social services it is the decentralization of authority rather than the ownership of services that is being sought. To avoid a highly regressive pattern of taxation in financing these services it is necessary to regionalize or federalize the sources of funds, while localizing decisions. Education and medical care are examples.

In the area of medical care for the aged and for the medically indigent, American social policy is based on a voucher system in which the patient selects the service of his choice and the vendor is paid directly by government for the service so purchased. Alan Gartner, the associate director of the New Careers Development Center of New York University, proposed that this policy could be used to win "Community Control of the Human Resources."[28] If the users would elect to purchase their care from selected vendors, and if a group of doctors would agree to limit their practices to this clientele, then a type of closed corporation could be formed. That doctors would agree in the present high demand, low supply market to an arrangement whereby a guaranteed patient load is exchanged for medical accountability to consumers, seems unlikely. However, in many communities where a limited number of physicians are already providing medical care for a large indigent population of medical care recipients concentrated in a limited geographic area, these clients could be organized to seek more control over the practice which is already dependent upon the purchase of the services. Where the public agencies already render the services directly, as they do in community health services, then the poor can serve on the boards of these agencies. But here we have only another example of participation in policy-making.

It is in the field of education, however, that a shift from participation in power to the transfer of power is being attempted. The outcome of the experiment is uncertain as illustrated by the clash in New York City between teachers seeking to protect their working conditions and neighborhood boards eager to have the freedom to select teachers of their own choosing.

In summary then, the argument for a transfer of power, whether by purchasing services from the profits of local corporations or by decentralizing authority, rests on the belief that the present principles of bureaucratic and professional accountability no longer are able to safeguard individual rights.

> . . . [I]n principle an administrator is responsible to government, and government to the people. The aggrieved citizen can protest through his representative against any intrusion on his rights. But a citizen grievance against bureaucracy cannot be simply and quickly dealt with . . . the bureaucracy . . . becomes increasingly autonomous. It is the judge of its own integrity; it controls the information by which its competence could be challenged; and it outlasts the politicians who depend upon it to execute their policies. It begins to seem an insidious threat to the whole concept of a democratic society.[29]

A professional's behavior, even in principle, is accountable not to clients but to professional colleagues who license and review the practice of other professionals. But while we cannot hope to dismantle bureaucracy or alter the essence of professional discretions, new mechanisms of accountability are being sought. Decentralization and the transfer of power to consumers represents an example of this trend. The issues of accountability have converged with the charge of welfare colonialism in the social services, and with the rise of black separatism.

CONCLUSIONS

The principle of citizen participation in public policy is not new in American political democracy. What is new, however, is the interpretation which says that citizens should be involved in the process. We are now preoccupied with finding ways of including the excluded citizens, especially the poor and the black. This trend must be reckoned as a significant move toward democracy in decision making, responsiveness of bureaucracies to consumer preferences, expansion of the concepts of rights and entitlement of public largess, and experimentation with new forms of protection against professional and administrative discretion. But at the same time this important step forward has generated much conflict, and it has substituted, at least in the short run, a struggle for power for the rendering of quality service. Moreover, it has in practice reduced democracy, as in the case where small cliques take over policy making without representing the interest of the majority of the residents in low income areas. Finally it has inhibited the use of professional wisdom and experience as citizens learn afresh the errors of past histories.

This brief history of citizen participation in the 1960's has reviewed the many different and simultaneously held interpretations about the form which such participation should take. Even in this short period, public policy has shifted its emphasis from one interpretation to another without abandoning or repudiating any view. Fadism has emerged as the conflicts and dilemmas of each approach have become evident, when vague ideals wrestle with practical implementation.

Our recital of difficulties and tensions in the unfolding of citizenship participation in the sixties could lead to the conclusion that it should be abandoned. That would be a grievous error. The idea of participation will be tremendously important in humanizing and democratizing institutions. It already reverberates in many fields—both students and welfare recipients assert that they have rights; legislation in many fields stipulates the involvement of the poor or the service recipient; the service bureaucracy is now viewed from the position of the user rather than the professional. Thus, the spillover effects have spread much beyond the community action programs which have been the focus of this article.

The theme of participation has fed the black revolution and, in turn, has been shaped by it. The course of race change is still uncertain; issues are still unsettled; ambiguity about goals and low faith in available means lead to stormy confrontations; the legitimacy of old and new Negro representatives and spokesmen is under challenge. These circumstances lead to the untidy situation of shifting focuses in citizenship participation. Since participation is not only a response to the issues of the past, but is constantly being assailed by the rapid cacophony of the unsettled struggle that is race relations today, it cannot be settled form.

While we see the shifting and refocusing as inevitable and recognize that experimentation is desirable, we fear that the end result is that no approach gets sufficient funding and support to have penetrating impact. Constantly changing gears may give the illusion of motion. In the next several years participation should shake down into a limited number of major models if it is to be powerful.

The other general concern we have about participation is the stress of many on its socio-therapeutic significance, which appears in many guises. It is our conclusion that the stress on socio-therapy leads to control rather than change, to spending small funds rather than large, and to presumed opportunity rather than to real opportunity.

Sometimes, groups seeking widely sweeping changes combine with more conservatively-minded groups emphasizing socio-therapy. This seems to be the case of the proposed community corporations legislation. Although strange bedfellows are sometimes the parents of effective new policies, often the end product may not be what one of the partners imagined. The partner with the broader agenda may hope to subtly influence the group with the narrow socio-therapeutic intent or to use it while yielding little of its own agenda. Our feeling is that more conservative public agendas win more than they lose to the more radical, and that if a socio-therapeutic orientation is not guarded against, it insidiously gains ascendancy. The black struggle of today may change this picture and reduce the likelihood of socio-therapy suppressing the drive for social change. But there is no assurance that protean socio-therapy will not dominate.

While the road is not easy or smooth, public policy cannot retreat from the course of expanding participation. "Maximum feasible participation" has ushered in a new era—stormy and hopeful—in the life of bureaucracy, professionalism and democracy.

NOTES

1. Economic Opportunity Act of 1964, 46 U.S.C. §§ 113(a)(6) (1964).
2. Harlem Youth Opportunities Unlimited, *Youth in the Ghetto* (1964) (report prepared for President's Committee on Delinquency and Youth Crime).
3. P. Marris and M. Rein, *Dilemmas of Social Reform,* 170 (1967).
4. *Id.* at 167.
5. P. Marris and M. Rein, *supra* note 3, at 185–187 reviews this debate.
6. M. Dumont, "A Model Community Mental Health Program for a Model Cities Area," August, 1967, (Center for Community Planners, H.E.W., Washington) (mimeo).
7. *Id.* at 3.
8. Glazer, "The Problem with American Cities," *New Society* (1968).
9. Long, "Politics and Ghetto Perpetuation," to appear in *Politics and the Ghetto* (R. Warren ed., New York: Atherton, 1969).
10. *Politics and the Ghetto* (R. Warren ed.).
11. Long, "Politics and Ghetto Perpetuation," *supra* note 9.
12. J. Cunningham, The Struggle of the American Urbidente for Freedom and Power, a report prepared for the Ford Foundation (1967).
13. *Id.*
14. *Id.* at 57–69.
15. The experience in Syracuse illustrates these tensions. *See also* S. Lipsky, "The Politics of Protest" (1967, Institute of Research on Poverty, University of Wisconsin, mimeo).
16. *New Careers Newsletter* (August 1967).
17. P. Marris and M. Rein, *supra* note 3, at 174.
18. Cloward and Piven, "A Strategy To End Poverty," *The Nation* 510 (May 2, 1966).
19. J. Dyckman, "The Organization of Metropolitan Social Planning 9" (September 1968, mimeo, National League of Cities and H.E.W., Chicago).
20. Leshner, "The Non-profit Corporation—A Neglected Step Child Comes of Age," 22 *Bus. Lawyer* 951, 957 (1967).
21. *Id.* at 966.
22. *Id.*
23. "Antipoverty, Community Corporations 3" *Colum. Journal of Law and Social Problems* 94, 98 (1967).
24. Tobier, "Cooperative Communities North and South: A Response to Poverty," 114 *Cong. Rec.* S. 971 (daily ed. July 24, 1968).

25. *See* S. 3875, S. 3876, H.R. 18709, H.R. 18715, H.R. 18976, H.R. 19201, H.R. 19205, 90th Cong., 2d Sess (1968); 114 *Cong Rec.* S. 9274 (daily ed. July 24, 1968).

26. S. 3875, 90th Cong., 2d Sess., Title II (1968).

27. S. 3875, 90th Cong., 2d Sess, Title I (1968).

28. Social Policy Notes 2 (July 1968, New York University, mimeo.).

29. P. Marris, "A Report on the Scandinavian Ombudsman and the British Citizen." Advice Bureau 2 (1966, mimeo, Ford Foundation).

Chapter 19

Barriers to Employment of the Disadvantaged

The disadvantaged workers still jobless or underemployed in this period of economic prosperity—who, in President Johnson's words, are ". . . blocked from productive employment by barriers rooted in poverty: lack of health, lack of education, lack of training, lack of motivation"[1] —are now the chief concern of manpower policy. If programs are to be shaped effectively to these workers' specific needs, deeper understanding of their problems and the obstacles to their employment is essential.

This chapter therefore explores the sociological, cultural, psychological, and economic barriers to employment of the disadvantaged in big city slums.[2] The introductory section sketches the major statistical dimensions of joblessness and underemployment in urban poverty areas. The chapter is concerned in the main, however, not with measurement and description of these problems but with exploration of their deep-rooted personal and environmental causes.

In this analysis, the barriers to employment are divided into those stemming from social-psychological characteristics and those access and institutional barriers which bar slum residents from otherwise available jobs. Since the special economic world that has developed in

Reprinted with permission of the co-author, S. M. Miller, from the *President's Manpower Report for 1968*.

slum areas greatly influences the residents' attitudes toward regular jobs, this "irregular economy" is analyzed briefly. And there is an illustrative discussion of one important group of the poor and underemployed—the mothers receiving assistance under the Aid to Families with Dependent Children (AFDC) program. The emphasis in this discussion is on the complex interrelationships between employment and welfare for these women, and the possible implications of the findings for the new Work Incentive Program aimed at equipping more AFDC mothers for regular jobs.

In conclusion, some important objectives in job creation and other manpower policies that bear directly on the barriers to employment of the disadvantaged are reviewed. Suggestions are also made as to the strategies and program improvements that would strengthen present efforts to overcome these barriers and enable the hard-core unemployed and marginal workers to obtain and hold steady, decently paid jobs.

THE SUB-EMPLOYED

The present measures of unemployment—limited, broadly, to persons who have no work at all and are actively seeking a job—are particularly inadequate for assessing the economic situation of disadvantaged workers in urban slums, and also rural areas. A broader, more useful concept for analysis of the problems of these groups—that of sub-employment—was introduced in 1967.

The concept of sub-employment broadens the traditional notions of attachment to the labor force and availability for work, and it introduces the issue of the quality of employment as represented by the level of wages. This is especially important for the development of manpower policy in poverty areas. The employed poor—with earnings below the poverty line even for fulltime work—now represent a larger problem, at least in terms of numbers, than the unemployed. Yet they are a group which has so far received comparatively little attention.

Separate consideration of the different kinds of people included among the sub-employed is also essential. The sub-employed are a diverse group, with varied problems requiring different remedial approaches. No one policy will deal effectively with the employment problems of all the sub-employed, nor with all aspects of their problems.

Some of the sub-employed are unable to get or keep a job because of social-psychological characteristics or low motivation. But such difficulties must not be considered as characteristic of all the sub-employed. Nor can social-psychological barriers to employment be analyzed apart from the context of available opportunities.

Two obvious but crucial questions are: What are the reasons for the continuing high sub-employment among Negroes and other minority groups in large cities? What can be done to decrease it further? Efforts to answer these questions are seriously hampered by the inadequacy of present information. Some leads can be obtained, however, by pulling together the scattered and fragmentary evidence at hand. This section gives some highlights of the available data on the numbers and characteristics of the subemployed in urban areas as a background for considering the barriers to their employment.

Unemployment and Sub-Employment in Poverty Areas

While unemployment is only a partial index of the deprivation of slumdwellers, it is concentrated among the same groups that suffer from low earnings and other forms of sub-employment. The differences in unemployment rates between people in and outside poverty areas illustrate the gap in economic conditions between slum residents and the American people as a whole.

Half a million persons were unemployed in the poverty areas of large Standard Metropolitan Statistical Areas (SMSA's) in March 1966, representing 7.5 percent of the poverty area work force. This unemployment rate was nearly double the national average rate at that time (4.0 percent).[3] One out of every 4 teenage workers (14 to 19 years old) in the poverty areas, and nearly 1 out of 10 nonwhites of all ages, were unemployed. Among nonwhite teenagers, nearly a third of the boys and nearly half of the girls were jobless. Furthermore, the geographic concentration of nonwhite unemployment was great; about 60 percent of the jobless nonwhites in the SMSA's were living in these poverty areas, four times the proportion for jobless white workers.

Startling as these figures are, they do not adequately represent the situation in some of the poorest city slums. The unemployment rate was 10 percent or more in the slum areas of ten of the thirteen cities for which information was obtained by the Department of Labor and cooperating State agencies in November 1966 (in three cities from independent studies).[4] In two of these city slums, the unemployment rate was above 15 percent.

Besides having high rates of unemployment, the workers in poverty areas were much more likely than others to be out of work for long periods (according to the March 1966 data). Above-average proportions of the men of normal working age were neither employed nor looking for work; many were unable to look for work because of poor health, and some had apparently been discouraged by their inability to find a job. In addition, many slum residents had been able to find only parttime work, and the jobs they had were very often unskilled and low paying.

The evidence is thus overwhelming that any meaningful count of the disadvantaged—the sub-employed—in poverty areas of the country's large metropolitan centers would greatly exceed the half million found to be unemployed there in March 1966. A reasonable, and probably minimal, estimate of sub-employment in these poverty areas would be 1.5 million.

Characteristics of Slum Residents

The residents of poverty areas include above-average proportions of older people; of widowed, divorced, and separated persons; of households headed by women; and of members of ethnic minority groups.

Nevertheless, white people outnumber nonwhites by three to two in urban poverty areas as a whole, according to the March 1966 survey. It is only in the very worst slums that nonwhites predominate in total numbers.[5] Because of their extremely high rate of unemployment, however, nonwhites represent a majority of all the poverty area unemployed.

Is poverty area unemployment primarily a youth problem, a conclusion reached by many observers? As shown by the figures already cited, the proportion of poverty area youth unemployed—and presumably alienated in many cases—is shockingly high. On the other hand, many men in the prime working ages are also jobless in these areas. And since there are not nearly as many teenagers as adult men, unemployed youth constitute a relatively small proportion of all unemployed males in poverty areas, as in the country generally.

A recent study in Newark confirms the finding that youth unemployment is not the numerically dominant type in poverty areas. The unemployment rate for Negro males 16 to 19 years of age in these slum areas was 33 percent, and for those aged 20 to 24 it was 13 percent. The group aged 25 and over had a lower unemployment rate (8 percent) but represented 60 percent of all unemployed Negro men.[6] Clearly, manpower policy must be as concerned with the employment needs of adult men in the ghettos as with those of jobless youth.

Public policy must also recognize the variations in social characteristics among slum residents. While detailed data on the sub-employed are not available, information on the general characteristics of the poverty area population strongly suggests the extent of variability. Accounts of social pathology in the slums frequently tend to obscure these important differences.

Although the proportion of families headed by women is higher in poverty areas than elsewhere, nearly two-thirds of the families in such areas in 1966 were headed by men. Contrary to a widely held notion, the proportion of large families was no higher there than in the country generally; the proportion of families with six or more members was about 15 percent in each case. Furthermore, although relatively more of the employed workers in poverty areas than of the country's work force as a whole were in service and laboring jobs, the proportion in such jobs was only 1 out of 3; the number in somewhat higher level occupations was twice as large.

There is, thus, some strength and stability in poverty areas, as well as considerable social pathology and disorganization. Neither the positive nor the negative aspects of the situation should be overlooked in policy development.

The variations from one ghetto area to another can also be considerable. A study of unemployed, out-of-school Negro youth in the Harlem and the Bedford-Stuyvesant areas of New York City, for example, showed sizable differences in outlook. Asked whether they expected to have the income they would need to support a family with two children within the next 5 to 10 years, 44 percent of Harlem youth, as contrasted with only 28 percent of those in Bedford-Stuyvesant, showed high expectations. The expectations of the youth in Harlem approached, though they did not quite equal, those of middle-class high school students.[7]

Relatively more of the Harlem than of the Bedford-Stuyvesant youth had been born in New York City or had come from the urban—instead of the rural—South. Consequently, the Harlem young people tended to be in better economic circumstances, as shown by their job histories and their families' earnings situation.

Probably the most important generalization that can be made about ghettos and poverty areas is their heterogeneity. No single program can reach all groups of slumdwellers.

BARRIERS TO EMPLOYMENT

The factors which produce sub-employment in big city poverty areas are as diverse as the characteristics of the people affected. They are also interrelated, mutually reinforcing, and difficult to disentangle. Social-psychological factors, lack of education and training, ill health, discrimination, and other employer practices with respect to selection of employees, and distance from available jobs are among the many barriers which contribute to joblessness, underemployment, and low earnings.

The following sections discuss three kinds of barriers to employment of the disadvantaged—social-psychological, access, and institutional.[8]

Social-Psychological Barriers

One interpretation of the high rates of joblessness and low earnings in city slums, increasingly cited as the general level of unemployment drops, stresses the presumed distinctive characteristics of the big city sub-employed —that they are less motivated to work, lack perseverance in working, and are generally alienated from the world of work. Although not fully supported, this explanation does have some validity. Reports by employers about men from poverty areas who were placed on jobs and then quit them seem to indicate that the work attitudes and motivation of the sub-employed of big cities are major barriers to their regular employment. Just how important these social-psychological factors are in the total complex of factors affecting the employment of disadvantaged workers is not certain, however. And the strategies that would be most effective in dealing with such factors are neither obvious nor free from controversy.

The social-psychological factors encompassed in explanations of the job behavior of low-income Negroes and others who have difficulty in getting and keeping jobs include attitudes, aspirations, motivation (especially achievement motivation), ability or willingness to defer gratification, and self-image. Most frequently, the individual's early family experiences are used to explain the development of this complex of attitudes and motivations. The basic assumption is that a person's perception of himself, his attitudes towards work, his motivation, and his ability to postpone gratifications affect his chances of getting and keeping a job.

The important considerations from the perspective of this analysis are the distribution, relevance, and causality of the various possible factors. Distribution denotes the extent to which a given factor or attribute, considered an important element in a positive orientation toward work, is found among the fully employed and not among the sub-employed. Relevance refers to the relationship between the particular factor and work-connected behavior—that is, how important the factor really is in work behavior. Causality concerns the genesis of the attribute: Is it a reaction to a particular set of job-related events, or does it have more deep-seated roots?

Distribution. Assuming that a complex of attitudes, aspirations, motivations, and identity orientation affects work behavior, does this lead, among the sub-employed, to crippling or otherwise inadequate outlooks toward work? Few studies on this general subject present data pertaining to the sub-employed as such; much more commonly they contrast Negroes with whites, or persons of lower socioeconomic status (as measured by income, occupation, education, or some combination of the three) with those of higher position. Before examining some findings of these studies, however, it is essential to note that neither the poor, nor the nonpoor, nor Negroes, nor whites are homogeneous. Furthermore, there is overlap in characteristics among groups. Some poor rank higher in social-psychological characteristics, no matter what the indicator, than some nonpoor. Consequently, public policy must be flexible and allow a variety of approaches if the sub-employed are to be aided effectively.

Although many studies show that relatively more people of high than of low socioeconomic status have positive work attitudes, this is far from a uniform finding. For example, a study of Job Corps enrollees concluded that the aspirations of the youth participating in this program did not differ substantially from those of youth in better circumstances.[9]

The aspiration data are complex. There is evidence, for example, that Negro parents often have very high educational aspirations for their children. These aspirations may be unrealistically high, as is often charged. But this is very different from the contention, also frequently made, that it is low aspirations which produce poor results in getting and keeping a job.

It has been suggested that the need to achieve is relatively low among persons at the poverty level, partly because early training in self-reliance may be less prevalent in poor families than in those in higher socioeconomic groups. Furthermore, several studies indicate that low-status Negroes have less need for achievement than low-status whites.[10] But there is conflicting evidence as well. For example, one sample of low-income Negro residents of a public housing project revealed that more than two-thirds agreed with the statement that "the most important qualities of a real man are determination and driving ambition."[11]

Aspiration is also relative to the expectation that one can achieve what one aspires to. This is shown by a study of Neighborhood Youth Corps enrollees (referred to previously). Only one-third of the unemployed Negro youth thought their chances of having enough income to support a family within 5 to 10 years were very good. When male freshmen and sophomores at a Catholic and a Negro university were asked the same question, the proportion reporting such expectations was twice as large (approximately 2 out of every 3). And more than one-half of a sample of Catholic high school students responded that their chances of being able to support a family within the indicated period were "very good."[12]

The findings of studies on deferred and delayed gratification also warrant careful attention. A number of studies investigating the ability to postpone gratification in order to gain a larger reward in the future have failed to indicate any uniform or striking differences between respondents in lower socioeconomic groups and those in higher positions.[13]

Relevance.   Social-psychological variables do not always have a clear-cut relationship to work behavior. The need to achieve has been offered as an important causal explanation of work behavior—workers who have a low need to achieve perform less satisfactorily. But in one study of unemployed males, a significant relationship between achievement motivation and job-finding success was not established. When Negroes and young workers (21 years old and under) were eliminated from the analysis, a stronger relationship was evident. Nevertheless, these findings suggest that, for certain groups at least, there is question about the importance of the need-achievement variable.[14]

Studies on a national scale also raise questions about the importance of achievement motivation. A comparative analysis of social mobility, for example, indicates that workers in France, the Netherlands, and Germany, characterized as having relatively low need-achievement,[15] do not differ markedly in mobility from workers in the United States and Britain, where need-achievement levels are higher.

Obviously, attitudes and values tend to intermingle with situational factors of opportunity and chance.

Causality. Attitudes and motivations can lead people to shun particular kinds of jobs or to handle them poorly. This is beyond question. But the chain of causality may move in the other direction also—unsatisfactory job experiences may lead to negative attitudes and motivations. Difficulty in getting a job, irregularity of employment, and inadequacy of wages may all contribute to low aspirations and expectations and inability to persevere on a job. Thus, ". . . the Negro youth starts out with determination to do a good job, but experience with a number of menial, low-paying, and insecure jobs quickly produces an erosion of his commitment to work."[16]

Moreover, failure to develop a work identity may lead to the development of an identity which competes with employment. The youth who lacks a work identity, as well as an identity as a husband and father, "must seek in other ways to construct a self which provides some measure of gratification of needs and earns some measure of recognition of one's self as a social being." The development of a "dramatic self" through adherence to the "expressive life style" provides an alternative identity.[17] If the youth is successful in establishing such an identity, it will provide him with the security, social participation, and feeling of status that he has failed to achieve through the worker-provider role. In dropping out of family life, he drops into a male-centered social world that provides a "strategy for survival," even though not centered about work.

Both early life experiences and those as a worker can contribute to the development of a life style which competes with an effective work identity. But once again, the chain of causality is not clear. The attitudes engendered by the family in early life can be reinforced, overturned, or modified as a result of later experiences.

In some respects, the behavior of the poor is less a reflection of basic values than an effort to cope with current situations. The mechanisms used for this purpose (such as dropping out of regular work and engaging instead in illicit activities) may have many negative consequences. But more important from the viewpoint of social policy is the question of whether these adjustive reactions, or "survival techniques," are responses to particular experiences and situations or the result of basic values learned at an early age and little affected by outside influences thereafter. Obviously, if later experiences, rather than early family life, have the more potent influence on work attitudes, changing these experiences may be a most important route to influencing workers' development.

This brief examination of a large and complicated body of literature suggests the following tentative conclusions:

1. Since the disadvantaged are not homogeneous, what may be characteristic of the most troubled individuals in this category may not be generally applicable to the disadvantaged.
2. The dividing line between employability and the lack of it is not fixed. In part, it reflects employers' judgments about individuals, made in the context of the general labor supply-and-demand situation. These relative judgments apply to the work attitudes and motivation of individuals as well as their levels of education and skill.
3. The extent to which these difficulties are the major factors in sub-employment is unclear. Still lacking is an adequate understanding of the connections between attitudes and work patterns. Attitudes are certainly significant, but it is not yet possible to say what the most relevant attitudes are, nor precisely how they influence actions.

The policy implications of the social-psychological factors are uncertain also. Two possible approaches are suggested. One emphasizes the necessity of direct efforts to modify the attitudes of the disadvantaged before introducing them to job situations. The other would bring the sub-employed into the job situation and then add the activities and services that may be needed to influence their attitudes and their ability to handle the demands of work.

The first approach is based on the principle of preparation—preparing people in advance for a change in environment. The latter approach seeks to provide supports for them after they have entered a different environment. The shift from preparation to support is an important change in the conception of the role of social services.

In the early 1960s, the emphasis was largely upon the first approach—through programs which aimed at motivating workers, especially the young, and which stressed prevocational activities and training in attitudes and social skills. More recently, however, emphasis has shifted to getting workers into jobs—based on the theory that "real life" work situations are those most likely to affect attitudes. The aim is to provide a setting in which a disadvantaged individual can perform adequately without a fully developed work identity and can then move in the direction of strengthening that identity. In some programs, traditional guidance and casework have been superseded by the development of racial pride and identity as a method of improving the capacity to take and hold a job.

This approach also implies the necessity for selective job development aimed at the particular groups to be served—which is one of the major new emphases in manpower programs. The cooperation of private industry is being sought in efforts to employ the disadvantaged in regular jobs. But projected job situations may be needed for a relatively small residual group (as further discussed later in this chapter).

Since low-income "families differ in background, in resources and skills, and in their ability to cope with the vicissitudes of a marginal existence,"[18] no one program will succeed with all. Nor should it be assumed that the same social-psychological factors are equally significant in every case.

Access and Institutional Barriers

The obstacles that stand between disadvantaged workers and jobs are partly personal, partly environmental and institutional. To consider the personal factors first, a great many ghetto residents—including Puerto Ricans and Mexican Americans as well as Negroes—do not have the basic education and command of standard English generally required for employment. Many more lack the work skills essential for the available jobs. Health problems and lack of adequate medical care are also pervasive difficulties. Police and bad debt records are further barriers to employment for significant numbers.

Besides these personal factors many sub-employed have an added difficulty: they do not look like "typical" employed workers. Differences in dress, hairstyle, and grooming make them less likely to be employed. "The style is the man" is an old saying which has some force, but its aptness may be overemphasized in judging fitness for work.

Undoubtedly, some sub-employed mirror in their personal appearance and behavior the kinds of difficulties they might have on the job—untidiness, inattention to detail, unreliability. For some, the usual employment situation may not be appropriate. But employers should realize that an unsatisfactory personal appearance is not necessarily indicative of inability to handle the usual work situation. An inadequate awareness of what jobs demand in terms of personal bearing may be involved. This lack of awareness can be overcome in many cases when the individuals' difficulties do not have deep psychological roots. In some cases, graded work experiences can help individuals adapt over time to job demands. The "strangeness" of some sub-employed should certainly not be regarded as typical of all of them. Nor should even those whose appearance is most disturbing to employers be rejected without exploration of their ability to adapt to work situations, given special help.

An additional obstacle to employment is the lack of adequate child-care facilities. This affects a significant number of women who want and need work.

The barriers discussed in this section are those relating to the job search, travel to jobs, institutional factors affecting hiring and promotion, and the current job structure.

The Job Search. Many disadvantaged persons, willing to work and looking for jobs, do not know how to go about the job search effectively. The slum resident is, to a large extent, confined to his own neighborhood. And jobs in outlying areas, or even in the central city of which the neighborhood is a part, are likely to be beyond his reach. Inadequate transportation, changes in occupational patterns, or shifts of industry from central cities to surrounding suburbs inhibit his search.

The disadvantaged youth or adult, then, starts on an active job hunt beset by problems. For the most part, the job does not come to him, although some efforts at recruiting within areas of concentrated poverty have been made in the last few years. The slum resident must search out available openings, and he may do this in a number of ways—through the nearest placement services; through newspaper ads; through direct application to plants, stores, or other possible locations of job openings; or through friends or relatives.

Learning about available jobs from friends and relatives is central to the job search, both in and outside poverty areas. But in the slums, this source of information is restricted by the limited connections which exist with the outside job world and also within the community. What little job information slum residents can get from friends and relatives usually pertains only to low-level occupations.

For people in poverty areas, social segregation and personal isolation act as barriers. Negro residential segregation has been increasing steadily over the past decade in cities throughout the United States, despite overall improvements in the socioeconomic status of Negroes.[19] This segregation has the effect of confining networks of informal communication to within the ethnic communities. Yet the lower the socioeconomic status of the community, the weaker the intracommunity network is likely to be, except where kin-group association is strong. Furthermore, unemployment contributes to social isolation; this is indicated by research conducted during the depression of the 1930s, as well as by more recent studies.[20]

Thus, in lower income communities, the long-term unemployed person often suffers the double burden of relative isolation within his own community, as well as segregation from the larger world of the metropolis. In some situations, such as that of the Pruitt-Igoe public housing project in St. Louis, most forms of interpersonal relationships are regarded with mistrust.[21]

The frequency with which informal information is relied upon in looking for jobs is made clear by a number of studies. A survey of workers affected by plant shutdowns in five communities revealed that from 31 to 53 percent of those who had been successful in finding new jobs had relied on informal information. In a sample of young labor force entrants, as many as 60 percent reported reliance upon friends or relatives.[22] Workers covered by these studies made relatively little use of the State Employment Service.

A nationwide survey of the 1962 graduates of vocational high schools showed Negro youth to be more dependent than white youth on informal sources of assistance in their job search. Half of all Negro students, as contrasted with about one-third of white students, depended upon friends or relatives to assist them in finding jobs. The Negroes received less help from the schools' job placement facilities than the white students. Though they relied more than whites on the State Employment Service, the importance of this service to them as a source of job referrals was limited, compared with their dependence on friends and relatives.[23]

Since dependence upon these informal sources of job information is so widespread, the accelerated movement of Negroes into technical and professional work, and into other white-collar and skilled manual jobs, should open up a new source of job information. The individuals entering such jobs should be channels of information to sub-employed friends and family members, not only about the job market in general but also about specific job openings.

The problem of bringing sub-employed slum residents within reach of information which would contribute to job-finding success is much larger than this, however. One approach to dissolving the communications barrier in the segregated ghetto lies in aiding the sub-employed to move to other neighborhoods. There are compelling reasons for this approach. But even if open housing policies come rapidly closer to meeting their objectives in this direction, people who move may continue to lack needed job information. Individuals and families whose social status or racial characteristics differ greatly from the majority in their neighborhood tend to remain isolated. Consequently, the need for increased efforts to get adequate job information to disadvantaged members of minority groups may extend to those in open housing.

Another approach is to improve the lines of communication to slum residents. One technique for doing this is to use workers from the poverty area to provide job information through personal contacts. In addition, community meeting places, such as churches and pool halls, may be used as information centers. Formal lines of communication can also be established through radio and television, which are more likely to reach lower income people than are newspapers and other written materials. And when placement services are brought into the slum areas, as has been done in the recent past, considerable improvement in job placements has occurred. The effectiveness of these techniques is limited, however, by the number of suitable jobs available, and the lack of inexpensive transportation to outlying areas may be a major obstacle.

A third approach is to bring jobs into ghetto areas. The visibility of new plants or business offices heightens the community's knowledge of available opportunities. In addition, it facilitates direct application to the company itself. The recent opening of a new tent factory in the Watts district of Los Angeles, for example, has demonstrated how effective this approach can be in informing workers about opportunities, even though only 300 of the 5,500 applicants for jobs at the plant could be hired.[24] Information about job availability must not, of course, be equated with employment, especially when jobs are in limited supply.

Transportation.   Metropolitan areas, of which slums and poverty areas are a part, are generally regarded as integrated job markets. But this generalization obscures the problems of specialized job markets and of the relationship between the location of a worker's home and the likelihood that he will be unemployed.

The isolation of slum residents, both youth and adults, from the larger urban area inhibits their participation in the broader job market, thus contributing to the problem of sub-employment. But there is another link between unemployment and slum residence, through the existence of a local and specialized juvenile job market, which warrants special attention. The situation has been described as follows:

> The teenage children of poor families desperately need after-school jobs; this work may . . . be a prerequisite to their remaining in school. But the demand for their services, for such things as baby-sitting, grass-cutting, snow-shoveling, lies largely in the middle- and upper-income neighborhoods . . . in the large urban area the supply of young labor may be many miles removed from the demand for it. In short, we . . . do not have an effective market for juvenile labor. . . . Slum children without part-time work may drop out of school, virtually ensuring a lifetime of low-grade employment at best and perhaps chronic unemployment.[25]

The lack of connections between young people who need part-time jobs and their potential employers is among the hidden social costs of the slum. It is one which the in-school program of the Neighborhood Youth Corps is specifically designed to offset—by generating within the ghetto opportunities for part-time employment of school youth. The alternative approach would be to bridge the gap between residence and place of employment through transportation strategies.

A similar gap separates adults in the slums from the areas of growing employment opportunity in their city's outskirts. Business and jobs are increasingly moving to the suburbs. While the suburbanite commutes to the city for his work, residents of central city slums seldom commute to jobs in the new and expanding plants in the outer suburban ring.

Here again, three solutions to the problem are possible—to bring jobs to the slums, to help slum residents move to the suburbs, or to accept a spatial separation between work and residence for many of these people and link the two by transportation. Each of the three solutions has both advantages and disadvantages. Bringing jobs to the ghetto will reinforce and solidify its elements of strength. Bringing slum residents to suburbia will weaken the ghetto and, if accompanied by open housing policies, will promote economic and racial integration. Arranging for people to commute to jobs from present slum areas will require coordination of job development and transportation programs, if sub-employment problems are not to be reduced at the cost of intensifying urban traffic crises.

As barriers to employment are identified and efforts are made to reduce them, it must not be assumed that each step in this direction will by itself lead to increased employment and higher income. For example, improvements in transportation aimed at enlarging employment opportunities for residents of poverty areas may not be effective in every case. Multiple strategies, rather than dependence upon a single one, will be necessary.

Institutional Barriers. Among the *institutional factors* which impede employment of slum residents—most of whom are members of ethnic minority groups and many of whom are old—discrimination is probably the most important. Discrimination not only in hiring but in access to promotion ladders dominates the life of many of the sub-employed.

The recruiting and hiring of workers is a selection process—although some critics have asserted that it is basically an exclusion process, which keeps out workers who do not fit personnel officers' conception of the model employee their company should have. Job applicants undergo a process of testing, interviewing, and credential scrutiny which operates to bar many of the sub-employed who might perform usefully on jobs.

Two types of errors are possible in the selection process—first, the rejection of persons who could handle satisfactorily the job to be filled and, second, the hiring of persons unable to perform the tasks involved at a satisfactory level. Much current hiring practice is concerned with preventing the second kind of error—a logical emphasis where the focus of concern is on the firm and its profits. But from a broader economic and social viewpoint, the first kind of error has become increasingly important, since it is one of the factors restricting job opportunities for the sub-employed.

The requirement of a high school diploma for many relatively low-skilled jobs is a particular obstacle to employment of disadvantaged workers— including large numbers of youth who are school dropouts. Employers argue that, in selecting employees, they must consider their potentiality for advancement to positions where the work demands a high school education, even if this is not necessary for the tasks involved in the entry jobs. But in view of the great need for enlarged opportunities for workers with limited education, this hiring policy should be reconsidered wherever possible.

The contention that a high school diploma has little relevance for many jobs is supported by several strands of evidence. For example, in a number of Western European countries—including France, Switzerland, Sweden, West Germany, and the Netherlands—workers from Southern Europe and Africa have done much useful factory work. Many of these foreign workers not only had less education than the sub-employed of the United States but could not speak the local language.

In this country, according to a recent study, few firms have ever systematically evaluated the performance of employees with different levels of education. Some data are available, however, on employees in private industry and government agencies, which compare the performance of workers at the same occupational level but with different amounts of education.[26] The indicators of performance used were of several types: Occasionally a direct productivity measure was utilized, but more often an indirect indicator such as absenteeism, employee turnover, or the rate of promotion was used. As might be expected, the results demonstrate that education is no guarantee of good performance. But more significantly, the opposite is suggested by some data. Thus, in many specific occupations, in a variety of industries and firms, the lower educated may do as well as, and often better than, workers with more formal training.

This information is by no means as definitive and comprehensive as would be desirable, since the occupations were not systematically sampled. But the clear implication is that the prevalent, mechanical requirement of a high school diploma or other certificate of education eligibility for a wide range of jobs may result in barring potentially useful workers.[27]

Many employers also use various kinds of paper-and-pencil tests to screen prospective employees. The use of objective tests in lieu of subjective judgment has the potential to work in favor of members of minority groups. However, all too often these tests are used without any evidence that they are related to performance on the job, and the same standard of test performance is applied to applicants for jobs of differing levels of skill within the same plant. The use of tests under these circumstances may result in excluding workers with low levels of education or limited command of English from jobs they could handle. Extensive efforts have been made, however, by the Department of Labor and other organizations to develop intelligence and aptitude tests which are free of cultural bias. It is important that these should continue, and also that great care should be used in the selection, administration, and interpretation of tests, in order to prevent unwarranted rejection of disadvantaged workers, especially those from ethnic minority groups.

The Job Structure.   So far, the discussion has been restricted to the barriers limiting opportunities for the sub-employed in existing jobs. But another question may be posed: Should the existing structure of jobs be regarded as given, or is it possible and desirable to change the context of some jobs so as to open more opportunities for the sub-employed?

The present division of tasks and responsibilities among occupations reflects both deliberate, rational allocation of tasks and more haphazard factors. This structure of jobs and occupations has been much influenced by tradition, interest groups, and accident, as well as by careful analysis of who could best perform a particular task and under what conditions.

No single pattern of division of labor by any means represents the only way the tasks could be divided. During World War II, for example, a considerable amount of job dilution occurred; people with less training than was formerly required did a great deal of essential work. And in more recent years, the distribution of tasks in the medical field has been shifting toward service workers (e.g., nurse aides) from middle-level professionals (e.g., nurses), who in turn have taken over some tasks from top professionals (physicians).

Many job openings in professional, technical, and skilled occupations are unfilled because of a lack of trained manpower. This may be due in part to demographic influences (i.e., the low birthrates of the 1930s), but it also reflects hiring requirements. Each occupation seeks the "best" people, although by definition the "best" can be only a few. Yet this general search for the best could build a permanent insufficiency of manpower able to meet hiring specifications.

The scarcity of qualified workers for many present jobs suggests that it may be desirable to reallocate tasks so that the best are not always necessary, and to recognize the likelihood that workers judged less than the best can do useful work. The development of more subprofessional jobs in health and related fields is a trend in this direction, but comparable developments have not occurred on a wide scale in other types of employment.

Opportunities for the sub-employed would be increased immediately by the opening of more unskilled jobs. But the number of unskilled jobs has not been growing, and there is little if any evidence of a "filtering down" to make jobs formerly the preserve of the more skilled workers available to the less skilled. Progress in this direction has been impeded partly by the frequent mingling of unskilled and skilled tasks in jobs labeled as skilled. But it also reflects employers' reluctance to take on a new kind of labor, unable to meet their traditional hiring requirements: they may prefer to have some unfilled job openings, rather than face the problems such a change would entail.

Altogether, the present job structure and placement processes bar many of the sub-employed from jobs—particularly from jobs which have some status and are relatively well paid. The job structure also retards the upgrading of workers whose previous positions could then be filled by the sub-employed, and it restricts the downgrading of jobs in order to open them to the sub-employed. The problems the sub-employed face in their job search are obviously created in major part by this rigid job structure. Strategies for aiding their entry into steady employment will have to be concerned, among other things, with provision of incentives for modifying jobs so that disadvantaged workers can qualify for them.

THE IRREGULAR ECONOMY OF POVERTY AREAS

The barriers which separate sub-employed slum residents, nonwhite or white, from the mainstream of economic and social life have resulted in the creation of a separate economic world, which differs vitally, and in many ways, from the middle-class world surrounding the slums. This world has its own special values, its own strategies for survival, its own moral standards, its own criteria of success or failure.

The sources of income of the poor and dependent—those at the bottom one-fifth of the income distribution—are varied, and public policy is directed at altering them in many ways. When income from employment is low, unstable, and unpredictable, the traditional distinctions between employment and unemployment, work and welfare become blurred, and extra-legal sources of income may be sought.

The contrasts between this irregular economy[28] of the slums and the country's regular economy are sharp. In the regular economy, work offers opportunities for vertical mobility, a reasonably predictable pattern of wage improvement with increasing seniority and skill, and the possibility of stable employment. Jobs can be classified in terms of status, skill requirements, and level and stability of earnings—as white- or blue-collar, skilled or unskilled, salaried or paying an hourly wage. By contrast, the irregular economy is characterized by horizontal mobility, erratic wage fluctuations, and overlap between the welfare and the wage systems. Jobs are better described as dead end, low wage, sporadic, extra-legal, and so forth.

The size, characteristics, and fluctuations of the irregular economy are not well known nor understood. How does this economy work? How does it overlap with the regular economy? What are its implications for public policy?

The irregular economy has many different income streams, which blend into economic sustenance for slumdwellers. Many people work in low-wage, parttime, marginal jobs that provide no ladder to better opportunities. The work may be physically exacting, job security low, and employment offered only on a shorttime basis. In some jobs, the employer pays so little that employees have great temptation to steal from him in order to supplement their earnings. Occasionally, a criminal activity may be the source of income, but the situation is seldom so clear cut. A man may have his own type of "hustle"—an easy way to money, sometimes legitimate, sometimes partly not, that puts him in a quasi-entrepreneurial role. For example, he may discover where he can get a watch cheap—a "hot" watch—and then sell it to someone on his block. A woman may be on welfare for some months of the year and work in other months;[29] or she may receive welfare and at the same time work covertly; or a man may be living with a woman receiving welfare. As another alternative, a man may enroll in one of the training programs which pay stipends, in order to get funds to tide him over a lean period. Or he may borrow money, to be repaid when he gets a job or a hustle. Or he may decide to retire temporarily from the "scuffle" for a livelihood, and so swell the ranks of the jobless. However, many ghetto residents show high motivation and unusual resourcefulness and persistence in efforts to earn a living.

A possible basis of life for marginal workers is thus provided by the irregular economy. The variations of this world, its occasional excitement and flexibility, may have more appeal to many such workers than do low-paid, demanding, regular jobs. According to a recent study:

> . . . the streetcorner man . . . knows the social value of the job by the amount of money the employer is willing to pay him for doing it. . . . every pay day, he counts . . . the value placed on the job by society at large. . . . Nor does the low-wage offer prestige, respect, interesting work, opportunity for learning or advancement, or any other compensation . . . [The low-wage job in the regular economy is] hard, dirty, uninteresting and underpaid. The rest of society . . . holds the job of the dishwasher or janitor or unskilled laborer in low esteem if not outright contempt. So does the streetcorner man. He cannot do otherwise. He cannot draw from a job those social values which other people do not put into it.[30]

The marginal economy develops a social psychology appropriate to its work world. As the streetcorner man views his future:

> It is a future in which everything is uncertain except the ultimate destruction of his hopes and the eventual realization of his fears. . . . Thus, when Richard squanders a week's pay in two days it is not because . . . he is . . . unaware of or unconcerned with his future. He does so precisely because he is aware of the future and the hopelessness of it all.[31]

Since the jobs typically available to slum residents have no attraction in terms either of income or of the nature of the work, it is not surprising that many of these jobs are rejected or held for only short periods. A taxing regular job must offer higher income than the economic activities of the irregular economy to appear preferable to them. And it must offer compensation also for the strain of regular hours of work day in and day out, often in physically demanding or boring work, and of accommodating to supervisors.

There is evidence that many from poverty areas do not stay, even on better jobs. They may not know how to behave on such jobs or find it difficult to maintain the routine; or too much may be expected of them too soon; or their off-job situation may make it difficult to keep the job. For such workers, placement in jobs in the mainstream economy may not be enough; they will need assistance in handling and adjusting to the new jobs.

Employers and supervisors need to develop increased understanding of these workers' problems and to learn how they can be handled. When jobs are opened up for the disadvantaged, changes in the customary work patterns and in supervisory relationships are likely to be essential if the workers are to succeed in, and stay on, the job.

Furthermore, manpower and social policy must be concerned with the ways in which work-training and welfare programs influence the irregular economy. The more differentiated and partial the benefit system, the more opportunities for integration of this system with the irregular economy's other income sources. Programs which provide only marginal increases in an individual's income tend to reinforce this economy.

To challenge it effectively, more attractive alternatives must be provided. This can be done by helping private employers open reasonably well-paying jobs in the regular economy to sub-employed workers. Many individuals who live in the irregular economy are eager to leave it, provided they have a chance to really advance their position in a society strongly oriented toward consumption. They would welcome an opportunity to move from a dead end job to a career opportunity, such as the New Careers program is designed to offer.

THE AFDC MOTHER—A CASE STUDY OF SUB-EMPLOYMENT

Mothers receiving assistance through the federal program of Aid to Families with Dependent Children (AFDC) provide an illustrative case study of one group of sub-employed in the irregular economy—their problems, their difficulties in meeting these problems, and the way in which they react not only to their individual situations but also to the economic opportunities available to them.

Many theories have been evolved, and myths created, about this relatively small group of the underprivileged. Recipients of AFDC have been widely regarded as caught in a chronic, static condition of dependency, handed down from one generation to the next. Welfare has been viewed as an alternative to work, increasingly unrelated to such economic factors as the general level of unemployment or the participation of women in the labor force. This discussion looks at some of these theories in the light of available evidence. Obviously, there are families whose members have been brought up with welfare support and then have gone on to raise their own families with such support. But there are also many families whose members are on welfare rolls for very short periods of time and never sever their connection with the labor force, even when they are on welfare.

AFDC recipients are encouraged by welfare agencies to find work. Their earnings are included in the total family income that is considered when the amount of welfare payment is determined. States may, however, disregard some part of the earnings of mothers in order to conserve them for the future needs of children.[32]

Data for the analysis that follows are drawn largely from the only two available national studies of AFDC caseloads. A study sponsored by the American Public Welfare Association was based on a one in three sample of cases closed during the first three months of 1961;[33] a study sponsored by the Department of Health, Education and Welfare (HEW) covered a 1 percent sample of the cases currently active during the last two months of 1961.[34] The situation has undergone changes since that time—one of the most notable being the continuing increase in the AFDC caseload, despite the marked reduction in the overall rate of unemployment. The increased caseload is the result of many factors, including an increase in the numbers of young children, of female-headed households, and of children in such households; a relaxation in eligibility requirements in many states; and wider knowledge of the existence of the AFDC program. However, more recent evidence, including several studies of local situations, in general bears out the conclusions reached in the two nationwide surveys.

Length of Time on Welfare

One way of exploring whether welfare is in fact a way of life, passed on from one generation to another, is to examine the length of time individual recipients remain on welfare. In 1961, the median length of time on AFDC was 27 months for currently active cases and 18 months for closed cases. But the length of time on assistance varied widely with both race and residence. For closed cases, the median time spent on assistance was higher for Negroes (22 months) than for whites (15 months) and lower in urban areas (16 months) than in rural areas (20 months). Periods of dependency tended to be longer in medium-sized cities (50,000 to 500,000) than in the largest cities. In general, however, the mothers in rural farm and nonfarm areas were those who spent the longest continuous periods of time on assistance.[35]

These figures on "continuous time" on assistance obscure the great turnover in the AFDC rolls. A recent analysis of case turnover showed that 584,000 cases were authorized and 508,000 cases were closed in calendar year 1966, while slightly more than 1 million were carried over from the preceding year. Averaged over the year, about 45,000 new families were added to the rolls each month, while 41,000 left. Certain families have repeated periods on relief; of the cases added in 1966, about 34 percent had received assistance previously.[36]

Since individuals do go on and off welfare, cumulative data showing the total time spent on welfare by an AFDC mother and her children are important in determining how welfare fits into their life cycle. According to the study of cases closed in 1961, 10 percent of the Negro and 7 percent of the white mothers had spent 9 or more years on welfare. Nevertheless, in absolute terms, white families outnumbered Negro families among the very small minority of AFDC cases on assistance for as long as this.[37]

The proportion of their adult life that women spend on AFDC is another significant measure of their dependence on this assistance. A study based on a 1 percent random sample of AFDC cases in Philadelphia (drawn in 1959, and followed through to 1962) showed that the majority (60 percent) had spent slightly less than half (47 percent) of their adult life on

welfare.[38] In at least one city, then, welfare was not a permanent or exclusive style of life for all of the women on AFDC during the time they
raised their children.

Finally, intergenerational dependency on welfare can also be measured.
In the cases closed during early 1961, less than a third both of the white
and of the Negro mothers had grown up in families in which their parents
had also been on assistance.[39] However, a study in the state of Washington
in 1964 yielded a substantially higher figure. About 43 percent of the
AFDC mothers in the sample reported that their parents had been on assistance—3 percent said their parents had been dependent for as long as
they could remember; 27 percent said that they had been dependent for
several years; and 13 percent said that they had received assistance for a
brief period.[40]

Altogether, the generalization that welfare becomes a permanent style
of life for all or most AFDC recipients is not supported by the available
evidence. The people on welfare are a varied group. Many of the families
are not involved in long-term or intergenerational dependency. It must be
recognized, however, that significant proportions of AFDC families do
represent a second generation on welfare. This is one of the problems to
which the program changes provided for by the 1967 amendments to the
Social Security Act are addressed.

Welfare and Work

Welfare and employment are widely regarded as alternative rather than
complementary or overlapping sources of income. The AFDC caseload is
generally seen as made up of nonworking mothers. This is consistent with
the theory of public assistance embodied in the original Social Security
Act of 1935, which assumed that social insurance protected members of
the labor force when their income was interrupted, while federally financed
social assistance was for the unemployable. The 1967 amendments to the
Social Security Act are directed at promoting economic independence—a
permanent or long-term break from the irregular economy—through a
program of social services, job training, and cash incentives.

The recent amendments are based on the assumption that AFDC mothers
have been entirely outside the labor force and that, if adequate child-care
facilities are made available, they can, through training and other services,
be enabled to care for themselves and their families. But, in fact, AFDC
mothers have frequently been active members of the sub-employed labor
force—the underemployed and low-wage workers. Public assistance often
served as a form of wage supplementation for the low-paid, partially employed worker. Welfare status did not necessarily represent a sharp break
with the labor force, as the theory of assistance would imply.

The study of AFDC cases closed in 1961 showed that about 26 percent of the white and 41 percent of the Negro children were in families where the mothers had maintained some degree of attachment to the labor force during the periods on AFDC. (See Table 1.) About half of the mothers had been regularly employed before receiving welfare and continued to be regularly employed after receipt of AFDC payments.[41]

Table 1. Percent Distribution of AFDC Children by Color and by Employment Status of Homemaker During Period on AFDC*

Employment status of homemaker	White	Negro
Total: Number	9,629	4,245
Percent	100.0	100.0
Employed	26.4	40.6
Full-time throughout period	3.0	5.4
Full-time most of period	4.5	4.4
Part-time throughout period	4.8	11.0
Part-time most of period	7.2	12.6
Other employment history	6.9	7.2
Not employed	73.2	58.8
Employment status unknown	.4	.6

* Based on a sample of cases closed in first 3 months of 1961; includes children born in wedlock only.

SOURCE: M. Elaine Burgess and Daniel O. Price, *An American Dependency Challenge* (Chicago: American Public Welfare Association, 1963), based on table on p. 268.

The HEW study of AFDC cases active in late 1961 showed the mother's employment status at a given point in time, rather than over a longer period. Of all AFDC mothers on the rolls at the time of the study, 14 percent were employed—including 11 percent of the white and 19 percent of the Negro mothers.[42]

The study of the AFDC caseload in Philadelphia in 1962 classified the work history of AFDC mothers in terms of their level of skill and job stability, based on information on their first job, their longest job, and their most recent job. About 40 percent of the women had a stable work history, and 47 percent an unstable one. Only 13 percent had no history of work. Of those with a work history, 40 percent had been been employed in skilled or semi-skilled jobs.

Thus, AFDC mothers can hardly be described as a group made up predominantly of "work-shy women" who inherited their welfare status. However, there appears to be a generational difference in these women's work histories. The older ones had the more stable work history but lower levels of skill, while the reverse was true for the younger women. These different work habits may have resulted from the nature of the job market at the time the women entered it. Older women had apparently been able to develop a pattern of stability in a job world which accepted their low level of skill, but younger women with higher education and somewhat more skill appeared unable to develop a pattern of work stability in the present, more demanding job market. In general, the women who were unskilled workers had spent less of their adult lives on assistance than had the more skilled.

In view of the generally higher overall rates of unemployment among unskilled than higher skilled workers, this is a rather significant finding. It underlines the special circumstances—social and psychological as well as economic—which affect the work situation of these sub-employed women and other groups in the irregular economy.

The type of locality in which these mothers lived also had a marked effect on their pattern of employment. According to the study of cases closed in early 1961, the proportion of mothers who had been employed was lowest in large cities. This was true of both white and Negro mothers, but geographic location had a greater effect on the employment pattern of Negro women than on that of whites. Only about one-fourth of the Negro women in cities of over half a million had worked while on welfare, as compared with nearly 3 out of every 4 of those on farms. (See Table 2.)

Table 2. Place of Residence and Employment Status of Homemaker During Period on AFDC, by Color*

Place of residence	All AFDC families** (percent distribution)	Percent with homemaker employed	
		White	Negro
Total	100.0	26.4	40.6
Metropolitan Counties			
City of 500,000 or more	25.3	16.4	23.5
City of 50,000 to 499,999	21.1	25.9	45.8
City of 2,500 to 49,999	7.5	25.8	44.4
Rural nonfarm	4.4	25.6	56.5
Nonmetropolitan Counties			
City of 2,500 to 49,999	19.4	33.2	57.6
Rural nonfarm	18.4	26.7	56.5
Farm	3.9	20.8	72.9

* Based on a sample of cases closed during first 3 months of 1961.
** A few families, 0.3 percent, were in farm areas of metropolitan counties.

SOURCE: M. Elaine Burgess and Daniel O. Price, *An American Dependency Challenge* (Chicago: American Public Welfare Association, 1963), based on tables on pp. 264, 265, and 268.

Some Implications and Program Developments

These findings cast some doubt on two of the dominant ideas which color much of the discussion about the public assistance program—that being on welfare generally becomes a permanent style of life and that the benefits it provides are an alternative to work. Employment and welfare are systems which mesh in complex ways. Welfare is a form of social provision when income is absent, interrupted, or inadequate, and not simply a cash transfer system operating outside the world of work.

Each state sets its own cost standards for living requirements under AFDC. But many states also set arbitrary ceilings on the amount of assistance that will actually be paid—often well below the amount of determined need.

Much more information is needed, however, about the interrelationships between work and welfare and, in particular, about why many AFDC mothers work. At present, there is no definitive information on this latter point. One can do little more than speculate regarding the factors that enter into the situation and even about how many mothers do and do not increase their total income through their work.

To throw light on these basic questions will require extensive study of the circumstances surrounding these women's employment, as well as analysis of their budgets. The need for such research is the more urgent because of the possible implications of the findings for current programs aimed at increasing employment of AFDC mothers.

It seems probable that, in many cases, monetary incentives may not be the crucial factor in the mothers' decisions to work. At the same time, it is likely to take more than minimum earnings to effect a real change in the status of AFDC recipients; this requires income adequate for upward mobility—for a takeoff from dependency to economic self-sufficiency.[43] Thus, programs of income incentives and work training may not reverse the upward trend in the welfare rolls, unless the training is designed to move clients to permanent employment at adequate wages. The Work Incentive Program established under the 1967 Social Security Act amendments is aimed at precisely this objective.

An expansion of child-care facilities is also provided for by these amendments, on the assumption that lack of such facilities has been one of the factors which prevent AFDC mothers from seeking employment. The total capacity of licensed child-care facilities in the United States is placed presently at only 310,000 to 350,000. So the proportion of working women using such facilities is necessarily small. According to a 1965 study, only about 5 percent of all working mothers placed their children in group care. Of those with low incomes (under $3,000), only 3 percent used such facilities.

In view of these findings, it is not clear how expansion of child-care facilities will affect the AFDC mother's entry into the labor force. But whether or not the number of such mothers who become economically self-sufficient increases markedly, the provision of more good facilities for child care should help both the mothers and the children who use them. It may reasonably be expected that such services will ease the tensions of work for these women and reduce their absences from the job. They will also improve the situation of the children, who will benefit socially and educationally from organized programs of care.

SOME CONSIDERATIONS AFFECTING MANPOWER POLICIES

Objectives in Job Development

To provide a satisfactory alternative to dependence on welfare or other sources of income in the irregular economy, a job must now offer more than mere subsistence. This is apparent from the foregoing discussion both of the irregular economy and of AFDC mothers' sometimes alternate, sometimes simultaneous reliance on work and welfare.

Jobs which furnish only subsistence for the worker and his family have become less and less satisfactory, as the majority of people in this country have achieved higher standards of living, and as the provision of minimum subsistence has become increasingly a function of public welfare. Little is yet known about the job "extras" which are most important to sub-employed workers, but the identification of these "extras" is crucial to a successful policy of job creation for the disadvantaged.

Two questions must be considered. The first relates to the amount of earnings: How much more than subsistence is a job expected to provide? The second involves the kinds of job extras which may be expected. While these two questions are not easily distinguished, their formulation may help clarify the problems manpower policy must confront.

Does the prospective jobholder see his job as one which should provide him with the means to subsistence, plus comfort and security? Or does he want a "career"—a reasonable expectation that he will be able to move upward, socially and economically?

A study of Negroes in Philadelphia illustrates the importance of income as opposed to status. Given a hypothetical choice between a high-status but relatively low-paid job and a low-status but higher paid job, those in the lowest socioeconomic group consistently chose the latter. But this was not true for respondents with higher status.[44]

Further evidence also suggests that among workers in low-income groups, the majority direct their job aspirations toward the goal of the "good American life"—of ability to provide for the comfort and security of their families. Both men and women respondents in a public housing project in St. Louis generally agreed that "a job should come first," and that "the most important thing a parent can do is to help his children get further ahead than he did."[45]

Thus, current concern about dead end jobs may not be valid for many sub-employed adults, since the first priority for those with family responsibilities is likely to be a job with wages high enough for adequate family support, and indirectly for the upward mobility of the children. For lower income respondents who have modest aspirations and who wish to provide for their families, the level of wages and job security become important in job creation. Members of this group want to be part of the stable working class, and they are not averse to menial jobs, if such jobs pay well.

At some point in the lives of many disadvantaged boys and men, aspirations for a job which would provide either "the good American life" or career success become frustrated. Made aware of these generally accepted objectives through mass communications media, if not through personal experience, these men often have a heightened sense of comparative deprivation as well as frustration.

One response to this frustration is retreat into despair and hopelessness; another is resort to illegitimate activity. The slum resident who frequently has even his modest aspirations frustrated also lives in a community environment which provides relatively easy access to illegitimate means for achieving those aspirations. As former Secretary of Labor Wirtz has said:[46]

> We realize all of a sudden the very intimate, sinister, complex interrelationship between crime and the unemployment that we have now. It is not only that unemployment produces crime. It is that crime, to a very considerable extent, complicates the motivational problem in the slums. I hate to say to you how many times we run into a boy who hesitates to take a training program with an allowance of perhaps $35 a week, when he could make five times that much peddling dope.

In dealing with the critical though small minority of the sub-employed engaged in activities such as peddling dope and picking up numbers, government job creation and training programs compete with the high monetary return of organized crime, as well as with other economic rewards of the irregular economy. Such illegitimate job substitutes also have other attractions for slum residents in addition to their monetary aspects, and these must be better understood also if the problems they present are to be met. Nevertheless, the inference is clear from several studies that people in lower income groups generally prefer less remunerative but secure jobs to high-paying, high-risk activities. Crime cannot provide the "extra" of job security; perhaps governmental policy can.

Finally, manpower and antipoverty programs may themselves contribute to frustration if they raise hopes which they fail to fulfill. These programs have done much to awaken dormant aspirations. For example, about two-thirds of Job Corps recruits already had jobs—generally at very low wages—but wanted to better their situation. If programs do not meet justified expectations, despair will intensify.

The dilemma is clear. Without aspirations and hope, little can be accomplished. But aspirations and hope are fragile, requiring reinforcement from life experience. To snuff out hope once it is kindled may leave a worse situation than before.

Social Objectives

If manpower policy is to serve social objectives with emphasis on the disadvantaged, these objectives must be better understood and articulated. The priorities assigned to different objectives—implicitly if not explicitly—greatly influence decisions as to how manpower resources should be allocated.

The three objectives selected for discussion here represent alternative approaches to the common goal of social integration and stability. They all bear directly on current efforts to help the sub-employed enter and adjust to regular jobs, and to overcome dependence on welfare or extra-legal activities. These related but also competing objectives are:

1. To substitute earned for unearned income, because of the therapeutic quality of work.
2. To contribute to family stability by concentrating on employment for men, while also considering the needs of women family heads.
3. To build self-respect and satisfaction by providing jobs which have "quality," either in terms of career potential or immediately satisfactory income.

Work as Social Therapy. The rationale for emphasizing work or earned income as a social objective lies in the constructive impact work has on behavior. In past years, theories of how to promote personal and social stability and reduce delinquency and crime placed reliance on remedial programs involving organized recreation, street clubs which combined play and counseling, and sound housing to replace dilapidated slums. But faith in these approaches has been slowly lost. Today, the opportunity theory of delinquency stresses the importance of removing barriers which inhibit low-income youth from sharing the employment and other benefits available in the broader society.

Loosely interpreted, this theory means programs which emphasize jobs and education. The Juvenile Delinquency and Youth Offenses Control Act of 1961 adopted this frame of reference in launching a series of new programs which emphasized the link between work and reduction of social disorganization. In the wake of riots and unrest in the central cities, the theory that work may reduce crime has been extended to include the idea that work may also reduce social unrest.

This theory of the therapeutic effects of work has led to policies aimed at getting as many of the sub-employed as possible into jobs—at substituting earned income for public relief or the hustle. Emphasis is on the importance of jobs as such; the quality of the jobs and the level of income they produce are regarded as secondary considerations.

The analysis earlier in this chapter of the demographic characteristics of the sub-employed and the social-psychological barriers to their employment lends some support to this approach by underlining the importance of entry jobs for these disadvantaged people. But the foregoing discussion also suggests the shortcomings of this thesis, which makes no allowance for the job "extras" many individuals may demand as offsets to the advantages of activities in the irregular economy, and in fulfillment of expectations as to an acceptable level of income in this affluent country.

Personal and Family Stability. Complementary to the theory of the social therapy of work is the objective of increasing family stability. This objective stresses the male-headed household, where the man can serve as the role model for young people as they develop. The quality of family life is assumed to generate motivation for work and social involvement. Accordingly, manpower and social policies must be directed at strengthening the family, which serves as the most effective instrument for social orientation of youth and for facilitating their entry into the job market.

With family stability a primary objective, manpower policy must be aimed not simply at expanding employment of the disadvantaged but also at determining which individuals are to get the available jobs. And on this point, the implication is clear: priority should be given to jobs for adult men—in the hope that this will have the double effect of keeping men who are already household heads in their homes and of encouraging those who have left the household to return. Men are not always the most disadvantaged members of the sub-employed. But if they are to achieve the same position in the world of the minority which they enjoy in that of the majority, they must become the principal wage earners and family providers.

At the same time, the many women who are household heads also deserve priority consideration. Families headed by women are among the most impoverished, include large numbers of children, and provide the only source of psychological and economic stability these children have. The disadvantaged women who carry the heavy burden of supporting a family have a high claim on training opportunities and other help in obtaining decently paid jobs.

The Quality of Work and Income. The third objective is "decent" work and adequate income. This approach emphasizes the link between the level of income and social stability. The quality of work and the amount of income are regarded as of prime importance (rather than the source of income, emphasized in the approach based on the therapeutic value of work). Work in itself may not be as critical as the amount of income it yields.

A project in Milwaukee designed to retrain AFDC mothers for employment illustrates this point. According to the data available, the mothers were enabled to get and presumably hold jobs, but their earnings were not appreciably higher than their welfare payments had been. The source of their income was changed without improving the quality of their life.

Such an outcome might be acceptable if it is assumed that welfare payments are stigmatizing. On this basis, substituting earned income for welfare would, by itself, enhance the individuals' dignity and improve the quality of their life. But it could be argued that the stigma might also be removed by developing alternative cash transfer programs—family allowances or a negative income tax, for example—which allocate income with dignity.

That the quality of work and the level of income earned may be crucial in promoting social stability is suggested by more direct evidence, however. The participants in recent urban riots apparently did not represent the most disadvantaged people in the slum areas involved. Indeed, "evidence about educational achievement suggests that the rioters were . . . slightly better educated than their peers . . . and . . . the great majority . . . were currently employed." The conclusion was that the Watts rioters were in "the mainstream of modern Negro urban life."[47] They were not simply seeking jobs, but better ones. This may indicate that, to a large group of rioters, jobs with dignity and power were more important than just being at work.

A Department of Labor study of 500 persons arrested in connection with the Detroit riots in July 1967 led to similar findings.[48] The typical prisoner was employed at the time of the riot—working in a manufacturing plant, where he earned an average of $120 a week. Two out of every five of the prisoners had a high school education or better, but only a few (probably around 1 out of 10) had a skilled or white-collar job, commensurate with this level of education. Furthermore, the rate of unemployment was high— 22 percent, about five times the average unemployment rate for the entire Detroit metropolitan area.

The kinds of tasks involved in a job and the conditions under which these are performed can be important also. A low-status job presumably affects the worker's attitudes about himself as well as his employment. In a society where the poor of a big city can constantly see the inequities of their situation, the issue is not merely jobs as against no jobs, but what kind of jobs they can get.[49] The quality of the jobs available to slum residents assumes steadily growing importance—measured in terms not only of income and stability but also of amenities such as decent treatment by supervisors and of the absence of strenuous labor. Freedom from hard physical work has become an important status symbol in the present-day nonagricultural economy, and the physical limitations of many of the sub-employed make heavy labor impossible for them.

From this perspective, it is not enough to get manpower services. They have also participated in the shift in manpower goals, during the last few years, to primary orientation toward the disadvantaged worker.

With this shift has come increased experimentation and exploration, but not yet a fully coordinated and interconnected system of programs and services. Problems of coordination of manpower programs at the federal level have been substantially worked out. However, the development of the best possible working relationships between federal, state, and local agencies is still unfinished business, although substantial progress has been made in this direction.

The characteristics of a fully developed manpower system are known—integrated, flexible, diversified, person-centered, coordinated, durable, and continuous. The difficulties lie in implementing these concepts, not only at the federal, state, and city levels, but even more critically at the neighborhood level. Development of responsibility and authority in the neighborhood is crucial, but to achieve this also requires allocation of responsibility and authority at higher levels in the city and above.

The structure of programs—involving many different public and private agencies, with separate funding and separate staffs—has been a major obstacle in efforts to forge an effective system. It has also had a direct effect on the quality of services provided. Just as the allocation of welfare expenditures often forces an individual to receive services based on the category into which he fits, rather than on his particular needs, so the divisions between manpower programs have hampered the provision of services tailored to the individual.[50]

Integration and coordination of activities, needed at all levels, are most important at the point of delivery of services. To be effective, efforts to increase coordination must be aimed directly at better service to the individuals involved.

Sub-employed individuals who are to be helped should each be assigned to a person who can call on services, obtain jobs, and the like. This person would make the important recommendations and arrange for the services. He should follow through on the entire process, so that there is clear-cut responsibility for the outcome.

Another important issue is the appropriate sorting of individuals into the various manpower programs. The program an individual goes into has depended to some extent on chance, partly because many cities have lacked a central agency in close contact with the variety of programs now available. It is now recognized as essential to assure that a person is routed into the appropriate activity, that he benefits from the program, and that he is enabled to move into a decent job.

In the past, the unit of manpower policy has been, to a large extent, the individual program rather than the individual person. But as many recent program developments emphasize, the need is for centering on the person and for assuring that he gets a job. Responsibility should not end there, however, since he may not stay on the job, especially if he is among the more disadvantaged workers. Responsibility for the worker must extend beyond the initial placement and even involve giving a second chance to those who quit.

To provide the organizational framework that would facilitate the exercise of effective and continuing concern for individuals is the objective of a number of major new programs—notably, the Cooperative Area Manpower Planning System and the Concentrated Employment Program. The new neighborhood centers in many areas also are aimed at bringing to individuals the constellation of services they need.

Steady improvements may be expected through these efforts to coordinate and concentrate programs. It should be recognized, however, that grave difficulties are often encountered and have to be overcome in bringing the needed program components together into an effective system.[51]

Toward Opening More Jobs for the Sub-Employed

The economic expansion of the past seven years has drawn many previously jobless workers into employment in cities and rural areas as well. But many of the sub-employed in city slums have not obtained jobs and will not get them without special help, even assuming continued rapid economic growth.

All too often, decent employment has not been available for relatively low-skilled workers under prevailing hiring standards. Employers are frequently unwilling to tolerate workers who do not quickly meet established standards of promptness, low absenteeism, and comportment. The key, then, is the development of more job situations suited to the needs of the disadvantaged, and designed to aid both the worker and the employer in what may be a difficult adjustment process.

Some of the sub-employed can work in standard jobs if hiring—and also retention—requirements are reduced. There has been, in fact, considerable movement in this direction in both the public and private sectors of the economy. Many government agencies have scaled down their educational requirements. In several cities, employers have begun to hire men whom they would previously have rejected. More than hiring appears to be necessary, however, in view of reports of frequently high turnover rates among disadvantaged workers in these standard jobs.

At least some standard jobs could be modified to provide more extensive and flexible induction processes on the job. Workers new to production-line activity or to steady, quality employment do not always rapidly accept and acquire the normal work practices and habits. While some of the disadvantaged have no problem in adjusting to a steady work pattern, experience shows that many do. To meet their special needs, the standard job might be modified in one of two ways—adaptation of traditional working arrangements, or increased and continued services and supervision. The former approach may involve longer work induction and training processes than are typically required for new recruits. In some cases, it may be desirable to assign disadvantaged workers, at least at the beginning, to units made up of formerly sub-employed workers who have adjusted to the work pattern.[52] It may be useful, also, to experiment with placing these workers throughout a plant as openings arise, or with mixed units including both disadvantaged and other workers. No one method is appropriate for all of the sub-employed, and a large plant employing many of the disadvantaged might utilize different methods—in each case selecting that which best fits the particular worker.

Separate work units for the formerly sub-employed—whether in plants to which they travel or in new firms near their homes—would facilitate adjusting their work day, if this appears necessary to keep these workers on the job. Is it essential that everyone work a regular eight hour day? A shorter working day (with less pay) might be possible, at least at the beginning, for workers who are the most difficult to retain. They would then gradually work toward a longer day. Another possibility is to have workers come in later in the morning—perhaps at 9 or 10 a.m.—rather than insisting that everyone get to work by 8 a.m. from the start. Such experiments would, obviously, require a high degree of cooperation and understanding on the part of the regular work force, and might prove feasible only in exceptional work situations.

Still another possibility might be an intensive program of education for workers already on the job, to enlist their help in the adjustment process of the newly hired sub-employed. A key element in the Concentrated Employment Program is the assignment of a "coach" to each new worker to help him adjust to the job, aid him with off-the-job problems, and also help managment adjust to these new workers. To be effective, coaches should work with only one or a few of the newly hired, so the system is expensive. It is not a magical solution to the problems of job adjustment and turnover, but in a positive job setting, it can make a substantial contribution.

In addition, supervisors of the formerly sub-employed may need training in working with this group, administrative support for their efforts, and time to spend on working with the new employees. Fitting a new kind of worker into a traditional work assignment may not be easy if the supervisor has this responsibility added to already heavy burdens. If supervisory aides could be provided, this would help to give new workers the kind and extent of supervision many of them need.

These kinds of changes in normal working arrangements would, of course, involve additional costs—and possibly heavy ones. Reimbursement of employers for these extra costs is, therefore, an essential feature of the new JOBS Program and also of several experimental programs already underway.

Besides special working arrangements in standard jobs, "protected" or "sheltered" employment will need to be developed for some of the sub-employed. An unknown but surely substantial number, have difficulty in adapting to even modified employment. "Motivational training" helps some of them; for Negroes, training programs tied to racial pride may be effective. But for others, training is not the answer; they need to be put directly into remunerative work producing a creditable output. The employment arrangements must be flexible, and the workers must recognize that these arrangements offer the possibility of successful movement into regular jobs.

This kind of graduated, special employment situation may have to continue for a considerable length of time before the worker may be able to manage a job elsewhere. The main purpose should be to provide meaningful, paid work experience for men, though some women will undoubtedly want and need this protected job situation also. There is, of course, danger that such an arrangement will become a permanent crutch for the workers involved. To prevent this will require good supervisors with time to give close attention to individual workers and a definite plan to help ease workers into a more independent role. Counseling and other services should also be available on and off the job.

The development of new types of standard jobs can help to meet the needs of another, less disadvantaged group of the sub-employed. There is need, for example, for rapid expansion of subprofessional occupations and particularly for increasing the number of men in this kind of work. Subprofessional positions have more interesting elements than most of the jobs open to the unskilled. They also have stature. And many subprofessional posts are in poverty areas—an important consideration, since one of the major issues in expanding the number of standard jobs available to the sub-employed is location. As suggested earlier, there is considerable merit in developing standard jobs in the slum neighborhoods where the sub-employed live; travel time is reduced, and attitudes toward work among neighborhood residents may be improved.

The total number of subprofessional jobs so far available to the poor is not large enough, however, to reduce hard-core unemployment significantly. Further expansion of such openings is needed and, along with this, training of and services for the sub-employed to enable them to qualify for these openings.

In many situations, both in government and private agencies, new funds would not be needed to augment the number of subprofessional jobs. Restructuring existing professional jobs (many of which cannot be filled because of shortages of qualified personnel) so that less trained people can take over part of the work would immediately increase the number of openings. While there has been some movement in this direction, so far only a small start has been made toward a potentially more rational allocation of tasks and personnel.

What is needed, then, is a multiple strategy—opening more traditional jobs to persons with limited education and also developing new kinds of jobs for them. Some of the sub-employed will be able to fill these jobs adequately from the start. For others, the jobs will have to be modified so that they can manage them more effectively; for this group, the provision of supporting services is important. For still others—the ones most difficult to keep on the job—even these steps may not be enough. A new and specially constructed employment situation may be needed for such individuals, without expectation of rapid solution of their work difficulties.

If a wide variety of job situations were available, the sub-employed could go into the one best suited to their needs at a particular stage in their development, and move on to other situations as these become appropriate for them. A variety of opportunities and individual treatment for each sub-employed person are crucially important.

Toward Adequate Resources

Manpower programs, to be effective in helping the most disadvantaged, will require large expenditures over an extended period. In the past, instability in funding and lack of assurance of funds from one year to another have sometimes been grave problems. But even more important, of course, is the amount of funds available. The President's recommended budget for fiscal 1969, which calls for an increase of 25 percent in manpower funds, clearly recognizes this fact.

To help a low-skilled worker get and keep a decent job is likely to involve costs beyond those which employers have customarily assumed. Thus, private employers may need financial help if they are to train low-skilled workers and prepare them for responsible, well-paying jobs (as already indicated), and this help may have to continue until the worker has reached reasonably high productivity.

Four factors which contribute to the high cost of helping the disadvantaged are the essentiality of adequate pay, the length of time during which services should be provided, the wide range of services likely to be required, and the need to open new sources of job opportunities in slum areas.

The target of providing men with satisfying jobs, and with earnings high enough to compete with the irregular economy and to support their families, requires that pay be substantially above the training stipends established in the past. Since these jobs are to be regarded as work rather than training, pay must be indicative of a regular job and not suggestive of a temporary, low training allowance.

If the goal is to insure not merely that the worker gets training or work experience but that he enters and stays in a decent job, it will be necessary to continue services to workers over a much longer period than has been usual in the past. Lengthening the period of responsibility, of course, means higher costs.

In addition, for many of the sub-employed in big cities who are particularly difficult to place, a variety of services will undoubtedly be needed—ranging from medical care to improved basic education, to employment and skill training, to provision of coaches who can facilitate work adjustment. More services for more workers over longer periods mean greater expenditures. But the expression "penny wise, pound foolish" applies particularly in the case of the most disadvantaged worker. If the choice is between giving some limited help to a greater number of the most disadvantaged (at a lower cost per person) or giving a smaller number more intensive services (at higher per-person cost), the latter may be the more desirable course. A little money spent on a greatly disadvantaged individual may serve only as a stopgap and, in the long run, be largely wasted.

A fourth cost factor is that some of the new job opportunities must be located in slum areas. The start-up funds needed for new firms run by neighborhood people will be considerable, as will the operating costs until the new firms become self-supporting.

Altogether, though sizable resources have already been invested by the government in manpower and job development efforts, the needs of the more disadvantaged workers have not yet been fully met. The President's budget recommendations for fiscal 1969 will make possible expanded programs to get the hard-core unemployed into jobs. Experience during the year will indicate whether still greater resources in providing employment opportunities for the sub-employed of big cities are essential.

Toward Progressive Improvement in Manpower Services

Finally, the efforts already underway to improve the quality of training and other manpower services and their relevance to the needs of the disadvantaged must be continued and strengthened. In training the sub-employed, manpower programs have, to some extent, taken on a function of education and skill development in which the schools have failed, and they have often had as trainees individuals with attitudes shaped by unhappy school experiences. Frequently, the trained personnel and the skill-educational designs needed to work effectively with the sub-employed have been lacking. Coupled with financing and organizational problems, these difficulties have sometimes resulted in low-quality programs, despite constant concern for preventing and remedying such deficiencies.

Clarification of the objectives of individual programs and their components is needed in some cases and is now the target of concerted efforts. Sometimes a program has moved in several directions at the same time. It may, for example, be predicated on the notion of working with the hard-core unemployed, but have an intricate recruiting and intake process. Or training may be oriented to increasing skills, yet a trainee may not be actively discouraged from dropping out of the program to take an available job no better than his previous one.

In seeking to eliminate such inconsistencies, it is recognized that different programs should have different objectives, within an overall manpower plan or system for the community (like that which the CAMPS program is designed to develop). But whatever its goal, a program must be internally consistent, and its various parts must reinforce each other. A "quality" program requires moving toward a clear objective in terms of who goes into the program and what the outcome for him is expected to be.

Difficulty in *recruiting qualified staff* and a high rate of staff turnover are major problems for many programs. Those funded on an annual basis find it hard to attract and keep good staff, although officials frequently have been ingenious in stabilizing funds for more than a year. As one evaluative report on several youth programs concludes: "It takes a new program several months to recruit staff; with the uncertainty of the program beyond the year, many of the staff begin to think of their next job shortly after they begin to work." New financing and staffing patterns are needed in many programs to facilitate recruiting, developing, and keeping a good staff.

Increased emphasis on *staff development*—including both organized training and upgrading arrangements—is another need in many manpower programs. The development of all kinds and levels of staff—counselors, crew chiefs, coaches, administrators—is needed, as the emphasis on improving the situation of the sub-employed adds complexity to the problems with which these staff members must deal.

In the next several years *the role of private business* in manpower development will increase. Large companies have recently begun to recruit disadvantaged workers for the first time in many years. It should not be assumed, however, that these companies' experiences with higher skilled workers automatically give them competence to work effectively with the sub-employed. Indeed, a sense of uncertainty about how to deal with those difficult to place and keep on the job may underlie the refusal by many personnel officers to employ the undereducated and unskilled. The development of staff capable of working effectively with these new employees may be of special importance to the success of the JOBS program and other efforts to expand opportunities for the disadvantaged in private employment.

Realization of the need for *special approaches in working with the sub-*

employed is also growing. Many individuals require programs that offer quick movement to a job, rather than a long process of intake, referral, rehabilitation, and training. Frequently, services must be built around the job, rather than preliminary to it; this may be especially true of remedial education. In general, a visible, concrete, immediate payoff is needed to help the disadvantaged make the initial step into the program. This is no less essential than incentives to stay with the program in the hope of larger returns in the future—the issue now stressed in many programs.

An articulated, quality manpower system should make low-level entry jobs transitional for as many of the sub-employed as possible. In particular, the low-level job should be only a beginning for young workers, which they leave after a short time. Manpower programs should emphasize *development* —not just getting an individual into a low-wage job but continuing the investment in him until he can move up to a more rewarding position.

Limitations on Manpower Objectives

The possibilities of a strong manpower policy should not obscure its limits. High employment will not, by itself, resolve all ghetto unrest, though it undoubtedly can make a strong contribution. Much anger arises from the feelings of ghetto people that they are politically powerless, exploited as consumers, denied decent housing and opportunities to move to better neighborhoods, and underprotected and overthreatened by police. Reduced unemployment and higher incomes would eliminate many but not all of these feelings. Manpower policy cannot be expected to handle all the tensions of life.

Nor should it be anticipated that all the sub-employed will get decent jobs. Nor should all the adult poor be employed. The relationship between work and welfare, for example, is more complicated than many realize. Many AFDC mothers already work; getting more of them into jobs may not always be either easy or desirable.

In other words, manpower policy must go hand in hand with economic, educational, welfare, and housing policies in efforts to solve the social and economic problems of the big cities and of the sub-employed.

NOTES

1. The President's message on Manpower, January 23, 1968, p. 2.
2. For a discussion of the equally urgent problems of the rural poor, see the chapter on Geographic Factors in Employment and Manpower Development; also *The People Left Behind* (Washington, D.C.: President's National Advisory Commission on Rural Poverty, September 1967).
3. The poverty area classification system used here was developed within the

Bureau of the Census for the Office of Economic Opportunity. A total of 193 neighborhoods in 100 (of the 101) Standard Metropolitan Statistical Areas (SMSA's) with a 1960 population of 250,000 or more were designated as "poverty areas" on the basis of an index of census tracts (reflecting 1960 income, education, skills, housing and proportion of broken homes), contiguity of tracts, and the effects of urban renewal. The 193 poverty areas included about 22 percent of the census tracts in the SMSA's. For a detailed discussion of the poverty area definition, see Current Population Reports, Series P–23, No. 19, August 24, 1966; and *1960 Census of Population,* Supplementary Reports, PC(S1)–54, November 13, 1967.

For a full discussion of the poverty area findings of March 1966, see James R. Wetzel and Susan S. Holland, "Poverty Areas of Our Major Cities," *Monthly Labor Review,* October 1966, pp. 1105–1110, reprinted as Special Labor Force Report No. 75.

4. For a discussion of these surveys and their findings, see *1967 Manpower Report,* pp. 74–75.
5. *1967 Manpower Report,* p. 76.
6. Jack Chernick, Bernard P. Indik, and George Sternlieb, *Newark-New Jersey: Population and Labor Force, Spring 1967* (New Brunswick, N.J.: Rutgers—The State University, December 1967), p. 12.
7. *Study of the Meaning, Experience, and Effects of the Neighborhood Youth Corps on Negro Youth Who are Seeking Work,* pt. I (New York: New York University, Center for the Study of Unemployed Youth, January 1967), pp. XIII and XIV, and pp. 149–150.
8. For a more extended review of the social science literature in which this classification is developed, see Chapter 21.
9. Sar A. Levitan, "Job Corps," *Examination of the War on Poverty* (Washington: 90th Congress, 1st session, U.S. Senate, Committee on Labor and Public Welfare, Subcommittee on Employment, Manpower, and Poverty, August 1967), Staff and Consultants Reports, Vol. 1, p. 26.
10. Thomas F. Pettigrew, "Negro American Personality: Why Isn't More Known?" *Journal of Social Issues,* April 1964, p. 13.
11. William Yancy, "Some Adaptations to Underemployment," paper prepared for the Southern Sociological Meeting in Atlanta, Ga., April 11–13, 1968.
12. *Study of the Meaning, Experience, and Effects of the Neighborhood Youth Corps on Negro Youth Who are Seeking Work, op. cit.,* pp. 149–150.
13. S. M. Miller, Frank Riessman, and Arthur A. Seagull, "Poverty and Self-Indulgence: A Critique of the Non-Deferred Gratification Pattern," in *Poverty in America,* Louis A. Ferman, Joyce L. Kornbluh, and Alan Haber, eds. (Ann Arbor, Mich.: University of Michigan Press, 1965), pp. 285–302.
14. Harold L. Sheppard and A. Harvey Belitsky, *The Job Hunt: Jobseeking Behavior of Unemployed Workers in a Local Economy* (Baltimore: The Johns Hopkins University Press, 1966), pp. 114 ff.
15. David C. McClelland, *The Achieving Society* (Princeton, N.J.: Van Nostrand, 1961), pp. 90 ff.; and Thomas Fox and S. M. Miller, "Intra-Country Variations: Occupational Stratification and Mobility," and Seymour Martin Lipset and Hans L. Zetterberg, "A Theory of Social Mobility" in Reinhard Bendix and

Seymour Martin Lipset, *Class, Status, and Power,* rev. ed. (New York: Free Press, 1967).

16. *Study of the Meaning, Experience, and Effects of the Neighborhood Youth Corps on Negro Youth Who are Seeking Work, op. cit.,* p. 182.

17. Lee Rainwater, "Work and Identity in the Lower Class," in *Planning for a Nation of Cities,* Sam Bass Warner, Jr., ed. (Cambridge, Mass.: The M.I.T. Press, 1966), pp. 105–123; and Lee Rainwater, "The Lessons of Pruitt-Igoe," *The Public Interest,* Summer 1967, pp. 116–126.

18. Helen Icken Safa, *An Analysis of Upward Mobility in Low Income Families; A Comparison of Family and Community Life Among American Negro and Puerto Rican Poor* (Syracuse, N.Y.: Syracuse University, Youth Development Center, 1967), p. 100.

19. Karl E. and Alma F. Taeuber, "The Negro as an Immigrant Group," *American Journal of Sociology,* January 1964, p. 378. For their nationwide study, see *Negroes in Cities* (Chicago: Aldine, 1965).

20. See Edward Wright Bakke, *Citizens Without Work* (New Haven: Yale University Press, 1940), p. 7; Mirra Komarovsky, *The Unemployed Man and His Family* (Morningside Heights, N.Y.: Institute of Social Research, 1940), p. 128; H. W. Singer, *Unemployment and the Unemployed* (London: P. S. King & Son, Ltd., 1940), p. 100; and H. Pope, "Economic Deprivation and Social Participation," *Social Problems,* Winter 1964, p. 291.

21. Lee Rainwater, "Fear and the House-as-Haven in the Lower Class," in *Urban Renewal; People, Politics, and Planning,* Jewell Bellush and Murray Hausknecht, ed. (New York: Doubleday, 1967).

22. Richard C. Wilcock and Walter H. Franke, *Unwanted Workers* (New York: Free Press, 1963), and Larry D. Singell, "Some Private and Social Aspects of the Labor Mobility of Young Workers," *Quarterly Review of Economics and Business,* Spring 1966, p. 21.

23. Max V. Eniger, *The Process and Product of T & I High School Level Vocational Education in the United States* (Pittsburgh: American Institutes for Research, September 1965), ch. 5, p. 41.

24. *The New York Times,* December 24, 1967, sec. A, p. 34.

25. Wilbur R. Thompson, *A Preface to Urban Economics* (Washington: Resources for the Future, Inc., 1965), p. 373.

26. A preliminary report on the findings of this study appears in Ivar Berg, "Educational Requirements for Jobs," *Manpower Strategics for the Metropolis,* Eli Ginzberg, ed. (New York: Columbia University Press, in press).

27. S. M. Miller, *Breaking the Credentials Barrier* (New York: The Ford Foundation, 1968).

28. The irregular economy is discussed by Louis A. Ferman in an unpublished paper titled, "The Irregular Economy: Informal Work Patterns in the Urban Ghetto" (Ann Arbor, Mich.: University of Michigan—Wayne State University, Institute of Labor and Industrial Relations, June 1967).

29. In 1966 about 12 percent of the case closings on AFDC were attributable to employment or increased earnings of the mothers.

30. Elliot Liebow, *Tally's Corner* (Boston: Little, Brown, 1967), pp. 57–59. This study describes the job and other experiences of the Negro marginal worker in a big city.

31. *Ibid.,* p. 66.
32. The 1967 amendments liberalize somewhat the amount of income which may be excluded in determining AFDC assistance. See *Summary of Social Security Amendments of 1967* (Washington, D.C.: 90th Congress, 1st Session, Committee on Finance of the U.S. Senate and Committee on Ways and Means of the U.S. House of Representatives, December 1967), p. 17.
33. M. Elaine Burgess and Daniel O. Price, *An American Dependency Challenge* (Chicago: American Public Welfare Association, 1963).
34. *Study of Recipients of Aid to Families With Dependent Children, November–December 1961; National Cross-Tabulations* (Washington, D.C.: U.S. Department of Health, Education and Welfare, Welfare Administration, August 1965).
35. Burgess and Price, *op. cit.,* p. 50.
36. Wilbur Cohen, testifying as Under Secretary of HEW, said that it would be a great mistake to think of the caseload as being static, with the same families continuing to receive assistance for long periods of time. *Social Security Amendments of 1967,* Hearings Before the Committee on Finance (Washington, D.C.: 90th Congress, 1st Session, U.S. Senate, Committee on Finance, 1967), H.R. 12080, pt. I, p. 254 and 730.
37. Burgess and Price, *op. cit.,* p. 49.
38. Jane C. Kronick, "Family Life and Economic Dependency, A Report to the Welfare Administration," October 27, 1965 (mimeo.). In addition, a special analysis of the relationship between welfare and work experience of AFDC families in Philadelphia was made for this report.

    The age of the mothers is important since a high proportion of adult life can mean a short period of time in the case of young mothers. In the Philadelphia study, the average age of the mothers was 35, and as only a small proportion of young mothers was included, age bias does not appear important in this case.
39. Burgess and Price, *op. cit.,* based on tables on pp. 258, 259, and 280.
40. *Public Welfare, Poverty—Prevention or Perpetuation* (New York: Greenleigh Associates, December 1964), p. 32.
41. Burgess and Price, *op. cit.,* pp. 28 and 250.
42. *Study of Recipients of Aid to Families with Dependent Children, November–December 1961: National Cross-Tabulations,* Table 25.
43. For a discussion of this issue, see Alvin L. Schorr, *Poor Kids* (New York: Basic Books, 1965).
44. Seymour Parker and Robert Kleiner, "Status Position, Mobility, and Ethnic Identification of the Negro," *Journal of Social Issues,* April 1964, pp. 85–102.
45. William Yancy, *op. cit.*
46. *Examination of the War on Poverty,* Hearings Before the Subcommittee on Employment, Manpower, and Poverty (Washington, D.C.: 90th Congress, 1st Session, U.S. Senate, Committee on Labor and Public Welfare, July 1967), S. 1545, pt. 10, p. 3237.
47. Robert M. Fogelson, "White on Black: A Critique of the McCone Commission Report on the Los Angeles Riots," *Political Science Quarterly,* September 1967, p. 346.
48. See *The Detroit Riot . . . A Profile of 500 Prisoners* (Washington, D.C.: U.S. Department of Labor), March 1968.

49. Herbert Gans, "Malemployment," *New Generation,* Spring 1968.
50. See Chapter 3.
51. For a detailed account of recent experience, see Peter Marris and Martin Rein, *Dilemmas of Social Reform* (New York: Atherton, 1966), pp. 70–92.
52. This arrangement would promote the development of group feeling and team spirit, which might facilitate adjustment to mainstream industrial life.

Part VI

Social Science and Social Policy

Chapter 20

Social Science and the Elimination of Poverty

The literature of the social sciences abounds in hypotheses concerning the noneconomic causes and consequences of poverty, although these are often more implicit than explicit. They tend to be organized around three quite different perspectives: resource allocation, social and personal theory, and institutional performance. Each perspective supports a different concept of what needs to be stressed in policy considerations—redistribution of resources, modification of people and the immediate groups of which they are members, and changing the performance of institutions which service the poor. Frequently use of these perspectives reflects biases based upon the personal beliefs of various investigators rather than on dispassionate social theory. When employed individually they suggest quite different priorities for action. *All* these perspectives are needed, and the desideratum in policy is mix, not choice of specific areas of intervention.

In the course of examining the literature related to poverty, it became evident that there is not only a lack of an appropriate framework within which to examine the problem, but also conflicting findings even within the same terms of reference. There is little attempt to

Reprinted by permission of the Journal of the American Institute of Planners (Vol. 33, No. 3, May 1967).

bring together or acknowledge contradictory evidence, let alone an attempt to reconcile differences in fact and interpretation. Moreover, there are few efforts made to explore the implications for social policy of what is known and accepted. This paper, then, is an effort to bring together contributions from selected areas of social science theory and research in order to explore the implications of various types of findings for the development of social policy. For purposes of organization, findings will be discussed within each of three different perspectives: resource allocation, social and personal theory, and institutional performance.

RESOURCE ALLOCATION

According to this perspective, material insufficiency in housing, in nutritional levels, and in income itself is not only an attribute of poverty but an independent variable contributing to the creation and perpetuation of poverty. With refreshing candor, Alvin Schorr has described this approach as the "nonculture of poverty" in order to contrast it with present preoccupation with life-style and social interaction.[1] It is a bold departure from most contemporary social science analyses which, in the fashion of the day, are largely concerned with interaction, motivation, social structure, and culture as explanatory variables. Most social scientists seem singularly uninterested in the effects of want and deprivation on the psychology of the poor, and upon their coping strategies and potential for occupational mobility.

Even the studies during the depression were largely concerned with status problems associated with loss of role as a result of unemployment. Impoverishment was regarded as a secondary consequence of unemployment and received little attention as a subject in its own right. Research was concerned with the loss of work, not the loss of money. As a subject of inquiry, impoverishment has continued to be grossly neglected, and when it is examined there are few attempts to assess its contribution with regard to other variables which are highly correlated with it. Since most such studies are correlational, it is difficult to separate cause and effect or to understand the underlying processes which link these variables to each other. Resource inadequacies are responsible for the way of life, while at the same time the way of life sponsors these insufficiencies.

Health and Nutrition

Although the literature seldom deals directly with deprivation, a number of hypotheses can be developed which deal with the impact of deprivation and insufficiency on health.

Some hypotheses have a strong biological bias and attempt to show that the malfunctioning of the body can lead to serious organic and social consequences. For example, prenatal nutritional deficiencies in mothers can lead to organic and mental defects in their children, leaving them physically and mentally disadvantaged and thereby increasing the likelihood that they will be unable to maintain an independent income in their adult life.[2] They are also more likely than otherwise to produce children who are handicapped at birth. Thus, the legacy of poverty and malnutrition in one generation is passed on to the following ones.

Other hypotheses consistent with this frame of reference do not posit either organic or intergenerational consequences. They assume that inadequate nutritional levels, clinically identifiable by a symptom such as low hemoglobin count, affect the capacity of the body to function by affecting energy levels. When a nutritional deficiency is sustained over a long period of time, it can lead to a chronic state of depression, apathy, lethargy, and low motivation. These psychological responses prevent individuals from participating in the world of work and in carrying out their functions as heads of families. This line of reasoning suggests that low income produces dietary inadequacies which in turn contribute to greater illness, and that the incapacities created by illness handicap the family's earning capacity while pressing it with high medical expenditures. This process has the effect of inhibiting upward social class mobility and increasing the likelihood of downward mobility.

This type of hypothesis appears reasonable, but surprisingly, when we examine the relationship between morbidity and poverty, we find that these anticipated relationships fail to emerge.

Some have begun to question the traditional assumptions that morbidity and poverty are related to each other and if they are related whether low income is the cause or the consequence of ill health. Kadushin in a provocative but not rigorous discussion asserts that "a review of the evidence . . . leads to the conclusion that in recent years . . . there is very little association between getting a disease and social class, although the lower class still feel sicker."[3] And he adds that he doubts "whether any of the scientists are even aware of their possible misrepresentation on the facts." Most of the studies he relies upon to make the case were done during the Depression in the U.S. or immediately after World War II in Britain. He does quote, however, one recent study of the prevalence of chronic illness in the U.S. in 1957 and 1958 in which the percent of persons with one or more chronic illnesses is unrelated to their annual income. Indeed for persons under age 45 "there is even a slightly positive relationship between income and the prevalence of chronic illness."[4] The higher the income the larger the percent of persons with chronic illness. For those in the 45 to 64 age bracket, however, the trend is reversed; chronic illness is more likely to occur in lower income groups, although the differences are by no means impressive.

Kadushin's argument does acknowledge that persons with low income complain more about illness and stay out of work longer for each illness; the consequence of illness for low income groups is generally more severe. It is not low income which causes the incidence of illness, but illness which serves to maintain or reduce the already poor capacity to maintain an independent income stream. This arises because the period of hospitalization for low income persons is longer, illnesses are more sustained, and income loss is more dramatic. The response of the poor to illness should not be confused with its causes. Kadushin urges that we distinguish more sharply between exposure to illness and reaction to illness. He concludes his provocative analysis with the observation that ". . . we should not be afraid of the consequences of our findings. Policy makers probably will not cease to support medical care for lower class persons because we say that they are not especially sick."[5]

In their study of schizophrenia, Brown and his colleagues offer some further evidence that illness causes low income and downward drift in occupational position. When we examine the occupational level of the patients before their first admission into a mental hospital, we find there is a disproportionate concentration in the semi-skilled and unskilled categories relative to the occupation of their fathers. When, however, one examines the highest occupation these patients ever attained, the distribution is very similar to the usual occupation of their fathers. The clear implication is that the illness which has eventually brought about their entry into the hospital has also been responsible for reducing their occupational level below what could be expected on the basis of their fathers' occupational level. As further evidence along this same line, among those with a first admission to the hospital at the end of a five-year period, over half the professional, clerical, and skilled workers had declined in their occupational level or were unemployed, and a third of the semi-skilled and unskilled were unemployed by the end of the period.[6]

This confusion regarding the direction of causality between income and health has been noticed as well by other social scientists. Recently, Victor Fuchs made the following insightful observation:

> One possible reason for the effect of income levels on health having been overestimated is that investigators often find a very high correlation between income and the health status of individuals. . . . There has been a tendency to assume that the latter was the result of the former, but some recent studies of schizophrenia and bronchitis suggest that the causal relationship may run the other way. There is evidence that illness causes a deterioration in occupational status (from a skilled job to an unskilled job and from an unskilled job into unemployment.) The evidence relates to the decline in occupational status from father to son (where the latter is a victim of the disease) and also within the patient's own history.[7]

Consider the body of literature on stress which also attempts to link insufficiency and ill health. Here again the evidence is unclear. The argument can be stated as follows: deprivation (adversity, hardship) produces stress and emotional instability as suggested by the physical analogy of a "heavy and unpleasant load applied to the body." Low income as a state of deprivation is assumed, often uncritically, to be inherently "stressful" without regard to the context of surrounding events. Stress created by the circumstances of a harsh environment is treated as an intervening variable to help account for poor physical and mental health. "The hypothesis that 'stress' is associated with disease is one of the most pervasive and tenaciously held in current thought."[8] Pasamanick and his colleagues, in their study of mental disease in the urban population, provide an illustration of the findings that the prevalance of psychoneurosis is concentrated in the lowest and highest income groups. They account for their finding as follows:

> . . . On the face it would appear that stress is greatest in the lowest and highest social economic strata, in the former due to deprivation and the frustrations consequent to deprivation and in the latter possibly due to various social and cultural inconsistencies and stress consequent to attempt to maintain status.[9]

Scattered evidence in support of these hypotheses can be found in the literature. Eisenberg and Lazarsfeld in their review of "The Psychological Effects of Unemployment" quote a number of studies which show the relationship between economic deprivation and emotional instability. Adversity saps morale so that those who suffer most can take suffering the least.[10] The dynamics which connect deprivation and personal instability are not made explicit. Yet some concept like stress, which forms a bridge between the level of external reality and personal response, is implied.

Cassel and his colleagues make the link explicit. They argue that stress is a crucial factor in producing pathology and that when it is not absorbed or managed by small groups and/or the personality system it will become manifest in increased rates of psychological, somatic, and social ill health. While the concept of stress is used as an intervening variable, the independent variable in this study is rural-urban migration rather than deprivation.

Dohrenwend distinguishes between internal and external constraints as factors in mental health.[11] Internal refers to factors which become part of the body through heredity or past experience (drives, desires, and internalized rules) and external refers to factors which act from without such as diet, climate, occupation, social class, and so forth. The internal and external are mediating factors which influence the response to agents which produce stress. Poor people endure illness as a result of situational stress which results from their low income and job insecurity. Hylan Lewis, from an intensive study of 66 families, 57 of whom were low income, asserts that deprivation affects life style. Deprivation is the source of stress and life style a protective or adjustive reaction to stress. "The behaviors observed in . . . low income families . . . appear as a broad spectrum of pragmatic adjustments to external and internal stresses and deprivations."[12] Lewis is one of the few writers that singles out deprivation as an independent variable which "causes" life style. His conclusion follows from his premise that we must intervene to change the conditions of deprivation. The preliminary report does not bring together the research findings to convincingly demonstrate how deprivation leads to the selection of a life style. What is crucial to this line of argument is the conclusion that "programming might best focus on the facts of deprivation, rather than by intervening in life style."[13]

In summary then, these hypotheses concern the direct and indirect effects on health of deprivation, adversity, and insufficiency, viewing them as sufficient conditions for strain and stress in the body, which in turn cause breakdown. But there is also an extensive literature which suggests that hardship seems to lead to stress only under certain social situations. Impoverishment by itself may have little adverse effect and may not lead to stress. According to this argument, man can withstand varying adversity; it is the sense of deprivation relative to the situation of others that produces stress.[14] Scotch, in a study of the relationship between stress and hypertension among the Zulu, observed that while people were poorer in the rural as compared to the urban areas, stress and hypertension were higher in the urban setting. "Stress is not inherent in a given social situation or behavior pattern." The social context is crucial. Stress in urban areas is associated with "not only poverty, but degradation and humiliation in the treatment of Africans by Europeans . . ."[15]

Housing

There is a long history of studies associating overcrowded and dilapidated housing conditions with loss of self-esteem, lack of privacy to permit concentration on school work, and loss of parental authority as children are forced to play unsupervised out-of-doors. Octavia Hill, social reformer in the 1880's in England, regarded better dwellings as "an instrument for building character." "Sewer socialism," popular at the turn of the century in the United States, was preoccupied with the consequences of a lack of physical amenities, and emphasized the relationship between housing and crime as well as housing and poverty. More recently the harsh limitations on movement and privacy are seen as contributing to low need for achievement and antisocial behavior. Schorr has reintroduced this tradition. In an analysis of social policy, he has admirably summarized the argument:

The following effects may spring from poor housing: a perception of one's self that leads to pessimism and possibly stress to which the individual cannot adapt, poor health, and a state of dissatisfaction . . . cynicism about people and organizations, a high degree of sexual stimulation without legitimate outlet, and difficulty in household management and child rearing . . .[16]

This line of reasoning, like the discussion of health, clearly implies that the poor are inadequately housed and that the consequences of these inadequacies produce a chain of events which lead to poverty. But these assumptions are questionable. According to the 1956 National Housing Survey, only one-third of the poorest families with incomes of under $2000 per annum residing in standard metropolitan statistical areas lived in substandard housing, leaving the startling conclusion that two-thirds of them reside in standard housing. Although the highest concentration of occupants of substandard housing is of the low income group, most of the poor do not live in substandard units. In a detailed analysis of these figures, Grigsby concludes: "It would seem that analysts who use the number of low-income families as the measure of housing need grossly exaggerate the housing problem of this group."[17] Wilner's extensive and rigorous study of housing and health in Baltimore concludes that improved housing has little effect on physical illness, with perhaps the exception of childhood communicable diseases and accident rates.[18] Extending these observations, Nathan Glazer concluded that "housing is not dynamic as an element in improving the general position of groups in society" because it is one of those social measures "that is not likely to have any multiplier effect in enabling families to rise in the social scale."[19] The contribution of housing to beneficial patterns of relationships, motivation, attitudes, and definition of self is a questionable proposition. Glazer suggests that we may in fact have confused the line of causal relationship.

A better case can actually be made for the proposition that it is social relationships and social solidarity that are more likely to affect housing utilization than the reverse. Cohesive families living in the slums of underdeveloped areas do not seem to be adversely affected by poor housing; indeed, they may not even regard themselves as living in slums. At the same time, the benefits of housing amenities can be nullified by the fragmented and incohesive family relationships which inhibit their adequate use.[20]

Insufficient Income

Insufficient income may serve as a stimulant to promote incentive, but where the disparity between needs and income grows too wide it leads to despair and abandonment of the struggle for self-maintenance. Income deficiency alone can lead to stress and strain, which in turn can lead to family tension and eventually to the dissolution of the family as a unit.

An income squeeze—lack of money to meet needs—can have one of two effects: it may lead to action designed to reduce need—controlling the number of children—and to paring down of family expenditures; and/or it can lead to mounting frustration. It must be acknowledged that the processes leading to one or the other course of action are not well understood. Studies during the Depression suggested that it was the internal strength of the family as a social unit before it experienced deprivation that was a key factor affecting its capacity to adjust and to accommodate to abrupt interruption of income.[21] Presumably, families lacking such strengths are unable to maintain a balance between available income and an adequate standard of living. But one can also argue that adequate income is a factor which strengthens the family as a unit. Bcton M. Fleisher, for example, finds a relationship between relatively small increments of income and family stability. He reports that statistically "A $500 increase in family income will cause a decline in the number of separated or divorced women over 14 by about 2.7 per 1000."[22] Income and family support affect each other, but the dynamics which link them are elusive and complex.

Some critics stress the limitations of the argument which connects income alone to poverty. Warren Haggstrom questions "whether the problems of the poor primarily result from a lack of money." He concludes that since the psychology of poverty is found only under certain circumstances, one cannot therefore use lack of income as an explanation for those psychological characteristics which are often but not invariably associated with low income. In support of his position he argues that comparable families receiving public assistance with similar needs but with marked differences in income because of sharp variation in welfare grants, nevertheless, have similar psychological orientations.[23]

Policy Implications

To the extent that it can be demonstrated that inadequate nutritional levels, housing, and income are not only attributes of poverty but contribute to its perpetuation, then it is argued that an improvement in material circumstances may lead to the reduction of economic poverty. According to this formulation, increased attention must be given to medical care, housing programs, and financial support. It argues that poverty can be reduced, not only by changing people, but by changing the severe circumstances of deprivation under which they live.

This review of the literature, however, is in many respects profoundly disturbing. It challenges traditional views and suggests that we have misinterpreted the causal link between poverty and health and that we have overestimated the extent that the poor are in ill health and occupy poor housing. This analysis raises questions concerning the validity of policies which assert that improved housing and medical care will reduce poverty by increasing the personal health and altering the physical environment of the poor, thus facilitating their capacity to earn and to maintain an independent and adequate income stream. There is little doubt that in the early stages of industrial development, housing and health were more closely associated with poverty than they are today. In part, then, the problem is one of historical lag, for we have failed to change our assumptions as the data have changed. To the extent that we justify increased expenditures for services in terms of increased long-run savings, we are reluctant to examine new data which force us to reconceptualize the rationale which supported medical and housing services for the poor. The theory that there is any economy in spending is justified if we accept the position that giving the poor more money will later save money, because the added input produces a qualitative change in the poor which increases their capacity to maintain an independent income. Social policy is seen as self-liquidating. Social services, including public housing and medical care, have only a residual function.

The provision of resources, however, while undoubtedly a necessary precondition, will undoubtedly not be a sufficient condition for the elimination of poverty. Economists like Kenneth Boulding have questioned the relevance of a poverty elimination policy; for some groups permanent subsidization is the only way out. Adequate social provision in an affluent society is a legitimate social goal, without attention to its contribution to reducing poverty.[24]

These scattered findings suggest an even more basic issue concerning the need to reconceptualize the social services not in terms of their remedial, therapeutic, and instrumental value for reducing poverty, but as an extension of income, as amenities in their own right. Certainly the poor need money if they are to command the resources which affect the quality of their lives. But increasingly poverty is not only a lack of income but a lack of the goods and services necessary to support a desired level of well-being. Medical care and housing will increasingly be provided through collective intervention which supersedes the market, for they are services which consumers cannot purchase with income alone.

Although a rather convincing case could be made for the inequitable distribution of medical care resources by income class, it is not at all clear from available data that improved medical services for low-income families will lead to the reduction of poverty. While we do know that lower income persons lose more work days due to illness or injury than other income groups, it is not certain that working more regularly would catapult these groups out of poverty to any substantial extent.

The expansion of adequate housing can also be supported on grounds other than its instrumental value in reducing poverty. The rationale for public housing programs can be based on the grounds of equity. If tax concessions are equated with direct subsidies, the top fifth in income received twice as much as the bottom fifth. Or, as Grigsby has observed, "the necessity to live in a slum environment when one can see on all sides vastly superior housing accommodations which are available to most of the population, may contribute to a feeling of being poor, or inadequate, or rejected, or part of an unfair social system."[25] Inequalities and loss of dignity are the crucial aspects of poor housing, and, as Schorr most recently observed: "It makes little difference whether housing is a result or cause of poverty, it is an integral part of being poor." Good housing and medical care are valid programs if poverty is conceptualized as the lack of these amenities: People are poor when they lack adequate housing and access to health services; by definition, adequate amenities means reduced poverty.

PERSONAL AND SOCIAL THEORY

The bulk of social science research deals with hypotheses which are derived from the personal and social frames of reference. Ordering so vast a body of information is indeed a formidable task, and the scheme presented is both preliminary and arbitrary. Selection is one problem, but equally disturbing from a policy perspective is how to reconcile, or at least to understand, the conflicting evidence and theories. Four general problems deserve comment.

First, quite dissimilar processes can lead to a similar end result; there are many different routes into poverty. The efforts to classify the types of families in poverty, especially over the life cycle of the family, are at a most primitive level. Moreover, poverty profiles suffer because the nature of the statistical evidence is limited; most analyses will either compare some selected characteristics of the poor with those of the nonpoor, or examine the proportion of people in poverty that have these characteristics. The selected characteristics are those believed to be poverty-linked, which too often is assumed to mean causes of poverty. But the important point is that in virtually all situations these analyses fail to describe what *most* of the poor are like. For example, female-based families are twice as often found among Negro families as compared to whites, but *most* Negro families (75 percent) in poverty are headed by a male. More people have short time perspective among the working class than among the middle class, but *most* working class people probably do not have short time perspective. Conflicting views may reflect only the diversity of the population at risk and/or the selective interpretation of statistics.

A second factor which helps account for the divergent theories in sociology is the vague meaning of the concept of poverty. A broad definition tends to lead to different theories about causes than does a narrower view. Consider the following definition: poverty is seen as the lack of resources needed to achieve a gratifying and acceptable life relative to prevailing norms. Those in poverty lack products, prestige, and power. Education, health, and personal welfare are regarded as *products* or the outputs needed to expand life opportunities to permit one to develop and expand his horizons and potential. The emphasis lies on outcomes, because the inputs of schooling, medical care, and income transfers may serve as poor proxy variables to measure the necessary prerequisites for an "economic takeoff." *Prestige* is the capacity to present oneself with confidence to strangers. The feeling of having prestige is reflective of the response of others to the way observables are presented—clothes, demeanor, color—to strangers. *Power* is the capacity to get what one wants more often than one is denied his preferences. It is partly reflected in the capacity to manage information, which facilitates an ability to control the environment.[26]

A third factor which affects the selection and interpretation of data is the value preferences of the investigator. Although the rhetoric of democracy insists on equality of opportunity as a central value, social scientists seem divided as to the consequences and hence the value of reducing inequalities in the opportunity structure.

There have been a number of attempts to treat the thesis of equal opportunity as an independent variable contributing to the reduction of personal maladjustment and social friction. Cloward and Ohlin argued that crime and delinquency are a function of blocked and therefore unequal available opportunity. Some interpretations of the Watts riots are in terms of an "envy hypothesis" which asserts that groups are resentful when the visibility of affluence dramatizes the disparity between the haves and the have nots. Such resentment or feeling of relative deprivation disrupts the social fabric. Those who accept this position argue that the expansion of opportunity is necessary to stabilize society. It is similar to the argument that a higher degree of equality is necessary if we are to prevent Marx's prediction of class warfare from coming true.

Social scientists have also argued that equalization of opportunity may actually intensify the problems of personal adjustment. Robert Lampman has noted that "a wide-spread belief in equality of opportunity heightens the subjective experience of failure and makes personal adjustment more difficult."[27] The more equal opportunities actually become, the more severe is the sense of personal failure, because then we have only ourselves to blame for our lack of achievement. These observations lead to the conclusion that "personal adjustments to the realities of individual differences in social needs will be furthered by establishing a set of differing, meaningful and reasonably obtainable goals, each of which carries status."[28]

There is, as Lampman has observed, a second argument against the equalization of opportunity. Complex societies must be socially and functionally differentiated. If people are to perform different occupational tasks, then it may be necessary that they acquire life styles which differ from the dominant middle class pattern, especially as reflected in the balance of value judgments concerning investments and consumption preferences. The argument then suggests that inequality is actually beneficial—it both reduces personal maladjustment and supports the functional differentiation essential for industrial society.

A fourth problem in understanding the implications of research findings is that different courses of action are suggested depending upon whether one concentrates on finding the causes for the various pathological aspects of poverty, or whether he seeks an understanding of the kinds of needs all people have at varying stages in their development. This distinction between pathology and developmental needs serves as a convenient, although admittedly arbitrary, way of organizing some of the main trends of thought within the general framework of social and personal theory.

Pathology

Mental Illness.   This approach accepts the assumption that mental illness is concentrated among the poor. Several conflicting hypotheses have been developed to account for this relationship. The drift hypothesis argues that people owe their poverty to their pathology. Emotionally sick individuals drift through the class structure and eventually are concentrated in the core of center cities—skid row and the ghetto. The validity of this approach depends on "whether it can be shown that persons who develop schizophrenia are found in the same class from birth onward."[29] An alternative position is that when individuals strive to break out of poverty with limited resources, the odds against them are so great that they succumb to mental illness. Another point of view is that upward mobility strivings (not just for the poor) are associated with mental illness. One study found vertical mobility "to be a factor in both schizophrenia and psychoneurosis," but cautiously added that "this does not necessarily mean that mobility is the only or even the principal causative factor."[30]

Another approach is less concerned with drawing causal or relational inferences, but attempts to define low income and unemployment as an attribute of mental illness, a component of an "inadequacy syndrome." In a study of families applying for help from major social agencies in Syracuse, Cumming finds that the majority of men in this population show a long-term inability to maintain a job or an adequate income. "These evidences of social inadequacy [are] viewed as symptoms of mental illness. The long term unemployed and those with insufficient income are defined as having inadequately organized egos, i.e., the executive portion of the ego which develops independent of the conflict between id and superego."[31]

Culture of Poverty.   There is not one culture of poverty theory but many, and each has different policy implications. The use of this concept to explain poverty can be invidious when it serves as a sophisticated version of the older and now discredited personal defect theory that poverty is caused by the inferior character, constitution, and intellect of the poor.

Character defects, in nineteenth-century social work thought, were regarded as the major cause of poverty. The poor were seen as improvident, ignorant, and intemperate. As a result they lacked the capacity to consume, in accordance with their meager but sufficient income, the goods and services which would rescue them from poverty. "Not alms, but a friend" captured the essentials of the argument which was more preoccupied with the supervision of consumption than with the adequacy of provision.[32]

This argument has its modern counterparts. It found expression in the recent controversial analysis of the relationship between race and poverty. Moynihan puts the argument as follows:

> At the heart of deterioration of the fabric of Negro society is the deterioration of the Negro family. . . . Three centuries of injustice have brought about deep-seated structural distortions in the life of the Negro American. At this point the present tangle of pathology is capable of perpetuating itself without assistance from the white world. The cycle can be broken only if these distortions are set right. In a word, a national effort toward the problems of Negro Americans must be directed towards the question of family structure.[33]

At root is the assumption that this tangle of pathology prevents people from responding to opportunities.[34] Oscar Lewis and Michael Harrington have done much to popularize this concept of a culture of poverty. They view the life style of the poor as a cultural deficiency which sets in motion a self-perpetuating cycle of poverty. The theory of the poverty cycle tends, with some variation, to take the following form: Poverty is seen as self-perpetuating; deprivation in one generation leads, through cultural impoverishment, indifference, or misunderstanding of their children's educational needs to deprivation in the next; lacking the self-respect that comes from earning an adequate living, the young men cannot sustain the responsibilities of marriage and so they hand down to their children the same burden of ignorance, broken homes, and apathy by which they were themselves crippled.

The theory of the poverty cycle stresses the apathy of the poor and their incapacity, because of apathy and social disengagement, to exploit opportunities which are available. This argument neglects or rejects the position that the level of living contributes to the development of character and life style as well. It assumes that the tangle of pathology must be treated first. But the attribution of a causal link is unsupported, thus the order of priority which places rehabilitation before attack on the inequities in the distribution of resources seems arbitrary.

In addition to some methodological questions concerning the empirical basis for this view, this emphasis on deficiency, disorganization, and disruption as the central theme of poverty has been sharply criticized on substantive grounds. Broadly speaking, the critics share in common a more positive view of the values of lower class sub-culture. Frank Riessman views the thesis of the culture of poverty as a packaging of negative attributes, whose negative character is derived from an invidious comparison with presumably better middle-class standards. The resulting portrait is incomplete because it fails to take into account, for example, the equally valid observation that the poor have a rich and imaginative language and that they are quite verbal. Moreover, the focus on limitations in many situations leads to a neglect of opportunities for constructive action based on the positive qualities which the poor have.[35] Riessman's emphasis on the strength of the poor directs attention to the need for educational reform in the techniques of teaching.

Walter Miller, revising his earlier emphasis on family socialization as the major support for the lower class life style, developed the thesis of occupational enculturation. As long as society continues "to require" low skilled jobs (Miller estimates 10 million such jobs are needed in todays economy) a child-rearing pattern will develop that is suited to training individuals to hold these jobs. "The female-based child rearing unit is a prime source of this essential pool of low-skilled laborers. It brings them into the world and it furnishes them the values, the aspirations, and the psychic make-up that low-skill jobs require (e.g., high toleration of recurrent unemployment; high boredom tolerance; . . . capacity to find life gratification outside the world of work)."[36] The argument is curiously similar to the Marxian view that a capitalist economy needs the poor, only as an anthropologist Miller sees the same process operating through the abstract entity called society of which the economy is only a part.

Other ideas and concepts are consistent with the culture of poverty's emphasis on apathy and a cycle of poverty, but lead to other policy implications and therefore warrant some brief comment in their own right.

Powerlessness. One of the recurrent explanations in social science of the nature of industrial society is that of alienation—that man is detached or estranged "from the more complex institutions that presumably serve but are more likely to manipulate him."[37] Seeman has recently developed five categories to describe the many forms of alienation. One of his categories is powerlessness. "The expectancy . . . held by the individual that his own behavior cannot determine the occurrence of the outcomes, or reinforcements, he seeks."[38]

Powerlessness has received a great deal of public attention as an explanation of the cause and consequences of poverty, especially as it affects the Negro. Charles Silberman of *Fortune* magazine summarizes the argument: "For apathy and aimlessness—the lack of 'motivation' which characterize the Negro poor, and the self-hatred that in some measure afflicts all Negroes—stem in the last analysis from their sense of dependency and powerlessness."[39] Haryou, the beleaguered community action program in Harlem, built its rationale on this theme. According to its first report, the destruction of culture can be understood as "the consequence of powerlessness." The lack of power derives from the dependency of the Negro on the white, and as a result Negroes are unable to control the events which shape their lives. In a discussion of the Negro's crippling dependency on the white community to improve education of the children of the ghetto, the Haryou report notes:

> . . . and then the black man goes back home again and says, "I can't solve my problem unless I have a white person at my side; but I can't fight and make a change in this system unless I have a white person at my side; I can't be a man and not ask but take what is mine unless I have a white person by my side." And so he sees that he is, in fact, less than a man. To reduce the demoralizing consequences of this form of welfare colonialism the vitality, anger and energy of youth must be harnessed. Haryou must not attempt to teach the young person . . . but Haryou must be taught by the young person in Harlem.[40]

The confidence and self-respect of the Negro was to be achieved through his own involvement and participation in shaping and creating his own life. The more the Negro controlled the strategic institutions in ghetto life, the more he would be able to reject welfare colonialism and substitute a vitality of independence and self-respect, which by definition would reduce poverty.

Cognitive Defects.   In this explanation of the dynamics of the cycle of poverty, intellectual impairment emerges as one major factor inhibiting the adjustment of low income children to the school's performance standards.[41] Cognitive defects are the result of stimulus deprivation which is the product of child-rearing patterns among the poor. The child fails to develop the tactile and auditory discriminations which permit him to learn from and respond to his environment. Basil Bernstein, in his studies of English working class children, while observing the same cognitive deficiencies, emphasizes the difference between formal and informal or public language. Formal language is developed in middle class homes when parents communicate with their children with a differentiated, personal, and qualified language. An effort is made by the mother to explain to a child why he is expected to behave in a special way, thus offering a model for logically connecting command and purpose. Public language tends to develop when authority is exerted by status—all children must behave in a certain way. Public speech has its origins in a special form of social relationship which develops in closed communities and is "based upon some extensive set of closely shared identifications self-consciously held by the members"; prisons, combat units in the Armed Forces, and adolescents. The speech will tend to be fast, fluent, "condensed, dislocated, and local to the relationship." Thirty percent of the labor force, Bernstein estimates, is limited to this restricted speech code and has no other. This speech pattern is a handicap in acquiring an education in public schools.[42]

Policy Implications. These various themes of apathy, impotence, incapacity, and incompetence lead to rehabilitative strategies of intervention. Advocates of this approach regard the conflicting evidence as a challenge rather than a repudiation of the thesis. They do not doubt the validity of the thesis but believe that more research is needed to determine the causal line between illness and pathology. Although their major assumptions seem to be drawn from many different fields of social science—psychology, anthropology, education, and sociology—rehabilitative strategies share a common if implicit conception of social services. Services are essentially to be self-liquidating, instrumental, and facilitative. In principle, if the poor had greater capacity to exploit available opportunity in the educational, health, employment and political arenas, these facilitative services would not be necessary. In this sense they can also be regarded as self-liquidating, for the task is to make people sufficiently independent so that they will be able to effectively use established institutions. What is at issue is the capacity to use institutions, rather than the relevance of the functions which these institutions carry out. Unlike the view of services as amenities, as new forms of income which extend well-being, in this context services are instrumental, a means for changing the competence of people.

The policy implication of the poverty cycle argument can be understood by an examination of the types of programs stimulated by the Community Action Program:

First, comprehensiveness. The theory allows for a very flexible strategy, since it sets no order of priority. If the causes of poverty are circular, then intervention at any point may be effective, and the more the better. Community Action Programs encourage variety rather than a concentration on one preferred program. The effort to coordinate these multiple interventions in order to break the poverty cycle provides the rationale which supports much of the current emphasis on comprehensiveness. At the same time, neglect of any one aspect of the problem can be excused by the claim that it is indirectly influenced by other interrelated programs. By this argument the projects were able to focus on youth and to largely ignore the aged and the fully employed low-wage earners with large families who account for two-thirds of those who are poor.

Employability is a second program focus. The logic of the poverty cycle argument does not lead to a focus on job creation, for youth have been ill-prepared to accept work. Nor is there a focus on income, which might be dissipated because the poor lack the capacity to consume. Emphasis is on preparatory training programs on the assumption that poor youth need to acquire stronger motivation and an acceptable demeanor before they can take their place in the world of work. Consequently, such programs are less concerned with technical skills than with adjustment of individuals to the demands of employment. They reject social work techniques, hoping to inspire motivation and to teach deportment through work experience. The Neighborhood Youth Corps and the Job Corps are examples of pre-training programs.

Remedial programs are another important concern. These programs are in principle similar to those of employability but with techniques and activities appropriate to the world of school rather than the world of work. One emphasis is on the importance of compensatory education where the school acts as a substitute family to the child, compensating him for earlier stimulus deprivation and providing him with a person rather than a status oriented relationship. One of these programs tries to reach the child early in his development through an enriched program outside of the home which will permit him to better negotiate the school system. Pre-school programs like Operation Headstart are its prototypes. The child is taught skills which hopefully will enable him to make better use of the opportunity structure. Change in the school is assumed to be less crucial. The competence of the child to use the school is the focus.

The final central concern is participation, which embraces those programs which are designed to promote social inclusion by providing families with a stake in society through encouraging their participation in social action. Powerlessness is regarded as a cause of retreat and apathy and is thus one of the key forces which set the poverty cycle in motion. If poverty is the lack of power to command events which affect one's life, then the redistribution of power is necessary to change people. Participation in social action generates power—the capacity to alter and control events in one's life. As individuals go through the process of acquiring power and seeking to change their world, they change as well. Social action is thus a form of social therapy to treat apathy and social disintegration through self-help.

The failure of people to help themselves leads to a weakening of the integrative functions of community life and to a breakdown in the machinery of social control. The emphasis on participation in the poverty program was largely inspired by the programs initiated by the President's Committee on Juvenile Delinquency and Youth Crime which had as its mandate the prevention of delinquency and crime. As the goals shifted from delinquency prevention to poverty reduction the programs remained largely the same. Both poverty and crime can be seen as conditions which arise because of individual defect. James Reston offered a penetrating insight into these assumptions when he described the goals of the poverty program—"to take poverty out of the people, rather than the old New Deal technique of merely taking the people out of poverty by handouts."[43]

A program cannot promote self-respect and dignity when it regards poverty as a social-psychological problem "inherent in those who are demoralized, rather than as a moral problem, inherent in the society which humiliated them."[44] The lack of jobs, the lack of income, and lack of resources for the institutions which service the poor may prove more significant as an explanation of poverty than the culture of poverty thesis. If we regard the war on poverty as an experimental test of the validity and relevance of remediation as a national policy to reduce poverty, then negative results may in the end serve a positive role.

Developmental Needs

Scheduling. Work and family each has its own cycle of development. The timing of the critical transitions within these two spheres has received little systematic study. The common sense theory about scheduling is that there is a preferred order for timing significant life events, and that occupational identity should precede psychosocial intimacy in marriage. Early marriage is to be discouraged as a premature assumption of responsibility. Several important recent studies of college marriages challenge these assumptions and suggest that "early marriers tend to be more mature, to be better academic performers, and to display fewer indications of marital disruptions than students who were single or married after graduating from college."[45] The studies imply that the order in which the events are scheduled is *not* as significant as the capacity to cope with the circumstances surrounding simultaneous status transitions. However, this research was not directed at low income families.

Is scheduling important, however, for those who have a job rather than a career, when they have little promise for sequential development and increased economic rewards, since over time their income actually declines with age? For these families there appears to be little incentive to postpone marriage; delay seems to have little real value. Yet the consequences of the failure to schedule seem quite severe. Schorr's analysis of the relationship between family cycle and income developments tells the grim story. Early marriage seems to affect the number and spacing of children, producing more children both early and late. (The pattern does not seem to apply to the Negro.) Husbands are pressed to take the first job they can secure, and with limited educational achievement the first job affects future jobs and determines a chaotic pattern of employment. Moreover, since the husband is young, the risk of unemployment is high and the likelihood of a low income seems assured. But these risks come at the very moment when family size is expanding family need, with needs outstripping resources. Frustration leads to the abandonment of the roles of husband and breadwinner as family breakup and unstable work history follows with disturbing regularity.[46]

The relationship between work and family can be seen from yet another perspective. Alex Inkeles has suggested that there is a general tendency in industrial societies toward isomorphism—a similar behavior pattern in both life spheres.[47] Raymond Smith's study of the West Indian Negro family provides evidence to show that instability in the male's occupation is represented by instability in the family situation.[48] There is, however, also some evidence to the contrary. Geismar's study of stable and unstable families in a housing project reports that malfunctioning in intrafamilial relations does not appear to be related to malfunctioning in the world of work.[49] Economic stability—earning a low income but having the ability to hold a job—does not significantly distinguish between problem and stable families.

Critical Life Cycle Transitions. This approach assumes that there are critical stages in the life cycle when intervention is most effective. Special ceremonies or "rites of passage," accompany these transition points—the birth of a child, adolescence, retirement, death. In addition to normal developmental changes such as these, transitional crisis may be brought about by: (1) traumatic events, such as, premature birth, surgery, loss of income through urban renewal or disasters; and (2) points of resocialization such as entry or release from prison or a mental hospital.[50] Psychiatrists and sociologists have developed the hypothesis that status transition points provide the greatest point of leverage for purposive intervention to produce change.

There is a two-sided nature to crisis—it is a sign of danger as well as opportunity. Old patterns of adjustment are being challenged, while new forms of adaptation have not yet emerged. Because the system is fluid, the potential for growth is greatest.[51] Observers who have studied this process have suggested that the period of "heightened susceptibility" is quite short, lasting only a few weeks or at most two months before new patterns are crystallized.[52]

Policy Implications. The focus on scheduling and life cycle transitions suggests that intervention is possible at any stage of development. Significant changes in a child's performance in school can be achieved at any point of transition—from home to school as illustrated by the pre-school program, during puberty and in junior high school programs like the Banneker project in St. Louis, and from high school to college as in Upward Bound. The range of preferred points of intervention seen in terms of the life cycle is optimistically widened. This perspective permits us to abandon the demanding principle that early intervention is always preferred for the more flexible view that the occurrence of significant events rather than age is the crucial factor in promoting change.

When maturation and developmental change rather than pathology and alienation serve as the terms of reference for policy development, a new set of assumptions concerning the nature and purpose of social services seems to be necessary. Remedial strategies for the disengaged, apathetic, and sick are replaced by strategies which facilitate crisis and transition, risks which all people encounter over the course of the life cycle. Thus universal services for all citizens rather than isolated services for the alienated are appropriate.

For those who leave school early, the transition from school to work falls most heavily on those least mature and least skilled to perform the tasks it implies. If the postponement and scheduling of transitions seems necessary, it points to the need for new social inventions which serve the same functions that many colleges offer for the middle classes—aging vats which permit youth to experiment with living at relatively low cost to their future development.

Even adulthood is characterized by continuing periods of transition and change. Women marry and complete the task of raising their children when they are still relatively young. They are thus in search of new careers as they experience the transition from home to work. In a period of rapid technological change occupational shifts are common as we discover with the obsolescence of knowledge we are all no longer educated for the world we come to live and work in. This dramatizes the need for continuous education and retraining throughout the life cycle. The discoveries of modern science make recovery from illness more certain; thus many experience transition from dependency to self-care. Finally, in the transition from work to retirement we are catapulted into a crisis when the activity which provides meaning and dignity to life must be found in areas other than work.

Among many the risk of falling into poverty is present at each stage of development and transition. Increasingly the family no longer performs the functions which facilitate transition over the life cycle and the market is indifferent or unable to create the kind of personal service needed. As we have suggested, new social inventions are needed to extend and enrich the quality of life in an affluent society. Seen in this light social services take on a new meaning as universal provision to expand choices rather than reduce pathology.

Periods of transition can be sustained by a variety of direct and indirect policies: intervening outside of the family, increasing job stability, educational opportunity, or the size and stability of income transfers. One approach creates incentives for postponement of work and the development of a family. Some economists have proposed universal student stipends which in effect pay students to continue in school. The in-school program of the Neighborhood Youth Corps is a reluctant educational subsidy still tied to the assumption that the stipend is contingent on work performed. As the work standard is relaxed the importance of the subsidy is more evident. The success of the postponement approach depends on our inventing new forms of socially approved dependency. Whereas the GI Bill was seen as payment for services rendered, student subsidies will need to be justified on some other principle such as the right to develop, based on a common citizenship in society. Peter Marris has recently proposed the creation of liberal arts colleges for the poor, with a focus on broadening and deepening life experiences and, in the same spirit of a liberal arts education without attention to future job placement. The educational curriculum need not be bound by tradition—travel as well as reading can be stressed.

Another approach discounts the issues of scheduling and attempts to reduce the pressure from the family squeeze, the divergence of income, and family growth.[53] It is directed not at the future generation but at the parents and their young children. Three programs are illustrative: the expansion of income through a family or children's allowance, the reduction of need by a program of birth control and abortion, the increase in income by altering the pattern of expenditures—low cost or housing subsidies, saving on food cost, supermarkets in the slums, and protection against salary garnishing or loan sharking.

Finally, we can concentrate on the relationship between employment and the capacity to fulfill the adult role of wage earner. Rainwater's interesting analysis of the policy implications of the problem of identity in lower class youth suggests how work and growth affect each other. He argues that a loss of identity comes about when the self we presented to others fails to be acknowledged or accepted by others. "The major validation of self for men is expected to stem from performance in the occupational world."[54] For the blue collar worker, career opportunities are limited. He must rely on the goal of being a good provider, oriented to providing adequate income rather than occupational mobility. Lower class youth tend to reject both the career and the provider roles and rely for their identity on a life style variously called action-seeking, cats and kicks syndrome, or expressive style. "The available rewards of the expressive life style are greatest for the young and seem to decrease rapidly with age." Since earlier forms of adaptation no longer suffice, we would expect that the personality system is most fluid and open for change. Rainwater suggests that job continuity—holding a job without being fired—can validate the role of good provider. But during the period of transition, employers will need to tolerate behavior which interferes with job performance. A tight labor market for unskilled workers naturally lowers the performance standards of employers. It is chiefly in a labor surplus market that new devices are needed, both in and outside of the market, such as work experience programs to contribute to easing youth from one stage of development to another. Job continuity can only be achieved by significantly expanding the volume of low skilled jobs. Economic and social policy cannot be arbitrarily isolated from each other.

INSTITUTIONAL PERFORMANCE

The major assumption of this approach is that social institutions function in such a way so as to support and nurture poverty. In the nineteenth century it was assumed that organized charity encouraged people to become paupers by interfering with the functioning of the market and destroying the incentive system. In Victorian England philanthropists were enjoined against giving alms indiscriminately. These ideas still influence our thinking.

Perhaps the most important theory about the consequences of institutional performance is that the largesse of public and private institutions benefits most those who need it least. Our social institutions operate on the implicit principle of a double standard, rejecting and blocking for the poor the opportunity for participation in the larger society, while rewarding those with an established position in society with the opportunities for further advancement. Those who hold this position argue that we are confronted with a major institutional crisis in law and the courts, education and social welfare, for they all serve as instruments of degradation and control of the poor, inhibiting lower class achievement.

Institutions have developed a variety of mechanisms which permit them to allocate rewards and services differentially by social class. For example, IQ tests in school and GATBY tests in state employment service have served as instruments of social discrimination and social disadvantage for the poor. More recently attention has been called to the broader problem where labeling by the helping institutions exacerbates social problems by stigmatizing their self-esteem.

Why has opportunity been blocked? To list but a few of a great many theories which have been advanced: professional technology and ideology support the middle class client and reject the poor; bureaucratic rigidity acts to prevent institutions from adapting rapidly to changing social and economic conditions. No mechanism exists in welfare which performs the corrective function of the market. A harsher explanation is found in the conflict of interests between classes and races: the status of the middle class requires that "the poor be kept in their place"; or racial discrimination blocks opportunity.[55]

Inequities in the use of services are in part related to how they are distributed. Here we are confronted with a dilemma in the choice of strategies of delivering services. Universal services designed to reach all members of a specified category, for example, all school age children through universal public education, tend to "cream," or allocate resources so as to benefit most those who are better off economically. On the other hand, selective programs designed to reach the poor and the disadvantaged tend to stigmatize those they seek to aid. Titmuss incisively comments on this delivery problem:

> There is, I think, no escaping the conclusion that if we are effectively to reach the poor . . . we must differentiate and discriminate, individually and collectively. We have to do so if we wish to channel proportionately more economic resources to aid the poor and the handicapped . . .
>
> The problem then is not whether to differentiate in access, treatment, giving, and outcome but *how* to differentiate; . . . how in some respects to treat equals unequally and in other respects unequals equally. We cannot now disengage ourselves from the challenge of distributing social rights without stigma.[56]

Policy Implications

Two broad approaches can be identified: resource redistribution and institutional reform. The former is embodied in the principle of positive discrimination in favor of low income groups. The Elementary and Secondary Education Act of 1965 makes such discrimination national policy. Yet in many large urban areas it is not enough to only allocate more resources to social service institutions. Their purposes, assumptions, and practice must change as well. According to this perspective, changing people so that they can more effectively negotiate the system is not adequate where, for example, an income transfer system stigmatizes its recipients and undermines their self-esteem and dignity. It must be frankly recognized that we know much less about the processes by which institutions change than we do about the source of resistance to change. The literature on purposive social change has been built largely on an educational model which assumes that communication failures are a major source of institutional resistance. More recently the limitations of this view have been recognized, and change is being examined in terms of interest groups and conflict. It has become clear that the politics of promoting change needs to be separated from the agenda of change—the specific institutional reforms which are necessary.

The Community Action Program provides one example of an attempt to change institutions as a means to reduce poverty. While the rationale behind Community Action is subject to a number of interpretations, there is little doubt that in its early history it was committed to institutional change on the assumption that institutions needed to become more relevant to the needs of the poor. It devised a strategy to fit its theory that social service bureaucracies had become more preoccupied with loyalty to procedure at the expense of their functions, and had drifted into a self-regarding posture which made them insensitive to the needs of those they served.[57] First, Community Action emphasized innovation and experimentation. Disturbed about lack of professional interest in serving the poor, it insisted that programs be willing to make use of nonprofessionals. Not only did this provide employment opportunities for the poor, but the intrusion of indigenous personnel into a rigid bureaucracy could force self-examination and propel the organization to change. Programs were also to be innovative in the sense that they search out new techniques for reaching, training, and educating the poor. But the heart of the strategy assumed that the problem was the arbitrary jurisdictional boundaries established by agencies and the crucial reform that was needed was reorganization of the total framework of splintered and unrelated social services. While change in isolated bureaucracies was necessary, it was not sufficient. The total welfare delivery system needed to be integrated and made more coherent through coordination. The theory of the poverty cycle led to an emphasis on comprehensiveness which embraced a broad range of varied activities; but with limited resources, this meant that no single program would receive very many funds. The rhetoric of CAP programs emphasized linkage, integration, coordination, and coherence. "The strengthening of the central planning capability and increased control over resource allocations are absolutely essential to effective local program development," the chief of Research and Program Development for CAP resolutely declared.[58] Finally, the poor should be involved in policy decisions, not so much to reduce their apathy, which was the argument for social action, but to press for institutional change and to guard against the retreat by CAP into bureaucratic irrelevance. *Innovation*, *coordination*, and *participation* are the three major themes of the CAP program.

A great deal of attention is also being directed at specific reforms related to the performance of welfare institutions and the pattern by which their services are organized and distributed. They are addressed to such topics as consumer protection, the quality and relevance of social services, the machinery of their allocation and distribution. An ombudsman has been proposed to protect recipients from the very services which are designed to aid them. Decentralized delivery systems have been recommended which are accountable to the citizens who are the consumers of social services. Voucher payments, which will permit students to buy education, thus forcing educational institutions into competition with each other, have been boldly proposed.[59] A nationalized public assistance system has been recommended by the 1966 Advisory Council on Public Assistance, because the present system inflicts stigma and is itself a cause of poverty. The virtues of a negative income tax are being debated, its proponents arguing that it can reduce stigma by distributing income through the socially approved institution of the federal income tax system, while at the same time limiting the distribution of cash to those in need.

CONCLUDING OBSERVATIONS

This review has arbitrarily excluded the economic literature and has treated the social factors in a fragmentary way, examining each of three perspectives isolated from each other and from economic forces. But clearly the task is more complex. If we accept the view that each perspective contributes something to our understanding about the causes of poverty and the means to overcome them, then all of these factors must somehow be related to each other and brought together into some coherent national policy. But how are we to assess the relative importance of each perspective —redistribution, personal intervention, institutional reform, and economic growth? It is not only a question of priority, for the simultaneous pursuit of these strategies may conflict with each other. Diverting more resources to the poor may impede economic growth, while increasing the absolute level of living of groups in society such as the Negro may also increase inequalities by widening their relative positions. Rising expectations and increased relative deprivations encourage social instability, as the long hot summers have demonstrated.

Can cost-benefit analysis rescue us from the dilemma of setting priorities and making choices by identifying an optimum strategy for the allocation of scarce resources by subjecting various combinations of programs to a rigorous assessment of effectiveness in relation to cost? Social planning seldom lends itself to such orderly analysis. There is an intrinsic difficulty in submitting social decisions to an impartial cost-benefit analysis. Decisions have different consequences for different interest groups. Consider the example of an urban renewal project. The net gains and losses of those who are displaced by renewal and those who are presumed to benefit cannot be measured on a single yardstick. We have no common standards for making interpersonal comparisons of utility and not all gains and losses can be converted into monetary terms.[60] Confronted with this dilemma some have argued that the social scientist or planner must serve as an advocate for a particular point of view. Titmuss has argued that we can see the problem of poverty as the "social pathology of other people's progress."[61] According to this point of view economic activity as well as technological and scientific changes is accompanied by social costs or disservices which can threaten the earning power and health of families. The increase of private wealth and increased benefits of scientific progress creates social problems for others. Policy oriented research cast within these terms of reference is an attempt to document the costs of social change. It implies a view of social policy as an instrument of social justice, compensating those who are victimized by the progress of others. This perspective takes the consumers' point of view as contrasted with the cost-benefit framework which seeks a value neutral optimum. Its social arithmetic is based on the implicit value assumption that increments to earnings are a benefit and earnings foregone a cost. The importance of this approach lies in its creative reinterpretation of the measurement of costs and benefits and not in the discovery of a tool for substituting science for judgment. But both perspectives neglect the fact that policy tends to be concerned with multiple goals, each of which is desirable in itself, but all of which can conflict when pursued simultaneously and where there is no single yardstick which permits us to rank these goals hierarchically. But it is just such complex problems which most need rational assessment.

Some interesting work is being done in this area. For example in the case of two aims in partial conflict one can be treated as a goal and the other as a constraint. Thus, one may be willing to accept X percent economic growth, but only on the condition that it is accompanied by Y percent redistribution. Another approach sees the process in long range terms arguing that policies follow some pattern of time phasing, economic growth for X years, to be followed by redistribution, and then repeating the cycle. The choice of goals and constraints and the selection of acceptable time periods in the pursuit of complementary goals cannot be solved by rational analysis alone, although the nature of the choices which must be made can by such procedures become clearer. Here we must frankly acknowledge the limits of the contribution that social science can make to policy.

We must in the end make brute personal, political, and value choices about what we regard as desirable public policy. These choices cannot be made without some conception of what is the good society. Thus, the more ruthlessly we pursue the path of technology the more we come to acknowledge the role of ideology in the selection among policy alternatives.

NOTES

1. Alvin L. Schorr, "The Non Culture of Poverty," *American Journal of Ortho Psychiatry,* XXXIV (1964) 907–912.
2. See, for example, the research of A. Keys, "Caloric Deficiency and Starvation," and Frederick Tisdall, "The Relation of Nutrition to Health," reported in Norman Jolliffee, F. F. Tisdall, and Paul R. Canon, (eds.) *Clinical Nutrition* (New York: Harper and Brothers, 1950) and Benjamin Pasamanick, Abraham Lilienfeld, and Martha E. Rogers, *Prenatal and Paranatal Factors in the Development of Childhood Behavior Disorders* (Baltimore: The Johns Hopkins University School of Hygiene and Public Health, n.d.).
3. Charles Kadushin, "Health and Social Class," *New Society* (December 24, 1964) p. 14. See also, Thomas Arie, "Class and Disease," *New Society* (January 27, 1966). Arie tries to refute Kadushin's thesis by the argument that if mortality rates are higher among the poor, morbidity must be as well.
4. *Ibid.,* p. 12.
5. *Ibid.,* p. 13.
6. G. W. Brown *et al., Schizophrenia and Social Care,* A Comparative Follow-up Study of 339 Schizophrenic Patients (London: Oxford University Press, 1966) pp. 86–87.
7. Victor Fuchs, "The Contribution of Health Services to the American Economy," (Washington, D.C.: National Bureau of Economic Research, February 1966, mimeo), p. 31.
8. Norman A. Scotch and Sol Levine, "Stress as a Variable," a paper read at the 57th annual meeting of the American Sociological Association, September, 1962.
9. Benjamin Pasamanick *et al.,* "A Survey of Mental Disease in an Urban Population: Prevalence by Race and Income," reprinted in Frank Riessman *et al., Mental Health of the Poor* (New York: The Free Press of Glencoe, 1964), p. 47.
10. Philip Eisenberg and Paul Lazarsfeld, "The Psychological Effects of Unemployment," *Psychological Bulletin,* XXXV (1935), 358–390.

11. Bruce Dohrenwend, "The Social Psychological Nature of Stress," *Journal of Abnormal and Social Psychology,* LXII (1961).

12. Hylan Lewis, "Child Rearing Practices Among Low Income Families in the District of Columbia," paper presented at the National Conference on Social Welfare, 1961, p. 9.

13. *Ibid.*

14. W. C. Runciman, *Relative Deprivation and Social Justice,* A Study of Attitudes to Social Inequality in Twentieth-Century England (London: Routledge and Kegan, 1966).

15. See Norman A. Scotch and H. Jack Geiger, "The Epidemiology of Essential Hypertension," *Journal of Chronic Diseases,* XVI (November, 1963). The classic work on relative deprivation is found in Stouffer's study of the American soldier and Merton's reanalysis of his findings and the development of reference group theory. Robert K. Merton, *Social Theory and Social Structure* (Glencoe: The Free Press, 1961).

16. Alvin Schorr, *Slums and Social Insecurity,* Research Report No. 1, Division of Research and Statistics, Social Security Administration (Washington: U.S. Government Printing Office, 1963), pp. 31–32.

17. William Grigsby, *Housing Markets and Public Policy* (Philadelphia: University of Pennsylvania Press, 1963), p. 27.

18. David M. Wilner *et al., The Housing Environment and Family Life* (Baltimore: The Johns Hopkins Press, 1962).

19. Nathan Glazer and Davis McEntire (eds.), *Studies in Housing and Minority Groups* (Berkeley: University of California Press, 1960).

20. Nathan Glazer, "Slum Dwellings Do Not Make a Slum," *New York Times Magazine Section,* Nov. 21, 1965.

21. E. Wight Bakke, "The Cycle of Adjustment to Unemployment," reprinted in Norman W. Bell and Ezra F. Vogel (eds.), *A Modern Introduction to the Family* (Glencoe, Illinois: Free Press, 1960).

22. Beton M. Fleisher, "The Effect of Income on Delinquency," Center for Social Organizational Studies, Working Paper No. 40 (University of Chicago, January, 1965).

23. Warren Haggstrom, "The Power of the Poor," reprinted in Riessman et al. (eds.), *The Mental Health of the Poor, op. cit.*

24. Kenneth A. Boulding, "Reflections on Poverty," *The Social Welfare Forum* (New York: Columbia University Press, 1961), p. 51.

25. William Grigsby, unpublished memo on housing and poverty.

26. I am indebted to Robert S. Weiss, sociologist at Brandeis University, for these observations.

27. Robert J. Lampman, "Recent Thoughts on Equalitarianism," *The Quarterly Journal of Economics,* Vol. LXXI (May, 1957), 252.

28. *Ibid.*

29. H. Warren Dunham, Patricia Phillips, and Barbara Srinivasan, "A Research Note on Diagnosed Mental Illness and Social Class," *American Sociological Review,* XXXI (April, 1966), 223.

30. Evelyn Ellis, "Social Psychological Correlates of Upward Mobility Among Unmarried Career Women," *American Sociological Review,* 17 (1952), 563.

31. John Cumming, "The Inadequacy Syndrome," mimeo.

32. Roy Lubove, "Social Work and the Life of the Poor," *The Nation,* (May 23, 1966).

33. Daniel P. Moynihan, "The Negro Family: The Case for National Action," (Office of Planning and Research, U.S. Department of Labor, March, 1966), pp. 5 and 47.

34. The interpretation of the Moynihan report and the controversy which developed around it has been thoughtfully analyzed by Lee Rainwater and William L. Yancy in "Black Families and the White House," *Trans-Action* (July-August, 1966). See also correspondence between Steve Polgar and Lee Rainwater in *Trans-Action* (December, 1966) pp. 55–56.

35. Frank Riessman, "Lower Income Culture: The Strengths of the Poor," *Journal of Marriage and the Family* (November, 1964).

36. Walter Miller's introduction in Sidney E. Bernard, *Fatherless Families: Their Economic and Social Adjustment* (Brandeis University, Papers in Social Welfare, No. 7, 1964).

37. Norman MacKenzie, "Concepts of Alienation," *New Society* (February, 1964).

38. Melvin Seeman, "On the Meaning of Alienation," *American Sociological Review,* XXIV, No. 6 (December, 1959).

39. Charles Silberman, "Is Education Enough?" mimeo (May, 1965).

40. *Youth in the Ghetto,* Haryou (1964), pp. 348–49.

41. Martin Deutsch, "The Disadvantaged Child and the Learning Process," in A. Harry Passow (ed.), *Education in Depressed Areas* (New York: Teachers College, Columbia University, 1963), pp. 163–179.

42. Basil Bernstein, "Social Class, Speech Systems and Psychotherapy," in Riessman, *The Mental Health of the Poor, op. cit.*

43. *New York Times, International Edition,* January 16, 1967.

44. Peter Marris and Martin Rein, *Dilemmas of Social Reform: Poverty and Community Action in the United States* (New York: Atherton Press, 1967) p. 189.

45. Robert and Rhona Rapaport, "Work and Family in Contemporary Society," *American Sociological Review,* XXX, No. 3 (June, 1965).

46. This argument is developed in a forthcoming book where it is presented as a rationale in support of a children's allowance program. Alvin Schorr, *Poor Kids* (New York: Basic Books, 1967).

47. Alex Inkeles in an unpublished paper quoted in Rappaport, "Work and Family in Contemporary Society." *op. cit.*

48. Raymond Smith, *The Negro Family in British Guiana* (London: Routledge and Paul, 1956).

49. Ludwig L. Geismar and Michael A. La Sorte, *Understanding the Multi-Problem Family: A Conceptual Analysis and Exploration in Early Identification* (New York: Association Press, 1964).

50. The importance of crisis and transition as normal events experienced during the life cycle has been proposed by a number of investigators. See, for example, Orville Brim, "Socialization Through the Life Cycle," mimeo; Rhona Rappaport, "Normal Crisis, Family Structure and Mental Health," *Family Process,* II (March, 1963); and Gerald Caplan, *Principles of Preventive Psychiatry* (New York: Basic Books, 1964).

51. Bertram Gross, *The Managing of Organizations* (New York: The Free Press, 1964), p. 792.
52. Rappaport, *op. cit.,* p. 389.
53. See Schorr, *op. cit.,* for an analysis of how different types of income transfer schemes affect the family squeeze.
54. Lee Rainwater, "Work and Identity and the Lower Class Male," mimeo.
55. The literature on this perspective is fragmented. Research and analysis of how institutional defects affect poverty are not readily available. It is for this reason that we have only presented the argument without reference to the literature.
56. Richard Titmuss, "Social Policy and Economic Progress," paper presented at the National Conference on Social Welfare, Chicago, June, 1966, p. 12.
57. A. Peter Marris and Martin Rein, *Dilemmas of Social Reform, op. cit.*
58. Sanford Kravitz, "Community Action Programs: Past, Present and Future," *American Child,* XLVII, (November, 1965), 4.
59. Christopher Jenks, "Are the Public Schools Obsolete?" *The Public Interest,* I, No. 2 (1966).
60. For a fuller discussion of these issues, see Martin Rein and Peter Marris, "Poverty and the Community Planner's Mandate," in Bernard J. Frieden and Robert Morris (eds.), *Urban Planning and Social Policy* (New York: Basic Books, 1968), pp. 423–431.
61. Richard Titmuss, "Social Policy and Economic Progress," *op. cit.,* p. 20.

Chapter 21

Problems in the Definition and Measurement of Poverty

The problems of how to define and measure poverty cannot proceed until we clarify the conception of poverty we wish to employ. Three broad concepts of poverty can be identified. Poverty may be regarded as subsistence, inequality, or externality. *Subsistence* is concerned with the minimum of provision needed to maintain health and working capacity. Its terms of reference are the capacity to survive and to maintain physical efficiency. *Inequality* is concerned with the relative position of income groups to each other. Poverty cannot be understood by isolating the poor and treating them as a special group. Society is seen as a series of stratified income layers and poverty is concerned with how the bottom layers fare relative to the rest of society. Hence, the concept of poverty must be seen in the context of society as a whole. The study of the poor then depends on an understanding of the level of living of the rich, since it is these conditions relative to each other that are critical in the conception of inequality. To understand the poor

Reprinted by permission of the publisher from *Poverty in America: A Reader* (revised edition), Louis A. Ferman, *et al.*, eds. (Ann Arbor, Michigan: The University of Michigan Press, 1968).

we must then study the affluent. *Externality* is concerned with the social consequences of poverty for the rest of society rather than in terms of the needs of the poor. The poverty line should serve "as an index of the disutility to the community of the persistence of poverty."[1]

People must not be allowed to become so poor that they offend or are hurtful to society. It is not so much the misery and plight of the poor but the discomfort and cost to the community which is crucial to this view of poverty. We have a problem of poverty to the extent that low income creates problems for those who are now poor. Poverty then is social problems which are correlated with low income. Hence only when income-conditioned problems are randomized can poverty be eliminated. To improve the level of living of the poor without reducing disutility to the rest of community is insufficient.

Each of these concepts presents numerous problems of definition and measurement. Should we define poverty only in terms of economic insufficiency, economic inequality, and economic diseconomy, or should the definition be broadened to embrace non-economic variables such as prestige, power, and social services? For example, Titmuss has insisted that "we cannot . . . delineate the new frontiers of poverty unless we take account of the changing agents and characteristics of inequality."[2] Although the concept of poverty Titmuss holds is that of inequality, he is posing the broader question that poverty is more than the lack of income.

When a more encompassing view of poverty is accepted which extends beyond the distribution of income, two critical issues emerge—where to establish the cut-off points which separate the poor from the non-poor, and which non-economic conditions should be taken into account.

Paradoxically, we measure poverty in subsistence terms, but the programs and policies we have evolved to reduce poverty in America are based on a broader conception of the dimensions of well-being for which no systematic statistical information is available. These include the lack of accepted minima, or inequalities in the distribution of power, education, and legal justice. These dimensions of the level of living are not included in the goods and services which make up a minimum personal market basket, on which the measurement of poverty is based, because these items cannot be purchased by the individual with low income in the market. However, little organized effort has been directed at conceptualizing and measuring a conception of poverty which is more closely related to the programs we have developed, or at developing a program to reduce poverty (cash transfers) which is more closely tied to the concept of poverty we employ—the lack of minimum income for subsistence.

However, a small body of literature is being developed which does attempt to spell out the non-economic dimensions of poverty. Townsend, influenced by Titmuss, defines poverty as inequities in the distribution of seven resources,[3] including income, capital assets, occupational fringe benefits, current public services, and current private services, occupational and living environment and facilities. A national study of poverty in England based on an empirical investigation of the distribution of these items is now being undertaken by Townsend and Abel-Smith. Miller and Rein, also influenced by Titmuss, have drawn up a somewhat different list of items which, in being more responsive to the American context, pays attention to the political, legal, and educational components of well-being.[4]

But broadening the definition only confounds the problem of where to draw the cut-off points which distinguish those in poverty from the rest of the population. For a solution to this dilemma we return again to relative, absolute, and disutility conceptions of poverty. Are we interested in establishing standards which will enable us to define minimum powers, social honor, environmental health, and justice? Our search for such standards is illusory and no viable definition can be found which does not depend on inequalities in the distribution of these resources which comprise our level of living. Grigsby and Baratz suggest that the cut-off points may be established at that point or region where the relationship between income and social and personal problems is statistically randomized.[5] This formulation of where to establish the division between poor and non-poor draws on the externality conception of poverty, for it is concerned with the consequences of being poor or with the bottom of an income distribution.

The extensive reliance by governmental bodies such as the Office of Economic Opportunity and the Council of Economic Advisers on estimates of poverty which are based upon data concerning the cost of subsistence in the United States suggests that we have what is in effect an official American definition of poverty. As such, it deserves the closest scrutiny. This paper examines some of the problems inherent in the current "official" definition of poverty. Some attempt is made to place the analysis in a historical context, although no systematic historical review is attempted.

A SUBSISTENCE DEFINITION OF POVERTY

A definition of poverty in terms of subsistence levels of living has had wide acceptance because it seems to accord with common sense and appears to be divorced from personal values of either harshness or compassion. It seeks to describe poverty objectively as lack of the income needed to acquire the minimum necessities of life. Those who lack the necessities to sustain life are by definition poor. But how should "minimum" be defined? Agreement on the meaning of minimum is crucial to the development of standards which will permit the establishment of a dividing line separating the poor from the non-poor. Much of the history of the study of poverty can be understood as an effort to establish a non-subjective or "scientific" poverty line, the standard for which was equated with subsistence—the amount needed to sustain life. But like the search for the philosopher's stone, the efforts to discover an absolute and value-free definition of poverty based on the concept of subsistence proved abortive.

Rowntree was the first investigator to attempt a rigorous definition of poverty in subsistence terms.[6] In his classic study of poverty in the city of York, he wrote:

> My primary poverty line represented the minimum sum on which physical efficiency could be maintained. It was a standard of bare subsistence rather than living. In calculating it the utmost economy was practised . . . "A family living upon the scale allowed for in this estimate must . . . be governed by the regulation, 'Nothing must be bought but that which is absolutely necessary for the maintenance of physical health, and what is bought must be of the plainest and most economical description.' "[7]

Thus, a standard of bare subsistence could be supported if all human passions for frivolity, the relief of monotony, and even irresponsibility were ruthlessly suppressed. Only expenditures which provided physical health were permissible. The failure or the incapacity to conduct one's daily affairs according to these severe regulations brought the family into a state of secondary poverty. Secondary poverty existed when income was adequate to maintain a subsistence level, but the family failed to spend its income to purchase the necessities to sustain life and health. According to Rowntree, a defect of moral character or native intelligence, rather than an insufficiency of resources, distinguishes primary from secondary poverty. For his definition of "the minimum necessaries for the maintenance of mere physical efficiency," Rowntree drew upon the research of the American nutritionist, Atwater, who had devised a minimum diet based on research undertaken on American convicts. Atwater had estimated minimum caloric intake per day by determining the amount of food which was required to prevent prisoners from either gaining or losing weight. Estimating variations for men and women and determining the market value of the food which satisfied these minimum requirements, Rowntree arrived at a low-cost food plan which served as the basis for his definition of poverty.[8]

Present procedures for estimating minimum nutritional requirements have progressed beyond these primitive beginnings, but they still depend on a judgment of nutritional need which takes into account both actual consumption patterns and a definition of minimum caloric intake based on an independent assessment of nutritional adequacy. The basic technique is operationalized in the U.S. Department of Agriculture's economy food plan which forms the basis for several subsistence estimates of poverty. But the minimum amount of money needed to achieve minimum nutritional standards tells us nothing about the cost of clothing, shelter, and other items necessary to maintain life. Some means of converting expenditure for food into total expenditures is needed. Engel had observed in 1857 that there was an inverse relationship between income and the percentage of total expenditure spent for food. By examining the proportion of the family budget spent for food in various income classes an Engel coefficient[9] can be computed, which, when multiplied by food expenditure, provides an estimate of the total minimum budget required to keep a family out of poverty.[10]

An alternative to an aggregate estimate of all non-food expenditures through the use of the Engel coefficient is the development of an itemized budget for each consumption item necessary for subsistence—shelter, medical care, clothing, etc. This procedure assumes that minimum requirements can be specified for each item and that these can serve as cut-off points separating adequate consumption from inadequate. To illustrate the procedure, we can consider how minimum clothing needs may be defined.

During the 1930s, Dorothy Brady devised an imaginative scheme based on the principle of income elasticity of demand whereby the number of units of clothing purchased, rather than total expenditures, was crucial. As income rises, a family reaches a critical point where the number of additional units purchased declines and the price paid per unit increases. That is to say, instead of buying more and more clothes, they begin buying items of higher quality. That point is defined as the clothing poverty line. For each consumption item a cut-off point which represents some combination of utilization pattern and arbitrary standard of adequacy can be similarly determined, and the collection of points becomes the basis for drawing a poverty line. In the case of clothing, with increased affluence the elasticity threshold is reached at a comparatively low income and thus is increasingly less useful in differentiating the poor from the non-poor, but the concept still has considerable merit.

As we might expect, there have been many attempts to define the minimum subsistence basket with reference not only to food essentials, but other necessities as well. Some of the earliest attempts to estimate minimum living costs, such as the studies undertaken by the Factory Investigating Commission of New York State in 1915, were based on estimates of the amount of money needed to achieve both an adequate diet and sanitary housing.[11] It proved very difficult, however, to establish rigorous standards of adequacy for any of the essentials of living except food. J. Murray Luck, analyzing the definition of poverty after World War II, put the matter as follows:

> The wants to be considered here are the recognized biological necessities—food and drink. Little will be said about housing. The need for shelter varies according to locale and to social custom: it cannot be accurately measured. Fuel is essential for survival in a cold environment, but this too is a regional and variable necessity. A similar consideration applies to clothing. The conventional biological definition of a necessity . . . excludes, except for reproduction, almost everything except food and water.[12]

More recently, Orshansky has noted that "there is no generally acceptable standard of adequacy for essentials of living except food."[13] Actually, as will be demonstrated below, even in the estimates of minimum food requirements accepted standards are lacking. This fact raises a serious question as to the usefulness of any attempt to measure an absolute standard of adequacy which the term subsistence implies.

A DEFINITION OF POVERTY BASED ON NUTRITIONAL ADEQUACY

Poverty is defined by the Social Security Administration (SSA) as nutritional inadequacy. This definition clearly implies some standard for determining the minimum cost of an adequate diet. During the depression the National Research Council undertook intensive work in developing a recommended dietary allowance which served as a basis for defining minimal nutritional requirements for calories and essential nutrients. All foods were sorted into eleven categories on the basis of the nutrients they contained. An estimate was then made of the quantities of food needed in each of these food groups, by individuals of different age and sex. As it turned out, if the recommended quantities of food were purchased in the most economical way and without regard to dietary habits, the cost of the food plan would be extremely low. Stigler, for example, estimated that if the minimum number of calories were purchased in the cheapest bulk market basket, the total cost to purchase the food needed for an adequate diet would come to about $40 per year in 1944.[14] Even allowing for a tripling of prices since that date, the present cost would come to less than $120 per annum. Unfortunately, as Stigler sought to demonstrate by this calculation, persons in American society simply do not consume the lowest-cost food items. Thus, a realistic definition of poverty requires that attention be given to actual consumption patterns. "Even with food," Orshansky acknowledges, "social conscience and custom dictate that there be not only sufficient quantity but sufficient variety to meet recommended nutritional goals and conform to customary eating patterns. Calories alone will not be enough."[15] Yet food alone provides the best basis for measuring minimum requirements; however, the definition must therefore be based on both customary behavior and expert definition of nutritional adequacy.

Reflecting this fact, a household food consumption survey undertaken by the U.S. Department of Agriculture was divided into four levels of cost: economy, low, moderate, and liberal. The cost of a standard family food plan is developed at each of these levels. If, however, only prevailing consumption patterns were taken as a standard, without attention to an independent definition of adequacy, there would be no objective way of establishing a cut-off point which distinguishes an adequate from an inadequate diet. When the food plan was developed for each income group, therefore, it was based on expert judgment regarding an acceptable tradeoff between nutritional standards and consumption patterns.[16]

The SSA procedure for measuring poverty is based on the cost of USDA's "economy" food plan, which is adapted to the pattern of food expenditures of those in the lowest third of the income range. It is designed for "temporary or emergency use when funds are low" and costs about 75–80 percent of the low-cost plan.[17] It was adopted in about 1960 when a food plan was needed which was consistent with actual food budgets already developed for families receiving public assistance. The existing standards of welfare assistance served to define the food consumption needs of the poor.

In estimating costs, the Department of Agriculture assumed that housewives make average choices within each food group and average prices are paid for each food item in the basket. Each year these average prices are adjusted for changes in the price level. It is further assumed that all family members under the plan prepare all of their food at home, including lunches which they may eat at work.

To determine the minimum total income requirements for a family an Engel coefficient is needed. A Department of Agriculture survey conducted in 1955 was used to determine the proportion of total family income among low-income family units that was spent for food.[18] Actually, three different coefficients were used: 0.27 for two-person families; 0.33 for families of 3 or more; and for unattached individuals, a special estimate based on approximately 80 percent of the total requirements of a two-person family. The last is based on the assumption that when income is low, the cost of living for a single person is only slightly less than for a couple.

The SSA procedure for defining and measuring poverty is especially vulnerable to the criticism that when a choice among alternative estimating procedures was necessary the rationale for selection was arbitrary, but not necessarily unreasoned. The extent and character of this arbitrariness will be examined in four substantive areas: the size of the Engel coefficient; the diversity of nutritional need; the disparity between actual consumption patterns and expert judgment as to the ingredients of an adequate diet; and the insistence on an economical market basket.

The Size of the Engel Coefficent

The size of the Engel coefficient obviously affects estimates of the extent of poverty. However, an Engel coefficient is not used by the SSA to determine minimum budget requirements for persons living alone. The requirements of an unattached individual living alone are estimated indirectly as a proportion of the expenditures for a couple. The explanation offered is that "the consumption data are hard to interpret because of the heavy representation of aged individuals not shown separately."[19] Although this procedure seems reasonable, there appears to be no firm evidence on which to estimate the needs of one aged person as a proportion of the needs of an aged couple. In an early report Orshansky notes that, "pending further research, the relationship of the cost of living for a single individual to that of a couple must remain something everyone talks about but about which little is known."[20] The deficiency is serious, because, as Orshansky explains, the correction for single-person households is "by far the most important adjustment"[21] which is necessary in making an estimate of the budgetary needs of elderly persons. The extent of poverty among the aged could drop, perhaps sharply, if an estimate of 60 or 70 percent were used, instead of 80 percent.[22]

If we consider the size of the coefficient used, even more serious objections can be raised to the procedures followed by SSA. As has been said, the lower the coefficient, the larger the number of impoverished. In estimating the income-food-expenditure relationship Orshansky had available two surveys, the Department of Agriculture consumption survey of 1955,[23] and a 1960–61 Bureau of Labor Statistics survey of urban families.[24]

The BLS survey found that about 25 percent of the income of all families regardless of size goes for food, whereas the Agriculture survey found substantial variations by family size and an average expenditure for food of 33 percent for families with two or more members. The BLS data are based on interviewer estimates of annual outlays for food, while the Department of Agriculture figures are derived from a detailed checklist of foods consumed during the week in which the survey was held. The Social Security Administration used the Agriculture study. Haber criticizes this choice.

> It was suggested (by Orshansky) that the BLS study tended to understate food expenditures; but this would affect ratio figures only if it also tended to overstate or not similarly understate other expenditures. This was not demonstrated and since the study collected data on expenditures in all categories, not just food, there would seem to be an internal check on the relative figures. Furthermore, comparison of 1950 to 1960–61 BLS studies reflected a decline of 5.6 percent in the ratio within the same methodology. The earlier USDA figure is almost certain to be overstated.[25]

Recalculating the poverty cut-off point with a coefficient of .30 rather than .33 for a four-person urban family and taking into account gross income rather than income after taxes, Haber arrives at a $3,474 poverty line "for the deceptive economy plan and a truer $4,263 for the low-cost plan," compared with a $3,130 line using Agriculture data.[26]

Rose Friedman also criticizes the "official" definition of poverty but on different grounds. Using estimates based on actual consumption and a higher Engel coefficient, she is able to cut the poverty population in half.

The nutritive adequacy definition of poverty . . . gives an income of $2,200 as the poverty line for a nonfarm family of four. The cost of food implied by the $3,000 income for a family of four . . . is $5.00 per person per week. The amount actually spent for food, on the average, by a family of four with an income of $2,200 was over $6.00 per person per week, because the fraction of income spent on food at this level was about 60 percent and not 33 percent.

It should be emphasized that the difference between the Council's estimate that 20 percent of families were poor . . . and my estimate that 10 percent were poor results neither from a different basic criterion of poverty nor from the use of different data. Both use nutrition to separate the poor from the not-poor; both use the same standard of nutritive-adequacy; both use the same statistical data.[27]

It is interesting to speculate on how political realities affect technical decisions. The first working definition of poverty used by the Council of Economic Advisers established the extent of American poverty at about 34 million persons, or roughly one-fifth of the population. More refined estimates, if they were to be politically acceptable, had to be consistent with CEA's estimate of the size of the problem. It was all right for a new definition to change the character of poverty, but not its size. As a consequence, technical decisions regarding definition of income or the size of the Engel coefficient or the choice of a survey on food consumption, all of which can significantly alter the estimated extent of poverty, have come to reflect not only our understanding of the meaning of subsistence but also the political views and realities which provide the framework for professional judgments.

What is important in all these controversies is not who is right and who is wrong but that even where presumably objective measures are available, the selection of minimum standards is of necessity arbitrary. This point is expanded upon in the following section.

The Diversity of Nutritional Need

Another example of arbitrariness concerns the adjustments which are made for differential nutritional needs based on age and sex groupings, but not upon the level of activity. Adequate caloric intake comes to about 3,000 calories a day for a male age 18 to 64, while a child under ten requires 1,200 to 1,800 calories. However, the level of physical activity appears to be as important as age. A farmer, for example, may require as many as 4,500 calories.[28]

Physical fitness is not a precisely definable condition. One has first to ask fitness for what? A bank clerk in the best of health might be unfit to work on a trolley or in a coal mine. A woman able to bear two or three children without endangering her health might well prove unfit for the demands of motherhood in a society where families of seven or eight children were the rule. Secondly, standards of physical fitness vary over time, as well as between country and country . . . class and class.[29]

Townsend estimates that when sedentary and manual occupations are compared, the number of calories needed per hour may differ from 30 to as much as 450. Since age and sex are taken into account in estimating minimal caloric need, one would think that the level of physical activity would be regarded as equally important, the more so because the poor are more likely than the non-poor to be employed in manual and unskilled jobs requiring physical exertion.

Townsend is sharply critical not only of the neglect of activity levels, but also of other factors involved in nutritional standards. In expressing his criticism, he offers an analysis of the formidable barriers to scientifically determined subsistence diets.

> There are real difficulties in estimating nutritional needs. The nutritionist has not subtly broken up the different needs of individuals; they have made overall estimates. These estimates are not even based on studies of the intake of persons in different occupations. Beyond a certain minimum (somewhere, perhaps, between 1,000 and 1,500 calories), the number of calories a man needs . . . depends upon the society in which he lives. Even his dietary needs depend upon climate, the kind of housing he lives in, the kind of job he has, and the kind of leisure activities he follows. In other words, estimates of need, even nutritional needs, cannot be absolute; they must be relative to the kind of society in which a man is living.[30]

The estimates of caloric requirements at one time did take into account level of activity, but nutritionists have dropped this variable, perhaps because they were not primarily concerned with the problem of poverty. Caloric estimates lack the scientific rigor which is claimed for them, for they depend on global and aggregate judgments which underestimate the diversity of human need. But endless refinement of details is not the appropriate answer to the problem, the standards which emerge will become so complex and detailed as to add new dimensions of unreality. Moreover, there is no way of defining minimum levels of activity for work and leisure, even though caloric needs depend on energy spent.

These criticisms of estimates of caloric levels may seem somewhat overdrawn, since caloric requirements alone can be met quite cheaply. It is achieving a balance of vitamins, minerals, and other nutrients that is most problematic for the poor. Further, disagreements over minimum caloric requirements are not nearly so important as disagreements over what constitutes an adequate diet generally and whether minor deviations from prescribed diets affect performance—the capacity to learn and work. Still further, it is doubtful whether getting more refined estimates would affect the numbers of those in poverty to the same extent as does a change in the estimate of the size of the Engel coefficient. On the other hand, the issue of level of physical activity does highlight value problems by undermining the nutritionist claim for objectivity and by dramatizing the difficulties of measurement.

The Disparity Between Actual Behavior and Expert Judgment

An examination of actual consumption patterns reveals great variation among low-income families. On the average, families in the $2,999 income group in 1958 were spending more for food per person than the low-cost food plan of the Department of Agriculture calls for, but equally interesting was the fact that 28 percent of families were spending less than the amount suggested. Some of this spread is due simply to regional variations. In 1959, for example, the United States' average weekly food consumption for a family consisting of a mother, father, and two children under age twelve was $24.00, but expenditures ranged from $19.80 in the South to $26.50 in the Northeast, a difference of 35 percent.[31]

There were also wide variations in expenditures by the aged. Orshansky estimates that there was a 20 percent spread in cost of living for the aged in the 20 largest cities and suburbs of the United States, ranging from $2,641 in Houston to $3,366 in Chicago. How these variations in the cost of living affect the cost of the low-cost food plan is by no means clear. On one hand, it is plausible to argue that at subsistence levels there is much less room for significant variations in actual budgets, and there is therefore little variability in actual expenditures. On the other hand, there are wide variations in actual expenditures for the income group which is expected to follow the low-cost food plan. If we consider one item—consumption of food at home—the range of expenditures seems to be impressively large, from $711 for an elderly couple in Houston to $900 in Boston.

These variations raise questions about the use of a single food plan to estimate poverty. Another reason for skepticism has to do with the fact that the economy food and low-cost plans assume an efficient housekeeper who secures an adequate diet for the family within the cost of the plan. This seems unlikely, partly because the low-income housewife is likely to be a less informed consumer and partly because the quality of the food she purchases may be inferior and higher priced in comparison with food purchased by higher-income shoppers. A recent study by the Bureau of Labor Statistics concluded that the poor pay more for food than consumers in higher-income areas, but that food stores do not charge more in low-income areas.[32] It is not that the poor are overcharged, but that they cannot exploit the economics of bulk purchase. For example, the poor tend to buy flour in two-pound rather than five-pound sacks, even though "the price for flour ranged from 14 percent a pound higher in New York to 35 percent higher in Chicago when purchased in two-pound sacks." Similar differentials hold for milk, sugar, and other food items.[33]

In light of the above, it is not surprising to learn that many persons who have resources sufficient to live only at the level prescribed by the economy or low-cost food plan will also fail to meet a prescribed minimum diet. But to what extent should the experts be forced to revise their estimates of the cost of a minimum diet to reflect actual consumption patterns? If the budget needed to achieve minimum dietary adequacy is defined as less than what families apparently do spend to achieve this minimum, it is difficult to determine whether the experts are wrong in where they have placed the poverty line, or whether the prevailing pattern of consumption is an inappropriate criterion because the poor lack the capacity to consume. More important, to the extent that standards are based on actual consumption there is a circularity in the analysis.[34] Orshansky in a discussion with the author made a similar observation that there are no extrinsic standards for determining minimum nutritional needs.

The Economical Market Basket

The cost of the market basket of food items needed to prevent nutritional poverty is computed so that it is the most economic basket possible. The concern for least cost is at conflict with the desire to take account of actual consumption patterns and introduces a note of unreality into the definition of the poverty line. Rowntree recognized this when he observed that "no housewife without a considerable knowledge of the nutritive value of different food-stuffs and considerable skill in cooking, would be likely to choose a menu at once so economically and so comparatively attractive as the one upon which I base my costs."[35] Orshansky makes the same observation, "the lower the level of cost, the more restricted the kinds and qualities of food must be and the more skill in marketing and food preparation is required."[36] But those in poverty clearly have the least skills in marketing, knowledge of nutrition, and resourcefulness in cooking to meet the stringent demands of economy. The failure to meet the nutritional standards set by the poverty budget is assumed to reflect the incapacity of the poor to consume, that is, secondary poverty. If the diet is to be based on actual consumption, and if it is to avoid building into its definition a confusion between primary and secondary poverty, then the standards of economy must be relaxed and a more realistic assumption of human error be accepted. The effect of this intrusion of reality into budgeting will be to raise the poverty level and increase the amount of poverty.

SUMMARY

I have tried to demonstrate that the subsistence-level definition of poverty is arbitrary, circular, and relative. The definition of poverty based on nutritional requirements is dependent not only on expert definition but also on actual levels and patterns of living. Thus, no extrinsic standard to measure food adequacy is available and the subsistence definition of poverty is, therefore, circular. But this procedure imposes a number of arbitrary judgments which rob the nutritional approach of its claim that it is based on scientific rigor with minimum attention to value judgments. To take account of customary behavior requires that we know in advance the relevant income group which distinguishes the poor from the non-poor. Thus the procedure for measuring poverty is based on a circular argument from which it cannot retreat. The result is that those who hold different value judgments concerning how stringent or lenient the poverty standard should be, can use the same data to demonstrate that poverty is either a significant or trivial problem. All of the procedures in establishing a tradeoff between consumption standards and expert judgment have an arbitrary quality which can be challenged by those who wish to see the standards of poverty defined more harshly or more leniently. On the other hand, the criterion that the budget should be *most* economical forces the expert to accept an unrealistic assumption of a no-waste budget, and extensive knowledge in marketing and cooking. An economical budget must be based on knowledge and skill which is least likely to be present in the low income groups we are concerned with. The result is that a stubborn and continuing ambiguity between primary and secondary poverty is built into the very procedures by which the minimum nutritional standard is determined. If we cannot distinguish between the capacity to consume and the adequacy of the resource base for consumption, there is no independent standard for questioning and revising expert judgment.

Almost every procedure in the subsistence-level definition of poverty can be reasonably challenged. The estimates are based on the consumption pattern of the entire low-income third instead of subgroups of this population. The estimates of nutritional needs take age and sex into account but not physical activity. Average price and average consumption are used as the standard for constructing the low-cost food plan, rather than actual behavior. The economy food plan is an arbitrary derivative (approximately three-quarters) of the low-cost plan. We must conclude that subsistence measures of poverty cannot claim to rest solely on a technical or scientific definition of nutritional adequacy. Values, preferences, and political realities influence the definition of subsistence. Yet once a biological definition is abandoned and actual consumption is taken into account, no absolute measurement of poverty in subsistence terms is possible.[37] The other conceptions of poverty reviewed at the beginning of this paper deserve more attention and developments.

NOTES

1. Eugene Smolensky, "Investment in the Education of the Poor: A Pessimistic Report," *American Economic Review*, Supplement LV, May 1966.
2. Richard Titmuss, *Income Distribution and Social Change* (London: George Allen and Unwin, 1962), p. 187.
3. Peter Townsend, "Measures and Explanations of Poverty in High Income and Low Income Countries: The Problems of Operationalizing the Concepts of Development, Class and Poverty," a paper presented at the International Seminar on Poverty, University of Essex, April 3–6, 1967.
4. S. M. Miller, Martin Rein, *et al.*, "Poverty, Inequality and Conflict," *The Annals*, September 1967.
5. William Grigsby and Merton Baratz, with Martin Rein, "Conceptualization and Measurement of Poverty," mimeo, 1967.
6. Benjamin S. Rowntree, *Poverty and Progress: A Second Social Survey of York* (London: Longmans, Green, 1941).
7. *Ibid.*, pp. 102–3.
8. Peter Townsend, "The Meaning of Poverty," *British Journal of Sociology*, XVIII, 3 (September 1962), 215 ff.
9. For a discussion of Engel Coefficient see, E. J. Hobsbawm, "Poverty," in *New International Encyclopedia of the Social Sciences*, 1969.
10. The relationship can be expressed by the following equation: $C=ME$ where C is equal to the cost of total consumption of a household, M equals expenditures for a minimum food basket, and E equals the size of the Engel coefficient. See, Koji Taira, *Country Report No. 6 on Japan*. International Trade Union Seminar on Low Income Groups and Methods of Dealing with their Problems, Social Affairs Division of The Organization for Economic Co-operation and Development.
11. These studies grew out of an interest in determining how to estimate minimum wage requirements. See, Helen H. Lamale, "Changes in Concepts of Income Adequacy in the Last Century," *American Economic Review*, XLVII (May 1958), 291–99.
12. J. Murray Luck, *The War on Malnutrition and Poverty* (New York: Harper, 1946), p. 15.
13. Mollie Orshansky, "Counting the Poor: Another Look at the Poverty Profile," *Social Security Bulletin*, XXVIII, 1 (January 1965), 5.
14. George J. Stigler, "The Cost of Subsistence," *Journal of Farm Economics*, XXVII (1945), 311 ff.
15. Orshansky, *op. cit.*
16. *Ibid.*, p. 5.

17. *Ibid.,* p. 6.
18. U. S. Department of Agriculture, Household Food Consumption Survey, 1955. *Dietary Evaluation of Food Used in Households in the United States,* Report No. 16, November 1961.
19. Orshansky, *op. cit.,* p. 9.
20. Mollie Orshansky, "Budget for an Elderly Couple: Interim Revision by the Bureau of Labor Statistics," *Social Security Bulletin,* XXIII, 12 (December 1960), 31.
21. *Ibid.,* p. 28.
22. *Ibid.,* pp. 11–13.
23. U. S. Department of Agriculture, Household Food Consumption Survey, *op. cit.*
24. U. S. Bureau of Labor Statistics, *Consumer Expenditures and Income, Urban U. S. 1960–61.* Supplement 3–Part A to BLS Report 237–38, Table 29A, July 1964.
25. Alan Haber, "Poverty Budgets: How Much is Enough," *Poverty and Human Resources Abstracts,* I, 3 (Ann Arbor, 1966), 6.
26. *Ibid.,* p. 7.
27. Rose D. Friedman, *Poverty: Definition and Perspective* (Washington, D.C.: American Enterprise Institute for Public Policy Research, 1965), p. 35.
28. These caloric estimates are discussed in Luck, *op. cit.,* pp. 15 ff.
29. Tony Lynes, *National Assistance and National Prosperity.* Occasional Papers on Social Administration (Wellyn, England: Vedicite Press, 1962), pp. 9–10.
30. Peter Townsend, "The Scale and Meaning of Poverty in Contemporary Western Society," *Dependency and Poverty, 1963–1964.* Colloquium Series Paper, Brandeis University, July 1965, p. 15.
31. See, "Low-Cost Food Plans—New Regional Estimates," *Research and Statistics,* 28, Social Security Administration (October 1959), 5. What is often overlooked is that migration between regions seems to affect food costs, because food consumption patterns are not instantly abandoned. A report on nutrition of Negroes states: "The food habits of Southern Negroes in the North . . . appear to be particularly erratic, with a substantial amount of money being spent to acquire Southern food which has a very limited nutritional value, such as fatback and grits." Jean Mayer, "The Nutritional Status of American Negroes," *Nutrition Review,* XXIII, 6 (June 1965), 163.
32. *New York Times,* June 12, 1966, p. 56.
33. *Ibid.* The study did not, however, examine why chain stores tend to stay out of low income areas.
34. Orshansky, "Counting the Poor," *op. cit.,* p. 8.
35. Rowntree, *op. cit.,* p. 112.
36. Orshansky, "Counting the Poor," *op. cit.,* p. 6.
37. In the light of these observations it is rather surprising to note Kolko's insistence on the validity of an absolute measure of subsistence. He asserts: "The maintenance budget is a synthesis of what families actually spend, modified to include what they must have to meet minimum health criteria. It is *not* a relative or changing standard such as that employed by 'social workers' (who) will call a person 'underprivileged' whose scale of living is considerably below the average." Gabriel Kolko, *Wealth and Power in America* (New York: Praeger, 1962), p. 96.

Chapter 22

Research and the Development of Social Policy

Much of the literature on the relationship between research and action is directed at evaluative research—the assessment of policies already established.[1] This essay, by contrast, is concerned with the contribution of research to the development of social policy. It examines three types of research: needs-resources studies designed to measure the size of the gap between a specific need and the resources required to meet it; distributional research which examines the distribution of resources (money, men, and material) within a specific program; and allocative research which is addressed to alternative programs to achieve a stated goal or reduce a specific problem. Each framework raises different questions and provides different information on which to make policy recommendations. The choice of a framework, even before the information is in hand, affects the kinds of policy proposals which are likely to be made. Thus, the policy maker needs to know what kinds of policies he is prepared to pursue before commissioning research. Research provides a rationale for programs which are chosen by other criteria.

NEEDS-RESOURCE RESEARCH

A good deal of policy-oriented research in the 1940s and 1950s generated by Health and Welfare Councils throughout the United States tended to use the needs-resource framework. This type of research attempted to identify the disparity between needs and resources. Resources were defined with reference to the established pattern of professional services and community facilities, and the distinction between needs and preferences was obscured. Not surprisingly, with unflagging regularity these studies concluded that there was a need for casework, mental health, group work, or whatever community service was the focus of the inquiry. Such studies were mired in a conceptual confusion from which they could not be rescued. Casework and mental health and other services are presumably solutions to a problem. First the researchers assumed that the service did what it claimed to do; so if they found a need, they justified the service. They also neglected to recognize that for any given problem, a variety of different programs or interventions can be generated. But to start with the intervention and to neglect the problem left the research with a self-contained framework, a circular logic which failed to separate the task from its solutions. Means and ends became blurred as the service itself came to be regarded as the social aim. But to insist on explicating the concrete goals of each service intervention was to present a daunting challenge. Few programs could provide a statement of objectives that would satisfy researchers embarked on evaluative research. The research progressed without clarifying the tough question of social purposes which was a precondition for demonstrating that intervention could meet the problem.

For example, what are the social objectives of public recreation? To link recreation to a social problem like delinquency would imply that the program might be repudiated if it failed to reduce delinquency rates significantly. This approach fails to take into account that individuals would still demand recreation even if it contributed nothing to the reduction of deviant behavior. The framework of problem solving implies that needs are bounded and residual, and that the rendering of adequate services would reduce demands, a premise they assumed but did not test. The research model carried an implicit requirement that services be regarded as self-liquidating. Since many social problems were associated with low income, it was assumed that as incomes rose the need for social programs would decline. But as income rose, the cost of welfare programs also expanded. We can account for this anomaly if services are viewed as a response to consumer preferences rather than to problems; they can then be seen as amenities which expand choice and enhance the quality and level of living. Accordingly, resources will always fail to meet needs, since needs are indefinitely expansive. Moreover, needs grow, rather than decline, with increased affluence, as society has the economic capability to respond to the expanding consumer demand for publicly distributed services.

Inadvertently such studies also tended to have an inherent, but unrecognized, political conservatism because they seem to have relied upon a design which reaffirmed the importance of maintaining the form and structure of the established pattern for delivering local social services. This happened because resources were inventoried, not evaluated. Hence, they supported a type of planning which led to social service aggrandizement in that it sought to expand resources to permit growth of the prevailing service pattern. They hoped, in short, to create a bigger pie without reallocating its sections by function, auspice, or purpose.

Other reasons, besides a limited perspective, explain why prescriptions to relieve social ailments recommended more of the same social medicine. Professional commitments limit vision, political obstacles impel planners to avoid conflict, and intellectual problems make it difficult to develop innovative proposals.

DISTRIBUTIVE RESEARCH

Distributive research is directed at the reallocation rather than the expansion of the resources of money, personnel, and facilities within the programmatic sectors of housing, education, manpower, health, and so forth. It does not necessarily reject the importance of more resources, but assigns to it a lower priority on the assumption that the defects lie in the performance of the system. Hence it is necessary to search out the underlying principles on which the system of services is rendered, to challenge their plausibility and validity, and to examine the consequences of pursuing programs based on these principles. Distributive studies tend to be oriented toward changing the service structure and framework, while needs-resources studies tend to support and expand the established allocative system. Ideally distributive studies are best conducted where the disparity between needs and resources is least problematic, so that they can direct their attention to the administrative, structural, professional, and organizational issues.

William Ryan's study of mental health services in metropolitan Boston illustrates how research within this framework contributes to the development of policy. Ryan makes unusually explicit the assessment by the researcher that the problem rests with the organization and distribution of resources (personnel) rather than with their accretion. He explains:

> . . . [the] supply of out-patient psychiatric resources exceeds by over one-third the number generally considered as an ideal goal . . . these sobering facts raise

some serious questions, first of all about the direction in which solutions should be sought to some of these problems. It seems quite unrealistic, for example, to think of increasing quantities of mental health personnel as a reasonable solution, even if dramatically larger supplies of money and gross manpower were actually available.[2]

If more resources offer no solution, then policy must turn to strategies of redistribution. It is clear, then, that this study is chiefly concerned with the problem of distribution of personnel. The research findings enable Ryan to highlight the anomalies in the distribution of tasks and resources among agencies and professionals who service those who are in emotional distress.

ALLOCATIVE RESEARCH

The third type of study designed to contribute to the development of policy is concerned with choice and priority among alternative programs to reach a stated objective. Whereas distributive research focuses on organizational changes within a program, allocative research is concerned with the problem, with program outputs, and with the pattern of distributing resources among sectors. It tries to identify the size and nature of the problem (which is related to how the problem is conceptualized and defined, and for whom is the condition regarded as problematic), its distribution (including both composition and incidence data), and its causes and consequences on the assumption that such study will help clarify policy choices. Allocative research is directed at program outcomes where the inputs to be evaluated are broader than the program itself. This approach is consistent with its problem orientation. Such studies proceed on the untested assumption that there is a graceful movement from problem analysis to programmatic implications, rather than an abrupt leap and an awkward transition. Yet the critical task of allocative research is to explicate this transition from problem to program or from program output to policies, for the analysis of the problem or program must somehow clarify the policy choices. There is, I believe, by and large, no instant policy where merely examining the data logically impels the researcher to accept certain policy implications and to reject others. Consider a specific example: in the effort to reduce poverty, should we focus on social services (participation, legal aid, training, counseling, etc.), or on cash transfers (treating cash transfers as an incentive or investment which will facilitate an economic takeoff), or on expanding the volume and quality of jobs (especially selective economic policies which affect the available number of jobs for special groups)? We may, of course, prefer a mix rather than a single choice among these programs. If so, the issue of priority becomes critical. Hopefully, allocative research helps to provide a rationale for the selection among these programmatic options to achieve some stated goal.

In summary, research which is concerned with the development of policy seems to start with different problems: the needs or preferences for a *specific program,* or the redistribution of resources *within a specific program,* or the nature of the problem *without reference to a program.* The first framework leads to policies which seem to require more resources; this tends to be the approach of professionals who are responsible for specific programs. The second approach demands reform and change in the structure of services; this tends to be the style of the sociologist. The third type of research is concerned with choice among competing alternatives; this tends to be the framework of the economist. The choice of one or another of these frameworks affects not only the kinds of research questions which are pursued, but it also affects the level at which policy recommendations can be made if the data are to serve as a constraint on these recommendations. These approaches offer diverging and clashing frameworks because they are based upon different interpretations of what is the policy puzzle which needs to be solved. They are not complementary in the sense of yielding additive insights which, when brought together in some form of collaborative interdisciplinary research, facilitates the solution of the problem about which there is common agreement. Perhaps the best way to illustrate this thesis is to examine briefly three different types of policy recommendations in one area, education, in order to show the relationship between research and policy development.

One type of recommendation focuses on the need for more resources in the ghetto. Studies that offer evidence of inequities in the per capita expenditures among center city and suburban schools provide the data for the case for more resources (both absolute and relative). The classic study in this framework has been done by Conant.[3] If the children of the poor receive less educational resources and if the marginal rate of increase of new resources is greater among the nonpoor than the poor, then poor children not only get less, but are handicapped in the competition for the same occupational positions which now increasingly require greater educational achievement. Moreover, if the poor start school with an educational disadvantage, then to equalize their unequal conditions, unequal amounts of resources are needed. The logic is clear: needs are great and resources are limited; hence, the disparity between needs and resources must be filled by larger outlays of funds. Various ingenious research designs can be developed which focus on inequalities in the distribution of resources or needs for service, but such designs lead inevitably to policies which are directed at the amount of resources needed.

The needs-resource approach assumes that there is a relationship between the input (school) and the outcome (education). It views outcome failures as a function of input limits. Distributional research assumes that the use of available resources within a program sector is problematic, hence substantial increase in educational achievement can be brought about by altering the distribution, rather than the amount, of resources by using them more efficiently or effectively. The task of this type of research is to show that resources are being poorly used. One dramatic way to demonstrate this is to show that they are actually hurtful. Rosenthal's study of the relationship between teacher expectation and student performance tries to demonstrate that the teacher's anticipation of low performance levels produces low student achievement. Expectation, rather than intellectual ability, affects educational performance. Changes in teacher expectation should produce corresponding changes in student achievement, especially for young children.[4] The "service," education, has become an "anti-service," inflicting hurt rather than achieving gains. A large change in educational achievement might be expected by promoting institutional change in the way the teacher sets about the task of teaching. Such research takes organizational variables as their terms of reference. Other studies within this framework may try to redistribute authority (decentralization), or alter teaching tasks (nonprofessionals), or change morale (distribution of rewards).

Finally, research may be directed at alternative approaches to secure educational achievement. Here the focus is on the problem—low educational achievement—rather than on the specific program—the educational system. More specifically this type of research gives attention not to a comparison of inputs as the measure of the quality of service, but to the more basic question of outputs—educational achievement. James Coleman's study in the United States[5] and the Plowden Report in England are examples of this type of research. Both studies seek to answer the question of what is the relative importance of educational and family background, school facilities, curriculum, teacher characteristics, and student body characteristics for educational achievement. Standardized multiple regression coefficients are developed for different clusters of variables and then these are related to various measures of educational achievement. The findings of studies conducted in this framework seem to suggest that the school resources inputs, other than the characteristics of teachers, are less important as instruments of learning than are the attributes of the child's own family and the social characteristics of the student body in his grade. One inference is that to stimulate educational achievement more can be gained by intervention outside the education system.

The findings secured from a research design which examines the contribution of alternative inputs to educational achievement facilitate making this kind of inference. But the policy inference to be drawn from these data are by no means self-evident, for there is no graceful immediate translation of facts into policies. It is just as reasonable to conclude that since the lack of variability among schools contributes to the findings of no relationship between educational inputs and pupil performance more investment in schooling is needed. The function of the schools is to educate, and if they fail to do so we must find new ways of getting the educational system to function properly.

One type of study urges that the schools need more resources, another that the resources be redistributed, and the third that intervention outside the schools may be more important for the achievement of educational goals than either more resources for schools or educational reforms.

Most policy-oriented research starts with an implicit programmatic conclusion and seeks to support or repudiate that conclusion with convincing data. Thus, the objectives of action form and shape the research design; hence, policy preferences are integral to the design. What factors should influence the choice of research questions? Ideological, technical, and pragmatic considerations all play their respective roles as the researcher tries to study what he believes is right. He may seek to exploit the tools that he is most familiar with, or he may be impelled by a commitment to be relevant to policy makers, that is, his findings should not only be "right," but be useful.

I want to explore more fully the problem of research's relevance to policy and the consequent utilization of research findings. Freeman has argued that researchers should select those variables to which the established policy or decision-making systems will respond. Accordingly, the researcher has "an obligation to understand both the organizational needs of these systems and the ways in which research must be structured because of these needs."[6] According to this formulation, research would have to respond to, but not challenge, the needs and orientation of the decision-making and implementing systems of policy. This conception of the role of research as handmaiden to established power can be understood as a strategy to maximize its relevance and hence to enhance its utilization. But distributive and allocative research do not accept this definition of the task of policy-oriented research; they challenge, rather than accept, the premise on which the policy and operating systems operate. What effect will research as social criticism of established power have on its utilization? To examine this question we need to give some consideration to the present state of knowledge about the utilization of sponsored or commissioned research.[7]

THE UTILIZATION OF RESEARCH

In the past sociologists did not give great attention to this problem. Their avoidance of this issue may be symptomatic of some diffidence about the extent to which research is used. There has, however, been some work which has sought to specify factors associated with research utilization. Gouldner believes that in order for research to be effective, it must address itself to the client's real difficulties, which may be different from the requests the client at first presents.[8] This means acting as a clinician and trying to discover what is truly problematic in the situation, rather than acting simply as a technician and responding to the client's own formulation of the problem. This emphasis on trying to understand the deeper dynamics of the client system is found in the work of those followers of Kurt Lewin who have done research in industry, the community, and elsewhere.[9] In this tradition, Blum[10] talks about the introduction of change into industry, and Lippitt[11] searches for common elements in the introduction of planned change into the community, the group, and the individual. In this model, the client's difficulties are perceived as a disease and the researcher is perceived as a clinician skilled in diagnosing the malaise, although the researcher is perhaps more skilled in convincing the patient to act on the diagnosis and in overcoming the client's resistance to change. Gouldner sees the need for a clinical sociology "which can aid in mending the rift between the policy maker and social scientist."[12] The important element in this approach is the assumption that research is utilized insofar as the sociologist has been insightful enough to direct his efforts to the key problem of the client system.

Quite another approach considers research to be effective when it gets the proper backing within the client system. Such an approach considers the question of where the sociologist has entered the organization, or, essentially, how powerful is his backing within the organization. It is generally thought by those who follow this line of argument that the proper way of entering an organization is with the backing of all relevant groups—the social work professionals, the social work executives, and the board. Closely related to the issue of support and entry is the nature of the organizational tie between the client and the researcher. The importance of the organization context for research utilization has been noted by Merton.[13] A generally accepted working hypothesis is that when the organization is the object of the study, utilization of research information increases when the researcher is part of an independent agency. A corollary to this position is that the greater the prestige of the outside agency, and the greater the reputation of the researcher, the greater is the likelihood that the information produced will be utilized.

Still a third approach to the question of how best to achieve research utilization involves how research is presented to the client. Here concern is directed to the feedback operation and to the proper ways of enlisting the client's motivation to absorb information and use it in his organizational behavior. Thus, some members of the University of Michigan Survey Research Center have concerned themselves not so much with the centrality of the problem they have dealt with, nor the level on which they have entered the organization, but with the extent to which their research information has been incorporated by their client audience and with the development of techniques, especially near-therapeutic group meetings, which maximize a client's response to and incorporation of the material.[14]

To summarize, interest in this area has developed around these three ways in which the sociologist can maximize utilization of his research: first, by working on the right problem; second, by getting the appropriate relationship to the organization; third, by the way in which he involves the client in the process of receiving the information.

Each view assumes that utilization is somehow dependent on the sociologist; whether he has the right sponsorship, the right relationship to the organization, directs his research toward the right problem, or introduces his results in the proper manner. I would like to suggest an alternative view, which is not original but has not been given the attention it deserves: the possibility that research will be used by an organization to the extent that it does *not* bear on the central problems of the organization and to the extent that it avoids implications which deal with the organization's most central dynamics. (Of course, during internal power struggles, research may be picked up and used selectively.)

Though this may seem paradoxical when stated for organizations, it is almost a truism in regard to individuals. One hardly expects to change individual behavior which is deeply motivated and central to the personality simply by communicating information to the individual. Much research and experience support the view that individuals select information to support their basic commitments, and that where they cannot select, they distort or deny. Information may help an individual choose means to goals so long as he has no emotional stake in any set of means, but information alone is unlikely to affect goals. The same processes seem to hold true in organizations. Research produces only information and cannot alone change the basic direction of organizational behavior. Organizational goals and basic policies or strategies for meeting these goals are molded by values and by the vested interests of key personnel, and these are typically unchangeable by information. Thus, to increase the likelihood that research findings will be used, researchers must avoid challenging the system's operating premises in any fundamental way; when possible, these premises should be affirmed by providing a rationale to support their validity. But in our efforts to be useful, we have surrendered the role of social analysis for short term relevance.

Consider the example of a project I directed in the field of social welfare, concerned with learning the ways in which certain kinds of child welfare services may be improved.[15] The project was inspired by an agency's desire to become professional and by the wish of the top staff to be able to identify with professional service. In writing up research findings and recommendations, I wanted to suggest that professionalization was not, at least in this case, appropriate. However, had my report noted that professional workers are not the best for the organization's particular clientele, it seemed likely that the organization would change its clientele rather than change its professionalizing goal. There was also the chance, of course, that the organization would reject the research findings as incompetent and irrelevant or simply ignore them. It is almost certain that any recommendation that the agency not be professionalized would be disregarded. So, I tried to suggest ways in which the agency could continue to do the job that it did in its non-professional past after it became professionalized.

Does research which deals with basic organizational problems or which challenges rather than accommodates the predetermined preferences of those who are the subject of the inquiry ever get used? Must we assume that the Ryan study will be disregarded because it searched too deeply and questioned too openly the tenets on which the mental health system rested? I believe there is no need for such a skeptical conclusion. Such research can be used, since there are undoubtedly many ways in which action yields to criticism. One example can be seen in the experience of a study[16] commissioned by a mental hospital. This hospital asked a sociologist and a psychiatrist to study possible therapeutic and nontherapeutic effects of the hospital system and the ward atmosphere on its patient population. The final report resulted in minimal changes within the structure of the organization which had commissioned the report. It was felt to be too threatening to the existing individually focused therapeutic ideology and to the organizational position and prestige of present high-level staff. The report suggested a much more sociological, milieu-oriented approach, rather than the strictly psychiatric approach which had been the keynote of the organization. The result was a complete failure to utilize the findings of the research in terms of bringing about changes in the organization's operation.

However, what happened subsequently is of interest. The research report was picked up by the field. It has become something of a classic in its area and has affected thinking in other organizations and among the entering staff and the new executives of these organizations. It has contributed significantly to the changes in the climate within which mental hospitals exist. As a result, it has had a great deal of effect, though not directly on the organization which commissioned the research. The cumulative effect of this and other studies has been to produce information which has entered the mainstream of thought and become part of the conceptual apparatus of individuals who will staff organizations in the future. These studies will have a very real impact on organizations of the kind which originally sponsored the research.

THE RELATIONSHIP BETWEEN ALLOCATIVE AND DISTRIBUTIONAL RESEARCH

Thus far I have treated research as alternatives; to choose a research framework is to go a long way in establishing in advance of the findings the kinds of policy recommendations which can be made. But this position overstates the case. The questions we have considered can be interrelated and reinforced. An effective social policy often requires more resources, reorganized along different principles, and reallocated among different sectors. I should like, therefore, to illustrate how distributive research can lead to asking allocative questions, by using as an example research in the mental health field.

Let me briefly review the findings of two distributional studies: the research of Elaine Cummings in the city of Syracuse and of William Ryan in the city of Boston. Both studies are concerned with the distribution of mental health personnel as these relate to the distribution of mental health problems.

Cummings studied 275 men over 25 years of age who had approached various social service agencies for assistance; she found that an average of 16 percent had a previous history of mental hospitalization. The highest rates of previous hospitalization were found among sheltered workshops and charitable services for transients (20 percent); prior hospitalization rates in public assistance were somewhat lower (about 15 percent); while medical clinics and family services experienced the lowest rates (about 6 percent). She concluded that:

> It appears that the psychotic . . . is allocated or allocates himself to the community services whose workers have the lowest level of training for helping the mentally ill . . . in all, a principle of allocation on which all agents appear to have a relatively high level of consensus in that the poorer, the more ignorant and the sicker the patient, the more eligible he is for treatment by the less trained and less professional practitioner.[17]

If there are such inequities in the relationship between distribution of professional skill and problem severity, then, Cummings declares, we must be prepared to face "some vexing questions about the system itself."

The Ryan study does not deal with previously hospitalized individuals, but with the more diffuse concept of emotional disability, since he is unable to make statements regarding the relationship between severity of illness and the distribution of professional service. He is, however, able to show convincingly that different social service gatekeepers have differential contacts with persons who exhibit what these gatekeepers define as emotional disabilities that presumably handicap their social functioning. His most important conclusion is that nonpsychiatric personnel and agencies handle by far most of the emotional disability in the city of Boston. The greatest concentration of emotional disability is found in the caseloads of the family doctor and other nonpsychiatric physicians. Like Cummings, Ryan concludes that the distribution of the higher status professional skills seems to be inversely related to the social and economic situation of individuals who are believed to have symptoms of emotional disability.

Nonpsychiatric personnel try to direct these patients to psychiatric professionals and facilities, which—although adequate by national standards—are nevertheless insufficient to accommodate the estimated 25 percent of the population who present such emotional disabilities.[18] Hence, there is a great deal of motion and activity in which individuals are referred from one part of the social service sector to another, but because of scarcity the process does not yield services. The problems of routing are documented in a special followup referral study of 140 emotionally disturbed individuals. Ryan notes that only a "small number of clients . . . were counted as having received significant help as a result of the referral process." But even these "were by no means provided with all the services required for the problems with which they were coping."[19]

What inferences can be drawn from these suggestive findings? Clearly nonprofessionals work with clients having emotional disabilities and they rely on a defective referral system, where few people receive the services for which they were sent. To improve the present referral system would place even greater demands on psychiatric facilities and personnel, yet it seems unreasonable to opt for further growth when Boston's resources already exceed national standards and still appear unable to meet the demands placed upon them. With most communities having dramatically fewer psychiatric resources than Boston, the strategy of expansion cannot seriously be presented as a viable national solution. Both studies wish to strengthen the nonpsychiatric system and weaken psychiatric control by the breakup of the medical model.

The medical model can be challenged in at least two ways. First, the principle of the distribution of skilled manpower to treat those with emotional disabilities of different intensities can be questioned. How shall scarce resources (the skill of the psychiatrists) be distributed among those in need? Second, the concept of emotional disability and the meaning of a mental health problem can be reassessed. Here we are forced to rethink the nature of the problem, and to accept the possibility that programs other than the intervention of skilled mental health personnel may be necessary to reduce the problem. This latter approach starts with the problem and asks what programs are relevant; the former approach starts with the program and asks how its resources should be redistributed among different clienteles.

We consider each of these questions. Take the case for the distribution of scarce resources. What directions should these changes take? Distributive research, although it dramatizes the need for change much as needs-resource studies documented the need for more resources, does not systematically provide principles on which redistribution of resources might be developed. The assumption is that the number of persons suffering from disability appears to be so large that it is altogether unrealistic to expect that there will be enough fully trained psychiatric personnel to reach all those who are afflicted with this "illness." Here the argument is clear but inconclusive.

Scarcity of personnel requires a more effective system of rationing. But what criteria for rationing might be used? The most skilled personnel could be allocated to those most in need (severity), or to those populations which have the highest prevalence of the problem (presumably low-income groups), or to those who are most capable of using the treatment (presumably, middle-income groups who do not have severe disabilities). Clearly the selection of the principle of rationing—severity, prevalence, or the ability to benefit from treatment—can either challenge or support the present pattern of distributing services.

Distribution research while it calls attention to the need for change does not offer rules for change. But because scarcity of skilled resources is endemic and the size of the problem is formidable, with one-fourth of the adult population so defined, those who undertake distributional studies in the hope of restructuring the pattern of services are forced to reexamine the nature of the problem. I believe, then, that they are forced into this position because of the logic of scarcity and because they are willing to accept the political constraint that it is neither desirable nor feasible to approach the problem by expanding the volume of skilled psychiatric manpower. Hence, they are led to the position that the less skilled must work with the most disabled. For example, Ryan asserts:

> . . . [it is] necessary to abandon the myth of medical responsibility and to adapt to the fact that, now and in the foreseeable future, most mental health problems involving social disorders—and probably most mental health problems of poor people—are, properly and explicitly, the responsibility of non-psychiatric interests.[20]

Thus, an examination of the distribution of services permits Ryan to raise policy questions concerning the mental health system and its central premise of medical responsibility. Welfare workers and school teachers have the largest proportion of cases with emotional disability. It is therefore necessary to upgrade the personnel of welfare departments and Boards of Education, even if this requires forgoing the expansion of the budget of mental health personnel. But this approach tries to convert the teacher and the welfare worker into a mental health worker, who in turn must be educated under the supervision of the psychiatrist. Curiously, then, such a proposal extends the power of the psychiatrist, enlarges the size of the mental health system, and reinforces the medical model. Although intervention in other sectors is stressed, the effect is to strengthen the mental health sector through a subtle form of sectoral imperialism. Moreover, such an approach can change the character of welfare and education systems, by undermining the relative importance of cash vs. personnel in the cash transfer system, and altering the priorities of counseling vs. teaching in the educational sector. These types of policy proposals are all within the framework of distributional research, that is, reform by reorganization. It is only when the concept of mental health itself is challenged, forcing a reexamination of the problem, that we move toward allocative research.

The concept of emotional or mental disability is quite vague. Presumably, emotional disabilities concern not only the nature of the hurt, but its origins. The concept of emotional disability might imply that if a random sample of individuals were placed in the same situation of stress or deprivation, the healthy individuals' responses would not be as severe as those in the sample who are emotionally disabled, since the disabled person's response is in terms of personal rather than situational factors. The Ryan study offers an example of a woman whose depression is "a condition which might seem quite natural in view of what is happening to her."

He argues that her emotional disturbance and her marital difficulties "are discovered in the context of serious social disturbance and are only parts of an inter-locking system of problems." He concludes that "she does not have a psychiatric problem,". . . if she is to receive help at all, she must receive help for her total situation.[21]

> The direct relationship between social problems in mental health is not only becoming more and more clear, but is increasingly becoming a matter of concern . . . Stressful effects of poverty, poor housing, unemployment, racial discrimination, and inadequate schools are entered into many instances of emotional disturbance.[22]

The problem to be solved seems to be inherently ambiguous because there is no operational way to distinguish emotional from situational disability. Perhaps, then, no workable definition of emotional disability can be developed for people who are subjected to overwhelming environmental stress.[23]

The policy implications of this analysis suggest that if emotional disability may be better understood as response to environmental stress, then it may be better relieved by intervention from outside the mental health system and not by training outside personnel to be mental health workers.

Allocative research makes it possible to ask whether goals in a particular area may be best reached by means outside that area. But there are formidable difficulties in city government and other governmental units in organizing research to ask such a question. Planning bodies tend to be organized around special purposes—housing, health, poverty. The definition of their mission limits the range of vision and the choice of policies. Allocative research is rare and often limited to universities. Government tends to be conservative in its research and planning, simply because everyone does his best on behalf of his own program. A planning department is needed which has no specific mission, but rather is concerned with the questions of allocative research. Mental health and other specialized planning are thus repudiated as models to be replaced by a more encompassing ideal of social planning. But we have not yet resolved the administrative, political, conceptual, and moral issues which such a centralized approach requires. And perhaps in the end, there may be no solutions, but only problems—which the Europeans regard as something to be endured as contrasted with the American position which views problems as conditions to be eliminated.

NOTES

1. There are, of course, exceptions to this generalization. See, for example, Irving Louis Horowitz, "Social Science and Public Policy: An Examination of the Political Foundations of Modern Research," *International Quarterly*, XI, 1 (March 1967); and Lee Rainwater, "Policy Research, Applied Research and Lower Class Culture," Occasional Paper No. 26 (Washington University at St. Louis, May, 1967) (mimeo.).
2. William Ryan, ed., *Distress in the City* (Cleveland: Case Western Reserve Press, 1969), p. 49.
3. James Conant, *Slums and Suburbs* (New York: McGraw-Hill, 1961), p. 3. Many wealthy suburbs spend $1,000 per pupil annually and provide a staff of 70 professionals per 1,000 students. Slum schools, by contrast, spend only half as much and provide more meager staff as well—40 professionals or less per 1,000 students.
4. Robert Rosenthal and Lenore Jacobson, "Pygmalion in the Classroom," *The Urban Review*, Vol. 3, No. 1 (September 1968). The authors conclude that "the results of our own study suggest that after one year, fifth graders may not show the effects of teacher expectations, though first and second graders do." (p. 20.)
5. James Coleman *et al.*, "Equality of Educational Opportunity" (Washington, D.C.: Office of Education, U. S. Department of Health, Education and Welfare, U. S. Government Printing Office, 1966). For a major criticism of the Coleman report see the paper by Kain and Hanushek. They support a different type of research design, which is a variant of what I have called the "needs-resources" framework. Kain and Hanushek argue that different kinds of measurements are needed for each of the three different purposes of the Coleman report—the measurement of differential resource inputs of the schools, the measurement of student achievements, and the study of the relationship between inputs and outputs. They feel that a choice should have been made among these alternative designs and they would have supported a study which carefully documented the inequalities in resource inputs between schools attended by Negro and white children. Such a study would have highlighted the contribution of discrimination in the schooling experienced by Negroes, prima facie evidence for the differential educational achievement of Negroes and whites. Coleman rejects a study of inequalities of inputs in favor of one which also tries to relate the traditional measures of inputs (per pupil expenditure, class size, teacher salary, age of building and equipment, etc.) to output measures of achievement. He explains that policy should not seek to eradicate "irrelevant inequalities."
   See, John F. Kain and Eric A. Hanushek, "On the Value of Equality of

Educational Opportunity as a Guide to Public Policy." Program on Regional and Urban Economics, Discussion paper Number 16, Harvard University, May, 1968. For the response to this criticism, see, James S. Coleman, "The Evaluation of Equality of Educational Opportunity." The Johns Hopkins University, The Center for the Study of Social Organization of Schools, Report Number 25, August, 1968.

6. Howard Freeman, "The Strategy of Social Policy Research," in *The Social Welfare Forum, 1963* (New York: Columbia University Press, 1963), p. 156.

7. To call policy-oriented research "applied" research as is the fashion is misleading because it begs the question of whether the findings of the study will be applied. The terms "commissioned" or "sponsored" research indicate only that someone has called for a study—not how the research is used, misused, abused, or disregarded. The observations in this discussion are based on an unpublished paper by Martin Rein and Robert Weiss.

8. Alvin W. Gouldner, "Explorations in Applied Social Science," in Alvin W. Gouldner and S. M. Miller, eds., *Applied Sociology: Opportunities and Problems* (New York: Free Press, 1965), pp. 17–21.

9. Kurt Lewin, *Resolving Social Conflicts* (New York: Harper & Brothers, 1948); see especially his discussion of "The Function and Position of Research within Social Planning and Action," pp. 205–208.

10. Fred Blum, "Toward a Democratic Work Place: The Hormel Packing House, Workers Experiment," *Harpers, 1953.*

11. Ronald Lippitt, Jeanne Watson, and Bruce Westley, *Dynamics of Planned Change* (New York: Harcourt, Brace, 1958); and "Consulting with Groups and Organizations," J. R. Gibb and Ronald Lippitt, eds., special issue, *Journal of Social Issues,* XV, 2 (1959).

12. Gouldner, *op. cit.*

13. Robert K. Merton, "The Role of Applied Social Science: A Research Memorandum," *Philosophy of Science,* 16, 3 (July 1949), 161–181.

14. See, for example, H. H. Halpert, "Communication as a Basic Tool in Promoting Utilization of Research Findings," *Community Mental Health Journal* (1966), pp. 231–236; and Robert K. Kahn and Floyd C. Mann, "Uses of Survey Research in Policy Determination," *Proceedings of the Ninth Annual Meeting of the Industrial Relations Research Association,* held December 1956, in Cleveland, Ohio; pp. 256–274.

15. Martin Rein, *The Network of Community Agencies Providing Child Protective Services in Massachusetts* (Boston: Graduate School for Advanced Study in Social Welfare, Brandeis University, 1962).

16. Alfred H. Stanton and Morris S. Schwartz, *The Mental Hospital* (New York: Basic Books, 1954). I am indebted to Morris Schwartz for calling my attention to this illuminating example.

   A study of the Planned Parenthood Federation of America illustrates how, as the political environment changed and national pressure emerged to enhance the organization's effectiveness, an organization can embrace policy recommendations which it earlier rejected. See chapter 9.

17. Elaine Cummings, "Allocation of Care to the Mentally Ill, American Style," in Mayer N. Zald, ed., *Organizing for Community Welfare* (Chicago: Quadrangle Books, 1967), pp. 144–145.

18. Presumably a more stringent and precise definition would decrease the size of the population, while a more relaxed one would substantially increase it. But, surprisingly, Ryan's conclusion that one-fourth of the population is emotionally disabled is supported by the findings of the Mid-Town Manhattan survey, an epidemiological study which relied upon six graded categories for the classification of symptom formation. According to this study, only 18.5 percent of the noninstitutional adult population were found to be "free of significant symptoms of mental pathology," while at the other end of the continuum 23 percent of the population was classified as impaired (Leo Srole *et al., Mental Health in the Metropolis: The Midtown Manhattan Study* [New York: McGraw-Hill, 1962], Vol. 1). When studies show that 80 percent or more of the population shows some symptoms of mental pathology, the concept of illness itself must be seriously questioned. For a discussion by Srole and his colleagues of the credibility of their findings, see p. 139ff.
19. Ryan, *op. cit.*, p. 23.
20. Ryan, *op. cit.*, p. 48.
21. *Ibid.*, p. 44.
22. *Ibid.*, p. 56.
23. For a discussion of the interrelationship between social environment and individual personality, see Marc Fried, "Social Problems and Psychopathology," in *Urban America and the Planning of Mental Health Services*, Vol. V, Symposium No. 10, held November 1964 (Group for the Advancement of Psychiatry), pp. 403–446.

Index

Abel-Smith, Brian, 23, 81, 488
Access, 229–30, 426
  to employment, 383–87
  problem of, 35–37
Accountability, 151, 296
ADC, *see* Aid to Families of Dependent Children
Advocacy planning, 196–97, 208, 212, 268
AFDC, *see* Aid to Families of Dependent Children
Aggregative economic measures, 228–29
Aggressive imperialism, 12
Agriculture, Department of (USDA), 449, 451–53, 456
Aid to Families of Dependent Children (AFDC) (ADC), 254, 311–20, 402
  extension of, 311–12
  sub-employed AFDC mothers, 315, 375, 392–98, 410
Aims, *see* Goals
Alinsky, Saul, 149, 209, 293
Allocation
  allocative decisions, 24–28
  to eliminate poverty, 418–26
  politics of, 28–31
  to reduce poverty, 231–41
  of services, xv–xvi
Allocative research, 464–67, 470–75
Ambiguity of strategy, 225, 227–28
Amenities, 17, 225, 327, 332
  access to, 229–30, 426
  redistribution of, 347–48
  See also Child care; Education; Housing; Medical care; Therapy
American Birth Control League, 169
Ancillary services, 334, 337–38
Apathy
  innovative change of, 154, 156–57
  poverty as, 354–56
Atlanta Employment and Evaluation Service Center, 118
Authority, 175, 194–98, 213
  bureaucratic, 195–96, 198–99
  consumer, 196–97
  decentralization of, *see* Decentralization
  of expertise, 194–95
  of professional values, 197–98

Banfield, Edward, 184, 243
Beckman, Norman, 195
Benefits-in-kind, 322–23
Birth Control Federation, 170
Black capitalism, 252, 273, 277–78, 368
Black ghettos, 375, 377–85, 398, 402, 406, 431
Black power, 271, 276, 278–79
Black separatism, 366, 368, 370
Blacks, 148, 189, 204, 229–30, 252–53, 271–281
  class antagonisms of, 275–76
  employment of, 151, 229, 254, 277–78, 331, 375, 377–85, 398, 402, 406
  as institutional reformers, 79–80
  militant, 209, 271, 281, 368
  Negro children, 119, 132–33, 254
  Negro families, 52, 154, 222–24, 393, 395–96, 426, 429, 434–35
  participation by, 354–55, 358–59, 363
  powerlessness of, 430–31
  in protest movement, 66
  radical social work with, 290, 294–96
  urban renewal affecting, 86, 257
Boulding, Kenneth, 425
Budget, Bureau of the, 38, 40, 314
Buell, Bradley, 33, 112–13
Bureaucratic cycle, 158–59
  policy implications of, 159
  theory of, 158
Burns, Eveline, 25, 239–40

CAMPS, *see* Cooperative Area Manpower Planning System
CAP, *see* Community Action Programs
Carter, Genevieve, 182
Casework
  aggressive, 113
  defined, 15–16
  radical, 290–92, 298

479

Casework (*continued*)
  traditional, 288–90, 296
Cash grants, 315
Cash transfers, 305–6, 308–10, 327–29, 343
  duplication of, 109
  income maintenance via, 254–55, 310–311
  as intervention strategy, 226–27
Catholics, 166, 170–72
Change, xvi
  without choice, 310–15, 320
  need for, 332–37
  theories of, 286–88
  See also Community change; Institutional change; Social change; Social reform; Strategies of change
Charity Organization Society, 58, 109, 203, 255, 284, 344
Chicago Area Project, 293
Child care, 314, 323, 383
  duplication of services for, 110–11
  expansion of, 397
  failure of, 94–95
  incoherent, 123–24
Child welfare, 130
  child neglect, 110
  foster care, 119–22, 132
  for Negro children, 119, 132–33
Choice, 121–22, 220–414
  case studies of, 304–414
  change without, 310–15, 320
  conservative, 262–63, 271–80, 287
  of equally ultimate ends, 250
  intervention strategies for, 224–28, 286–295
  radical, 260, 281–301
  reduction of, 105, 107–8, 129–34
  social, 80–81
  of social objectives, 220–301
Cicourel, A. V., 72
Citizen participation
  as legal protection, 363–64
  as policy development, 364–66
  by the poor, 353–73
  in social planning, 30
  as strategy for change (reform), 207–210, 336, 340
Citizen rights, 348
"Citizenship and Social Class" (Marshall), 252–53
City planning, *see* Urban planning
Civil Service Commission, 276–77
Clark, Kenneth, 354

Class structure, *see* Social class
Client advocacy, 16
Clinical Research Bureau, 169–70
Cloward, Richard A., 113, 294, 322, 333, 427
  on law enforcement, 73
  on MFY programs, 238
  on participation, 160–61, 209, 363
  on political powerlessness, 228
  on service agencies, 53–54
Coleman, James, 287, 466
Committee on Local Authority and Allied Personal Social Services, *see* Seebohm Committee
Community Action Agencies, 41, 360, 365
Community Action Programs, 36, 82, 117, 131, 208, 274, 432
  duplication of, 148
  institutional reform via, 439–40
  as instruments of change, 153–64
  as redistributive mechanism, 162–63
  reform of, 341–42
  sociotherapeutic value of, 292, 296
  See also Haryou; Head Start
Community agencies, 36–37
  conflicting perspectives on, 48–50
  coordination of, 110–11, 116
  goals of, 179–81
  residential vs., 60
Community change, 178–92
  through community leaders, 183–85
Community corporations, 367–69
Community Development Boards, 274, 368
Community Development Corporation (C.D.C.), 368–369
Community development programs, 256
Community Mental Health Facilities Act of 1964, 39
Community organization
  described, 15–16
  as sociotherapy, 293, 356–59
Community Progress Inc., 341
Community Research Associates, 62
Community Self-Determination Act of 1968, 208, 271, 273, 368–69
Comprehensive CAP programs, 155–56, 159, 432
Concentrated Employment Program, 404–405
Conflicts
  community, 166, 172–73
  goal, 126–28, 249–70

Conflicts (*continued*)
  between rights and services, 255
  of sources of legitimacy, 199, 205
  value, 174–76, 202, 239–45
Consensus
  of elites, 200–3
  over goals, 182–83, 187, 189–90
Consumer interests, servicing of, 250–54
Continuity of care, 39
Control, 26–27
"Cooling the Mark Out" (Goffman), 93
Cooperative Area Manpower Planning
  System, 404, 409
Cooperative rationality planning, 182–
  185, 187
Coordination, planning for, 31–41
  planning structures, 41
  service inundation in, 33–35
Coordination, service of, 34
Coordination strategy, 159, 161–62
Cost-benefit analysis, 441
  importance of values in, 241–44
  for urban renewal, 28–29
Council of Economic Advisers (CEA), 64,
  92, 257, 448, 454
Cumming, Elaine, 51, 57, 333, 428, 471

Davidoff, Paul, 196–97, 244
Decentralization, 295, 368–70
  of social services, 114–15
Decision-making, 295
  on child welfare, 120–21
  technicians' approach to, 9–10
Demonstration Cities and Metropolitan
  Act of 1966, 199, 327
Demonstration cities program, 25
Demonstration-research, 138–52
  assessment of, 63–67
  criteria for success of, 142–43
  liabilities of, 141–42
Detroit riots (1967), 343, 402
Disadvantaged groups, 255, 374–414
  distribution of attitudes of, 379–80
  HEW study of, 392–93, 395
  survival techniques of, 381, 390
  See also Low-income earners; Poverty
Discontinuity
  described, 38–40, 105–7
  of related functions, 116–22
Disengagement, 54
Distributive research, 463–67, 470–75
Donnison, David V., 8, 256

on child care, 110, 123–24
on institutionalization, 58–59
on social welfare, 21, 26
on voluntary service, 49
Dumont, M., 357–58
Duplication problem, 105–6, 109–16
Duplication strategy, 148–49, 203
Dyckman, John, 5, 196, 221

East Central Citizens Organization
  (ECCO), 367
Eckstein, Harry, 10
Economic approach, 4–5
Economic development, 259
Economic disservices, 88–89
Economic growth, 329–32
  goal of, 18, 231, 257
  investment theory of, 329–30
Economic independence, 318–19, 326–52
  of AFDC mothers, 397–98
  goal of, 345
  legislation promoting, 344
Economic market, 262–65
Economic Opportunity Act of 1964, 36,
  78, 199, 223, 296, 306–8, 344
  funds available under, 339
  maximum participation under, 208, 353–
  354
  Scheuer amendment of, 307–8
  Work Experience Program of, 316
  work-training programs under, 227
  See also Community Action Program;
  War on poverty
Economist, The (journal), 97–98
Education, 80–81, 285, 312
  academic disciplines, 6–11
  coordinated programs of, 104–5, 123–
  124, 127
  decentralization of, 295, 369
  of disadvantaged groups, 380, 387
  failure of, 95
  innovative change of, 129–31, 146–47,
  156, 203
  postponement of, 436
  for poverty reduction, 225, 237–39, 254–
  255
  remedial, 62–63
  research on, 465–67
  school drop-outs, 92–93
  as social service, 18, 23, 329–30
  tracking system of, 40
  vocational training, 77, 80, 129, 203

Elberfield system, 255, 284
Elementary and Secondary School Act of
  1965, 28, 80–81, 128, 439
Elites
  as board members, 172
  as city planners, 200–3
  non-elites, 175, 207
  power, 359
  as social planners, 207, 209
Employability strategy, 155–57, 432–33
Employment, 27, 90–93, 151, 277–79
  coherent programs for, 237–39
  coordination of employment services,
    117–18
  of the disadvantaged, 374–414
  other goals conflicting with, 254, 257–59
  of indigenous personnel, 361–63
  job continuity, 437
  job development (creation), 254, 307–8,
    398–400, 404–7
  quality of, 401–2
  social-psychological barriers to, 378–89
  technology and, 90-92
  work and welfare interdependence, 311–
    322, 324, 394–98
  See also Job Corps; Sub-employment;
    Unemployment; WIN
Engel coefficient, 450, 452–54, 456
England, 34, 223, 254, 310, 431, 437
  duplication problem in, 110–16
  incoherence problem in, 124–25
  Labour Government of, 239, 322
  output studies in, 466
  personal social services in, 348
  professional rigidity in, 55–56
  supplementary programs in, 316
  wage stoppage in, 321–22
  as welfare state, 23, 346
"Envy hypothesis," 427
Equality
  goal of, 229–30
  of opportunity, 427

Family Service Association of America,
  178, 180
Federal Task Force on Organization of
  Social Services in the U.S., 114
Fleisher, Beton M., 424
Ford Fondation, 58, 148, 165
  Grey Area Projects of, 62, 126, 153,
    306
  matching funds for, 145

Frankel, Charles, 80, 149
Friedman, Rose, 453–54
FSAA, *see* Family Service Association of
  America
Fuchs, Victor, 420
Functional dispersion problem, 105–6,
  109–16

Galbraith, John Kenneth, 13, 139, 263,
  331
Gans, Herbert, 11, 96, 196, 281, 333
Girls at Vocational High School, 333–34
Glazer, Nathan, 78–80, 232–33, 423
  missing middleman thesis of, 272, 358
  on social policy, 253
Goals, 18, 125–28
  conflicting, 126–28, 249–70
  of demonstration-research, 143, 147,
    149–51
  displacement of, 188
  economic independence as, 345
  goal-constraint strategy, 267
  organizational, 165, 174, 179–92
  planning, 59–63
  of poverty reduction, 229–31, 235, 239–
    240, 254–56
  "preamble aims," 66
Goffman, Erving, 251
Gorham, William, 260–61
Gouldner, Alvin W., 57, 200–1, 211, 467–
  468
  on adoption agencies, 291
  on sociology, 281–82, 468
Greenleigh studies (1965), 347
Grigsby, William G., 230, 233–34, 423,
  426, 448
Group work, 235
  described, 15–16
  as production-delivery system, 50
  recreation as, 364
Guaranteed employment, 307, 343
Guaranteed income, 98, 254, 343–44

Haber, Alan, 227, 453
Haggstrom, Warren, 424
Harrington, Michael, 429
Hartman, Chester, 86
Haryou, 292, 354–55, 430–31
Head Start, 18, 127, 242, 326
  change of, 359–60
  as demonstration project, 143–44

Head Start (*continued*)
  as remediation program, 155–56
  as social service, 329
Health, 23
  poverty related to, 231–35, 418–25
  public health movement, 202
  See also Medical care; Mental illness;
    Nutrition
Health and Welfare Councils, 462
High-school graduation, 237, 387
  See also School drop-outs
Hirschman, Albert O., 268
House Ways and Means Committee, 312
Housing, 18, 95, 329, 347
  benefits, distribution of, 22–23
  policy, 422–26
  public, 323, 384
  quality of, 231–35
  relocation, 256
  services, coordination of, 118–19, 123
  subsidies, 98, 229–30
Human resources approach (investment
  in human capital), 225, 329–30, 334–
  335, 345
Humility, need for, 12

Identity, confusion of, 12
Ideology
  defined, 244
  end of, 204
  of social work, 288
Illegitimacy, 52
Illness, *see* Health
Impatience, sense of, 12
Incentive system, 313, 318–20
  See also WIN
Incoherence, 105, 122–25
  described, 107
Income, 343–44
  coordination of income programs, 118–
    119
  equalization of, 346
  guaranteed, 98, 254, 343–44
  level of, 319, 401–2
  redistribution of, 97, 226, 259
  transfer, 254–55, 310–11
  See also Low-income earners
Incrementalism, welfare, 82–83, 160
Indian Affairs, Bureau of, 263–64
Indians, American, 30, 105
Indigenous workers, 361–63

Individual rationality planning, 184–85,
  187, 190–91
Individualistic bias, 56–57
Industry Incentives program, 308
Inequality, 234, 251–53, 426, 438
  poverty as, 446–47
Infiltration strategy, 147–48
Institutional barriers, 387–88
Institutional change, 65–66, 70–84
  planning for, 78–83
  social action and protest for, 359–61
Institutional performance, 437–40
Institutional reform, 439–40
Institutionalization, 58–60, 66–67
Integrative organizations, 187–90
Intelligence testing (IQ tests), 72, 75–76,
  90, 92, 388, 438
Intervention strategies, 113, 286–95, 432–
  437
  outlines of, 224–29, 432–34
Investment programs, 231–35, 327
  investment in human capital, 225,
    329–30, 334–35, 345
Involvement, 202, 228
  See also Citizen participation; Participa-
    tion strategy
Iron Law of Social Welfare, 94–98
Irregular economy, 375, 389–92

Job Corps, 14, 80, 225, 354, 400
  aspirations of enrollees in, 379
  cost of, 77
  discontinuity in, 38–40
  innovative change through, 127, 131,
    155–56
  as pretraining program, 433
  technical progress and, 91
Jobs, *see* Employment
"Jobs Now" program, 336–37
JOBS Program, 406, 409
Joint Commission on Mental Health and
  Illness, 57, 95
Joint Economic Committee, 17, 261, 345
Juvenile Delinquency and Youth Offenses
  Control Act of 1961, 37, 78, 199,
  356, 400

Kadushin, Charles, 233, 419–20
Kahn, Alfred J., 74, 296
  on drop-outs, 92
  on "social utilities," 225
  on "urban-child care crisis," 95

Kitsuse, John I., 72
Klarman, Herbert E., 238
Klein, Philip, 227
Knowledge, 11
  as strategy, 144, 146–47
  strategy, power of, 203–7, 211
Kuusi, Peka, 13, 345

Labor, Department of, 62, 117, 388, 402
Labor market, 312
Labor Statistics, Bureau of (BLS), 453,
  456
Lampman, Robert J., 22–23, 310, 427
Legal services, 309, 348, 363–65
Legitimacy, 193–217
  dilemmas in search for, 210–12
  of goals, 183
  new source of, 196
  strategies of, 199–210
Levitan, Sar A., 226
Lewis, Hylan, 422
Lewis, Oscar, 429
Lewis, W. Arthur, 266–67
Lichtenberg, Philip, 291
Life cycle
  scheduling, 434–37
  transitions, 435
Lipsky, Michael, 209–10
Litwak, Eugene, 189, 211
Locality-responsive strategy, 167–71, 174–
  175
  components of, 167–68
Long, Norton, 272, 358
Low-income earners, 311, 379–84, 400–2,
  419–24, 439
  family stability of, 401
  health of, 233, 383, 419–22
  housing of, 384, 422–23
  identity of, 381
  mental illness of, 420–22
  See also Disadvantaged groups; Poverty
Low-skilled workers, 407, 430
Luck, J. Murray, 450

McEwen, William J., 173
Manpower Development and Training Act
  (1962), 38, 78, 117, 131, 155, 238, 320,
  327
Manpower policies, 308, 377, 398–410
  adequate resources for, 407–8
  improvement of manpower services,
  408–10

limited objectives of, 410
social objectives of, 400–4
Manpower Report of the President (1968),
  254
Manpower training programs, 203, 254
Margaret Sanger Clinic, 170
Marris, Peter, 140, 436
Massachusetts Society for the Prevention
  of Cruelty to Children, 48, 55–56, 123
MDTA, *see* Manpower Development and
  Manpower Development and Train-
  ing Act
Means-tested programs, 262, 311
Medical care, 329, 425–26
  decentralization of, 369
  planning for, 60-61
  quality of, 94
Mental illness
  poverty and, 224, 420–22, 428
  psychosis (schizophrenia), 74–75, 420,
  428
  treatment of, *see* Psychiatry
Merriam, Ida C., 22
Merton, Robert K., xi, 468
Meyerson, Martin, 196, 243
MFY, *see* Mobilization for Youth
Miller, Herman, 226
Miller, S. M., 277, 448
Miller, Walter, 235, 430
Mills, C. Wright, 359
Mobility, 230, 380–81
Mobilization for Youth, 141, 165, 236–37,
  336
  citizen participation in, 356–58, 363
  criticism of, 64
  discontinuity in, 40–41
  pressure strategy of, 149
  sociotherapeutic value of, 293
  storefront multi-service center of, 309
  youth training programs of, 238
Model Cities Program, 126, 208, 211, 293
  development of, 306
Morbidity, *see* Health
Morgan, James N., 94, 223
Moynihan, Daniel Patrick, 94, 154, 223,
  276–77, 357, 429
MSPCC, *see* Massachusetts Society for the
  Prevention of Cruelty to Children
Myrdal, Gunnar, 3, 13, 330
  on economic progress, 231
  on perversion of policy, 78, 94
  on poverty levels, 340

NAACP (National Association for the Advancement of Colored People), 181, 185, 188
National Foundation for Infantile Paralysis, 170, 175, 178, 185
National Housing Survey (1956), 233, 423
National Institute of Mental Health, 60, 293
National Urban Coalition, 271–72, 275
National Urban Development Bank, 271
Needs
  developmental, 434–37
  nutritional, 454–56
  services neglecting greatest, 53–55
  services relevant to, 333–34
Needs-resource research, 462–63, 465
Negroes, *see* Blacks
Neighborhood organization, 356–59
Neighborhood Service Stations, 160
Neighborhood Youth Corps, 27, 38, 155, 225, 386
  aspirations of enrollees in, 380
  in-school program of, 436
  as pretraining program, 433
New Careers program, 307–8
New Poor Law of 1834, 155, 318, 344
New York City Planning Commission, 194–95, 198
New York City Youth Board, 34, 104
  Gang Project of, 293
NIMH, *see* National Institute of Mental Health
Nonprofessionals, 290, 336, 361–63, 471–72
Norms, 71
  See also Standards
North Carolina Fund, 154
Nutrition, 323, 449–58
  adequate, 451–57
  minimal standards of, 449–50, 458
  resources allocated to, 418–22

OEO (Office of Economic Opportunity), 18, 149, 354–55, 362, 367, 448
  Federal Assistance Programs of, 107
  legal services of, 348, 364–65
  rehabilitation program of, 227
  See also Head Start; Job Corps
O.J.T. (On-the-Job Training programs), 307–8
Operation Head Start, *see* Head Start
Opportunities Industrialization, 148

Optimality, principle of, 5, 213
Organization delivery, 76–78
Organizational strategy
  selection of, 167
  for social change, 165–77
Organizational structures, 178–92, 201
  two types of, 185–86
Orshansky, Mollie, 451, 453, 457

Parallelism, 37, 79–80
Pareto, Wilfred, 5, 213
Participation
  citizen, *see* Citizen participation
  as social-service function, 328
Participation strategy
  for change, 145, 156, 159–62
  of intervention, 227–28, 433
Pasamanick, Benjamin, 421
Pathology of poverty, 428–34
Peacock, Allan, 263
Pechman, Joseph, 258–59
Perloff, Harvey, 64, 142
Physical renewal, *see* Urban renewal
Piven, Frances Fox, 160–61, 209, 322, 363
Planned Parenthood Federation of America, Inc., 166-74, 181, 188
  Board of Directors of, 167
  controversy over, 166, 172–74
  local affiliates of, 168–73
Planning, 267–68
  See also Social planning; Urban planning; Welfare planning
Planning organizations, 65–66, 201, 204
Planning-Programming-Budgeting System 260–61
Plowden Report, 466
Polish Peasant (Znaniecki and Thomas), 292–93
Political feasibility, 222, 224, 332
Political partisanship, 265–67
Pool, De Sola, 7–8
Poor Law, 133, 255, 314, 337
Poor Law Commissions
  1905, 124–25, 129
  1909, 310–11
Poor Law Reform of 1834 (New Poor Law), 155, 318, 344
Poor People's Campaign (1968), 275
Poverty, 113–14, 305–8, 338–42, 417–60
  as black phenomenon, 272
  "case," 331
  causes of, 224, 417

Poverty (*continued*)
  characteristics of the poor, 222–24
  definitions of, 222, 229, 446–60
  dependence and, 96–98
  as distribution problem, 162–63
  elimination of, 296–97, 417–45
  job creation and, 307–8
  levels of, 340
  measurement of, 446–60
  minimal nutritional standards and, 449–450, 458
  participation of the poor, 353–73
  as powerlessness, 228, 354–56
  primary and secondary, 449
  See also War on poverty; Welfare system; Working poor
Poverty areas, 384
  irregular economy of, 389–92
  unemployment in, 376–78
  See also Urban ghettos
Poverty culture theories, 223, 232, 242, 428–30
  criticism of, 429–30
Poverty cycle, 93, 154-58, 356, 430–34
  program implications of, 155–56, 432–434
  vicious cycle, 154
Poverty reduction, 125, 221–48, 250–56
  coherent programs of, 237–39
  effective programs of, 235–37
  programs most reducing poverty, 254–256
  six strategies for, 224–29
  via cash transfers, 305–6
Power, 194, 257, 276–79, 295–96
  black, 271, 276, 278–79
  defined, 427
  established power groups, 359, 361
  of knowledge strategy, 203–7, 211
  of the people strategy, 207–10
  transfer of, 366–67, 370
Powerlessness, 228, 354–56
PPBS, *see* Planning-Programming-Budgeting System
President's Committee on Juvenile Delinquency and Youth Crime, 58, 61, 293, 359
  innovative change and, 126, 143, 145–146, 153, 165, 191, 203–4, 208
  politicies developed by, 306, 433
Pressure strategy, 149–50
Price stability, 231, 257–59, 308
Procurement, problem of, 35–36

Professionals, 183, 388–89
  as organizational executives, 168, 175–76
  performance by, 121
  radicalization of, 281–301
  rigidity of, 55–56
  services dispensed by, 51–55, 95–97
  standards of, 76
  values of, 197–98
  See also Nonprofessionals
Project Camelot, 11
Project Head Start, *see* Head Start
Proliferation, defined, 31
Proxmire, William, 258, 276
Psychiatry, 74–75
  community, 39
  coordination of psychiatric services, 113, 116
  failure of, 95
  for "hopeless" cases, 55
  research on psychiatric services, 471–74
"Psychological Effects of Unemployment, The" (Eisenberg and Lazarsfeld), 421
Public assistance, *see* Welfare system
Public policy, 13–15, 257–58

Race, 251
  institutional racism, 279
  racial integration, 181, 257
  racial segregation, 384, 438
  as urban problem, 295–96
  See also Blacks; Indians
Race Relations and Social Change (Coleman), 287
Rainwater, Lee, 335, 339, 437
Rational analysis, 203, 259-62, 267
Rational objectives, 222–24
Rational planning, 182–85, 187, 190–91
Rationality, limits of, 224
Rationality testing, 89–90
Redistribution
  goal of, 127, 259
  of income, 97, 226, 259
  for institutional change, 80–81
  of jobs, 308
  of power, 295
  redistribution mechanism and poverty, 162–63
  of resources, 268
  of social services, 374–79
Referrals, 335
  to birth-control agencies, 166, 171
  job, 151, 314

Reform, *see* Social reform
Rehabilitation programs, 230, 240
   effectiveness of, 235–37
Rehabilitation strategy, 227
Remediation strategy, 155–57, 203,
   433–35
Renewal and Rehabilitation Corporation,
   367
Research
   evaluative, 461–62
   policy development through, 267–68
   on social policy, 8–10, 461–77
   as strategy for change, 205–6, 211
   utilization of, 467–70
   See also Demonstration-research
Resources
   allocation (distribution) of, *see* Alloca-
      tion
   competition for, 37–38, 205
   inadequate, 407–8
   needs-resource research, 462–63, 465
   redistribution of, 268
Riessman, Frank, 76, 430
Ritualism, 188–89
Robb, J. H., 49
Roman Catholics, 166, 170–72
Rowntree, Benjamin S., 449, 457
Ryan, William, 120, 130, 463–64, 470–74

San Francisco Community Action Agency,
   360
Sanger, Margaret, 169
Shlesinger, Arthur, Jr., 331
School drop-outs, 92–93
Schorr, Alvin, 23, 232, 234, 244, 434
   on insufficiency, 418, 422–23, 426
Schultz, Theodore W., 225
Schwartz, Morris S., 39
Scotch, Norman A., 422
Scribner, Sylvia, 293–94
Seebohm Committee, 34, 114, 348
Seeley, John R., 74, 253, 282
Seldon, Arthur, xii
Selective economic measures, 228–29
Self-help, 209–10, 277, 287, 292–93
Self-sufficiency, 127, 277, 397-98
Serial continuity, defined, 117
Shriver, Sargent, 296, 335, 339
Sills, David, 168, 170, 175
Slums, *see* Urban ghettos
Smolensky, Eugene, 222–23

SMSA's, *see* Standard Metropolitan Statistical Areas
Social action, 340
   for institutional change, 359–61
   therapeutic value of, 292–94
   See also Community Action Programs
Social administration, *see* Social policy
Social change, 250
   organization strategy for, 165–177
   See also Social reform
Social choice, 80–81
Social class, 75–77, 272-79, 294, 437–38
   class warfare, 427
   lower-class behavior, 75–76
   lower-class culture, 272–73, 430
   lower-class identity, 437
   social policy based on, 274–79
   social unrest based on, 272–74
   See also Elites
Social control, 26–27
Social Costs of Private Enterprise, The
   (Knapp), 89
Social decency goal, 229
Social elites, *see* Elites
Social inclusion, 230–31
Social insurance, 255, 311
Social mobility, 230, 380–81
Social planning, 193–212
   urban, 194–98
Social policy, xv, 3–20, 294–97
   defined, 3–6
   development of, 461–77
   of eliminating poverty, 296–97, 417–45
   perversion of, 78, 94
   planning of, 211–14
   radical, 294–95, 297
   social purposes and, 9–12
   socioeconomic policy, 345–46
Social policy goals
   conflicting, 249–70
   goal management, 259–67
Social-psychological states, 287
   as barriers to employment, 378–83
   housing affecting, 232–33
   See also Apathy; Powerlessness
Social reform, 16, 296–97, 308–10
   legitimate, 201–2, 204–7
   liberal, 276–77
   See also Change
Social science, 214, 417–45
   personal and social theory of, 426–37
   value-free, 203–5
   See also Sociology

Social Security Act (1935), 67, 311, 315, 366
  1962 amendments to, 37, 88, 144, 227, 261, 327, 344, 347
  1965 amendments to, 78
  1967 amendments to, 15, 104, 312–13, 347, 394, 397
Social Security Administration, 85, 326
  fiscal estimates of, 22
  poverty defined by, 451–53
Social service network
  competing views of, 50–53
  defined, 47–48
Social service problems, 76–78
  "cashing in" as, 76
  "creaming off" as, 62–63, 78, 83, 113
  problems of organization, 103–34
Social services, xv–xvi, 46–99, 312–13, 326–352
  allocations among, 27
  control of, 295–96
  coordination of, 103–37
  crisis in, 47–69
  criticism of, 332–35
  decentralization of, 368–70
  definitions of, 3–4, 47, 327–29
  functions of, 328
  labelling of service users, 50–53
  local, defined, 47
  objectives of, 9
  personal, 15–18, 348
  public dependence on, 85–99
  purpose of, 21–22
  reform of, 306, 338–46
  reorganization of, 57–58
  "sickness" model of, 334
  social use of, 346–49, 438
  See also Cash transfers; Social work; Welfare system
Social stability, 18
  in black ghettos, 271–80
  as goal, 230, 240
Social stratification, 73
  See also Social class
Social structure, 57
Social therapy, *see* Sociotherapy
Social welfare system, *see* Welfare system
Social work, 176, 334–35
  goals of, 178–80
  immediate aims of, 294
  origin of, 109
  radical, 281–301
  social policy related to, 15–18
  See also Casework

Social workers' creeds, 283–84, 288–98
  four major, 288–95
Society for the Prevention of Cruelty to Children, 48, 55–56, 123–24
Sociology, 281–82, 468
  as discipline, 7
  radical, 11
Sociotherapy, 371–72
  community, 292–94
  neighborhood organization for, 296, 356–59
  work as, 400–1
SPCC, *see* Society for the Prevention of Cruelty to Children
Speenhamland system, 254, 315
Sprout, W. J. M., 7
SSA, *see* Social Security Administration
Standard Metropolitan Statistical Areas, 233, 376
Standards
  of client behavior, 284–86, 290, 294
  for institutional change, 71–78
  stated vs. actual, 75–76
  See also Norms
Stigler, George J., 451
Stigma
  elegibility and, 240, 252
  standards and, 73–74
Strategies of change, 63–67, 288
  appropriate to goal achievement, 179
  British, 110-16, 124–25
  change of poverty cycle, 155–56
  defined, 181
  innovative change, 63, 102–212
  institutional change, 79–83
  strategies of reform, 338–46
Subculture, 157
Sub-employment, 286–87, 375–78, 387, 389, 403–10
  of AFDC mothers, 315, 375, 392–98
  job creation and, 404–7
  in poverty areas, 376–78
  "strangeness" of subemployees, 383
  See also Unemployment
Subsistence levels, 446, 448–51, 458
Sundquist, James, 307, 311–12
Supplementary Benefits Commission, 316
Survival, problem of, 189–90, 201
Syracuse Community Development Association, 149

ten Broek, Jacobus, 240

Therapy, 51, 209–10
  See also Psychiatry; Sociotherapy
Thompson, James D., 173
They Shall Not Pass (Black), 76
Timms, Noel, 283
Titmuss, Richard, 4, 55–57, 67, 82, 98,
  229–30, 250, 441
  on casework, 289
  on coordinated services, 104, 125
  criticism of, xii
  on delivery problem, 438
  on disservices, 89
  on inequality, 447–48
  on professionals, 55–56, 95
  on social administration, 8–9
  on social services, 21–22
  on "Territorial Welfare Justice," 337
  on values, 244, 284
Tobin, James, 239
Townsend, Peter, 448, 455
Transfer payments, *see* Cash transfers
Transportation and employment, 383–87

Unemployment, 93, 228–29, 331–32
  automation affecting, 90
  nonwhite, 77
  in poverty areas, 376–78
  price stability vs., 257
  rising rate of, 86
  welfare and, 27
  unemployment benefits, 98, 311–14
Unified Social Service Center (New Haven),
  336
United Fund, 30, 168, 190
United Nations, 28–29, 128
Universal dependency, 87–89
Universal programs (services), 262, 438
Urban ghettos, 256–57, 266, 271–80, 431
  characteristics of slum residents, 377–78
  class structure of, 272–79
  disadvantaged ghetto residents, 374–414
Urban League, 189, 227
Urban planning, 194–99
  academic study of, 12
  sources of authority for, 194–98
Urban problems, 295–98
Urban renewal, 18, 86, 256–57
  innovative, 58
  resource allocations for, 25, 28–29
Utility maximization, 262, 265

Values, 18, 212–14

conflict of, 174–76, 202, 239–45
consensus of, 190–91, 212
legitimate, 197–98
of social workers, 283–84, 290
value-free science, 203–5
value preferences, 222–24
Verstehen, defined, xi
Vidich, Arthur, 30
Vietnam War, 13, 276, 279, 308
Voluntary institutions, 200
Voluntary service organizations, 49, 109,
  207

Wage supplementation, 254, 315, 322
War on poverty, 115, 126, 434
  resources of, 27, 30
  Senate hearings on, 331
  as slogan, 161
  value choices of, 244–45
  See also Community Action Programs;
    Economic Opportunity Act of 1964
Watts riot (Los Angeles, 1965), 27, 402,
  427
Webb, Beatrice, 124–25, 310, 337
Webb, Sidney, 124–25, 310, 337
Webber, Melvin, 126, 241
Weber, Max, xi, 10
Welfare colonialism, 126, 271, 293–94, 370
Welfare incrementalism strategy, 82–83,
  160
Welfare planning, 21–43
  institutional change in, 70–84
  planning process, 24
  social, economic, and physical, 25–27
Welfare policy, 13–14, 17–18
Welfare Rights Movement, 294, 309, 363–
  64
Welfare system, xv–xvi, 305–25, 343, 392–
  398
  benefit levels under, 316–22
  failure of, 94
  intergenerational dependency on, 311,
    394
  integration of, 180–81, 189
  iron law applied to, 96–97
  length of time on, 393–94
  principles of deterrence and elegibility
    of, 240
  as substitutive system, 310–15
  as supplementary system, 310, 315–18,
    322–23
  withering-away doctrine of, 310

Welfare system (*continued*)
  work and welfare interdependence, 311–322, 324, 394–98
  See also Aid to Families of Dependent Children; Cash transfers; Child welfare; Social services
Wickenden, Elizabeth, 224, 230, 294
WIN, *see* Work Incentive Program

Wirtz, Willard, 331, 361, 399
Wootton, Barbara, 88, 147, 235–36
  on service agencies, 49, 51
Work Incentive Program, 313–14, 316, 375, 397
Working poor, 254, 310, 313, 315
World Population Emergency Campaign, 170

ABOUT THE AUTHOR

Martin Rein is a Professor at Bryn Mawr College in the Graduate School of Social Work and Social Research. He has published numerous monographs and articles. He is co-author of *Dilemmas of Social Reform* (1967) and co-editor with S. M. Miller of a series on Social Policy to be published by Random House. In September 1970, he will join the faculty of the Massachusetts Institute of Technology as Professor of Social Policy.